Public

DATE DUE

Return Material Promptly

VOLUME I: BEGINNINGS TO 1900

PUBLIC WOMEN, PUBLIC WORDS

A Documentary History of
American Feminism

Edited by Dawn Keetley & John Pettegrew

MADISON HOUSE

Madison 1997

Keetley, Dawn & John Pettegrew
Public Women, Public Words
A Documentary History of American Feminism
VOLUME I: BEGINNINGS TO 1900

LIBRARY OF CONGRESS
CATALOGING-IN-PUBLICATION DATA

Keetley, Dawn Elizabeth, 1965–
       Public women, public words : a documen-
tary history of American feminism / edited by
Dawn Elizabeth Keetley & John Charles
Pettegrew.
          p.   cm.
       Includes bibliographical references and
       index. Contents: v. 1. Beginnings to 1900.
          ISBN 0-945612-44-3 (alk. paper).—
       ISBN 0-945612-45-1 (pbk. : alk. paper)
          1. Feminism—United States—History—
       18th century—Sources.   2. Feminism—
       United States—History—19th century—
       Sources.   I. Pettegrew, John Charles, 1959– .
HQ1410.K444 1997
305.42'0973—dc21   97–3580
                                              CIP

Printed in the United States of America
on acid-free paper.

Published by Madison House Publishers, Inc.
P. O. Box 3100, Madison, Wisconsin 53704

FIRST EDITION

Contents

PART THREE
Early Rights Consciousness in Antebellum America

PART FOUR
The Post-Civil War Struggle for Political and Social Equality   231

I. *Suffrage and Other Essential Rights*   233

INTRODUCTION

Splitting Differences: Conceiving of American Feminism

THIS COLLECTION OF DOCUMENTS traces the development of feminist thought from colonial North America through United States political and popular culture of the late-twentieth century. A primary goal of the book is to offer an intellectual history of American feminism: that is, to examine not only the *conceptual* composition of the subject, but also to study how women have used ideas *practically* to gain power within specific historical circumstances. We understand feminism as a process, an activity, a social movement that has flourished through the polypragmatic expression of women's needs in public-political discourses and institutions. Feminism describes *enactments* of thought meant to improve social-sexual relations.

Overview

Many of the following documents reflect our interest in revealing the confluence between thought and action in American feminism. For example, Frances Wright—a founding figure of the early-nineteenth century women's rights movement—not only wrote and lectured throughout the 1820s but also established the utopian community of Nashoba in Tennessee. Maintaining that "mankind must reasonably hesitate to receive as truths, theories, however ingenious, if unsupported by experiment," Wright instituted greater freedom for women at Nashoba than any other American community of its time, nullifying all marriage laws and further declaring that no woman entering the community would "forfeit individual rights and her independent existence." Insisting on "liberty" and "equality" for every individual, Wright infused immediate substance into these ideals by founding Nashoba.

A second principal goal of this collection is to represent the diversity of American feminism. Rather than rendering feminism as the battle of a homogeneous group of women in the name of a single cause such as suffrage or equal rights with men, we discuss feminism specific to various races, ethnicities, classes, regions, and sexualities and seek to illuminate the distinct interests that have sprung from these social groups. We document, in other words, a history that has been varied, multiple, and far from unified. But even while concentrating on the contested nature of American feminism, we do not want to rule out the possibility of locating shared concerns and common actions among women of different orientations. Our selection of texts attempts to establish a middle ground between arguments for, on one side, the dispersion of an infinite number of feminisms and, on the other side, the overarching unanimity of American feminism.

This effort to represent both the diversity and the common purposes of feminism is reinforced by our use of an eclectic mix of published documents, including speeches and manifestos, fiction and poetry, articles in radical, popular and middle-brow magazines, underground newspapers, professional and academic journals, and courtroom transcripts and records of other official proceedings. Such published texts may be used historically to connect ideas and actions to specific groups of people. Attention to the author of a feminist tract, for example, places that woman and her thoughts within a certain time and place and suggests further the identities and mind sets and circumstances of the women for whom she wrote. Close examination of a document, then, may reveal not only textual meaning regarding specific principles of feminist thought but also crucial information about the context of its production. We have tried to include documents—the 1794 commencement oration to the Young Ladies Academy of Philadelphia, for instance, or the 1971 preamble to *Asian Women*, a feminist newspaper published at the University of California–Berkeley—that help locate and detail women's institutional organization and political activism.

It should be emphasized that this collection is meant to chronicle the activism of different groups of American women. We are concerned with the interrelationship between ideas and the circumstances of social change, between words and political action. We have a bias for documents that place women in specific public contexts. Some texts provide official record of feminist activism, as in the trial transcript of the United States government's case against Susan B. Anthony for voting in the Congressional election of 1872. This account of Anthony's willful defiance of federal law, along with her impassioned and insistent courtroom defense of the "fundamental privilege" of female citizenship, offer dramatic evidence of how feminists have publicly opposed state-sanctioned subordination of women.

Feminist activism, of course, has not been limited to legal proceedings; public opposition to women's subordination can be found in every one of the texts in this collection. In fact, we see literature itself as a form of activism. Even though writing and reading are often understood as acts of private or personal dimension, literature should also be seen, ideally, as something that happens between people. We hope readers of this book will consider the following documents as types of public speech. American feminism has developed in the form of argument; it has been produced with the self-conscious intention of persuasion. This includes feminist fiction, autobiography, and poetry—work, which, in its own way, has been written to change minds.

In contrast to the battle for legal rights, undertaken in more formal arenas such as the courtroom or the political convention, "creative" writing demonstrates how feminism has also been concerned with the subjective development of diverse women. These forms of feminist literature attempt to displace fixed ideas of the female self, conceptions that support women's subordinate position in the work place, the family, and, more generally, in relationships with men and male-dominated structures of power. Finally, feminist fiction, autobiography, and poetry is historically valuable because it allows the reader to compare subjectivities among different racial, ethnic, and class-based groups of American women, reminding one that a woman's identity is determined through a number of factors, not just sexuality and gender.

Competing Definitions of Feminism

Despite the fact that no common identity exists among American women, there is philosophical support for the idea that in some ways women have been united by historical circumstance. There has been a type of "synchronicity" involved in the female experience of living in cultures and societies similarly influenced by masculine interests: social institutions, relations, and practices have, as the theorist Iris Marion Young describes, situated women "serially," placing them within sexually-determined "limits and restraints"; "enforced heterosexuality," for instance, and the "sexual division of labor," work to "collectivize" women's conceptions of how they have been individually constrained by male-based systems of power. Young is quick to point out that this shared history of women is not the same thing as *feminism*, which she defines as an explicit attempt to improve women's conditions. Feminism is "a particularly reflexive impulse of women grouping," Young emphasizes, "women grouping in order to change or eliminate the structures that serialize them."[1] This distinction is crucial to understanding the specific scope and purpose of this book. It explains the difference between the history of American women and the history of American feminism. Feminist thought and activism—the organizing theme of the following collection of documents—is only a small (albeit crucial) part of the history of women in colonial North America and the United States. Both women's history and feminism depend on female subjectivity: the felt experience of being a woman. But another, essential element of feminism is the deliberate creation of solidarity among women: it is a self conscious effort to connect with others for the express purpose of more effectively challenging sexual inequality.

One problem, though, with defining feminism through the idea of solidarity is that the history of feminism, at least among women in the United States, is anything but one of unity. In both its theory and practice, American feminism has embraced exclusion, in some ways matching the social divisiveness found in United States history at large. African-American female thinkers have made clear how racial bias has been written into non-black feminist politics. White feminist thought, as bell hooks explains, is often produced "from a standpoint that ignores black women's experiences and thus reinforces white supremacist thinking by viewing white women's experiences as the universal standard for evaluating gender status and identity."[2] By concentrating purely on issues of sexism, many white feminists extend the prejudices of a dominant race, failing to realize their own implication in and to some extent responsibility for the subjugation of other women.

Consider Charlotte Perkins Gilman, who—as author of "The Yellow Wallpaper" (1892), *Women and Economics* (1898), her own monthly journal *The Forerunner* (1909–16), and voluminous other writings of social science, literary criticism, utopian fiction, autobiography, and poetry—is rightfully considered to be one of the most intellectually productive feminists in

United States history. Gilman also adopted, however, some of the most conservative racial views of her day—prejudices that necessarily "color" the value of her feminist thought. Gilman openly described blacks as an "inferior" race, adding that their current "degenerative" status caused a drag on "human evolution," inevitably slowing the social progress of white America. In typical fashion, Gilman offered a comprehensive answer to the "negro problem," suggesting that the least evolved blacks be separated out of society and placed in a compulsory state-run corps until they could pass out of that group. This class of black internees would include, of course, a large number of "women," the same group Gilman insisted, in other contexts, needed to "set ourselves free" and whose independence determined overall "human development."[3] This contradiction in Gilman's thought is an extreme example of racism within feminism—of course not all white feminists have believed these things—but the point should by now be clear: if feminism involves the coming together of women (a process of "grouping"), then it needs to be realized that the social dynamics of that process have brought diversity as well as consensus, exclusion as well as solidarity, and opposition as well as unity.

The intellectual history of feminism—how the movement developed conceptually and theoretically, as a body of political thought, as an "ism"—is also largely a story of conflict and schism. Consider, for instance, the origins of the word "feminism" in the United States. As Nancy Cott has explained, "feminism" did not appear regularly in print or public speech until the 1910s, with common usage beginning in 1913.[4] And yet by 1914 one could read in the popular magazine *Current Opinion* that, in addition to the immediate rise of anti-feminist thought, "[n]ow it appears that there are two emergent forces in the feminist movement itself." The article goes on to cite Charlotte Perkins Gilman in *The Forerunner*, who distinguished between "Female Feminists"—those who believe fundamental differences exist between the sexes and that women need the opportunity for full expression of their distinct attributes—and "Human Feminists"—those who minimize sexual difference and emphasize that women should be allowed to develop themselves as people, free from pre-existent notions of proper feminine identity and behavior.

Notice how these two strands of feminism are, as *Current Opinion* recognized, "not only distinct but opposed."[5] The prefixes "human" and "female" do not signify variations of a common definition of feminism; they are, rather, set against each other as opposites, involving wholly different formulations of female self-identity and suggesting competing agendas for political mobilization. American feminism—before and after the word entered the national lexicon—has had no true "essence," except perhaps this one of opposition and duality. This point, as paradoxical as it is, needs to be considered in any intellectual history of American feminism: American feminist thought has developed through the creation of a series of mutually exclusive categories, usually organized in a series of either–or choices, or what some theorists would call "binary oppositions."

Keep this point in mind while studying the documents. To recognize the binate nature of feminist thought is to gain critical distance on the intellectual limitations of American feminism. This distancing is not necessarily in order to transcend these dualisms, or even to try always to move past them. If we return to Gilman's delineation of "Female" and "Human" feminists we can see how this binary (and its many variations) is ingrained in generations of American feminist discourse. In 1855, for instance, we find Elizabeth Cady Stanton debating

Antoinette Brown in the women's journal *The Una* about the existence of "natural" differences between the sexes. And this same core issue—whether women should deem themselves not only equal to but also fundamentally the same as men—still constitutes the most basic division in late-twentieth century feminist theory. What Gilman called "human" feminism is commonly known today as "equality" feminism: it urges the full integration of women into society, demanding women's equal rights, equal work, equal pay, and, generally, equal status and treatment in private and public relations; equality feminism bases itself on an ideal of the autonomous human individual, aiming ultimately to erase most if not all distinctions based on sex. And what Gilman labeled "Female" feminism is now known as "difference" feminism: it values women's unique perspective and envisions a society in which women are not subject to male-dominated institutions, values, and individualist-based standards of self-identity; instead of pushing for a sexually-integrated society, difference feminism envisions an autonomous female world, one that ultimately separates the concepts of femininity and masculinity.

Attention to this and other categories within feminist thought, then, is crucial to understanding the intellectual history of American feminism: dualisms help us reconstruct ideas as they were thought at the time under study; they also help locate continuities in feminism, giving it a visible and "usable past." We can see something of a tradition, for instance, running from Anne Hutchinsons's battle to realize equal status of men within the Puritan church, through Mary Gove Nichols's strong, wide-ranging assertions in the 1850s of women's sexual freedom, up to Naomi Wolf's problematic lifestyle feminism or "power feminism," in which individualist-minded women succeed in corporate America and simply have "fun." We can also recognize a counter-tradition, from Catharine Beecher's mid-nineteenth century insistence that women's power to effect social reform, including abolition of slavery, lay exclusively in her private feminine influence, to Camille Paglia's assertion of absolute differences between active male sexuality and a passive female sex principle.

We want to urge readers here, though, to guard against accepting the equality-difference split as a complete accounting of American feminism. Dualisms, while historically edifying, have always been far too schematic. The categorization of feminism into sets of either–or decisions obscures the full range of ways women have formulated their opposition to male-based systems of power. To draw mutually exclusive lines of feminist thought is to overlook how individual feminists have mixed and matched categories, refusing the confines of neatly delineated binaries.

Once again, the expansive thought of Charlotte Perkins Gilman provides a good example. Even though she recognized (and thereby promoted) the equality-difference split—and even though she identified with the equality or "Human" side of the equation—much of her thought advanced the difference or "Female" tradition of feminism. Gilman recognized distinctive female characteristics, as in her utopian novel *Herland* (1915), which presents a separate society of women who have a strong commitment to mothering and who have banished "masculine" values of competition.

In general terms, dualisms work against appreciation of the multiplicity of feminist perspectives. To assert an either–or vision of feminism not only lessens the ability to recognize those women who choose both (or neither) poles, but it can finally narrow that vision until only one side of the equation is illuminated. Most dualistic accounts of feminism privilege one viewpoint or the other as the essence of feminism, representing it as the most productive for contemporary feminism and, in less than objective hindsight, the one that has predominated historically. This is a pivotal point at which unnecessary exclusion begins in feminist theorizing. The act of defining "true feminism" involves subordinating those outside of the fold. While categorical systems of thought have made it easier to tell who is a feminist, they have also made it easier to identify who is *not* a feminist—a concern, in some feminist discourses, that eclipses attention to the different ways women subvert male power. Indeed, this is another problem of dualistic thinking: one's politics are determined by and, ultimately, confined to what one opposes; one is defined, in other words, in the negative—by what one is not rather than what one is.

In light of the dangers of essentializing feminism, some women's historians and other scholars have fashioned an explicitly inclusive and self-consciously anti-theoretical formulation of the movement. This effort begins with finding an "unrestrictive definition of feminism" itself, as Nancy Cott has written, one that "dispense[s] with totalizing, either/or questions (was she a feminist or not?)." One definition that Cott favors is offered by Linda Gordon: "Feminism is a critique of male supremacy, formed and offered in the light of a will to change it, which in turn assumes a conviction that it is changeable."[6] Gordon's definition has been central to our project, as it values action over essence, circumventing rigid, dualistic tests of true feminism. Moreover, this conception of feminism not only eliminates the need to choose one side or another of a binary opposition, it goes one step further in suggesting the benefit of holding equality-difference, individualism-community, and other dualisms in creative and productive tension. The conceptual umbrella of feminism is broad enough to contain diverse and even contradictory elements, allowing women to choose the ideas that best apply to the political exigencies of the time; they are thus not always constrained by an overarching and predetermined agenda that dictates choices without regard to context and consequences.

"Feminism" or "Feminisms"?

This broad-based, non-exclusive conceptualization of feminism is pluralist in nature: it is most concerned with practical details of activism, focusing on specific strategies of political organization and local sites of resistance.

But does feminism comprise nothing more or less than a sequence of local acts of resistance? As suggested above, some feminists (Iris Marion Young and Nancy Cott, for example) believe that a necessary part of the movement has been the recognition of "women acting as women"—that is, a self-consciousness of womanhood and of one's connection to that community. Who, though, are the "women" who have self-consciously acted as women? With what women have they tried to connect? And in the name of which "women" has the feminist movement acted? Historically, mainstream feminist thought has too often relied uncritically on the concept of "women" as a legitimating and cohesive category, while in practice including only a few social groups and racial types within its rubric. The utopian female intersubjectivity—women acting as, with, and for women—that has undergirded so much feminist discourse has in fact been imperfect, excluding and omitting large numbers of American women.

As articulated by middle-class white women, feminism has more often than not served the needs and interests of those women alone, women who have often been unable to recognize that the "sisterhood" of women extended also to women of color. For instance, both before and after the Civil War some women's rights activists debated whether or not they should work for the abolition of slavery and for the rights of black women during Reconstruction—about whether or not, in other words, the rights of African-American women were "woman's rights." A century later, Betty Friedan's *The Feminine Mystique* centered its analysis on the plight of upper middle-class housewives, women confined to the home and a life of mindless leisure. Clearly not accounting for variables of race and class, Friedan omitted the majority of women who had neither the money nor the ideological impetus to leave the paid work force and stay at home. To the extent that African-American women—to name just one marginalized group—have been less than supportive of mainstream or white American feminism, it is because, as Pauline Terrelonge Stone has argued, "[r]acism is . . . so entrenched among many white women, that black females have been reluctant to admit that anything affecting the white female could also affect them."[7] Women of all races have both perceived and construed the category of "women" as a bar to collective action as much as they have seen it as the foundation of feminist collectivity.

In addition to disagreeing over the identity of feminist subjects, marginalized groups of women have also pointed out the propensity of the movement to fix exclusively on issues of sexual inequality. Deborah King describes this singleminded agenda as "monist": it illuminates only one form of domination, insisting that "social relations can be reduced to one factor" of gender.[8] For an illustrative case of monism in practice, consider how the debate over the extension of suffrage after the Civil War routinely asserted that either black men or white women could gain the vote—but not both. Black women found themselves torn between former anti-slavery organizations, which sought to extend the franchise to blacks (i.e., black men), and the woman's rights movement, which sought the vote for women (i.e., white women). In such an either–or situation, black women fell into a middle-ground of non-identity; neither black men nor white women, they were asked to support causes that did not include them.

The liminal situation of African-American women reveals how the subjugation of most women has arisen not simply from an ingrained sexism but also from intersecting forms of oppression such as racism, heterosexism, and class inequality. Women who are oppressed by other systems as well as the sex/gender system are necessarily oppressed *differently* by sexism: a poor, black woman does not experience sexual inequality in the same way that a wealthy white woman does. As a consequence, women who are not white, middle-class, and heterosexual, while not denying the importance of fighting sexism, have refused to grant that it is paramount. Many black feminists, for instance, will not make a choice between race or gender as the predominant category that structures their resistance, insisting on the need to hold both within the same world view.

The phenomenon of monism among American feminists results from a failure to conceptualize adequately the relation between sexism and forms of oppression based on categories other than gender. When they have theorized the relation between race and feminism at all, white feminists have traditionally done so mostly through analogy, claiming that oppression on the grounds of race is structurally equal to oppression on the grounds of sex and is experienced in the same way. When Mary Gove Nichols argued in 1857 that white women are "enslaved" by marriage laws as inexorably as the African-American is by slavery, she implied not only that institutionalized racism and sexism are analogous but also that racism is secondary, serving merely to illuminate the horrors of sexism. In fact, Nichols adds, slavery is only "*nearly* parallel in its evils" to marriage. This method of integrating race into theories of feminism works to subsume race into gender—making race invisible at the very moment it is ostensibly being rendered visible.

Recently, feminist theorists of color have moved beyond the confines of the race-sex analogy, employing first the concept of the "double jeopardy" of race and sex oppression and then of the "triple jeopardy" of racism, sexism, and classism. Deborah King has called for a move even beyond the "triple jeopardy" model, which, while it does recognize the different kinds of discrimination women of color face, does so in an additive way: the effects of race and class are simply appended to the effects of sex. The model of triple jeopardy presupposes that each variable—race, sex, and class—has a "single, direct, and independent effect on status." King, on the other hand, thinks that the effects are not independent of each other, proposing an "interactive model," which she calls "multiple jeopardy." The term "multiple" incorporates "not only . . . several, simultaneous oppressions" but also the "multiplicative relationships among them as well. In other words," she continues, "the equivalent formulation is racism multiplied by sexism multiplied by classism."[9] This model recognizes the multiple linkages between different forms of structural inequality and also the "multiplicative"—as opposed to additive—oppressive effect that such linkages bring to bear on an individual.

Our collection—our historical vision of American feminism, as it were—is fundamentally shaped by the theorizing of women of color in terms of the multiple ways in which women have been oppressed and by the similarly multiple and contextualized positions from which women have acted to challenge their oppression. These positions are always gendered somehow—or they could not be considered "feminism"—but gender is not the only or even always the principal point of critique or site of resistance. For women of all races—including white—those disempowering systems that support male privilege often also support class privilege, heterosexual privilege, or white privilege. When one subverts a certain racist practice, then, one may also be subverting sexism at the same time. For instance, when Harriet Jacobs exposed in her autobiography the evils of slavery, she also exposed the sexual and economic power that white men had over both white and black women.

In light of the wholesale critique of the category "women" as it has historically been employed by the mainstream feminist movement, the word has lost its status as a unified concept fixed in a simple binary opposition to "men." It can best be understood, instead, as a dispersed, fluid, and contested category. This is not to say, however, that a woman's self-conscious belief that she is as a part of the collective group "women" is no longer important to a definition of feminism. Philosopher Judith Butler has argued that it is precisely "the rifts among women over the content of the term ["women"] that ought to be affirmed as the ungrounded ground of feminist theory."[10] While continuing to act for "women," feminists should constantly question their own internal preconceptions and biases about what that entails.

This collection of documents demonstrates that there has indeed been a history of such self-questioning; it reveals both a lack of and a struggle toward consensus about who the "women" are in whose name feminism has spoken, written, and acted. These rifts need not be wholly divisive but can be, rather, the basis of a self-aware, flexible, and contingent community of feminist interests.

Women and the Public

Our conception of the public nature of American feminism is influenced by two key points. The first is the imbrication of public spheres of feminist activism with the private realm of women's lives. "The personal is political"—a stock phrase of mid- to late-twentieth-century feminism—still provides an important reminder that, in contrast to the traditionally masculine world of electoral politics, feminist politics has always concerned itself with so-called private issues of domestic labor, sexuality, family, and the like. Feminists have strived continually to transform personal power relations between men and women into the stuff of politics, taking what often occurs "behind closed doors" and exposing it to the vicissitudes of public analysis and opinion-making. Integral to this understanding of a feminist public, as Sara Evans has pointed out, is the history of American women's voluntary associations.[11] Organizations such as moral reform and temperance societies have provided an essential link between the lived daily experience of women and opportunities for political change, collapsing the border between public and private worlds.

A second critical idea concerning women's public sphere involves the political value of those feminist institutions, discourses, and strategies, that are separate from and opposed to dominant social and cultural forces. Women's integration into masculine sources of power and prestige—from labor unions to elite social clubs, from schools and colleges to the United States Congress—is certainly a central component of American feminism; but we also mean to emphasize the "contestatory function" of what Nancy Fraser calls "subaltern counterpublics"—"parallel discursive arenas where members of subordinated social groups invent and circulate counterdiscourses, which in turn permit them to formulate oppositional interpretations of their identities, interests, and needs." Counterpublics, as Fraser points out, have a dual purpose: they provide "spaces of withdrawal and regroupment" for those already located outside of the fold of power; at the same time, though, they "function as bases and training ground for agitational activities directed towards wider publics."[12] In as much as feminist counterpublics are separate enclaves, then, they also foster communication for the purpose of disseminating their oppositional message. Many of the feminist words and deeds represented in this collection originated from such public associations of activism and subversion—counterpublics of women created both to provide a separate source of strength and purity of feminist purpose but also meant to connect with and change the institutional powers that be.

This documentary history does not pretend to provide the impossible—a coherent, comprehensive narrative of integrative and "counterpublic" American feminism; but we do, however, want to close by tracing the various key institutions, both separatist and integrated, into which women have entered at specific historical periods.

Women's voices were first heard within the church, as they intermittently challenged traditional religious practices in the colonies. In particular, women questioned their place within the Puritan establishment, drawing for their dissent on more marginal religions, such as Quakerism, or on their own material experiences as women.

In the post-Revolutionary period, some women not only had available, for the first time, some kind of systematic formal education, but they also started to found separate female academies. The subsequent rise in women's literacy rates led at the end of the eighteenth century to the creation of a distinctly feminine literary culture, which included the first women's magazines and the first popular women's fiction—novels of seduction and sentiment.

Beginning in the late 1830s and 1840s, American women became active in a variety of reform movements, notably anti-slavery, from which the nineteenth century women's rights movement grew. Central to this key development were woman's rights conventions, which proliferated in the middle of the century; while not formal institutions, the conventions established networks and communities of activist women and inculcated strategies of organization building—not the least of which was the art of public speaking. Drawing on organizational skills acquired in the early years of the women's rights movement, feminists in the second half of the nineteenth century created a number of women's institutions—from middle-class women's clubs to trade unions and suffrage associations. While women had first gained entry into the medical profession, as physicians, in the 1840s, it was not until the 1870s and 1880s that women's encroachment into the previously male bastions of the elite professions such as the law and higher education became discernable.

With the dramatic increase in immigration and the rapid growth of an urban industrial social environment at the turn of the twentieth century, American feminism became markedly more diverse and complex. Along with mass immigration to the United States, a more regionally, racially, and ethnically diverse group of American women started to challenge forms of masculine dominance. This variegated feminist consciousness shaped itself during and in conjunction with the rise of modern mass culture and media, including widely circulated popular magazines and newspapers, many of which represented the interests of specific populations such as Chinese-Americans in California or Jews in New York. White middle-class women made still greater inroads within the university, gaining a foothold in both white-collar professions and academia itself, hence adding to the burgeoning intellectual class in New York and other large cities.

While many historians continue to characterize the period between the passage of the Nineteenth Amendment (which, in 1920, gave all women the vote) and the 1960s as a time in which feminism remained dormant, we trace the continued activity of women within already established institutions such as trade unions, voluntary clubs, and professional associations. These four decades were a particularly active period for those women interested in women's labor rights, in part because of women's massive entry into the paid labor force during two world wars. The period is also marked by heightened socialist consciousness, and some feminists even attempted a union between feminist activism and communism.

The late 1960s saw what has been called the "second-wave" of American feminism, a re-emergent, broad-based, and coherent movement for women's "liberation" akin to that of the 1850s. Just as the "first-wave" of American feminism had grown from the anti-slavery movement, the "second-wave" was historically interwoven with African-Americans' struggle for civil rights. Along with the founding of mainstream organizations such as the National Organization of Women (NOW), the '60s and '70s also saw the large-scale emergence of women's small groups and collectives, each centered on experiences of oppression and communal responses including radical plans for liberation.

In the late twentieth century, during a time of a "backlash" against feminism and a retrenchment of the movement, women have continued to assert themselves in public life, attaining increasingly influential positions in business, the university, and in the government. Perhaps in part as a result of the success of some highly visible women, some have heralded a "postfeminist" age, claiming that feminism is obsolete and should be either abandoned or radically revised. Feminism has thus become still more fragmented and contentious, producing internally conflicted and opposing views of itself and its potential role in women's lives. While the rhetoric of the 1990s puts feminism in a unprecedented state of crisis, our book aims to show that such contention has not only always been present but is, perhaps, feminism's grounding premise. In other words, American feminism continues.

Notes

1. Iris Marion Young, "Gender As Seriality: Thinking About Women as a Social Collective," *Signs* 19 (Spring 1994), 728, 736.

2. bell hooks, "Black Students Who Reject Feminism," *The Chronicle of Higher Education*, July 13, 1994, A44.

3. Charlotte Perkins Gilman, "A Suggestion on the Negro Problem," originally published in *The American Journal of Sociology* 14 (July 1908), 78–85, reprinted in *Charlotte Perkins Gilman: A Nonfiction Reader*, ed. Larry Ceplair (New York: Columbia University Press, 1991), 176–83; Charlotte Perkins Gilman, "Our Androcentric Culture; or the Man-Made World," *The Forerunner* 1 (June 1910), 20.

4. Nancy F. Cott, *The Grounding of Modern Feminism* (New Haven: Yale University Press, 1987), 13.

5. "The Conflict Between 'Human' and 'Female' Feminism," *Current Opinion* 56 (1914), 9.

6. Nancy F. Cott, "What's In a Name? The Limits of 'Social Feminism': or, Expanding the Vocabulary of Women's History," *Journal of American History* 76 (1989), 826; Linda Gordon, "What's New in Women's History" in *Feminist Studies/Critical Studies*, ed. Teresa De Lauretis (Bloomington: Indiana University Press, 1986), 29.

7. Pauline Terrelonge Stone, "Feminist Consciousness and Black Women" in *Women: A Feminist Perspective*, ed. Jo Freeman (Palo Alto: Mayfield, 1979), 583.

8. Deborah K. King, "Multiple Jeopardy, Multiple Consciousness: The Context of a Black Feminist Ideology," *Signs* 14 (1988), 51.

9. Ibid., 46–47.

10. Judith Butler, "Contingent Foundations: Feminism and the Question of 'Postmodernism'" in *Feminist Theorize the Political*, ed. Judith Butler and Joan Scott (New York: Routledge, 1992), 16.

11. Sara M. Evans, "Women's History and Political Theory: Toward a Feminist Approach to Public Life," in *Visible Women: New Essays On American Activism*, ed. Nancy A. Hewitt and Suzanne Lebstock (Urbana: University of Illinois Press, 1993), 119–39; also important is Mary P. Ryan, *Women in Public: Between Banners and Ballots, 1825–1880* (Baltimore: The Johns Hopkins University Press, 1990).

12. Nancy Fraser, "Rethinking the Public Sphere: A Contribution to the Critique of Actually Existing Democracy," in *Between Borders: Pedagogy and the Politics of Cultural Studies*, ed. Henry A. Giroux and Peter McLaren (New York: Routledge, 1994), 84–85.

PART I

Identities Through Adversity: Women in Colonial North America

THE FIRST EUROPEAN SETTLERS IN NEW ENGLAND brought with them family structure that vested authority unambiguously in the hands of the father. Woman's place in this "patriarchal" institution was clearly delimited; less autonomous individuals than wives and mothers, women throughout the North American colonies were subject to an intricately organized hierarchy that placed them below father, husband, brothers, and even adult sons. Unable to inherit either the land or the offices of their fathers, women became virtually invisible in the public life of the thirteen colonies. With its strict gender stratification and divisions of labor, the patriarchal family served as a model for and basis of social and political relations and institutions. In the 1637 trial of Anne Hutchinson for dissent from the Puritan church, for instance, the issue of Hutchinson's revolt against the subordinate status of women was inextricable from her religious rebellion. As one of her accusers proclaimed: "You have rather bine a Husband than a Wife and a preacher than a Hearer; and a Magistrate than a subject"—thus drawing a direct line between Hutchinson's religious unruliness and her perceived political and sexual disorder.

Patriarchal power in the colonies was not absolute, however. Due to the centrality of the household in an agrarian, primarily subsistence economy, women did create important economic and social roles for themselves. The case of Margaret Brent illustrates both how women could gain some power in the political sphere of colonial life, and also how the law inevitably circumscribed that power. In 1648, Brent petitioned the Maryland Assembly for the right to vote, an unprecedented act that was nevertheless in keeping with Brent's active legal and political career. She never married and frequently served as her brothers' business advisor and legal representative. A major landowner in her own right, Brent also represented herself in court cases, and for her acumen she was named the executrix of Maryland's governor—a close friend—when he died in 1657. It was on the grounds of her legal right to protect the former governor's interests that Brent sought the vote. Although her request was denied, the record shows that Brent "protested."

Aside from the economic and legal actions of a handful of prominent, land-owning women, the first stirrings of feminism in the colonies were the individual acts of rebellion against one institution—the Puritan church. Dissenting women, however, necessarily challenged those other institutions from which religion was inseparable, notably family and gender. Paradoxically, these early feminists drew their power to challenge established religion and the sexual hierarchies it instituted from Puritanism itself. Religious dissenters in New England carried the Puritan idea of the "aloneness" of believers in their relation with God so far that even the ministry became an obstacle to faith. "Grace," which was located within the self, accrued liberating possibilities in that it potentially challenged the hegemony of the clergy—the powerful elite of both church and state. The radical potential of the individual and its corollary—the spiritual equality of each individual regardless of sex—caused tensions in a society based on female subordination and finally created an avenue for women to question that subordination. The assertion of one's inner feeling of God's grace, of a distinctly personal revelation, could be used to justify rebellion against any and all of the authoritarian structures in which the individual was situated. Conversely, any woman who questioned the church was also perceived to be disavowing her place in secular and family life, of transgressing even her sex. In subsequent centuries it was this "wayward" and radically individualistic Puritan *woman* who would become an icon of the feminist individual, challenging a culture that on the one hand celebrates individualism and on the other hand limits, by gender and race, its realization.

One major strand of dissent was the Antinomian heresy, in which Anne Hutchinson played a central part. Antinomianism placed the private experience of religion above the formal rules of orthodox Puritanism, stressing that questions of salvation were decided between an individual and God, without the intervention of ministers. Hutchinson came under attack from the Puritan clergy of the Massachusetts Bay Colony precisely because of her defiance of their authority; she held meetings in her home every Sunday to discuss the day's sermon, even as rumors began to circulate that both the religious and political leadership were being criticized. Ordered to appear before a convocation of ministers, Hutchinson was ultimately excommunicated and banished; she and five of her six children were killed by Indians five years later on Long Island.

Another strand of religious dissent in colonial North America was Quakerism. Like the Antinomians, the Quakers believed in the "Inner Light"—rather than the authoritarian, institutional structures of the church—as a means to truth and salvation. The Society of Friends empowered women through their belief in spiritual equality and also in the development of co-equal status in church organization, including encouraging women to preach. The women's movement of the nineteenth-century was in part made possible by the legacy of Quaker women in the seventeenth and eighteenth centuries; indeed, a large number of the first nationally-known women's rights advocates were Quakers, including Sarah and Angelina Grimké, Lucretia Mott, and Susan B. Anthony.

One of the most prominent of early Quaker women was Mary Dyer, who exemplified the Quaker belief in religious freedom and also nonviolence, two values that would persist and flourish within the women's movement. Like Hutchinson, Dyer was tried and convicted in Massachusetts for religious dissent; she became the only woman executed for defying the Puritan authorities. Dyer protested, specifically, the 1658 Massachusetts law that banished all Quakers from the colony on pain of death. She had come to Boston after the passage of the law in order to support two friends who were imprisoned; after being banished twice by the authorities, Dyer returned to Boston, refusing to leave peacefully after the magistrates executed her friends and fellow Quakers. Accusing the magistrates of "disobedience," Dyer warned them in a letter of 1659 of the dire consequences of their sins. She paid for her challenge to Puritan authority and for her convictions about the freedom of conscience with her life.

When trying dissenters, Massachusetts courts inevitably delivered a sentence of banishment, forcing "heretics" into areas beyond the bounds of the Puritan theocracy such as Rhode Island and Pennsylvania. In a sense, this banishment functions as a metaphor for a second legacy that early American rebellious women bequeathed to subsequent generations of feminists: an oppositional or "liminal" impulse—an unruly existence, in other words, beyond the pale of established structures. Whether by choice (as in the case of the religious dissenters) or not (as in the case of Mary Rowlandson, forcibly removed from her town by Indians), some colonial women lived outside the confines of patriarchal society. While they spoke from beyond the literal and institutional borders of their culture, however, these women shaped and changed that culture, contributing in part to the loosening of oppressive hierarchies.

Perhaps the epitome of the liminal woman—of her social marginality, of her occupation of the borders of society—is the figure of the witch. Accusations of witchcraft reflect the anxiety of a culture that anticipates its own dissolution and thus demonizes and expels that which it fears is the cause of incipient social breakdown. Often that "culprit" in colonial New England was the independent, unmarried woman, more frequently the victim of witch-hunting than any other group. Carol Karlsen has added that "witches" were often women without brothers or sons—women, that is, who "stood in the way of the orderly transmission of property from one generation of males to another."[1] Clearly having gained enough power to provoke such deep-seated fears in the first place, the "witch" was at the same time a victim of those social processes that she defied.

Both Susannah Martin and Martha Carrier were victims of the Salem witchcraft "hysteria," which began in 1692 when a group of adolescent girls claimed to be possessed and began naming several of their neighbors as having consorted with the devil. Out of the 200 people (mostly women) who were accused of witchcraft in Salem during the course of the summer of 1692, thirteen women and six men were finally executed.

Some of the women executed as witches at Salem were clearly nontraditional women who did not conform to ideals of Puritan womanhood. A contemporary, Thomas Maule, for instance, estimated that two-thirds of the accused in the Salem witchcraft trials had either rebelled against their parents or committed adultery. Certainly, women accused of witchcraft were often on the margins of society, frequently unmarried and sometimes with a history of outspokenness. Susannah Martin had been involved in altercations with her neighbors; she expressed anger toward her accusers at her trial, using her own reading of the Bible to try to discredit them. Martha Carrier, charged with at least thirteen murders, had argued with neighbors over land and threatened a male antagonist with physical violence; in her examination, she charged the magistrate as the only "black [i.e., satanic] man" she had seen and insisted that she be believed over a group of hysterical girls. Like Mary Dyer, Martin and Carrier died because of their integrity; the public legacy of all three women helped to ensure that the execution of "deviant" women in New England would not last.

That women began to develop a distinct identity and voice in colonial America was a prerequisite for the subsequent emergence of a collective and public feminist movement.

---

1. Carol F. Karlsen, *The Devil in the Shape of a Woman: Witchcraft in Colonial New England* (New York: Norton, 1987), 116, 213.

Only as women began to define and represent themselves could they start to transcend gender roles imposed from without by the state, the church, the law, and other social and cultural forms. Women in America first found a public voice and identity through religion, again discovering, paradoxically, a certain amount of freedom in the system that also oppressed them. Puritanism incorporated an emphasis on self-scrutiny, often in the form of written conversion narratives and spiritual autobiographies, in which one would detail personal struggles on the path to salvation. At a time when women had virtually no social or institutional frameworks within which to express themselves, written or spoken words of religious introspection and nascent subjectivity became the first step to subverting patriarchal discourse and power.

Two of the earliest autobiographies by women in America were those of Mary Rowlandson and Elizabeth Ashbridge, both of which began to shape women's distinct consciousness and individuality. Published in Boston in 1682, Mary Rowlandson's narrative tells the story of her three-month long captivity by the Naragansett tribe of Native Americans. Rowlandson's account of her experience with the Naragansetts is one of the earliest of the captivity narratives, regarded by some as the first distinctively "American" literary genre. In her account, Rowlandson is clearly directed by the Puritan belief in the providential nature of the colonists' encounter with the Indians; she interprets each event as part of God's divine plan to test his "chosen people" through their encounter with the "evil" natives. Placed in exigent circumstances, however, Rowlandson's individuality—separate from the Puritan orthodoxy—starts to emerge; she finds her own food, makes things to trade with her captors, and even shifts her opinion about Indians, refusing to recognize them as simply evil.

Elizabeth Ashbridge quite literally creates herself anew in her autobiography of 1774; there is virtually no record of her other than that which her own hand transcribes. Evidence suggests that Ashbridge was authorized by her local Quaker meeting at Goshen, Pennsylvania, to travel and to preach and that it was generally acknowledged that she spoke with an increasingly authoritative voice. Ashbridge's text is a spiritual autobiography—the story of her struggle to achieve grace and a divine life, a story given symbolic expression in the dream she has of a woman bearing a lamp. As a Quaker, Ashbridge's "lamp" is, of course, the Quaker "Inner Light" that Mary Dyer died for over a century earlier; it is also the light of personal faith for which Anne Hutchinson was excommunicated. Like both Dyer and Hutchinson, Ashbridge's story is not just a quest for *spiritual* freedom though; her text, makes explicit her challenge to patriarchal institutional authority in secular areas of life such as the family, a challenge that was more covert in the religious struggles of Hutchinson and Dyer. Ashbridge's search for her personal truth is undertaken not just in the face of male-dominated religion but also in the face of tyrannical social and sexual relations, and her trials include, an exploitative master and a coercive, abusive husband. Finally, Ashbridge does achieve not only freedom of conscience but also a relatively autonomous identity.

Another literary genre at which women excelled in the colonial period was poetry, which was originally a distinctly masculine discourse in Puritan New England. Women poets not only stepped into the public sphere themselves, giving future women writers intellectual forebears, but they also carried on women's cultural work of defining their own subjectivity, making their own preoccupations part of the store of public knowledge. Anne Bradstreet first encroached on that terrain in 1650 when her book of poems, *The Tenth Muse,* was published in London, the first book of original poetry written in America. Publicly challenging the preconception that poetry was a masculine endeavor, Bradstreet asserts in "The Prologue" that "I am obnoxious to each carping tongue / Who says my hand a needle better fits." In both "The Prologue" and "The Author to Her Book," Bradstreet reflects on and defends her own role as a woman poet. Like proponents of women's education in the late-eighteenth century, Bradstreet insists that her intellectual work is not incompatible with domestic duties and child-rearing.

About a century after Bradstreet issued her volume of poetry, Phillis Wheatley became the first Africa-American to publish a poetic work, her *Poems on Various Subjects, Religious and Moral* (1773). Wheatley's poetry was a distinct assertion of subjectivity at a time when most Anglo-Americans believed that African-Americans had none; there was even a "hearing" shortly after publication to determine if Wheatley was in fact the writer of the poems, since intellectual output from a black woman and a slave at that time was considered scarcely credible. Wheatley's writing, then, began to replace the patriarchal constructions of women—especially African-American women—with their own authentic self-constructions. Wheatley's poetry, however, contributed to political issues other than the subjectivity of women and slaves. "On Being Brought from Africa to America" expresses a spiritual vision that necessitates an equality between the races inimicable to the institution of slavery. And "The Right Honourable William, Earl of Dartmouth" reflects Wheatley's interest in the politics of the pre-Revolutionary ferment. Her poetry represents, albeit somewhat obliquely, the first entry of an African-American woman into the political issues of slavery and British imperialism.

To write about "feminism" in the colonial period is to commit somewhat of an anachronism; and those few historians who have even broached the topic of feminism in early America do so tentatively. The "disorder" of colonial women was not, after all, directed self-consciously against the collective situation of women *as* women. Anne Hutchinson is probably closest to such an ideal, as she did specifically argue for the right of women to exercise religious freedom and as she drew a crowd of largely female followers. (A contemporary of Hutchinson wrote that "'the weaker sex' set her up as 'a Priest' and 'thronged' after her.")[2] But these early rebels and intellectuals laid the groundwork for future feminist action—daring to transgress their allotted place, daring to oppose patriarchal authority within the institutions of the church and the family, and daring to move into masculine literary territories. Colonial women developed, in great adversity, an individuality that they expressed publicly.

2. Lyle Koehler, "The Case of the American Jezebels: Anne Hutchinson and Female Agitation During the Years of Antinomian Turmoil, 1636–1640," *William and Mary Quarterly* 31 (1974): 61.

1

The Examination of Anne Hutchinson (1637)

Mr. Winthrop, governor. Mrs. Hutchinson, you are called here as one of those that have troubled the peace of the commonwealth and the churches here; you are known to be a woman that hath had a great share in the promoting and divulging of those opinions that are causes of this trouble, and to be nearly joined not only in affinity and affection with some of those the court had taken notice of and passed censure upon, but you have spoken divers things as we have been informed very prejudicial to the honour of the churches and ministers thereof, and you have maintained a meeting and an assembly in your house that hath been condemned by the general assembly as a thing not tolerable nor comely in the sight of God nor fitting for your sex, and notwithstanding that was cried down you have continued the same, therefore we have thought good to send for you to understand how things are, that if you be in an erroneous way we may reduce you that so you may become a profitable member here among us, otherwise if you be obstinate in your course that then the court may take such course that you may trouble us no further, therefore I would intreat you to express whether you do not assent and hold in practice to those opinions and factions that have been handled in court already, that is to say, and factions that have been handled in court already, that is to say, whether you do not justify Mr. Wheelwright's sermon and the petition.

Mrs. Hutchinson. I am called here to answer before you but I hear no things laid to my charge.

Reprinted by permission of the publishers from *The History of the Colony and Province of Massachusetts-Bay* by Thomas Hutchinson, ed. Lawrence Shaw Mayo (Cambridge, Mass.: Harvard Univ. Press, 1936), 366–372, 375, 376, 383–384, 388, 391.

Gov. I have told you some already and more I can tell you.

Mrs. H. Name one Sir.

Gov. Have I not named some already?

Mrs. H. What have I said or done?

Gov. Why for your doings, this you did harbour and countenance those that are parties in this faction that you have heard of.

Mrs. H. That's matter of conscience, Sir.

Gov. Your conscience you must keep or it must be kept for you.

Mrs. H. Must not I then entertain the saints because I must keep my conscience.

Gov. Say that one brother should commit felony or treason and come to his brother's house, if he knows him guilty and conceals him he is guilty of the same. It is his conscience to entertain him, but if his conscience comes into act in giving countenance and entertainment to him that hath broken the law he is guilty too. So if you do countenance those that are transgressors of the law you are in the same fact.

Mrs. H. What law do they transgress?

Gov. The law of God and of the state. . . .

Mrs. H. What law have I broken?

Gov. Why the fifth commandment.

Mrs. H. I deny that for he saith in the Lord.

Gov. You have joined with them in the faction.

Mrs. H. In what faction have I joined with them?

Gov. In presenting the petition.*

Mrs. H. Suppose I had set my hand to the petition what then?

Gov. You saw that case tried before.

Mrs. H. But I had not my hand to the petition.

Gov. You have councelled them.

Mrs. H. Wherein?

Gov. Why in entertaining them.

Mrs. H. What breach of law is that Sir?

Gov. Why dishonouring of parents.

Mrs. H. But put the case Sir that I do fear

*The Antinomian party presented a petition to the General Court in March, 1637 (editors' note).

the Lord and my parents, may not I entertain them that fear the Lord because my parents will not give me leave?

Gov. If they be the fathers of the commonwealth, and they of another religion, if you entertain them then you dishonour your parents and are justly punishable.

Mrs. H. If I entertain them, as they have dishonoured their parents I do.

Gov. No but you by countenancing them above others put honor upon them.

Mrs. H. I may put honor upon them as the children of God and as they do honor the Lord.

Gov. We do not mean to discourse with those of your sex but only this; you do adhere unto them and do endeavor to set forward this faction and so you do dishonour us.

Mrs. H. I do acknowledge no such thing neither do I think that I ever put any dishonour upon you.

Gov. Why do you keep such a meeting at your house as you do every week upon a set day?

Mrs. H. It is lawful for me so to do, as it is all your practices and can you find a warrant for yourself and condemn me for the same thing? The ground of my taking it up was, when I first came to this land because I did not go to such meetings as those were, it was presently reported that I did not allow for such meetings but held them unlawful and therefore in that regard they said I was proud and did despise all ordinances, upon that a friend came unto me and told me of it and I to prevent such aspersions took it up, but it was in practice before I came therefore I was not the first.

Gov. For this, that you appeal to our practice you need no confutation. If your meeting had answered to the former it had not been offensive, but I will say that there was no meeting of women alone, but your meeting is of another sort for there are sometimes men among you.

Mrs. H. There was never any man with us.

Gov. Well, admit there was no man at your meeting and that you was sorry for it, there is no warrant for your doings, and by what warrant do you continue such a course?

Mrs. H. I conceive there lyes a clear rule in Titus, that the elder women should instruct the younger and then I must have a time wherein I must do it.

Gov. All this I grant you, I grant you a time for it, but what is this to the purpose that you Mrs. Hutchinson must call a company together from their callings to come to be taught of you?

Mrs. H. Will it please you to answer me this and to give me a rule for them I will willingly submit to any truth. If any come to my house to be instructed in the ways of God what rule have I to put them away?

Gov. But suppose that a hundred men come unto you to be instructed will you forbear to instruct them?

Mrs. H. As far as I conceive I cross a rule in it.

Gov. Very well and do you not so here?

Mrs. H. No Sir for my ground is they are men.

Gov. Men and women all is one for that, but suppose that a man should come and say Mrs. Hutchinson I hear that you are a woman that God hath given his grace unto and you have knowledge in the word of God I pray instruct me a little, ought you not to instruct this man?

Mrs. H. I think I may.—Do you think it not lawful for me to teach women and why do you call me to teach the court?

Gov. We do not call you to teach the court but to lay open yourself.

Mrs. H. I desire you that you would then set me down a rule by which I may put them away that come unto me and so have peace in so doing.

Gov. You must shew your rule to receive them.

Mrs. H. I have done it.

Gov. I deny it because I have brought more arguments than you have.

Mrs. H. I say, to me it is a rule.

Mr. Endicot, an assistant. You say there are some rules unto you. I think there is a contradiction in your own words. What rule for your practice do you bring, only a custom in Boston.

Mrs. H. No Sir that was no rule to me but if

you look upon the rule in Titus it is a rule to me. If you convince me that it is no rule I shall yield.

Gov. You know that there is no rule that crosses another, but this rule crosses that in the Corinthians. But you must take it in this sense that elder women must instruct the younger about their business and to love their husbands and not to make them to clash.

Mrs. H. I do not conceive but that it is meant for some publick times.

Gov. Well, have you no more to say but this?

Mrs. H. I have said sufficient for my practice.

Gov. Your course is not to be suffered for, besides that we find such a course as this to be greatly prejudicial to the state, besides the occasion that it is to seduce many honest persons that are called to those meetings and your opinions being known to be different from the word of God may seduce many simple souls that resort unto you, besides that the occasion which hath come of late hath come from none but such as have frequented your meetings, so that now they are flown off from magistrates and ministers and this since they have come to you, and besides that it will not well stand with the common wealth that families should be neglected for so many neighbours and dames and so much time spent, we see no rule of God for this, we see not that any should have authority to set up any other exercises besides what authority hath already set up and so what hurt comes of this you will be guilty of and we for suffering you.

Mrs. H. Sir I do not believe that to be so.

Gov. Well, we see how it is we must therefore put it away from you or restrain you from maintaining this course.

Mrs. H. If you have a rule for it from God's word you may.

Gov. We are your judges, and not you ours and we must compel you to it.

Mrs. H. If it please you by authority to put it down I will freely let you for I am subject to your authority.

Mr. Bradstreet, an assistant. I would ask this question of Mrs. Hutchinson, whether you do think this is lawful? for then this will follow that all other women that do not are in a sin.

Mrs. H. I conceive this is a free will offering.

Bradstreet. If it be a free will offering you ought to forebear it because it gives offence.

Mrs. H. Sir, in regard of myself I could, but for others I do not yet see light but shall further consider of it.

Bradstreet. I am not against all women's meetings but do think them to be lawful.

Mr. Dudley, deputy governor. Here hath been much spoken concerning Mrs. Hutchinson's meetings and among other answers she saith that men come not there, I would ask you this one question then, whether never any man was at your meeting?

Gov. There are two meetings kept at their house.

Dep. Gov. How; is there two meetings?

Mrs. H. Ey Sir, I shall not equivocate, there is a meeting of men and women and there is a meeting only for women.

Dep. Gov. Are they both constant?

Mrs. H. No, but upon occasions they are deferred.

Mr. Endicot. Who teaches in the men's meetings none but men, do not women sometimes?

Mrs. H. Never as I heard, not one.

Dep. Gov. I would go a little higher with Mrs. Hutchinson. Abut three years ago we were all in peace. Mrs. Hutchinson from that time she came hath made a disturbance, and some that came over with her in the ship did inform me what she was as soon as she was landed. I being then in place dealt with the pastor and teacher of Boston and desired them to enquire of her, and then I was satisfied that she held nothing different from us, but within half a year after, she had vented divers of her strange opinions and had made parties in the country, and at length it comes that Mr. Cotton and Mr. Vane were of her judgment, but Mr. Cotton hath cleared himself that he was not of that mind, but now it appears by this woman's meeting that Mrs. Hutchinson hath so forestalled the minds of many by their resort to her meeting that now she hath a potent party in the country. Now if all these things have endangered us as from that foundation and if she in particular hath disparaged all our ministers in the land that they have preached a covenant of works, and only Mr. Cotton a covenant of grace, why this is not to be suffered, and therefore being driven to the foundation and it being found that Mrs. Hutchinson is she that hath depraved all the ministers and hath been the cause of what is fallen out, why we must take away the foundation and the building will fall.

Mrs. H. I pray Sir prove it that I said they preached nothing but a covenant of works.

Dep. Gov. Nothing but a covenant of works, why a Jesuit may preach truth sometimes.

Mrs. H. Did I ever say they preached a covenant of works then?

Dep. Gov. If they do not preach a covenant of grace clearly, then they preach a covenant of works.

Mrs. H. No Sir, one may preach a covenant of grace more clearly than another, so I said.

Dep. Gov. We are not upon that now but upon position.

Mrs. H. Prove this then Sir that you say I said.

Dep. Gov. When they do preach a covenant of works do they preach truth?

Mrs. H. Yes Sir, but when they preach a covenant of works for salvation, that is not truth.

Dep. Gov. I do but ask you this, when the ministers do preach a covenant of works do they preach a way of salvation?

Mrs. H. I did not come hither to answer to questions of that sort.

Dep. Gov. Because you will deny the thing.

Mrs. H. Ey, but that is to be proved first.

Dep. Gov. I will make it plain that you did say that the ministers did preach a covenant of works.

Mrs. H. I deny that.

Dep. Gov. And that you said they were not able ministers of the new testament, but Mr. Cotton only.

Mrs. H. If ever I spake that I proved it by God's word.

Court. Very well, very well.

Mrs. H. If one shall come unto me in private, and desire me seriously to tell them what I thought of such an one. I must either speak false or true in my answer.

Dep. Gov. Likewise I will prove this that you said the gospel in the letter and words holds forth nothing but a covenant of works and that all that do not hold as you do are in a covenant of works.

Mrs. H. I deny this for if I should so say I should speak against my own judgment.

Mr. Endicot. I desire to speak seeing Mrs. Hutchinson seems to lay something against them that are to witness against her.

Gov. Only I would add this. It is well discerned to the court that Mrs. Hutchinson can tell when to speak and when to hold her tongue. Upon the answering of a question which we desire her to tell her thoughts of she desires to be pardoned.

Mrs. H. It is one thing for me to come before a public magistracy and there to speak what they would have me to speak and another when a man comes to me in a way of friendship privately there is difference in that.

Gov. What if the matter be all one.

Mr. Hugh Peters, Minister of Salem. That which concerns us to speak unto as yet we are sparing in unless the court command us to speak, then we shall answer to Mrs. Hutchinson notwithstanding our brethren are very unwilling to answer.

Gov. This speech was not spoken in a corner but in a public assembly, and though things were spoken in private yet now coming to us, we are to deal with them as public.

Mr. Peters. We shall give you a fair account of what was said and desire that we may not be thought to come as informers against the gentlewoman, but as it may be serviceable for the country and our posterity to give you a brief account. This gentlewoman went under suspicion not only from her landing, that she was a woman not only difficult in her opinions, but also of an intemperate spirit. What was done at her landing I do not well remember, but as soon as Mr. Vane and ourselves came this controversy began yet it did reflect upon Mrs. Hutchinson and some of our brethren had dealt with her, and it so fell out that some of our ministry doth suffer as if it were not according to the gospel and as if we taught a covenant of works instead of a covenant of grace. Upon these and the like we did address ourselves to the teacher of that church, and the court then assembled being sensible of these things, and this gentlewoman being as we understood a chief agent, our desire to the teacher was to tell us wherein the difference lay between him and us, for the spring did then arise as we did conceive from this gentlewoman, and so we told him. He said that he thought it not according to God to commend this to the magistrates but to take some other course, and so going on in the discourse we thought it good to send for this gentlewoman, and she willingly came, and at the very first we gave her notice that such reports there were that she did conceive our ministry to be different from the ministry of the gospel, and that we taught a covenant of works, &c. and this was her table talk and therefore we desired her to clear herself and deal plainly. She was very tender at the first. Some of our brethren did desire to put this upon proof, and then her words upon that were. The fear of man is a snare why should I be afraid. These were her words. I did then take upon me to ask her this question. What difference do you conceive to be between your teacher and us? She did not request us that we should preserve her from danger or that we should be silent. Briefly, she told me there was a wide and a broad difference between our brother Mr. Cotton and our selves. I desired to know the difference. She answered that he preaches the covenant of grace and you the covenant of works and that you are not able ministers of the new testament and know no more than the apostles did before the resurrection of Christ. . . .

Dep. Gov. I called these witnesses and you deny them. You see they have proved this and you deny this, but it is clear. You said they preached a covenant of works and that they were not able ministers of the new testament; now there are two other things that you did affirm which were that the scriptures in the letter of them held forth nothing but a covenant of works and likewise that those that were under a covenant of works cannot be saved.

Mrs. H. Prove that I said so.

Gov. Did you say so?

Mrs. H. No Sir it is your conclusion.

Dep. Gov. What do I do charging of you if you deny what is so fully proved.

Gov. Here are six undeniable ministers who say it is true and yet you deny that you did say that they did preach a covenant of works and that they were not able ministers of the gospel, and it appears plainly that you have spoken it, and whereas you say that it was drawn from you in a way of friendship, you did profess then that it was out of conscience that you spake and said The fear of man is a snare, wherefore shall I be afraid, I will speak plainly and freely.

Mrs. H. That I absolutely deny, for the first question, was thus answered by me to them. They thought that I did conceive there was a difference between them and Mr. Cotton. At the first I was somewhat reserved, then said Mr. Peters I pray answer the question directly as fully and as plainly as you desire we should tell you our minds. Mrs. Hutchinson we come for plain dealing and telling you our hearts. Then I said I would deal as plainly as I could, and whereas they say I said they were under a covenant of works and in the state of the apostles why these two speeches cross one another. I might say they might preach a covenant of works as did the apostles, but to preach a covenant of works and to be under a covenant of works is another business.

Dep. Gov. There have been six witnesses to prove this and yet you deny it.

Mrs. H. I deny that these were the first words that were spoken. . . .

(THE NEXT MORNING)

Gov. We proceeded the last night as far as we could in hearing of this cause of Mrs. Hutchinson. There were divers things laid to her charge, her ordinary meetings about religious exercises, her speeches in derogation of the ministers among us, and the weakening of the hands and hearts of the people towards them. Here was sufficient proof made of that which she was accused of in that point concerning the ministers and their ministry, as that they did preach a covenant of works when others did preach a covenant of grace, and that they were not able ministers of the new testament, and that they had not the seal of the spirit, and this was spoken not as was pretended out of private conference, but out of conscience and warrant from scripture alledged the fear of man is a snare and seeing God had given her a calling to it she would freely speak. Some other speeches she used, as that the letter of the scripture held forth a covenant of works, and this is offered to be proved by probable grounds. If there be any thing else that the court hath to say they may speak. . . .

Dep. Gov. They affirm that Mrs. Hutchinson did say they were not able ministers of the new testament.

Mr. Cotton, teacher at Boston church. I do not remember it.

Mrs. H. If you please to give me leave I shall give you the ground of what I know to be true. Being much troubled to see the falseness of the constitution of the church of England, I had like to have turned separatist; whereupon I kept a day of solemn humiliation and pondering of the thing; this scripture was brought unto me—he that denies Jesus Christ to be come in the flesh is antichrist—This I considered of and in considering found that the papists did not deny him to be come in the flesh, nor we did not deny him—who then was antichrist? Was the Turk antichrist only? The Lord knows that I could not open scripture; he must by his prophetical office open it unto me. So after that being unsatisfied in the thing, the Lord was pleased to bring

this scripture out of the Hebrews. He that denies the testament denies the testator, and in this did open unto me and give me to see that those which did not teach the new covenant had the spirit of antichrist, and upon this he did discover the ministry unto me and ever since, I bless the Lord, he hath let me see which was the clear ministry and which the wrong. Since that time I confess I have been more choice and he hath left me to distinguish between the voice of my beloved and the voice of Moses, the voice of John Baptist and the voice of antichrist, for all those voices are spoken of in scripture. Now if you do condemn me for speaking what in my conscience I know to be truth I must commit myself unto the Lord.

Mr. Nowel, an assistant. How do you know that that was the spirit?

Mrs. H. How did Abraham know that it was God that bid him offer his son, being a breach of the sixth commandment?

Dep. Gov. By an immediate voice.

Mrs. H. So to me by an immediate revelation.

Dep. Gov. How! an immediate revelation.

Mrs. H. By the voice of his own spirit to my soul. I will give you another scripture, Jer. 46. 27, 28—out of which the Lord shewed me what he would do for me and the rest of his servants.—But after he was pleased to reveal himself to me I did presently like Abraham run to Hagar. And after that he did let me see the atheism of my own heart, for which I begged of the Lord that it might not remain in my heart, and being thus, he did shew me this (a twelvemonth after) which I told you of before. Ever since that time I have been confident of what he hath revealed unto me. . . . I was then much troubled concerning the ministry under which I lived, and then that place in the 30th of Isaiah was brought to my mind. Though the Lord give thee bread of adversity and water of affliction yet shall not thy teachers be removed into corners any more, but thine eyes shall see thy teachers. The Lord giving me this promise and they being gone there was none then left that I was able to hear, and I could not be at rest but I must come hither. Yet that place of Isaiah did much follow me, though the Lord give thee the bread of adversity and water of affliction. This place lying I say upon me then this place in Daniel was brought unto me and did shew me that though I should meet with affliction yet I am the same God that delivered Daniel out of the lion's den, I will also deliver thee.—Therefore I desire you to look to it, for you see this scripture fulfilled this day and therefore I desire you that as you tender the Lord and the church and commonwealth to consider and look what you do. You have power over my body but the Lord Jesus hath power over my body and soul, and assure yourselves thus much, you do as much as in you lies to put the Lord Jesus Christ from you, and if you go on in this course you begin you will bring a curse upon you and your posterity, and the mouth of the Lord hath spoken it.

Dep. Gov. What is the scripture she brings?

Mr. Stoughton, an assistant. Behold I turn away from you.

Mrs. H. But now having seen him which is invisible I fear not what man can do unto me.

Gov. Daniel was delivered by miracle do you think to be deliver'd so too?

Mrs. H. I do here speak it before the court. I look that the Lord should deliver me by his providence.

Mr. Harlakenden, an assistant. I may read scripture and the most glorious hypocrite may read them and yet go down to hell.

Mrs. H. It may be so. . . .

Dep. Gov. These disturbances that have come among the Germans have been all grounded upon revelations, and so they that have vented them have stirred up their hearts to take up arms against their prince and to cut the throats of one another, and these have been the fruits of them, and whether the devil may inspire the same into their hearts here I know not, for I am fully persuaded that Mrs. Hutchinson is deluded by the devil, because the spirit of God speaks truth in all his servants.

Gov. I am persuaded that the revelation she brings forth is delusion. All the court but some two or three ministers cry out we all believe it—we all believe it.

Mr. Endicot. I suppose all the world may see where the foundation of all these troubles among us lies.

Mr. Eliot, Minister of Roxbury. I say there is an expectation of things promised, but to have a particular revelation of things that shall fall out, there is no such thing in the scripture.

Gov. We will not limit the word of God.

Mr. Collicut, a deputy. It is a great burden to us that we differ from Mr. Cotton and that he should justify these revelations. I would intreat him to answer concerning that about the destruction of England.

Gov. M. Cotton is not called to answer to any thing but we are to deal with the party here standing before us.

Mr. Bartholomew, a deputy for Salem. My wife hath said that Mr. Wheelwright was not acquainted with this way until that she imparted it unto him.

Mr. Brown, a deputy for Watertown. Inasmuch as I am called to speak, I would therefore speak the mind of our brethren. Though we had sufficient ground for the censure before, yet now she having vented herself and I find such flat contradiction to the scripture in what she saith, as to that in the first to the Hebrews—God at sundry times spake to our fathers—For my part I understand that scripture and other scriptures of the Lord Jesus Christ, and the apostle writing to Timothy saith that the scripture is able to make one perfect—therefore I say the mind of the brethren—I think she deserves no less a censure than hath been already past but rather something more, for this is the foundation of all mischief and of all those bastardly things which have been overthrowing by that great meeting. They have all come out from this cursed fountain.

Gov. Seeing the court hath thus declared itself and hearing what hath been laid to the charge of Mrs. Hutchinson and especially what she by the providence of God hath declared freely without being asked, if therefore it be the mind of the court, looking at her as the principal cause of all our trouble, that they would now consider what is to be done to her.— . . .

Gov. The court hath already declared themselves satisfied concerning things you hear, and concerning the troublesomeness of her spirit and the danger of her course amongst us, which is not to be suffered. Therefore if it be the mind of the court that Mrs. Hutchinson for these things that appear before us is unfit for our society, and if it be the mind of the court that she shall be banished out of our liberties and imprisoned till she be sent away, let them hold up their hands.

(All but three)

Those that are contrary minded hold up yours,

(Mr. Coddington and Mr. Colborn, only)

Mr. Jennison, a deputy of Ipswich I cannot hold up my hand one way or the other, and I shall give my reason if the court require it.

Gov. Mrs. Hutchinson, the sentence of the court you hear is that you are banished from out of our jurisdiction as being a woman not fit for our society, and are to be imprisoned till the court shall send you away.

Mrs. H. I desire to know wherefore I am banished?

Gov. Say no more, the court knows wherefore and is satisfied.

2

MARGARET BRENT
Petition to the Maryland Assembly Requesting the Right to Vote (1648)

Came Mistress Margarett Brent and requested to have vote in the howse for her selfe and voyce

From *Proceedings and Acts of the General Assembly of Maryland, January 1637/8–September 1664* (Baltimore: Maryland Historical Society, 1883), 215.

allso for that att the last Court 3rd Jan: it was ordered that the said Mrs Brent was to be lookd uppon and received as his Lordships Attorney. The Governor denyed that the said Mrs Brent should have any vote in the howse. And the said Mrs Brent protested against all proceedings in this present Assembly, unlesse shee may be present and have vote as aforesaid.

3

MARY DYER
Letter to the Massachusetts General Court Protesting the Persecution of Quakers (1659)

"To the General Court now in Boston.

"Whereas I am by many charged with the Guiltiness of my own Blood; if you mean, in my coming to Boston, I am therein clear, and justified by the Lord, in whose Will I came, who will require my Blood of you, be sure, who have made a Law to take away the Lives of the Innocent Servants of God, if they come among you, who are called by you, *Cursed Quakers;* altho' I say, and am a living Witness for them and the Lord, that he hath Blessed them, and sent them unto you: Therefore be not found Fighters against God, but let my Counsel and Request be accepted with you, To Repeal all such Laws, that the Truth and Servants of the Lord may have free Passage among you, and you be kept from shedding Innocent Blood, which I know there are many among you would not do, if they knew it so to be: Nor can the Enemy that stirreth you up thus to destroy this Holy Seed, in any measure countervail the great Damage that you will by thus doing procure: Therefore, seeing the Lord hath not hid it from me, it lyeth upon me, in Love to your Souls, thus to persuade you: I

From Horatio Rogers, *Mary Dyer of Rhode Island: The Quaker Martyr That Was Hanged on Boston Common, June 1, 1660* (Providence: Preston and Rounds, 1896), 84–90.

have no self-ends, the Lord knoweth, for if my Life were freely granted by you, it would not avail me, nor could I expect it of you, so long as I should daily hear or see the Sufferings of these People, my dear Brethren and Seed, with whom my Life is bound up, as I have done these two Years; and now it is like to encrease, even unto Death, for no evil Doing, but coming among you: Was ever the like Laws heard of, among a People that profess Christ come in the Flesh? And have such no other Weapons, but such Laws, to fight against Spiritual Wickedness withall, as you call it? Wo is me for you! Of whom take you Counsel? Search with the Light of Christ in ye, and it will shew you of whom, as it hath done me and many more, who have been disobedient and deceived, as now you are; which Light, as you come into, and obeying what is made manifest to you therein, you will not Repent, that you were kept from shedding Blood, tho' it were from a woman: It's not mine own Life I seek (for I chuse rather to suffer with the People of God, than to enjoy the Pleasures of Egypt) but the Life of the Seed, which I know the Lord hath Blessed; and therefore seeks the Enemy thus vehemently the Life thereof to Destroy, as in all Ages he ever did: Oh! hearken not unto him, I beseech you, for the Seed's sake, which is one in all, and is dear in the sight of God; which they that touch, touch the Apple of his Eye, and cannot escape his Wrath; whereof I having felt, cannot but perswade all Men that I have to do withal, especially you who name the Name of Christ, to depart from such Iniquity, as shedding Blood, even of the Saints of the Most High . . . Therefore I leave these Lines with you, Appealing to the faithful and true Witness of God, which is one in all Consciences, before whom we must all appear; with whom I shall eternally Rest, in everlasting Joy and Peace, whether you will hear or forbear: With him is my Reward, with Whom to live is my Joy, and to dye is my Gain, tho' I had not had your forty eight Hours warning, for the Preparation to the Death of Mary Dyar.

"And know this also, That if through the En-mity you shall declare your selves worse than Ahasuerus, and confirm your Law, tho' it were but by taking away the Life of one of us, That the Lord will overthrow both your Law and you, by his righteous Judgments and Plagues poured justly upon you, who now whilst you are warned thereof, and tenderly sought unto, may avoid the one, by removing the other: If you neither hear nor obey the Lord nor his Servants, yet will he send more of his Servants among you, so that your end shall be frustrated, that think to restrain them, yo call *Cursed Quakers,* from coming among you, by any Thing you can do to them; yea, verily, he hath a Seed here among you, for whom we have suffered all this while, and yet Suffer; whom the Lord of the Harvest will send forth more Labourers to gather (out of the Mouths of the Devourers of all sorts) into his Fold, where he will lead them into fresh Pastures, even the Paths of Righteousness, for his Names sake: Oh! let none of you put this good Day far from you, which verily in the Light of the Lord I see approaching, even to many in and about Boston, which is the bitterest and darkest professing Place, and so to continue so long as you have done, that ever I heard of; let the time past therefore suffice, for such a Profession as brings forth such Fruits as these Laws are. In Love and in the Spirit of Meekness I again beseech you, for I have no Enmity to the Persons of any; but you shall know, That God will not be mocked, but what you sow, that shall you reap from him, that will render to everyone according to the Deeds done in the Body, whether Good or Evil; Even so be it, saith

"Mary Dyar."

4

The Examinations of Susannah Martin and Martha Carrier for the Crime of Witchcraft (1692)

(EXAMINATION OF SUSANNAH MARTIN)

The Examination of Susan: Martin. 2. May

As soon as she came in many had fits.

Do you know this Woman

Abigail: Williams saith it is Goody Martin she hath hurt me often. Others by fits were hindered from speaking.

Elizabeth: Hubbard said she hath not been hurt by her. John Indian said he hath not seen her. Mercy Lewes pointed to her & fell into a little fit. Ann Putman threw her Glove in a fit at her. The examinant laught.

What do you laugh at it?

Well I may at such folly.

Is this folly? The hurt of these persons.

I never hurt man woman or child.

Mercy Lewes cryed out she hath hurt me a great many times, & pulls me down

Then Martin laught againe

Mary Walcot saith this woman hath hurt me a great many times.

Sus: Sheldon also accused her of afflicting her.

What do you say to this?

I have no hand in Witchcraft.

What did you do? Did not you give your consent?

No, never in my life.

What ails this people?

I do not know.

But what do you think?

I do not desire to spend my judgment upon it.

Do not you think they are Bewitcht?

No. I do not think they are.

Tell me your thoughts about them.

From *The Salem Witchcraft Papers: Verbatim Transcripts of the Legal Documents of the Salem Witchcraft Outbreak of 1692*, 2 vols., Paul Boyer and Stephen Nissenbaum, ed. (New York: Da Capo Press, 1977), 1:184–186, 2:550–552.

Why my thoughts are my own, when they are in, but when they are out they are anothers.

You said their Master who do you think is their Master?

If they be dealing in the black art, you may know as well as I.

Well what have you done towards this?

Nothing.

Why it is you, or your appearance.

I cannot help it.

That may be your Master.

I desire to lead my self according to the word of God.

Is this according to Gods word?

If I were such a person I would tell you the truth.

How comes your appearance just now to hurt these.

How do I know?

Are not you willing to tell the Truth?

I cannot tell: He that appeared in sams shape a glorifyed saint can appear in any ones shape.

Do you beleive these do not say true?

They may lye for ought I know

May not you lye?

I dare not tell a lye if it would save my life.

Then you will speak the Truth.

I have spake nothing else, I would do them any good.

I do not think you have such affections for them, whom just now you insinuated had the Devill for their Master. . . .

You have been a long time coming to the Court to day, you can come fast enough in the night, said Mercy Lewes.

No, sweet heart, said the examinant, And then Mercy Lewes, & all, or many of the rest, were afflicted

John Indian fell into a violent fit, & said it was that woman, she bites, she bites, and then she was biting her lips

Have you not compassion for these afflicted?

No, I have none

Some cryed out there was the black man with her, & Goody Bibber who had not accused her before confirmed it

Abig: William upon trial could not come near her—Nor Goody Bibber. Nor Mary Walcot. John Indian cryed he would Kill her if he came near her, but he was flung down in his approach to her

What is the reason these cannot come near you?

I cannot tell. It may be the Devil bears me more malice than an other

Do not you see how God evidently discovers you?

No, not a bit for that.

All the congregation think so.

Let them think what they will.

What is the reason these cannot come near you?

I do not know but they can if they will, or else if you please, I will come to then.

What is the black man whispering to you?

There was none whispered to me

(EXAMINATION OF MARTHA CARRIER)
The Examination of Martha Carrier. 31.May.

Abigail Williams who hurts you?
Goody Carrier of Andover.

Elizabeth: Hubbard who hurts you?
Goody Carrier

Susan: Sheldon, who hurts you?

Goody Carrier, she bites me, pinches me, & tells me she would cut my throat, if I did not signe her book

Mary Walcot said she afflicted her & brought the book to her.

What do you say to this you are charged with?

I have not done it.

Sus: Sheldon cried she looks upon the black man.

Ann Putman complained of a pin stuck in her.

What black man is that?

I know none

Ann Putman testifyed there was.

Mary Warrin cryed out she was prickt.

What black man did you see?

I saw no black man but your own presence.

Can you look upon these & not knock them down?

They will dissemble if I look upon them.

You see you look upon them & they fall down

It is false the Devil is a liar.

I lookt upon none since I came into the room but you

Susan: Sheldon cryed out in a Trance I wonder what could you murder. 13. persons?

Mary Walcot testifyed the same that there lay. 13. Ghosts.

All the afflicted fell into most intollerable out-cries & agonies.

Elizabeth: Hubbard & Ann Putman testifyed the same that she had killed 13. at Andover.

It is a shamefull thing that you should mind these folks that are out of their wits.

Do not you see them?

If I do speak you will not believe me?

You do see them, said the accusers.

You lye, I am wronged.

There is the black man wispering in her ear said many of the afflicted.

Mercy Lewes in a violent fit, was well upon the examinants grasping her arm.

The Tortures of the afflicted was so great that there was no enduring of it, so that she was ordered away & to be bound hand & foot with all expedition the afflicted in the mean while almost killed to the great trouble of all spectators Magistrates & others.

Note. As soon as she was well bound they all had strange & sodain ease.

Mary Walcot told the Magistrates that this woman told her she had been a witch this. 40. yeares.

5
ANNE BRADSTREET
Poems

The Prologue (1650)

1

To sing of Wars, of Captains, and of Kings,
Of Cities founded, Common-wealths begun,
For my mean pen are too superiour things:
Or how they all, or each their dates have run
Let Poets and Historians set these forth,
My obscure Lines shall not so dim their worth.

2

But when my wondring eyes and envious heart
Great Bartas sugar'd lines, do but read o're
Fool I do grudg the Muses did not part
'Twixt him and me that overfluent store;
A Bartas can, do what a Bartas will
But simple I according to my skill.

3

From school-boyes tongue no rhet'rick we ex-
    pect
Nor yet a sweet Consort from broken strings,
Nor perfect beauty, where's a main defect:
My foolish, broken, blemish'd Muse so sings
And this to mend, alas, no Art is able,
'Cause nature, made it so irreparable.

4

Nor can I, like that fluent sweet tongu'd Greek,
Who lisp'd at first, in future times speak plain
By Art he gladly found what he did seek
A full requital of his, striving pain
Art can do much, but this maxime's most sure
A weak or wounded brain admits no cure.

From *The Works of Anne Bradstreet* in *Prose and Verse*, John Harvard Ellis, ed. (Charlestown: Abram E. Cutter, 1867), 100–102, 389–390.

5

I am obnoxious to each carping tongue
Who says my hand a needle better fits,
A Poets pen all scorn I should thus wrong,
For such despite they cast on Female wits:
If what I do prove well, it won't advance,
They'l say it's stoln, or else it was by chance.

6

But sure the Antique Greeks were far more mild
Else of our Sexe, why feigned they those Nine
And poesy made, Calliope's own Child;
So 'mongst the rest they placed the Arts divine,
But this weak knot, they will full soon untie,
The Greeks did nought, but play the fools & lye.

7

Let Greeks be Greeks, and women what they
    are
Men have precedency and still excell,
It is but vain unjustly to wage warre;
Men can do best, and women know it well
Preheminence in all and each is yours;
Yet grant some small acknowledgement of ours.

8

And oh ye high flown quills that soar the Skies,
And ever with your prey still catch your praise,
If e're you daigne these lowly lines your eyes
Give Thyme or Parsley wreath, I ask no bayes,
This mean and unrefined ore of mine
Will make you glistring gold, but more to shine.

The Author to Her Book (1678)

Thou ill-form'd offspring of my feeble brain,
Who after birth did'st by my side remain,
Till snatcht from thence by friends, less wife
    then true
Who thee abroad, expos'd to publick view,
Made thee in raggs, halting to th' press to trudg,
Where errors were not lessened (all may judg)
At thy return my blushing was not small,
My rambling brat (in print) should mother call,
I cast thee by as one unfit for light,
Thy Visage was so irksome in my sight;

Yet being mine own, at length affection would
Thy blemishes amend, if so I could:
I wash'd thy face, but more defects I saw,
And rubbing off a spot, still made a flaw.
I stretcht thy joynts to make thee even feet,
Yet still thou run'st more hobling then is meet;
In better dress to trim thee was my mind,
But nought save home-spun Cloth, i'th' house I
   find
In this array, 'mongst Vulgars mayst thou roam
In Critics hands, beware thou dost not come;
And take thy way where yet thou art not known,
If for thy Father askt, say, thou hadst none:
And for thy Mother, she alas is poor,
Which caus'd her thus to send thee out of door.

6

MARY ROWLANDSON
Captivity, Sufferings, and
Removes (1682)

On the 10th of February, 1675, the Indians, in
great numbers, came upon Lancaster. Their first
coming was about sun-rising; hearing the noise
of some guns, we looked out; several houses
were burning, and the smoke ascending to
heaven. There were five persons taken in one
house, the father, the mother, and a sucking child
they knocked on the head; the other two they
took and carried away alive.——There were two
others, who being out of the garrison upon occasion, were set upon; one was knocked on the
head, the other escaped: another there was, who
running along, was shot and wounded, and fell
down; he begged of them his life, promising
them money, (as they told me) but they would
not hearken to him, knocked him on the head,
stripped him naked, and ripped open his bowels. Another, seeing many of the Indians about
his barn, ventured out, but was quickly shot

From *A Narrative of the Captivity, Sufferings, and Removes, of Mrs. Mary Rowlandson* (n.p.: Chapman Whitcomb,
1682), 3–7, 8–9. 18–21, 22–24, 54.

down. There were three others belonging to the
same garrison, who were killed; the Indians getting up on the roof of the barn, had advantage
to shoot down upon them over their fortifica-
tion. Thus these murderous wretches went on
burning and destroying all before them.

At length they came and beset our own
house, and quickly it was the dolefulest day that
ever mine eyes saw. . . . Now is the dreadful
hour come, that I have often heard of (in the
time of the war, as was the case with others) but
now mine eyes see it. Some in our house were
fighting for their lives, others wallowing in their
blood, the house on fire over our heads, and the
bloody heathen ready to knock us on the head if
we stirred out. Now might we hear mothers and
children crying out for themselves and one another, *Lord what shall we do!* Then I took my children (and one of my sisters her's) to go forth
and leave the house: but as soon as we came to
the door, and appeared, the Indians shot so thick,
that the bullets rattled against the house, as if
one had taken an handful of stones and threw
them, so that we were forced to give back. We
had six stout dogs belonging to our garrison,
but none of them would stir, tho at another time,
if an Indian had come to the door, they were
ready to fly upon him and tear him down. The
Lord hereby would make us the more to acknowledge his hand, and to see that our help is
always in him.——But out we must go, the fire
increasing, and coming along behind us, roaring, and the Indians gaping before us with their
guns, spears, and hatchets, to devour us. No
sooner were we out of the house, but my
brother-in-law (being before wounded, in de-
fending the house, in or near the throat) fell
down dead, whereat the Indians scornfully
shouted, and hallooed, and were presently upon
him, stripping off his cloaths. The bullets flying
thick, one went thro my side, and the same (as
it would seem, thro the bowels and hand of my
poor child in my arms. One of my elder sister's
children (named William) had then his leg broken, which the Indians perceiving, they knocked
him on the head. Thus were we butchered by

those merciless heathens, standing amazed, with the blood running down to our heels. My elder sister being yet in the house, and seeing those woeful sights, the infidels hauling mothers one way, and children another, and some wallowing in their blood: and her eldest son telling her that her son William was dead, and myself wounded, she said, *Lord, let me die with them.*—which was no sooner said than she was struck with a bullet, and fell down dead over the threshold. I hope she is reaping the fruit of her good labours, being faithful to the service of God in her place. In her younger years she lay under much trouble upon spiritual accounts, till it pleased God to make that precious scripture take hold of her heart, 2 Cor. xii. 9. And he said unto me, My Grace is sufficient for thee. More than twenty years after, I have heard her tell how sweet and comfortable that place was to her. But to return; the Indians laid hold on us, pulling me one way, and the children another, and said, Come, go along with us: I told them they would kill me; they answered, If I were willing to go along with them, they would not hurt me.

Oh! the doleful sight that now was to behold at this house! Come behold the works of the Lord, what desolations he has made in the earth. Of thirty seven persons who were in this one house, none escaped either present death, or a bitter captivity, save only one, who might say as in Job 1. xv. And I only am escaped alone to tell the news. There were twelve killed, some shot, some stabbed with their spears, some knocked down with their hatchets. When we are in prosperity, ho, the little that we think of such dreadful sights, to see our dear friends and relations lie bleeding out their hearts blood upon the ground.—There was one who was chopped into the head with a hatchet and stripped naked, and yet was crawling up and down. It is a solemn sight to see so many christians lying in their blood, some here and some there, like a company of sheep torn by wolves. All of them stripped naked by a company of hell hounds, roaring, singing, ranting and insulting, as if they would have torn our very hearts out; yet the

Lord, by his almighty power, preserved a number of us from death, for there were twenty four of us taken alive and carried captive.

I had often before this said, that if the Indians should come, I should choose rather to be killed by them, than taken alive: but when it came to the trial, my mind changed; their glittering weapons so daunted my spirits, that I chose rather to go along with those (as I may say) ravenous bears, than that moment to end my days. And that I may the better declare what happened to me during that grievous captivity, I shall particularly speak of the several Removes we had up and down the wilderness.

The First Remove

Now away we must go with those barbarous creatures, with our bodies wounded and bleeding, and our hearts no less than our bodies. About a mile we went that night, up upon a hill within sight of the town, where they intended to lodge. There was hard by a vacant house, (deserted by the English before, for fear of the Indians) I asked them whether I might not lodge in the house that night to which they answered, What, will you love Englishmen still. This was the dolefulest night that ever my eyes saw. Oh, the roaring, and singing, dancing, and yelling of those black creatures in the night, which made the place a lively resemblance of hell: and as miserable was the waste that was there made, of horses, cattle, sheep, swine, calves, lambs, roasting pigs, and fowls, (which they had plundered in the town) some roasting, some lying and burning, and some boiling, to feed our merciless enemies, who were joyful enough, though we were disconsolate. To add to the dolefulness of the former day, and the dismalness of the present night, my thoughts ran upon my losses, and sad bereaved condition. All was gone, my husband gone, (at least separated from me, he being in the bay; and to add to my grief, the Indians told me they would kill him as he came homeward) my children gone, my relations and friends gone, our house and home, and all our comforts within door and without, all were gone, (except my life) and I knew not but the next moment that might go too.

There remained nothing to me but one poor wounded babe, and it seemed at present worse than death, that it was in such a pitiful condition, bespeaking compassion, and I had no refreshing for it, nor suitable things to revive it. Little do many think, what is the savageness and bruitishness of this barbarous enemy . . .

The Third Remove

The morning being come, they prepared to go on their way: one of the Indians got up on a horse, and they set me up behind him, with my poor sick babe in my lap. A very wearisome and tedious day I had of it; what with my own wound, and my child being so exceedingly sick, and in a lamentable condition with her wound, it may easily be judged what a poor feeble condition we were in, there being not the least crumb of refreshment that came within either of our mouths from Wednesday night to Saturday night, except only a little cold water. This day in the afternoon, about an hour by sun, we came to the place where they intended, viz. an Indian town called Wenimesset, northward of Quabang. When we were come, Oh the number of pagans (our merciless enemies) that there came about me! I might say as David, Psal. xxvii 1 3 . *I had fainted, unless I had believed, &c.* The next day was the sabbath: I then remembered how careless I had been of God's holy time; how many Sabbaths I had lost and misspent, and how evilly I had walked in God's sight; which lay so closely upon my spirit that it was easy for me to see how righteous it was with God to cut off the thread of my life, and cast me out of his presence forever. Yet the Lord still shewed mercy to me, and helped me; and as he wounded me with one hand, so he healed me with the other. This day there came to me one Robert Pepper, (a man belonging to Roxbury) who was taken at Capt. Beers's fight; and had been now a considerable time with the Indians, and up with them

almost as far as Albany, to see King Philip, as he told me, and was now very lately come with them into these parts. Hearing that I was in this Indian town, he obtained leave to come and see me. He told me he himself was wounded in the leg at Capt. Beers's fight; and was not able for some time to go, but as they carried him, and that he took oak leaves and laid on his wound, and by the blessing of God, he was able to travel again. Then I took oak leaves and laid on my side, and with the blessing of God, it cured me also; yet before the cure was wrought, I might say as it is in Psai. xxxviii 5, 6, *My wounds stink and are corrupt, I am troubled, I am bowed down greatly, I go mourning all the day long.*—I sat much alone with my poor wounded child in my lap, which moaned night and day, having nothing to revive the body, or cheer thee spirits of her; but instead of that, one Indian would come and tell me one hour, your master will knock your child on the head; and then a second, and then a third, your master will quickly knock your child on the head. . . .

The Seventh Remove

After a restless and hungry night there, we had a wearisome time of it the next day. The swamp, by which we lay, was as it were a deep dungeon, and a very high and steep hill before it. Before I got to the top of the hill, I thought that my heart, legs, and all would have broken, and failed me. What through faintness and soreness of body, it was a grievous day of travel to me. As we went along, I saw a place where English cattle had been; that was comfort to me, such as it was. Quickly after that, we came to an English path, which so took with me, that I thought I could there have freely lain down and died. That day, a little after noon, we came to Squauheag, where the Indians quickly spread themselves over the deserted English fields, gleaning, what they could find: some picked up ears of wheat, that were crickled down; some found ears of Indian corn; some found groundnuts, and others sheaves of wheat, that were frozen together in the shock, and went to thresh-ing them out. I got two ears of Indian corn, and whilst I did but turn my back, one of them was stolen from me, which much troubled me. There came an Indian to them at that time, with a bas-ket of horse-liver; I asked him to give me a piece. What, (says he) can you eat horse-liver? I told him I would try, if he would give me a piece, which he did; and I laid it on the coals to roast; but before it was half ready, they got half of it away from me; so that I was forced to take the rest and eat it as it was, with the blood about my mouth, and yet a savoury bit it was to me, for to the hungry soul every bitter thing is sweet.—A solemn sight I thought it was, to see whole fields of wheat and Indian corn forsaken and spoiled, and the remainders of them to be food for our merciless enemies. That night we had a mess of wheat for our supper.

The Eight Remove

On the morrow morning we must go over Con-necticut river to meet with king Philip; two ca-noes full they had carried over; the next turn I was to go; but as my foot was upon the canoe to step in, there was a sudden out-cry among them, and I must step back; and instead of going up the river, I must go four or five miles farther northward. Some of the Indians ran one way, and some another. The cause of this rout was, as I thought, their espying some English scouts, who were thereabouts. In this travel, about noon the company made a stop, and sat down, some to eat and others to rest them. As I sat amongst them, musing on things past, my son Joseph un-expectedly came to me: we asked of each other's welfare, bemoaning our doleful condition, and the change that had come upon us; we had had husband, and father, children, and sisters, friends, and relations, house and home, and many comforts of this life; but now might we say with Job, *Naked came I out of my mother's womb, and naked shall I return: The Lord gave, and the Lord hath taken away, blessed be the name of the Lord. . . .*

But to return: We travelled on till night,

and in the morning we must go over the river to Philip's crew. When I was in the canoe, I could not but be amazed at the numerous crew of pa-gans that were on the bank on the other side. When I came ashore, they gathered all about me, I sitting alone in the midst; I observed they asked one another questions, and laughed, and rejoiced over their gains and victories. Then my heart began to fail, and I fell a weeping; which was the first time, to my remembrance, that I wept before them; although I had met with so much affliction and my heart was many times ready to break, yet could I not shed one tear in their sight, but rather had been all this while in a maze, and like one astonished; but now I may say as Psal. cxxxii. 1. *By the River of Babylon, there we sat down, yea, we wept when we remembered Zion.* There one of them asked me, why I wept? I could hardly tell what to say; yet I answered, they would kill me. No, said he, none will hurt you.—Then came one of them, and gave me two spoonfuls of meal, to comfort me; and another gave me half a pint of peas, which was more worth than many bushels at another time. Then I went to see King Philip; he bade me come in, and sit down; and asked me whether I would smoke it? (an usual compliment now-a-days, among saints and sinners): But this no way suited me. For though I had formerly used tobacco, yet I had left it ever since I was first taken. It seems to be a bait the devil lays, to make men lose their pre-cious time. I remember with shame, how for-merly, when I had taken two or three pipes, I was presently ready for another; such a bewitch-ing thing it is: but I thank God, he has now give me power over it; surely there are many who may be better employed, than to sit sucking a stinking tobacco pipe. . . .

During my abode in this place, Philip spake to me to make a shirt for his boy, which I did; for which he gave me a shilling; I offered the money to my master, but he bade me keep it, and with it I bought a piece of horse flesh. Af-terward he asked me to make a cap for his boy, for which he invited me to dinner: I went, and he gave me a pancake, about as big as two fingers; it was made of parched wheat, beaten, and fried in bear's grease, but I thought I never tasted pleasanter food in my life. There was a squaw who spake to me to make a shirt for her sannup; for which she gave me a piece of bear. Another asked me to knit a pair of stockings, for which she gave me a quart of peas. I boiled my peas and bear together, and invited my master and mistress to dinner; but the proud gossip, because I served them both in one dish, would eat nothing, except one bit that he gave her upon the point of his knife. . . .

The Ninth Remove

But instead of going either to Albany or homeward, we must go five miles up the river, and then go over it. Here we abode a while. Here lived a sorry Indian, who spake to me to make him a shirt; when I had done it, he would pay me nothing for it. But he lived by the river side, where I often went to fetch water; I would often be putting him in mind, and calling for my pay; at last he told me, if I would make another shirt for a papoos not yet born, he would give me a knife, which he did, when I had done it. I carried the knife in, and my master asked me to give it to him, and I was not a little glad that I had any thing that they would accept of, and be pleased with. . . .

My son being now about a mile from me, I asked liberty to go and see him; they bade me go, and away I went; but quickly lost myself, travelling over hills and thro swamps, and could not find the way to him. And I cannot but admire at the wonderful power and goodness of God to me in that tho I was gone from home, and met with all sorts of Indians, and those I had no knowledge of, and there being no Christian soul near me, yet not one of them offered the least imaginable miscarriage to me. I turned homeward again, and met my master, and he shewed me the way to my son. When I came to him I found him not well; and withal he had a boil on his side, which much troubled him: we bemoaned one another a while, as the Lord helped us, and then I returned again. When I was returned, I found myself as unsatisfied as I was before. I went up and down mourning and lamenting, and my spirit was ready to sink with the thoughts of my poor children. My son was ill, and I could not but think of his mournful looks, having no Christian friend near him, to do any office of love for him, either for soul or body. And my poor girl, I knew not where she was, nor whether she was sick or well, alive or dead. I repaired under these thoughts to my bible, (my great comforter in that time) and that scripture came to my hand, *Cast thy burden upon the Lord, and he shall sustain thee.* Psal. lv. 22.

But I was fain to go and look after something to satisfy my hunger; and going among the wigwams, I went into one, and there found a squaw who shewed herself very kind to me, and gave me a piece of bear, I put it into my pocket, and came home; but could not find an opportunity to broil it, for fear they should get it from me; and there it lay all that day and night in my stinking pocket. In the morning I went again to the same squaw, who had a kettle of ground-nuts boiling: I asked her to let me boil my piece of bear in the kettle, which she did, and gave me some ground-nuts to eat with it, and I cannot but think how pleasant it was to me. I have sometimes seen bear baked handsomely among the English, and some liked it; but the thoughts that it was bear, made me tremble: But now that was savoury to me that one would think was enough to turn the stomach of a brute creature.

One bitter cold day, I could find no room to sit down before the fire: I went out, and could not tell what to do, but I went into another wigwam, where they were all sitting around the fire; but the squaw laid a skin for me and bade me sit down, and gave me some ground-nuts, and bade me come again; and told me they would buy me, if they were able; and yet these were strangers to me that I never knew before. . . .

[Rowlandson, along with her son and daughter, were finally redeemed from the Indians and allowed to return home.]

Our family being now gathered together, the south church in Boston hired an house for us; Then we removed from Mr. Shepard's (those cordial friends) and went to Boston, where we continued about three quarters of a year. Still the Lord went along with us, and provided graciously for us. I thought it somewhat strange to set up house-keeping with bare walls; but, as Solomon says, *Money answers all things:* And that we had, thro the benevolence of christian friends, some in this town, and some in that, and others; and some from England, so that in a little time we might look and see the house furnished with love. The Lord hath been exceedingly good to us in our low estate, in that, when we had neither house nor home, nor other necessaries, the Lord so moved the hearts of these and those towards us, that we wanted neither food nor raiment for ourselves nor ours. Prov. xv.ii. 24. *There is a friend that sticketh closer than a brother.* And how many such friends have we found, and now live among! . . .

7

Phillis Wheatley
Poems (1773)

On being brought from AFRICA to AMERICA

'Twas mercy brought me from my *Pagan* land,
Taught my benighted soul to understand
That there's a God, that there's a *Saviour* too:
Once I redemption neither sought nor knew.
Some view our sable race with scornful eye,
"Their colour is a diabolic die."
Remember, *Christians, Negros,* black as *Cain,*
May be refin'd, and join th' angelic train.

From *Poems on Various Subjects, Religious and Moral* (London: A. Bell, 1773), 18, 73–75.

To the Right Honourable WILLIAM, Earl of Dartmouth, His Majesty's Principal Secretary of State for North America, &c.

Hail, happy day, when, smiling like the morn,
Fair *Freedom* rose *New-England* to adorn:
The northern clime beneath her genial ray,
Dartmouth, congratulates thy blissful sway:
Elate with hope her race no longer mourns,
Each soul expands, each grateful bosom burns,
While in thine hand with pleasure we behold
The silken reins, and *Freedom's* charms unfold.
Long lost to realms beneath the northern skies
She shines supreme, while hated *faction* dies:
Soon as appear'd the *Goddess* long desir'd,
Sick at the view, she languish'd and expir'd;
Thus from the splendors of the morning light
The owl in sadness seeks the caves of night.

   No more, *America,* in mournful strain
Of wrongs, and grievance unredress'd complain,
No longer shall thou dread the iron chain,
Which wanton *Tyranny* with lawless hand
Had made, and with it meant t' enslave the land.
   Should you, my lord, while you peruse my song,
Wonder from whence my love of Freedom sprung,
Whence flow these wishes for the common good,
By feeling hearts alone best understood,
I, young in life, by seeming cruel fate
Was snatch'd from *Afric's* fancy'd happy feat:
What pangs excruciating must molest,
What sorrows labour in my parent's breast?
Steel'd was that soul and by no misery mov'd
That from a father seiz'd his babe belov'd:
Such, such my case. And can I then but pray
Others may never feel tyrannic sway?
   For favours past, great Sir, our thanks are due,
And thee we ask thy favours to renew,
Since in thy pow'r, as in thy will before,
To sooth the griefs, which thou did'st once deplore.
May heav'nly grace the sacred sanction give
To all thy works, and thou for ever live

Not only on the wings of fleeting *Fame,*
Though praise immortal crowns the patriot's
    name,
But to conduct to heav'ns refulgent fane,
May fiery coursers sweep th' ethereal plain,
And bear thee upwards to that blest abode,
Where, like the prophet, thou shalt find thy God.

8

ELIZABETH ASHBRIDGE
Uncommon Occurrences (1774)

My life having been attended with many uncommon occurrences, I have thought proper to make
some remarks on the dealings of divine goodness with me. I have often had cause, with David,
to say, 'It is good for me that I have been afflicted; and most earnestly I desire that they who
read the following lines may take warning, and
shun the evils into which I have been drawn.

I was born at Middlewich, in Cheshire, in
the year 1713, of honest parents, named Thomas and Mary Sampson. My father bore a good
character, but he was not so strictly religious as
my mother, who was a pattern of virtue to me.
I was my father's only child; but my mother had
a son and a daughter by a former husband. Soon
after I was born, my father went to sea, and following his profession, which was that of a sur-
geon, made many long voyages. He continued
in his sea-faring course of life till I was twelve
years old, so that the care of the early part of
my education devolved upon my mother; and
she discharged her duty, in endeavoring to im-
bue my mind with the principles of virtue. I have
had reason to be thankful that I was blest with
such a parent; her good advice and counsel to
me have been as bread cast upon the waters. She
was an instructive example to all who knew her,

From *Some Account of the Early Part of the Life of Elizabeth Ashbridge. Written by Herself* (Concord, N.H.: Cooledge
and Hough, 1810), 3–5, 8–11, 20, 21–25, 28–29, 30–
31, 33.

and generally beloved; but, alas! as soon as the
time came, when she might reasonably expect
the benefit from her labors, and have had comfort in me, I deserted her. In my childhood I had
an awful regard for religion and religious people,
particularly for ministers, all of whom I believed
to be good men and beloved of God, which I
earnestly wished to be my own case. . . .

I observed that there were several different
religious societies; this I often thought of, and
wept with desires that I might be directed to
the one which it would be best for me to join.
In this frame of mind passed my younger years.
I was sometimes guilty of the faults common
among children, but was always sorry for what
I had done amiss; and, till I was fourteen years
of age, I was as innocent as most children. About
this time, my sorrows (which have continued,
for the greatest part of my life, ever since) began, by my giving way to a foolish passion, in
setting my affections on a young man, who, without leave of my parents, courted me till I consented to marry him; and, with sorrow of heart,
I relate, that I suffered myself to be carried off
in the night. We were married: My parents made
all possible search for me, as soon as I was missing, but it was in vain. This precipitate act
plunged me into much sorrow. I was soon smitten with remorse for thus leaving my parents,
whose right it was to have disposed of me to
their content, or who, at least, ought to have
been consulted. But I was soon chastised for my
disobedience, and convinced of my error. In five
months, I was stripped of the darling of my
heart, and left a young and disconsolate widow.
I was now without a home. My husband had
derived his livelihood only from his trade, which
was that of a stocking weaver; and my father was
so displeased that he would do nothing for me.
My dear mother had some compassion for me,
and kept me among the neighbors. Afterwards,
by her advice, I went to a relation of hers, at
Dublin. We hoped that my absence would soften
my father's rigor; but he continued inflexible:
he would not send for me back, and I dared not
to return unless he did. . . .

[Ashebridge meets a "gentlewoman" who agrees to pay her passage to America; ignorant of the nature of an indenture, Ashbridge has actually been bound as a servant.]

On the 15th of the 7th month, which was nine weeks after we left Dublin, we arrived at New York. Here I was betrayed by the very men whose lives I had preserved. The captain caused an indenture to be made, and threatened me with a gaol, if I refused to sign it. I told him that I could find means to satisfy him for my passage without becoming bound. He replied, that I might take my choice, either to sign the indenture he showed me, or the one I had signed in Ireland should be in force. In a fright, I signed the former; for I had, by this time, learned the character of the woman who first induced me to think of going to America; she was a vile creature, and I feared that, if I fell into her hands, I should be used ill.

In two weeks I was sold. At first I had not much reason to complain of the treatment I received; but, in a short time, a difference, in which I was innocent, happened, that set my master against me, and rendered him inhuman. It will be impossible for me to convey an adequate idea of the sufferings of my servitude. Though my father was not rich, yet in his house I lived well, and I had been used to little but my school; but, now, I found it would have been better for me if I had been brought up with less indulgence. I was not allowed decent clothes; I was obliged to perform the meanest drudgery, and even to go barefoot in the snow. I suffered the utmost hardship that my body was able to bear, and the effect produced on my mind had nearly been my ruin forever.

My master seemed to be a very religious man, taking the sacrament (so called) regularly, and praying every night in his family; unless his prayer-book could not be found, for he never prayed without it to my knowledge. His example, however, made me sick of his religion: for, though I had but little religion myself, I had some idea of what religious people ought to be.

Respecting religion, my opinions began to waver; I even doubted whether there was any such thing; and began to think that the convictions I had felt from my infancy, were only the prejudices of education. These convictions seemed now to be lost; and, for some months, I do not remember to have felt them. I became hardened, and was ready to conclude that there was no God. The veneration I had felt for religious men, in my infancy, was entirely gone; I now looked upon them in a very different manner. My master's house was a place of great resort for the clergy; and, sometimes, those who came from a distance lodged with him. The observations I made on their conduct confirmed me in my atheistical opinions. They diverted themselves, in the evening, with cards and songs, and, a few moments after, introduced prayers and singing psalms to Almighty God. Often did I say to myself, "If there be a God, he is a pure Being, and will not hear the prayers of polluted lips."

But he who hath, in an abundant manner, shown mercy to me, (as will be seen in the sequel) did not long suffer my mind to be perplexed with doubts; but, in a moment, when my feet were on the brink of the bottomless pit, plucked me back.

To one woman, and to no other, I told the nature of the difference which had happened, two years before, between my master and me. By her means he heard of it, and, though he knew it was true, he sent for the town's whipper to correct me. I was called in. He never asked me whether I had told any such thing, but ordered me to strip. My heart was ready to burst. I would as freely have given up my life, as have suffered such ignominy. "If," said I, "there be a God, be graciously pleased to look down on one of the most unhappy creatures, and plead my cause; for thou knowest that, what I have related, is the truth;" and, had it not been for a principle more noble than he was capable of I would have told it to his wife. Then, fixing my eyes on the barbarous man, I said, "Sir, if you have no pity on me, yet for my father's sake, spare me from this shame; (for he had heard several ways of my parents) and, if you think I deserve such punishment, do it yourself." He took a turn over the room, and bade the whipper go about his business. Thus I came off without a blow; but my character seemed to be lost. Many reports were spread, which I bless God were not true. I suffered so much cruelty that I could not bear it; and was tempted to put an end to my miserable life. I listened to the temptation, and, for that purpose, went into the garret to hang myself. Now it was I felt convinced that there was a God. As I entered the place, horror and trembling seized me; and, while I stood as one in amazement, I seemed to hear a voice saying, "There is a hell beyond the grave." I was greatly astonished, and cried, "God be merciful, and enable me to bear whatsoever thou, in thy providence, shall bring or suffer to come upon me." I then went down stairs, but let no one know what I had been about.

Soon after this I had a dream; and, though some make a ridicule of dreams, this seemed very significant to me, and therefore I shall mention it. I thought I heard a knocking at the door, by which, when I had opened it, there stood a grave woman, holding in her right hand a lamp burning who, with a solid countenance, fixed her eye upon me and said, "I am sent to tell thee, that if thou wilt return to the Lord thy God, who created thee, he will have mercy on thee, and thy lamp shall not be put out in obscurity." Her lamp then flamed in an extraordinary manner; she left me and I awoke. . . .

[Ashbridge travels to Pennsylvania where she stays with her aunt, a Quaker preacher. One night, while asleep, Ashbridge is warned by the "enemy of mankind" not to be deluded by the Quakers.]

Warned in this manner, (from the right source as I thought) I resolved to be aware of those deceivers [Quakers], and, for some weeks, did not touch one of their books. The next day, being the first of the week, I was desirous of going to church, which was distant about four miles; but, being a stranger, and having no one to go with me, I gave up all thoughts of that, and, as most of the family were going to meeting, I went there with them. As we sat in silence, I looked over the meeting, and said to myself, 'How like fools these people sit; how much better would it be to stay at home, and read the Bible, or some good book, than come here and go to sleep.' As for me I was very drowsy; and, while asleep, had nearly fallen down. This was the last time I ever fell asleep in a meeting. I now began to be lifted up with spiritual pride, and to think myself better than they; but this disposition of mind did not last long. It may seem strange, that after living so long with one of this society at Dublin, I should yet be so much a stranger to them. In answer, let it be considered, that while I was there, I never read any of their books, nor went to a meeting; besides, I had heard such accounts of them, as made me think, that, of all societies, they were the worst. But he who knows the sincerity of the heart, looked on my weakness with pity; I was permitted to see my error, and shown that these were the people I ought to join. . . .

Of these things I let no one know. I feared discovery, and did not even appear like a friend.

I now hired to keep a school, and hearing of a place for my husband, I wrote, and desired him to come, though I did not let him know how it was with me.

I loved to go to meetings, but did not love to be seen going on week-days and therefore went to them from my school, through the woods. Notwithstanding all my care, the neighbors, (who were not friends) soon began to revile me with the name of Quaker; adding, that they supposed I intended to be a fool, and turn preacher. Thus did I receive the same censure, which, about a year before, I had passed on one of the handmaids of the Lord in Boston. I was so weak, that I could not bear the reproach. In order to change their opinion, I went into greater excess of apparel than I had freedom to do, even before I became acquainted with friends. In this condition I continued till my husband came, and then began the trial of my faith.

Before he reached me, he heard I was turned Quaker; at which he stamped, and said, "I had rather have heard she was dead, well as I love her; for, if it be so, all my comfort is gone. He then came to me; it was after an absence of four months; I got up and said to him, "My dear, I am glad to see thee." At this, he flew into a great rage, exclaiming 'The devil thee, thee, thee, don't thee me.' I endeavored, by every mild means, to pacify him; and, at length, got him fit to speak to my relations. As soon after this as we were alone, he said to me, "And so I see your Quaker relations have made you one;" I replied, that they had not, (which was true) I never had told them how it was with me. He said he would not stay amongst them; and having found a place to his mind, hired and came directly back to fetch me, walking, in one afternoon, thirty miles to keep me from meeting the next day, which was first day. He took me, after testing this day, to the place where he had hired, and to lodgings he had engaged at the house of a churchwarden. This man was a bitter enemy of Friends, and did all he could to irritate my husband against them.

Though I did not appear like a friend, they all believed me to be one. When my husband and he used to be making their diversions and reviling, I sat in silence, though now and then an involuntary sigh broke from me; at which he would say, 'There did not I tell you your wife was a Quaker, and she will become a preacher.' On such an occasion as this, my husband once came up to me, in a great rage, and shaking his hand over me, said, "You had better be hanged in that day." I was seized with horror, and again plunged into despair, which continued nearly three months. . . .

In the night, when, under this painful distress of mind, I could not sleep, if my husband perceived me weeping, he would revile me for it. At length, when he and his friend thought themselves too weak to overset me, he went to the priest at Chester, to inquire what he could

do with me. This man knew I was a member of the church, for I had shown him my certificate. His advice was, to take me out of Pennsylvania, and settle in some place where there were no Quakers. My husband replied, he did not care where we went, if he could but restore me to my natural liveliness of temper. As for me, I had no resolution to oppose their proposals, nor much cared where I went. I seemed to have nothing to hope for. I daily expected to be made a victim of divine wrath, and was possessed with the idea that this would be by thunder.

When the time of removal came, I was not permitted to bid my relations farewell; and, as my husband was poor, and kept no horse, I was obliged to travel on foot. We came to Wilmington, 15 miles, and from thence to Philadelphia by water. Here we stopt at a tavern, where I became the spectacle and discourse of the company. My husband told them his wife had become a Quaker, and he designed, if possible to find out a place where there were none: (thought I) I was once in a condition to deserve that name, but now it is over with me. O that I might, from a true hope, once more have an opportunity to confess the truth; though I was sure of all manner of cruelties, I would not regard them. Such were my concerns, while he was entertaining the company with my story, in which he told them that I had been a good dancer, but now he could get me neither to dance or sing. One of the company then started up, and said, "I'll fetch a fiddle, and we'll have a good dance;" a proposal with which my husband was pleased. When the fiddle was brought my husband came and said to me, "My dear, shake off that gloom, and let us have a civil dance; you would, now and then, when you were a good churchwoman, and that's better than a stiff Quaker." I had taken up the resolution not to comply with his request, whatever might be the consequence; this I let him know, though I durst say little, for fear of his choleric temper. He pulled me round the room, till the tears fell from my eyes, at the sight of which the musician stopt, and said, "I'll play no more; let your wife alone." There was a person in company that came from Freehold, in East Jersey, who said, "I see your wife's a Quaker, but if you'll take my advice you need not go so far as you intend; come and live with us; we'll soon cure her of her Quakerism, and we want a schoolmaster and schoolmistress too." He consented, and a happy turn it was for me, as will shortly be seen. The answer of peace was afforded me, for refusing to dance; I rejoiced more than if I had been made mistress of much riches, and, with tears, prayed, "Lord, I dread to ask, and yet without thy gracious pardon; I am miserable. I therefore fall down before thy throne, imploring mercy at thy hand. O Lord, once more, I beseech thee, try my obedience, and then, in whatsoever thou commandest, I will obey thee, and not fear to confess thee before men." My cries were heard, and it was shown to me, that he delights not in the death of a sinner. My soul was again set at liberty, and I could praise him. . . .

By the end of the week, we got settled in our new situation. We took a room, in a friend's house, one mile from each school, and eight from the meetinghouse. I now deemed it proper to let my husband see I was determined to join with Friends. When first day came, I directed myself to him in this manner "My dear, art thou willing to let me go to meeting?" He flew into a rage, and replied, "No you sha'n't." Speaking firmly, I told him, 'That, as a dutiful wife, I was ready to obey all his lawful commands; but, when they imposed upon my conscience, I could not obey him. I had already wronged myself, in having done it too long: and though he was near to me, and, as a wife ought, I loved him; yet God, who was nearer than all the world to me, had made me sensible that this was the way in which I ought to go. I added, that this was no small cross to my own will; but I had given up my heart, and I trusted that he who called for it would enable me, for the remainder of my life, to keep it steadily devoted to his service; and I hoped I should not, on this account, make the worse wife. I spoke, however, to no purpose; he continued inflexible.

I had now put my hand to the plough, and resolved not to draw back; I therefore went without leave. I expected he would immediately follow and force me back, but he did not. I called at the house of one of the neighbors, and, getting a girl to show me the way I went on rejoicing and praising God in my heart. . . .

Finding that all the means he had yet used could not alter my resolutions, he several times struck me with severe blows. I endeavored to bear all with patience, believing that the time would come when he would see I was in the right. Once he came up to me, took out his penknife, and said, "If you offer to go to meeting to-morrow, with this knife I'll cripple you, for you shall not be a Quaker." I made him no answer. In the morning I set out as usual; he did not attempt to harm me. . . .

[Ashbridge goes to a Quaker meeting and confesses her faith in public.]

This day, as usual, I had gone to meeting on foot. While my husband (as he afterwards told me) was lying on the bed, these words crossed his mind:—"Lord, where shall I flee to shun thee," &c. upon which he arose, and seeing it rain, got the horse and set off to fetch me, arriving just as the meeting broke up. I got on horseback as quickly as possible, lest he should hear I had been speaking; he did hear of it nevertheless, and, as soon as we were in the woods, began with saying, "Why do you mean thus to make my life unhappy? What, could you not be a Quaker, without turning fool in this manner?" I answered in tears, "My dear, look on me with pity, if thou hast any; canst thou think that I, in the bloom of my days, would bear all that thou knowest of, and much that thou knowest not of, if I did not feel it my duty?" These words touched him, and he said, "Well, I'll e'en give you up; I see it wont avail to strive; if it be of God I cannot overthrow it; and, if of yourself, it will soon fall." I saw the tears stand in his eyes, at which I was overcome with joy, and began already to reap the fruits of my obedience. . . .

We lived in a small house by ourselves, which though mean, and though we had little to put in it our bed being no better than chaff, I was truly content. The only desires I had were for my own preservation, and to be blessed with the reformation of my husband. He was connected with a set of men whom he feared would make game of him, which indeed they already did; asking him when he designed to commence preacher, for they saw he intended to turn Quaker, and seemed to love his wife better since she became one, than before. They used to come to our house, and provoked him to sit up and drink with them, sometimes till near day, while I have been sorrowing in a stable. Once, as I sat in this condition I heard him say to his company, "I can't bear any longer to afflict my poor wife in this manner; for whatever you may think of her, I do believe she's a good woman." He then came to me and said: . . . 'Come in my dear, God has given thee a deal of patience; I'll put an end to this practice.' That was the last time they sat up late at night.

Suggestions for Further Reading

Bacon, Margaret Hope. *Mothers of Feminism: The Story of Quaker Women in America*. San Francisco: Harper and Row, 1986.

Burke, Helen M. "The Rhetoric and Politics of Marginality: The Subject of Phillis Wheatley." *Tulsa Studies in Women's Literature* 10 (1991): 31–46.

Dexter, Elizabeth. *Colonial Women of Affairs: Women in Business and the Professions in America before 1776*. New York: Houghton Mifflin, 1931.

Dunn, Mary Maples. "Saints and Sisters: Congregational and Quaker Women in the Early Colonial Period." *American Quarterly* 30 (1978): 582–601.

Edkins, Carol. "Quest for Community: Spiritual Autobiographies of Eighteenth-Century Quaker and Puritan Women in America." In *Women's Autobiography: Essays in Criticism,* ed. by Estelle Jelinek. Bloomington: Indiana Univ. Press, 1980. pp. 39–52.

Evans, Sara M. *Born for Liberty: A History of Women in America*. New York: The Free Press, 1989.

Foster, Frances Smith. *Written by Herself: Literary Production by African American Women, 1746–1892*. Bloomington: Indiana Univ. Press, 1993.

George, Carol V. R. "Anne Hutchinson and the 'Revolution Which Never Happened.'" In *"Remember the Ladies": New Perspectives on Women in American History,* ed. Carol George. Syracuse: Syracuse Univ. Press, 1975. pp. 13–37.

Karlsen, Carol F. *The Devil in the Shape of a Woman: Witchcraft in Colonial New England*. New York: W. W. Norton, 1987.

Kibbey, Ann. "Mutations of the Supernatural: Witchcraft, Remarkable Providences, and the Power of Puritan Men." *American Quarterly* 34 (1982): 125–48.

Koehler, Lyle. "The Case of the American Jezebels: Anne Hutchinson and Female Agitation During the Years of Antinomian Turmoil, 1636–1640." *William and Mary Quarterly*, 31 (1974): 55–78.

———. *A Search for Power: The "Weaker Sex" in Seventeenth-Century New England*. Urbana: Univ. of Illinois Press, 1980.

Lang, Amy Schrager. *Prophetic Woman: Anne Hutchinson and the Problem of Dissent in the Literature of New England*. Berkeley: Univ. of California Press, 1987.

Martin, Wendy. *An American Triptych: Anne Bradstreet, Emily Dickinson, Adrienne Rich*. Chapel Hill: Univ. of North Carolina Press, 1984.

Matthews, Glenna. *The Rise of Public Woman: Woman's Power and Woman's Place in the United States, 1630–1970*. New York: Oxford Univ. Press, 1992.

Norton, Mary Beth. "The Evolution of White Women's Experience in Early America." *American Historical Review* 89 (1984): 593–619.

Spruill, Julia Cherry. *Women's Life and Work in the Southern Colonies*. New York: W. W. Norton, 1975.

Ulrich, Laurel Thatcher. *Good Wives: Image and Reality in the Lives of Women in Northern New England, 1650–1750*. New York: Alfred A. Knopf, 1982.

PART II

Of Education and Virtue: Women's Thought in the Revolutionary and Early National Periods

I. *Revolutionizing the Family and Relations Between the Sexes*

FEMINISM IN THE NEWLY CREATED UNITED STATES began with the American Revolution; the celebrated origin of "America" also witnessed the beginning of a more covert revolution of the nation's social relations. To support the war effort, many American women refused to drink tea and spun their own cloth thus effecting political action through domestic activities. Other women—in Philadelphia, New Jersey, Maryland, and Virginia—organized to raise money for the soldiers. The broadside, "Sentiments of an American Woman" (1780), written by Esther DeBerdt Reed, initiated the first national women's organization, enlisting support not just from the women of Philadelphia but of all thirteen new states. The document signals the collective entry of American women into politics and, in its claim that women are "at least equal . . . in our love for the public good," ushered them into the world of national politics. In substantiating her assertion that women were the active enemies of political tyranny, Reed traces a tradition of public, even sovereign and military women, drawing on the history of Antiquity, of Europe, and on the Bible for strong female forebears.

While the Revolution and the founding of the United States did afford some women political rights (New Jersey, for instance, allowed white women who owned property to vote until 1807 and Virginia explicitly made white women citizens for a short time), the framers of the Constitution and the state legislatures did not heed Abigail Adams's call to "remember the ladies," did not, in other words, acknowledge women's citizenship within the new republic.

Of course, most African-American women suffered the additional hardship and degradation of involuntary servitude, as the nation failed to resolve the awful contradiction between life under slavery and the ideals of the Revolution. Paradoxically, though, the language of individual rights, equality, and personal freedom—which at least on its surface was ungendered—could be adopted by even the most disenfranchised. Belinda, a slave, petitioned the legislature of Massachusetts in 1782 in order to win an allowance from the estate of her late master; her argument indicts the United States for casting off the "lawless dominion" of England and thus ending American "vassalage" while at the same time perpetuating both evils in the institution of slavery.

Other women invoked the Revolution in order to advance their own cause, using the war, like Belinda did, as an analogy for the struggle against a patriarchal society. While Belinda fixed on the social depravity of slavery, other women focused on the debauchery and licen-

37

tiousness of men and on how those evils led to the suffering of women. (Significantly, the effort to abolish the system of slavery and to reform the morals of the nation, begun after the Revolution, would impel women's first efforts at mass public organizing in the earliest decades of the nineteenth century.) In her pamphlet, "Women Invited to War," (1787) Hannah Adams claims that, as men's spiritual equals, women have a responsibility to be first in the battle against the pervasive moral "sin" that has "done more harm already, than all the armies of Britain have done," adding that men are the first to succumb to destructive vices such as intemperance. The satirical "Humble Address of Ten Thousand Federal Maids" (1791) charges that women have, by default, become the defenders of civic liberty—soldiers in a war against vice which men have deserted, subsequently becoming the enemy. Since women are the prime movers in the defense of national freedom, health, and happiness, they deserve the consequent rights of citizenship such as holding public office. In both of these documents, the writers adopt the language of the Revolution in imagining an egalitarian republic, one that would reflect and preserve the distinct values of women.

Anglo-American women of the early national period also drew from the egalitarian rhetoric of the Revolution to challenge the balance of power in marriage and, more generally, to reform the social structure of the family. It is important to note, however, that radically different family structures were already present in North America. Some Native American tribes, such as the Iroquois, were both matrilineal (descent was determined through the mother) and matrilocal (a man lived with his wife's family). In part because of their central position in the family, some Native American women had a considerable amount of public power; Cherokee women, for instance, tried to prevent the disposition of tribal land by the Cherokee government in the late-eighteenth and early-nineteenth centuries. In her "Letter to President Benjamin Franklin" (1787), Katteuha draws on the respect that she expects and demands as a mother to try to ensure peace between whites and Cherokees, despite battles over land.

White women, just starting to revise the patriarchal family structure, began by publicly questioning the idea of men's superiority to women, arguing instead for a non-hierarchical relationship between husband and wife. The anonymous writers of both "On the Supposed Superiority of the Masculine Understanding" (1791) and "On Matrimonial Obedience" (1792) reject the notion that women owe absolute obedience to their husbands, a concept that produces despotism and "slavery" rather than a loving relationship of mutual respect and equality. The belief in marriage as a contract between equals necessarily entails women's becoming better educated: both these two writers argue, that men's interests will be served by having an intelligent partner whose sound advice and good sense he can depend on, as opposed to a mindless slave both to himself and to the typical feminine pursuits of fashion and leisure.

In terms of the reform of family relations, ideas of human equality converged with Enlightenment emphasis on the malleability of a child's mind and belief in noncoercive education, resulting in a shift, as Glenna Matthews has pointed out, from the authoritative patriarchal structure of the family to an increasingly natural model of affection: "fathers would surrender some of their power and authority to mothers, and both parents would strive to be loved rather than feared."[1] The author of "A Second Vindication of the Rights of Women" (1801)

1. Glenna Matthews, *The Rise of Public Woman: Woman's Power and Woman's Place in the United States, 1630–1970* (New York: Oxford Univ. Press, 1992), 54–55.

articulates the belief in the increasingly sympathetic father, who would never "subjugate" his daughters to "lordly imposition"; by extension, the writer continues, nor should he subjugate his wife.

As the role of the father changed, so too did the complementary role of mother. As a child's early training became increasingly central to his or her role as a citizen of the republic, women began to acquire power *as* mothers. Linda Kerber has coined the phrase "Republican Motherhood" to express the new complex of values, at the end of the eighteenth century, that connected women's private work in the home with the national interest: "The woman now claimed a significant political role, though she played it in the home. This new identity," Kerber continues, "had the advantage of appearing to reconcile politics and domesticity; it justified continued political education and political sensibility."[2] And, indeed, the writer of "On the Supposed Superiority of the Masculine Understanding" uses the role of motherhood—of a woman's "making the first impressions on the infant minds of the whole human race"—as the cornerstone of her argument for women's equality with men in both education and politics.

A couple of decades later, Hannah Crocker wrote an exemplary statement of Republican Motherhood in her "On the Real Rights of Women" (1818), a document that consistently refers to the "mutual rights" and the "equal judgment" of men and women and to the power of mothers to "make better subjects for a republican government." Using metaphors that extend women's influence beyond the walls of the home and into the larger public sphere, Crocker argues for a woman's right to rule over a "family government." She thus conflates the private and the public realm, claiming their interdependence and even inseparability: the "public faith and confidence in the government," Crocker asserts, "commence[s] in the private faith and confidence of individuals." And in Crocker's opinion women both are, and are essential in shaping, those "individuals" that found the republic.

Within their late-eighteenth-century reformulations of family relations, most women writers were reluctant to suggest that women should abandon the institutions of the home, marriage, and motherhood; a notable exception, though, is the anonymously authored "Lines, Written by a Lady, Who Was Questioned Respecting Her Inclination to Marry" (1794). In this poem, the speaker compares herself to a republic that "abhors" the "tyrannical systems and modes" of marriage; furthermore, she portrays the state of the unmarried woman, the "old maid," as a "republic of freedom and ease." This document fleetingly highlights the potential of egalitarian rhetoric to reject rather than to reform the institution of marriage: implicit within the poem is the radical notion that republican ideals of equality and freedom and eighteenth-century laws and conventions of marriage are irreconcilable—that they cannot function in the complementary fashion so many other writers envisioned. Indeed, the doctrine of coverture persisted through the social upheaval of the Revolution, as women remained invisible—"covered" by their husband's economic, legal, and political state—from the moment they married.

The limited effectiveness of republican rhetorics of rights, freedom, equality, and reciprocity to change existing legal and social institutions became increasingly evident around the turn into the nineteenth century. Consider, for instance, the concept of feminine virtue. At

2. Linda Kerber, *Women of the Republic: Intellect and Ideology in Revolutionary America* (New York: Norton, 1980), 11.

the time of the Revolution, the term bridged the public and private realms, functioning like Republican Motherhood to tie women's domestic and familial activities to wider ideals of national and political service. By around 1800, though, "virtue" lost its political meaning and began to signify a somehow eternal and essential feminine trait of moral purity and goodness. "Virtuous" women thus became further removed from the public sphere and also from the possibility of directly agitating for the transformation of the public institutions in and under which they lived.

On the one hand, demonstrating how women's virtue had become confined to the home and to the domestic sphere by the early nineteenth century, "The Criterion of Virtue" (1802) also reveals how the new discourse of feminine virtue ushered in a distinct kind of feminist thought based on woman's moral superiority. Instead of pushing for equality with men, some women thinkers emphasized the distinct character of the sexes and urged that women maintain their different qualities, a nexus of virtues that included sympathy, humility, selflessness, and duty. As the nineteenth century began, women's virtue became the most important and most *visible* feminine quality—hence the emphasis in "The Criterion of Virtue" on physical manifestations of virtue: the writer insists, for instance, that a virtuous woman is always able to "drop a tear of compassion." For women, the power of being marked as virtuous meant that, while they did not have any direct power to change their circumstances, they did (in theory at least) have the power of influence and of "moral suasion," and could thus convince men to act according to their dictates.

9

ESTHER DeBERDT REED
Sentiments of an American
Woman (1780)

On the commencement of actual war, the Women of America manifested a firm resolution to contribute as much as could depend on them, to the deliverance of their country. Animated by the purest patriotism they are sensible of sorrow at this day, in not offering more than barren wishes for the success of so glorious a Revolution. They aspire to render themselves more really useful; and this sentiment is universal from the north to the south of the Thirteen United States. Our ambition is kindled by the fame of those heroines of antiquity, who have rendered their sex illustrious, and have proved to the universe, that, if the weakness of our Constitution, if opinion and manners did not forbid us to march to glory by the same path as the Men, we should at least equal and sometimes surpass them in our love for the public good. I glory in all that which my sex has done great and commendable. I call to mind with enthusiasm and with admiration, all those acts of courage, of constancy and patriotism, which history has transmitted to us: The people favoured by Heaven, preserved from destruction by the virtues, the zeal and the resolution of Deborah, of Judith, of Esther! The fortitude of the mother of the Macchabees, in giving up her sons to die before her eyes: Rome saved from the fury of a victorious enemy by the efforts of Volumnia, and other Roman ladies: So many famous sieges where the Women have been seen forgetting the weakness of their sex, building new walls, digging trenches with their feeble hands; furnishing arms to their defenders, they themselves darting the missile weapons on the enemy, resigning the ornaments of their apparel, and their

Broadside, printed by John Dunlap in Philadelphia, June 10, 1780.

fortunes to fill the public treasury, and to hasten the deliverance of their country; burying themselves under its ruins; throwing themselves into the flames rather than submit to the disgrace of humiliation before a proud enemy.

Born for liberty, disdaining to bear the irons of a tyrannic Government, we associate ourselves to the grandeur of those Sovereigns, cherished and revered, who have held with so much splendour the scepter of the greatest States, The Batildas, the Elizabeths, the Maries, the Catharines, who have extended the empire of liberty, and contented to reign by sweetness and justice, have broken the chains of slavery, forged by tyrants in the times of ignorance and barbarity. The Spanish Women, do they not make, at this moment, the most patriotic sacrifices, to encrease the means of victory in the hands of their Sovereign. He is a friend to the French Nation. They are our allies. We call to mind, doubly interested, that it was a French Maid who kindled up amongst her fellow-citizens, the flame of patriotism buried under long misfortunes; It was the Maid of Orleans who drove from the kingdom of France the ancestors of those same British, whose odious yoke we have just shaken off; and whom it is necessary that we drive from this Continent.

But I must limit myself to the recollection of this small number of achievements. Who knows if persons disposed to censure, and sometimes too severely with regard to us, may not disapprove our appearing acquainted even with the actions of which our sex boasts? We are at least certain, that he cannot be a good citizen who will not applaud our efforts for the relief of the armies which defend our lives, our possessions, our liberty? The situation of our soldiery has been represented to me; the evils inseparable from war, and the firm and generous spirit which has enabled them to support these. But it has been said, that they may apprehend, that, in the course of a long war, the view of their distresses may be lost, and their services be forgotten. Forgotten! never; I can answer in the name of all my sex. Brave Americans, your disinterestedness, your courage, and your constancy will always be dear to America, as long as she shall preserve her virtue.

We know that at a distance from the theatre of war, if we enjoy any tranquility, it is the fruit of your watchings, your labours, your dangers. If I live happy in the midst of my family; if my husband cultivates his field, and reaps his harvest in peace; if, surrounded with my children, I myself nourish the youngest, and press it to my bosom, without being affraid of seeing myself separated from it, by a ferocious enemy; if the house in which we dwell; if our barns, our orchards are safe at the present time from the hands of those incendiaries, it is to you that we owe it. And shall we hesitate to evidence to you our gratitude? Shall we hesitate to wear a cloathing more simple; hair dressed less elegant, while at the price of this small privation, we shall deserve your benedictions. Who, amongst us, will not renounce with the highest pleasure, those vain ornaments, when she shall consider that the valiant defenders of America will be able to draw some advantage from the money which she may have laid out in these; that they will be better defended from the rigours of the seasons, that after their painful toils, they will receive some extraordinary and unexpected relief; that these presents will perhaps be valued by them at a greater price, when they will have it in their power to say: *This is the offering of the Ladies.* The time is arrived to display the same sentiments which animated us at the beginning of the Revolution when we renounced the use of teas, however agreeable to our taste, rather than receive them from our persecutors; when we made it appear to them that we placed former necessaries in the rank of superfluities, when our liberty was interested; when our republican and laborious hands spun the flax, prepared the linen intended for the use of our soldiers; when exiles and fugitives we supported with courage all the evils which are the concomitants of war. Let us not lose a moment; let us be engaged to offer the homage of our gratitude at the altar of military valour, and you, our brave deliverers, while

mercenary slaves combat to cause you to share with them, the irons with which they are loaded, receive with a free hand our offering, the purest which can be presented to your virtue.

10

BELINDA

Petition of an African Slave (1782)

To the honourable the senate and house of representatives, in general court assembled:

The petition of Belinda, an African, Humbly shews,

That seventy years have rolled away, since she, on the banks of the Rio de Valta, received her existence. The mountain, covered with spicy forests—the vallies, loaded with the richest fruits, spontaneously produced—joined to that happy temperature of air, which excludes excess, would have yielded her the most complete felicity, had not her mind received early impressions of the cruelty of men, whose faces were like the moon, and whose bows and arrows were like the thunder and the lightning of the clouds. The idea of these, the most dreadful of all enemies, filled her infant slumbers with horror, and her noon-tide moments with cruel apprehensions! But her affrighted imagination, in its most alarming extension, never represented distress equal to what she has since really experienced: for before she had twelve years enjoyed the fragrance of her native groves and ere she realized that Europeans placed their happiness in the yellow dust, which she carelessly marked with her infant footsteps—even when she, in a sacred grove, with each hand in that of a tender parent, was paying her devotion to the great Orisa, who made all things, an armed band of white men, driving many of her countrymen in

"Petition of an African Slave, to the Legislature of Massachusetts," Boston, February, 1782, *The American Museum or Repository of Ancient and Modern Fugitive Pieces, &c. Prose and Poetical* 1 (June 1787).

chains, rushed into the hallowed shades! Could the tears, the sighs, and supplications, bursted from the tortured parental affection, have blunted the keen edge of avarice, she might have been rescued from agony, which many of her country's children have felt, but which none have ever described. In vain she lifted her supplicating voice to an insulted father, and her guiltless hands to a dishonoured deity! She was ravished from the bosom of her country, from the arms of her friends, while the advanced age of her parents, rendering them unfit for servitude, cruelly separated her from them forever.

Scenes which her imagination had never conceived of, a floating world, the sporting monsters of the deep, and the familiar meetings of billows and clouds, strove, but in vain, to divert her attention from three hundred Africans in chains, suffering the most excruciating torment; and some of them rejoicing that the pangs of death came, like a balm to the wounds.

Once more her eyes were blest with a continent: but alas! how unlike the land where she received her being! Here all things appeared unpropitious. She learned to catch the ideas, marked by the sounds of language, only to know that her doom was slavery, from which death alone was to emancipate her. What did it avail her, that the walls of her lord were hung with splendor, and that the dust trodden under foot in her native country, crouded his gates with sordid worshippers! The laws rendered her incapable of receiving property: and though she was a free moral agent, accountable for her own actions, yet never had she a moment at her own disposal! Fifty years her faithful hands have been compelled to ignoble servitude for the benefit of an Isaac Royall, until, as if nations must be agitated, and the world convulsed, for the preservation of that freedom, which the Almighty Father intended for all the human race, the present war commenced. The terrors of men, armed in the cause of freedom, compelled her master to fly, and to breathe away his life in a land, where lawless dominion sits enthroned, pouring blood and vengeance on all who dare to be free.

The face of your petitioner is now marked with the furrows of time, and her frame feebly bending under the oppression of years, while she, by the laws of the land, is denied the enjoyment of one morsel of that immense wealth, a part whereof hath been accumulated by her own industry, and the whole augmented by her servitude.

Wherefore, casting herself at the feet of your honours, as to a body of men, formed for the extirpation of vassalage, for the reward of virtue, and the just returns of honest industry— she prays that such allowance may be made her, out of the estate of colonel Royall, as will prevent her, and her more infirm daughter, from misery in the greatest extreme, and scatter comfort over the short and downward path of their lives: and she will ever pray.

Belinda.

11

KATTEUHA
Letter to President Benjamin Franklin (1787)

Brother,

I am in hopes my Brothers and the Beloved men near the water side will heare from me. This day I filled the pipes that they smoaked in piece, and I am in hopes the smoake has Reached up to the skies above. I here send you a piece of the same Tobacco, and am in hopes you and your Beloved men will smoake it in Friendship—and I am glad in my heart that I am the mother of men that will smoak it in piece.
Brother,

I am in hopes if you Rightly consider it that woman is the mother of All—and that Woman Does not pull Children out of Trees or Stumps nor out of old Logs, but out of their Bodies, so that they ought to mind what a woman says, and

From Samuel Hazard, ed., *Pennsylvania Archives 1787*, vol. 11, (Philadelphia, 1852–56), 181–82.

look upon her as a mother—and I have Taken the privelage to Speak to you as my own Children, and the same as if you had sucked my Breast—and I am in hopes you have a beloved woman amongst you who will help to put her Children right if they do wrong, as I shall do the same—the great men have all promised to Keep the path clear and white so that the Messengers shall go and come in safety Between us—the old people is never done Talking to their Children—which makes me say so much as I do. The Talk you sent to me was to talk to my Children, which I have done this day, and they all liked my Talk well, which I am in hopes you will heare from me Every now and then that I keep my children in piece—tho' I am a woman giving you this Talk, I am in hopes that you and all the Beloved men in Congress will pay particular Attention to it, as I am Delivering it to you from the Bottom of my heart, that they will Lay this on the white stool in Congress, wishing them all well and success in all their undertakings—I hold fast the good Talk I Received from you my Brother, and thanks you kindly for your good Talks, and your presents, and the kind usage you gave to my son.

From KATTEUHA
The Beloved Woman of Chota

12

Hannah Adams
Women Invited to War (1787)

Preface

The Writer of the following Address to the Women, is one who is, and has been for some years past, very much concerned for the happiness and welfare of the people of America, especially upon a spiritual account.

And although she is sensible that a great many

From *Women Invited to War, or a Friendly Address to the Honourable Women of the United States. By a Daughter of America* (Boston: Edes and Son, 1787), 2–4, 10–12

of those to whom she writes, are her Superiors in grace and knowledge; yet she hopes it may not be thought amiss that she has put them in mind of some things that seem to be too little regarded among us.

Several Ministers of the Gospel advised, and desired her, to write an Exhortation to the People: And some Reverend Ministers and other Religious Persons, have perused her Writings; they commend the Book, and approve of the Publication of it.

O ye ladies of honour, worthy women, and honourable daughters of America,—Although it is our lot to live in a time of remarkable difficulty, trouble and danger; a time wherein we have heard the confused noise of the warrior, and seen garments rolled in blood: yet blessed by God, we have had the honour and favour of seeing our friends and brethren exert themselves valiantly in the defence of life and liberty.

And the Lord of Hosts gave them courage, fortitude, prudence and zeal in a good cause, and continued the same, and made them instrumental of defeating many of the designs of our enemies until the destructive war has been brought to an end. But alas! my dear friends, there is another powerful enemy spread through America, and is daily increasing among us, and threatens our destruction. This enemy has done more harm already, than all the armies of Britain have done or ever will be able to do. This dangerous and ruining enemy that is in the midst of us, has almost got the victory over America, and we shall all be destroyed or brought into captivity, if the women as well as the men, do not oppose, resist, and fight against this destructive enemy.

This enemy is deceitful and cruel, and many thousands have been deceived and destroyed thereby: and verily it has caused many of our dear friends to fall: and we are all in danger every hour, of being either slain or wounded by this enemy. And there are many among us, who entertain this enemy as if it were a friend: and they seem to be as unconcerned and insensible of their danger, as if they were fast a sleep: therefore they take no suitable care to prevent their own ruin, nor the destruction of America: and so by stupidity and carelessness, our danger is increased.

Now if any of you inquire, saying, What enemy is this by whom we are in danger of being destroyed?

I answer, Truly my friends, we are in great danger of being overcome and destroyed by SIN, which is the worst of all enemies. This enemy does more harm than Satan is able to do: though he is a subtle and powerful enemy, and is striving to lead us into the destructive ways of sin, yet if we resist him as we ought, he can never destroy us. . . .

But perhaps some of you may say, there are some very heinous sins, which our sex are not so commonly guilty of, as the men are; in particular the vile sin of drinking to excess, and also prophane swearing and cursing, and taking the great and holy Name of God in vain, are practiced more by men than by women, in some parts of America: and these sins are some of the destructive enemies that should be immediately resisted and overcome. Now if it be so, if the men have in these, or any other instances, been more out of the way than we have been: then let us at present, leave them to mend their own errors, and let us speedily and carefully endeavour to find out, and reform what is amiss in ourselves. Now if I should ask you, What is your mind concerning this matter? I doubt not but you would all say, There ought to be a speedy reformation among us, and you think it is high time to fight against our spiritual enemies: But I fear there are some who are not yet sensible of the greatness of their danger, and therefore they will postpone the great work of striving to overcome the enemy: and it may be, they will endeavour to excuse their delay, by saying, it belongs to the men to be leaders in religious affairs; therefore let them rise up first and shew their zeal and courage in fighting against the worst of enemies!

And truly it may be said, Every man in his own house, and the officers in the christian church, ought to be leaders in the external performance of many religious duties; and I hope there are to be found among them, some who are zealous for their GOD, and by the help of His spirit and grace are now striving to overcome the worst of all enemies; and are diligent also in their endeavours to excite and persuade others to engage in this great work of opposing and resisting the enemy. But this warfare is of a spiritual nature: and the Lord Jesus Christ himself is the leader of all those who engage in his service, and fight against his enemies: he is captain of the Lord's host, and he has overcome our spiritual enemies; he has got the victory over all the powers of darkness; he has broke the snare of the enemy, wherein all mankind were taken, and has opened a way for our escape: and all the ends of the earth are called upon to look unto him, and be saved. And whereas the woman was first overcome by the enemy, and brought into bondage to Sin and Satan, it becomes the women now to be foremost (if it be possible) in fleeing to Christ for deliverance from their spiritual bondage; and in striving by the help of his grace and spirit, to overcome the temptations of Satan, and to get the victory over every Sin.

Now concerning the Men,—Though there may be many of them who are not yet engaged in battle against their spiritual enemies, this should no way discourage or hinder the women from going forward in their spiritual warfare; but should rather excite them to be more zealously engaged in this good cause.

But it may be, some will enquire, saying, Is not the Female the inferior sex, and shall inferiors set out before their superiors, in this great and important affair?—To which it may be replied, that in this spiritual warfare, an inferior may go before a superior without acting contrary to the rules of religion, decency or good manners. And as to one sex being superior to the other, let it be considered that our first parents were made, the one as well as the other of them, in the image of GOD, and that they had equal dominion over the creatures: And as some writers have observed, The woman was not made out of Man's head to rule him, nor out of his feet to be trampled upon by him, but of his side, to be equal. Though it is acknowledged, that as the Man was first formed, and as the Woman was first in the transgression, therefore the male is in civil respects to be considered as the superior sex. But still, in the rights of religion and conscience, and in point of salvation, there is neither male nor female, but all are one in Christ, and joint-heirs of the promise: for with God there is no respect of persons. And therefore the superiority of the Male can be no bar to hinder the Female from being either the first engaged, or more zealous and courageous in proceeding in this spiritual warfare. And the Women as well as the Men, are invited to inlist themselves into the service of Christ, and fight against his enemies. And it is required of those who are engaged in the cause of Christ, that they be strong in the Lord, and in the power of his might: also that they put on the whole armour of God, that they may be able to stand against the wiles of the Devil. And if called thereunto, they must resist even unto blood, striving against sin. They must be steadfast, unmovable, always abounding in the work of the Lord. They must be diligently following every good work, and abstain from all appearance of evil.

13
The Humble Address of Ten Thousand Maids (1791)

To the Honorable CONGRESS of the UNITED STATES.
The humble Address of ten thousand Federal Maids.

With a blush of female modesty, we present this respectful address, in hopes that our federal voice may in some degree soften the clamour of discontent that stuns your ears. We are grieved to see, that a glorious empire ce-

From *The General Advertiser and Political, Commercial and Literary Journal*, 24 January 1791.

mented by the blood of gallant fellow-citizens, fathers and brothers, is yet in danger from licentious discord; and we make you a solemn tender of all the aid that *faithful female hearts* can give. Phlegmatic pedants and flirting beaus may ridicule this language as the effusion of enthusiasm; we scorn the paltry beings who never felt the sublimity and ardour of *our country's sacred love*. We repeat again, command our utmost efforts for the public good. If the men will not suffer your excise to touch their *darling grog*, excess in which does every year destroy thousands, brings many hundred families to beggary, and breaks the hearts of many amiable wives—tax then freely our favorite tea, our caps, bonnets, cushions, bishops, every piece of ornamental dress. If still more is wanted, tax our very under-petticoats. If our young men will not learn how to defend their liberty and property, their hoary sire, the mother who bore and suckled them—then order us into the field. We shrink indeed from violence; some of us cannot without pain kill a chicken: But alas! the sword is yet in this civilized era, the *ultima ratio*. This charming country may invite bold invaders; it may breed vipers in its bosom. This land of liberty must be defended against foreign and domestic foes. Some of us are of the society called *Friends*, and we all respect the civil virtues of this society; but we cannot believe that a man does please the righteous judge of mankind, and father of mercies, by suffering a savage to *scalp his child, or burn the wife of his bosom in slow fires*. We all know the value of national industry; but *gold must be defended by steel*. Independence must not be hazarded merely to make an apprentice work some *additional* days more in the year for his master. Learning is both useful and ornamental to nations: But do not our scholars know, that *Minerva was the Goddess of arms as well as arts*? Some of us will never marry a fellow who cannot protect his sweet-heart, although he could chant all the battles of Homer in Greek.

Your petitioners revere the rights of conscience. They know also that general regulations require modification; but every good citizen will chearfully bear his portion of the public burden; if he cannot fight, he will pay; if he drinks a great deal, he will not grudge the price of his enjoyment.

Finally, as those that sow have a right to reap, your petitioners request with due submission a few small privileges: as *an order of female heroism*, like that of the *Cincinnati*; the right of election to all public offices; and especially an *absolute command over non-paying and non-fighting husbands.*

TEN THOUSAND FEDERAL MAIDS.

14
On the Supposed Superiority of the Masculine Understanding (1791)

The mind of man no sooner expands itself into action, than it is impressed with the passions of vanity, and a love of power. An indulgence of these passions, and a supine inattention to first causes, aided by a tame submission to whatever receives the authority of hereditary usage, have combined to sanction absurdities, and establish laws which nature never designed.——However inconsistent the hypothesis, if it flatters ambition, or promises dominion, it will have its votaries, and be handed down by the ignorant and designing, until it becomes sacred by prescription.

From these, and various combining circumstances, we may trace the source of that assumption of superiority, by which the men claim an implicit obedience from our sex: a claim which they support on the vain presumption of their being assigned the most important duties of life, and being intrusted by nature with the guardianship and protection of women. Let the daily victims of their infidelity speak how worthy they are of the boasted title of protectors. But it is in us that Heaven hath reposed its supreme confidence; to us it hath assigned the care of making

From *The Universal Asylum and Columbian Magazine* 7 (July 1791).

the first impressions on the infant minds of the whole human race, a trust of more importance than the government of provinces, and the marshalling of armies; as on the first impression depends more than on the discipline of the schools, the grave lectures of divines, or the future terrors of the laws.

But the duties imposed by this important despot, disqualify us for the exercises necessary for the acquisition of that corporeal strength, which might fit us for advantageous occupations, which accumulate wealth, the immediate source of power. Hence is derived the imputation of our imaginary inability; hence the opportunity, of which those men seldom fail to take the advantage, of arrogating to themselves all power and authority; which is too often displayed, in making us wretched, and rendering themselves ridiculous.

The daily follies committed by men, leave it unnecessary to prove the imbecility of their *minds;* and as to what strength of *body* they possess superior to the women, this may be chiefly attributed to the exercise permitted and encouraged in their youth; but forbidden to us, even to a ridiculous degree.

Nothing gives muscular strength but exercise. In the nursery, strength is equal in the male and female. Education soon draws on those distinctions with which nature is charged. A boy no sooner goes to school than his fellows dare him to fight: he has no alternative, he must fight or be wretched. He soon learns to whip a top, run after a hoop, and jump over a rope. These exercises promote health and spirits; strengthen his whole frame, and often rectify those enormous errors committed in the nursery (*that baneful prison with a fashionable name!*) the consequences of which are rather confirmed than relaxed by the future education of girls; committed to illiterate teachers, and as illiterate school-mistresses, ignorant of manners, books, and men.——With these tyrants, they are cooped up in a room, confined to needle-work, deprived of exercise, reproved without being faulty, and schooled in frivolity, until they are reduced to mere automatons in the most active and best part of their lives: at a time when they possess a redundancy of spirits, which were given by nature to establish a proper strength and activity of constitution, but which if once forfeited, the loss draws on consequences which never after can be eradicated. These are some of the many disadvantages we are doomed to suffer, while the boys are encouraged in activity, instructed in sciences and languages, and rendered familiar with the best authors, by which they may refine their taste, improve their judgment, and form a system of morals that may ensure their happiness ever after.

When an intelligent and reflecting mind views and contemplates such a combination of facts, all tending to advance one sex and depress the other, such a mind will be struck with horror, but not with surprise, at the pale-faced, decrepid, weak, deformed women, daily presented to view, who have been tortured into a debility which renders their existence wretched, and leaves them only the melancholy hope that a friendly consumption may relieve them, by death, from their unhappy situation.

Thus, it is the united folly of parents which has brought on so wide a distinction of the sexes; not the impartial wisdom of the creator, who must equally delight in seeing all his creatures wise and happy.

But so tyrannic is custom, that if a *woman* of distinguished abilities rises superior to all her disadvantages, and, like the sun, bursts through the cloud, and shines from amidst the mists she has scattered by her rays, she is received like a noxious comet; she is the dread of her own sex, and envied by every male dunce within whose sphere she may happen to move. Different, it is true, is the conduct of men of learning and genius! they hourly lament the misfortune of being confined to ignorance; while they are possessing beauty. A man of sense soon grows weary of saying silly things: he finds himself in a state of solitude when the same object daily presents herself to his senses, without affording any entertainment to the mind; and he deplores that

he must drag on a weary life with a woman he can neither forsake nor enjoy.

Men contribute to their own wretchedness when they neglect the culture of our minds. They are our mental qualities that give their truest enjoyment; and men are seldom brutish to such a degree, as long to enjoy the company of women who can only gratify the lowest appetite. Those cloistered drones who effect to despise the society of women, grow timid, sullen, and suspicious; while those, as the French, who for all their pleasurable parties in the company of women, retain their vivacity, and enjoy life to its latest period. This mixture in society improves both the sexes. Boys brought up under mothers form respectable ideas of women; and girls, early introduced into mixed company, always behave with much propriety. Nothing makes so ridiculous a figure as an ignorant coquette, just released from the unnatural restraint of a boarding-school. She is a stranger to all decorum; she is either grossly rude through reserve, or disgustingly familiar through uncultivated vivacity, and generally falls in love with the first coxcomb who affects to admire her.

But with all our disadvantages, it is to the judgment of women that the world is indebted for some of the greatest characters among men. Ben Jonson, Newton, Locke, and Henry the Great of France, were all left to the guardianship of women. Equal advantages may be hoped from the instructions of our sex in the present century, since we have women who excel in the sciences of commerce, government, poetry, and history; and in the various branches of the polite arts.

Voltaire said, the minds of women were capable of whatever was performed by those of the men; and refused the invitation of the king of Prussia for the company of Madame de Chatelot, telling the king, that (between philosophers) he loved a lady better than a king. This lady knew by heart most of the beautiful passages in Horace, Virgil, and Lucretius, and all the philosophical works of Cicero; could write Latin elegantly, and speak all the languages of

Europe: was perfectly conversant with the works of Locke, Newton, and Pope, and was particularly fond of the mathematics and metaphysics. When she died, the king of Prussia gave Voltaire a second invitation: it was accepted, and he went and lived with the king. Does this not draw conviction, that we possess faculties which are by no means inferior to the greatest ornaments of the other sex; and that the highest felicity man can possess must arise from the society of well educated women.

But what must be the sentiments of such women, when they hear from the lips of an idiot husband, that men are created their lords and masters? when then they find themselves united to those who know not their worth? and discover, that where they looked up for protection, they are quickly taught submission? When they find the fawning slave of yesterday the tyrant of to-day; and having resigned *themselves,* they are given to understand that they have neither liberty nor property—like the lion in the fable, all is his by right of lion—can the soul subdue its feelings, and not revolt against the hidden baseness? Disappointment chills the heart, stagnates affection, and draws on that morbid indifference which we often observe in the married state. Yet how often do we see the hapless female, with patient virtue, smothering concealed wretchedness, and enduring her afflictions, with a fortitude which would do honour to the greatest hero that was ever drawn by the hand of fiction.

Thus, then, the superiority of man consists only in that strength which he pretends is needful for our protection; and his boasted protection resembles that of a ruffian, who should guard you from a pick-pocket, only that himself might do you a more selfish and more irreparable injury. Let them withdraw their injuries, and we shall easily spare their protection; but did our education disencumber them from our dependence, they could not as readily dispense with the assistance of our solicitudes.

15
On Matrimonial Obedience (1792)

GENTLEMEN,

THE following Letter having been generally admired, though at first published in a very confined circle, I send it to your Magazine, not doubting but that it will be acceptable to your female subscribers. I am, your's,

COLLECTOR.

TO LOVE, CHERISH, AND OBEY.
Matrimonial Service, Common Prayer.

SIR,

I happened to be lately in company with a few select and agreeable friends, who met on a holiday occasion, when, near the hour of parting, the conversation happened to turn on the Matrimonial Service appointed by the church; how the subject was started I do not now recollect; but it soon seemed to take this turn, that the word *obey,* in the promise or vow to be made by the *woman* was very improper, and ought not to be. It was strenuously contended by a very amiable lady present, that the obliging women to make a *vow* to *obey* their husbands, was in a manner obliging them to perjure themselves; as a thousand instances might occur, in which her obedience would be exceedingly improper.

I need not tell you, that a subject of this kind, started in a company consisting partly of married persons, and partly of single, would occasion a good deal of debate. The lady, however, who gave the above opinion, evidently had the advantage; and it is in defence of that opinion, that I now address a few words to you.

I object to the word *obey* in the marriage-service, (and I dare say many ladies have objected to it on the same account) because it is a general word, without limitation or definition. My dictionary tells me what it is *to obey,* and the word

From *Lady's Magazine, and Repository of Entertaining Knowledge* 1 (July 1792).

in our marriage-service, admits of no exceptions: it is *obey* in its fullest sense. The bride, who should pronounce the word *obey* with mental reservations, would certainly deceive herself, if she supposed she would not be guilty of a species of perjury; for where I have sworn, or even promised to obey any man, I must on honour consider myself as having sworn or promised to obey him in all things, and at all times. In a word, I have bound myself to be his *slave,* until he is pleased to release me, which in the matrimonial word, is an occurrence that I believe seldom happens. And in doing this, I think it will not be denied that I am a slave to all intents and purposes; intents in which I have no design, and purposes in which I have no interest, and from which I derive no happiness.

But we are not accustomed in this liberal age to consider the marriage engagement as a contract of this kind. Why, therefore, is the word *obey* still preserved in our service, when it would be so easy to leave it out; and when, in fact, we know that it is virtually left out by nine out of ten who enter into that holy state? You may say, perhaps, that the word *obey* means only, that the wife is to obey in all things lawful.—Yes—But can you prove that *obey,* as it appears in our service, will admit of this restrictive interpretation?—Can you also prove, that husbands in general, will admit of the very favourable construction you are pleased to put upon it? I am afraid not. And on these accounts, I repeat it, I wish that the words, "love and cherish" remained alone, and the word *obey* should be omitted, but understood to be implied as far as proper, in the preceding words. . . .

The obedience between man and wife, I conceive, is, or ought to be mutual. It ought to be mutual for the sake of their interest, inasmuch as two free opinions conjoined, are much more likely to produce a wise decision, than one haughty and exclusive. And it ought to be mutual for the sake of their happiness; for I believe it will be acknowledged, with conviction on all hands, that whatever miseries arise in the married state, arise from the assumption on one side

or other of absolute power. Marriage ought never to be considered as a contract between a superior and an inferior, but a reciprocal union of interest, an implied partnership of interests, where all differences are accommodated by conference; and where the decision admits of no retrospect. Separate privileges there may be on both sides; but like the houses of lords and commons, tenacious as they are of their privileges, they should, in all disputed points, meet each other half way, and like those houses too, when a question of privilege occurs, always clear the galleries, that there may be no witnesses of the dispute. . . .

To enforce obedience by a promise before marriage, from one party and not from the other, does not seem to be very just; it certainly will produce no good effect and to persist in exacting that obedience after marriage, can only produce the very worst effects. Suppose we leave out of our consideration the many women of superior judgment, of our acquaintance, it will still be allowed that there is no woman whose understanding is so very barren, but that she may at sometime take the lead in command, with a better effect than her husband. In a word, sir, begging pardon for detaining you so long, let men take care that they do not marry for beauty or riches only, and they may in this world, find it not difficult to procure a wife whose love will alleviate their cares, whose advice will promote their interest, and whose understanding they may be proud to consult.
I am, your's

A Matrimonial Republican.

16

Lines, Written by a Lady, Who Was Questioned Respecting Her Inclination to Marry (1794)

With an heart light as cork, and a mind free as
    air,
Unshackled I'll live and I'll die, I declare;
No ties shall perplex me, no fetters shall bind,
That innocent freedom that dwells in my mind.
At liberty's spring such draughts I've imbib'd,
That I hate all the doctrines by wedlock
    prescrib'd;
Its laws of obedience could never suit me,
My spirit's too lofty, my thoughts are too free.
Like an haughty republic my heart with disdain,
Views the edicts of Hymen and laughs at his
    chain,
Abhors his tyrannical systems and modes,
His bastiles, his shackles, his maxims, and codes;
Inquires why women consent to be tools,
And calmly conform to such rigorous rules;
Inquires in vain, for no reasons appear,
Why matrons should live in subjection and fear.
But round freedom's fair standard I've rallied
    and paid,
A vow of allegiance to die an old maid.
Long live the republic of freedom and ease,
May its subjects live happy and do as they please.

17

A Second Vindication of the Rights of Women (1801)

The appellation of Father, one may naturally suppose must impress the mind with a knowledge
of the claims that are incontestibly connected
with it.—Reason has no certain standard to ar-

Document 16 from *Massachusetts Magazine*, September 1794.

Document 17 from *Ladies Monitor* 1 (August 1801).

gue from, it seems subordinate to opinion, to
the fluctuations of fancy, and to the flights of
imagination; but those ties which subsist between parent and child must have their eternal
and invariable standard in the laws of nature.
The claims that a daughter has upon the protection of a father, are vast and extensive: a more
weighty charge devolves on him than merely the
provision of meat, drink and cloathing; but it is
too common to observe that when that duty is
discharged the generality of fathers think themselves amply detached from every other claim,
and leave the formation of the character either
to the child itself or the tutor, who seldom has
ascendency enough over the mind to bend the
twig consistently with its better growth. From
a weak effeminate indulgence of mothers the
temper of children is mostly obstinate and perverse ere they are sent to school, and then the
tuition of the respective lessons is more the object of the tutor than the formation of the qualities of the heart. To begin to remedy any
wide-spread evil, or rather the most effectual
mean to eradicate it is to grasp at the root. Mothers would hardly act with that inconsistency in
the formation of their daughter's temper which
must infallibly make them disagreeable to themselves, and burdensome to those whom they are
connected with, if they had in their childhood
been taught otherwise by their own parents.
Women are more effeminate from custom than
nature: If the daughter be taught aright, when
in the course of human events she becomes a
mother, she will know how to act aright. Man's
avocations in business, either in public or private life demand most of his time and attention;
yet, as a pleasing relaxation, even he might appropriate some moments to a secondary object,
and impress his daughters with a knowledge of
the dignified sphere they were intended to move
in, and the performances of such duties as naturally devolve on them. Refinement of manner,
and of the toilet have long since arrived at their
zenith, the meridian splendor of a full dressed
woman may dazzle the sight, and encapture the
heart momentarily, but it never can give lasting

pleasure to the understanding.—This frivolity in women is attended with more serious consequence than a foolish display of their own vanity; but it is merely a substitute for other employment. A truly sensible woman was never known to be extravagantly fond of dress, but as the impression is made in childhood it mostly continues to womanhood, and unless a different direction is given to the youthful mind, the mind matured in frivolity will still remain a subject of derision to the moralist and philosopher, and it will be a plea with men to hold women under subjection to the government of men, when from men we may trace every source that has long since conducted to the perversion of the female character.

Let this essay be directed to the hearts of fathers. Can it be supposed that there exists a father who is not solicitous for the welfare of his daughter? Is it natural to think that a father would, with impunity, subjugate his child to lordly imposition? Does not every passion of the soul rebel in vengeance against the seducer of an innocent daughter? And though all men are liable to be fathers, yet almost all men infringe the rights of women! Daughters must consequently partake of the mother's fate. The calls of nature make a father wish to see his daughter exempted from many troubles that attend life, when at the same time, he can with careless indifference be accessary in the same troubles to his wife. When through the powers of a natural genius a daughter has had her judgment consolidated, and she becomes eventually connected in marriage with a man whose mental powers may not be equally capacious with her own, who wantonly trifles with her feelings by treating her with scorn and contempt, and renders her acquisitions a subject of hatred to herself, can a father brook such treatment to a darling daughter with placidness and composure? No. Yet husbands do inconsiderately make themselves guilty of this fault toward their wives. In short, fathers must suffer the same corroding anxieties for daughters until a reformation takes place in the conduct of husbands towards their wives. All

wives must first be daughters, therefore no daughter would ever cost a father any anxiety if the father-in-law's daughter would meet with affectionate treatment from the husband. Much may be said on this subject, but we will defer our sentiments of it to a future essay.

18
The Criterion of Virtue (1802)

It is, I believe extremely common, in the appropriation of words to ideas, to give them erroneous significations, or attribute greater latitude to general terms than they were originally intended to express; and as I have often, though vainly, wished to see the criterion of virtue, as it respects our sex, properly established, it shall be the employment of a serious hour to assign, with as much precision as my slender knowledge will admit, the distinct and proper claims of the highest grace a woman can possess, and ascertain how far she may be justified in arrogating to herself the character of a *woman of virtue;* also in what instances, although *"chaste as unsunned snow,"* that character can be deficient. "Chaste, yet not virtuous!—this is surely an inexplicable paradox," observes the decorous female, on whose spotless name no mildew of calumny ever fixed. "Were this thesis established, it must totally remove the boundaries of good and evil, and damp, if not destroy, the praiseworthy attempt at moral strictness, besides effectually repelling the advances of the equivocally virtuous to a more perfect reputation."—A moment's indulgence, dear Madam, while I endeavor to prove, that Chastity, (although the fairest ornament our sex can boast, and without which no woman can be estimable) is yet but a *single* virtue, and may be sullied by a variety of culpable errors. She whose consciousness of integrity can give a decided affirmative

From *The Weekly Visitor, or, Ladies Miscellany* 1 (November 1802).

to the following interrogatories, is, indisputably, possessed of that exalted characteristical excellence.

"When, in conversation with the giddy and unfeeling, the faults of an unhappy female are exposed with unnecessary severity, do I remain silent, when to *speak* would be to condemn; or if I do speak, is it to deduce, from the representation before me, instructive lessons for the advantage of a thoughtless and youthful audience? Do I extenuate, with a cautious benevolence, the unauthorised condemnation of an absent fellow creature? Do I, when solicited by one of those very wretched beings for the assistance my finances will allow, extend the hand of mercy, perhaps drop a tear of compassion for what, strictly speaking, is *merited* distress? Do I leave to others the office of emblazoning those virtues which an inward consciousness appropriates to my own character; and seek rather to exalt the graces of another, than presumptuously detail my own as objects of imitation? Do I practice, as nearly as human imperfection will admit, those duties more immediately relative to my situation?"

From this little categorical sketch of what a *woman of virtue ought* to be, may our sex determine with true precision what they really are.

Virtue, if I understand its implication rightly, is a combination, not a solitary grace, when meant to include female excellence; and it is as possible for a woman to be chaste without being good, as for a man to be industrious without being honest. Certainly every amiable propensity is a degree of virtue; but when the term is made use of as above, it is an aggregate, and contains the sum of human goodness.

But while thus attempting to settle the claims of Chastity, and in what degree its professors may be deficient, I would carefully avoid giving the smallest suffrage to those who possess not this charming quality: deprived of that, the sweetest features lose their brilliancy in an equal degree that the plainest countenance acquires a comparative loveliness from its influence. How dreadful to consider, that, like those planets which derive their brightness from the sun, every secondary grace becomes, if not extinct, yet faint and almost imperceptible, from the absence of that glorious emanation, which heightens, illustrates, and irradiates the lesser virtues of the soul. Even the gift of Charity loses some of its effect from being tendered by the hand of impurity; and however the liberal and truly virtuous mind may appreciate the bounty of a thoughtless wanton, it cannot reject a sentiment of contempt. Let urbanity of disposition, placidity of temper, the practice of economy, and unbounded benevolence, meet in that mind and character, undignified by Chastity, and too often the lovely attributes are depreciated by a severe, and perhaps unjust, degradation of their usefulness.

O ye, my dear and once amiable fellow-creatures, could you but estimate your loss in the proportion you do your falsely-named pleasures—could you give a moment's attention to the suggestions of a wounded conscience, and draw aside the gaudy veil which conceals the slow but *sure* operations of that awful monitor,—callous and deplorably unfeeling, indeed, must be the heart which such a retrospect would not soften.—Your very excellencies, while in such a situation, make against you. Contracted in their usefulness, sullied by continual error, what are they (in the estimation of the illiberal, who can give no credit to them while contaminated by impurity) but splendid sins? Are you daughters, wives, mothers? Have you tasted the sweets of relative affection? Have you been innocent, unsuspicious, beloved, and esteemed? And can you submit to be degraded, despised, classed with the unhappy creatures you once, it may be, pitied; neglected too, by those whose hearts your shameful conduct has keenly pierced? Reflect—repent—return to virtue! And should there be *one* harsh judge, to whom your wish of returning to the respectable society you once quitted appears improper, and who can reject the earnest petition, *she* cannot establish herself as a *woman of virtue*.

19

HANNAH MATHER CROCKER
On the Real Rights of Women with Their Appropriate Duties (1818)

It must be the appropriate duty and privilege of females, to convince by reason and persuasion. It must be their peculiar province to sooth the turbulent passions of men, when almost sinking in the sea of care, without even an anchor of hope to support them. Under such circumstances women should display their talents by taking the helm, and steer them safe to the haven of rest and peace, and that should be their own happy mansion, where they may always retire and find a safe asylum from the rigid cares of business. It is woman's peculiar right to keep calm and serene under every circumstance in life, as it is undoubtedly her appropriate duty, to sooth and alleviate the anxious cares of man, and her friendly and sympathetic breast should be found the best solace for him, as she has an equal right to partake with him the cares, as well as the pleasures of life.

It was evidently the design of heaven, by the mode of our first formation, that they should walk side by side, as mutual supports in all times of trial. There can be no doubt, that, in most cases, their judgment may be equal with the other sex; perhaps even on the subject of law, politics or religion, they may form good judgment, but it would be morally improper, and physically very incorrect, for the female character to claim the statesman's birth, or ascend the rostrum to gain the loud applause of men, although their powers of mind may be equal to the task.

We find among men, that their powers of mind are not equal in all cases; if the wise au-

From *Observations on the Real Rights of Women, with Their Appropriate Duties, Agreeable to Scripture, Reason and Common Sense* (Boston: Printed for the Author, 1818), 15–21, 54–55, 62–63, 65, 67–68.

thor of nature has been graciously pleased to endow all men with the same powers of mind, they do not all improve them to the same advantage; or from some imperfection in the organization of the human frame, the powers or faculties cannot operate on all alike. Some minds are so enfeebled that they are rendered incapable of judging right from wrong; therefore it appears necessary, from the very order of nature, that there should be a distinction in society, and that those whose minds are more expanded should be looked up to, as guides, to the general mass of the citizens. Females have equal right with the male citizen, to claim the protection, friendship and the approbation of such a class of men. As she is now restored to her original right by the blessing of the christian system, no longer is she the slave, but the friend of man. From the local circumstances, and the domestic cares in which most females are involved, it cannot be expected they should make so great improvement in science and literature, as those whose whole life has been devoted to their studies. It must not be expected that the reputable mechanic will rival the man of letters and science, neither would it well suit the female frame or character, to boast of her knowledge in mechanism, or her skill in the manly art of slaughtering fellow-men. It is woman's appropriate duty and peculiar privilege to cultivate the olive branches around her table. It is for her to implant in the juvenile breast the first seed of virtue, the love of God, and their country, with all the other virtues that shall prepare them to shine as statesmen, soldiers, philosophers and christians. Some of our first worthies have boasted that they imbibed their heroic principles with their mother's milk; and by precept and example were first taught the love of virtue, religion, and their country. Surely they should have a right to share with them the laurel, but not the right of conquest; for that must be man's prerogative, and woman is to rejoice in his conquest. There may be a few groveling minds who think woman should not aspire to any further knowledge than to obtain enough of the cymical art to enable them to compound a good pudding, pie, or cake, for her lord and master to discompound. Others, of a still weaker class, may say, it is enough for woman scientifically to arrange the spinning-wheel and distaff, and exercise her extensive capacity in knitting and sewing, since the fall and restoration of woman these employments have been the appropriate duties of the female sex. The art of dress, which in some measure produced the art of industry, did not commence till sin, folly and shame, introduced the first invention of dress, which ought to check the modest female from every species of wantonness and extravagance in dress; cultivate the mind, and trifling in dress will soon appear in its true colours.

To those who appear unfriendly to female literature let me say, in behalf of the sex, they claim no right to infringe on any domestic economy; but those ladies, who continue in a state of celibacy, and find pleasure in literary researches, have a right to indulge the propensity, and solace themselves with the feast of reason and knowledge; also those ladies who in youth have laid up a treasure of literary and scientific information, have a right to improve in further literary researches, after they have faithfully discharged their domestic duties. . . .

Women have an equal right, with the other sex, to form societies for promoting religious, charitable and benevolent purposes. Every association formed for benevolence, must have a tendency to make man mild, and sociable to man; an institution formed for historical and literary researches, would have a happy effect on the mind and manners of the youth of both sexes. As the circulating libraries are often resorted to after novels by both sexes for want of judgment to select works of more merit, the study of history would strengthen their memory, and improve the mind, whereas novels have a tendency to vitiate the mind and morals of the youth of each sex before they are ripe for more valuable acquisitions. Much abstruse study or metaphysical reasoning seldom agrees with the natural vivacity or the slender frame of many females,

therefore the moral and physical distinction of the sex must be allowed; if the powers of the mind are fully equal, they must still estimate the rights of men, and own it their prerogative exclusively to contend for public honours and preferment, either in church or state, and females may console themselves and feel happy, that by the moral distinction of the sexes they are called to move in a sphere of life remote from those masculine contentions, although they hold equal right with them of studying every branch of science, even jurisprudence.

But it would be morally wrong, and physically imprudent, for any woman to attempt pleading at the bar of justice, as no law can give her the right of deviating from the strictest rules of rectitude and decorum. No servile dependence on men can be recommended under the christian system, for that abolished the law of slavery, and left only a claim on their friendship; as the author of their nature originally intended, they should be the protectors of female innocence, and not the fatal destroyers of their peace and happiness. They claim no right at the gambling table, and to the moral sensibility of females how disgusting must be the horse-race, the bull-bate, and the cock-fight. These are barbarous scenes, ill suited to the delicacy of females.

It must be woman's prerogative to shine in the domestic circle, and her appropriate duty to teach and regulate the opening mind of her little flock, and teach their juvenile ideas how to shoot forth into well improved sentiments. It is most undoubtedly the duty and privilege of woman to regulate her garrison with such good order and propriety, that the generalissimo of her affection, shall never have reason to seek other quarters for well disciplined and regulated troops, and there must not a murmur or beat be heard throughout the garrison, except that of the heart vibrating with mutual affection, reciprocally soft. The rights of woman displayed on such a plan, might perhaps draw the other sex from the nocturnal ramble to the more endearing scenes of domestic peace and harmony.

The woman, who can gain such a victory, as to secure the undivided affection of her generalissimo, must have the exclusive right to shine unrivalled in her garrison.

Without love even diligence is ungrateful, and submission itself has the air of disobedience. Mutual trust and confidence are the great bonds of society, without which it cannot possibly subsist. Mutual love must be founded on the basis of mutual friendship, without which life will have but few charms. The only things which can render friendship sure and lasting, are virtue, purity of manners, and perfect integrity of heart. With an elevated soul, it is highly proper that we should distinguish the friend from the companion. A conformity of taste for pleasure, and for any thing besides virtue, may constitute a club, but cannot make a society of friends. We must commence life with a religious determination, that "as for me and my house, we will serve the Lord"; and by a mutual agreement and sympathy, cemented by friendship, secure the right of mutual affection, on which connubial happiness very much depends.

The surest foundation to secure the female's right, must be in family government, as without that, women can have no established right. This must be the touchstone of the matrimonial faith; and on this depends very much the safety and happiness of a free republic. Family government should, in some measure, resemble a well regulated garrison; there should be sentinels continually on the watch-tower, and general orders should be given for the day, and these should be attended with the morning and evening orisons, that should ascend like holy incense, with gratitude of soul, for the divine care and protection. Women have a right to join in the family prayer and praise. Family worship must be mutual, as any jar or animosity will disorder the whole garrison, and a mutiny may ensue and throw the whole into confusion, and thus frustrate the cause of religion and virtue, and the demon of discord may enter, with all the accumulated miseries of Pandora's box, and perhaps storm and carry the garrison. . . .

From the same principle of benevolence, women may reasonably become equal with men in patriotism and disinterested love of country, which embraces all its citizens, and produces that universal benevolence and philanthropy, which extends its influence to all nations. This idea leads us to an important subject, that is, the moral and political, which Russell says, consists in regulating ourselves and others. He says, to compare the advantages and disadvantages of the sexes, with regard to this object, it would be necessary to observe the same talent on society, and as applied to government, the women in society being continually upon the look-out. From the motive of curiosity and policy they must have perfect knowledge of men; they must be able to disentangle all the folds of self-love, and discover all their secret weaknesses; the false modesty, and the false grandeur; what man is, and what he should be. They must know and distinguish character. They must know the diffidence which proceeds from character or vice; from misfortune or from the mind; in short, they must know all their sentiments and all their shades. As women set a high value on opinion, they must reflect much on what will produce it: They must know how far one can direct without appearing to be interested, and how far one may presume upon that art after it is known; in what estimation they are held by those with whom they live, and to what degree it is necessary to serve them, that they may govern them, in all cases of business. Women know the great affairs which are produced by little causes; they know how to captivate by praises those who deserve them, and sometimes raise a blush by bestowing them where they are not due.

These delicate sciences are the leading strings by which women conduct the men; men have less time for observation and can hardly be possessed of such a crowd of little notices, and those polite attentions, which are every moment necessary in the commerce of life. Therefore men's calculations in society must be more slow and less sure than women's, as applied to government. . . .

As it appears from scripture and reason there is a just, and right equality of the sexes, common sense must teach the propriety of a union of the sexes in sentiments and opinions respecting the rights of women. Very little has been written on the subject in America; and perhaps it has not been necessary in a land where the rights of women have never appeared a bone of much contention. It may naturally be supposed, the ideas of a free independent people, will be more liberal and expanded respecting the sexual rights.

Under this impression, the writer has ventured to pen this small system or statement of the mutual rights and appropriate duties of the sexes with the most philanthropic wish, that the parties concerned may mutually agree to support the real orthodox principle of a mutual dependence on each other, which will promote peace, harmony and happiness; for without harmony and affection subsist between the sexes, society must soon become a mere nuisance to itself. . . .

It is almost impossible that those, who reside under a despotic or monarchical government, can imbibe as liberal sentiments as those, who reside under the more temperate zone of a free, federal republican government, which admits of free discussion of sentiments among all classes of the citizens. Such a government requires more sense and judgment to preserve it from disorder and disunion; therefore the union and right understanding of the sexes will have a tendency to strengthen, confirm and support such a government, and common sense must allow women the right of mutual judgment, and joining with the other sex in every prudent measure for their mutual defence and safety.

It may be seen by the fatal fall of Greece and Rome how much depends on public faith and confidence in the government, which must commence in the private faith and confidence of individuals.

From the universal benevolence, conspicuous in every section of the union, there is reason to anticipate our future greatness and respectability. The various institutions, for benevolent and charitable purposes, have a tendency to promote the kind affections, and make man mild and sociable to man; women shine preeminent in most of them, and have an equal right to establish schools of industry and economy, which must have a happy effect on the community. There is nothing can make better subjects for a republican government, than to give children an early education, and train them in habits of prudence and industry. Every day produces some proofs how much we are the creatures of habit; the juvenile mind requires continual occupation, for the vivacity of youth is such, that if not constantly employed in some valuable pursuit, there is danger of their resorting to some evil propensity, for want of regular occupation; for such is the natural depravity of the human heart. As women generally have the forming of the infant mind, it is necessary their own minds should be cultivated, that they may be capable of enlarging the mind of their pupils; as the first seeds implanted in their breast, if virtuous and noble, will prepare them for some important station in life. Children's constitution and capacities differ so very much, that it requires the affection, tenderness and care of a prudent woman to mould and model the tender olive-branch, as there is hardly a human being, though of very inferior abilities, but will discover a genius for some particular employment, and that ought to be cultivated, and the bent of their genius should be always consistent.

II. Education and Women's Literary Culture

ONE OF THE FOREMOST ACHIEVEMENTS OF WOMEN in the early national period was both the creation of a rationale for female education and the founding (between 1790 and 1830) of nearly 400 private academies and seminaries for girls and women. While domestic service remained the single largest category of female employment until well into the twentieth century, school teaching rapidly became the next most important profession for women in the early decades of the nineteenth century, as proliferating female academies both produced and employed an increasing number of women scholars.

From the 1790s onward, women writers and thinkers began contributing to the ongoing debate about women's capacity for learning—seeking, as educator Sarah Pierce put it, to "vindicate the equality of the female intellect."[1] In 1792, British feminist Mary Wollstonecraft published *A Vindication of the Rights of Woman*, a treatise that attacked the current system of educating girls on the ground that it distorted women's minds and bodies and created a helpless, dependent, and useless class of people. Like Wollstonecraft, writers in the United States similarly deplored the pernicious effects of women's training solely in superficial matters of fashion, manners, and gossip. The most sustained and complex of such arguments, Judith Sargent Murray's "On the Equality of the Sexes" (1790), not only pre-dates Wollstonecraft's *Vindication*, but also anticipates twentieth-century feminist arguments that gender difference is not innate but the product of culture—that it is, more specifically, the effect of stratified educational practices.

Murray's essay responds to a central question debated avidly by her contemporaries: are women's minds equal to men's? Answering in the affirmative, Murray drew on the widely-accepted ideas of the eighteenth-century Enlightenment, notably the primacy of reason and John Locke's theory of the human mind as a *tabula rasa*, an essentially "blank" entity determined by culture and not predetermined by nature. Both precepts led to the conclusion that women were rational beings; furthermore, to the extent that women were not rational, they were the products of debased educational and cultural conventions. As Murray points out, the "needle and kitchen . . . leave the intelligent principle vacant." Arguing that very young boys and girls are fundamentally similar in their abilities, Murray claims that girls are "early confined and limited" and that custom produces a "second nature" which is subsequently deemed to be woman's "nature." Brilliantly apprehending how the effects of training can be mistaken for "nature," Murray insists that girls should receive the same education as boys—including astronomy, geography, and natural philosophy—and that such an education would effectively narrow the intellectual gap between the sexes.

The call of those women engaged in vindicating the female intellect was answered in the many academies for girls that sprang up in the late-eighteenth and early-nineteenth centuries. This shift from the dearth of formal education for girls in the colonial period was not uncon-

---

1. Quoted in Mary Beth Norton, *Liberty's Daughters: The Revolutionary Experience of American Women, 1750–1800* (Boston: Little, Brown, 1980), 271.

tested, and conflict centered particularly around the curriculum of the new schools. Academies were expected to inscribe female difference in their classrooms; they were expected not to teach girls, in other words, what boys were taught. The Philadelphia Young Ladies Academy, which was founded in 1787 and which proclaimed itself the first female academy chartered in the United States, was unique in excluding needlework from its curriculum and in encouraging public speaking; nevertheless, in a necessary compromise, the school was committed to upholding traditional values at the same time that it emphasized the intellect.

The problem of whether young women should learn to speak in public epitomized the problem of women's education: why should young women acquire such a skill? for whom would they practice it? would it deleteriously affect their "feminine" qualities? While each of the speakers at the Philadelphia Young Ladies Academy in 1793 defends their right to speak in public, most qualify their claim by specifying appropriate audiences (not a "promiscuous and indiscriminate one," Molly Wallace points out) and by circumscribing their topics. Wallace goes on to argue explicitly that women should not "harangue at the head of an Army, in the Senate, or before a popular Assembly." Disclosing how conflicted the physical and discursive space of the academy was, however, another speaker, disagrees. In her oration, Priscilla Mason insists not only on women's right to speak in public but also for their right to employ their oratorical skills in the "Church, the Bar, and the Senate"—institutions, she adds, that are closed to women for no good reason.

The problem debated by the women at the Philadelphia Young Ladies Academy was debated beyond its walls as well: would women become "masculine" if they acquired what was formerly deemed a man's education? Would they want to usurp "man's place" within, as Mason puts it, the "Church, the Bar, and the Senate"? In 1801 an anonymous woman, known only as "The Female Advocate," published a pamphlet of the same name that unequivocally defends women's right to the same education and the same pursuits as men; her analysis has been called perhaps the most lucid and sustained critique of the social order of the early republic as it affected women. "The Female Advocate" debunks the widely-held belief that educated women are "masculine" by pointing out that her culture's system of gender relations had declared all superiority, including intellectual excellence, as masculine; therefore, any woman who aspired to superior intellectual skills was inevitably and unfairly deemed masculine. Trying to demonstrate the arbitrariness of expectations for the respective sexes, "The Female Advocate" suggests that the doors of America's seminaries be shut to men and open to women; intellectual superiority would not long be considered "masculine," she argues, when men were denied access to formal education.

If "The Female Advocate" strenuously champions equality and women's right to be learned no matter what their objective, most women writers were more cautious. They tended to defend women's public, scholarly activities on the grounds that they furthered women's unique function within the home; they were careful, in other words, to assure their readers that educated women would remain "feminine" and would not encroach on men's intellectual and professional territory. Both Judith Sargent Murray and Emma Willard, thinkers who, respectively, opened and closed the republican period, argued that the new nation should educate women in order to create better wives and mothers. This argument for women's education on the grounds of their cultural uniqueness arose from the writers' pragmatic recognition that women's social roles and duties were considered to be different from men's and that their intellect could thus most effectively be vindicated if that difference were acknowledged.

In the preface to her three-volume history of the American Revolution (1805), Mercy Otis Warren clearly feels compelled to justify her writing the first substantial work of history by an American woman. Warren had written, moreover, not simply a history but a political and military history, apparently entering "the more peculiar province of masculine strength," a province in which men not only waged war but wrote about it afterwards. While Warren admits that men and women each have certain "appropriate duties," she also claims that women are as patriotic as men and thus their "duties" should of necessity include such patriotic acts as writing about their nation's birth. Strategically addressing and calming men's fears, Warren nevertheless goes on to extend women's intellectual realm until it is virtually equal to men's.

Despite its detractors, formal education for girls and young women flourished throughout the end of the eighteenth and beginning of the nineteenth centuries. By 1819, when Emma Willard published her "An Address to the Public, Proposing a Plan for Improving Female Education," the terms of the debate were no longer whether women should be educated but how their education might best be effected. (Willard put her "Plan" into action when she opened the Troy Female Seminary in 1821.) Pointing out the inconsistencies and biases inevitable in a strictly privatized system of education, Willard urged the creation of large, state-supported female academies; she wanted for young women's schooling the same "public authority" and "permanency" as that received by young men. Willard, moreover, wanted to train women not only so that they would be better mothers but also so that they could become teachers, hence expanding women's as-yet limited professional opportunities.

The debate over women's intellect and the founding of hundreds of female academies and seminaries had the inevitable effect of improving literacy rates among women. White female literacy, as Mary Kelley has pointed out, lagged behind that of males during the colonial period. That changed in the decades following the end of the Revolution, however: one historian estimates that white middle-class women's literacy rates rose from 60 percent in the early 1780s to nearly 80 percent for the decade from 1787 to 1796.[2] Rising female literary rates coincided with the advent of the novel in America, a genre that, in its earliest forms, spoke particularly to women's concerns and interests. The boom in novel-reading at the turn of the eighteenth century not only gave a few women another area of public employment—as writers; it also gave all women, as readers, access to a broadening social and cultural arena. Novels provided a way for both the writers and consumers of fiction to shape political discourse, to direct what was talked about in the public sphere.

It was no accident, then, that the first popular fictional genre written and read in America was the novel of seduction, a genre with an intrinsic political relevance for women. The novel of seduction expressed women's fear about their own vulnerability to licentious "rakes" and about the sexual double standard. Women, in the plots of this genre, were punished over and

2. Mary Kelley, "'Vindicating the Equality of Female Intellect': Women and Authority in the Early Republic," *Prospects* 17 (1992): 21.

over again for the sins of men: they were seduced by men, abandoned by men, and then ostracized by society, while their seducers remained unpunished. Susanna Rowson's *Charlotte Temple*, published in England in 1791 and in America in 1794, was the biggest best-seller in American history before Harriet Beecher Stowe's *Uncle Tom's Cabin* (1852). The sad fate of Charlotte, seduced and left to die in childbirth by her betrayer, galvanized the young nation— sending thousands of Americans to the purported grave of "poor Charlotte" to leave momentos such as flowers and verse. *Charlotte Temple*, like sentimental women's novels throughout the nineteenth century, moved America by appealing to the emotions; it addressed a real social and political issue, but it made Americans think about the issue by first making them *feel* it. Rowson also appeals to women as a group—urging them to band together and help each other, encouraging them to rescue rather than to abandon seduced women. Rowson thus anticipates the first organizational efforts of women in the nineteenth century, who formed voluntary associations precisely to reform morality, sexual practices, and prostitution.

Hannah Webster Foster used the vehicle of the seduction novel to indict not just individual seducers but also more radically the institution of marriage. In *The Coquette* (1797), Foster condemns a societal system that allows women no choice but marriage. Her protagonist, Eliza Wharton, is an intelligent woman who, recognizing the daunting fact that her life will be defined by the man she marries, is rightfully wary of the constraints of marriage and domestic life. Eliza's tragedy is that she can find no viable means to pursue the freedom she desires; in envisioning her future, she is not allowed to see past or around those men who want to marry her.

Eliza's story is a powerful metaphor for the situation of women in the late-eighteenth and early-nineteenth centuries. The more loudly Eliza proclaims her right to be free, the more her friends and family insist that she should marry. Like Eliza, women after the Revolution increasingly protested their situation, thus moving from their relative public *invisibility* in the colonial period to an increasing *visibility* after the Revolution. They formed organizations and worked for patriotic causes; they wrote for magazines, loudly demanding their rights; they published histories, newspapers, pamphlets and novels; and they founded, attended, and taught in schools. Women's increasing visibility, like Eliza's protestations, evoked a countering reaction from their society, which responded by insisting more and more vociferously that women should remain in their "place." Thus, at the very time that women were enjoying more public power, the sexes became increasingly hierarchized, and what was "appropriate" for women was more fervently urged. One of the primary challenges launched by feminists of the nineteenth century would be against the increasingly entrenched definitions of "woman's nature" and "woman's sphere," definitions that grew in force as women's public presence and power emerged in the years after the Revolution.

20

JUDITH SARGENT MURRAY
On the Equality of the Sexes
(1790)

The following Essay *is yielded to the patronage of Candour.—If it hath been anticipated, the testimony of many respectable persons, who saw it in manuscript as early as the year 1779, can obviate the imputation of plagiarism.*

On the EQUALITY of the SEXES.

THAT minds are not alike, full well I know,
This truth each day's experience will show;
To heights surprising some great spirits soar,
With inborn strength mysterious depths ex
      plore;
Their eager gaze surveys the path of light,
Confess it stood to Newton's piercing sight.
    Deep science, like a bashful maid retires,
And but the *ardent* breast her worth inspires;
By perseverance the coy fair is won.
And Genius, led by Study, wears the crown.
    But some there are who wish not to im
      prove,
Who never can the path of knowledge love,
Whose souls almost with the dull body one,
With anxious care each mental pleasure shun;
Weak is the level'd, enervated mind,
And but while here to vegetate design'd.
The torpid spirit mingling with its clod,
Can scarcely boast its origin from God;
Stupidly dull—they move progressing on—
They eat, and drink, and all their work is done.
While others, emulous of sweet applause,
Industrious seek for each event a cause,
Tracing the hidden springs whence knowledge
      flows,
Which nature all in beauteous order shows.
    Yet cannot I their sentiments imbibe,

From *Massachusetts Magazine* 2 (March and April 1790).

Who this distinction to the sex ascribe,
As if a woman's form must needs enrol,
A weak, a servile, an inferiour soul;
And that the guise of man must still proclaim,
Greatness of mind, and him, to be the same:
Yet as the hours revolve fair proofs arise,
Which the bright wreath of growing fame sup-
      plies;
And in past times some men have *sunk* so *low,*
That female records nothing *less* can show.
But imbecility is still confin'd,
And by the lordly sex to us consign'd;
They rob us of the power t' improve,
And then declare we only trifles love;
Yet haste the era, when the world shall know,
That such distinctions only dwell below;
The foul unfetter'd, to no sex confin'd,
Was for the abodes of cloudless day design'd.
    Mean time we emulate their manly fires,
Though erudition all their thoughts inspires,
Yet nature with *equality* imparts,
And *noble passions,* swell e'en *female hearts.*

    Is it upon mature consideration we adopt the idea, that nature is thus partial in her distributions? Is it indeed a fact, that she hath yielded to one half of the human species so unquestionable a mental superiority? I know that to both sexes elevated understandings, and the reverse, are common. But, suffer me to ask, in what the minds of females are so notoriously deficient, or unequal. May not the intellectual powers be ranged under these four heads—imagination, reason, memory and judgment. The province of imagination hath long since been surrendered up to us, and we have been crowned undoubted sovereigns of the regions of fancy. Invention is perhaps the most arduous effort of the mind; this branch of imagination hath been particularly ceded to us, and we have been time out of mind invested with that creative faculty. Observe the variety of fashions (here I bar the contemptuous smile) which distinguish and adorn the female world; how continually are they changing, insomuch that they almost render the wise man's assertion problematical, and we are ready to say, *there is something new under the sun*. Now what a playfulness, what an exuberance of fancy, what strength of inventi[v]e imagination, doth this continual variation discover? Again, it hath been observed, that if the turpitude of the conduct of our sex, hath been ever so enormous, so extremely ready are we, that the very first thought presents us with an apology, so plausible, as to produce our actions even in an amiable light. Another instance of our creative powers, is our talent for slander; how ingenious are we at inventive scandal? what a formidable story can we in a moment fabricate merely from the force of a prolifick imagination? how many reputations, in the fertile brain of a female, have been utterly despoiled? how industrious are we at improving a hint? suspicion how easily do we convert into conviction, and conviction, embellished by the power of eloquence, stalks abroad to the surprise and confusion of unsuspecting innocence. Perhaps it will be asked if I furnish these facts as instances of excellency in our sex. Certainly not; but as proofs of a creative faculty, of a lively imagination. Assuredly great activity of mind is thereby discovered, and was this activity properly directed, what beneficial effects would follow. Is the needle and kitchen sufficient to employ the operations of a soul thus organized? I should conceive not. Nay, it is a truth that those very departments leave the intelligent principle vacant, and at liberty for speculation. Are we deficient in reason? we can only reason from what we know, and if an opportunity of acquiring knowledge hath been denied us, the inferiority of our sex cannot fairly be deduced from thence. Memory, I believe, will be allowed us in common, since every one's experience must testify, that a loquacious old woman is as frequently met with, as a communicative old man; their subjects are alike drawn from the fund of other times, and the transactions of their youth, or of maturer life, entertain, or perhaps fatigue you, in the evening of their lives. "But our judgment is not so strong—we do not distinguish so well."—Yet it may be questioned, from what doth this superiority, in this

determmining faculty of the soul, proceed. May we not trace its source in the difference of education, and continued advantages? Will it be said that the judgment of a male of two years old, is more sage than that of a female's of the same age? I believe the reverse is generally observed to be true. But from that period what partiality! how is the one exalted, and the other depressed, by the contrary modes of education which are adopted! the one is taught to aspire, and the other is early confined and limited. As their years increase, the sister must be wholly domesticated, while the brother is led by the hand through all the flowery paths of science. Grant that their minds are by nature equal, yet who shall wonder at the *apparent* superiority, if indeed custom becomes *second nature;* nay if it taketh place of nature, and that it doth the experience of each day will evince. At length arrived at womanhood, the uncultivated fair one feels a void, which the employments allotted her are by no means capable of filling. What can she do? to books she may not apply; or if she doth, *to those only of the novel kind,* left the merit the appellation of a *learned lady;* and what ideas have been affixed to this term, the observation of many can testify. Fashion, scandal, and sometimes what is still more reprehensible are then called in to her relief; and who can say to what lengths the liberties she takes may proceed. Meantime she herself is most unhappy; she feels the want of a cultivated mind. Is she single, she in vain seeks to fill up time from sexual employments or amusements. Is she united to a person whose soul nature made equal to her own, education hath set him so far above her, that in those entertainments which are productive of such rational felicity, she is not qualified to accompany him. She experiences a mortifying consciousness of inferiority, which embitters every enjoyment. Doth the person to whom her adverse fate hath consigned her, possess a mind incapable of improvement, she is equally wretched, in being so closely connected with an individual whom she cannot but despise. Now, was she permitted the same instructors as her brother, (with an eye however to their particular departments) for the employment of a rational mind an ample field would be opened. In astronomy she might catch a glimpse of the immensity of the Deity, and thence she would form amazing conceptions of the august and supreme Intelligence. In geography she would admire Jehovah in the midst of his benevolence; thus adapting this globe to the various wants and amusements of its inhabitants. In natural philosophy she would adore the infinite majesty of heaven, clothed in condescension; and as she traversed the reptile world, she would hail the goodness of a creating God. A mind, thus filled, would have little room for the trifles with which our sex are, with too much justice, accused of amusing themselves, and they would thus be rendered fit companions for those, who should one day wear them as their crown. Fashions, in their variety, would then give place to conjectures, which might perhaps conduce to the improvement of the literary world; and there would be no leisure for slander or detraction. Reputation would not then be blasted, but serious speculations would occupy the lively imaginations of the sex. Unnecessary visits would be precluded, and that custom would only be indulged by way of relaxation, or to answer the demands of consanguinity and friendship. Females would become discreet, their judgments would be invigorated, and their partners of life being circumspectly chosen, an unhappy Hymen would then be as rare, as is now the reverse.

Will it be urged that those acquirements would supersede our domestick duties. I answer that every requisite in female economy is easily attained; and, with truth I can add, that when once attained, they require no further *mental attention.* Nay, while we are pursuing the needle, or the superintendency of the family, I repeat, that our minds are at full liberty for reflection; that imagination may exert itself in full vigor; and that if a just foundation is early laid, our ideas will then be worthy of rational beings. If we were industrious we might easily find time to arrange them upon paper, or should avoca-

tions press too hard for such an indulgence, the hours allotted for conversation would at least become more refined and rational. Should it still be vociferated, "Your domestick employments are sufficient"—I would calmly ask, is it reasonable, that a candidate for immortality, for the joys of heaven, an intelligent being, who is to spend an eternity in contemplating the works of Deity, should at present be so degraded, as to be allowed no other ideas, than those which are suggested by the mechanism of a pudding, or the sewing the seams of a garment? Pity that all such censurers of female improvement do not go one step further, and deny their future existence; to be consistent they surely ought.

Yes, ye lordly, ye haughty sex, our souls are by nature *equal* to yours; the same breath of God animates, enlivens, and invigorates us; and that we are not fallen lower than yourselves, let those witness who have greatly towered above the various discouragements by which they have been so heavily oppressed; and though I am unacquainted with the list of celebrated characters on either side, yet from the observations I have made in the contracted circle in which I have moved, I dare confidently believe, that from the commencement of time to the present day, there hath been as many females, as males, who, by the *mere force of natural powers,* have merited the crown of applause; who, *thus unassisted,* have seized the wreath of fame. I know there are who assert, that as the animal powers of the one sex are superiour, of course their mental faculties also must be stronger; thus attributing strength of mind to the transient organization of this earth born tenement. But if this reasoning is just, man must be content to yield the palm to many of the brute creation, since by not a few of his brethren of the field, he is far surpassed in bodily strength. Moreover, was this argument admitted, it would prove too much, for occular demonstration evinceth, that there are many robust masculine ladies, and effeminate gentlemen. Yet I fancy that Mr. Pope, though clogged with an enervated body, and distinguished by a diminutive stature, could nevertheless lay claim to greatness of soul; and perhaps there are many other instances which might be adduced to combat so unphilosophical an opinion. Do we not often see, that when the clay built tabernacle is well nigh dissolved, when it is just ready to mingle with the parent soil, the immortal inhabitant aspires to, and even attaineth heights the most sublime, and which were before wholly unexplored. Besides, were we to grant that animal strength proved any thing, taking into consideration the accustomed impartiality of nature, we should be induced to imagine, that she had invested the female mind with superior strength as an equivalent for the bodily powers of man. But waving this however palpable advantage, for *equality only,* we wish to contend.

I am aware that there are many passages in the sacred oracles which seem to give the advantage to the other sex; but I consider all these as wholly metaphorical. Thus David was a man after God's own heart, yet see him enervated by his licentious passions! behold him following Uriah to the death, and shew me wherein could consist the immaculate Being's complacency. Listen to the curses which Job bestoweth upon the day of his nativity and tell me where is his perfection, where his patience—*literally* it existed not. David and Job were types of him who was to come; and the superiority of man, as exhibited in scripture, being also emblematical, all arguments deduced from thence, of course fall to the ground. The exquisite delicacy of the female mind proclaimeth the exactness of its texture, while its nice sense of honour announceth its innate, its native grandeur. And indeed, in one respect, the preeminence seems to be tacitly allowed us, for after an education which limits and confines, and employments and recreations which naturally tend to enervate the body, and debilitate the mind; after we have from early youth been adorned with ribbons, and other gewgaws, dressed out like the ancient victims previous to a sacrifice, being taught by the care of our parents in collecting the most showy materials that the ornamenting our exteriors

ought to be the principal object of our attention; after, I say, fifteen years thus spent, we are introduced into the world, amid the united adulation of every beholder. Praise is sweet to the soul; we are immediately intoxicated by large draughts of flattery, which being plentifully administered, is to the pride of our hearts the most acceptable incense. It is expected that with the other sex we should commence immediate war, and that we should triumph over the machinations of the most artful. We must be constantly upon our guard; prudence and discretion must be our characteristics; and we must rise superiour to, and obtain a complete victory over those who have been long adding to the native strength of their minds, by an unremitted study of men and books, and who have, moreover, conceived from the loose characters which they have seen portrayed in the extensive variety of their reading, a most contemptible opinion of the sex. Thus unequal, we are, notwithstanding, forced to the combat, and the infamy which is consequent upon the smallest deviation in our conduct, proclaims the high idea which was formed of our native strength; and thus, indirectly at least, is the preference acknowledged to be our due. And if we are allowed an equality of requirement, let serious studies equally employ our minds, and we will bid our souls arise to equal strength. We will meet upon even ground, the despot man; we will rush with alacrity to the combat, and, crowned by the success, we shall then answer the exalted expectations which are formed. Though sensibility, soft compassion, and gentle commiseration, are inmates in the female bosom, yet against every deep laid art, altogether fearless of the event, we will set them in array; for assuredly the wreath of victory will encircle the spotless brow. If we meet an equal, a sensible friend, we will reward him with the hand of amity, and through life we will be assiduous to promote his happiness; but from every deep laid scheme for our ruin, retiring into ourselves, amid the flowery paths of science, we will indulge in all the refined and sentimental pleasures of contemplation: And should it still be urged, that the studies thus insisted upon would interfere with our more peculiar department, I must further reply, that *early hours,* and close application, will do wonders; and to her who is from the first dawn of reason taught to fill up time rationally, both the requisites will be easy. I grant that niggard fortune is too generally unfriendly to the mind, and that much of that valuable treasure, time, is necessarily expended upon the wants of the body; but it should be remembered; that in embarrassed circumstances our companions have as little leisure for literary improvement, as is afforded to us; for most certainly their provident care is at least as requisite as our exertions. Nay, we have even more leisure for sedentary pleasures, as our avocations are more retired, much less laborious, and, as hath been observed, by no means require that avidity of attention which is proper to the employments of the other sex. In high life, or, in other words, where the parties are in possession of affluence, the objection respecting time is wholly obviated, and of course falls to the ground; and it may also be repeated, that many of those hours which are at present swallowed up in fashion and scandal, might be redeemed, were we habituated to useful reflections. But in one respect, O ye arbiters of our fate! we confess that the superiority is indubitably yours; you are by nature formed for our protectors; we pretend not to vie with you in bodily strength; upon this point we will never contend for victory. Shield us then, we beseech you, from external evils, and in return *we* will transact *your* domestick affairs. Yes, *your,* for are you not equally interested in those matters with ourselves? Is not the elegancy of neatness as agreeable to your sight as to ours; is not the well favoured viand equally delightful to your taste; and doth not your sense of hearing suffer as much, from the discordant sounds prevalent in an ill regulated family, produced by the voices of children and many *et ceteras?*

CONSTANTIA.

21
Orations Delivered to the Young Ladies Academy of Philadelphia (1793)

Ann Loxley, *Valedictory Oration*

When I reflect on my appearing in public, and consider my years, I tremble at the task I now undertake: but flatter myself, that such polite characters, as this audience consists of, will silently pass over, and give allowance for the foibles my age is accustomed to. But when I inform you, that it is nearly two years since I have been a member of this seminary, and now am about to leave it, trust that all who are present, will with candour excuse my undertaking. It appears from the little experience I have had, and the best information I can collect, that the female sex, in point of scholastic education, in some measure, have been neglected. But now daily experience and common observation teach us, that the paths of science are laid open and made plain to us—that no age, sex, or denomination, are deprived of the means whereby an ample and sufficient knowledge of the different branches of the arts and sciences may be acquired. I believe it be the opinion of the public in general, that the plan of female education, now in vogue, is the most eligible of any hitherto practised; and that the veil of female ignorance will be laid aside, and our tender intellects be gently led forth by our kind instructor, in the flowery fields of knowledge, where they shall ripen with golden fruit; which I may venture to say, is the sincere wish of every friend to literature.

From *The Rise and Progress of the Young-Ladies' Academy of Philadelphia* (Philadelphia: Stewart and Cochran, 1794), 39–40, 49–50, 73–75, 90–95.

Eliza Shrupp, *Valedictory Oration*

RESPECTABLE AUDIENCE,

To reflect on my appearance in public, at this time must fill a mind (so unexperienced) with terrors unfelt before. But, relying on the candour of good and great minds, I shall not hesitate to obey the authority of my superiors, or decline the task assigned me. They will do me the justice to believe nothing but a sense of duty, could overcome the diffidence of my tender years. The wise and benevolent Author of all beings, has inspired parents with an instinctive fondness for their offspring. They are ready to sacrifice many of the comforts of life, to meliorate our condition. If we make an estimate of the condition of many nations, where ignorance sways her leaden sceptre, we shall recollect, with gratitude, many precious seasons allotted us for acquiring a sufficient competency of human learning. Where the mind is given up to vanity, or neglected in the early stages of its existence, it is not easily disincumbered of ignorance and prejudice. The immortal inhabitant within would soon loose sight of those objects, that constitute our chief happiness, while the passions, unsubdued by reason and law, might precipitate us into the gulph of ruin. The transition, from a state of ignorance, is neither so sudden or miraculous, as to preclude the use of books or instructors. Whatever has been the infelicity of former ages, the present possess the most ample means, and exhibit the best models for education. Many benefits are derived to mankind from improvements in grammar, geography, philosophy, and the polite arts: And as the accent is rendered smooth and easy, shall not our sex be ambitious of gaining the summit?

Molly Wallace, *Valedictory Oration*

The silent and solemn attention of a respectable audience, has often, at the beginning of discourses intimidated, even veterans, in the art of public elocution. What then must my situation be, when my sex, my youth and inexperience all conspire to make me tremble at the talk which I have undertaken? But the friendly encouragement, which I behold in almost every countenance, enables me to overcome difficulties, that would otherwise be insurmountable. With some, however, it has been made a question, whether we ought *ever* to appear in so public a manner. Our natural timidity, the domestic situation to which, by nature and custom we seem destined, are, urged as arguments against what I have now undertaken:—Many sarcastical observations have been handed out against female oratory: But to what do they amount? Do they not plainly inform us, that, because we are females, we ought therefore to be deprived of what is perhaps the most effectual means of acquiring a just, natural and graceful delivery? No one will pretend to deny, that we should be taught to read in the best manner. And if to read, why not to speak? For surely it cannot be a less necessary qualification for a young Lady to speak properly, than for her to read so, since she will, perhaps, rarely have occasion to read in public; tho' she may almost every day be obliged to speak, not only in the circle of her friends and acquaintance, but even before strangers, who will not often make the allowances, which an awkward and uncouth mode of elocution would necessarily require. But yet it may be asked, what, has a female character to do with declamation? That she should harangue at the head of an Army, in the Senate, or before a popular Assembly, is not pretended, neither is it requested that she ought to be an adept in the stormy and contentious eloquence of the bar, or in the abstract and subtle reasoning of the Senate;—we look not for a female Pitt, Cicero, or Demosthenes.

There are more humble and milder scenes than those which I have mentioned, in which a woman may display her elocution? There are numerous topics, on which she may discourse without impropriety, in the discussion of which, she may instruct and please others, and in which she may exercise and improve her own understanding. After all, we do not expect women should become perfect orators. Why then should they be taught to speak in public? This question may possibly be answered by asking several others.

Why is a boy diligently and carefully taught the Latin, the Greek, or the Hebrew language, in which he will seldom have occasion, either to write or converse? Why is he taught to demonstrate the propositions of Euclid, when during his whole life, he will not perhaps make use of one of them? Are we taught to dance merely for the sake of becoming dancers? No, certainly. These things are commonly studied, more on account of the habits, which the learning of them establishes, than on account of any important advantages which the mere knowledge of them can afford. So a young lady, from the exercise of speaking before a properly selected audience, may acquire some valuable habits, which, otherwise she can obtain from no examples, and that no precept can give. But, this exercise can with propriety be performed only before a select audience: a promiscuous and indiscriminate one, for obvious reasons, would be absolutely unsuitable, and should always be carefully avoided.

Priscilla Mason, Salutatory Oration

Venerable Trustees of the Seminary[,] Patrons of the improvement of the female mind; suffer us to present the first fruits of your labours as an offering to you, and cordially to salute you on this auspicious day. . . .

A female, young and inexperienced, addressing a promiscuous assembly, is a novelty which requires an apology, as some may suppose. I therefore, with submission, beg leave to offer a few thoughts in vindication of female eloquence.

I mean not at this early day, to become an advocate for that species of female eloquence, of which husbands so much, and so justly, stand in awe,—a species of which the famous Grecian orator, Xantippe, was an illustrious example. Although the free exercise of this natural talent, is a part of the rights of woman, and must

be allowed by the courtesy of Europe and America too; yet it is rather to be *tolerated* than *established;* and should rest like the sword in the scabbard, to be used only when occasion requires.—Leaving my sex in full possession of this prerogative, I claim for them the further right of being heard on more public occasions—of addressing the reason as well as the fears of the other sex.

Our right to instruct and persuade cannot be disputed, if it shall appear, that we possess the talents of the orator—and have opportunities for the exercise of those talents. Is a power of speech, and volubility of expression, one of the talents of the orator? Our sex possess it in an eminent degree.

Do personal attractions give charms to eloquence, and force to the orator's arguments? There is some truth mixed with the flattery we receive on this head. Do tender passions enable the orator to speak in a moving and forcible manner? This talent of the orator is confessedly ours. In all these respects the female orator stands on equal,—nay, on *superior* ground.

If therefore she should fail in the capacity for mathematical studies, or metaphysical profundities, she has, on the whole, equal pretensions to the palm of eloquence. Granted it is, that a perfect knowledge of the subject is essential to the accomplish'd Orator. But seldom does it happen, that the abstruse sciences, become the subject of eloquence. And, as to that knowledge which is popular and practical,—that knowledge which alone is useful to the orator; who will say that the female mind is incapable?

Our high and mighty Lords (thanks to their arbitrary constitutions) have denied us the means of knowledge, and then reproached us for the want of it. Being the stronger party, they early seized the scepter and the sword; with these they gave laws to society; they denied women the advantage of a liberal education; forbid them to exercise their talents on those great occasions, which would serve to improve them. They doom'd the sex to servile or frivolous employments, on purpose to degrade their minds, that they themselves might hold unrivall'd, the power and pre-eminence they had usurped. Happily, a more liberal way of thinking begins to prevail. The sources of knowledge are gradually opening to our sex. Some have already availed themselves of the privilege so far, as to wipe off our reproach in some measure.

A McCaulley, a Carter, a Moore, a Rowe, and other illustrous female characters, have shown of what the sex are capable, under the cultivating hand of science. But supposing now that we possess'd all the talents of the orator, in the highest perfection; where shall we find a theatre for the display of them? The Church, the Bar, and the Senate are shut against us. Who shut them? *Man;* despotic man, first made us incapable of the duty, and then forbid us the exercise. Let us by suitable education, qualify ourselves for those high departments—they will open before us. They *will,* did I say? They have done it already. Besides several Churches of less importance, a most numerous and respectable Society, has display'd its impartiality.——I had almost said gallantry in this respect. With *others,* women forsooth, are complimented with the wall, the right hand, the head of the table,—with a kind of mock pre-eminence in small matters: but on great occasions the sycophant changes his tune, and says, "Sit down at my feet and learn.["] Not so the members of the enlightened and liberal Church. They regard not the anatomical formation of the body. They look to the soul, and allow all to teach who are capable of it, be they male or female.

But Paul forbids it! Contemptible little body! The girls laughed at the deformed creature. To be revenged, he declares war against the whole sex: advises men not to marry them; and has the insolence to order them to keep silence in the Church—: afraid, I suppose, that they would say something against celibacy, or ridicule the old bachelor.

With respect to the bar, citizens of either sex, have an undoubted right to plead their own cause there. Instances could be given of females being admitted to plead the cause of a friend, a husband, a son; and they have done it with energy and effect. I am assured that there is nothing in our laws or constitution, to prohibit the licensure of female Attornies; and sure our judges have to much gallantry, to urge *prescription* in bar of their claim. In regard to the senate, prescription is clearly in our favour. We have one or two cases exactly in point.

Heliogabalus, the Roman Emperor; of blessed memory, made his grand-mother a senator of Rome. He also established a senate of women: appointed his mother President; and committed to them the important business of regulating dress and fashions. And truly methinks the dress of our own country, at this day, would admit of some regulation, for it is subject to no rules at all—It would be worthy the wisdom of Congress, to consider whether a similar institution, established at the seat of our Federal Government, would not be a public benefit. We cannot be independent, while we receive our fashions from other countries; nor act properly, while we imitate the manners of governments not congenial to our own. Such a Senate, composed of women most noted for wisdom, learning and taste, delegated from every part of the Union, would give dignity, and independence to our manners; uniformity, and even authority to our fashions.

It would fire the female breast with the most generous ambition, prompting to illustrious actions. It would furnish the most noble Theatre for the display, the exercise and improvement of every faculty. It would call forth all that is human—all that is *divine* in the soul of woman; and having proved them equally capable with the other sex, would lead to their equal participation of honor and office.

22

Susanna Rowson

The Death of Charlotte Temple (1794)

Author's Preface

For the perusal of the young and thoughtless of the fair sex, this Tale of Truth is designed; and I could wish my fair readers to consider it as not merely the effusion of Fancy, but as a reality. The circumstances, on which I have founded this novel, were related to me some little time since, by an old lady who had personally known Charlotte, though she concealed the real names of the characters, and likewise the place where the unfortunate scenes were acted: yet as it was impossible to offer a relation to the public in such an imperfect state, I have thrown over the whole a slight veil of fiction, and substituted names and places according to my own fancy. The principal characters in this little tale are now consigned to the silent tomb: it can therefore hurt the feelings of no one; and may, I flatter myself, be of service to some who are so unfortunate as to have neither friends to advise, or understanding to direct them, through the various and unexpected evils that attend a young and unprotected woman in her first entrance into life.

While the tear of compassion still trembled in my eye for the fate of the unhappy Charlotte, "I may have children of my own," said I, "to whom this recital may be of use." "And if to your own children," said Benevolence, "why not to the many daughters of Misfortune, who, deprived of natural friends, or spoilt by a mistaken education, are thrown on an unfeeling world without the least power to defend themselves from the snares not only of the other sex, but from the more dangerous arts of the profligate of their own?"

From *Charlotte Temple, A Tale of Truth*, 5th American ed. (Harrisburgh: Carey, 1802), iii–iv, 105–110.

Sensible as I am, that a novel writer, at a time when such a variety of works are ushered into the world under that name, stands but a poor chance for fame in the annals of literature, but conscious that I wrote with a mind anxious for the happiness of that sex whose morals and conduct have so powerful an influence on mankind in general; and convinced that I have not written a line that conveys a wrong idea to the head, or a corrupt wish to the heart, I shall rest satisfied in the purity of my own intentions, and if I merit not applause, I feel that I dread not censure.

If the following tale should save one hapless fair one from the errors which ruined poor Charlotte, or rescue from impending misery the heart of one anxious parent, I shall feel a much higher gratification in reflecting on this trifling performance, than could possibly result from the applause which might attend the most elegant finished piece of literature, whose tendency might deprave the heart, or mislead the understanding. . . .

[Charlotte Temple is lured away from boarding school by Montraville, a handsome soldier. Betrayed not only by her lover but also by one of her teachers, the unsuspecting Charlotte goes with Montraville to America, believing that they will be married when they arrive. Her hopes are unfounded, however, as Montraville has no intention of marrying her.]

Chapter XVIII. Reflections

"And am I indeed fallen so low," said Charlotte, "as to be only pitied? Will the voice of approbation no more meet my ear? and shall I never again possess a friend, whose face will wear a smile of joy, whenever I approach? Alas! how thoughtless, how dreadfully imprudent have I been! I know not which is most painful to endure, the sneer of contempt, or the glance of compassion, which is depicted in the various countenances of my own sex: they are both equally humiliating. Ah! my dear parents, could you now see the child of your affections, the daughter whom you so dearly loved, a poor solitary being, without society, here wearing out her heavy hours in deep regret and anguish of heart, no kind friend of her own sex to whom she can unbosom her griefs, no beloved mother, no woman of character to appear in her company; and, low as your Charlotte is fallen, she cannot associate with infamy."

These were the painful reflections which occupied the mind of Charlotte. Montraville had placed her in a small house, a few miles from New-York: he gave her one female attendant, and supplied her with what money she wanted; but business and pleasure so entirely occupied his time, that he had little to devote to the woman whom he had brought from all her connections and robbed of innocence. Sometimes, indeed, he would steal out at the close of evening, and pass a few hours with her; and then so much was she attached to him, that all her sorrows were forgotten while blest with his society: she would enjoy a walk by moonlight, or sit by him in a little arbour at the bottom of the garden, and play on the harp, accompanying it with her plaintive, harmonious voice. But often, very often, did he promise to renew his visits, and, forgetful of his promise, leave her to mourn her disappointment. What painful hours of expectation would she pass! She would sit at a window which looked toward a field he used to cross, counting the minutes, and straining her eyes to catch the first glimpse of his person, till, blinded with tears of disappointment, she would lean her head on her hands, and give free vent to her sorrows: then catching at some new hope, she would again renew her watchful position, till the shades of evening enveloped every object in a dusky cloud: she would then renew her complaints, and, with a heart bursting with disappointed love and wounded sensibility, retire to a bed which remorse had strewed with thorns, and court in vain that comforter of weary nature (who seldom visits the unhappy) to come and steep her senses in oblivion.

Who can form an adequate idea of the sorrow that preyed upon the mind of Charlotte? The wife, whose breast glows with affection for her husband, and who in return meets only indifference, can but faintly conceive her anguish. Dreadfully painful is the situation of such a woman; but she has many comforts, of which our poor Charlotte was deprived. The duteous, faithful wife, though treated with indifference, has one solid pleasure within her own bosom: she can reflect that she has not deserved neglect-that she has ever fulfilled the duties of her station with the strictest exactness; she may hope, by constant assiduity and unremitted attention, to recall her wanderer, and be doubly happy in his returning affection; she knows he cannot leave her to unite himself to another: he cannot cast her out to poverty and contempt. She looks around her, and sees the smile of friendly welcome, or the tear of affectionate consolation, on the face of every person whom she favors with her esteem; and from all these circumstances, she gathers comfort; but the poor girl, by thoughtless passion led astray, who, in parting with her honor, has forfeited the esteem of the very man to whom she has sacrificed every thing dear and valuable in life, feels his indifference to be the fruit of her own folly, and laments her want of power to recall his lost affection: she knows, there is no tie but honor, and that, in a man who has been guilty of seduction, is but very feeble; he may leave her in a moment to shame and want; he may marry and forsake her forever; and should he do so, she has no redress, no friendly soothing companion to pour into her wounded mind the balm of consolation, no benevolent hand to lead her back to the path of rectitude; she has disgraced her friends, forfeited the good opinion of the world, and undone herself. She feels herself a poor solitary being in the midst of surrounding multitudes; shame bows her to the earth, remorse tears her distracted mind, and guilt, poverty, and disease close the dreadful scene; she sinks unnoticed to oblivion. The finger of contempt may point out, to some passing daughter of youthful mirth, the humble bed where lies this frail sister of mortality: and will she, in the unbounded gaiety of her heart, exult in her own unblemished fame, and triumph over the silent ashes of the dead? Oh no! she has a heart of sensibility, she will stop, and thus address the unhappy victim of folly: . . .*

"Thou hadst thy faults; but surely thy sufferings have expiated them: thy errors brought thee to an early grave; but thou wert a fellow-creature . . . . thou hast been unhappy . . . . then be those errors forgotten."

Then, as she stoops to pluck the noxious weed from off the sod, a tear will fall, and consecrate the spot to Charity.

For ever honored be the sacred drop of humanity: the angel of mercy shall record its source, and the soul from whence it sprang shall be immortal.

My dear Madam, contract not your brow into a frown of disapprobation. I mean not to extenuate the faults of those unhappy women who fall victims to guilt and folly; but surely, when we reflect how many errors we are ourselves subject to, how many secret faults lie hid in the recesses of our hearts, which we should blush to have brought into open day (and yet those faults require the lenity and pity of a benevolent judge, or awful would be our prospect of futurity) I say, my dear Madam, when we consider this, we surely may pity the faults of others.

Believe me, many an unfortunate female, who has once strayed into the thorny paths of vice, would gladly return to virtue, was any generous friend to endeavour to raise and re-assure her; but alas! it cannot be, you say; the world would deride and scoff. Then let me tell you, Madam, 'tis a very unfeeling world, and does not deserve half the blessings which a bountiful Providence showers upon it.

Oh, thou benevolent giver of all good! how shall we, erring mortals, dare to look up to thy mercy in the great day of retribution, if we now

uncharitably refuse to overlook the errors, or alleviate the miseries, of our fellow-creatures.

[Montraville soon falls in love with another woman—an heiress—and he grows more distant from Charlotte. He finally marries the heiress, and the story ends as Charlotte dies delivering his child.]

23

Hannah Webster Foster
The Coquette (1797)

[Eliza Wharton, to please her parents, had agreed to marry a man she did not love. He dies unexpectedly before they marry, and the novel opens as Eliza, enjoying her new-found freedom, insists that she does not want to get married any time soon. She is pursued vigorously, however, by Major Sanford, a charming rake, and the Reverend Boyer, an honorable but dull man. Eliza is dissatisfied with both suitors—and with the seemingly inevitable prospect of marriage.]

Letter V.

TO MISS LUCY FREEMAN.

New Haven.

These bewitching charms of mine have a tendency to keep my mind in a state of perturbation. I am so pestered with these admirers! Not that I am so very handsome neither; but I don't know how it is, I am certainly very much the taste of the other sex. Followed, flattered, and caressed, I have cards and compliments in profusion. But I must try to be serious; for I have, alas! one serious lover. As I promised you to be particular in my writing, I suppose I must proceed methodically. Yesterday we had a party to dine. Mr. Boyer was of the number. His at-

---

*This ellipsis, and the following two ellipses, are all in the original document (editors' note).

From *The Coquette; or, the History of Eliza Wharton* (Boston: Fetridge & Co., 1855), 42–44, 60–62, 66–71, 90–92, 100–103, 105–106, 281–284.

tention was immediately engrossed; and I soon perceived that every word, every action, and every look was studied to gain my approbation. As he sat next me at dinner, his assiduity and politeness were pleasing; and as we walked together afterwards, his conservation was improving. Mine was sentimental and sedate—perfectly adapted to the taste of my gallant. Nothing, however, was said particularly expressive of his apparent wishes. I studiously avoided every kind of discourse which might lead to this topic. I wish not for a declaration from any one, especially from one whom I could not repulse and do not intend to encourage at present. His conversation, so similar to what I had often heard from a similar character, brought a deceased friend to mind, and rendered me somewhat pensive. I retired directly after supper. Mr. Boyer had just taken leave.

Mrs. Richman came into my chamber as she was passing to her own. "Excuse my intrusion, Eliza," said she. "I thought I would just step in and ask you if you have passed a pleasant day?"

"Perfectly so, madam; and I have now retired to protract the enjoyment by recollection." "What, my dear, is your opinion of our favorite, Mr. Boyer?" "Declaring him your favorite, madam, is sufficient to render me partial to him. But to be frank, independent of that, I think him an agreeable man." "Your heart, I presume, is now free?" "Yes, and I hope it will long remain so." "Your friends, my dear, solicitous for your welfare, wish to see you suitably and agreeably connected." "I hope my friends will never again interpose in my concerns of that nature. You, madam, who have ever known my heart, are sensible that, had the Almighty spared life in a certain instance, I must have sacrificed my own happiness or incurred their censure. I am young, gay, volatile. A melancholy event has lately extricated me from those shackles, which parental authority had imposed on my mind. Let me, then, enjoy that freedom which I so highly prize. Let me have opportunity, unbiased by opinion, to gratify my natural disposition in a participation of those pleasures which youth and inno-

cence afford." "Of such pleasures, no one, my dear, would wish to deprive you; but beware, Eliza! Though strewed with flowers, when contemplated by your lively imagination, it is, after all, a slippery, thorny path. The round of fashionable dissipation is dangerous. A phantom is often pursued, which leaves its deluded votary the real form of wretchedness." She spoke with an emphasis, and taking up her candle, wished me a good night. I had not power to return the compliment. Something seemingly prophetic in her looks and expressions, cast a momentary gloom upon my mind; but I despise those contracted ideas which confine virtue to a cell. I have no notion of becoming a recluse. Mrs. Richman has ever been a beloved friend of mine; yet I always thought her rather prudish. Adieu.

Eliza Wharton.

Letter XII.

TO MISS LUCY FREEMAN.

New Haven.

The heart of your friend is again besieged. Whether it will surrender to the assailants or not I am unable at present to determine. Sometimes I think of becoming a predestinarian, and submitting implicitly to fate, without any exercise of free will; but, as mine seems to be a wayward one, I would counteract the operations of it, if possible.

Mrs. Richman told me this morning that she hoped I should be as agreeably entertained this afternoon, as I had been the preceding; that she expected Mr. Boyer to dine and take tea and doubted not but he would be as attentive and sincere to me, if not as gay and polite, as the gentleman who obtruded his civilities yesterday. I replied that I had no reason to doubt the sincerity of the one or the other, having never put them to the test, nor did I imagine I ever should. "Your friends, Eliza," said she, "would be very happy to see you united to a man of Mr. Boyer's worth, and so agreeably settled, as he has a prospect of being." "I hope," said I, "that my friends are not so weary of my company, as to wish to dispose of me. I am too happy in my present connections to quit them for new ones. Marriage is the tomb of friendship. It appears to me a very selfish state. Why do people in general, as soon as they are married, centre all their cares, their concerns, and pleasures in their own families? Former acquaintances are neglected or forgotten; the tenderest ties between friends are weakened or dissolved; and benevolence itself moves in a very limited sphere." "It is the glory of the marriage state," she rejoined, "to refine, by circumscribing our enjoyments. Here we can respose in safety. . . . True, we cannot always pay that attention to former associates which we may wish; but the little community which we superintend is quite as important an object, and certainly renders us more beneficial to the public. True benevolence, though it may change its objects, is not limited by time or place. Its effects are the same, and, aided by a second self, are rendered more diffusive and salutary." . . .

Eliza Wharton.

Letter XIV.

TO MISS LUCY FREEMAN.

New Haven.

I have received, and read again and again, your friendly epistle. My reason and judgment entirely coincide with your opinion; but my fancy claims some share in the decision: and I cannot yet tell which will preponderate. This was the day fixed for deciding Mr. Boyer's cause. . . .

With all the candor and frankness which I was capable of assuming, I thus answered his long harangue, to which I had listened without interrupting him." Self-knowledge, sir, that most important of all sciences, I have yet to learn. Such have been my situations in life, and the natural volatility of my temper, that I have looked but little into my own heart in regard to its future wishes and views. From a scene of constraint and confinement, ill suited to my years and inclination, I have just launched into society. My heart beats high in expectation of its fancied joys. My sanguine imagination paints, in

alluring colors, the charms of youth and freedom, regulated by virtue and innocence. Of these I wish to partake. While I own myself under obligations for the esteem which you are pleased to profess for me, and, in return, acknowledge, that neither your person nor manners are disagreeable to me, I recoil at the thought of immediately forming a connection which must confine me to the duties of domestic life, and make me dependent for happiness, perhaps, too, for subsistence, upon a class of people who will claim the right of scrutinizing every part of my conduct, and by censuring those foibles which I am conscious of not having prudence to avoid, may render me completely miserable. While, therefore, I receive your visits, and cultivate towards you sentiments of friendship and esteem, I would not have you consider me as confined to your society, or obligated to a future connection. Our short acquaintance renders it impossible for me to decide what the operations of my mind may hereafter be. You must either quit the subject, or leave me to the exercise of my free will, which, perhaps may coincide with your present wishes." "Madam," said he, "far is the wish from me to restrain your person or mind. In your breast I will repose my cause. It shall be my study to merit a return of affection; and I doubt not but generosity and honor will influence your conduct towards me. I expect soon to settle among a generous and enlightened people, where I flatter myself I shall be exempt from those difficulties, and embarrassments to which too many of my brethren are subject. The local situation is agreeable, the society refined and polished; and if, in addition, I may obtain that felicity which you are formed to bestow in a family connection, I shall be happy indeed." . . .

He tarried to supper, and took his leave. I retired immediately to my chamber, to which I was followed by Mrs. Richman. I related to her the conversation and the encouragement which I had given Mr. Boyer. She was pleased; but insisted that I should own myself somewhat engaged to him. This, I told her, I should never do to any man before the indissoluble knot was tied. "That," said I, "will be time enough to resign my freedom." She replied, that I had wrong ideas of freedom and matrimony; but she hoped that Mr. Boyer would happily rectify them.

I have now, my dear friend, given you an account of my present situation, and leave you to judge for yourself concerning it. Write me your opinion, and believe me ever yours,

Eliza Wharton.

Letter XV.

TO MISS ELIZA WHARTON.

Hartford.

I congratulate you, my dear Eliza, on the stability of your conduct towards Mr. Boyer. Pursue the system which you have adopted, and I dare say that happiness will crown your future days. You are indeed very tenacious of your freedom, as you call it; but that is a play about words. A man of Mr. Boyer's honor and good sense will never abridge any privileges which virtue can claim.

When do you return to embellish our society here? I am impatient to see you, and likewise this amiable man. I am much interested in his favor. By the way, I am told that Major Sanford has been to look at the seat of Captain Pribble, which is upon sale. It is reported that he will probably purchase it. Many of our gentry are pleased with the prospect of such a neighbor. "As an accomplished gentleman," say they, "he will be an agreeable addition to our social parties; and as a man of property and public spirit, he will be an advantage to the town." But from what I have heard of him, I am far from supposing him a desirable acquisition in either of these respects. A man of vicious character cannot be a good member of society. In order to that, his principle and practice must be uncorrupted; in his morals, at least, he must be a man of probity, and honor. Of these qualifications, if I mistake not, this gallant of yours cannot boast. But I shall not set up for a censor. I hope neither you nor I shall have much connection with him. . . .

Lucy Freeman.

Letter XXIII.

TO THE REV. J. BOYER.

New Haven.

. . . It is said she has many admirers, and I conceive it very possible that this [Major Sanford] may be one of them; though, truly, I do not think that she would esteem such a conquest any great honor. I now joined in the general topic of conversation, which was politics; Mrs. Richman and Miss Wharton judiciously, yet modestly, bore a part; while the other ladies amused themselves with Major Sanford, who was making his sage remarks on the play, which he still kept in his hand. General Richman at length observed that we had formed into parties. Major Sanford, upon this, laid aside his book. Miss Laurence simpered, and looked as if she was well pleased with being in a party with so fine a man; while her mother replied that she never meddled with politics. "Miss Wharton and I," said Mrs. Richman, "must beg leave to differ from you, madam. We think ourselves interested in the welfare and prosperity of our country; and, consequently, claim the right of inquiring into those affairs, which may conduce to, or interfere with the common weal. We shall not be called to the senate or the field to assert its privileges and defend its rights, but we shall feel for the honor and safety of our friends and connections who are thus employed. If the community flourish and enjoy health and freedom, shall we not share in the happy effects? If it be oppressed and disturbed, shall we not endure or proportion of the evil? Why then should the love of our country be a masculine passion only? Why should government, which involves the peace and order of the society of which we are a part, be wholly excluded from our observation?" Mrs. Laurence made some slight reply, and waved the subject. The gentlemen applauded Mrs. Richman's sentiments as truly Roman, and, what was more, they said, truly republican. . . .

T. Selby.

Letter XXVI

TO MISS LUCY FREEMAN

New Haven.

. . . "Pardon me, my dear Eliza," said he [Major Sanford], "if I am impertinent; it is my regard for you which impels me to the presumption. Do you intend to give your hand to Mr. Boyer?" "I do not intend to give my hand to any man at present. I have but lately entered society, and wish, for a while, to enjoy my freedom, in the participation of pleasures suited to my age and sex." "These," said he, "you are aware, I suppose, when you form a connection with that man, you must renounce, and content yourself with a confinement to the tedious round of domestic duties, the pedantic conversation of scholars, and the invidious criticisms of a whole town." "I have been accustomed," said I, "and am therefore attached to men of letters; and as to the praise or censure of the populace, I hope always to enjoy that approbation of conscience which will render me superior to both. But you forget your promise not to talk in this style, and have deviated far from the character of a friend and brother, with which you consented to rest satisfied." "Yes, but I find myself unequal to the task. I am not stoic enough tamely to make so great a sacrifice. I must plead for an interest in your favor, till you banish me from your presence, and tell me plainly that you hate me." We had by this time reached the gate, and as we dismounted, were unexpectedly accosted by Mr. Selby, who had come, agreeably to his promise, to dine with us, and receive my letter to Mr. Boyer.

Major Sanford took his leave as General Richman appeared at the door. The general and his lady rallied me on my change of company, but very prudently concealed their sentiments of Major Sanford, while Mr. Selby was present. Nothing material occurred before and during dinner; soon after which Mr. Selby went away. I retired to dress for the assembly, and had nearly completed the labor of the toilet, when Mrs. Richman entered. "My friendship for you, my dear Eliza," said she, "interests me so much in your affairs that I cannot repress my curiosity to know who has the honor of your hand this evening." "If it be any honor," said I, it will be confered on Major Sanford." "I think it far too great to be thus bestowed," returned she. "It is perfectly astonishing to me that the virtuous part of my sex will countenance, caress, and encourage those men whose profession it is to blast their reputation, destroy their peace, and triumph in their infamy." "Is this, madam, the avowed design of Major Sanford?" "I know not what he avows, but his practice too plainly bespeaks his principles and views." "Does he now practice the arts you mention? or do you refer to past follies?" "I cannot answer for his present conduct; his past has established his character." "You, madam, are an advocate for charity; that, perhaps, if exercised in this instance might lead you to think it possible for him to reform, to become a valuable member of society, and, when connected with a lady of virtue and refinement, to be capable of making a good husband." "I cannot conceive that such a lady would be willing to risk her all upon the slender prospect of his reformation. I hope the one with whom I am conversing, has no inclination to so hazardous an experiment." "Why, not much." "Not much! If you have any, why do you continue to encourage Mr. Boyer's addresses?" "I am not sufficiently acquainted with either, yet, to determine which to take. At present, I shall not confine myself in any way. In regard to these men, my fancy and my judgment are in scales; sometimes one preponderates, sometimes the other; which will finally outweigh, time alone can reveal." "O my cousin, beware of the delusions of fancy! Reason must be our guide, if we would expect durable happiness." At this instant a servant opened the door, and told me that Major Sanford waited in the parlor. Being ready, I wished Mrs. Richman a good evening, and went down. Neither General Richman nor his lady appeared. He therefore handed me immediately into his phaeton, and we were soon in the assembly room. . . .

What shall I say now, my friend? This man, to an agreeable person has superadded graceful manners, an amiable temper, and a fortune sufficient to ensure the enjoyments of all the pleasing varieties of social life. Perhaps a gay disposition and a lax education may have betrayed him into some scenes of dissipation. But is it not an adage generally received, that *"a reformed rake makes the best husband"*? My fancy leads me for happiness to the festive haunts of fashionable life. I am at present, and know not but I ever shall be, too volatile for a confinement to domestic avocations and sedentary pleasures. I dare not, therefore, place myself in a situation where these must be indispensable. Mr. Boyer's person and character are agreeable. I really esteem the man. My reason and judgment, as I have observed before, declare for a connection with him, as a state of tranquility and rational happiness. But the idea of relinquishing those delightful amusements and flattering attentions, which wealth and equipage bestow is painful. Why were not the virtues of the one and the graces and affluence of the other combined? I should then have been happy indeed. But, as the case not stands, I am loath to give up either; being doubtful which will conduce most to my felicity.

Pray write me impartially; let me know your real sentiments, for I rely greatly upon your opinion. I am, &c.,

Eliza Wharton.

[Eliza, remaining ambivalent about marriage rejects Boyer's proposal and soon finds herself alone when both Sanford and Boyer marry other women. Her attraction for the charming and dangerous Sanford continues—and continues to be reciprocated despite Sanford's marriage. Eliza finally enters into an illicit relationship with him. Becoming pregnant, she leaves her family and friends and dies in childbirth, alone in a roadside inn.]

Letter LXXIII.

TO MISS JULIA GRANBY.

Boston.

A melancholy tale have you unfolded, my dear Julia; and tragic indeed is the concluding scene.

Is she then gone? gone in this most distressing manner? Have I lost my once-loved friend? lost her in a way which I could never have conceived to be possible?

Our days of childhood were spent together in the same pursuits, in the same amusements. Our riper years encreased our mutual affection, and maturer judgment most firmly cemented our friendship. Can I, then, calmly resign her to so severe a fate? Can I bear the idea of her being lost to honor, to fame, and to life? No; she shall still live in the heart of her faithful Lucy, whose experience of her numerous virtues and engaging qualities has imprinted her image too deeply on the memory to be obliterated. However she may have erred, her sincere repentance is sufficient to restore her to charity.

Your letter gave the first information of this awful event. I had taken a short excursion into the country, where I had not seen the papers, or, if I had, paid little or no attention to them. By your directions I found the distressing narrative of her exit. The poignancy of my grief, and the unavailing lamentations which the intelligence excited, need no delineation. To scenes of this nature you have been habituated in the mansion of sorrow, where you reside.

How sincerely I sympathize with the bereaved parent of the dear, deceased Eliza, I can feel, but have not power to express. Let it be her consolation that her child is at rest. The resolution which carried this deluded wanderer thus far from her friends, and supported her through her various trials, is astonishing. Happy would it have been had she exerted an equal degree of fortitude in repelling the first attacks upon her virtue. But she is no more, and Heaven forbid that I should accuse or reproach her.

Yet in what language shall I express my abhorrence of the monster, whose detestable arts have blasted one of the fairest flowers in creation? I leave him to God and his own conscience. Already is he exposed in his true colors. Vengeance already begins to overtake him. His sordid mind must now suffer the deprivation of those sensual gratifications beyond which he is incapable of enjoyment.

Upon your reflecting and steady mind, my dear Julia, I need not inculcate the lessons which may be drawn from this woe-fraught tale; but for the sake of my sex in general, I wish it engraved upon every heart, that virtue alone, independent of the trappings of wealth, the parade of equipage, and the adulation of gallantry, can secure lasting felicity. From the melancholy story of Eliza Wharton, let the American fair learn to reject with disdain every insinuation derogatory to their true dignity and honor. Let them despise and for ever banish the man who can glory in the seduction of innocence and the ruin of reputation. To associate is to approve; to approve, is to be betrayed.

I am, &c.,

Lucy Sumner [formerly Freeman].

24
The Female Advocate (1801)

. . . We read in the 7th chapter of Genesis, that when Noah entered the Ark, there went in two and two of all flesh, that had the breath of life, male and female.

As GOD in his great, good, and just Providence, has seen fit for many wise and obvious reasons, that the world should consist of male and female, I would ask the unprejudiced, the wise and the candid, how has Providence designed that they should conduct themselves toward each other:—As master and servant, or as companion and yoke-fellow? Do you not generously answer, and say, surely the latter! Why

From *The Female Advocate* (New Haven, Ct.: n. p., 1801), 14–17, 20–21, 23–24, 26–27, 30–32, 39.

ought the one half of mankind, to vaunt, and lord it, over the other. The scripture saith, the man is not without the woman; nor the woman without the man. But as the world is already filled with books and the greatest authors, sacred and profane, have displayed their talents, and geniuses, from Moses down to the present day, perhaps in the estimation of many, it will appear folly and arrogance for an aged matron, one too, who belongs to a class, whose weakness is become quite proverbial among the self sufficient lords of this lower world, if she should attempt to say any thing, in behalf of her own sex, or a single word on the long exploded subject of female merit. But the sensations of my mind are so wounded, when I hear my sex treated, as I think, with contempt, when I see them viewed by some, with self-distant superiority, and when I behold too many, seemingly adopt the sentiment of a titled nobleman, to his natural son, that women are destitute of sense and judgment, I expect, if not from this description of men, yet, at least, from the judicious and candid, a ready apology will be found, for what may be attempted in the following lines.

Perhaps a strong motive, which induced me to make choice of this subject, and to collect what arguments might meet my mind, in the moments of contemplative leisure, was hearing it observed by one of the arrogant assumers of male merit, what appeared to me totally devoid of every foundation, and even the semblance of justice, that our sex arrived at its zenith of improvement, at the age of twenty-one. . . .

But hush such fruitless disagreeable thoughts, on the ingratitude and reproaches of others. Why is it, said I, that we are so much more admired, adored and caressed, by the gentlemen, while in our youth, than at any other age? Doth it indicate wisdom, virtue, piety and worth; or doth it point out weakness, folly and levity. The age most admired by the other sex, is the very age, which, by that admiration, proves, not what they would wish to demonstrate, but *their* folly and *our* superior wisdom. It is an age, in which we are much the most addicted to foibles, and fondest of dress, gaiety and folly; yet this devotedness to vanity, pleases and captivates the other sex, and at once delineates their weakness. If that which is the very weakness of woman will effectually captivate the man of assumed superiority, and cause even a tyrant to forget his savage nature as we read in the Apocrypha, does it not prove, that the former possesses not only superior charms, but a mental quality which, though in youth, rises paramount to the boasted reason of the assuming lords of this world. The man boasts of his power, and talents and dominion; but the woman, with all her imagined weakness, will silently command their power, their wisdom and their authority, to yield themselves, an obsequious victim to female merit, and cause them to pay obeisance, like the elder brethren of an ancient family, in scripture, to the superior genius of the younger brother. . . .

Without wishing, or intending, to give any offence to the young gentlemen, I shall now endeavor to make it appear, that an aged, pious and venerable matron, who has been full of good works all her days, is to be highly valued; that such a one, though passed over by the unprincipled part of mankind, is incalculably more worthy of being stiled, "Angelic," than that gay, and volatile age, which has the epithet usually conferred upon it.

Governed in my sentiments by the best of rules, the unerring guide of sacred writ, we find that in the days of our Saviour, and his Apostles, the aged ladies had a just preference, not only to youth, but to the other sex, in fidelity, affection and piety. How different then from the present day, in which men engross all the emoluments, offices, honours and merits of church and state. Not so was it in the primitive church, and ecclesiastical communities. St. Paul directs Timothy to admit them, under just conditions, as freely as the men, to offices of honour and public utility; and that too, at an age when, by modern thinkers, they have past the season of usefulness. "At the age of three score years," he writes, "let them be taken into the number,"—

that is, into the number of Deaconnesses. It is well known to all conversant in the sacred writings, that such offices were filled by the female sex in the primitive and purest days of the church. But in modern times, instead of admission to office, they are not permitted even to speak in public, or to have a voice in the church. . . .

I hope, says a very pious and justly celebrated author, that I shall give no offence, by observing the following sentiments. "I am very serious in saying, that the frequent mention, which is made in the Evangelists, of the generous and courageous zeal of some pious women, in the service of Christ, and especially in their faithfulness and resolute constancy, with which they attended him in those last scenes of his sufferings, might, very possibly, be intended to obviate that senseless contempt, which the pride of men, often irritated by those vexations, to which their own irregular passions have exposed them, has in all ages, affected to throw on that sex, which probably in the sight of God, constitute by far the better half of mankind, and to whose care and tenderness, the wisest and best of men, generally owe and ascribe much of the daily comforts and enjoyments of life."

Enough, cries my satisfied soul! Let the wise and pious but concede an equality between the sexes; let them reprove the vain, the arrogant and assuming advocates for female exclusion, and we are contented with less than the concessious of the above pious defender of female worth, "*that women constitute the better half of mankind.*" I aspire to nothing more than the just rank, which God and nature designed, that equality of talents, of genius, of morals, as well as intellectual worth, which, by evident traits, does exist between the sexes; but of which the arrogance of modern self-sufficiency would totally divest us had it the power. . . .

Now for a moment, let me turn your attention to the young, while in the years of tender adolescence. Can it be said, that Chesterfield has no pupils in the world; no infidel wretches, who are assiduously practicing the art of gallantry and seduction, and taking the advantage of the credulous, unsuspecting, unexperienced, young and tender minds? Is it not true that when by art, under the soft appellation of gallantry, or the fine feelings of sentimental affection; when by that cruel, wicked, artifice of flattery, and lying, they have made a conquest of innocence, they straightway go and boast of that, which ought to be the greatest blot in their character. And yet the consequence of this injurious conduct is, that the villain is admitted to honors and emoluments, at least it becomes no impediment to his promotion, while the injured fair one, once innocent and beloved by her parents, receives a stain, by one act of indiscretion, which she can never obliterate, or fully wear away. Why is it, that woman must forever suffer reproach for a single crime, though deceived by the superior artifice of a man of the world, who has learned the art of gallantry, as one would a trade, while the latter, though far more criminal, as much more so, as the deceiver than the deluded, shalt, notwithstanding one or a hundred similar villainies, be caressed, esteemed and admitted to honorary employments. . . .

Much and often has the world exclaimed against masculine women. Before I offer any sentiment on this exclamation, I would wish to hear the word properly and fairly defined. If by the epithet "Masculine," be meant a bold, assuming, haughty arrogant, all sufficient, dogmatical, temper and spirit, I would wish totally and entirely to discard it from the society of the fair sex. I would wish the term to be applied, where I think it is appropriate, by long established custom. I am quite willing that the other sex should share it altogether to themselves. But if by the word "Masculine," be meant a person of reading and letters, a person of science and information, one who can properly answer a question, without fear and trembling, or one who is capable of doing business, with a suitable command over self; this I believe to be a glory to the one sex, equally with the other.——The sole reason why the epithet is disgraceful, in the estimation of many, is because custom, which is not

infallible, has gradually introduced the habits of seeing imaginary propriety, that all science, all public utility, all superiority, all that is intellectually great and astonishing, should be engrossed exclusively by the male half of mankind.——But may I not securely say, that it is a point of great consequence, that we should have an equal share in science, or that degree of education, at least, which enables us, in some measure, to have command over ourselves, and become superior to those base artifices of the many, by which numerous females, through the want of suitable privileges in education, have been the dupes of men inferior to themselves, in every other respect but this single advantage, of education.

Are we not sensible, my female friends, and have we not often heard it observed, by the other sex, as an objection to our possessing peculiar advantages for scientific improvements, that they cannot so easily command the ascendancy over us; but why should we wish them to have this dominion, if we are sensible that that is often, and, may I not say, almost always, the reason and foundation of our ruin. A young lady of the greatest purity of mind, yet uneducated, is frequently a victim to the arts of seductions: differently advantaged by knowledge, the seducer would have respected her virtues, and conducted with becoming deference. Thus, a second advantage would be the consequence of female education. It would reform the men, or at least prevent, or restrain, many of those artifices, which are now too successfully used, with innocent, uneducated, and unsuspecting females. . . .

Why then may not all the seeming difference between the sexes, be imputed solely to the difference of their education and subsequent advantages?——Here let us draw a just and plain parallel between the education of a sister and her brother. Perhaps they are sent to the same school, till the age of ten or twelve years. Here the advantages of their improvement are the same, and their actual augmentation of mind is equal, unless there be a real superiority of genius, in the female youth, which is a case not unusual. Behold the arbitrary distinctions which are, next, made between them. The brother is taken from a common school, and transmitted to an academy, or a collegiate life; next becomes a divine, a lawyer or physician; the whole term of time, including usually from seven to nine years. But how is the time of his sister occupied, after she is taken from her early school. Immediately she is removed from every mean of literary improvement, and almost as effectually immured in a house, as a roman catholic Nun. She is admitted to walk in no road of preferment, and has before her, no incentives to aspire to public utility, by superior enlargement of mind. No! that is not the path for her to walk. Science and public utility are exclusively appropriated to the males.—See the invariable sister's fate! If she be not sent to a nunnery, she is at least confined to domestic labor, and utterly secluded from all public concerns.

If not thus limited, she must have what the world calls a polite education: such as dancing, music, embroidering, altering and adjusting the fashion of her apparel. I have heard it, and I think very justly, observed, as an apology for females when frequently conversing, and being more disposed than the men, to talk of fashion, dress, amusements and the polite customs of the fair world, that the former were precisely following the natural and almost necessary effect of their appropriate education. A young Miss is taught to esteem it of the utmost consequence to her success in life, that she be dressed fashionably, and observe the external graces. It requires but a small share of sagacity, for her to discern, that unless she pay more attention to outward ornaments, than intellectual endowments, she will not be noticed by the other sex, on whom is her dependence for a partner, or, shall I say, "master," for life. For high intellectual endowments, she would rather be avoided, in the view of a connexion for life, as these would be qualities incompatible with that arbitrary sovereignty, which the man would wish to have fully established in his domestic empire. To such a man, when she is united by the dearest ties, how are the best of her days, and the prime of her life to be devoted?—In a way truly, which I acknowledge to be highly beneficial; in the employments of the house and the nursing of children, and imbruing their tender minds with the early precepts of true wisdom. But beneficial as it may be, does not this confined mode of living, and devoting our rolling years, afford sufficient arguments, why females do not advance in literary acquisitions, and the knowledge of men and manners, and the concerns of more public utility so far as the other sex.

Let us farther, in the pursuit of the general arguments of the subject before us, descant for a moment on a class of our fellow men, who have for ages been holden in the vilest bondage:—I mean the African race. Divested of almost every advantage for intellectual improvement, we may perhaps derive a good additional argument for the elucidation of the equality of intelligence naturally between the sexes. In this class of human beings, we may fairly see the force of nature, unaided by art or cultivation, as it respects the male and the female. Do we find in these human souls, that distinction of intelligence, which is contested among the whites? If there be a difference in point of natural talents, between the sexes in the African race, is not that difference evidently in favour of the females? What African has displayed a greater share of genius, and stronger mental powers, than the justly celebrated Phillis Wheatley, whose poetical writings are so much read and applauded. How long had the world been accustomed to believe this despised race to be really inferior? How unjust in making no allowance between their children, and those of the whites, in early education, early ideas of liberty in the one, and of slavery, which never fails to depress the mind in the other. But in returning from the regions of slavery, which are at this day irradiating, by the all cheering sun of liberty, will not the last observations enable us to discern, that the only cause of the discrimination between the sexes, in the Christian world, arises from the early difference in education, and total distinction of future temporal prospects as to pubic utility.

Let us for a moment advance the supposition, that this distinction were reversed in favour of the females. What would be the consequence, if the doors of our seminaries were as effectually shut against the gentlemen, as they now are against the other sex;—and colleges and superior schools of scientific improvement, were appropriately open to the benefit of the female world. I ask what would then be the consequence? Would it not be a *complete reverse* of superiority in the sexes. Methinks I see some of my sex smilingly say, surely the result is indisputably true. The scale of literature would soon preponderate in our favour, and the gentlemen become of course, the same ignorant, weak and pitiable beings, as they now view the females. May I not add? "And *a little more awkward too.*"— But hush, I will say no more, lest I should give offence. It is not my design, if in my power to enter the lists as a candidate for a paper battle; I wish only to be indulged in a little railery on the other sex, in return for far more bitter things, and much severer satire, which they have long uttered against female talents. Thus much I will add for their consolation, they need not ever fear the most distant probability of our soaring above them so long as domestic confines, and the nursery of children are our destiny and employment all the prime of our lives, and the best of our days. But what I desire of them is that they lay no more on us, than God in his providence has designed. . . .

Perhaps these lines may chance to meet the eye of one, whose soul may yet be troubled, notwithstanding all his stock of science, with the spleen of criticism, and prejudiced jealousy against our sex. Surely such will say, what miserable language is this! what bad grammar! surely she does not round her periods! She had better been at her needle work, or the distaff! Friend, I will spare you all this labor of criticism. I acknowledge all my want of literary improvement; but yet I am not willing to ascribe it to want of mental powers, but the disadvantages attending my education. I have not been brought up at the feet of Gamaliel, but like Martha, have

been cumbered with much serving. Should any presume to say, that some man of letters has sitten, behind the curtain, to guide the movements of my pen, this I shall positively deny, and subjoin with the Authoress of the "Gleaner," "My nearest friend is totally ignorant of this performance, and is an utter stranger to every line, till he may see it from the press."

25
Mercy Otis Warren
On Writing a Political History of the American Revolution (1805)

At a period when every manly arm was occupied, and every trait of talent or activity engaged, either in the cabinet or the field, apprehensive, that amidst the sudden convulsions, crowded scenes, and rapid changes, that flowed in quick succession, many circumstances might escape the more busy and active members of society, I have been induced to improve the leisure Providence had lent, to record as they passed, in the following pages, the new and unexperienced events exhibited in a land previously blessed with peace, liberty, simplicity, and virtue.

As circumstances were collected, facts related, and characters drawn, many years antecedent to any history since published, relative to the dismemberment of the colonies, and to American independence, there are few allusions to any later writers.

Connected by nature, friendship, and every social tie, with many of the first patriots, and most influential characters on the continent; in the habits of confidential and epistolary intercourse with several gentlemen employed abroad in the most distinguished stations, and with others since elevated to the highest grades of rank and distinction, I had the best means of

From preface to *History of the Rise, Progress and Termination of the American Revolution*, vol. 1 (Boston: Manning and Loring, 1805), iii–vii.

information, through a long period that the colonies were in suspense, waiting the operation of foreign courts, and the success of their own enterprising spirit.

The solemnity that covered every countenance, when contemplating the sword uplifted, and the horrors of civil war rushing to habitations not inured to scenes of rapine and misery; even to the quiet cottage, where only concord and affection had reigned; stimulated to observation a mind that had not yielded to the assertion, that all political attentions lay out of the road of female life.

It is true there are certain appropriate duties assigned to each sex; and doubtless it is the more peculiar province of masculine strength, not only to repel the bold invader of the rights of his country and of mankind, but in the nervous style of manly eloquence, to describe the blood-stained field, and relate the story of slaughtered armies.

Sensible of this, the trembling heart has recoiled at the magnitude of the undertaking, and the hand often shrunk back from the task; yet, recollecting that every domestic enjoyment depends on the unimpaired possession of civil and religious liberty, that a concern for the welfare of society ought equally to glow in every human breast, the work was not relinquished. The most interesting circumstances were collected, active characters portrayed, the principles of the times developed, and the changes marked; nor need it cause a blush to acknowledge, a detail was preserved with a view of transmitting it to the rising youth of my country, some of them in infancy, others in the European world, while the most interesting events lowered over their native land.

Conscious that truth has been the guide of my pen, and candor, as well as justice, the accompaniment of my wishes through every page, I can say, with an ingenious writer, "I have used my pen with the liberty of one, who neither hopes nor fears, nor has any interest in the success or failure of any party, and who speaks to posterity—perhaps very far remote."

The sympathizing heart has looked abroad and wept the many victims of affliction, inevitably such in consequence of civil feuds and the concomitant miseries of war, either foreign or domestic. The reverses of life, and the instability of the world, have been viewed on the point of both extremes. Their delusory nature and character, have been contemplated as becomes the philosopher and the christian: the one teaches us from the analogies of nature, the necessity of changes, decay, and death; the other strengthens the mind to meet them with the rational hope of revival and renovation.

Several years have elapsed since the historical tracts, now with diffidence submitted to the public, have been arranged in the present order. Local circumstances, the decline of health, temporary deprivations of sight, the death of the most amiable of children, "the shaft flew thrice, and thrice my peace was slain," have sometimes prompted to throw by the pen in despair. I draw a veil over the woe-fraught scenes that have pierced my own heart. "While the soul was melting inwardly, it has endeavoured to support outwardly, with decency and dignity, those accidents which admit of no redress, and to exert that spirit that enables to get the better of those that do."

Not indifferent to the opinion of the world, nor servilely courting its smiles, no further apology is offered for the attempt, though many may be necessary, for the incomplete execution of a design, that had rectitude for its basis, and a beneficent regard for the civil and religious rights of mankind, for its motive.

The liberal-minded will peruse with candor, rather than criticise with severity; nor will they think it necessary, that any apology should be offered, for sometimes introducing characters nearly connected with the author of the following annals; as they were early and zealously attached to the public cause, uniform in their principles, and constantly active in the great scenes that produced the revolution, and obtained independence for their country, truth precludes that reserve which might have been proper on less important occasions, and forbids to pass over in silence the names of such as expired before the conflict was finished, or have since retired from public scenes. The historian has never laid aside the tenderness of the sex or the friend, at the same time, she has endeavoured, on all occasions, that the strictest veracity should govern her heart, and the most exact impartiality be the guide of her pen. . . .

Before this address to my countrymen is closed, I beg leave to observe, that as a new century has dawned upon us, the mind is naturally led to contemplate the great events that have run parallel with, and have just closed the last. From the revolutionary spirit of the times, the vast improvements in science, arts, and agriculture, the boldness of genius that marks the age, the investigation of new theories, and the changes in the political, civil, and religious characters of men, succeeding generations have reason to expect still more astonishing exhibitions in the next. In the mean time, Providence has clearly pointed out the duties of the present generation, particularly the paths which Americans ought to tread. The United States form a young republic, a confederacy which ought ever to be cemented by a union of interests and affection, under the influence of those principles which obtained their independence. These have indeed, at certain periods, appeared to be in the wane; but let them never be eradicated, by the jarring interests of parties, jealousies of the sister states, or the ambition of individuals! It has been observed, by a writer of celebrity,* that "that people, government, and constitution is the freest, which makes the best provision for the enacting of expedient and salutary laws." May this truth be evinced to all ages, by the wise and salutary laws that shall be enacted in the federal legislature of America!

26

EMMA WILLARD

An Address to the Public, Proposing a Plan for Improving Female Education (1819)

The object of this Address, is to convince the public, that a reform, with respect to female education, is necessary; that it cannot be effected by individual exertion, but that it requires the aid of the legislature; and further, by shewing the justice, the policy, and the magnamity of such an undertaking, to persuade the body to endow a seminary for females, as the commencement of such reformation.

The idea of a college for males will naturally be associated with that of a seminary, instituted and endowed by the public; and the absurdity of sending ladies to college, may, at first thought, strike every one to whom this subject shall be proposed. I therefore hasten to observe, that the seminary here recommended, will be as different from those appropriated to the other sex, as the female character and duties are from the male. The business of the husbandman is not to waste his endeavours, in seeking to make his orchard attain the strength and majesty of his forest, but to rear each, to the perfection of its nature.

That the improvement of female education will be considered by our enlightened citizens as a subject of importance, the liberality with which they part with their property to educate their daughters, is a sufficient evidence; and why should they not, when assembled in the legislature, act in concert to effect a noble object, which, though dear to them individually, cannot be accomplished by their unconnected exertions.

From *An Address to the Public; Particularly to the Members of the Legislature of New-York, Proposing a Plan for Improving Female Education* (Middlebury, Ct.: J.W. Copeland. 1819), 5–6, 7–8, 9–10, 15, 32–34.

*Paley's *Moral Philosophy.*

If the improvement of the American female character, and that alone, could be effected by public liberality, employed in giving better means of instruction; such improvement of one half of society, and that half, which barbarous and despotic nations have ever degraded, would of itself be an object, worthy of the most liberal government on earth; but if the female character be raised, it must inevitably raise that of the other sex: and thus does the plan proposed, offer, as the object of legislative bounty, to elevate the whole character of the community.

As evidence that this statement does not exaggerate the female influence in society, our sex need but be considered, in the single relation of mothers. In this character, we have the charge of the whole mass of individuals, who are to compose the succeeding generation; during that period of youth, when the pliant mind takes any direction, to which it is steadily guided by a forming hand. How important a power is given by this charge! yet, little do too many of my sex know how, either to appreciate or improve it. Unprovided with the means of acquiring that knowledge, which flows liberally to the other sex—having our time of education devoted to frivolous acquirements, how should we understand the nature of the mind, so as to be aware of the importance of those early impressions, which we make upon the minds of our children?—or how should we be able to form enlarged and correct views, either of the character, to which we ought to mould them, or of the means most proper to form them aright?

Considered in this point of view, were the interests of male education alone to be consulted, that of females becomes of sufficient importance to engage the public attention. Would we rear the human plant to its perfection, we must first fertilize the soil which produces it. If it acquire its first bent and texture upon a barren plain, it will avail comparatively little, should it be afterwards transplanted to a garden. . . .

Civilized nations have long since been convinced that education, as it respects males, will not, like trade, regulate itself; and hence, they have made it a prime object to provide that sex with everything requisite to facilitate their progress in learning: but female educattion has been left to the mercy of private adventurers; and the consequence has been to our sex, the same, as it would have been to the other, had legislatures left their accomodations, and means of instruction, to chance also.

Education cannot prosper in any community, unless, from the ordinary motives which actuate the human mind, the best and most cultivated talents of that community, can be brought into exercise in that way. Male education flourishes, because, from the guardian care of legislatures, the presidencies and professorships of our colleges are some of the highest objects to which the eye of ambition is directed. Not so with female institutions. Preceptresses of these, are dependent on their pupils for support, and are consequently liable to become the victims of their caprice. In such a situation, it is not more desirable to be a preceptress, than it would be, to be a parent, invested with the care of children, and responsible for their behaviour, but yet, dependending on them for subsistence, and destitute of power to enforce their obedience. . . .

It is impossible that in these schools such systems should be adopted and enforced, as are requisite for properly classing the pupils. Institutions for young gentlemen are founded by public authority, and are permanent; they are endowed with funds, and their instructors and overseers, are invested with authority to make such laws, as they shall deem most salutary. From their permanency, their laws and rules are well known. With their funds they procure libraries, philosophical apparatus, and other advantages, superior to what can elsewhere be found; and to enjoy these, individuals are placed under their discipline, who would not else be subjected to it. Hence the directors of these institutions can enforce, among other regulations, those which enable them to make a perfect classification of their students. They regulate their qualifications for entrance, the kind and order of their studies, and the period of their remaining at the seminary. Female schools present the reverse of this. Wanting permanency, and dependent on individual patronage, had they the wisdom to make salutary regulations, they could neither enforce nor purchase compliance. The pupils are irregular in their times of entering and leaving school; and they are of various and dissimilar acquirements.

Each scholar, of mature age, thinks she has a right to judge for herself respecting what she is to be taught; and the parents of those, who are not, consider that they have the same right to judge for them. Under such disadvantages, a school cannot be classed, except in a very imperfect manner. . . .

Another errour [in female education] is, that it has been made the first object in educating our sex, to prepare them to please the other. But reason and religion teach, that we too are primary existencies; that it is for us to move, in the orbit of our duty, around the Holy Centre of perfection, the companions, not the satellites of men; else, instead of shedding around us an influence, that may help to keep them in their proper course, we must accompany them in their wildest deviations.

I would not be understood to insinuate, that we are not, in particular situations, to yield obedience to the other sex. Submission and obedience belong to every being in the universe, except the great Master of the whole. Nor is it a degrading particuliarity to our sex, to be under human authority. Whenever one class of human beings, derive from another the benefits of support and protection, they must pay its equivalent, obedience. . . .

The inquiry, to which these remarks have conducted us is this- What is offered by the plan of female education, here proposed, which may teach, or preserve, among females of wealthy families, that purity of manners, which is allowed, to be so essential to national prosperity, and so necessary, to the existence of a republican government. . . .

By being enlightened in moral philosophy, and in that, which teaches the operations of the mind, females would be enabled to perceive the nature and extent, of that influence, which they possess over their children, and the obligation, which this lays them under, to watch the formation of their characters with unceasing vigilance, to become their instructors, to devise plans for their improvement, to weed out the vices from their minds, and to implant and foster the virtues. . . .

Thus, laudable objects and employments, would be furnished for the great body of females, who are not kept by poverty from excesses. But among these, as among the other sex, will be found master spirits, who must have pre-eminence, at whatever price they acquire it. Domestic life cannot hold these, because they prefer to be infamous, rather than obscure. To leave such, without any virtuous road to eminence, is unsafe to community; for not unfrequently, are the secret springs of revolution, set in motion by their intrigues. Such aspiring minds, we will regulate, by education, we will remove obstructions to the course of literature, which has heretofore been their only honorable way to distinction; and we offer them a new object, worthy of their ambition; to govern, and improve the seminaries for their sex.

Suggestions for Further Reading

Allen, Paula Gunn. "Who Is Your Mother? Red Roots of White Feminism." In *The Graywolf Annual Five: Multi-Cultural Literacy*, ed., Rick Simonson and Scott Walker. Saint Paul, Minn.: Graywolf Press, 1988. 13–27.

Applewhite, Harriet B. and Darline G. Levy, ed. *Women and Politics in the Age of Democratic Revolution*. Ann Arbor: Univ. of Michigan Press, 1990.

Baker, Paula. "The Domestication of Politics: Women and American Political Society, 1780–1920." *American Historical Review* 89 (1984): 620–47.

Baym, Nina. "From Enlightenment to Victorian: Toward a Narrative of American Women Writers Writing History." In *Feminism and American Literary History*. New Brunswick: Rutgers Univ. Press, 1992.

Blackwood, Evelyn. "Sexuality and Gender in Certain Native American Tribes: The Case of Cross-Gender Females." *Signs* 10 (1984): 27–42.

Bloch, Ruth H. "The Gendered Meanings of Virtue in Revolutionary America." *Signs* 13 (1987): 37–58

Boylan, Anne M. "Women and Politics in the Era Before Seneca Falls." *Journal of the Early Republic* 10 (1990): 363–82.

Brown, Judith K. "Economic Organization and the Position of Women Among the Iroquois." *Ethnohistory* 17 (1970): 151–67.

Cohen, Lester H. "Mercy Otis Warren: The Politics of Language and the Aesthetics of Self." *American Quarterly* 35 (1983): 481–98.

Cott, Nancy. *The Bonds of Womanhood: "Woman's Sphere" in New England, 1780–1835*. New Haven: Yale Univ. Press, 1977.

Davidson, Cathy N. *Revolution and the Word: The Rise of the Novel in America*. New York: Oxford Univ. Press, 1986.

De Pauw, Linda Grant. *Founding Mothers: Women in America in the Revolutionary Era*. Boston: Houghton Mifflin, 1975.

Evans, Sara M. *Born for Liberty: A History of Women in America*. New York: The Free Press, 1989.

Foster, Frances Smith. *Written by Herself: Literary Production by African American Women, 1746–1892*. Bloomington: Indiana Univ. Press, 1993.

Giddings, Paula. *When and Where I Enter: The Impact of Black Women on Race and Sex in America*. New York: William Morrow, 1984.

Gordon, Ann D. "The Philadelphia Young Ladies Academy." In *Women of America: A History*, ed., Carol Berkin and Mary Beth Norton. Boston: Houghton Mifflin, 1979. 69–91.

Gunderson, Joan R. "Independence, Citizenship, and the American Revolution." *Signs* 13 (1987): 59–77.

Kaplan, Sidney. *The Black Presence in the Era of the American Revolution, 1770–1800*. Greenwich, CT: New York Graphic Press, 1973.

Kelley, Mary. "'Vindicating the Equality of Female Intellect': Women and Authority in the Early Republic." *Prospects* 17 (1992): 1–27.

Kerber, Linda. "The Republican Ideology of the Revolutionary Generation." *American Quarterly* 37 (1985): 474–95.

___. *Women of the Republic: Intellect and Ideology in Revolutionary America.* New York: W. W. Norton, 1986.

Lewis, Jan. "The Republican Wife: Virtue and Seduction in the Early Republic." *William and Mary Quarterly* 44 (1987): 689–721.

Matthews, Glenna. *The Rise of Public Woman: Woman's Power and Woman's Place in the United States, 1630–1970.* New York: Oxford Univ. Press, 1992.

Norton, Mary Beth. *Liberty's Daughters: The Revolutionary Experience of American Women, 1750–1800.* Boston: Little, Brown, 1980.

Perdue, Theda. "Cherokee Women and the Trail of Tears." *Journal of Women's History* 1 (1989): 14–30.

Schwager, Sally. "Educating Women in America." *Signs* 12 (1987): 333–72.

Zagarri, Rose Marie. "Morals, Manners, and the Republican Mother." *American Quarterly* 44 (June 1992): 192–215.

PART III

Early Rights Consciousness in Antebellum America

I. Contesting Woman's Nature and Woman's Sphere

AS COMMERCE AND INDUSTRY GREW IN THE UNITED STATES in the early to mid-nineteenth century, a system of production that had the home as its economic center was replaced as the realms of work and homelife became increasingly separate and increasingly gendered: while wage labor and masculinity combined in the burgeoning market economy, home and femininity were increasingly privatized as the sites of domestic activities and affections. What the ideology of separate spheres meant for literate, middle-class women was that their place, their role, and their work were circumscribed by the walls of the home and by the values that home—a haven in the market-driven world of antebellum America—was supposed to contain. Maria McIntosh's *Woman in America* (1850), one of the hundreds of treatises that defined woman's sphere and nature, articulates the way in which the functions of women and men were opposed, using the pervasive imagery of the interior to represent the former and the exterior to represent the latter: "But while all the outward machinery of government, the body, the thews and sinews of society, are man's, woman, if true to her own not less important or less sacred mission, controls its vital principle." McIntosh continues by elaborating the notion of woman's influence—that her power over the world should come from indirect and invisible persuasion rather than from direct, visible, and public action: woman is "[u]nseen herself, working, like nature, in secret." Like the vital organ of the heart, woman "regulates [society's] pulsations, and sends forth from its heart, in pure and temperate flow, the life-giving current."[1]

True womanly values emerged not only from the increasing division between public and private realms but also from the evangelical fervor of the Second Great Awakening, which reached its apex in the 1820s. The religious revivals that proliferated especially in the northern United States facilitated the greater public presence of women, and also validated the moral concerns and the power of feeling and sentiment with which women were becoming increasingly identified. The Great Awakening—with its insistence that the nation had become overly-secularized and morally bankrupt—legitimated women's role as the transmittor of religious values. As a bulwark against moral decay and economic excess, the true woman extended the function of the republican mother, instilling values in her children, indeed her whole family that could save the nation.

---

1. Maria J. McIntosh, *Woman in America: Her Work and Her Reward* (New York: Appleton, 1850), 23, 25.

The question of women preachers tested the limits of appropriate action for women. On the one hand, women who preached purveyed Christian virtues, thereby realizing woman's mission to inculcate morality; on the other hand, the idea of women speaking in public was widely condemned as unfeminine, in part because it involved direct exhortation—an "unseemly" public exhibition—rather than indirect and private influence. Jarena Lee, the first black woman to make a career of preaching, published an autobiography in 1836 that in part describes the resistance she encountered in following her calling. "My Call to Preach" describes the struggles Lee had with the African Methodist Episcopal Church, which at first would allow her only to exhort at prayer meetings not to preach. Lee also describes her internal struggles, first in having to give up her community to move with her husband and then in having to leave her children in the care of others while she worked as an itinerant preacher. Partaking of the evangelical belief in a person's individual relationship with God, Lee not only argues for women's right to preach, but also, in her condemnation of slavery, for women's right to enter the realm of secular politics.

Like Jarena Lee, Sarah Grimké—along with her sister Angelina—became one of the first American women to speak in public, defying the most entrenched dictate about woman's private place and nature; the Grimké sisters were, in fact, the first women to speak out systematically against slavery. Also like Lee, Grimké met resistance from the church, and in the selection from *Letters on the Equality of the Sexes* (1838), she responds to a pastoral letter that condemns any woman who speaks in public for transgressing scripture and God. Grimké, however, used her own interpretation of scripture to enlarge the realm of activity for women, claiming that almost everything written by her contemporaries on the "sphere of woman" has been due to an egregious misinterpretation of scripture and that the sphere God intended woman to move in is infinitely broader than that defined for her by men. Again drawing on scripture, Grimké argues for equality between the sexes, defying not just conventional wisdom about the opposition of men's and women's place but also the difference of their nature; labeling the heightening distinctions between the masculine and the feminine "anti-Christian," Grimké insists that only a "forgetfulness of sex" can purify the nation.

Not all public women in the antebellum period opposed the ideology of separate spheres, however; some women defined the political self-understanding and action of women as an extension of domesticity and a result of their moral nature. Centering themselves within the home and insisting on the domestic function of woman, they nevertheless expanded both the home and the domestic function, blurring the boundaries between private and public sphere and domestic and political activity. The writing of these women, "domestic feminists" as they have been called, is deeply conflicted, as they insist on both women's social subordination and her moral superiority, as they describe the utter inappropriateness of women's public visibility while themselves being nationally-known figures, actively engaging in work beyond the confines of the home.

Along with her sister Harriet Beecher Stowe, Catharine Beecher was the most prominent of the domestic feminists. Although she herself was active in women's education, founding schools and writing prolifically, Beecher insisted that women keep to their "sphere," an insistence that brought her into conflict with the Grimké sisters whom, she thought, pursued their goals in too public a fashion. The Grimkés and Beecher also disagreed over the issue of sexual distinction, since Beecher believed that women were inherently different from men. While adhering to the ideal of woman's separate sphere and nature, though, Beecher nevertheless managed to make both integral to the *public* world. In "The Importance of Domestic Economy" (1842), Beecher legitimates ideas of women's domestic function not only by systematizing that function but also by countering the democratic rights that define the public world of men with the Christian ethic of love that defines woman's place. While in the civic world, women are subordinate to men, the principles of Christianity secure to women a "lofty" position and a crucial "moral enterprise" on which the success of all democratic institutions depends.

In "A Woman-Thought, a Woman-Perception, a Woman-Intuition" (1851), Elizabeth Oakes Smith—a feminist speaker and writer—argues, like Beecher, that men and women are innately different; drawing on the ideas that undergirded the ideology of separate spheres, she claims that woman is more spiritual and man more material. While Oakes Smith believes in inherently feminine qualities, however, she does not believe that those qualities should be exercised solely within a narrowly-defined realm. In fact, she claims that women have been paralyzed precisely by being limited "to in-door thought only, to the degradation of in-door toil." Oakes Smith makes the sweeping claim that women should be limited solely by the "laws of her own existence," which alone dictate to her what her sphere of action should be. Unlike Grimké, who drew upon scripture to refute distinctions about duty based on sex, Oakes Smith draws on each person's right to "individuality," an argument that anticipates the feminist cult of individuality in the first decades of the twentieth century.

Although Oakes Smith lectured on women's rights, she was somewhat on the fringes of the movement; at the Second National Woman's Rights Convention in 1851, Elizabeth Cady Stanton denied Oakes Smith the presidency of the convention because of her elaborate New York dress. However, the conflict she embodies—as a feminist who nevertheless believed in somewhat conventional ideals of woman's separate nature—was reflected in the emerging women's rights movement. In "Are the Sexes Different?" (1855), Stanton presents her views on the relative abilities and aspirations of women and men. Her article is a response to feminist activist Antoinette Brown, who believed in what Stanton calls the "mysterious twaddle" of the divergent male and female "element." Stanton adds that not just "outsiders" but also many "friends of the cause" believe—unfortunately—in the inherently different nature of woman.

Despite the conflict between Stanton on the one hand and Brown and Oakes Smith on the other, in terms of defining woman's sphere, women's rights activists seemed to enjoy somewhat of a consensus. Indeed, among the resolutions passed at the Second National Woman's Rights Convention was a declaration that no part of the human race could decide for another part what their "proper sphere" should be. Women, like everyone else, should decide what "sphere she will fill" and what her occupation will be. This resolution is echoed by Lucy Stone's speech at the Woman's Rights Convention in Cincinnati in 1855, "Leave Women, Then, to Find Their Sphere." Stone discusses the real consequences of the ideology of woman's sphere: she points out that when certain women leave their "sphere"—the home—because they need to make an independent living, they instantly lose caste and are paid at vastly lower rates than men.

Prominent women's rights activists such as Stanton and Stone were not alone in contesting ideas of woman's proper sphere. Women at the margins of the movement—perhaps by choice or because of region or race—also spoke out against the limitations of popular under-standings of women. M. Farley Emerson's "Woman's Sphere, Woman's Nature" (1857) is a selection from her book *Woman in America*, published by the author in Cincinnati. The first part of the book presents numerous excerpts from newspapers that prescribe woman's "nature" or her "sphere," which Emerson follows with her scathing critique; in the second part of the book, Emerson describes her travels across the country—mostly the western and southern portions, describing the pernicious effects that widely-held ideals of womanhood have on real women. Emerson—who has been virtually forgotten by feminist history—translates the ide-ology of separate spheres into material conditions that inhibit and damage women's lives.

Frances Ellen Watkins Harper, while not a part of the woman's rights movement, was one of the leading anti-slavery activists, lecturing almost daily between 1854 and 1860 for the cause of African-American emancipation. Also a prominent literary figure, Harper published the first short story by an African-American in the *Anglo-African Magazine*. "The Two Offers" (1859) tells the stories of two cousins, women of unspecified race, one of whom devotes her life to marriage and to an unworthy husband while the other gives over her life to abolishing slavery. The story makes a clear argument for the inadequacy of marriage and for the necessity of an increase in choices for women.

27

JARENA LEE

My Call to Preach the Gospel
(1836)

. . . Between four and five years after my sancti-fication, on a certain time, an impressive silence fell upon me, and I stood as if some one was about to speak to me, yet I had no such thought in my heart. But to my utter surprise there seemed to sound a voice which I thought I distinctly heard, and most certainly understood, which said to me, "Go preach the Gospel!" I immediately replied aloud, "No one will believe me." Again I listened, and again the same voice seemed to say—"Preach the Gospel; I will put words in your mouth, and will turn your enemies to become your friends."

At first I supposed Satan had spoken to me, for I had read that he could transform himself into an angel of light, for the purpose of deception. Immediately I went into a secret place, and called upon the Lord to know if he had called me to preach, and whether I was deceived or not; when there appeared to my view the form and figure of a pulpit, with a Bible lying thereon, the back of which was presented to me as plainly as if it had been a literal fact.

In consequence of this, my mind became so exercised, that during the night following, I took a text, and preached in my sleep. I thought there stood before me a great multitude, while I expounded to them the things of religion. So violent were my exertions, and so loud were my exclamations, that I awoke from the sound of my own voice, which also awoke the family of the house where I resided. Two days after, I went to see the preacher in charge of the Afri-

From *The Life and Religious Experience of Jarena Lee, A Coloured Lady, Giving an Account of Her Call to Preach the Gospel. Revised and Corrected from the Original Manuscript, Written by Herself* (Philadelphia: Printed and Published for the Author, 1836), 12–15, 22–23.

can Society, who was the Rev. Richard Allen, the same before named in these pages, to tell him that I felt it my duty to preach the gospel. But as I drew near the street in which his house was, which was in the city of Philadelphia, my courage began to fail me; so terrible did the cross appear, it seemed that I should not be able to bear it. Previous to my setting out to go to see him, so agitated was my mind, that my appetite for my daily food failed me entirely. Several times on my way there, I turned back again; but as often I felt my strength again renewed, and I soon found that the nearer I approached to the house of the minister, the less was my fear. Accordingly, as soon as I came to the door, my fears subsided; the cross was removed, all things appeared pleasant—I was tranquil.

I now told him, that the Lord had revealed it to me, that I must preach the gospel. He replied, by asking, in what sphere I wished to move in? I said, among the Methodists. He then replied, that a Mrs. Cook, a Methodist lady, had also some time before requested the same privilege; who it was believed, had done much good in the way of exhortation, and holding prayer meetings; and who had been permitted to do so by the verbal license of the preacher in charge at the time. But as to women preaching, he said that our Discipline knew nothing at all about it—that it did not call for women preachers. This I was glad to hear, because it removed the fear of the cross—but not no sooner did this feeling cross my mind, than I found that a love of souls had in a measure departed from me; that holy energy which burned within me, as a fire, began to be smothered. This I soon perceived.

O how careful ought we to be, lest through our by-laws of church government and discipline, we bring into disrepute even the word of life. For as unseemly as it may appear now-a-days for a woman to preach, it should be remembered that nothing is impossible with God. And why should it be thought impossible, heterodox, or improper, for a woman to preach?

seeing the Saviour died for the woman as well as the man.

If the man may preach, because the Saviour died for him, why not the woman? seeing he died for her also. Is he not a whole Saviour, instead of a half one? as those who hold it wrong for a woman to preach, would seem to make it appear.

Did not Mary *first* preach the risen Saviour, and is not the doctrine of the resurrection the very climax of Christianity—hangs not all our hope on this, as argued by St. Paul? Then did not Mary, a woman, preach the gospel? for she preached the resurrection of the crucified Son of God.

But some will say, that Mary did not expound the Scripture, therefore, she did not preach, in the proper sense of the term. To this I reply, it may be that the term *preach,* in those primitive times, did not mean exactly what it is now *made* to mean; perhaps it was a great deal more simple then, than it is now:—if it were not, the unlearned fishermen could not have preached the gospel at all, as they had no learning.

To this it may be replied, by those who are determined not to believe that it is right for a woman to preach, that the disciples, though they were fishermen, and ignorant of letters too, were inspired so to do. To which I would reply, that though they were inspired, yet that inspiration did not save them from showing their ignorance of letters, and of man's wisdom; this the multitude soon found out, by listening to the remarks of the envious Jewish priests. If then, to preach the gospel, by the gift of heaven, comes by inspiration solely, is God straitened; must he take the man exclusively? May he not, did he not, and can he not inspire a female to preach the simple story of the birth, life, death, and resurrection of our Lord, and accompany it to, with power to the sinner's heart. As for me, I am fully persuaded that the Lord called me to labour according to what I have received, in his vineyard. If he has not, how could he consistently bear testimony in favour of my poor labours, in awakening and converting sinners?

In my wanderings up and down among men, preaching according to my ability, I have frequently found families who told me that they had not for several years been to a meeting, and yet, while listening to hear what God would say by his poor coloured female instrument, have believed with trembling—tears rolling down their cheeks, the signs of contrition and repentance towards God. I firmly believe that I have sown seed, in the name of the Lord, which shall appear with its increase at the great day of accounts, when Christ shall come to make up his jewels. . . .

At this place I continued to hold meetings about six months. During that time I kept house with my little son, who was very sickly. About this time I had a call to preach at a place about thirty miles distant, among the Methodists, with whom I remained one week, and during the whole time, not a thought of my little son came into my mind; it was hid from me, lest I should have been diverted from the work I had to do, to look after my son. Here by the instrumentality of a poor coloured woman, the Lord poured forth his spirit among the people. Though, as I was told, there were lawyers, doctors, and magistrates present, to hear me speak, yet there was mourning and crying among sinners, for the Lord scattered fire among them of his own kindling. The Lord gave his handmaiden power to speak for his great name for he arrested the hearts of the people, and caused a shaking amongst the multitude, for God was in the midst.

I now returned home, found all well; no harm had come to my child, although I left it very sick. Friends had taken care of it which was of the Lord. I now began to think seriously of breaking up housekeeping, and forsaking all to preach the everlasting Gospel. I felt a strong desire to return to the place of my nativity, at Cape May, after an absence of about fourteen years. To this place, where the heaviest cross was to be met with, the Lord sent me, as Saul of Tarsus was sent to Jerusalem, to preach the same gospel which he had neglected and despised before his conversion. I went by water, and on my passage was much distressed by sea sickness, so much so that I expected to have died, but such was not the will of the Lord respecting me. After I had disembarked, I proceeded on as opportunities offered, toward where my mother lived. When within ten miles of that place, I appointed an evening meeting. There were a goodly number came out to hear. The Lord was pleased to give me light and liberty among the people. After meeting, there came an elderly lady to me and said, she believed the Lord had sent me among them; she then appointed me another meeting there two weeks from that night. The next day I hastened forward to the place of my mother, who was happy to see me, and the happiness was mutual between us. With her I left my poor sickly boy, while I departed to do my Master's will. In this neighborhood I had an uncle, who was a Methodist, and who gladly threw open his door for meetings to be held there. At the first meeting which I held at my uncle's house; there was, with others who had come from curiosity to hear the coloured woman preacher, an old man, who was a deist, and who said he did not believe the coloured people had any souls—he was sure they had none. He took a seat very near where I was standing, and boldly tried to look me out of countenance. But as I laboured on in the best manner I was able, looking to God all the while, though it seemed to me I had but little liberty, yet there went an arrow from the bent bow of the gospel, and fastened in his till then obdurate heart. After I had done speaking, he went out, and called the people around him, said that my preaching might seem a small thing, yet he believed I had the worth of souls at heart. This language was different from what it was a little time before, as he now seemed to admit that coloured people had souls, as it was to these I was chiefly speaking; and unless they had souls, whose good I had in view, his remark must have been without meaning. He now came into the house, and in the most friendly manner shook hands with me, saying, he hoped God had spared him to

some good purpose. This man was a great slave holder, and had been very cruel; thinking nothing of knocking down a slave with a fence stake, or whatever might come to hand. From this time it was said of him that he became greatly altered in his ways for the better. At that time he was about seventy years old, his head as white as snow; but whether he became a converted man or not, I never heard.

28

SARAH GRIMKÉ
The Equality of the Sexes (1838)

Letter I.

THE ORIGINAL EQUALITY OF WOMAN.

Amesbury, 7th Mo. 11th, 1837.

MY DEAR FRIEND,—In attempting to comply with thy request to give my views on the Province of Woman, I feel that I am venturing on nearly untrodden ground, and that I shall advance arguments in opposition to a corrupt public opinion, and to the perverted interpretation of Holy Writ, which has so universally obtained. But I am in search of truth; and no obstacle shall prevent my prosecuting that search, because I believe the welfare of the world will be materially advanced by every new discovery we make of the designs of Jehovah in the creation of woman. It is impossible that we can answer the purpose of our being, unless we understand that purpose. It is impossible that we should fulfil our duties, unless we comprehend them; or live up to our privileges, unless we know what they are.

In examining this important subject, I shall depend solely on the Bible to designate the sphere of woman, because I believe almost ev-

From *Letters on the Equality of the Sexes and the Condition of Woman, Addressed to Mary S. Parker, President of the Boston Female Anti-Slavery Society* (1838; reprint New York: Burt-Franklin, 1970), 3–4, 14–20, 22–24, 46–49.

ery thing that has been written on this subject, has been the result of a misconception of the simple truths revealed in the Scriptures, in consequence of the false translation of many passages of Holy Writ. My mind is entirely delivered from the superstitious reverence which is attached to the English version of the Bible. King James's translators certainly were not inspired. I therefore claim the original as my standard, *believing that to have been inspired,* and I also claim to judge for myself what is the meaning of the inspired writers, because I believe it to be the solemn duty of every individual to search the Scriptures for themselves, with the aid of the Holy Spirit, and not be governed by the views of any man, or set of men. . . .

Letter III.

THE PASTORAL LETTER OF THE GENERAL ASSOCIATION OF CONGRESSIONAL MINISTERS OF MASSACHUSETTS.

Haverhill, 7th Mo. 1837.

DEAR FRIEND,—When I last addressed thee, I had not seen the Pastoral Letter of the General Association. It has since fallen into my hands, and I must digress from my intention of exhibiting the condition of women in different parts of the world, in order to make some remarks on this extraordinary document. I am persuaded that when the minds of men and women become emancipated from the thraldom of superstition and 'traditions of men,' the sentiments contained in the Pastoral Letter will be recurred to with as much astonishment as the opinions of Cotton Mather and other distinguished men of his day, on the subject of witchcraft; nor will it be deemed less wonderful, that a body of divines should gravely assemble and endeavor to prove that woman has no right to 'open her mouth for the dumb,' than it now is that judges should have sat on the trials of witches, and solemnly condemned nineteen persons and one dog to death for witchcraft.

But to the letter. It says, 'We invite your attention to the dangers which at present seem to threaten the FEMALE CHARACTER with wide-spread and permanent injury.' I rejoice that they have called the attention of my sex to this subject, because I believe if woman investigates it, she will soon discover that danger is impending, though from a totally different source from that which the Association apprehends,—danger from those who, having long held the reins of *usurped* authority, are unwilling to permit us to fill that sphere which God created us to move in, and who have entered into league to crush the immortal mind of woman. I rejoice, because I am persuaded that the rights of woman, like the rights of slaves, need only be examined to be understood and asserted, even by some of those, who are now endeavoring to smother the irrepressible desire for mental and spiritual freedom which glows in the breast of many, who hardly dare to speak their sentiments.

'The appropriate duties and influence of women are clearly stated in the New Testament. Those duties are unobtrusive and private, but the sources of *mighty power.* When the mild, *dependent,* softening influence of woman upon the sternness of man's opinions is fully exercised, society feels the effects of it in a thousand ways.' No one can desire more earnestly than I do, that woman may move exactly in the sphere which her Creator has assigned her; and I believe her having been displaced from that sphere has introduced confusion into the world. It is, therefore, of vast importance to herself and to all the rational creation, that she should ascertain what [are] her duties and her privileges as a responsible and immortal being. The New Testament has been referred to, and I am willing to abide by its decisions, but must enter my protest against the false translation of some passages by the MEN who did that work, and against the perverted interpretation by the MEN who undertook to write commentaries thereon. I am inclined to think, when we are admitted to the honor of studying Greek and Hebrew, we shall produce some various readings of the Bible a little difference from those we now have.

The Lord Jesus defines the duties of his followers in his Sermon on the Mount. He lays down grand principles by which they should be governed, without any reference to sex or condition:—'Ye are the light of the world. A city that is set on a hill cannot be hid. Neither do men light a candle and put it under a bushel, but on a candlestick, and it giveth light unto all that are in the house. Let your light so shine before men, that they may see your good works, and glorify your Father which is in Heaven.' I follow him through all his precepts, and find him giving the same directions to women as to men, never even referring to the distinction now so strenuously insisted upon between masculine and feminine virtues: this is one of the antichristian 'traditions of men' which are taught instead of the 'commandments of God.' Men and women were CREATED EQUAL; they are both moral and accountable beings, and whatever is *right* for man to do, is *right* for woman.

But the influence of woman, says the Association, is to be private and unobtrusive; her light is not to shine before men like that of her brethren; but she is passively to let the lords of the creation, as they call themselves, put the bushel over it, lest peradventure it might appear that the world has been benefitted by the rays of *her* candle. So that her quenched light, according to their judgment, will be of more use than if it were set on the candlestick. 'Her influence is the source of mightly power.' This has ever been the flattering language of man since he laid aside the whip as a means to keep woman in subjection. He spares her body; but the war he has waged against her mind, her heart, and her soul, has been no less destructive to her as a moral being. How monstrous, how anti-christian, is the doctrine that woman is to be dependent on man! Where, in all the sacred Scriptures, is this taught? Alas! she has too well learned the lesson which MAN has labored to teach her. She has surrendered her dearest RIGHTS, and been satisfied with the privileges which man has assumed to grant her; she has been amused with the show of power, whilst man has absorbed all the reality

into himself. He has adorned the creature whom God gave him as a companion, with baubles and gewgaws, turned her attention to personal attractions, offered incense to her vanity and made her the instrument of his selfish gratification, a plaything to please his eye and amuse his hours of leisure. 'Rule by obedience and by submission sway,' or in other words, study to be a hypocrite, pretend to submit, but gain your point, has been the code of household morality which woman has been taught. The poet has sung, in sickly strains, the loveliness of woman's dependence upon man, and now we find it reechoed by those who profess to teach the religion of the Bible. God says, 'Cease ye from man whose breath is in his nostrils, for wherein is he to be accounted of?' Man says, depend upon me. God says 'HE will teach us of his ways.' Man says, believe it not, I am to be your teacher. This doctrine of dependence upon man is utterly at variance with the doctrine of the Bible. In that book I find nothing like the softness of woman, nor the sternness of man: both are equally commanded to bring forth the fruits of the Spirit, love, meekness, gentleness, &c.

But we are told, 'the power of woman is in her dependence, flowing from a consciousness of that weakness which God has given her for her protection.' If physical weakness is alluded to, I cheerfully concede the superiority; if brute force is what my brethren are claiming, I am willing to let them have all the honor they desire; but if they mean to intimate, that mental or moral weakness belongs to woman, more than to man, I utterly disclaim the charge. Our powers of mind have been crushed, as far as man could do it, our sense of morality has been impaired by his interpretation of our duties; but no where does God say that he made any distinction between us, as moral and intelligent beings.

'We appreciate,' say the Association, 'the *unostentatious* prayers and efforts of woman in advancing the cause of religion at home and abroad, in leading religious inquirers TO THE PASTOR for instruction.' Several points here demand attention. If public prayers and public efforts are necessarily ostentatious, then 'Anna the prophetess, (or preacher,) who departed not from the temple, but served God with fastings and prayers night and day,' 'and spake of Christ to all them that looked for redemption in Israel,' was ostentatious in her efforts. Then, the apostle Paul encourages women to be ostentatious in their efforts to spread the gospel, when he gives them directions how they should appear, when engaged in praying, or preaching in the public assemblies. Then, the whole association of Congregational ministers are ostentatious, in the efforts they are making in preaching and praying to convert souls.

But woman may be permitted to lead religious inquirers to the PASTORS for instruction. Now this is assuming that all pastors are better qualified to give instruction than woman. This I utterly deny. I have suffered too keenly from the teaching of man, to lead any one to him for instruction. The Lord Jesus says,—'Come unto me and learn of me.' He points his followers to no man; and when woman is made the favored instrument of rousing a sinner to his lost and helpless condition, she has no right to substitute any teacher for Christ; all she has to do is, to turn the contrite inquirer to the 'Lamb of God which taketh away the sins of the world.' More souls have probably been lost by going down to Egypt for help, and by trusting in man in the early stage of religious experience, than by any other error. Instead of the petition being offered to God,—'Lead me in thy truth, and TEACH me, for thou art the God of my salvation,'—instead of relying on the precious promises—'What man is he that feareth the Lord? him shall HE TEACH in the way that he shall choose'—'I will instruct thee and TEACH thee in the way which thou shalt go—I will guide thee with mine eye'—the young convert is directed to go to man, as if he were in the place of God, and his instructions essential to an advancement in the path of righteousness. That woman can have but a poor conception of the privilege of being taught of God, what he alone can teach,

who would turn the 'religious inquirer aside' from the fountain of living waters, where he might slake his thirst for spiritual instruction, to those broken cisterns which can hold no water and therefore cannot satisfy the panting spirit. The business of men and women, who are ORDAINED OF GOD to preach the unsearchable riches of Christ' to a lost and perishing world, is to lead souls to Christ, and not to Pastors for instruction.

The General Association say, that 'when woman assumes the place and tone of man as a public reformer, our care and protection of her seem unnecessary; we put ourselves in self-defence against her, and her character becomes unnatural.' Here again the unscriptural notion is held up, that there is a distinction between the duties of men and women as moral beings; that what is virtue in man, is vice in woman; and women who dare to obey the command of Jehovah, 'Cry aloud, spare not, life up thy voice like a trumpet, and show my people their transgression,' are threatened with having the protection of the brethren withdrawn. If this is all they do, we shall not even know the time when our chastisement is inflicted; our trust is in the Lord Jehovah, and in him is everlasting strength. . . .

Letter IV.

SOCIAL INTERCOURSE OF THE SEXES.

Andover, 7th Mo. 27th, 1837.

MY DEAR FRIEND,—Before I proceed with the account of that oppression which woman has suffered in every age and country from her *protector,* man, permit me to offer for your consideration some views relative to the social intercourse of the sexes. Nearly the whole of this intercourse is, in my apprehension, derogatory to man and woman, as moral and intellectual beings. We approach each other, and mingle with each other, under the constant pressure of a feeling that we are of different sexes; and, instead of regarding each other only in the light of immortal creatures, the mind is fettered by the idea which is early and industriously infused into it, that we must never forget the distinction between male and female. Hence our intercourse, instead of being elevated and refined, is generally calculated to excite and keep alive the lowest propensities of our nature. Nothing, I believe, has tended more to destroy the true dignity of woman, than the fact that she is approached by man in the character of a female. The idea that she is sought as an intelligent and heaven-born creature, whose society will cheer, refine and elevate her companion, and that she will receive the same blessings she confers, is rarely held up to her view. On the contrary, man almost always addresses himself to the weakness of woman. By flattery, by an appeal to her passions, he seeks access to her heart; and when he has gained her affections, he uses her as the instrument of his pleasure—the minister of his temporal comfort. He furnishes himself with a housekeeper, whose chief business is in the kitchen, or the nursery. And whilst he goes abroad and enjoys the means of improvement afforded by collision of intellect with cultivated minds, his wife is condemned to draw nearly all her instruction from books, if she has time to peruse them; and if not, from her meditations, whilst engaged in those domestic duties, which are necessary for the comfort of her lord and master.

Surely no one who contemplates, with the eye of a Christian philosopher, the design of God in the creation of woman, can believe that she is now fulfilling that design. The literal translation of the word 'help-meet' is a helper like unto himself; it is so rendered in the Septuagint, and manifestly signifies a companion. Now I believe it will be impossible for woman to fill the station assigned her by God, until her brethren mingle with her as an equal, as a moral being; and lose, in the dignity of her immortal nature, and in the fact of her bearing like himself the image and superscription of her God, the idea of her being a female. The apostle beautifully remarks, 'As many of you have been baptized

into Christ, have put on Christ. There is neither Jew nor Greek, there is neither bond nor free, there is neither *male* nor *female;* for ye are all one in Christ Jesus.' Until our intercourse is purified by the forgetfulness of sex,—until we rise above the present low and sordid views which entwine themselves around our social and domestic interchange of sentiment and feelings, we never can derive that benefit from each other's society which it is the design of our Creator that we should. Man has inflicted an unspeakable injury upon woman, by holding up to her view her animal nature, and placing in the back ground her moral and intellectual being. Woman has inflicted an injury upon herself by submitting to be thus regarded; and she is now called upon to rise from the station where *man,* not God, has placed her, and claim those sacred and inalienable rights, as a moral and responsible being, with which her Creator has invested her. . . .

Letter VIII.

ON THE CONDITION OF WOMEN IN THE UNITED STATES.

Brookline, 1837.

. . . I shall now proceed to make a few remarks on the condition of women in my own country. . . .

There is another and much more numerous class in this country, who are withdrawn by education or circumstances from the circle of fashionable amusements, but who are brought up with the dangerous and absurd idea, that *marriage* is a kind of preferment; and that to be able to keep their husband's house, and render his situation comfortable, is the end of her being. Much that she does and says and thinks is done in reference to this situation; and to be married is too often held up to the view of girls as the sine qua non of human happiness and human existence. For this purpose more than for any other, I verily believe the majority of girls are trained. This is demonstrated by the imperfect education which is bestowed upon them, and the little pains taken to cultivate their minds, after they leave school, by the little time allowed them for reading, and by the idea being constantly inculcated, that although all household concerns should be attended to with scrupulous punctuality at particular seasons, the improvement of their intellectual capacities is only a secondary consideration, and may serve as an occupation to fill up the odds and ends of time. In most families, it is considered a matter of far more consequence to call a girl off from making a pie, or a pudding, then to interrupt her whilst engage in her studies. This mode of training necessarily exalts, in their view, the animal above the intellectual and spiritual nature, and teaches women to regard themselves as a kind of machinery, necessary to keep the domestic engine in order, but of little value as the *intelligent* companions of men.

Let no one think, from these remarks, that I regard a knowledge of housewifery as beneath the acquisition of women. Far from it: I believe that a complete knowledge of household affairs is an indispensable requisite in a woman' education,—that by the mistress of a family, whether married or single, doing her duty thoroughly and *understandingly,* the happiness of the family is increased to an incalculable degree, [a]s well as a vast amount of time and money saved. All I complain of is, that our education consists so almost exclusively in culinary and other manual operations. I do long to see the time, when it will no longer be necessary for women to expend so many precious hours in furnishing 'a well spread table,' but that their husbands will forego some of their accustomed indulgences in this way, and encourage their wives to devote some portion of their time to mental cultivation, even at the expense of having to dine sometimes on baked potatoes, or bread and butter. . . .

29

CATHARINE BEECHER
The Importance of Domestic Economy (1842)

. . . There are some reasons, why American women should feel an interest in the support of the democratic institutions of their Country, which it is important that they should consider. The great maxim, which is the basis of all our civil and political institutions, is, that "all men are created equal," and that they are equally entitled to "life, liberty, and the pursuit of happiness."

But it can readily be seen, that this is only another mode of expressing the fundamental principle which the Great Rule of the Universe has established, as the law of His eternal government. "Thou shalt love thy neighbor as thyself;" and "Whatsoever ye would that men should do to you, do ye even so to them," are the Scripture forms, by which the Supreme Lawgiver requires that each individual of our race shall regard the happiness of others, as of the same value as his own; and which forbid any institution, in private or civil life, which secures advantages to one class, by sacrificing the interests of another.

The principles of democracy, then, are identical with the principles of Christianity.

But, in order that each individual may pursue and secure the highest degree of happiness within his reach, unimpeded by the selfish interests of others, a system of laws must be established, which sustain certain relations and dependencies in social and civil life. What these relations and their attending obligations shall be, are to be determined, not with reference to the wishes and interests of a few, but solely with

From *A Treatise on Domestic Economy, for the Use of Young Ladies at Home, and at School* (Boston: Thomas H. Webb, 1842), 25–27, 33–34, 36–38, 48–51, 155–157.

reference to the general good of all; so that each individual shall have his own interest, as well as the public benefit, secured by them.

For this purpose, it is needful that certain relations be sustained, which involve the duties of subordination. There must be the magistrate and the subject, one of whom is the superior, and the other the inferior. There must be the relations of husband and wife, parent and child, teacher and pupil, employer and employed, each involving the relative duties of subordination. The superior, in certain particulars, is to direct, and the inferior is to yield obedience. Society could never go forward, harmoniously, nor could any craft or profession be successfully pursued, unless these superior and subordinate relations be instituted and sustained.

But who shall take the higher, and who the subordinate, stations in social and civil life? . . .

In most other cases, in a truly democratic state, each individual is allowed to choose for himself, who shall take the position of his superior. No woman is forced to obey any husband but the one she chooses for herself; nor is she obliged to take a husband, if she prefers to remain single. So every domestic, and every artisan or laborer, after passing from parental control, can choose the employer to whom he is to accord obedience, or, if he prefers to relinquish certain advantages, he can remain without taking a subordinate place to any employer.

Each subject, also, has equal power with every other, to decide who shall be his superior as a ruler. The weakest, the poorest, the most illiterate, has the same opportunity to determine this question, as the richest, the most learned, and the most exalted.

And the various privileges that wealth secures, are equally open to all classes. Every man may aim at riches, unimpeded by any law or institution which secures peculiar privileges to a favored class, at the expense of another. Every law, and every institution, is tested by examining whether it secures equal advantages to all; and, if the people become convinced that any

regulation sacrifices the good of the majority to the interests of the smaller number, they have power to abolish it. . . .

The tendencies of democratic institutions, in reference to the rights and interests of the female sex, have been fully developed in the United States; and it is in this aspect, that the subject is one of peculiar interest to American women. In this Country, it is established, both by opinion and by practice, that woman has an equal interest in all social and civil concerns; and that no domestic, civil, or political, institution, is right, which sacrifices her interest to promote that of the other sex. But in order to secure her the more firmly in all these privileges, it is decided, that, in the domestic relation, she take a subordinate station, and that, in civil and political concerns, her interests be intrusted to the other sex, without her taking any part in voting, or in making and administering laws. . . .

It appears, then, that it is in America, alone, that women are raised to an equality with the other sex; and that, both in theory and practice, their interests are regarded as of equal value. They are made subordinate in station, only where a regard to their best interests demands it, while, as if in compensation for this, by custom and courtesy, they are always treated as superiors. Universally, in this Country, through every class of society, precedence is given to woman, in all the comforts, conveniences, and courtesies, of life.

In civil and political affairs, American women take no interest or concern, except so far as they sympathize with their family and personal friends; but in all cases, in which they do feel a concern, their opinions and feelings have a consideration, equal, or even superior, to that of the other sex.

In matters pertaining to the education of their children, in the selection and support of a clergyman, in all benevolent enterprises, and in all questions relating to morals or manners, they have a superior influence. In such concerns, it would be impossible to carry a point, contrary to their judgement and feelings; while an enterprise, sustained by them, will seldom fail of success.

If those who are bewailing themselves over the fancied wrongs and injuries of women in this Nation, could only see things as they are, they would know, that, whatever remnants of a barbarous or aristocratic age may remain in our civil institutions, in reference to the interests of women, it is only because they are ignorant of them, or do not use their influence to have them rectified; for it is very certain that there is nothing reasonable, which American women would unite in asking, that would not readily be bestowed.

The preceding remarks, then, illustrate the position, that the democratic institutions of this Country are in reality no other than the principles of Christianity carried into operation, and that they tend to place woman in her true position in society, as having equal rights with the other sex; and that, in fact, they have secured to American women a lofty and fortunate position, which, as yet, has been attained by the women of no other nation. . . .

The success of democratic institutions, as is conceded by all, depends upon the intellectual and moral character of the mass of the people. If they are intelligent and virtuous, democracy is a blessing; but if they are ignorant and wicked, it is only a curse, and as much more dreadful than any other form of civil government, as a thousand tyrants are more to be dreaded than one. It is equally conceded, that the formation of the moral and intellectual character of the young is committed mainly to the female hand. The mother forms the character of the future man; the sister bends the fibres that are hereafter to be the forest tree; the wife sways the heart, whose energies may turn for good or for evil the destinies of a nation. Let the women of a country be made virtuous and intelligent, and the men will certainly be the same. The proper education of a man decides the welfare of an individual; but educate a woman, and the interests of a whole family are secured.

If this be so, as none will deny, then to American women, more than to any others on earth, is committed the exalted privilege of extending over the world those blessed influences, which are to renovate degraded man, and "clothe all climes with beauty."

No American woman, then, has any occasion for feeling that hers is an humble or insignificant lot. The value of what an individual accomplishes, is to be estimated by the importance of the enterprise achieved, and not by the particular position of the laborer. The drops of heaven which freshen the earth, are each of equal value, whether they fall in the lowland meadow, or the princely parterre. The builders of a temple are of equal importance, whether they labor on the foundations, or toil upon the dome.

Thus, also, with those labors which are to be made effectual in the regeneration of the Earth. And it is by forming a habit of regarding the apparently insignificant efforts of each isolated laborer, in a comprehensive manner, as indispensable portions of a grand result, that the minds of all, however humble their sphere of service, can be invigorated and cheered. The woman, who is rearing a family of children; the woman, who labors in the schoolroom; the woman, who, in her retired chamber, earns, with her needle, the mite, which contributes to the intellectual and moral elevation of her Country; even the humble domestic, whose example and influence may be moulding and forming young minds, while her faithful services sustain a prosperous domestic state;—each and all may be animated by the consciousness, that they are agents in accomplishing the greatest work that ever was committed to human responsibility. It is the building of a glorious temple, whose base shall be coextensive with the bounds of the earth, whose summit shall pierce the skies, whose splendor shall beam on all lands; and those who hew the lowliest stone, as much as those who carve the highest capital, will be equally honored, when its top-stone shall be laid, with new rejoicings of the morning stars, and shoutings of the sons of God. . . .

Having pointed out the peculiar responsibilities of American women, and the peculiar embarrassments which they are called to encounter, the following suggestions are offered, as remedies for their difficulties.

In the first place, the physical and domestic education of daughters should occupy the principal attention of mothers, in childhood; and the stimulation of the intellect should be very much reduced. As a general rule, daughters should not be sent to school before they are six years old; and, when they are sent, far more attention should be paid to their physical developement, than is usually done. They should never be confined, at any employment, more than an hour at a time; and this confinement should be followed by sports in the open air. Such accommodations should be secured, that, at all seasons, and in all weathers, the teacher can every half hour send out a portion of her school, for sports. And still more care should be given to preserve pure air in the schoolroom. The close stoves, crowded condition, and poisonous air, of most school-rooms, act as constant drains on the health and strength of young children.

In addition to this, much less time should be given to school, and much more to domestic employments, especially in the wealthier classes. A little girl may begin, at five or six years of age, to assist her mother; and, if properly trained, by the time she is ten, she can render essential aid. From this time, until she is fourteen or fifteen, it should be the principal object of her education to secure a strong and healthy constitution, and a thorough practical knowledge of all kinds of domestic employments. During this period, though some attention ought to be paid to intellectual culture, it ought to be made altogether secondary in importance; and such a measure of study and intellectual excitement, as is now demanded in our best female seminaries, ought never to be allowed, until a young lady has passed the most critical period of her youth, and has a vigorous and healthful constitution fully established. The plan might be adopted, of having schools for young girls kept only in the afternoon; that their mornings might be occupied in domestic exercise, without interfering with school employments. Where a proper supply of domestic exercise cannot be afforded, the cultivation of flowers and fruits might be resorted to, as a delightful and unfailing promotive of pleasure and health. . . .

A second method of promoting the same object, is, to raise the science and practice of Domestic Economy to its appropriate place, as a regular study in female seminaries. The succeeding chapter will present the reasons for this, more at large. But it is to the mothers of our Country, that the community must look for this change. It cannot be expected, that teachers, who have their attention chiefly absorbed by the intellectual and moral interests of their pupils, should properly realize the importance of this department of education. But if mothers generally become convinced of this, their judgement and wishes will meet the respectful consideration they deserve, and the object will be accomplished. . . .

The discussion of the question of the equality of the sexes, in intellectual capacity, seems frivolous and useless, both because it can never be decided, and because there would be no possible advantage in the decision. But one topic, which is often drawn into this discussion, is of far more consequence; and that is, the relative importance and difficulty of the duties a woman is called to perform.

It is generally assumed, and almost as generally conceded, that woman's business and cares are contracted and trivial; and that the proper discharge of her duties, demands far less expansion of mind and vigor of intellect, than the pursuits of the other sex. This idea has prevailed, because women, as a mass, have never been educated with reference to their most important duties; while that portion of their employments, which is of least value, has been regarded as the chief, if not the sole, concern of a woman. The covering of the body, the conveniences of residences, and the gratification of the appetite, have been too much regarded as the sole objects, on which her intellectual powers are to be exercised.

But, as society gradually shakes off the remnants of barbarism, and the intellectual and moral interests of man rise, in estimation, above the merely sensual, a truer estimate is formed of woman's duties, and of the measure of intellect requisite for the proper discharge of them. Let any man, of sense and discernment, become the member of a large household, in which, a well-educated and pious woman is endeavoring systematically to discharge her multiform duties; let him fully comprehend all her cares, difficulties, and perplexities; and it is probable he would coincide in the opinion, that no statesman, at the head of a nation's affairs, had more frequent calls for wisdom, firmness, tact, discrimination, prudence, and versatility of talent, than such a woman.

She has a husband, to whose peculiar tastes and habits she must accommodate herself; she has children, whose health she must guard, whose physical constitutions she must study and develope, whose temper and habits she must regulate, whose principles she must form, whose pursuits she must direct. She has constantly changing domestics, with all varieties of temper and habits, whom she must govern, instruct, and direct; she is required to regulate the finances of the domestic state, and constantly to adapt expenditures to the means and to the relative claims of each department. She has the direction of the kitchen, where ignorance, forgetfulness, and awkwardness, are to be so regulated, that the various operations shall each start at the right time, and all be in completeness at the same given hour. She has the claims of society to meet, calls to receive and return, and the duties of hospitality to sustain. She has the poor to relieve; benevolent societies to aid; the schools of her children to inquire and decide about; the care of the sick; the nursing of infancy; and the endless miscellany of odd items, constantly recurring in a large family.

Surely, it is a pernicious and mistaken idea, that the duties, which tax a woman's mind, are petty, trivial, or unworthy of the highest grade of intellect and moral worth. Instead of allowing this feeling, every woman should imbibe, from early youth, the impression, that she is training for the discharge of the most important, the most difficult, and the most sacred and interesting duties that can possibly employ the highest intellect. She ought to feel, that her station and responsibilities, in the great drama of life, are second to none, either as viewed by her Maker, or in the estimation of all minds whose judgement is most worthy of respect.

She, who is the mother and housekeeper in a large family, is the sovereign of an empire, demanding more varied cares, and involving more difficult duties, than are really exacted of her, who, while she wears the crown, and professedly regulates the interests of the greatest nation on earth, finds abundant leisure for theatres, balls, horseraces, and every gay pursuit. . . .

30

ELIZABETH OAKES SMITH

A Woman-Thought, a Woman-Perception, a Woman-Intuition (1851)

. . . Whatever difference of opinion may exist amongst us as to the *propriety* of the recent Conventions held in our Country, called "Woman's Rights," the fact stands by itself, a handwriting on the wall, proclaiming a sense of wrong, a sense of something demanding redress, and this is fact enough to *justify the movement* to all candid eyes. Indeed enough to render it praiseworthy. For one, I am glad to see that our Republic has produced a class of women, who, feeling the Need of a larger sphere and a better recognition, have that clearness of intellect and strength

From *Woman and Her Needs* (New York: Fowlers and Wells, 1851), 10–11, 16–17, 19–24, 26–29.

of purpose by which they go to work resolutely to solve the difficulty. They might stay at home and fret and dawdle; be miserable themselves and make all within their sphere miserable likewise; but instead of this, they meet and talk the matter over, devise plans, explain difficulties, rehearse social oppressions and political disabilities, in the hope of evolving something permanently good.

All this is well, and grows naturally from the progress of institutions like our own, in which opinions are fearlessly discussed, and all thought traced home to its source. It isn't in the nature of things that any class in our midst should be long indifferent to topics of general interest; far less that such should feel the pressure of evils without inquiring into the best means of abatement. When our Fathers planted themselves upon the firm base of human freedom, claimed the inalienable rights of life, liberty, and the pursuit of happiness, they might have foreseen that at some day their daughters would sift thoroughly their opinions and their consequences, and daringly challenge the same rights.

For myself, I may not sympathize with a Convention—I may not feel *that* the best mode of arriving at truth to my own mind—I may feel that its singleness of import would be lost to me while standing in the solid phalanx of associated inquiry; but these objections do not apply to the majority of minds, and I reverence their search in their own way, the many converging lights of many minds all bent upon the same point, even although I myself peer about with my solitary lantern. . . .

The world needs the action of Woman thought in its destinies. The indefinite influence springing from the private circle is not enough; this is shaded away into the graceful lights of feminine subserviency and household endearment; blessing the individual husband, or ennobling the one group at the family altar, but the world goes on with its manifold wrongs, and woman has nothing but tears to bestow—the outrages that may wring either her own heart or that of others, are perpetrated before her

eyes, and she can only wring helpless hands, or plead with ideal remonstrance, while her lord and master tells her these things are quite beyond her comprehension; she can not see how unavoidable it is, but it is not the less unavoidable, and she must shut her eyes and ears, and "mind her spinning." Or, if blessed with a large share of manly arrogance, he will tell her, as did the captain of a militia company of a country town, who, in practising in the court of his house those martial evolutions that were to electrify the village upon parade, accidentally stepped down the trap-door of the cellar. His wife rushed out to succor her liege lord, when she was met with, "Go in, woman; what do you know about war?"

Sure enough, what does she? But this directness of sympathy, this promptitude to relieve, makes her fruitful in resource in small matters, and why should it not in large? If an evil come under her own inspection, she at once casts about for redress, and good comes of it. There is no reason why she should not enlarge her sphere in this way, and no fear of her being the less feminine or endearing by the process. . . .

I have said the world needs the admixture of Woman thought in its affairs; a deep, free, woman-souled utterance *is needed*. It is the disseverance of the sexes, the condemning of the one to *in-door* thought only, to the degradation of in-door toil, far more limiting in its nature than that of the out-door kind, beneath the invigorations of air and sky, that has done so much in our country to narrow and paralyze the energies of the sex. Excessive maternity, the cares and the labors consequent upon large families, with inadequate support (when we consider the amount of general intelligence amongst us) have conspired to induce the belief that the most entire domestic seclusion is the only sphere for a woman. Our republic has hitherto developed something akin to a savage lordliness in the other sex, in which he is to usurp all the privileges of freedom, and she is to take as much as she can get, after he is served.

Now, a woman may or may not be adapted to an in-door life exclusively. There is as much difference in us in that respect as there is in men. The expanse of earth and sky have unquestionably worked enlargement upon the mind of the other sex; and, in our own, have developed for the poor serving girl of the Inn of Domremy, inured to the toils of the stable, the chivalric and enthusiastic Joan of Arc. It is the making woman a creature of luxury—an object of sensuality—a vehicle for reproduction—or a thing of toil, each one, or all of these—that has caused half the miseries of the world. She, as a soul, has never been recognized. As a human being, to sin and to suffer, she has had more than an acknowledgment. As a human being, to obey her God, to think, to enjoy, men have been blind to her utmost needs.

She has been treated always as subservient; and yet all and the most entire responsibility has been exacted of her. She has had no voice in the law, and yet has been subjected to the heaviest penalties of the law. She has been denied the ability to make or enforce public opinion, and yet has been outraged, abandoned, given over to degradation, misery, and the thousand ills worse than a thousand deaths, by its terrible action. Even her affections—those arbitrary endowments imparted by the Most High for her own safeguard, and for the best being of society—have been warped and crushed by the action of masculine thought upon their manifestations, till their unadulterated play is well nigh lost.

Men have written for us, thought for us, legislated for us; and they have constructed from their own consciousness an effigy of a woman, to which we are expected to conform. It is not a Woman that they see; God forbid that it should be; it is one of those monsters of neither sex, that sometimes outrage the pangs of maternity, but which expire at the birth: whereas the distorted image to which men wish us to conform, lives to bewilder, to mislead, and to cause discord and belittlement where the Creator designed the highest dignity, the most complete

harmony. Men have said we should be thus and thus, and we have tried to be in accordance, because we are told it is womanly. . . .

Let woman learn to take a woman's view of life. Let her feel the need of a woman's thought. Let her search into her own needs—say, not what has the world hitherto thought in regard to this or that, but what is the *true* view of it from the nature of things. Let her not say, what does my husband, my brother, my father think—wise and good and trustworthy though they be—but let her evolve her own thoughts, recognize her own needs, and judge of her own acts by the best lights of her own mind.

Let her feel and understand that there is a difference in the soul as in the bodies of the sexes—a difference designed to produce the most beautiful harmony. But let her not, in admitting this, admit of inferiority. While the *form* of a man is as it were more arbitrary, more of a fact in creation, more distinct and uniform, a sort of completeness of the material, and his mind also more of a fixture, better adapted to the exactitudes of science, and those protracted labors needful to the hardier developments of the understanding, let her bear in mind that this fixedness, this patience of labor, this steadiness of the understanding, are in conformity with his position as *Lord of the material Universe,* to which God has appointed him; whereas she was an after-creation, with something nearer allied to the heavenly. In her shape there is a flexibility, a variety, more graceful, etherial, and beautiful, appealing more intimately to that something within the soul of man, that goes onward to the future and eternal—a softening down of the material to the illusions of the unseen—her mind, also, when unstinted and unadulterated, has in it more of aspiration, more of the subtle and intuitive character, that links it to the spiritual; she is impatient of labor, because her wings are nearly freed of the shell of the chrysalis, and prompt to a better element; she cares less for the deductions of reason, because she has an element in herself nearer to the truth than reason can ever reach, by which she *feels* the approaches of the true and the beautiful, without the manly wrestlings all night of the Patriarch to which the other sex are subjected. She does not need the ladder of Bethel, the step by step of the slow logician, because her feet are already upon the first rung of that mystic pass-way; this is why she is bid by the arrogance of apostolic injunction to veil her head in public, "because of the Angels." She is a step nearer them than her *material* lord and master. The angels recognize her as of nearer affinity. . . .

Would that women should learn to recognize their own individuality—their own singleness of thought. Let them not feel disparaged at the difference which I have recognized; it is a difference that crowns them with a new glory. We give the material Universe to men, and to those of our own sex who, from whatever cause, approximate to their standard; to such let us yield ungrudgingly the way; but it is no less certain that there is a woman-thought, a woman-perception, a woman-intuition, altogether distinct from the same things in the other sex; and to learn what these are, and to act from these, is what women must learn, and when they have so learned and impressed themselves thus through these upon the world, it will be regenerated and disenthralled. . . .

Women must recognize their unlikeness, and then understanding what needs grow out of this unlikeness, some great truth must be evolved. Now they busy themselves with methods of thought, springing, it is true, from their own sense of something needed, but suggested altogether by the masculine intellect. Let us first shake ourselves of this pupilage of mind by which our faculties are dwarfed, and courageously judge for ourselves. In doing this, I see no need of Amazonian strides or disfigurements, or a stentorian lungs. The more deeply and earnestly a woman feels the laws of her own existence, the more solemn, reverent, and harmonious is her bearing. She sees what nature designed in her creation, and her whole being falls gracefully into its allotted sphere. If she be a simple, genial, household divinity, she will bind garlands around the altar of the Penates, and worship in content. If more largely endowed, I see no reason why she should not be received cordially into the school of Arts, or Science, or Politics, or Theology, in the same manner as the individual capacities of the other sex are recognized. They do not all square themselves to one standard, and why should we? They have a very large number engaged in sewing, cooking, spinning, and writing very small articles for very small works, designed for very small minds.

The majority are far from being Platos, or Bayards, or Napoleons. When so very large a portion of the other sex are engaged in what is regarded as unmanly, I see no reason why those of ours who have a fancy to tinker a constitution, canvass a county, or preach the Gospel, should not be permitted to do so, provided they feel this to be the best use of their faculties. I do not say this is the best thing for them to do; but I see no reason, if their best intelligence finds its best expression in any such channel, why they should not be indulged.

Our right to individuality is what I would most assert. Men seem resolved to have but one type in our sex. They recognize the prerogative of the matter-of-fact Biddy to raise a great clamor, quite to the annoyance of a neighborhood, but where's the use of Nightingale? The laws of stubborn utilitarianism must govern us, while they may be as fantastic as they please. They tell much about a "woman's sphere"—can they define this? As the phrase is used, I confess it has a most shallow and indefinite sense. The most I can gather from it is, the consciousness of the speaker, which means something like the philosophy of Mr. Murdstone's firmness; it is sphere by which every woman creature, of whatever age, appending to himself, shall circle very much within his own—see and hear through his senses, and believe according to his dogmas, with a sort of general proviso, that if need be for his growth, glorification, or well-being, in any way, they will instantly and uncompromisingly become extinct.

There is a Woman's sphere—harmonious,

holy, soul-imparting; it has its grades, its laws from the nature of things, and these we must seek out. The pursuits of men vary with their capacities—are higher or lower, according to age; why should not those of women vary in the same way? The highest offices of legislation are filled by men of mature age, whose judgments are supposed to be consolidated by years. Among the Mohawks, a woman, who has so trained a boy that he became *elected* to the office of Chief—for this honor was not hereditary—was received into the Councils of the Nation. The Spartan women emulated the men in the terseness of their language and the hardihood of their patriotism. Often and often do we see the attributes of the sexes reversed; the woman becoming the protector and, in fact, the *bond* of the house, without a shadow of infringement upon the appropriateness or beauty of her womanhood. It is late in the day to be thrown upon the defensive. I see no way in which harmony can result in the world without entire recognition of differences, for surely nothing is gained upon either side by antagonism merely. Women cannot be so very ridiculous and absurd in their honest, hearty truth-searchings; for such are the Mothers of the Republic; and he who casts contempt upon them, endorses his own shame. If the members of his own household are exempt from solemn truth-askings, he should beware how he exults over such evidence of commonplace dullness or frivolity.

31
Resolution on "Woman's Sphere," at the Second Woman's Rights Convention in Worcester (1851)

. . . 7. *Resolved,* That we deny the right of any portion of the species to decide for another portion, or of any individual to decide for another individual what is and what is not their "proper sphere"; that the proper sphere for all human beings is the largest and highest to which they are able to attain; what this is, can not be ascertained without complete liberty of choice; woman, therefore, ought to choose for herself what sphere she will fill, what education she will seek, and what employment she will follow, and not be held bound to accept, in submission, the rights, the education, and the sphere which man thinks proper to allow her.

32
LUCY STONE
"Leave Women, Then, To Find Their Sphere," Address to the Woman's Rights Convention in Cincinnati (1855)

. . . The question of Woman's Rights is a practical one. The notion has prevailed that it was only an ephemeral idea; that it was but women claiming the right to smoke cigars in the streets, and to frequent bar-rooms. Others have supposed it a question of comparative intellect; others still,

Document 31 from Elizabeth Cady Stanton, Susan B. Anthony, and Matilda Joslyn Gage, eds., *History of Woman Suffrage, Vol. 1, 1848–1861* (New York: Fowler and Wells, 1881), 826.

Document 32 from Elizabeth Cady Stanton, Susan B. Anthony, and Matilda Joslyn Gage, eds., *History of Woman Suffrage, Vol. 1, 1848–1861* (New York: Fowler and Wells, 1881), 165–67.

of sphere. Too much has already been said and written about woman's sphere. Trace all the doctrines to their source and they will be found to have no basis except in the usages and prejudices of the age. This is seen in the fact that what is tolerated in woman in one country is not tolerated in another. In this country women may hold prayer-meetings, etc., but in Mohammaden countries it is written upon their mosques, "Women and dogs, and other impure animals, are not permitted to enter." Wendell Phillips says, "The best and greatest thing one is capable of doing, that is his sphere." I have confidence in the Father to believe that when He gives us the capacity to do anything He does not make a blunder. Leave women, then, to find their sphere. And do not tell us before we are born even, that our province is to cook dinners, darn stockings, and sew on buttons. We are told woman has all the rights she wants; and even women, I am ashamed to say, tell us so. They mistake the politeness of men for rights—seats while men stand in this hall to-night, and their adulations; but these are mere courtesies. We want rights. The flour-merchant, the house-builder, and the postman charge us no less on account of our sex; but when we endeavor to earn money to pay all these, then, indeed, we find the difference. Man, if he have energy, may hew out for himself a path where no mortal has ever trod, held back by nothing but what is in himself; the world is all before him, where to choose; and we are glad for you, brothers, men, that it is so. But the same society that drives forth the young man, keeps woman at home—a dependent—working little cats on worsted, and little dogs on punctured paper; but if she goes heartily and bravely to give herself to some worthy purpose, she is out of her sphere and she loses caste. Women working in tailor-shops are paid one-third as much as men. Some one in Philadelphia has stated that women make fine shirts for twelve and a half cents apiece; that no woman can make more than nine a week, and the sum thus earned, after deducting rent, fuel, etc., leaves her just three and a half cents a day for bread. Is it a wonder that women are driven to prostitution? Female teachers in New York are paid fifty dollars a year, and for every such situation there are five hundred applicants. I know not what you believe of God, but I believe He gave yearnings and longings to be filled, and that He did not mean all our time should be devoted to feeding and clothing the body. The present condition of woman causes a horrible perversion of the marriage relation. It is asked of a lady, "Has she married well?" "Oh, yes, her husband is rich." Woman must marry for a home, and you men are the sufferers by this; for a woman who loathes you may marry you because you have the means to get money which she can not have. But when a woman can enter the lists with you and make money for herself, she will marry you only for deep and earnest affection.

I am detaining you too long, many of you standing, that I ought to apologize, but women have been wronged so long that I may wrong you a little. (Applause). A woman undertook in Lowell to sell shoes to ladies. Men laughed at her, but in six years she has run them all out, and has a monopoly of the trade. Sarah Tyndale, whose husband was an importer of china, and died bankrupt, continued his business, paid off his debts, and has made a fortune and built the largest china warehouse in the world. (Mrs. Mott here corrected Lucy. Mrs. Tyndale has not the largest china warehouse, but the largest assortment of china in the world). Mrs. Tyndale, herself, drew the plan of her warehouse, and it is the best plan ever drawn. A laborer to whom the architect showed it, said: "Don't she know e'en as much as some men!" I have seen a woman at manual labor turning out chair-legs in a cabinet-shop, with a dress short enough not to drag in the shavings. I wish other women would imitate her in this. It made her hands harder and broader, it is true, but I think a hand with a dollar and a quarter a day in it, better than one with a crossed ninepence. The men in the shop didn't use tobacco, nor swear—they can't do those things where there are women, and we owe it to our brothers to go wherever they work to keep them decent. The widening of woman's sphere is to improve her lot. Let us do it, and if the world scoff, let it scoff—if it sneer, let it sneer—but we will go on emulating the example of the sisters Grimke and Abby Kelly. When they first lectured against slavery they were not listened to as respectfully as you listen to us. So the first female physician meets many difficulties, but to the next the path will be made easy. . . .

33

ELIZABETH CADY STANTON
Are the Sexes Different? (1855)

"A great deal has been said of the original difference of capacity between men and women; as if women were more quick, and men more judicious,—as if women were more remarkable for delicacy of association, and men for stronger powers of attention. All this we confess appears to us very fanciful. That there is a difference in the understandings of the men and the women we every day meet with, every body, we suppose, must perceive; but there is none, surely, which may not be accounted for by the difference of circumstances in which they have been placed, without referring to any conjectural difference of original conformation of mind. As long as boys and girls run about in the dirt, and trundle hoops together, they are both precisely alike. If you catch up one half of these creatures, and train them up to a particular set of actions and opinions, and the other half to a perfectly opposite set, of course their understandings will differ, as one or the other sort of occupations has called this or that talent into action.

"There is surely no occasion to go into any deeper or more abstruse reasoning, in order to explain so very simple a phenomenon." Here is the opinion of the Rev. Sydney Smith, the dis-

tinguished English Essayist and Divine. To speak of a natural mental difference in the sexes, was an absurdity to him fifty years ago. To speak of their identity is an absurdity to the Rev. Antoinette Brown in 1855. In her recent speech at Albany before a legislative committee, she said she would institute no comparison between men and women. "As well," she said, "you may ask which is the largest, a railroad or a steamboat; which the longest, a boa constrictor or a day in June." Now I beg leave to differ entirely with Antoinette Brown. I think boys and girls, men and women, can be compared. As moral and intellectual beings, does not all history prove them the same? There is no end to speculations or theories on any subject, and there is no way of combating visions or shadows. But of those things of which the evidences of our senses attest, we may reason and judge. Well, then, to let pass that indescribable something, in which it is said that all men and women differ, and to come down to what we see, and hear, and feel, what have we?

Man eats and drinks and sleeps, and so does woman. He runs and walks, laughs and cries, feels joy and sorrow, pleasure and pain, and so does woman. He loves, hates, is angry, sorry, impatient, unreasonable, tyrannical, and so is woman. He is religious, penitent, prayerful, dependent, and so is woman. He is courageous, bold, self-reliant, enduring, and so is woman. He is ambitious, loves glory, fame, power, and so does woman. He loves to think, reason, write, speak, debate, declaim, and so does woman. In fact what has man ever done, that woman has not done also?—what does he like, that she does not like too? Are not our hopes and fears for time and eternity the same? What virtue or vice, what aspiration or appetite has ever crowned or clouded the glory of manhood, that we have not seen in woman too, its beauty or its blight. The physical differences we see between some men and women, produced by different employments, may be seen also between man and man. Contrast the farmer with the man who has led a sedentary, scholastic life. Contrast those women

From *The Una: A Paper Devoted to the Elevation of Woman* 3 (May, 1855).

who have been developed by labor or accident, with some of your puny metropolitans who have never seen the sun rise or set. Theory may say that if man and woman from the beginning were educated precisely alike, man would still be the larger, the stronger. When the experiment is fully made, it will be time enough to admit the assumption. But suppose we admit that man is physically larger than woman, what do you gain by the admission? Among men the athletic, the muscular, the brawny, are by no means the great men in the best sense of that word, neither are they the strongest physically. The sight of a small man whipping a large one is not uncommon. The force of will has much more to do with strength than the size of the frame, the impelling organs of the brain than the size of the arm and chest. By far the greater proportion of distinguished men, of generals, statesmen, and philosophers, have been small men of fine nervous organization and exquisite sensibilities. Look at Napolean, Lord Nelson, Guizot, Hamilton, Burr, Adams, Channing, Emerson and Seward. So, should we grant man the superiority of the ox, we should but prove him an inferior order of being.

. . . Men and women are not so unlike in person either, but by skilful dressing the one may pass for the other. George Sand, the assumed name of the distinguished Madame Dudevant, has travelled incognito in man's attire through many countries and observed society in all its phases in Parisian life. There are many instances of men escaping from prison in women's attire, undiscovered, and of women disguised as soldiers fighting in the hottest of the battle, side by side with those they loved. In children's plays, boys and girls are constantly seen wrestling, running, climbing, comparing their strength and swiftness. I never heard it hinted in the play-ground or the school-room, that boys and girls were not legitimate subjects of comparison. When a girl, I have gone many a time from our Academy gate to the belfry, snowball in hand, to punish a boy for washing my face. The girls in my native village not only tried strength with

boys in the play-ground, but we measured lances with them, in the sciences, languages, and mathematics. In studying Algebra and Geometry, in reading Virgil or the Greek Testament, I never found out the difference in the male and female mind. In those days there was no feminine way of extracting the cube root of x, y, z; no masculine way of going through all the moods and tenses of the verbs Amo and Tupto. We have had so much sentimental talk in all our woman's conventions, by the friends of the cause, about the male and female element, and by outsiders, on woman's sphere, her mission, her peculiar duties, &c., that I should like to have all this mysterious twaddle thoroughly explored; all these nice shades of differences fully revealed. It is not enough to assert that there always has been, is, and always will be a difference. The question is, What is it?

34

M. FARLEY EMERSON
Woman's Sphere, Woman's Nature (1857)

. . . The New York *Post,* in speaking of *marriage,* comes right out plain and speaks of it as a business, an employment, a calling, a something that one class of people follow as the means of livelihood; as the easiest, the most agreeable, the most convenient, and the *very best* profession for that class. But in this sense, and in this connection why does he call it "sphere?" we do not say that Dr. Smith is in Washington following his *sphere,* though we may, with propriety, say that Dr. Smith is in Washington practicing medicine; nor do we say that Physics is the only *proper sphere* for Dr. Smith, because, according to our notions of things, he is disqualified for every other profession.

From *Woman in America: Her Character and Position as Indicated by Newspaper Editorials, and Sustained by American Social Life. By an American Woman* (Cincinnati: The Author, 1857), 16–21, 213–15.

Why does he not say, marriage is the only occupation a woman can, or should follow? Because he had rather use the term *sphere*. He can *live* a fact, and he can see all his female friends existing in a reality so disgusting to the modest ear, that he will not speak of it in plain terms. And he can live on thus, year after year without blushing and without shame. And yet, he seems to think that on the whole, it is rather foolish to try to conceal what is so generally understood. Everybody knows that the only thing girls can do, is to get married, therefore he thinks mothers very foolish to maneuver and waste time and the health of their daughters; they should do all openly, in a fair business style; that their daughters *must marry* and can do nothing else, excepting, may be, sew a little, or teach school a little, just to pass away the time while they are in waiting for this new profession; that this being their only pursuit, is so well known and understood, he thinks it exceedingly foolish to be so *sly* about it[.]

. . . [W]oman is just no more nor less than man allows her to become; that man's influence over woman is *efficient, absolute,* while her influence is infinitely smaller, not sufficient to command his reverence; not sufficient to prevent his licentiousness; not even sufficient to make his licentiousness look odious in society; an influence that falls back on self, and says, in effect, *we* must be very pure, but *men* have a right to be impure; *we* must be very virtuous and keep ourselves for men, but *they* have a right to be immoral and licentious. Now, this is not being virtuous for *virtue's* sake, but for *men's* sake; were it for virtue's sake, there would be as much talk about good, pure, moral men, as about good, pure, and moral women; it is not so, on the contrary it is quite unpopular with ladies to say any thing about virtuous men, or to expect men to be virtuous. An influence that says in effect, *we* must look about ourselves with great care, always, whether we stay in, or walk out, we must see that we do nothing improper, we must not look to the right or left as we pass along, but look straight forward, and if we can slily peep

round occasionally, and chance to see something funny, we must show how wise we are by putting on our knowing looks, and displaying our powers of ridicule. If we pass along the walk and see posters out for people to read, we must not stop to read, we must feel *above* that, for men as well as women are watching us, and afterwards, when in the company of gentlemen in conversation, if we are likely to appear ignorant, we must put on our meek, still looks, and become all at once, too *proud* to take part in gentlemen's conversation, we must feel *above* knowing what to say, when gentlemen discuss questions abstruse. We must watch ourselves, and watch each other incessantly; gentlemen also have a right to keep an eye on us, to see that no one shall get out of her sphere, to see that not one of us shall dare try to act like a man; but gentlemen have a right to do as they please; we must not take away their rights, nor watch their conduct as though we were their dictators, but *they* have a right to mark *our* conduct, and criticise the same, therefore we must not look to one side nor the other, as we pass along, but straight forward, thinking about ourselves all the time, as to how pretty we look, and of the propriety of our deportment, that never turns aside, nor sees any thing at all except by stealth.

. . . And then the gentlemen would say to themselves, Oh, what happy men we are! When we're in the halls of Congress, we have only to look into the galleries, and there behold numerous *pretty little shows,* on purpose for us to see, free gratis; when we walk out, lo! on every hand are plenty more *pretty little shows,* dodging about here and there, with downcast, modest looks, for *all,* or *any one,* to see who will look,—these are also free of charge. And then, whenever we're in the hotels, or wherever we may be, there we find more *pretty little shows* placed right in our way; and they're so fascinating, too,— how delightful to think of them! Those who can excite our passions most, by their winning ways, have most *power;*—this is woman's *power,* and we must please and satisfy such charming creatures,—talk much about their *power,* and make up large sermons, founded on quotations concerning *woman's nature,* and enlarge upon these for pastime whenever we have leisure.

There is nothing said about *men's nature,* in society, anywhere. I do not remember of having seen the phrase in print at any time in my life,—but I do think I have seen the term *woman's nature* in print, *millions* of times. It is expected that God has given men a nature that they know, without any to tell them what it is,—that if they are ambitious and spirited, they will do just as much as they *can do;* but from the time a female is born, she hears nothing, only about what is her *nature;* about this particular thing, and that particular thing she must not do, because she's a female; this way or that way that she must not look,—this thought or that thought that she must not have,—this motion or that motion that she must not make, because she's a female.

Thus every little girl is pursued, and worried, and hunted, till her intellectual life is dead, and then, of course, genius *dare not live,* and the soul is abject. And, for fear lest she may revive, there's constantly kept astir more large and knowing talk, about her *nature* and many beautiful little sayings about how *lovely* she is in weakness and dependence; and, instead of associating her spirit with the eagle motherbird, whom no male of their tribe excels in the bold grandeur of her lofty flights,—who is said to be more fearless, and longer on the wing, than the male,—she is likened to the hen, who clucks about patiently, just to suit the convenience of the rooster. . . .

35
FRANCES ELLEN WATKINS [HARPER]
The Two Offers (1859)

"What is the matter with you, Laura, this morning? I have been watching you this hour, and in that time you have commenced a half dozen letters and torn them all up. What matter of such grave moment is puzzling your dear little head, that you do not know how to decide?"

"Well, it is an important matter: I have two offers for marriage, and I do not know which to choose."

"I should accept neither, or to say the least, not at present."

"Why not?"

"Because I think a woman who is undecided between two offers, has not love enough for either to make a choice; and in that very hesitation, indecision, she has a reason to pause and seriously reflect, lest her marriage, instead of being an affinity of souls or a union of hearts, should only be a mere matter of bargain and sale, or an affair of convenience and selfish interest."

"But I consider them both very good offers, just such as many a girl would gladly receive. But to tell you the truth, I do not think that I regard either as a woman should the man she chooses for her husband. But then, if I refuse, there is the risk of being an old maid, and that is not to be thought of."

"Well, suppose there is, is that the most dreadful fate that can befall a woman? Is there not more intense wretchedness in an ill-assorted marriage—more utter loneliness in a loveless home, than in the lot of the old maid who accepts her earthly mission as a gift from God, and strives to walk the path of life with earnest and unfaltering steps?"

"Oh! what a little preacher you are. I really believe that you were cut out for an old maid;

From *The Anglo-African Magazine* 1 (September and October, 1859).

that when nature formed you, she put in a double portion of intellect to make up for a deficiency of love; and yet you are kind and affectionate. But I do not think that you know anything of the grand, over-mastering passion, or the deep necessity of woman's heart for loving."

"Do you think so?" resumed the first speaker; and bending over her work she quietly applied herself to the knitting that had lain neglected by her side, during this brief conversation; but as she did so, a shadow flitted over her pale and intellectual brow, a mist gathered in her eyes, and a slight quivering of the lips, revealed a depth of feeling to which her companion was a stranger.

But before I proceed with my story, let me give you a slight history of the speakers. They were cousins, who had met life under different auspices. Laura Lagrange, was the only daughter of rich and indulgent parents, who had spared no pains to make her an accomplished lady. Her cousin, Janette Alston, was the child of parents, rich only in goodness and affection. Her father had been unfortunate in business, and dying before he could retrieve his fortunes, left his business in an embarrassed state. His widow was unacquainted with his business affairs, and when the estate was settled, hungry creditors had brought their claims and the lawyers had received their fees, she found herself homeless and almost penniless, and she who had been sheltered in the warm clasp of loving arms, found them too powerless to shield her from the pitiless pelting storms of adversity. Year after year she struggled with poverty and wrestled with want, till her toil-worn hands became too feeble to hold the shattered chords of existence, and her tear-dimmed eyes grew heavy with the slumber of death. Her daughter had watched over her with untiring devotion, had closed her eyes in death, and gone out into the busy, restless world, missing a precious tone from the voices of earth, a beloved step from the paths of life. Too self reliant to depend on the charity of relations, she endeavored to support herself by her own exertions, and she had succeeded. Her path

for a while was marked with struggle and trial, but instead of uselessly repining, she met them bravely, and her life became not a thing of ease and indulgence, but of conquest, victory, and accomplishments. At the time when this conversation took place, the deep trials of her life had passed away. The achievements of her genius had won her a position in the literary world, where she shone as one of its bright particular stars. And with her fame came a competence of worldly means, which gave her leisure for improvement, and the riper developement of her rare talents. And she, that pale intellectual woman, whose genius gave life and vivacity to the social circle, and whose presence threw a halo of beauty and grace around the charmed atmosphere in which she moved, had at one period of her life, known the mystic and solemn strength of an all-absorbing love. Years faded into the misty past, had seen the kindling of her eye, the quick flushing of her cheek, and the wild throbbing of her heart, at tones of a voice long since hushed to the stillness of death. Deeply, wildly, passionately, she had loved. Her whole life seemed like the pouring out of rich, warm and gushing affections. This love quickened her talents, inspired her genius, and threw over her life a tender and spiritual earnestness. And then came a fearful shock, a mournful waking from that "dream of beauty and delight[.]" A shadow fell around her path; it came between her and the object of her heart's worship; first a few cold words, estrangement, and then a painful separation; the old story of woman's pride—digging the sepulchre of her happiness, and then a new-made grave, and her path over it to the spirit world; and thus faded out from that young heart her bright, brief and saddened dream of life. Faint and spirit-broken, she turned from the scenes associated with the memory of the loved and lost. She tried to break the chain of sad associations that bound her to the mournful past; and so, pressing back the bitter sobs from her almost breaking heart, like the dying dolphin, whose beauty is born of its death anguish, her genius gathered strength from suffering and wondrous power and brilliancy for the agony she hid within the desolate chambers of her soul. Men hailed her as one of earth's strangely gifted children, and wreathed the garlands of fame for her brow, when it was throbbing with a wild and fearful unrest. They breathed her name with applause, when through the lonely halls of her stricken spirit, was an earnest cry for peace, a deep yearning for sympathy and heart-support.

But life, with its stern realities, met her; its solemn responsibilities confronted her, and turning, with an earnest and shattered spirit, to life's duties and trials, she found a calmness and strength that she had only imagined in her dreams of poetry and song. We will now pass over a period of ten years, and the cousins have met again. In that calm and lovely woman, in whose eyes is a depth of tenderness, tempering the flashes of her genius, whose looks and tones are fully of sympathy and love, we recognize the once smitten and stricken Janette Alston. The bloom of her girlhood had given way to a higher type of spiritual beauty, as if some unseen hand had been polishing and refining the temple in which her lovely spirit found its habitation; and this had been the fact. Her inner life had grown beautiful, and it was this that was constantly developing the outer. Never, in the early flush of womanhood, when an absorbing love had lit up her eyes and glowed in her life, had she appeared so interesting as when, with a countenance which seemed overshadowed with a spiritual light, she bent over the death-bed of a young woman, just lingering at the shadowy gates of the unseen land.

"Has he come?" faintly but eagerly exclaimed the dying woman. "Oh! how I have longed for his coming, and even in death he forgets me."

"Oh, do not say so, dear Laura, some accident may have detained him," said Janette to her cousin; for on that bed, from whence she will never rise, lies the once-beautiful and light-hearted Laura Lagrange, the brightness of whose eyes has long since been dimmed with tears, and whose voice had become like a harp whose every chord is tuned to sadness—whose faintest thrill and loudest vibrations are but the variations of agony. . . . And yet, earth had one object so very dear to her weary heart. It was her absent and recreant husband; for, since that conversation, she had accepted one of her offers, and become a wife. But, before she married, she learned that great lesson of human experience and woman's life, to love the man who bowed at her shrine, a willing worshipper. He had a pleasing address, raven hair, flashing eyes, a voice of thrilling sweetness, and lips of persuasive eloquence; and being well versed in the ways of the world, he won his way to her heart, and she became his bride, and he was proud of his prize. Vain and superficial in his character, he looked upon marriage not as a divine sacrament for the soul's development and human progression, but as the title-deed that gave him possession of the woman he thought he loved. But alas for her, the laxity of his principles had rendered him unworthy of the deed and undying devotion of a pure-hearted woman; but, for awhile, he hid from her his true character, and she blindly loved him, and for a short period was happy in the consciousness of being beloved; though sometimes a vague unrest would fill her soul, when, overflowing with a sense of the good, the beautiful, and the true, she would turn to him, but find no response to the deep yearnings of her soul—no appreciation of life's highest realities—its solemn grandeur and significant importance. Their souls never met, and soon she found a void in her bosom, that his earth-born love could not fill. He did not satisfy the wants of her mental and moral nature—between him and her there was no affinity of minds, no intercommunion of souls.

Talk as you will of woman's deep capacity for loving, of the strength of her affectional nature. I do not deny it; but will the mere possession of any human love, fully satisfy all the demands of her whole being? You may paint her in poetry or fiction, as a frail vine, clinging to her brother man for support, and dying when deprived of it; and all this may sound well enough to please the imaginations of school-girls, or love-lorn maidens. But woman—the true woman—if you would render her happy, it needs more than the mere development of her affectional nature. Her conscience should be enlightened, her faith in the true and right established, and scope given to her Heaven-endowed and God-given faculties. The true aim of female education should be, not a development of one or two, but all the faculties of the human soul, because no perfect womanhood is developed by imperfect culture. Intense love is often akin to intense suffering, and to trust the whole wealth of a woman's nature on the frail bark of human love, may often be like trusting a cargo of gold and precious gems, to a bark that has never battled with the storm, or buffeted the waves. Is it any wonder, then, that so many life-barks go down, paving the ocean of time with precious hearts and wasted hopes? that so many float around us, shattered and dismasted wrecks? that so many are stranded on the shoals of existence, mournful beacons and solemn warnings for the thoughtless, to whom marriage is a careless and hasty rushing together of the affections? Alas that an institution so fraught with good for humanity would be so perverted, and that state of life, which should be filled with happiness, become so replete with misery. And this was the fate of Laura Lagrange. For a brief period after her marriage her life seemed like a bright and beautiful dream, full of hope and radiant with joy. And then there came a change—he found other attractions that lay beyond the pale of home influences. The gambling saloon had power to win him from her side, he had lived in an element of unhealthy and unhallowed excitements, and the society of a loving wife, the pleasures of a well-regulated home, were enjoyments too tame for one who had vitiated his tastes by the pleasures of sin. There were charmed houses of vice, built upon dead men's loves, where, amid a flow of song, laughter, wine, and careless mirth, he would spend hour after hour, forgetting the cheek that was paling through his neglect, heedless of the tear-dimmed eyes, peering

anxiously into the darkness, waiting, or watching his return.

. . . Home should always be the best school for the affections, the birthplace of high resolves, and the altar upon which lofty aspirations are kindled, from whence the soul may go forth strengthened, to act its part aright in the great drama of life, with conscience enlightened, affections cultivated, and reason and judgment dominant. But alas for the young wife. Her husband had not been blessed with such a home. When he entered the arena of life, the voices from home did not linger around his path as angels of guidance about his steps; they were not like so many messages to invite him to deeds of high and holy worth. The memory of no sainted mother arose between him and deeds of darkness; the earnest prayers of no father arrested him in his downward course: and before a year of his married life had waned, his young wife had learned to wait and mourn his frequent and uncalled-for absence. More than once had she seen him come home from his midnight haunts, the bright intelligence of his eye displaced by the drunkard's stare, and his manly gait changed to the inebriate's stagger; and she was beginning to know the bitter agony that is compressed in the mournful words, a drunkard's wife.

. . . Year after year she wrestled with agony, and strove with despair, till the quick eyes of her brother read, in the paling of her cheek and the dimming eye, the secret anguish of her worn and weary spirit. On that wan, sad face, he saw the death-tokens, and he knew the dark wing of the mystic angel swept coldly around her path. "Laura," said her brother to her one day, "you are not well, and I think you need our mother's tender care and nursing. You are daily losing strength, and if you will go I will accompany you." At first, she hesitated, she shrank almost instinctively from presenting that pale sad face to the loved ones at home. That face was such a tell-tale; it told of heart-sickness, of hope deferred, and the mournful story of unrequited love. But then a deep yearning for home sympathy woke within her a passionate longing for love's kind words, for tenderness and heart-support, and she resolved to seek the home of her childhood, and lay her weary head upon her mother's bosom, to be folded again in her loving arms, to lay that poor, bruised and aching heart where it might beat and throb closely to the loved ones at home. A kind welcome awaited her. All that love and tenderness could devise was done to bring the bloom to her cheek and the light to her eye; but it was all in vain; her's was a disease that no medicine could cure, no earthly balm would heal. It was a slow wasting of the vital forces, the sickness of the soul. The unkindness and neglect of her husband, lay like a leaden weight upon her heart, and slowly oozed away its life-drops. And where was he that had won her love, and then cast it aside as a useless thing, who rifled her heart of its wealth and spread bitter ashes upon its broken altars? He was lingering away from her when the death-damps were gathering on her brow, when his name was trembling on her lips! lingering away! when she was watching his coming, though the death films were gathering before her eyes, and earthly things were fading from her vision. "I think I hear him now," said the dying woman, "surely that is his step;" but the sound died away in the distance. Again she started from an uneasy slumber, "that is his voice! I am so glad he has come." Tears gathered in the eyes of the sad watchers by that dying bed, for they knew that she was deceived. He had not returned. For her sake they wished his coming. Slowly the hours waned away, and then came the sad, soul-sickening thought that she was forgotten, forgotten in the last hour of human need, forgotten when the spirit, about to be dissolved, paused for the last time on the threshold of existence, a weary watcher at the gates of death. "He has forgotten me," again she faintly murmured, and the last tears she would ever shed on earth sprung to her mournful eyes, and clasping her hands together in silent anguish, a few broken sentences issued from her pale and quivering lips. . . . Her cousin turned from that death-bed a sadder and wiser woman. She resolved more earnestly than

ever to make the world better by her example, gladder by her presence, and to kindle the fires of her genius on the altars of universal love and truth. She had a higher and better object in all her writings than the mere acquisition of gold, or acquirement of fame. She felt that she had a high and holy mission on the battle-field of existence, that life was not given her to be frittered away in nonsense, or wasted away in trifling pursuits. She would willingly espouse an unpopular cause but not an unrighteous one. In her the down-trodden slave found an earnest advocate; the flying fugitive remembered her kindness as he stepped cautiously through our Republic, to gain his freedom in a monarchial land, having broken the chains on which the rust of centuries had gathered. Little children learned to name her with affection, the poor called her blessed, as she broke her bread to the pale lips of hunger. Her life was like a beautiful story, only it was clothed with the dignity of reality and invested with the sublimity of truth. True, she was an old maid, no husband brightened her life with his love, or shaded it with his neglect. No children nestling lovingly in her arms called her mother. No one appended Mrs. to her name; she was indeed an old maid, not vainly striving to keep up an appearance of girlishness, when departed was written on her youth. Not vainly pining at her loneliness and isolation: the world was full of warm, loving hearts, and her own beat in unison with them. Neither was she always sentimentally sighing for something to love, objects of affection were all around her, and the world was not so wealthy in love that it had no use for her's; in blessing others she made a life and benediction, and as old age descended peacefully and gently upon her, she had learned one of life's most precious lessons, that true happiness consists not so much in the fruition of our wishes as in the regulation of desires and the full development and right culture of our whole natures.

II. Women's Reform Movements

PERHAPS THE MOST SIGNIFICANT PUBLIC ROLE FOR WOMEN in the antebellum period, particularly during the 1830s and '40s, was that of reformer. Drawing on the moral fervor of the religious revivals of the Second Great Awakening, women crusaded for the reordering of society and for a revolution in personal habits and in public institutions. Most reformers were middle-class white women, although the cause of labor reform drew working women, while the cause of abolition enlisted African-Americans. The primary strategy of reformers was that of "moral suasion": they attempted to shape public policy by convincing an ever-widening circle of people, beginning with relatives and friends but extending to politicians, to improve their behavior simply because it was the right thing to do. A specific public strategy involved circulating petitions to present to state legislatures, collecting signatures for a variety of purposes—from repealing laws allowing the sale of alcohol to ending slavery. Reformers thus inhabited the threshold between woman's traditional private role—attempting to enact social change through the power of moral influence—and a more public role—directly addressing and challenging the laws and policies of the country's political institutions.

The change social reformers wanted to effect was primarily directed at the personal habits of men, but they ended up necessarily criticizing the pervasive and systematic power that men wielded over women. In targeting male drunkenness and debauchery, for instance, crusaders for moral reform and temperance also targeted the structure of the family (in which the husband had virtually absolute power, including the power to ruin his family) and the sexual double standard (in which men could pursue their sexual inclinations with impunity). In their challenge to fundamental gender inequality, then, women reformers evolved into some of the first organized feminists.

A symbol of the pervasive reform of the antebellum era was the utopian community, many of which were established in the 1830s and '40s. "The Nashoba Experiment" (1828) by Frances Wright describes the efforts by one of the most notorious women in the nineteenth century—who, among many other accomplishments, founded a utopian community outside of Memphis. Wright took to the lecture platform in the United States in the late 1820s, years before more conventional women like Angelina and Sarah Grimké made women's public speaking relatively acceptable. Vilified by the press, religious leaders, and even other reformers, Wright was daringly outspoken on the evils of slavery, marriage, capitalism, and authoritarian religion. Wright wanted Nashoba to execute her ideas on these issues, and so in 1825 she secured a piece of land to develop a self-help colony for a group of slaves. Wright insisted that her utopian commune would be not only a haven from slavery but also from marriage law, which she declared "of no force" within the bounds of Nashoba. The community failed within a few years, in part because Wright had no agricultural experience and because most of the slaves associated with it were women and children. After the failure, Wright personally financed the move of thirty black colonists to Haiti in 1830.

Wright's radical plan of reform proved to be an anomaly in its attempt to revolutionize, simultaneously, relations of race, gender, and economics. The mainstream women's reform movements, which finally wielded a much wider influence, had much more limited goals. Mainstream reform essentially began in 1834, with the inception of the New York Female Moral Reform Society. By 1839, having well over 400 female auxiliaries, mostly in New England, the Society decided to redefine itself as a national organization, the American Female Moral Reform Society. As "An Appeal to the Wives, Mothers, and Daughters of Our Land" (1836) illustrates, the moral reformers challenged the sexual double standard and the male license that it condoned. Many reformers targeted prostitution, attempting to shift society's condemnation away from the prostitutes and toward the men who bought their services. They entered brothels to chastise men, and the organ of the Female Moral Reform Society, the *Advocate of Moral Reform*, printed the names of men who frequented disreputable houses. The Society also established a network of women and insisted that its members reform those around them, making it a condition of membership that each woman exclude licentious people of both sexes from her company.

The aim of moral reformers is illustrated by a New York criminal case of 1843, in which Amelia Norman stabbed Henry Ballard, a man who had seduced her and abandoned her to prostitution. Although Ballard did not die, Norman was tried for assault with intent to kill. The Female Moral Reform Society took up the case as support for their efforts to reform sexual laws and practices, and several articles appeared in the *Advocate* arguing that seduced women like Norman would not be driven to crime if the original crime—that of seduction— were punishable by law. Lydia Maria Child, best known for her work in the abolition movement, also took up Norman's case. In "Amelia Norman's Innocence" (1844), Child insists that women's essentially pure nature was being violated by men's unrestrained sexuality—and also that Norman, a fallen woman, could be rehabilitated. In "Who Is Guilty in the Case of Amelia Norman?" (1850), Margaret Fuller indicts not only licentious men but also the social training of women that leads them to value men's flattery, fashion, and excitement. Both documents undermine both male power and the cultural denunciation of fallen women and prostitutes as the sole cause of the nation's decaying moral fabric.

Like the Female Moral Reform Society, the numerous female temperance associations that sprang up in the 1830s and '40s were attempts by women to use their alleged moral and spiritual superiority to control male behavior. Men's abuse of alcohol was an issue integral to the woman's rights movement from its inception. An alcoholic husband was a serious liability for women and their children because of the legal status of married women: the law refused to recognize the rights or property claims of married women. In virtually all states throughout the antebellum period, a man controlled not only the family property but also inheritance and his wife's wages; consequently, a wife had almost no legal recourse if her drunken husband lost all their joint property and even spent her own income.

While temperance organizations canvassed for signatures and sent petitions to state legislatures to prohibit the sale of alcohol, other women found ways outside of voluntary association to wage war on alcoholism. Emma C. Embury's short story "The Ruined Family" (1839) reflects a key strategy in women's fight against male alcoholism and the debauchery to which it seemingly inevitably led: sentimental fiction. Like countless other stories, Embury's "The

Ruined Family" portrays a husband's descent into licentiousness and the havoc that he wreaks on his family. Like other antebellum literary figures, such as Frances Ellen Watkins Harper and Harriet Beecher Stowe, Embury sought to change public policy by swaying and thus enlisting the nation's *feelings* to her cause.

Women's crusades against alcohol were often officially led by men—businessmen and ministers who were not necessarily sympathetic to the demand for woman's rights. Thus the temperance movement was sometimes divided on issues of gender, a fact evidenced by Lucy Stone's "Woman and Temperance" (1853), an address to about 3,000 people who had gathered in the Broadway Tabernacle in New York to demonstrate not only for the cause of temperance but also against the sexism of the World's Temperance Convention. Earlier in the year, official delegates of a state temperance society were asked to leave the apparently inclusive "world's" convention because they were women. Lucy Stone, one of the delegates who was expelled, voices her outrage at the temperance organization's sexual discrimination during a meeting organized to plan a "Whole World's Convention" that—unlike its predecessor—was true to its name.

While moral reform, temperance, dress reform, and abolition were primarily the work of the middle-class woman, working-class women, along with their male counterparts, formed associations that constituted the foundation of the labor movement. The mill-workers' attempts to reform their working conditions took two primary forms. One was represented by the *Lowell Offering*, a magazine written by and for the mill girls of Lowell, Massachusetts—the heart of American textile production. "The Aim of the Offering" (1845), written by the magazine's editor, Harriet Farley, articulates the goal of wiping out the prejudice toward working women by printing stories and articles, written by the factory women of Lowell, which demonstrate their "mental and moral condition." The *Lowell Offering* primarily functioned, like middle-class women's reform, as a kind of moral uplift for the factory workers, while at the same time vindicating both the workers' character and, perhaps most importantly, the worth of women's paid labor. Accused by some, as Farley's editorial indicates, of idealizing the stark realities of factory life, the *Lowell Offering* emphasized the beneficial aspects of factory life for women rather than its degradations.

Farley's decision to exclude labor controversies from her paper came under increasing attack through the 1840s, particularly as the movement to limit the working-day to ten hours gained momentum. In 1845 a labor paper called the *Voice of Industry* appeared in Lowell and the *Lowell Offering* collapsed, reappearing only in 1847 after the failure of the ten-hour movement. The *Voice of Industry* represented the more militant views of the Lowell Female Labor Reform Association and one of its leaders, Sarah Bagley. Bagley's "Speech on Behalf of the Female Labor Reform Association of Lowell" represents the coalition of female and male labor reformers in their attempt to legislate a humane working-day for factory laborers. Bagley was more interested in improving the concrete realities of women's working lives than in legitimating—by idealizing—those lives.

Jane Sophia Appleton's "Sequel to the 'Vision of Bangor in the Twentieth Century'" (1848) contributes to the reform of both labor and gender relations through realizing a utopian society in fiction. The story (set in 1978) is a response to a utopian sketch that denigrates women's ability to function outside the home; countering this vision, Appleton shows how well the whole society functions when women are released from the necessity of domestic work. Instead of depicting women laboring within private homes, Appleton presents a society in which people buy their food at "eating houses," prepared by paid workers who have chosen that particular line of work. Other women are thus free to choose their own line of paid work and are given the time to improve themselves intellectually. Anticipating late nineteenth-century thinkers such as Charlotte Perkins Gilman, Appleton raises an issue that was often overlooked by labor reformers in the antebellum period: the exploitation of women's unpaid labor in the service of their families.

Perhaps the least influential reform movement—but also the one that most directly intersected with the woman's rights movement—was dress reform. Early feminists understood that women's restrictive clothing was both a cause and an effect of larger societal limitations. Symbolic of the dress reform movement was the outfit that was variously called the "reform dress," the "American costume," and "bloomers." While Amelia Jenks Bloomer was not the first to wear bloomers, she popularized the dress in her temperance newspaper, the *Lily*, in 1849 and was inundated with requests for sewing instructions. Bloomer thus took up the cause of the shortened skirt that was worn over Turkish trousers or pantaloons. For a few years the leadership of the woman's rights movement (Stanton, Stone, and Anthony, for instance) took up the cause of dress reform and wore the reform dress. It was a disastrous experiment, however, and speakers at conventions were heckled simply for their appearance. The leadership of the movement decided to subordinate the issue of dress and to return to their long dresses, fearing that their message about women's economic and legal position would be overlooked as their dress was being ridiculed.

It was this retreat of the leaders of the woman's rights movement from dress reform that led to the exchange represented by Lydia Hasbrouck, "Traitors to the Cause of Dress Reform" (1857) and Lucy Stone, "Dress a Consequence of Woman's Vassalage—Not Its Cause" (1857), both published in *The Sibyl*. *The Sibyl: A Review of the Tastes, Errors, and Fashions of Society* was edited by dedicated dress reformer Lydia Hasbrouck between 1856 and 1864. Hasbrouck believed that the abdication of feminist leaders from dress reform—the most fundamental injustice with which women were forced to live, in her opinion—rendered them ineffective proponents of women's rights. Lucy Stone retorts, however, that as long as women must face severe legal and economic inequality, they are in no position to concern themselves with the relatively superficial matter of dress. Despite its marginalization by the mainstream woman's rights movement, dress reform did have a fervent following—evidenced by the numerous letters from women across the country printed regularly in *The Sibyl*, letters such as "Short Hair and Short Dresses" (1857), in which ordinary women testify to how a reformed fashion changed their lives.

36

FRANCES WRIGHT
The Nashoba Experiment
(1828)

This Institution was founded in the autumn of
1825, in the western district of the state of Tennessee, North America, by Frances Wright.

The object of the founder was to attempt
the practice of certain principles, which in
theory had been frequently advocated. She had
observed that the step between theory and practice is usually great,—that while many could
reason, few were prepared to proceed to action,
and that yet mankind must reasonably hesitate
to receive as truths, theories, however ingenious,
if unsupported by experiment. In the individual
who should first attempt an experiment opposed
to all existing opinions and practice, she believed
two requisites to be indispensable,—mental
courage, and, as some writers have defined it, a
passion for the improvement of the human race.
She felt within herself these necessary qualifications; and, strongly convinced of the truth of
the principles, which, after mature consideration, her heart and head had embraced, she
determined to apply all her energies, and to
devote her slender fortune, to the building up
of an institution which should have those principles for its base, and whose destinies,
she fondly hoped, might tend to convince mankind of their moral beauty and practical utility.
Actuated, from her earliest youth, by a passionate interest in the welfare of man, she had peculiarly addressed herself to the study of his past
and present condition. All her observations
tended to corroborate the opinion which her
own feelings might possibly, in the first instance,
have predisposed her to adopt,—*that men are
virtuous, in proportion as they are happy, and happy
in proportion as they are free.* She saw this truth
exemplified in the history of modern as of an-

From *The New-Harmony Gazette*, January and February 1828.

cient times. Every where knowledge, mental
refinement, and the gentler, as the more ennobling, feelings of humanity, have kept pace, influx or reflux, with the growth or depression of
the spirit of freedom.

. . . Political liberty may be said to exist in
the United States of America, and (without adverting to the yet unsettled, though we may
fondly trust secured republics of America's
southern continent) *only there.* Moral liberty
exists *no where.*

By political liberty we may understand the
liberty of speech and of action without incurring the violence of authority or the penalties
of law. By moral liberty may we not understand
the *free exercise of the liberty of speech and of action,*
without incurring the intolerance of popular
prejudice and ignorant public opinion! To secure
the latter where the former liberty exists, what
is necessary "but to will it." Far truer is the assertion as here applied to moral liberty than as
heretofore applied to political liberty. To free
ourselves of thrones, aristocracies and hierarchies, of [indecipherable word] and armies, and
all the arrayed panoply of organized despotism,
it is *not* sufficient to will it. We must fight for it,
and fight for it too with all the odds of wealth,
and power, and position against us. But when
the field is won, to use it is surely ours; and if
the possession of the right of free action inspire
not the courage to exercise the right, liberty has
done but little for us. It is much to have the fetters broken from our limbs, but yet better is it
to have them broken from the mind. It is much
to *have declared* men free and equal, but it shall
be more when they are rendered so; when means
shall be sought and found, and employed to develope all the intellectual and physical powers
of all human beings, without regard to sex or
condition, class, race, nation or color; and when
men shall learn to view each other as members
of one great family, with equal claims to enjoyment and equal capacities for labor and instruction, admitting always the sole differences arising
out of the varieties exhibited in individual organization.

. . . The founder of Nashoba looks not for the conversion of the existing generation; she looks not even for its sympathy. All that she ventures to anticipate is, the cooperation of a certain number of individuals acknowledging the same views with herself; a similar interest in the improvement of man, and a similar intrepidity, to venture all things for his welfare. To these individuals, now scattered throughout the world, and unknown probably to each other, she ventures to address herself. From their union, their cooperation, their exertions, she ventures to expect a successful experiment in favor of human liberty and human happiness. Let them unite their efforts (their numbers will not be too many) and in a country where human speech and human action are free, let them plant their standard in the earth—declare fearlessly their principles, however opposed to the received opinions of mankind, and establish their practice accordingly, with consistence and perseverance.

This has been attempted at Nashoba: not in a spirit of hostility to the practice of the world, but with a strong moral conviction of the superior truth and beauty of that consecrated by the legal act of the founder. By a reference to that act it will be seen that the principles on which the institution is based are those of human liberty and equality without exceptions or limitations,—*and its more especial object, the protection and regeneration of the race of color, universally oppressed and despised in a country self-denominated free.* This more immediate object was selected and specified by the founder, first, because her feelings had been peculiarly enlisted in behalf of the negro; and secondly, because the aristocracy of color is the peculiar vice of the country which she had chosen as the seat of her experiment.

. . . The limits of the present address will not admit of a detailed defence of the principle, and explanation of the practice of cooperative labor. And however great their advantages, the founder of Nashoba views them as entirely subordinate to the one great principle of human liberty, which she believes them calculated to further and secure. She sees in the cooperative system, as it has been termed, *the means,—not the end.* But after mature consideration of its theory and some observation of its practice, believing it the best means yet discovered for securing the one great end, that of human liberty, and equality,—she has for that reason and that reason only, made it the base of the experiment at Nashoba.

The Institution of Nashoba being thus founded on the broad basis of human liberty and equality, every provision made by the legal act of the founder, as well as the subsequent regulations of the trustees are shaped in accordance with it. It will be seen by a reference to that public record, of which it is recommended to attach a copy to this address, that the personal independence of each individual member of the society is effectually secured, and that without disputing the established laws of the country, the institution recognizes *only within its bosom* the force of its own principles.

It is declared in the deed of the founder, that no individual can be received as member, but after a noviciate of six months, and then only by a *unanimous* vote of the resident proprietors. It is also provided that the admission of a husband shall not involve that of a wife, nor the admission of a wife that of a husband, nor the admission of either or both of the parents that of the children *above the age of fourteen.* Each individual must pass through a separate trial, and be received or rejected on the strength of his or her merits or demerits. And, as, in the reception of members, the individual character is the only one recognized, so, by the principles of the society that character can never be forfeited. The marriage law existing without the pale of the Institution, is of no force within that pale. No woman can forfeit her individual rights or independent existence, and no man assert over her any rights or power whatsoever, beyond what he may exercise over her free and voluntary affections; nor, on the other hand, may any woman assert claims to the society or peculiar protection of any individual of the other sex, beyond what mutual inclination dictates and sanctions, while to every individual member of either sex is secured the protection and friendly aid of all.

The tyranny usurped by the matrimonial law over the most sacred of the human affections, can perhaps only be equalled by that of the unjust public opinion, which so frequently stamps with infamy, or condemns to martyrdom the best-grounded and most generous attachments, which ever did honor to the human heart, simply because unlegalized by human ceremonies, equally idle and offensive in the form and mischievous in the tendency.

This tyranny, as now exercised over the strongest and at the same time, if refined by mental cultivation, the noblest of the human passions, had probably its source in religious prejudice, or priestly rapacity, while it has found its plausible and more philosophical apology in the apparent dependence of children on the union of the parents. To this plea it might, perhaps, be replied, that the end, how important soever, is not secured by the means. That the forcible union of unsuitable and unsuited parents can little promote the happiness of the offspring; and supposing the protection of children to be the real source and object of our code of morals and of our matrimonial laws, what shall we say of the effects of these humane provisions on the fate and fortunes of one large family of helpless innocents, born into the world in spite of all prohibitions and persecutions, and whom a cruel law, and yet more cruel opinion, disown and stigmatize. But how wide a field does this topic embrace! How much cruelty—how much oppression of the weak and the helpless does it not involve! The children denominated illegitimate, *or natural,* (as if in contradiction of others who should be *out of nature,* because *under law*) may be multiplied to any number by an unprincipled father, easily exonerated by law and custom from the duties of paternity, while these duties, and their accompanying shame, are left to a mother but too often rendered desperate by misfortune! And should we follow out our review of the law of civilized countries, we shall find the offspring

termed legitimate, with whom honor and power and possession are associated, adjudged, in case of matrimonial dissensions to the father, who by means of this legal claim, has not unfrequently, bowed to servitude the spirit of a fond mother, and held her, as a galley slave, to the oar.

But it is not here that this subject can be discussed in all its bearings. The writer of this article will, however, challenge all the advocates of existing institutions and existing opinions to test them by the secret feelings of their own bosoms, and then to pronounce on their justice. She will challenge them to consider the wide field of human society as now existing, to examine its practice and to weigh its theory, and to pronounce on the consistency of the one and the virtue of the other. She will challenge them to determine how many of the moral evils and numerous family of physical diseases, which now torture the human species, have not their source in the false opinion and vicious institutions which have perverted the best source of human happiness—the intercourse of the sexes—into the deepest source of human misery. Let us look into our streets, our hospitals, our asylums; let us look into the secret thoughts of the anxious parent trembling for the minds and bodies of sons starting into life, or mourning over the dying health of daughters condemned to the unnatural repression of feelings and desires inherent in their very organization and necessary alike to their moral and physical well-being. Or let us look to the victims—not of pleasure, not of love, nor yet of their own depravity, but of those ignorant laws, ignorant prejudices, ignorant code of morals, which condemn one portion of the female sex to vicious excess, another to as vicious restraint, and all to defenceless helplessness and slavery, and generally the whole of the male sex to debasing licentiousness, if not to loathsome brutality.

. . . It is considered that the peculiar object of the founder, *the benefit of the negro race,* may best be consulted by the admission and incorporation of suitable individuals of that and the mixed race on the same principles of equality which guide the admission of all members; and further, that such individuals may best be found, among the *free citizens of color* who form no inconsiderable, and, frequently, a very respectable body in the American population, more especially in that of the southern cities.

As it was the object of the founder to attempt the peaceful influence of example, and silently to correct the practice, and reach the laws through the feelings and the reason of the American people, she carefully forbore from outraging any of the legal provisions in the slave state in which she ventured to attempt her experiment, or those of any of the slave states with which she is acquainted, and trusted confidently to the national good sense, and to the liberality fostered by the national institutions for the safety of any experiment however opposed to the national prejudices, which should be undertaken in a spirit of kindliness to all men, and conducted within the limits of private, or, as in the present case, of *associate* property.

It is not supposed that (with some rare exceptions) human beings raised under the benumbing influence of brutal slavery can be elevated to the level of a society based upon the principles of moral liberty and voluntary cooperation. The experiment therefore as respects the *slave* population, it is intended to limit, at Nashoba, to the first purchase of the founder, excepting in cases where planters becoming members, may wish to place their negroes under the protection of the Institution. And looking to effect the more especial object of the Institution through the present free race of color, and, more especially, by the education of colored children, the founder judged that she should best conciliate the laws of the southern states and the popular feeling of the whole union, as well as the interests of the emancipated negro, by providing for the colonization of all slaves emancipated by the Society in a free country without the limits of the United States. Personal observation had taught her the danger of la[u]nching a freed slave into the midst of an in-

imical population. And if unfit, as he must of necessity be, for incorporation into the society as a free proprietor, it appeared consistent with justice and humanity to enforce his being sent to a country of safety for his color when ejected from the protection of the Institution.

While fondly looking to the regeneration of America's citizens of color, the writer of this address believes that *slavery* may safely be left to work its own ruin.

37

THE NEW YORK FEMALE MORAL REFORM SOCIETY
An Appeal to the Wives, Mothers, and Daughters of Our Land (1836)

BELOVED SISTERS:—

We come before you now, not to ask your assistance in an untried experiment, but to give you the high privilege of becoming fellow-laborers with us, in a cause which is already triumphing, and is *destined* to triumph, until the floods of pollution are stayed, and the whole earth purified by the Spirit of the Lord.

In our efforts hitherto, we have had to contend not *only,* or *mainly,* with ignorance and vice.—They are our natural foes, and we had counted the cost of their opposition, and made up our minds accordingly. But we had a right to expect the co-operation of the virtuous and intelligent, of all who are seeking to effect the removal of sin and suffering, and the universal prevalence of purity and holiness. Our Society has these great objects expressly in view. It would save the inexperienced by warning them of their danger; and if it has failed to secure the entire

From *An Appeal to the Wives, Mothers and Daughters of Our Land, In the City and the Country, Earnestly and Affectionately Presented, by the Ladies of the New-York Female Moral Reform Society* (New-York: H. R. Piercy, 1836), 3–5, 7–9, 11.

confidence and approbation of any portion of the Christian community, we are confident it is because its claims have been overlooked or misunderstood by them. . . .

The Duty of Mothers to their Children.

MOTHER! while you are hesitating about your duty in reference to this matter, or it may be, totally *regardless* of it, think not that the future destiny of the children you so tenderly love will be uninfluenced by your decision. You may consider them safe beneath your sheltering wing, and guarded by your vigilant eye; but *facts* have taught us the contrary. They are exposed to corrupting influences where you least suspect it, and their minds may be incurably tainted in very early childhood. If our limits permitted, we could lay before you instances of deep and thrilling interest, which show the dangers to which even infant purity is constantly exposed. To *you,* as Mothers, is committed in a special manner the formation of the character of your children; you are their best and safest friend, and to you they look for counsel and example. We ask you, then, in the name of Him to whom you are responsible for this interesting charge, is it not a *paramount* duty to fortify their minds against the temptations to which they will inevitably be exposed? Ought you not in the *nursery* to sow the seeds of chastity and virtue, and to build up a wall of principle around these little ones, which shall stand in coming years, to beat back the surges of corruption? Say not, "The subject is so delicate we dare not meddle with it, lest we should do more harm than good in the attempt." You are not at *liberty* to keep back any part of the counsel of God against this sin. He has spoken plainly, and if you refuse to repeat his instructions, it is as palpable an act of disobedience as the transgression of the command, "Thou shalt not kill." How many have been ruined by disease, and covered with infamy, who might now have been ornaments to society, had their minds been early strengthened against temptation by the prayerful instructions of a tender and judi-

cious mother! The unhappy young man who is charged with murdering his wretched paramour in cold blood, and has thus exposed himself to the penalty of his country's violated law, was once an innocent boy—the pride and hope of the parents who must now go down mourning to the grave. Mother! what shall secure your child from the snares into which so many have fallen? . . .

Claims of the Cause.

We would likewise earnestly and affectionately ask your support and assistance in the arduous work to which we are devoted; and, beloved sisters, we are confident we shall not ask in vain. When you remember the 15,000 females annually sacrificed on the altar of lust, and the dreadful career of crime which reduces the period of their existence to an average of about five years, you must, you *will* feel the importance of united and vigorous exertion, to roll back this deadly flood, which is threatening to overwhelm all that is dear and valuable. As a Society, we need your influence in the cause of Moral Reform[.] . . .

Duty of Unmarried Females.

Upon your regard and attention, dear young friends, we feel that this cause has great and special claims. You belong to the class particularly exposed to the artifices of the destroyer, and in your hands are the principal weapons of defence. While you smile on the fashionable libertine—while you admit him to your presence, and receive his proffered attentions—our efforts to effect a reformation in public sentiment, will be comparatively in vain. Would you associate familiarly with one whom you know to be a thief, or a murderer? You turn away with disgust from the mere supposition; and is it then in your estimation a crime of less magnitude to steal from the trusting female, the priceless gem of honor and virtue, and expose her immortal soul to all the horrors of the second death?

Away with that sickly sentimentalism, which spends all its energies in weeping over fictitious woes, while it looks with utter indifference on the sin and suffering by which it is surrounded. Let us call things by their right names, and shun vice in its alluring, as well as in its most disgusting forms. Much is now depending on the stand taken by young ladies, individually and collectively, upon the question of Moral Reform. If you come boldly out on the side of purity and virtue, your influence will be felt to the remotest corners of our country. . . .

When the ignorance and prejudice of community are enlightened and subdued, and the overwhelming *facts* which daily come to our knowledge, are laid before them, we can safely leave the cause to make its own way to their hearts and consciences. For this purpose we commend to your attention the "ADVOCATE OF MORAL REFORM," and request you not only to take it yourselves, but to assist us in extending its circulation. We do this, believing it to be the most efficient way in which your assistance can at present be given, and one which falls peculiarly within your province. Every day brings fresh testimony from all quarters, to the value and usefulness of this paper; and by making it known still more widely, you may do much to reclaim and bless mankind.

Endeavor, as far as your influence extends to form Auxiliary Societies.

We need not enlarge on the superior advantages of organized effort over individual exertion. The minds of the community are in some degree awake to the importance of the subject, and our hearts are cheered by the frequent intelligence of the formation of new societies. Still, while we thank God and take courage, we would not disguise the fact, that comparatively *little* has yet been done. The field is wide enough for the exercise of the most expanded benevolence, for it is literally, "THE WORLD."

CONSTITUTION OF THE NEW-YORK FEMALE MORAL REFORM SOCIETY

Whereas, The sin of licentiousness has made fearful havoc in the world, "corrupting all flesh," drowning souls in perdition, and exposing us to the vengeance of a holy God, whose law in this respect has been trampled on almost universally, not only by actual transgression, but by the tacit consent of the virtuous, and by the almost perfect silence of those whom He has commanded to "cry aloud and spare not;"

And whereas, It is the duty of the virtuous to use every consistent moral means to save our country from utter destruction: We do, therefore, form ourselves into a Society for this ob[j]ect, to be governed by the following[:]

Article I

This Society shall be called "THE NEW-YORK FEMALE MORAL REFORM SOCIETY," auxiliary to the "American Society for promoting the observance of the Seventh Commandment."

Article II

This Society shall have for its object the prevention of licentiousness, by diffusing light in regard to the existence and great extent of the sin; by showing its fearfully immoral and soul-destroying influence; by pointing out the numberless lures and arts practised by the unprincipled destroyer, to seduce and ruin the unsuspecting; by excluding from social intercourse with us, all persons of both sexes who are known to be of licentious habits; and by such other means as the Society shall from time to time deem expedient.

Article III

This Society shall consist of those ladies who cordially approve of its object, sign its Constitution, and pledge themselves not to admit into their society any persons of either sex known to be licentious, and who statedly contribute to its funds. . . .

38

LYDIA MARIA CHILD
Amelia Norman's Innocence (1844)

The conduct of the prisoner, during the trial, was marked by a beautiful propriety. Sad and subdued, she made no artificial appeals to sympathy, and showed no disposition to consider herself a heroine of romance. When the verdict was given, she became very faint and dizzy, and for some time after seemed stunned and bewildered. Her health is much shattered by physical suffering and mental excitement; but her constitution is naturally good, and under the influence of care and kindness the process of renovation goes rapidly on. She is evidently a girl of strong feelings, but quiet, reserved, and docile to the influences of those she loves. A proper education would have made her a noble woman. I sometimes fear that, like poor Fleur de Marie, she will never be able to wash from her mind the "stern inexorable Past." It pains her to speak or think of her child. The fountain of maternal love has been poisoned at the source. I shall never forget the mournful smile with which she said, "I don't know as it was worth while to try to make any thing of me. I am nothing but a wreck." "Nay, Amelia," replied I, "noble vessels may be built from the timbers of a wreck."

The more I see of her, the more my hope is strengthened that her native energies and strong affections may be restored and purified, to aid and bless society, instead of being returned a danger and a curse, as she would have been had she been sent to Sing Sing. As for a pardon, in case an unfavorable verdict had been rendered, I had little hope that it would have been obtained,

From the *New York Post,* February 1, 1844.

though Mr. Sandford held out that idea to the jury. The strenuous effort to make her appear a great deal worse than she ever was, assuredly did not proceed entirely from a regard to public order. Ballard [her seducer and the plaintiff] had friends likely to exert a strong influence with the ruling powers; and their active opposition to her being released for a while on bail showed that it would be no fault of theirs if she were not safely locked up in prison for a long time.

The public sympathy manifested in this case has cheered my hopes, and increased my respect for human nature. When the poor girl returned to her cell, after her acquittal, some of the judges, several of the jury, her lawyers, and the officers of the prison gathered around her to express congratulation and sympathy. There was something beautiful in the compassionate respect with which they treated this erring sister, because she was unfortunate and wretched. . . .

The hours I spent in that hateful building [the Tombs], awaiting the opening of this case, were very sad to me. It was exceedingly painful to see poor, ragged beggars summarily dismissed to the penitentiary, for petit larcenies [sic]; having the strong conviction ever present in my mind, that all society [was] carrying on a great system of fraud and theft, and that these poor wretches merely lacked the knowledge and cunning necessary to keep theirs under legal protection.

The Egyptian architecture, with its monotonous recurrence of the straight line and the square, its heavy pillars, its cavernous dome of massive rings, its general expression of overpowering strength, is well suited to a building for such a purpose. But the graceful palm leaves, intertwined with lotus blossoms, spoke soothingly to me of the occasional triumph of the moral sentiments over legal technicalities, and of beautiful bursts of eloquence from the heart. Moreover, I remember that time had wrought such changes in opinion, that thousands of convents have been converted into manufactories and primary schools; and I joyfully prophesied the day when regenerated society would have no more need of prisons. The Tombs, with its style of architecture too subterranean for picture galleries or concert rooms, may then be reserved for fossil remains and mineralogical cabinets.

39

MARGARET FULLER
Who Is Guilty in the Case of Amelia Norman? (1850)

Soon after, I met a circle of women, stamped by society as among the most degraded of their sex. "How," it was asked of them, "did you come here?" for, by the society that I saw in the former place, they were shut up in a prison. The causes were not difficult to trace: love of dress, love of flattery, love of excitement. They had not dresses like the other ladies, so they stole them; they could not pay for flattery by distinctions, and the dower of a worldly marriage, so they paid by the profanation of their persons. In excitement, more and more madly sought from day to day, they drowned the voice of conscience.

Now I ask you, my sisters, if the women at the fashionable house be not answerable for those women being in the prison?

As to position in the world of souls, we may suppose the women of the prison stood fairest, both because they had misused less light, and because loneliness and sorrow had brought some of them to feel the need of better life, nearer truth and good. This was no merit in them, being an effect of circumstance, but it was hopeful. But you, my friends (and some of you I have already met), consecrate yourselves without waiting for reproof, in free love and unbroken energy, to win and to diffuse a better life. Offer beauty, talents, riches, on the altar; thus shall ye keep spotless your own hearts, and be visibly or invisibly the angels to others.

From *Woman in the Nineteenth Century* (London: George Slater, 1850), 138–140.

I would urge upon those women who have not yet considered this subject, to do so. Do not forget the unfortunates who dare not cross your guarded way. If it do not suit you to act with those who have organized measures of reform, then hold not yourself excused from acting in private. Seek out these degraded women, give them tender sympathy, counsel, employment. Take the place of mothers, such as might have saved them originally.

If you can do little for those already under the ban of the world, and the best considered efforts have often failed, from a want of strength in those unhappy ones to bear up against the sting of shame and the prejudices of the world, which makes them seek oblivion again in their old excitements, you will at least leave a sense of love and justice in their hearts that will prevent their becoming utterly embittered and corrupt. And you may learn the means of prevention for those yet uninjured. There will be found in a diffusion of mental culture, simple tastes, best taught by your example, a genuine self-respect, and, above all, what the influence of man tends to hide from woman, the love and fear of a divine, in preference to a human, tribunal.

But suppose you save many who would have lost their bodily innocence (for as to mental, the loss of that is incalculably more general) through mere vanity and folly; there still remain many, the prey and spoil of the brute passions of man. For the stories frequent in our newspapers outshame antiquity, and vie with the horrors of war.

As to this, it must be considered that, as the vanity and proneness to seduction of the imprisoned women represented a general degradation in their sex, so do these acts a still more general and worse in the male. When so many are weak, it is natural there should be many lost, where legislators admit that ten thousand prostitutes are a fair proportion to one city, and husbands tell their wives that it is folly to expect chastity from men, it is inevitable that there should be many monsters of vice.

I must in this place mention, with respect

and gratitude, the conduct of Mrs. Child in the case of Amelia Norman. The action and speech of this lady was of straight-forward nobleness, undeterred by custom or cavil from duty towards an injured sister. She showed the case and the arguments the counsel against the prisoner had the assurance to use, in their true light to the public. She put the case on the only ground of religion and equity. She was successful in arresting the attention of many who had before shrugged their shoulders, and let sin pass as necessarily a part of the company of men. They begin to ask whether virtue is not possible, perhaps necessary, to man as well as to woman. They begin to fear that the perdition of a woman must involve that of a man. This is a crisis. The results of this case will be important.

40
EMMA C. EMBURY
The Ruined Family (1839)

One of the most picturesque spots in the United States, is the little village of Malden. . . .

Among the many pretty dwellings which adorned the village was a low-roofed farmhouse, built on the gentle slope of a hill, and so completely embosomed in trees, that, when seen from the distant winding road, it almost seemed suspended, between the green sward and the foliage. This peculiarity in its appearance, together with its sheltered and secluded situation, had obtained for it the fanciful appellation of the Bird's Nest; and never was a title more appropriately bestowed: for at the time when I first beheld it, harmony and love were indeed its gentle habitants. I had been spending a few days in the neighbourhood of Malden, and had been much attracted by the beauty of the spot, when my interest was still further heightened by the discovery that the mistress of the Bird's Nest

From *Religious Souvenir* (New York: Scofield and Voorhies, 1839).

cottage was an early schoolmate and friend. We hastened to renew our early acquaintance; and I was no less pleased than surprised to find the laughing, merry-hearted hoyden of my recollection, transformed into the quiet, gentle wife and careful mother. I shall never forget the hours I spent in that sweet cottage. Mrs. Morison possessed exceeding beauty of person, and her four children resembled her very strongly; so that when her husband, a fine looking, farmerlike man, took his seat among them, a more perfect family group could scarcely be imagined. I never looked at the sweet face of the mother as she pressed to her bosom her youngest darling, without being involuntarily reminded of Raphael's Madonna. Of Mr. Morison I saw but little, for his daily labours in the field left him so little time to enjoy his domestic pleasures, that I felt they ought to be sacred from the intrusion of a stranger. What I have since learned of his character, and the after fortunes of the family, has been derived from other sources than personal observation.

During three generations the Bird's Nest cottage had been in the possession of the Morison family; and though its inmates had not escaped the misfortunes which ever await humanity—though its doors had been opened for the funeral procession as well as for the bridal—though its chambers had echoed to the moan of bodily suffering and the wail of sorrow, as well as to the ringing laugh of childhood, and the merry song of light-hearted youth, still the spirit of piety dwelt ever within its walls, and faith in the wisdom of Almighty providence had soothed every sorrow and heightened every joy. At the time of his father's death, Frank Morison had scarcely attained the age of manhood; but the precepts of that pious father had not been uttered to a regardless ear. Possessed of talents superior to the most of his companions, and an affectionate heart filled with the most generous impulses; guided, too, by the recollection of his father's noble nature, and by the watchful tenderness of his widowed mother, Frank Morison entered upon the duties of life with the fairest prospect of success. But as the stateliest tree often bears within its bosom the germ of its own destruction, so there was one defect in his character which threatened to neutralize all his higher qualities. This fault was indecision. His good-nature made it almost impossible for him to judge impartially of men and things. Persuasion was an irresistible weapon when exerted against him, and therefore it happened that, notwithstanding his good principles and his deep reverence for religion, his facile and vacillating temper constantly led him into error. Whatever might have been his defects of judgment, he was certainly not deceived in his choice of a wife. The orphan daughter of a country clergyman, she united the natural gift of beauty and the acquired graces of education with the habits of industry and order, so essential to man's household comforts. She loved her husband with a deep and earnest affection, which, while it did not prevent her from seeing his faults, led her upon all occasions to conceal, and at proper seasons to correct them. Her influence over him was never exerted, except to guard him against himself; and but for the occurrence of circumstances which all her foresight could not prevent, Frank Morison might have gone down to his grave without dreaming of the latent evil which was garnered in his heart. Alas! who of us can say to the transgressor, "stand aside, for I am holier than thou?" who can be sure that he would have resisted the temptation before which his neighbour fell? who may dare assert that he could have touched pitch, and not borne away the defilement of the open sinner?

Twelve years of wedded happiness had glided away so rapidly that, but for the little ones who gathered around his board, Frank Morison would scarcely have realized their number. His mother, enjoying a green old age, still occupied the "ingle nook;" his wife, scarcely less fair than in the days of her girlhood, still ministered to the comfort of all, and diffused her influence among them as gently as the night-dew dispenses freshness. Respected by all his neighbours for his uncompromising integrity; beloved for his

yielding, good nature, which, though a failing, still "leaned to virtue's side;" happy in his domestic circle and prosperous in his worldly affairs, Morison felt that God had indeed dealt to him "blessings with a full hand."

Unfortunately for many a family, a tavern, bearing the enticing name of the Farmer's Retreat, was at this time established on the outskirts of the village. The landlord, an idle, thriftless, but good-natured fellow; one of those men who are to be found in all communities, and are regarded with a sort of contemptuous pity, as "nobody's enemy but their own," was well known to the inhabitants, among whom his social qualities had unhappily made him a general favourite. His house soon became a place of frequent resort; and although the Farmer's Retreat, standing in the midst of a naked field, with its unsheltered porch and scarlet curtained windows, seemed but little inviting to those who were accustomed to seek repose beneath their own roof-tree, still many were found who, from their mental vacuity, sought companionship, and who knew no other relaxation from toil, than in dissipation.

Frank Morison had never entered the doors of a tavern in his life; for he was not a man to seek out evil, though too apt to yield to temptation if it beset him in the way. He was at first excessively annoyed at the establishment of such a place in the village, and declared in the most positive terms, that nothing should induce him to countenance it. Unluckily for his good resolutions, it became convenient to hold the assemblages for public business within its walls, and as he occupied a prominent station among the chief men of the village, he felt himself obliged to go with the multitude. How many there are, who by their daily virtues, have climbed [a prominence] which crumbles beneath their feet, because it is formed only of the sand of this world's wilderness! How many are there, who owe their final ruin to the self-reliance which they learned in the absence of temptation! It was during a season of political excitement that Morison first found himself resorting to the tavern, not for the transaction of business, but to hear the news. He felt that he was doing wrong, and he resolved to desist as soon as *the election was over*. The old stratagem of the enemy, procrastination, was put in force; and satisfying his conscience with a belief in his own good intentions, he persevered in the paths of danger. The influence of his wife and mother was now exerted in vain. Led away by political excitement, he fancied that his duty as a patriot demanded the sacrifice of his time and thoughts, to the petty concerns of the narrow circle within which he moved.

At length the hour of weakness came. The tempter was at hand, and Morison put the poisoned cup to his lips. Unaccustomed to the potent draught, his senses were soon overpowered, and he was persuaded to taste a second time. That night he was borne to his home in a state of helpless intoxication.

Words cannot describe the pangs of the wife and mother, at such a spectacle. Alas! what language could depict the bitter shame, the agonizing grief of her who had vowed to *honour* that humbled being; or worse, far worse, the utter misery of the mother who had purchased that child almost with her life; who had regarded him as the joy of her young years, and the stay of her old age, when she beheld him thus degraded to the level of the beasts that perish! Many a time had sorrow abode within that cottage, but never before had its inmates sat down with shame as their companion. It was a bitter trial, and the accents of prayer were uttered that night in the voice of agony. When Morison awoke next morning from the deep sleep which had enchained all his faculties, he was overwhelmed with sorrow and remorse. His aching head and languid frame forbade him to seek his healthful task in the fields, and, confined to the seclusion of his own chamber, he had time for reflection, even to madness. If simple penitence could cleanse one from the defilement of evil, Frank Morison would have been pure as the little one that clasped his knees; but, alas! he trusted too much in his own strength, forgetting that the "race is

not to the swift nor the battle to the strong," and that "by strength shall no man prevail."

What human eye can discern—what human hand portray, the gradual progress of evil in the heart of man? Who can mark the various gradations, from the first transgression, to the crowning sin? the weakness which yields to the guilt of others? the evil propensities which, once gratified, demand a second indulgence? the rapid hardening of the feelings? the dominant selfishness? the oblivion of all social affections? and finally the total abandonment of body and soul to the demon power of the besetting sin? Such a research is like groping among the festering corses of the dead, to trace the causes of the pestilence: the very contact is pollution.

It was on a peaceful Sabbath evening, just three years after the scene I have just described, that Frank Morison reaped the first-fruits of his repeated sins. Stretched on the bed of death, lay his aged mother. Heartsickness and sorrow, had done the work which time delayed to perform. Life was almost extinct, yet her restless eye wandered over the group which gathered round her pillow, as if it found not the object it most sought. There stood Mrs. Morison, pale and emaciated, bearing in her arms a puny infant; while four children, from the thoughtful little girl of twelve years, to the little one of three summers, silently gazed on the beloved countenance of the departing. But he, who should have closed the glazing eye—he, who should have heard the latest whisper of maternal love—the son—was not there. Wildly and sadly did the dying woman call upon her child, while the spirit seemed only lingering in its earthly tenement to bestow on him a blessing. At length he came; with the bloated form, the bloodshot eye, and reeling gait of habitual intemperance, he staggered into the room. His mother's dying blessing fell upon his dull ear and not yet hardened heart, like drops of molten fire; he retired from the chamber of death with all the horrors of an awakened conscience, and drained the poisoned cup of oblivion, until reason was again overthrown.

The death of his mother removed the only barrier which lay between him and destruction. During her life, the farm and cottage were unalienable; but he had already borrowed money upon it to its full value; so that no sooner was she laid in her grave than his creditors came forward and took immediate possession. The comforts which once belonged to the sweet spot had long since vanished. Every thing that could procure money to purchase selfish gratification had disappeared; and Mrs. Morison prepared to leave her home of happier years, with a calmness almost approaching to despair. With a heavy heart, but an unmoved countenance, she took her babe in her arms, and set out on her melancholy journey towards another shelter. Her half-clothed children bore the little that remained of all their many comforts, while her husband walked on in sullen and dogged silence; or only opened his lips to utter an impatient oath. Once, and only once, did her feelings overpower her. An aged wayfarer, struck with the singular appearance of the little group, paused to question them, and minister to their necessities. While Mrs. Morison lingered, one of the little ones stooped to pluck the wild flowers that grew beside the road. The soothing words of the old man; the sense of her desolate condition, and the utter unconsciousness of her helpless little ones, struck upon her heart with irresistible force, and she burst into a passion of tears.

"God made the country, and man made the town;" and O! how different do the evils of life appear, when viewed from among the beneficent gifts of Providence or the selfish works of man. The physical frame may suffer as acutely from want, in one place, as in another; but the squalid misery which surrounds poverty in a great city, is certainly not its concomitant in the country. There the poor have at least the free air and light of heaven; the fresh green sward, and the pure waters as they well up from the depths of the earth. But in the haunts of wretchedness which are appropriated to them, among the works of man, even those free gifts of heaven are denied; and surrounded by a thousand luxurious comforts which they cannot buy, the poor learn new lessons of selfishness. A miserable hovel in the suburbs of a neighbouring town was now the abode of the ruined family; and Mrs. Morison sought, by the labour of her hands, to supply the necessities of her famishing children.

In order that he might obtain the means of intoxication, Frank Morison became the attendant upon a tavern in the neighbourhood, and thus, as his wife thought, filled up the measure of his degradation. For many a weary month did the unhappy woman toil, to save her children from starvation. Sometimes weeks would elapse without any tidings of her husband; and he never came home except to demand her hard earnings, to supply his thirst after the intoxicating draught. The early principles of morality and piety in his heart had been like the seed sown by the way-side, which the fowls of the air devoured. Love for his family had long since been forgotten, in selfish gratification and sinful indulgence. His wife had learned to tremble at his approach, and his children, they who were wont to greet his coming with the kiss of innocent affection, now cowered into a corner, terrified at his rough caresses or harsh rebukes.

But the final harvest of sin was not yet gathered in. "He that, being often reproved, hardeneth his neck, shall suddenly be destroyed, and that without remedy." Mrs. Morison had resigned herself to suffering, and vainly thought that it would be impossible to add fresh bitterness to the cup of shame and sorrow which she was drinking to the dregs; but she was destined to a far greater trial than any she had yet encountered. One dark and stormy night, as she sat lulling to sleep her sick babe, and watching the disturbed slumbers of her hungry children as they tossed restlessly upon their wretched beds, she was startled by her husband's sudden entrance. To her great surprise, he was perfectly sober, but his countenance was frightfully pale, and his eyes glared with a light that seemed almost like insanity. Totally regardless of her anxious inquiries, he flung himself on the bed, beside his children, and slept, or feigned sleep. But in less than an hour afterwards the room was filled with fierce and angry faces; the voice of indignation aroused him, and he started up to find himself in the midst of the officers of justice, branded as a robber and murderer! Who could have foreseen such a result of one false step? Who would have supposed the mantling cup of pleasure would so soon have been exchanged, for the black and poisoned chalice of guilt?

For six weeks, Morison lay in prison awaiting his trial. When the appointed day arrived, one of his two confederates, and (as it generally happens) by far the most guilty, turned state['s] evidence, and detailed the whole affair. It appeared that a plan had been concerted by two well known villains, to rob the house of a rich old gentleman, who was known to have always a large sum of money about him. To make sure of their booty, they required another companion, and Morison was selected. They effected an entrance into the house, but met with more resistance than they had expected. A shot was fired, and at the same moment Morison's pistol accidentally went off. The old man was killed, but, whether by the unintentional discharge of Frank's pistol, or the deadly aim of his companion, could never be ascertained. The guilt of the robbery, however, was too evident to admit of a doubt; and the sentence of the court condemned him to solitary imprisonment for one year, and confinement at hard labour for the remainder of his life.

Debarred from the pernicious stimulants which had been, as it were, the nutriment of his wretched life, he was now fully sensible of the awful reaction, which must ever come upon the shattered nerves and weakened mind of the intemperate. Shut up in utter solitude, with nothing save the Bible to win him from his dreadful recollections, he seemed to take a strange delight in seeking out from its sacred pages all the most fearful denunciations against sinners. The promises of God were to him as idle words; his threatenings were like two-edged swords. This terrible conflict of feeling, "this fearful looking-for of judgment and fiery indignation," were too

much for the enfeebled brain of the wretched drunkard. He was removed from the cells of guilt, only to become the tenant of a madhouse. To the ravings of insanity succeeded the quiet and hopeless imbecility, which yields to no human skill. He lingered for more than ten years an *idiot,* and then sunk to death as a child would fall asleep; totally unconscious of the awful change which awaited him. Such was the fate of the affectionate, the kindhearted, but weak-principled Frank Morison; and while we shrink from his errors and his crimes, let us bless God, who has sheltered us from similar temptations, and strengthened us in the hour of need.

Mrs. Morison and her children found, in the far west, a refuge from poverty and disgrace. The prosperity of her later years may remind her sometimes of the happiness of early days; but alas! nothing can obliterate from her mind the remembrance of blighted affections and blasted youth. To her, "sorrow" had indeed been knowledge, and she had learned to say, in the language of the prophet:

"Although the fig tree shall not blossom, neither shall fruit be in the vines; the labour of the olive shall fail, and the field yield no meat; the flock be cut off from the fold, and there be no herd in the stalls: yet I will rejoice in the Lord, I will joy in the God of my salvation."

41

LUCY STONE

Woman and Temperance, Address to the Whole World's Temperance Convention (1853)

The speaker who preceded me said he did not dream, coming up from a slave-holding state, that, when we met in Brick Church Chapel the other morning, to call a World's Temperance

From *The Whole World's Temperance Convention, Held at Metropolitan Hall in the City of New York, September 1st and 2nd, 1853* (New York: Fowlers and Wells, 1853), 66–70.

Convention, that any such issue would take place. It is not for me to say what I dreamed of, or thought of. We were there as those who have a deep interest in the cause of Temperance. We went there without any claim beyond that allowed us by the call; and when a noble man nominated noble women to serve on a Committee, throughout the audience were heard cries of "Order!" and motions to "adjourn." Women, they said, had no business there. Women! the sisters of those who were the wives of drunkards. Women! the sisters of those who were the daughters of drunkards. Women! the sisters of those who, by all natural ties, were bound to men who despised them, and had involved them in ruin; these Women were there, and were told by Doctors of Divinity that it was no place for them! (Applause.) We didn't moot the question of Women's Rights; we simply asked that when the whole world came together Women should be recognized as part of the world, and have a right to meet in council with our brothers there. And one grey-haired Minister, the Rev. Dr. Hewitt, who, if he is present, will not be ashamed to have me repeat what he said, if he was not ashamed to say it, began discussing the question of Woman's Rights—and said, it was "improper," &c., for woman to take part in these proceedings; quoted Paul—said, that all usage was against us; that it was not easy for him to change from what he has always thought and taught. I know it is not easy for an old man, who has not kept his soul open to God's sun-shine and rain-drops, to change. But if he did not believe we had any right there, he should not in the call, have invited *all friends of Temperance* to come together.

. . . One man said: "we value woman, and we could not do without her." When we went to Metropolitan Hall, I found *how* they value us—namely, just as they value their horses, or their oxen, for the work they can get out of us. (Laughter.) At that convention, when there came to be a resolution voted upon, Dr. Patten said, that he hoped gentlemen and *ladies* would all vote."Yes, they valued us there, because we could

give strength to their resolutions. And we were also told that our *contributions* were highly valued! So after having voted us out of the Brick Church—after having insulted every man's mother and sister—they came to Metropolitan Hall, and asked ladies to contribute in their behalf! Yes, this is the way they value us, to raise funds to pay their salaries—and what other bills I don't know.

. . . I presume I look upon no person here who has not seen the face of the drunkard's wife or daughter, who, when the fire had gone out on her hearth-stone, the light of hope in her soul presented indeed a spectacle for the pity and sympathy of the world. I saw the wife of a drunkard, who was so cruelly beaten by her husband, that she was blackened all over with blows; that woman, when telling her sad tale of woe to a friend, spite of herself, found the big tear drops rolling down her cheeks, and the great grief of her heart in vain endeavoring to find utterance. This woman, and others in her circumstances, comes to the Brick Church, and asks to be saved from this brutal treatment, from these cruel blows; but Mayor Barstow says, in reply to her, you cannot sit in this body; and Dr. Hewitt tells her she is out of her place.

. . . I say when a man sees thirty thousand drunkards go down to an unhonored grave every year; when he sees their wives and children; when he sees a society like ours, endeavoring to do away with these evils, and he says "No; let the widow wail on, And the child shall remain the child of a drunkard"—what do you think of the sincerity of such a man? (Applause.) Whoever is the friend of a cause is glad of helpers from any source, and he who is true to his convictions as a temperance advocate, will even accept the aid of children. He who is a real friend of the cause, will say welcome, thrice welcome to those who come to put out the fire that burns in the distillery, and destroys the lives of our brothers and husbands. Why this opposition, then, to women? Does it not come from those who are opposed to reform, and who would stay the progress of the race. They say that there is

no precedent for Woman's interference in public affairs. Are we to have nothing but what we
have a precedent for? There was a time when
we had no precedents for steam or railroads;
and, certainly, as there was no precedent from
discoveries in her time, Isabella was a naughty
fool to have assisted Columbus—for, had she
not, America might never have been discovered,
nor would we be disputing about precedents in
a land which was discovered against all precedent. "My soul is not a palace of the past; I have
no fear of what is called for by the instinct of
the race."Whoever opens his ears, hears everywhere the cry for reform; it comes over the
ocean from every village and hamlet of the Old
World; the newspaper is scarcely dry, before the
reform it records is followed on its heels by another; and while every reform is rendering
woman more free, she shall not come to the
World's Convention as a helper, if Mayor
Barstow, who thinks "more of women than most
men," can prevent her. I know there are men
who are willing to ignore the existence of
woman and her rights, making them inferior to
their own; but they are not *men* who act in that
way, and we will appeal from them to those who
are willing to treat us justly, and to whom we
shall not appeal in vain, when we show that there
are sad hearts to be comforted, and erring minds
to be reformed. Now, I say, men and women of
New York, or from whatever quarter of the
world you come, whether you like it or not—
whether you say "God bless" or "God curse"—
whether you give us the right hand of fellowship,
or turn your back in scorn—whether you write
us down as unwomanly women, and unfit to live,
or what you please; so long as there is one
mother that leads by the hand a drunkard, and
the child of a drunkard; so long as one tear-drop
comes from her eye; so long as one man cannot
feel enough reverence for his own soul to stay
away from the wine cup, so long will we, in season and out of season, in highways and byways,
in public and private places, wherever we can
find an ear to hear, we will there speak; (tre-

mendous applause) and no man, or set of men,
no woman or set of women shall ever hinder us.

42

HARRIET FARLEY
The Aim of the *Offering* (1845)

THE AIM OF THE OFFERING. What is the aim
of the Offering? is a question frequently asked,
and one which we have often answered. But, as
the commencement of each volume brings us
in communion with a large proportion of new
patrons, we trust our old friends will not be
impatient if they then meet with a "twice-told
tale."

"What the object is, which we would fain
accomplish, need not be particularly specified.
All our readers are aware of the prejudice, which
has long existed, against the manufacturing females of New England—a prejudice which, in
this country, should never have been harbored
against any division of the laboring population,
and that many circumstances, and the exertions
of many different classes of individuals, had contributed to strengthen this prejudice. We were
not surprised that, when THE OFFERING first
appeared, so many were astonished; but we were
surprised that so many should, for so long a time,
withold from it their confidence. In spite of
these, however, THE OFFERING has done
much good. The involuntary blush does not so
often tinge the faces of our operatives, when
mingling with strangers, as when they claimed
no place amid the worthy, and the educated."

Thus we wrote more than two years since,
and, as then stated, our aim was to remove unjust prejudice—to prove that the female operatives of Lowell were, as a class, virtuous and
intelligent; this could not be done more effectually than by publishing not only their own
opinions relative to their peculiar occupation,

From "Editorial," the *Lowell Offering* 5 (1845).

but also their thoughts and feelings with regard to life in any of its real or imagined aspects. Their little essays and stories may not be, intrinsically, of any great value or interest, but, as indications of the mental and moral condition of a large class of females, they cannot be without a meaning. The Offering may be looked upon as a sort of intellectual barometer, though the complaint has been made that it always tells of "fair weather."

The charge of deception is not a light one, but we trust it is unmerited—wilfully we certainly have not erred. If we have pictured the fair side, it was because, to us, that *overshadowed* the darker phase. . . . We have published all the fault-finding communications which have been sent us, have expressed our readiness to receive more, and have even desired our contributors to write freely their own views of the wants, evils and temptations to which they and their companions are subjected, hoping always that subjects like these would be treated by females with good temper and good taste. . . .

But if by our writings we have misled any, and caused our distant readers to believe that Lowell is an Eden, and that we are all—not Eves, nor angels, but—Sapphos, then have we been deceptive in the impression created. Yet no error of this kind can more than offset the false impressions of a darker hue that have long existed.

Still, may we not guard against false impressions of any kind? We do not think our local stories have idealized factory life so much as fiction generally does its subject. We have had but few of these stories. One of our contributors, when asked to furnish something of this sort, replied, "I never think of factory life as distinct from other life, and of factory operatives as distinct from other laborers. We are just like others. We come here and stay awhile, and then go back to the little world, or little out-of-the-world, from which we came. Our hopes, fears, joys and sorrows are those to which all are subject."

There are , however, evils and temptations peculiar to our life, and causes for fear of a darker

future. Why have we not treated of them? When we first wrote for "the august public," it was sufficient for us that we wrote. The choice of a subject, and that a familiar one, must be our own. We were not adequate to a judicious treatment of philosophical subjects, and, in truth, thought little about them. We could have written of some petty grievances, but these are not the ones which are of paramount importance even to us. The great evils from which we suffer, are those which press upon the laborer in all other occupations, in this and every other country. The great thoughts upon this subject which, within a few years, have been promulgated, and rapidly circulated, were at first very new to us. Some views we could quickly apprehend, but how to reconcile the constitutional rights of the capitalist, and the natural rights of the operative, was more difficult. With time our powers of vision increased, but Alps on Alps would still arise; though our horizon receded, its limit was still a dim distant expanse.

But some things we know, and "know certain," and some neglected subjects shall yet receive our attention. Our aim is the good of our fellow-operatives in particular, and of all operatives in general; and it gratifies us exceedingly to learn that THE LOWELL OFFERING is creating deep interest in other countries, and that those who hail it the most joyfully are the reformers and philanthropists; those whose thoughts and lives are dedicated to the welfare of their fellow-men. We have incidentally advocated the doctrines of the dignity of labor, the benefits of universal education, the elevating tendencies of republican institutions, and the idea that respectability is to be conferred upon our employments, not received from them. We have incidentally done this; we can also do it directly, and, in future numbers, will treat of the topics not yet discussed. . . .

43

Sarah G. Bagley

Speech on Behalf of the Female
Labor Reform Association of
Lowell (1845)

. . . Friends of the Association: the usages of
society are such that those before whom we appear on this occasion may expect an apology,
and yet we are not disposed to offer one directly.
To those accustomed to pursue the same avocation as we are, and have seen so much of oppression, and have heard so many cries of
hopeless misery, it would seem extravagant to
hear us say anything that has the least resemblance of an apology. . . . For the last half a century, it has been deemed a violation of woman's
sphere to appear before the public as a speaker;
but when our rights are trampled upon and we
appeal in vain to legislators, what shall we do
but appeal to the people? Shall not our voice be
heard, and our rights acknowledged here; shall
it be said again to the daughters of New England,
that they have no political rights and are not
subject to legislative action? It is for the workingmen of this country to answer these questions—what shall we expect at your hands in
future?

Will ye not be the recording angel who shall
write on the walls of those who refuse to protect your daughters and sisters, as the angel did
on the walls of Belshazer.

Let your future action be peaceful, but firm
and decided, lest the silent statute of the immortal Washington, (which has been permitted
to keep sentinel at the doors of your Capitol)
utter a severer reproof than the thundertones
of his voice were accustomed to when the inspiration of other days fired his soul and beamed
from his eyes.

We came here to-day as the Representatives
of the Female Labor Reform Association of
Lowell, and in their behalf we present you this
simple but sincere token of their fidelity to the
cause in which you are engaged. We give it as a
token of their strong confidence in ultimate success. We give it as a motto, around which you
may safely rally; and if any discordant spirits shall
be found in your ranks, that they may be hushed
by the warning implied in its motto—"*Union
for Power.*"—and may no minor differences ever
arise to check the great work so well commenced.

We do not expect to enter the field as soldiers in this great warfare; but we would like
the heroines of the Revolution, be permitted to
furnish the soldiers with a blanket or replenish
their knapsacks from our pantries.

We claim no exalted place in your delib-
erations, nor do we expect to be instrumental
of any great re[v]olutions, yet we would not sit
idly down and fold our hands and refuse to do
the little that we may and ought to. We expect
to see the revolution commenced, recorded
among the revolutions of the past, and the name
of a Channing, Brisbane, Rykeman, Ripley,
Owen, Walsh, and a host of others, recorded
with that of Franklin, Jefferson and Washington,
on the pages of History. We do not expect this
banner to be borne away by the enemy as as a
trophy of our defeat, but although the conflict
may be long, our perseverance will overcome
all obstacles that might seem to stand in our way,
and a victory worthy a severe conte[s]t be ours.
If Oberlin with a few of the peasantry of his
country, could cut his way through one of the
mountains of Switzerland, shall we abandon our
enterprise with an army like the one before us,
or like those of which these are only the representatives? No! let your course be onward, ever
onward and adhere here strictly to your motto,
Union for Power. Learn to bless humanity and
you shall bequeath a lasting blessing to our race
and a complete victory crown your efforts.
Applause.

From the *Voice of Industry* 1 (June, 1845).

44

JANE SOPHIA APPLETON
Sequel to the "Vision of Bangor in the Twentieth Century" (1848)

[The narrator has a dream in which he is transported to a society over a century into the future. Among other changes, he finds out that "gallantry" and "flattery" are now obsolete, and a woman to whom he expresses his profuse admiration laughs uncontrollably at him. As his guide tells him: "*Your* age *fondled* woman. *Ours* honors her. You gave her *compliments. We* give her *rights.*"]

. . . "What is the standard of intellectual cultivation among women now."

"Culture of the broadest kind is considered necessary to both men and women, to fit them for their entrance into the cares and toils of life."

"But how do women find time for this? They could not do so in my day."

"You know the old adage, 'where there's a will, there's a way.' Since woman has awoke to the importance of self-culture, the means are found quite practicable. And besides, there are the increased facilities for domestic labor, to be considered in this matter. The household arrangements of this age are somewhat different from those of yours, I imagine. At this moment, you may see an exemplification of it, in the gay groups of people which you notice yonder, just filling the streets, as they go to their eating houses." . . .

[The guide continues that community eating houses are just one way in which each woman is allowed the freedom "to pursue her individual taste."]

From *Voices from the Kenduskeag* (Bangor: David Bugbee, 1848), 253, 255–58.

". . . Let me tell you, my good friend, that things have indeed changed with woman. As to 'clothing and food,' she provides them, (when necessity or inclination prompts) by her own hands or head, and what is more, can follow the impulses of her heart, in maintaining a feeble brother or sister, or an aged parent. She is therefore not obliged to enter the marriage state, as a harbor against poverty. And as for 'genteel society,' riches neither admit nor exclude from that, but man and woman both mingle in the circle for which talent or cultivation fit them, and take their places as easily as flowers turn to the light, or fold their leaves in the shade. And for this progress, we are mainly indebted to the genius of Charles Fourier, who, by his profound insight into the evils of society, induced such changes as gave due compensation to all industry, whether in man, woman or child. Coöperation substituted for competition, has in a great measure removed indigence from society, and division of labor in domestic art has increased the facilities of housekeeping as much as electricity has that of conveying news. Yet the labor of woman was lightened more reluctantly than other improvements, and the natural patience of that sex, and the selfishness of ours, might have made the eternal track of household labor go on as of old, but for the impossibility of getting female domestics for an occupation which brought so much social degradation and wear and tear of body and clothes! The factory, the shop, and the field even, came to be preferred before it, and men found that they must either starve, or contrive some better way of being fed.

"True, there are no 'Associations' properly, and many things that the genius of Fourier dreamed of, have never been realized. The reformer's plans seldom *are* fulfilled, as he foresees them, but much that that great man taught has been heeded, and men now bless his labor, and respect his name.

"Taking the hint from him, the poor first combined to purchase their supplies at shops established expressly for them, that their small parcels might come to them at wholesale prices. Rich men built comfortable, cheap dwellings, with the privilege for each tenant of [a] certain right in a common bakery, school, etc. Other changes followed. Philanthropists guided legislation in the poor man's behalf, till he gradually lost sight of his poverty, while the *hoarder* became unable to heap up wealth from the sweat of his less prosperous brother.

"True, we do not live in the 'phalanx,' but you have noticed the various houses for eating which accommodate the city. Covered passages in some of the streets, the arcade style of building generally adopted in others, and carriages for the more isolated and wealthy residences, make this a perfectly convenient custom, even in our climate, and 't is so generally adopted by our people, that only now and then a fidgety man, or a *peremptory woman,* attempts anything like the system of housekeeping in your day. Nothing but extraordinary wages enables a man now to have a little tea, a little cake, a little meat, a little potato, cooked under his own roof, served all by itself, on a little table for him especially. But the recluse and monk will be found in all ages.

"You would hardly recognize the process of cooking in one of our large establishments. Quiet, order, prudence, certainty of success, govern the process of turning out a ton of bread, or roasting an ox!—as much as the weaving a yard of cloth in one of our factories. No fuming, no fretting over the cooking stove, as of old! No 'roasted lady' at the head of the dinner table! Steam, machinery, division of labor, economy of material, make the whole as agreeable as any other toil, while the expense to pocket is as much less to man, as the wear of patience, time, bone and muscle, to woman.

"Look at that laundry establishment on the other side of the old Penobscot! See the busy boys and girls bearing to and fro the baskets of snowy linen, in exchange for the rolled and soiled bundle of clothes. There is a little fellow, now, just tumbling his load into this end of the building;—by the time he fairly walks round to the other side, it will be ready to place on his shoulders, clean, starched, and pressed with mirror-like polish! Ah, you did not *begin to live* in your benighted nineteenth century! Just think of the absurdity of one hundred housekeepers, every Saturday morning, striving to enlighten one hundred girls in the process of making pies for one hundred little ovens! (Some of these ovens remain to this day, to the great glee of antiquarians.) What fatigue! What vexation! Why, ten of our cooks, in the turning of a few cranks, and an hour or so of placing materials, produce pies enough to supply the whole of this city;—rather more than all your ladies together could do, I fancy. Window cleansing, carpet shaking, moving, sweeping, and dusting, too, are processes you would never know now, though, by the way, there is much less of this to do than there used to be, owing to a capital system of laying the dust by artificial showers which has long been used. . . ."

"I asked a while ago, how women could find *time* for the culture you were speaking of, but I am constrained to change my question now, and ask, what, for mercy's sake, is there left for them to do?" said I, indignantly, thinking of the unceasing turmoil of "washing-day," baking and ironing day, which my poor wife had always been obliged to submit to. "How lazy your women must be!"

"Lazy! why they take part in all these very processes. Labor no longer makes them fear to lose caste, and they join in hand or head work as they please, and from having greater variety of employments, those which were deemed more exclusively theirs, such as sewing or teaching, not being crowded, command as high remuneration as any. No, woman is not made lazy by this social progress. She finds abundance of work and freedom to do it. In every station, pecuniary independence is her own. Her duties as mother and daughter are now more faithfully fulfilled than ever, as freedom is more favorable to the growth of the affections than coercion, while in the marriage relation the change is too great to describe. No longer induced to enter it as a refuge from the ennui of unoccupied faculties, free also from the injurious public opinion which makes it necessary to respectability to wed, woman as well as man may go to her grave single if she pleases, without being pitied for having failed of the great end of her existence. Marriage is therefore seldom entered, except from mutual choice and strong affection."

45

Lydia Hasbrouck

Traitors to the Cause of Dress Reform (1857)

Mrs. Hasbrouck—Seeing in The Sibyl for December 1st, an account of the National Woman's Rights Convention, recently held in New York, I was minded to make this inquiry: How many of the advocates of Women's Rights, there present, wear the Reform Dress? It was reported in the papers, some time ago, that Lucy Stone Blackwell had gone back to the long dress. And of late I hear that Mrs. Stanton, Susan B. Anthony, and most of those who were earnest in wearing the short dress some three or four years ago, have laid it aside, and taken to the long dress again. If they adopted the short dress upon PRINCIPLE then, upon what PRINCIPLE do they lay it aside now?

We would not assume to question the right of any one to put on or take off at their pleasure. But we could see more consistency in our sisters demanding some rights which now they have not, if they would show themselves capable of using the rights they have. If females cannot stem the tide of prejudice and ignorance, and overcome the opposition to the short dress, it is hardly to be expected that they can use the right of suffrage creditably to themselves and their brothers.

—F.

From *The Sibyl—For Reforms*, January 1857.

Remarks.

We shall not suppress the truth your "inquiry" elicits, but expose, as their weakness merits, those who have proved *traitors* to an espoused principle which they themselves at one time declared was the foundation stone of all freedom to women. At the National Woman's Rights Convention, recently held in New York, we saw no representative of the Reform Dress save our humble self. We heard that another true to the cause was there, but failed to see her.

Lucy Stone Blackwell and Miss Anthony no longer appear in public thus dressed, but on the contrary have returned to all the absurd requirements of fashion; and none sported more sweeping sleeves and trailing skirts at the Convention than they. How they harmonize their course with the demands they make upon women to be true to the principles of right and humanity, of course we fail, alike with yourself, to discern.

They both declared they adopted the Reform Dress from principle, but a weak principle we think it must have been that could only sustain them in the right for two or three years; and it seems to us that persons of such frail powers to sustain principles, are not very reliable to stand as leaders of such important reforms as are embodied in the Woman's Rights movement of the day. We do not see but that, after a short time, if they fail to accomplish the desired good, they will prove equally faulty in this department of reform.

We happened to meet with Lucy Stone a few months before she was married, when she first commenced to wear long hair and long dresses, and she gave as an excuse, that she thought the merits of the Reform Dress were not sufficient to counteract the obstacles she was forced to meet in wearing it. We, knowing that she had worn it through seasons when it was far more difficult to sustain than at that time, could not fail to be somewhat startled at this information; but were far better prepared to learn from her now sister-in-law, Miss Antoinette Brown, that "Mr. Blackwell was not favorable to her wearing the dress in public, though she *might* do so as a home dress." This was a *poser;* the great champion of woman's independence and freedom of action, yielding this grand principle, the foundation of her wrongs, for the sake of getting—and pleasing when got—a *husband.* Lucy sank about twenty degrees below zero at that time, in our estimation, and no act of her's since has ever elevated her to the genial latitude she before occupied. This we find is the merited desert she has received from many a truthful laborer in reform; and the good she professedly hoped to gain toward the Woman's Rights movement, has been but a withering blight instead of vantage ground, which years of labor on her part can never redeem.

Lucy Stone has proved weak to the trust reposed in her. She has been an Arnold in the camp, and has fallen from an altitude she can never regain. As we viewed her at the convention, clad in her false robes, or saw her walking the streets with both hands engaged in the vain effort of protecting her flowing drapery from the swabbing of the wet streets and dripping rain, a feeling akin to contempt animated our breast toward her, in lieu of the pleasant one of warm admiration which her presence had before given; and this we found was not shared by us alone, for persons around, strangers to ourselves, were also remarking it. We saw with regret how slight a hold her floating drapery, unsustained by principle, had upon the mass in comparison to the free, noble principle she had the credit of maintaining with so much honor in meeting the obstacles which surrounded her in the Reform Dress. . . .

The same may be said of Miss Anthony and Mrs. Stanton. Whatever has caused either, after the stand they took in this branch of reform, to sustain it with so little faith, proves their lack of energy to properly fit them for reliable and responsible situations of trust. Vain will be their efforts to elevate others, when they show by their works they are powerless to elevate themselves. Vain will be their endeavors to incite others to action, when they show a spirit of cowering be-

hind the false phylacteries of society. It is not thus that bold and fearless commanders have reared the standard of reform, and carried it victorious over every obstacle. . . .

But thanks be to the Giver of all truth, not all who have taken this reform in charge, have proved false to the trust; but here and there, as may be seen by the letters in THE SIBYL, one and another have refused to bow the knee to the Baal of Fashion; and having gained strength instead of losing it, by the silly and contemptuous contest and persecution through which they have passed, are now newly equipped and full of vigor for whatever may arise. True, they may not be the *marked stars,* flashing before the eye of the world, but they are the strong and the true thinking and acting women in our rural districts, who will scorn to barter their faith for the smiles of the vulgar crowd. . . .

Talk of "Woman's Rights," and her strength to sustain herself amidst the contest of opposing influences, when she shows herself too weak to meet the words of scorn dropping from the lips of folly, although in defence of one of the noblest and most-needed reforms ever agitated before the world, and which must be triumphant ere woman can hope to take her equal and proper sphere side by side with man. If she would be successful in getting man to aid in her elevation, she must not falter to do what she may to elevate herself. If she prove true to herself and the principles for which she contends, then will her success be sure and merited; and not till then will humanity's rights be equalized. The women who are engaged in most of the reforms of the day, crush their own efforts by their half-developed powers of action—hence the need of new and truer laborers in the field, if we hope to accomplish the desired good.

46

Short Hair and Short Dresses (1857)

WAYNESVILLE, ILL., JAN. 26, 1857.

DEAR MADAM.—Enclosed I sent you $2, for which please send numbers of THE SIBYL to those I mention below. By accident I came across two numbers of your invaluable paper, for which I was very thankful, for it gave me the privilege of subscribing and getting subscribers.

I have worn the short dress for several years, and think it far superior to the long and heavy skirts that fashion demands. I have borne the insults of the people, and the salutes of the passers by, but have never felt my determination shaken. I feel that I am right, and mean to go ahead. I am the only one who wears the Reform Dress in this vicinity; so you can judge of the pleasure it was to me to meet with your paper. It seems like an old and tried friend; and with it to help me, I think that, with never-tiring zeal, I can accomplish something. I often meet with ladies who say that they 'glory in my spunk,' but they dare not come out and face public opinion.

I was glad to learn that I am not alone in wearing short hair, as I had supposed; I am very much opposed to long hair, but never could get any one to agree with me on that point. I have been told that I committed an unpardonable sin by wearing my hair short, because the Bible says that 'long hair is an ornament to woman;' but I believe in consulting nature as well as the Bible. Every one knows that when bathing the head, we have to suffer the inconvenience of letting the hair hang around the shoulders till dry, or twist it up wet, and let it sour and mould before it can dry thoroughly; and then, with the help of a half dozen hair pins to rust the hair, it is in a fine fix. I think there is a great need of reform in hair dressing. Wishing you success, I am yours,

E.E.S.

Remarks.

Daily are we in receipt of such letters. All agree in the opinion that THE SIBYL fills a niche in journalism vacant before its advent. . . .

. . . With respect to short hair, we cut ours off in the first place because it was rather thin, and troublesome to comb, brush and braid, as well as a painful annoyance—causing our head to ache with twisting and braiding, supported by combs and pins, none of which we intend ever to trouble ourselves with again, for the ease, lightness and relief we experience suits us much better than long hair. As to the Bible argument, it is an utter absurdity, being, like all other silly things said to be denounced in that book, merely distorted to suit the imagination of fanatics, who have no better occupation than to search for denunciations from its pages. The whole spirit of the Bible tends to uphold simplicity and neatness, while the braiding and plaiting of the hair, and the wearing of silly ornaments, now so common, are most strongly disapproved. Besides this, such arguments generally originate from minds having no real deference for truths anywhere found, save as they can present them as bugbears to frighten the weak and timid, among whom we are not one. And if those who pander to the silly and blighting fashions and falseness of the times, would only scan their own walk, and shape it more to the letter and spirit of the Bible, they would find need of a different walk and conversation from that they now indulge in, causing them to pause and reflect whether their course was one which tended toward the celestial city.—*Ed.*

From *The Sibyl—For Reforms*, February 1857.

47

LUCY STONE

Dress a Consequence of Woman's Vassalage—Not Its Cause (1857)

. . . I frankly confess that I do not expect any speedy or wide-spread change in the dress of women, until as a body they feel a deeper discontent with their present entire position. While they suffer "taxation without representation," and are thus placed, politically, lower than thieves, gamblers, and blacklegs, and bear it without a murmur; while, as wives, they quietly surrender the name their mother gave them, and prefer to be called by that of their legal owner, and to change it as often as they change husbands; while, as wives, in most of the states, they have

From *The Sibyl—For Reforms*, July 1857.

no right of personal property, or of earnings, and nowhere the right to the baby, warm nestling in their bosoms; nor even the right to themselves, and yet with exultant boast, iterate and reiterate that "they have all the rights they want;" believe me, they who can bear all this, are not in a condition to quarrel with the length of their skirts.

Her miserable style of dress is a consequence of her present vassalage, not its cause. Woman must become ennobled in the quality of her being. When she is so, and takes her place, clothed with the dignity which the possession and exercise of her natural human rights give, she will be able, unquestioned, to dictate the style of her dress.

With the best wishes for the good of the cause, yours, to help it as I am able.

LUCY STONE.*

*Is this *the* Lucy Stone? or, in other words, as called by the world, Lucy Stone Blackwell? . . . [—Ed.]

III. The Anti-Slavery Movement

WOMEN'S ORGANIZED EFFORTS TO END SLAVERY in the southern states of the union began in 1833, when several Quaker women of Philadelphia formed a Female Anti-Slavery Society. The members joined their male counterparts in circulating petitions to Congress, demanding an immediate end to slavery; by 1837 women's anti-slavery societies had proliferated, and the year saw a national meeting of anti-slavery women. The abolition movement is frequently credited with providing the framework for an emerging feminism, based on their similar quest for political rights: in their *History of Woman Suffrage*, Elizabeth Cady Stanton, Susan B. Anthony, and Matilda Joslyn Gage cite abolitionism "above all other causes" as the source of the woman's rights movement. Indeed, northern women learned both how to articulate an abstract critique of institutionalized oppression and how to attack it directly—using their right to petition legislatures and creating the right to lecture and write about a highly political issue. Women's anti-slavery work did not simply function as a kind of training ground for woman's rights activism, however; it was in and of itself feminist in that it launched a theoretical and pragmatic challenge to power relations between the races *and* the sexes. Abolitionist women's protests against the evils of slavery inevitably included denunciations of the sexual exploitation of slave women by white men, as well as of the ways in which white southern women were also oppressed by and often rendered complicit in a system that granted white men virtually unrestricted sexual license.

Despite historians' location of the origins of women's participation in the anti-slavery movement in 1833, Maria W. Stewart—a free, middle-class African-American woman from Connecticut—had done, a year earlier, what no American woman had ever done before: she delivered a public and political argument before a "promiscuous" audience of both men and women. Stewart, who had previously written for the abolitionist newspaper, *The Liberator*, was a pioneer black abolitionist and a champion of women's rights, though her public career lasted less than two years. Like many early reformers, she drew upon her religious faith to legitimate activity and beliefs that challenged law and social codes. Her "Why Sit Ye Here and Die?" (1832), delivered at Franklin Hall in Boston, begins by opposing the colonization movement, a plan to end the problems of United States slavery by expatriating certain black Americans to West Africa. Instead of black American emigration, Stewart exhorts her race to turn to "moral worth and intellectual improvement," pointing out that even free northern blacks were "enslaved" by ignorance and demeaning physical labor.

The most visible white women in the abolitionist movement were Angelina and Sarah Grimké, who had grown up in slave-holding South Carolina only to leave it and become anti-slavery activists. The Grimké sisters represented the powerful Garrisonian wing of the abolitionist movement, named for its leader William Lloyd Garrison. Garrisonian abolitionism was "perfectionist," identifying the sanctified individual conscience as the supreme moral standard and institutions as the source of corruption. A central Garrisonian belief was that a change in ideas—that is, a change in the moral conscience of every individual—must precede any revolution in social and legal structures. Angelina Grimké, in her numerous pamphlets and lectures on anti-slavery, espoused a perfectionist strategy—believing that the minds of southerners must be changed before slave laws could be repealed. In "An Appeal to the Christian Women of the South" (1836), Grimké sets out a plan of action for southern women that begins with private introspection and study and ends with public speech and action.

Catharine Beecher, an influential woman who wrote tirelessly about women's position in society, objected to the Grimké sisters' outspokenness, to their advocating that women should organize and speak publicly for the abolitionist cause, and also to their confrontational and coercive strategy directed at the entire white population of the South. Her "Essay on Slavery and Abolitionism" (1837), addressed to Angelina Grimké, argues that any activity which "throws woman into the attitude of a combatant, either for herself or others" lay outside "her appropriate sphere." Instead Beecher believes that change should be wrought through women's "influence," rather than through direct confrontation. Also, in her insistence that northerners could not force southerners to abandon any part of their social and economic structure against their will, she demonstrates her own persistent belief that women's efforts at social change should be limited to influencing the feelings and beliefs of a private circle of friends and relatives.

Beecher's advocating private influence as a force for social change is perfectly represented in the best-selling anti-slavery novel, *Uncle Tom's Cabin* (1852), written by her sister, Harriet Beecher Stowe. Enormously popular and controversial, *Uncle Tom's Cabin* may have sold as many as two and a half million copies in the years after its initial publication; banned in the South, the book was deemed so dangerous that it inspired over twenty countering southern novels that portrayed slavery positively. Like earlier literary figures, who had addressed the problem of the sexual double standard through the novel of seduction, Stowe used fiction to appeal to the *emotions* of her readers in order to effect the abolition of slavery.

The chapter "A Senator Is But a Man," from *Uncle Tom's Cabin,* demonstrates how Stowe attacked slavery by portraying the victimization of pure and noble-hearted slaves such as Eliza Harris, who is driven to escape from slavery only when her master threatens to take away her child. This excerpt also reveals Stowe's paradigm of white northern women's activism in the character of Mrs. Bird, who is not campaigning in public for the overthrow of slave laws, but who instead influences the *feelings* of her husband—a senator who has just helped pass the repressive Fugitive Slave Act; while the very law he helped pass should dictate that Senator Bird send Eliza back to her master in Kentucky, Mrs. Bird convinces him to sympathize with Eliza's plight and with her situation as a mother. Woman's job, Stowe insists, should be to influence the men who make laws not to try to make law herself; furthermore, her influence should appeal to the sentiments rather than to reason or logic.

The role that sentimental literature played in women's anti-slavery activism is also demonstrated in Lydia Maria Child's "The Quadroons" (1849). Although Child did not lead meetings or speak on abolitionism, she wrote prolifically in opposition to slavery, and between 1841 and 1843 she edited the weekly *National Anti-Slavery Standard*. After publishing factual accounts of slavery, which made her increasingly unpopular, Child decided to turn to fiction to try to broaden her audience. "The Quadroons" was her first attempt at a politicized fiction, as it embodies the wrongs of slavery in the archetype of the "tragic mulatta," a figure that indicted the hypocrisy of the South's sexual code. While Child herself did not feel "The Quadroons" effectively conveyed her political critique of slavery, it set the pattern for women's antislavery fiction, which would consistently focus on the pathetic and abandoned female slave caught in a coerced and dangerous "romance" with white slave-owners.

Along with the "tragic mulatta," another figure that women writers employed to personify the evils of slavery was the slave mother, torn between a natural love of her child and horror at the prospect of that child's future as a slave. Louisa J. Hall's "Birth in the Slave's Hut" (1849) and Frances Ellen Watkins (Harper's) "The Slave Mother" and "Eliza Harris" (1854) are different perspectives on the plight and the resources of the slave mother written, respectively, by a white and a black woman. Both writers use the cultural ideal of motherhood for political purposes, attempting to show that the ideal was impossible to sustain within slavery.

Aside from sentimental fiction, another literary form favored by abolitionists was the slave narrative—an ex-slave's truthful account of his or her experiences in slavery. Harriet Jacobs' *Incidents in the Life of a Slave Girl* (1861) was the most widely-read slave narrative written by a woman. "A Perilous Passage in a Slave Girl's Life" is a chapter in which Jacobs puts her own reputation at risk in order to expose to her white northern readers the horrors of slavery for African-American women. Harrassed for years by her master, Dr. Flint, Jacobs finally decides that the only way to avoid his increasingly abusive sexual advances is to give herself to another white man. Trying to assert her free will in an impossible situation, Jacobs reveals the inherent immorality of a system that makes her face such a choice—a system that had earlier denied her the right to marry and to receive the protection of a husband of her own race whom she loved. Like Hall and Harper in their poems on slave mothers, Jacobs insists that the ideals of virtuous and maternal womanhood held by Anglo-American culture were being daily defiled in the South, and that slave women—sexually exploited, denied the right to legal marriage and any legal claim to their children—were systematically precluded from being either virtuous or maternal; that slave women were either was due to their own will and in spite of white institutions.

Large-scale meetings would prove to be a more direct tactic for rallying support for the cause of abolitionism—a practice that quickly became integral to the woman's rights movement. Clearly, neither woman's rights conventions nor anti-slavery meetings were homogeneous spaces where a few celebrated speakers spoke for all those present. "Women Speak out at an Anti-Slavery Meeting in Philadelphia" (1853) reveals the diversity both of people and opinions joined together under the rubric of the anti-slavery cause. It also demonstrates the disagreements among those diverse people—including disagreements about the language of abolitionism, the place of scripture and of the Constitution in anti-slavery arguments, the extent to which they should conciliate rather than antagonize slave-holders, and the relevance of "the Woman question" to the anti-slavery movement.

When anti-slavery agitation reached its culmination in 1861 and Civil War broke out, women activists continued their activity to help the plight of slaves. Harriet Tubman, called Moses by African-Americans because she led her people to the "Promised Land" of the free North from the 1850s onward, spent the Civil War years continuing her work in the Underground Railroad, helping slaves out of the South. As "The Underground Railroad" (1863) exemplifies, Tubman was tireless not just in liberating slaves but then in trying to find them employment. Tubman was also a spy and a scout for Union troops, acquiring information from black informants behind Confederate lines.

Other women organized to help the Union in the war. The most overtly political wartime organization of northern women was the Loyal League, a group that combined women's anti-slavery and woman's rights activists with more moderate women who wanted to support Union troops. Having decided to postpone annual woman's rights meetings during the war, Elizabeth Cady Stanton and Susan B. Anthony put out the call for a meeting of the Loyal League on May 14, 1863, to which hundreds of women responded. The tension between the two groups of women whom the cause attracted—those committed to furthering slaves and women's rights and those interested in patriotic benevolence—is evident in "Loyal Women of the Nation Debate Their Role in a Time of War" (1863). The League passed several resolutions, most of them committing the association to working for the emancipation of slaves. The resolutions did not pass without rigorous debate, however, including protests like that voiced by Mrs. Hoyt of Wisconsin that "this meeting has been conducted in such a way as would lead one to suppose that it was an anti-slavery convention." One resolution, which was not unanimously passed, also introduced the political rights of women, which some women claimed was not in the least germane to the cause of preserving the Union. While the years of the Civil War did bring women such as Mrs. Hoyt into the public sphere and the historical record, they were, finally, years in which the more radical activity for African-American and women's rights was put on hold.

48

MARIA W. STEWART
Why Sit Ye Here and Die?
(1832)

Why sit ye here and die? If we say we will go to a foreign land, the famine and the pestilence are there, and there we shall die. If we sit here, we shall die. Come let us plead our cause before the whites: if they save us alive, we shall live—and if they kill us, we shall but die.

Methinks I heard a spiritual interrogation—'Who shall go forward, and take off the reproach that is cast upon the people of color? Shall it be a woman?' And my heart made this reply—'If it is thy will, be it even so, Lord Jesus!'

I have heard much respecting the horrors of slavery; but may Heaven forbid that the generality of my color throughout these United States should experience any more of its horrors than to be a servant of servants, or hewers of wood and drawers of water! Tell us no more of southern slavery; for with few exceptions, although I may be very erroneous in my opinion, yet I consider our condition but little better than that. Yet, after all, methinks there are no chains so galling as the chains of ignorance—no fetters so binding as those that bind the soul, and exclude it from the vast field of useful and scientific knowledge. O, had I received the advantages of early education, my ideas would, ere now, have expanded far and wide; but, alas! I possess nothing but moral capability—no teachings but the teachings of the Holy Spirit.

I have asked several individuals of my sex, who transact business for themselves, if providing our girls were to give them the most satisfactory references, they would not be willing to grant them an equal opportunity with others? Their reply has been—for their own part, they

From *Productions of Mrs. Maria W. Stewart, Presented to the First African Baptist Church and Society, of the City of Boston* (Boston: Published by Friends of Freedom and Virtue, 1835), 51–56.

had no objection; but as it was not the custom, were they to take them into their employ, they would be in danger of losing the public patronage.

And such is the powerful force of prejudice. Let our girls possess what amiable qualities of soul they may; let their characters be fair and spotless as innocence itself; let their natural taste and ingenuity be what they may; it is impossible for scarce an individual of them to rise above the condition of servants. Ah! why is this cruel and unfeeling distinction? Is it merely because God has made our complexion to vary? If it be, O shame to soft, relenting humanity! "Tell it not in Gath! publish it not in the streets of Askelon!" Yet, after all, methinks were the American free people of color to turn their attention more assiduously to moral worth and intellectual improvement, this would be the result: prejudice would gradually diminish, and the whites would be compelled to say, unloose those fetters!

Though black their skins are shades of night,
Their hearts are pure, their souls are white.

Few white persons of either sex, who are calculated for any thing else, are willing to spend their lives and bury their talents in performing mean, servile labor. And such is the horrible idea that I entertain respecting a life of servitude, that if I conceived of there being no possibility of my rising above the condition of a servant, I would gladly hail death as a welcome messenger. O, horrible idea, indeed! to possess noble souls aspiring after high and honorable acquirements, yet confined by the chains of ignorance and poverty to lives of continual drudgery and toil. Neither do I know of any who have enriched themselves by spending their lives as house-domestics, washing windows, shaking carpets, brushing boots, or tending upon gentlemen's tables. I can but die for expressing my sentiments; and I am as willing to die by the sword as the pestilence; for I am a true born American; your blood flows in my veins, and your spirit fires my breast.

I observed a piece in the Liberator a few months since, stating that the colonizationists had published a work respecting us, asserting that we were lazy and idle. I confute them on that point. Take us generally as a people, we are neither lazy nor idle; and considering how little we have to excite or stimulate us, I am almost astonished that there are so many industrious and ambitious ones to be found; although I acknowledge, with extreme sorrow, that there are some who never were and never will be serviceable to society. And have you not a similar class among yourselves? . . .

Again, continual hard labor irritates our tempers and sours our dispositions; the whole system becomes worn out with toil and fatigue; nature herself becomes almost exhausted, and we care but little whether we live or die. It is true, that the free people of color throughout these United States are neither bought nor sold, nor under the lash of the cruel driver; many obtain a comfortable support; but few, if any, have an opportunity of becoming rich and independent; and the employments we most pursue are as unprofitable to us as the spider's web or the floating bubbles that vanish into air. As servants, we are respected; but let us presume to aspire any higher, our employer regards us no longer. . . .

Most of our color have dragged out a miserable existence of servitude from the cradle to the grave. And what literary acquirements can be made, or useful knowledge derived, from either maps, books or charts, by those who continually drudge from Monday morning until Sunday noon? O, ye fairer sisters, whose hands are never soiled, whose nerves and muscles are never strained, go learn by experience! Had we had the opportunity that you have had, to improve our moral and mental faculties, what would have hindered our intellects from being as bright, and our manners from being as dignified as yours? Had it been our lot to have been nursed in the lap of affluence and ease, and to have basked beneath the smiles and sunshine of fortune, should we not have naturally supposed that we were never made to toil? And why are not our forms as delicate, and our constitutions as slender, as yours? Is not the workmanship as curious and complete? . . .

My beloved brethren, as Christ has died in vain for those who will not accept of offered mercy, so will it be vain for the advocates of freedom to spend their breath in our behalf, unless with united hearts and souls you make some mighty efforts to raise your sons and daughters from the horrible state of servitude and degradation in which they are placed. It is upon you that woman depends; she can do but little besides using her influence; and it is for her sake and yours that I have come forward and made myself a hissing and a reproach among the people; for I am also one of the wretched and miserable daughters of the descendants of fallen Africa. Do you ask, why are you wretched and miserable? I reply, look at many of the most worthy and interesting of us doomed to spend our lives in gentlemen's kitchens. Look at our young men, smart, active and energetic, with souls filled with ambitious fire; if they look forward, alas! what are their prospects? They can be nothing but the humblest laborers, on account of their dark complexions; hence many of them lose their ambition, and become worthless. Look at our middle-aged men, clad in their rusty plaids and coats; in winter, every cent they earn goes to buy their wood and pay their rents; their poor wives also toil beyond their strength, to help support their families. Look at our aged sires, whose heads are whitened with the frosts of seventy winters, with their old wood-saws on their backs. Alas, what keeps us so? Prejudice, ignorance and poverty. But ah! methinks our oppression is soon to come to an end; yea, before the Majesty of heaven, our groans and cries have reached the ears of the Lord of Sabaoth. As the prayers and tears of Christians will avail the finally impenitent nothing; neither will the prayers and tears of the friends of humanity avail us any thing, unless we possess a spirit of virtuous emulation within our breasts. Did the pilgrims, when they first landed on these shores, quietly compose themselves, and say, "the Britons have all the money and all the power, and we must continue their servants forever?" Did they sluggishly sigh and say, "our lot is hard, the Indians own the soil, and we cannot cultivate it?" No; they first made powerful efforts to raise themselves, and then God raised up those illustrious patriots, WASHINGTON and LAFAYETTE, to assist and defend them. And, my brethren, have you made a powerful effort? Have you prayed the Legislature for mercy's sake to grant you all the rights and privileges of free citizens, that your daughters may rise to that degree of respectability which true merit deserves, and your sons above the servile situations which most of them fill?

49

ANGELINA GRIMKÉ
An Appeal to the Christian Women of the South (1836)

It is because I feel a deep and tender interest in your present and eternal welfare that I am willing thus publicly to address you. Some of you have loved me as a relative, and some have felt bound to me in Christian sympathy, and Gospel fellowship; and even when compelled by a strong sense of duty, to break those outward bonds of union which bound us together as members of the same community, and members of the same religious denomination, you were generous enough to give me credit, for sincerity as a Christian, though you believed I had been most strangely deceived. . . . It is because you have known me, that I write thus unto you.

But there are other Christian women scattered over the Southern States, of whom a very large number have never seen me, and never heard my name, and feel *no* personal interest whatever in *me*. But I feel an interest in *you*, as

From "Appeal to the Christian Women of the South," *The Anti-Slavery Examiner* 1 (September, 1836).

branches of the same vine from whose root I daily draw the principle of spiritual vitality— Yes! Sisters in Christ I feel an interest in *you*, and often has the secret prayer arisen on your behalf, Lord "open thou their eyes that they may see wondrous things out of thy Law"—It is then, because I *do feel* and *do pray* for you, that I thus address you upon a subject about which of all others, perhaps you would rather not hear any thing; but, "would to God ye could bear with me a little in my folly, and indeed bear with me, for I am jealous over you with godly jealousy." Be not afraid then to read my appeal; it is *not* written in the heat of passion or prejudice, but in that solemn calmness which is the result of conviction and duty. It is true, I am going to tell you unwelcome truths, but I mean to speak those *truths in love* . . . I do not believe the time has yet come when *Christian women* "will not endure sound doctrine," even on the subject of Slavery, if it is spoken to them in tenderness and love, therefore I now address *you*. . . .

I have thus, I think, clearly proved to you seven propositions, viz.: First, that slavery is contrary to the declaration of our independence. Second, that it is contrary to the first charter of human rights given to Adam, and renewed to Noah. Third, that the fact of slavery having been the subject of prophecy, furnishes *no* excuse whatever to slaveholders. Fourth, that no such system existed under the patriarchal dispensation. Fifth, that *slavery never* existed under the Jewish dispensation; but so far otherwise, that every servant was placed under the *protection of law*, and care taken not only to prevent all *involuntary* servitude, but all *voluntary perpetual* bondage. Sixth, that slavery in America reduces a *man* to a *thing*, a "chattel personal," *robs him* of *all* his rights as a *human being*, fetters both his mind and body, and protects the *master* in the most unnatural and unreasonable power, whilst it *throws him out* of the protection of law. Seventh, that slavery is contrary to the example and precepts of our holy and merciful Redeemer, and of his apostles.

But perhaps you will be ready to query, why

appeal to *women* on this subject? *We* do not make the laws which perpetuate slavery. *No* legislative power is vested in *us*; *we* can do nothing to overthrow the system, even if we wished to do so. To this I reply, I know you do not make the laws, but I also know that *you are the wives and mothers, the sisters and daughters of those who do*; and if you really suppose *you* can do nothing to overthrow slavery, you are greatly mistaken. You can do much in every way: four things I will name. 1st. You can read on this subject. 2d. You can pray over this subject. 3d. You can speak on this subject. 4th. You can *act* on this subject. I have not placed reading before praying because I regard it more important, but because, in order to pray aright, we must understand what we are praying for; it is only then we can "pray with the understanding and the spirit also."

1. Read then on the subject of slavery. Search the Scriptures daily, whether the things I have told you are true. Other books and papers might be a great help to you in this investigation, but they are not necessary, and it is hardly probable that your Committees of Vigilance will allow you to have any other. The *Bible* then is the book. . . .

2. Pray over this subject. When you have entered into your closets, and shut the doors, then pray to your father, who seeth in secret, that he would open your eyes to see whether slavery is *sinful*, and if it is, that he would enable you to bear a faithful, open and unshrinking testimony against it, and to do whatsoever your hands find to do, leaving the consequences entirely to him, who still says to us whenever we try to reason away duty from the fear of consequences, *"What is that to thee, follow thou me."* Pray also for the poor slave, that he may be kept patient and submissive under his hard lot, until God is pleased to open the door of freedom to him without violence or bloodshed. . . .

3. Speak on this subject. It is through the tongue, the pen, and the press, that truth is principally propagated. Speak then to your relatives, your friends, your acquaintances on the subject of slavery; be not afraid if you are conscientiously

convinced it is *sinful*, to say so openly, but calmly, and to let your sentiments be known. If you are served by the slaves of others, try to ameliorate their condition as much as possible; never aggravate their faults, and thus add fuel to the fire of anger already kindled, in a master and mistress's bosom; remember their extreme ignorance, and consider them as your Heavenly Father does the *less* culpable on this account, even when they do wrong things. . . . Above all, try to persuade your husband, father, brothers and sons, that *slavery is a crime against God and man*, and that it is a great sin to keep *human beings* in such abject ignorance; to deny them the privilege of learning to read and write. . . .

4. Act on this subject. Some of you *own* slaves yourselves. If you believe slavery is *sinful*, set them at liberty, "undo the heavy burdens and let the oppressed go free." If they wish to remain with you, pay them wages, if not, let them leave you. Should they remain, teach them, and have them taught the common branches of an English education; they have minds, and those minds *ought to be improved*. . . .

But some of you will say, we can neither free our slaves nor teach them to read, for the laws of our state forbid it. Be not surprised when I say such wicked laws *ought to be no barrier* in the way of your duty, and I appeal to the Bible to prove this position. . . .

But some of you may say, if we do free our slaves, they will be taken up and sold, therefore there will be no use in doing it. Peter and John might just as well have said, we will not preach the gospel, for if we do, we shall be taken up and put in prison, therefore there will be no use in our preaching. *Consequences*, my friends, belong no more to *you*, than they did to these apostles. Duty is ours and events are God's. If you think slavery is sinful, all *you* have to do is to set your slaves at liberty, do all you can to protect them, and in humble faith and fervent prayer, commend them to your common Father. . . .

I know that this doctrine of obeying *God*, rather than man, will be considered as dangerous, and heretical by many, but I am not afraid openly to avow it, because it is the doctrine of the Bible; but I would not be understood to advocate resistance to any law however oppressive, if, in obeying it, I was not obliged to commit *sin*. If for instance, there was a law, which imposed imprisonment or a fine upon me if I manumitted a slave, I would on no account resist that law, I would set the slave free, and then go to prison or suffer the penalty. If a law commands me to *sin I will break it*; if it calls me to suffer, I will let it take its course *unresistingly*. The doctrine of blind obedience and unqualified submission to *any human* power, whether civil or ecclesiastical, is the doctrine of despotism, and ought to have no place among Republicans and Christians. . . .

The *women of the South can overthrow* this horrible system of oppression and cruelty, licentiousness and wrong. Such appeals to your legislatures would be irresistible, for there is something in the heart of man which *will bend under moral suasion*. There is a swift witness for truth in his bosom, which *will respond to truth* when it is uttered with calmness and dignity. If you could obtain but six signatures to such a petition in only one state, I would say, send up that petition, and be not in the least discouraged by the scoffs and jeers of the heartless, or the resolution of the house to lay it on the table. It will be a great thing if the subject can be introduced into your legislatures in any way, even by *women*, and *they* will be the most likely to introduce it there in the best possible manner, as a matter of *morals* and *religion*, not of expediency or politics. You may petition, too, the different ecclesiastical bodies of the slave states. Slavery must be attacked with the whole power of truth and the sword of the spirit. You must take it up on *Christian* ground, and fight against it with Christian weapons, whilst your feet are shod with the preparation of the gospel of peace. And *you are now* loudly called upon by the cries of the widow and the orphan, to arise and gird yourselves for this great moral conflict, "with the whole armour of righteousness on the right hand and on the left." . . .

50

CATHARINE BEECHER
An Essay on Slavery and Abolitionism (1837)

MY DEAR FRIEND,

Your public address to Christian females at the South has reached me, and I have been urged to aid in circulating it at the North. I have also been informed, that you contemplate a tour, during the ensuing year, for the purpose of exerting your influence to form Abolition Societies among ladies of the non-slave-holding States.

Our acquaintance and friendship give me a claim to your private ear; but there are reasons why it seems more desirable to address you, who now stand before the public as an advocate of Abolition measures, in a more public manner.

The object I have in view, is to present some reasons why it seems unwise and inexpedient for ladies of the non-slave-holding States to unite themselves in Abolition Societies; and thus, at the same time, to exhibit the inexpediency of the course you propose to adopt.

I would first remark, that your public address leads me to infer, that you are not sufficiently informed in regard to the feelings and opinions of Christian females at the North. Your remarks seem to assume, that the *principles* held by Abolitionists on the subject of slavery, are peculiar to them, and are not generally adopted by those at the North who oppose their *measures*. In this you are not correctly informed. In the sense in which Abolitionists explain the terms they employ, there is little, if any, difference between them and most northern persons. Especially is this true of northern persons of religious principles. I know not where to look for northern Christians, who would deny that every slave-holder is bound to treat his slaves exactly as he would claim that his own children

From *An Essay on Slavery and Abolitionism, with Reference to the Duty of American Females* (Philadelphia: Henry Perkins, 1837), 5–8, 97–104, 109, 128–29.

ought to be treated in similar circumstances; that the holding of our fellow men as property, or the withholding any of the rights of freedom, for mere purposes of gain, is a sin, and ought to be immediately abandoned; and that where the laws are such that a slave-holder cannot *legally* emancipate his slaves, without throwing them into worse bondage, he is bound to use all his influence to alter those laws, and, in the meantime, to treat his slaves, as nearly as he can, *as if* they were free.

I do not suppose there is one person in a thousand, at the North, who would dissent from these principles. They would only differ in the use of terms, and call this the doctrine of *gradual emancipation,* while Abolitionists would call it the doctrine of *immediate emancipation.*

As this is the state of public opinion at the North, there is no necessity for using any influence with northern ladies, in order that they may adopt your *principles* on the subject of slavery; for they hold them in common with yourself, and it would seem unwise, and might prove irritating, to approach them as if they held opposite sentiments.

In regard to the duty of making efforts to bring the people of the Southern States to adopt these principles, and act on them, it is entirely another matter. On this point you would find a large majority opposed to your views. Most persons in the non-slave-holding States have considered the matter of Southern slavery, as one in which they were no more called to interfere, than in the abolition of the press-gang system in England, or the tythe system of Ireland. Public opinion may have been wrong on this point, and yet have been right on all those great principles of rectitude and justice relating to slavery, which Abolitionists claim as their *distinctive* peculiarities.

[Beecher continues that she specifically objects to Grimké's belief that women should organize to protest slavery in public.]

. . . To appreciate more fully these objec-

tions, it will be necessary to recur to some general views in relation to the place woman is appointed to fill by the dispensations of heaven.

It has of late become quite fashionable in all benevolent efforts, to shower upon our sex an abundance of compliments, not only for what they have done, but also for what they can do; and so injudicious and so frequent, are these oblations, that while I feel an increasing respect for my countrywomen, that their good sense has not been decoyed by these appeals to their vanity and ambition, I cannot but apprehend that there is some need of inquiry as to the just bounds of female influence, and the times, places, and manner in which it can be appropriately exerted.

It is the grand feature of the Divine economy, that there should be different stations of superiority and subordination, and it is impossible to annihilate this beneficent and immutable law.

. . . In this arrangement of the duties of life, Heaven has appointed to one sex the superior, and to the other the subordinate station, and this without any reference to the character or conduct of either. It is therefore as much for the dignity as it is for the interest of females, in all respects to conform to the duties of this relation. And it is as much a duty as it is for the child to fulfil similar relations to parents, or subjects to rulers. But while woman holds a subordinate relation in society to the other sex, it is not because it was designed that her duties or her influence should be any the less important, or all-pervading. But it was designed that the mode of gaining influence and of exercising power should be altogether different and peculiar.

It is Christianity that has given to woman her true place in society. And it is the peculiar trait of Christianity alone that can sustain her therein. "Peace on earth and good will to men" is the character of all the rights and privileges, the influence, and the power of woman. A man may act on society by the collision of intellect, in public debate; he may urge his measures by a sense of shame, by fear and by personal interest; he may coerce by the combination of public sentiment; he may drive by physical force, and he does not outstep the boundaries of his sphere. But all the power, and all the conquests that are lawful to woman, are those only which appeal to the kindly, generous, peaceful and benevolent principles.

Woman is to win every thing by peace and love; by making herself so much respected, esteemed and loved, that to yield to her opinions and to gratify her wishes, will be the free-will offering of the heart. But this is to be all accomplished in the domestic and social circle. . . .

A woman may seek the aid of co-operation and combination among her own sex, to assist her in her appropriate offices of piety, charity, maternal and domestic duty; but whatever, in any measure, throws a woman into the attitude of a combatant, either for herself or others—whatever finds her in a party conflict—whatever obliges her in any way to exert coercive influences, throws her out of her appropriate sphere. If these general principles are correct, they are entirely opposed to the plan of arraying females in any Abolition movement; because it enlists them in an effort to coerce the South by the public sentiment of the North; because it brings them forward as partisans in a conflict that has been begun and carried forward by measures that are any thing rather than peaceful in their tendencies; because it draws them forth from their appropriate retirement, to expose themselves to the ungoverned violence of mobs, and to sneers and ridicule in public places; because it leads them into the arena of political collision, not as peaceful mediators to hush the opposing elements, but as combatants to cheer up and carry forward the measures of strife.

If it is asked, "May not woman appropriately come forward as a suppliant for a portion of her sex who are bound in cruel bondage?" It is replied, that, the rectitude and propriety of any such measure, depend entirely on its probable results. If petitions from females will operate to exasperate; if they will be deemed obtrusive, indecorous, and unwise, by those to whom they are addressed; if they will increase, rather than diminish the evil which it is wished to remove; if they will be the opening wedge, that will tend eventually to bring females as petitioners and partisans into every political measure that may tend to injure and oppress their sex, in various parts of the nation, and under the various public measures that may hereafter be enforced, then it is neither appropriate nor wise, nor right, for a woman to petition for the relief of oppressed females. . . .

But it may be asked, is there nothing to be done to bring this national sin of slavery to an end? Must the internal slave-trade, a trade now ranked as piracy among all civilized nations, still prosper in our bounds? Must the very seat of our government stand as one of the chief slave-markets of the land; and must not Christian females open their lips, nor lift a finger, to bring such a shame and sin to an end?

To this it may be replied, that Christian females may, and can say and do much to bring these evils to an end; and the present is a time and an occasion when it seems most desirable that they should know, and appreciate, and *exercise* the power which they do possess for so desirable an end. . . .

And is there not a peculiar propriety in such an emergency, in looking for the especial agency and assistance of females, who are shut out from the many temptations that assail the other sex,—who are the appointed ministers of all the gentler charities of life,—who are mingled throughout the whole mass of the community,—who dwell in those retirements where only peace and love ought ever to enter,—whose comfort, influence, and dearest blessings, all depend on preserving peace and good will among men?

In the present aspect of affairs among us, when everything seems to be tending to disunion and distraction, it surely has become the duty of every female instantly to relinquish the attitude of a partisan, in every matter of clashing interests, and to assume the office of a media-tor, and an advocate of peace. And to do this, it is not necessary that a woman should in any manner relinquish her opinion as to the evils or the benefits, the right or the wrong, of any principle or practice. But, while quietly holding her own opinions, and calmly avowing them, when conscience and integrity make the duty imperative, every female can employ her influence, not for the purpose of exciting or regulating public sentiment, but rather for the purpose of promoting a spirit of candour, forbearance, charity, and peace. . . .

51
LYDIA MARIA CHILD
The Quadroons (1849)

Not far from Augusta, Georgia, there is a pleasant place called Sand-Hills, appropriated almost exclusively to summer residences for the wealthy inhabitants of the neighbouring city. Among the beautiful cottages that adorn it was one far retired from the public roads, and almost hidden among the trees. It was a perfect model of rural beauty. . . .

The inhabitants of this cottage remained in it all the year round, and peculiarly enjoyed the season that left them without neighbours. To one of the parties, indeed, the fashionable summer residents, that came and went with the butterflies, were merely neighbours-in-law. The edicts of society had built up a wall of separation between her and them; for she was a quadroon. Conventional laws could not be reversed in her favour, though she was the daughter of a wealthy merchant, was highly cultivated in mind and manners, graceful as an antelope, and beautiful as the evening star. She had early attracted the attention of a handsome and wealthy young Georgian; and as their acquaintance increased, the purity and bright intelligence of her mind,

From *Fact and Fiction: A Collection of Stories* (New York: C. S. Francis, 1849), 61–76.

inspired him with far deeper interest than is ever excited by mere passion. It was genuine love; that mysterious union of soul and sense, in which the lowliest dew-drop reflects the image of the highest star.

The tenderness of Rosalie's conscience required an outward form of marriage; though she well knew that a union with her proscribed race was unrecognised by law, and therefore the ceremony gave her no legal hold on Edward's constancy. But her high poetic nature regarded the reality, rather than the semblance of things; and when he playfully asked how she could keep him if he wished to run away, she replied, "Let the church that my mother loved sanction our union, and my own soul will be satisfied, without the protection of the state. If your affections fall from me, I would not, if I could, hold you by a legal fetter."

It was a marriage sanctioned by Heaven, though unrecognised on earth. The picturesque cottage at Sand-Hills was built for the young bride under her own direction; and there they passed ten as happy years as ever blessed the heart of mortals. It was Edward's fancy to name their eldest child Xarifa; in commemoration of a quaint old Spanish ballad, which had first conveyed to his ears the sweet tones of her mother's voice. Her flexible form and noble motions were in harmony with the breezy sound of the name; and its Moorish origin was most appropriate to one so emphatically "a child of the sun." Her complexion, of a still lighter brown than Rosalie's, was rich and glowing as an autumnal leaf. The iris of her large, dark eye had the melting, mezzotinto outline, which remains the last vestige of African ancestry, and gives that plaintive expression, so often observed, and so appropriate to that docile and injured race.

Xarifa learned no lessons of humility or shame, within her own happy home; for she grew up in the warm atmosphere of father's and mother's love, like a flower open to the sunshine, and sheltered from the winds. But in summer walks with her beautiful mother, her young cheek often mantled at the rude gaze of the young men, and her dark eye flashed fire, when some contemptuous epithet met her ear, as white ladies passed them by, in scornful pride and ill-concealed envy.

Happy as Rosalie was in Edward's love, and surrounded by an outward environment of beauty, so well adapted to her poetic spirit, she felt these incidents with inexpressible pain. For herself, she cared but little; for she had found a sheltered home in Edward's heart, which the world might ridicule, but had no power to profane. But when she looked at her beloved Xarifa, and reflected upon the unavoidable and dangerous position which the tyranny of society had awarded her, her soul was filled with anguish. The rare loveliness of the child increased daily, and was evidently ripening into most marvellous beauty. The father rejoiced in it with unmingled pride; but in the deep tenderness of the mother's eye there was an indwelling sadness, that spoke of anxious thoughts and fearful forebodings.

When Xarifa entered her ninth year, these uneasy feelings found utterance in earnest solicitations that Edward would remove to France, or England. This request excited but little opposition, and was so attractive to his imagination, that he might have overcome all intervening obstacles, had not "a change come o'er the spirit of his dream." He still loved Rosalie, but he was now twenty-eight years old, and unconsciously to himself, ambition had for some time been slowly gaining an ascendency over his other feelings. The contagion of example had led him into the arena where so much American strength is wasted; he had thrown himself into political excitement, with all the honest fervour of youthful feeling. His motives had been unmixed with selfishness, nor could he ever define to himself when or how sincere patriotism took the form of personal ambition. But so it was, that at twenty-eight years old, he found himself an ambitious man, involved in movements which his frank nature would have once abhorred, and watching the doubtful game of mutual cunning with all the fierce excitement of a gambler.

Among those on whom his political success most depended, was a very popular and wealthy man, who had an only daughter. His visits to the house were at first of a purely political nature; but the young lady was pleasing, and he fancied he discovered in her a sort of timid preference for himself. This excited his vanity, and awakened thoughts of the great worldly advantages connected with a union. Reminiscences of his first love kept these vague ideas in check for several months; but Rosalie's image at last became an unwelcome intruder; for with it was associated the idea of restraint. Moreover Charlotte, though inferior in beauty, was yet a pretty contrast to her rival. Her light hair fell in silken profusion, her blue eyes were gentle, though inexpressive, and her delicate cheeks were like blush-rose-buds.

He had already become accustomed to the dangerous experiment of resisting his own inward convictions; and this new impulse to ambition, combined with the strong temptation of variety in love, met the ardent young man weakened in moral principle, and unfettered by laws of the land. The change wrought upon him was soon noticed by Rosalie. . . .

At length the news of his approaching marriage met her ear. Her head grew dizzy, and her heart fainted within her; but, with a strong effort at composure, she inquired all the particulars; and her pure mind at once took its resolution. Edward came that evening, and though she would have fain met him as usual, her heart was too full not to throw a deep sadness over her looks and tones. She had never complained of his decreasing tenderness, or of her own lonely hours; but he felt that the mute appeal of her heart-broken looks was more terrible than words. . . . At length, in words scarcely audible, Rosalie said, "Tell me, dear Edward, are you to be married next week?" He dropped her hand, as if a rifle-ball had struck him; and it was not until after long hesitation, that he began to make some reply about the necessity of circumstances. Mildly, but earnestly, the poor girl begged him to spare apologies. It was enough that he no longer loved her, and that they must bid farewell. Trusting to the yielding tenderness of her character, he ventured, in the most soothing accents, to suggest that as he still loved her better than all the world, she would ever be his real wife, and they might see each other frequently. He was not prepared for the storm of indignant emotion his words excited. Hers was a passion too absorbing to admit of partnership; and her spirit was too pure and kind to enter into a selfish league against the happiness of the innocent young bride.

At length this painful interview came to an end. They stood together by the Gothic gate, where they had so often met and parted in the moonlight. Old remembrances melted their souls. "Farewell, dearest Edward," said Rosalie. "Give me a parting kiss." Her voice was choked for utterance, and the tears flowed freely, as she bent her lips toward him. He folded her convulsively in his arms, and imprinted a long, impassioned kiss on that mouth, which had never spoken to him but in love and blessing.

With effort like a death-pang, she at length raised her head from his heaving bosom, and turning from him with bitter sobs, she said, "It is our *last*. God bless you. I would not have you so miserable as I am. Farewell. A *last* farewell." "The *last!*" exclaimed he, with a wild shriek. "Oh, Rosalie, do not say that!" and covering his face with his hands, he wept like a child.

Recovering from his emotion, he found himself alone. The moon looked down upon him mild, but very sorrowful; as the Madonna seems to gaze on her worshipping children, bowed down with consciousness of sin. At that moment he would have given worlds to have disengaged himself from Charlotte; but he had gone so far, that blame, disgrace, and duels with angry relatives, would now attend any effort to obtain his freedom. Oh, how the moonlight oppressed him with its friendly sadness! It was like the plaintive eye of his forsaken one; like the music of sorrow echoed from an unseen world. . . .

Poor Charlotte! had she known all, what a dreary lot would hers have been; but fortunately, she could not miss the impassioned tenderness she had never experienced; and Edward was the more careful in his kindness, because he was deficient in love. Once or twice she heard him murmur, "dear Rosalie," in his sleep; but the playful charge she brought was playfully answered, and the incident gave her no real uneasiness. The summer after their marriage, she proposed a residence at Sand-Hills; little aware what a whirlwind of emotion she excited in her husband's heart. The reasons he gave for rejecting the proposition appeared satisfactory; but she could not quite understand why he was never willing that their afternoon drives should be in the direction of those pleasant rural residences, which she had heard him praise so much. One day, as their barouche rolled along a winding road that skirted Sand-Hills, her attention was suddenly attracted by two figures among the trees by the way-side; and touching Edward's arm, she exclaimed, "Do look at that beautiful child!" He turned, and saw Rosalie and Xarifa. His lips quivered, and his face became deadly pale. His young wife looked at him intently, but said nothing. There were points of resemblance in the child, that seemed to account for his sudden emotion. Suspicion was awakened, and she soon learned that the mother of that lovely girl bore the name of Rosalie; with this information came recollections of the "dear Rosalie," murmured in uneasy slumbers. From gossiping tongues she soon learned more than she wished to know. She wept, but not as poor Rosalie had done; for she never had loved, and been beloved, like her, and her nature was more proud. Henceforth a change came over her feelings and her manners; and Edward had no further occasion to assume a tenderness in return for hers. Changed as he was by ambition, he felt the wintry chill of her polite propriety, and sometimes in agony of heart, compared it with the gushing love of her who was indeed his wife.

But these, and all his emotions, were a sealed book to Rosalie, of which she could only guess the contents. With remittances for her and her child's support, there sometimes came earnest pleadings that she would consent to see him again; but these she never answered, though her heart yearned to do so. She pitied his fair young bride, and would not be tempted to bring sorrow into their household by any fault of hers. . . . At last, the conflicts of her spirit proved too strong for the beautiful frame in which it dwelt. About a year after Edward's marriage, she was found dead in her bed, one bright autumnal morning. She had often expressed to her daughter a wish to be buried under a spreading oak, that shaded a rustic garden-chair, in which she and Edward had spent many happy evenings. And there she was buried; with a small white cross at her head, twined with the cypress vine. Edward came to the funeral, and wept long, very long, at the grave. Hours after midnight, he sat in the recess-window, with Xarifa folded to his heart. The poor child sobbed herself to sleep on his bosom; and the convicted murderer had small reason to envy that wretched man, as he gazed on the lovely countenance, which so strongly reminded him of his early and his only love.

From that time, Xarifa was the central point of all his warmest affections. He hired an excellent old negress to take charge of the cottage, from which he promised his darling child that she should never be removed. He employed a music master, and dancing master, to attend upon her; and a week never passed without a visit from him, and a present of books, pictures, or flowers. To hear her play upon the harp, or repeat some favourite poem in her mother's earnest accents and melodious tones, or to see her pliant figure float in the garland-dance, seemed to be the highest enjoyment of his life. Yet was the pleasure mixed with bitter thoughts. What would be the destiny of this fascinating young creature, so radiant with life and beauty? She belonged to a proscribed race; and though the brown colour on her soft cheek was scarcely deeper than the sunny side of a golden pear, yet was it sufficient to exclude her from virtuous society. He thought of Rosalie's wish to carry her to France: and he would have fulfilled it, had he been unmarried. As it was, he inwardly

resolved to make some arrangement to effect it in a few years, even if it involved separation from his darling child.

But alas for the calculations of man! From the time of Rosalie's death, Edward had sought relief for his wretched feelings in the free use of wine. Xarifa was scarcely fifteen, when her father was found dead by the road-side; having fallen from his horse, on his way to visit her. He left no will; but his wife, with kindness of heart worthy of a happier domestic fate, expressed a decided reluctance to change any of the plans he had made for the beautiful child at Sand-Hills.

Xarifa mourned her indulgent father; but not as one utterly desolate. True, she had lived "like a flower deep hid in rocky cleft;" but the sunshine of love had already peeped in upon her. Her teacher on the harp was a handsome and agreeable young man of twenty, the only son of an English widow. Perhaps Edward had not been altogether unmindful of the result, when he first invited him to the flowery cottage. Certain it is, he had more than once thought what a pleasant thing it would be, if English freedom from prejudice should lead him to offer legal protection to his graceful and winning child. Being thus encouraged, rather than checked, in his admiration, George Elliot could not be otherwise than strongly attracted toward his beautiful pupil. The lonely and unprotected state in which her father's death left her, deepened this feeling into tenderness. And lucky was it for her enthusiastic and affectionate nature; for she could not live without an atmosphere of love. In her innocence, she knew nothing of the dangers in her path; and she trusted George with an undoubting simplicity, that rendered her sacred to his noble and generous soul. . . .

Alas, the tempest was brooding over their young heads. Rosalie, though she knew it not, had been the daughter of a slave, whose wealthy master, though he remained attached to her to the end of her days, yet carelessly omitted to have papers of manumission recorded. His heirs had lately failed, under circumstances which greatly exasperated their creditors; and in an unlucky hour, they discovered their claim on Angelique's grand-child.

The gentle girl, happy as the birds in spring-time, accustomed to the fondest indulgence, surrounded by all the refinements of life, timid as a fawn, and with a soul full of romance, was ruthlessly seized by a sheriff, and placed on the public auction-stand in Savannah. There she stood, trembling, blushing, and weeping; compelled to listen to the grossest language, and shrinking from the rude hands that examined the graceful proportions of her beautiful frame. "Stop that!" exclaimed a stern voice. "I bid two thousand dollars for her, without asking any of their d—d questions." The speaker was probably about forty years of age, with handsome features, but a fierce and proud expression. An older man, who stood behind him, bid two thousand five hundred. The first bid higher; then a third, a dashing young man, bid three thousand; and thus they went on, with the keen excitement of gamblers, until the first speaker obtained the prize, for the moderate sum of five thousand dollars.

And where was George, during this dreadful scene? He was absent on a visit to his mother, at Mobile. But, had he been at Sand-Hills, he could not have saved his beloved from the wealthy profligate, who was determined to obtain her at any price. A letter of agonized entreaty from her brought him home on the wings of the wind. But what could he do? How could he ever obtain a sight of her, locked up as she was in the princely mansion of her master? At last, by bribing one of the slaves, he conveyed a letter to her, and received one in return. As yet, her purchaser treated her with respectful gentleness, and sought to win her favour, by flattery and presents; but she dreaded every moment, lest the scene should change, and trembled at the sound of every footfall. A plan was laid for escape. The slave agreed to drug his master's wine; a ladder of ropes was prepared, and a swift boat was in readiness. But the slave, to obtain a double reward, was treacherous. Xarifa had scarcely given an answering signal to the low

cautious whistle of her lover, when the sharp sound of a rifle was followed by a deep groan, and a heavy fall on the pavement of the court-yard. With frenzied eagerness she swung herself down by the ladder of ropes, and, by glancing light of lanthorns, saw George, bleeding and lifeless at her feet. One wild shriek, that pierced the brains of those who heard it, and she fell senseless by his side.

For many days she had a confused consciousness of some great agony, but knew not where she was, or by whom she was surrounded. The slow recovery of her reason settled into the most intense melancholy, which moved the compassion even of her cruel purchaser. The beautiful eyes, always pensive in expression, were now so heart-piercing in their sadness, that he could not endure to look upon them. For some months, he sought to win her smiles by lavish presents, and delicate attentions. He bought glittering chains of gold, and costly bands of pearl. His victim scarcely glanced at them, and her attendant slave laid them away, unheeded and forgotten. He purchased the furniture of the Cottage at Sand-Hills, and one morning Xarifa found her harp at the bedside, and the room filled with her own books, pictures, and flowers. She gazed upon them with a pang unutterable, and burst into an agony of tears; but she gave her master no thanks, and her gloom deepened.

At last his patience was exhausted. He grew weary of her obstinacy, as he was pleased to term it; and threats took the place of persuasion.

In a few months more, poor Xarifa was a raving maniac. That pure temple was desecrated; that loving heart was broken; and that beautiful head fractured against the wall in the frenzy of despair. Her master cursed the useless expense she had cost him; the slaves buried her; and no one wept at the grave of her who had been so carefully cherished, and so tenderly beloved.

52

HARRIET BEECHER STOWE
A Senator is But a Man (1852)

The light of the cheerful fire shone on the rug and carpet of a cosey parlor, and glittered on the sides of the teacups and well brightened teapot, as Senator Bird was drawing off his boots, preparatory to inserting his feet in a pair of new, handsome slippers, which his wife had been working for him while away on his senatorial tour. Mrs. Bird, looking the very picture of delight, was superintending the arrangements of the table, ever and anon mingling admonitory remarks to a number of frolicsome juveniles, who were effervescing in all those modes of untold gambol and mischief that have astonished mothers ever since the flood.

"Tom, let the door-knob alone,—there's a man! Mary! Mary! don't pull the cat's tail,—poor pussy! Jim, you must n't climb on that table,—no, no!—You don't know, my dear, what a surprise it is to us all, to see you here to-night!" said she, at last, when she found a space to say something to her husband.

"Yes, yes, I thought I'd just make a run down, spend the night, and have a little comfort at home. I'm tired to death, and my head aches!"

Mrs. Bird cast a glance at a camphor-bottle, which stood in the half-open closet, and appeared to meditate an approach to it, but her husband interposed.

"No, no, Mary, no doctoring! a cup of your good, hot tea, and some of our good, home living, is what I want. It's a tiresome business, this legislating!"

And the senator smiled, as if he rather liked the idea of considering himself a sacrifice to his country.

"Well," said his wife, after the business of

From *Uncle Tom's Cabin; or, Life Among the Lowly* (Boston and New York: Houghton Mifflin, 1891), 87–95, 99–100.

the tea-table was getting rather slack, "and what have they been doing in the Senate?"

Now, it was a very unusual thing for gentle little Mrs. Bird ever to trouble her head with what was going on in the house of the state, very wisely considering that she had enough to do to mind her own. Mr. Bird, therefore, opened his eyes in surprise, and said,—

"Not very much of importance."

"Well; but is it true that they have been passing a law forbidding people to give meat and drink to those poor colored folks that come along? I heard they were talking of some such law, but I did n't think any Christian legislature would pass it!"

"Why, Mary, you are getting to be a politician, all at once."

"No, nonsense! I would n't give a fig for all your politics, generally, but I think this is something downright cruel and unchristian. I hope my dear, no such law has been passed."

"There has been a law passed forbidding people to help off the slaves that come over from Kentucky, my dear; so much of that thing has been done by these reckless Abolitionists, that our brethren in Kentucky are very strongly excited, and it seems necessary, and no more than Christian and kind, that something should be done by our state to quiet the excitement."

"And what is the law? It don't forbid us to shelter these poor creatures a night, does it, and to give 'em something comfortable to eat, and a few old clothes, and to send them quietly about their business?"

"Why, yes, my dear; that would be aiding and abetting, you know."

Mrs. Bird was a timid, blushing little woman, about four feet in height, and with mild blue eyes, and a peach-blow complexion, and the gentlest, sweetest voice in the world; as for courage, a moderate-sized cock-turkey had been known to put her to rout at the very first gobble, and a stout house-dog, of moderate capacity, would bring her into subjection merely by a show of his teeth. Her husband and children were her entire world, and in these she ruled more by entreaty and persuasion than by command or argument. There was only one thing that was capable of arousing her, and that provocation came in on the side of her unusually gentle and sympathetic nature;—anything in the shape of cruelty would throw her into a passion, which was the more alarming and inexplicable in proportion to the general softness of her nature. Generally the most indulgent and easy to be entreated of all mothers, still her boys had a very reverent remembrance of a most vehement chastisement she once bestowed on them, because she found them leagued with several graceless boys of the neighborhood, stoning a defenceless kitten.

"I'll tell you what," Master Bill used to say, "I was scared that time. Mother came at me so that I thought she was crazy, and I was whipped and tumbled off to bed, without any supper, before I could get over wondering what had come about; and, after that, I heard mother crying outside the door, which made me feel worse than all the rest. I'll tell you what," he'd say, "we boys never stoned another kitten!"

On the present occasion, Mrs. Bird rose quickly, with very red cheeks, which quite improved her general appearance, and walked up to her husband, with quite a resolute air, and said, in a determined tone,—

"Now, John, I want to know if you think such a law as that is right and Christian?"

"You won't shoot me, now, Mary, if I say I do!"

"I never could have thought it of you, John; you did n't vote for it?"

"Even so, my fair politician."

"You ought to be ashamed, John! Poor, homeless, houseless creatures! It's a shameful, wicked, abominable law, and I'll break it, for one, the first time I get a chance; and I hope I *shall* have a chance, I do! Things have got to a pretty pass, if a woman can't give a warm supper and a bed to poor, starving creatures, just because they are slaves, and have been abused and oppressed all their lives, poor things!"

"But, Mary, just listen to me. Your feelings are all quite right, dear, and interesting, and I love you for them; but, then, dear, we must n't suffer our feelings to run away with our judgment; you must consider it's not a matter of private feeling,—there are great public interests involved,—there is such a state of public agitation rising, that we must put aside our private feelings."

"Now, John, I don't know anything abut politics, but I can read my Bible; and there I see that I must feed the hungry, clothe the naked, and comfort the desolate; and that Bible I mean to follow."

"But in cases where your doing so would involve a great public evil"—

"Obeying God never brings on public evils. I know it can't. It's always safest, all round, to *do as he* bids us."

"Now, listen to me, Mary, and I can state to you a very clear argument, to show"—

"Oh, nonsense, John! you can talk all night, but you would n't do it. I put it to you, John,—would *you,* now, turn away a poor shivering, hungry creature from your door, because he was a runaway? *Would* you, now?"

Now, if the truth must be told, our senator had the misfortune to be a man who had a particularly humane and accessible nature, and turning away anybody that was in trouble never had been his forte; and what was worse for him in this particular pinch of the argument was, that his wife knew it, and, of course, was making an assault on rather an indefensible point. So he had recourse to the usual means of gaining time for such cases made and provided; he said "ahem," and coughed several times, took out his pocket handkerchief, and began to wipe his glasses. Mrs. Bird, seeing the defenceless condition of the enemy's territory, had no more conscience than to push her advantage.

"I should like to see you doing that, John,—I really should! Turning a woman out of doors in a snow-storm, for instance; or, may be you'd take her up and put her in jail, would n't you? You would make a great hand at that!"

"Of course, it would be a very painful duty," began Mr. Bird, in a moderate tone.

"Duty, John! don't use that word! You know it is n't a duty,—it can't be a duty! If folks want to keep their slaves from running away, let 'em treat 'em well,—that's my doctrine. If I had slaves (as I hope I never shall have), I'd risk their wanting to run away from me, or you either, John. I tell you folks don't run away when they are happy; and when they do run, poor creatures! they suffer enough with cold and hunger and fear, without everybody's turning against them; and law or no law, I never will, so help me God!"

"Mary! Mary! My dear, let me reason with you."

"I hate reasoning, John,—especially reasoning on such subjects. There 's a way you political folks have of coming round and round a plain right thing; and you don't believe in it yourselves, when it comes to practice. I know *you* well enough, John. You don't believe it's right any more than I do; and you would n't do it any sooner than I."

At this critical juncture, old Cudjoe, the black man-of-all work, put his head in at the door, and wished "Missis would come into the kitchen;" and our senator, tolerably relieved, looked after his little wife with a whimsical mixture of amusement and vexation, and seating himself in the arm-chair, began to read the papers.

After a moment, his wife's voice was heard at the door, in a quick, earnest tone,—"John! John! I do wish you'd come here, a moment."

He laid down his paper, and went into the kitchen, and started, quite amazed at the sight that presented itself:—A young and slender woman, with garments torn and frozen, with one shoe gone, and the stocking torn away from the cut and bleeding foot, was laid back in a deadly swoon upon two chairs. There was the impress of the despised race on her face, yet none could help feeling its mournful and pathetic beauty, while its stony sharpness, its cold, fixed, deathly aspect, struck a solemn chill over him.

He drew his breath short, and stood in silence. His wife, and their only colored domestic, old Aunt Dinah, were busily engaged in restorative measures; while old Cudjoe had got the boy on his knee, and was busy pulling off his shoes and stockings, and chafing his little cold feet.

"Sure, now, if she an't a sight to behold!" said old Dinah, compassionately; "'pears like 't was the heat that made her faint. She was tol'able peart when she cum in, and asked if she could n't warm herse'f here a spell; and I was just a askin here where she cum from, and she fainted right down. Never done much hard work, guess, by the looks of her hands."

"Poor creature!" said Mrs. Bird, compassionately, as the woman slowly unclosed her large, dark eyes, and looked vacantly at her. Suddenly an expression of agony crossed her face, and she sprang up, saying, "Oh, my Harry! Have they got him?"

The boy, at this, jumped from Cudjoe's knee, and running to her side, put up his arms. "Oh, he's here! he's here!" she exclaimed.

"Oh, ma'am!" said she, wildly, to Mrs. Bird, "do protect us! don't let them get him!"

"Nobody shall hurt you here, poor woman," said Mrs. Bird, encouragingly. "You are safe; don't be afraid."

"God bless you!" said the woman, covering her face and sobbing; while the little boy, seeing her crying, tried to get into her lap.

With many gentle and womanly offices which none knew better how to render than Mrs. Bird, the poor woman was, in time, rendered more calm. A temporary bed was provided for her on the settle, near the fire; and, after a short time, she fell into a heavy slumber, with the child, who seemed no less weary, soundly sleeping on her arm; for the mother resisted, with nervous anxiety, the kindest attempts to take him from her; and, even in sleep, her arm encircled him with an unrelaxing clasp, as if she could not even then be beguiled of her vigilant hold.

Mr. and Mrs. Bird had gone back to the

parlor, where, strange as it may appear, no reference was made, on either side, to the preceding conversation; but Mrs. Bird busied herself with her knitting work, and Mr. Bird pretended to be reading the paper.

"I wonder who and what she is!" said Mr. Bird, at last, as he laid it down.

"When she wakes up and feels a little rested we will see," said Mrs. Bird.

"I say, wife!" said Mr. Bird, after musing in silence over his newspaper.

"Well, dear!"

"She could n't wear one of your gowns, could she, by any letting down, or such matter? She seems to be rather larger than you are."

A quite perceptible smile glimmered on Mrs. Bird's face as she answered, "We 'll see."

Another pause, and Mr. Bird again broke out,—

"I say, wife!"

"Well! what now?"

"Why, there 's that old bombazine cloak, that you keep on purpose to put over me when I take my afternoon's nap; you might as well give her that,—she needs clothes."

At this instant, Dinah looked in to say that the woman was awake, and wanted to see Missis.

Mr. and Mrs. Bird went into the kitchen, followed by the two eldest boys, the smaller fry having, by this time, been safely disposed of in bed.

The woman was now sitting up on the settle, by the fire. She was looking steadily into the blaze, with a calm heart-broken expression, very different from her former agitated wildness.

"Did you want me?" said Mrs. Bird, in gentle tones. "I hope you feel better now, poor woman!"

A long-drawn, shivering sigh was the only answer; but she lifted her dark eyes, and fixed them on her with such a forlorn and imploring expression, that the tears came into the little woman's eyes.

"You need n't be afraid of anything; we are friends here, poor woman! Tell me where you came from, and what you want," said she.

"I came from Kentucky," said the woman.

"When?" said Mr. Bird, taking up the interrogatory.

"To-night."

"How did you come?"

"I crossed on the ice."

"Crossed on the ice!" said every one present.

"Yes," said the woman, slowly, "I did. God helping me, I crossed on the ice; for they were behind me,—right behind,—and there was no other way!"

"Law, Missis," said Cudjoe, "the ice is all in broken-up blocks, a swinging and a teetering up and down in the water."

"I know it was,—I know it!" said she wildly; "but I did it! I would n't have thought I could,— I did n't think I should get over, but I did n't care! I could but die if I did n't. The Lord helped me; nobody knows how much the Lord can help em, till they try," said the woman, with a flashing eye.

"Were you a slave?" said Mr. Bird.

"Yes, sir; I belonged to a man in Kentucky"

"Was he unkind to you?"

"No, sir; he was a good master."

"And was your mistress unkind to you?"

"No, sir.—no! my mistress was always good to me."

"What could induce you to leave a good home, then, and run away, and go through such dangers?"

The woman looked up at Mrs. Bird with a keen, scrutinizing glance, and it did not escape her that she was dressed in deep mourning.

"Ma'am," she said, suddenly, "have you ever lost a child?"

The question was unexpected, and it was a thrust on a new wound; for it was only a month since a darling child of the family had been laid in the grave.

Mr. Bird turned around and walked to the window, and Mrs. Bird burst into tears; but, recovering her voice, she said,—

"Why do you ask that? I have lost a little one."

"Then you will feel for me. I have lost two,

one after another,—left 'em buried there when I came away and I had only this one left. I never slept a night without him; he was all I had. He was my comfort and pride, day and night; and, ma'am, they were going to take him away from me,—to *sell* him—sell him down south, ma'am, to go all alone,—a baby that had never been away from his mother in his life! I could n't stand it, ma'am. I knew I never should be good for anything, if they did; and when I knew the papers were signed, and he was sold, I took him and came off in the night; and they chased me,— the man that bought him, and some of Mas'r's folks,—and they were coming down right behind me, and I heard 'em. I jumped right on to the ice; and how I got across, I don't know,— but, first I knew, a man was helping me up the bank."

The woman did not sob nor weep. She had gone to a place where tears are dry; but every one around her was, in some way characteristic of themselves, showing signs of hearty sympathy.

The two little boys, after a desperate rummaging in their pockets, in search of those pocket-handkerchiefs which mothers know are never to be found there, had thrown themselves disconsolately into the skirts of their mother's gown, where they were sobbing, and wiping their eyes and noses, to their hearts content;— Mrs. Bird had her face fairly hidden in her pocket-handkerchief: and old Dinah, with tears streaming down her black, honest face, was ejaculating, "Lord have mercy on us!" with all the fervor of a camp-meeting;—while old Cudjoe, rubbing his eyes very hard with his cuffs, and making a most uncommon variety of wry faces, occasionally responded in the same key, with great fervor. Our senator was a statesman, and of course could not be expected to cry, like other mortals; and so he turned his back to the company, and looked out of the window, and seemed particularly busy in clearing his throat and wiping his spectacle-glasses, occasionally blowing his nose in a manner that was calculated to excite suspicion, had any one been in a state to observe critically. . . .

What a situation, now, for a patriotic senator, that had been all the week before spurring up the legislature of his native state to pass more stringent resolutions against escaping fugitives, their harborers and abettors!

Our good senator in his native state had not been exceeded by any of his brethren at Washington, in the sort of eloquence which has won for them immortal renown! How sublimely he had sat with his hands in his pockets, and scouted all sentimental weakness of those who would put the welfare of a few miserable fugitives before great state interests!

He was as bold as a lion bout it, and "mightily convinced" not only himself, but everybody that heard him;—but then his idea of a fugitive was only an idea of the letters that spell the word,—or, at the most, the image of a little newspaper picture of a man with a stick and bundle, with "Ran away from the subscriber" under it. The magic of the real presence of distress—the imploring human eye, the frail, trembling human hand, the despairing appeal of helpless agony,—these he had never tried. He had never thought that a fugitive might be a hapless mother, a defenceless child,—like that one which was now wearing his lost boy's little well-known cap; and so, as our poor senator was not stone or steel,—as he was a man, and a downright noble-hearted one, too,—he was, as everybody must see, in a sad case for his patriotism. And you need not exult over him, good brother of the Southern States; for we have some inklings that many of you, under similar circumstances, would not do much better. We have reason to know, in Kentucky, as in Mississippi, are noble and generous hearts, to whom never was tale of suffering told in vain. Ah, good brother! is it fair for you to expect of us services which your own brave, honorable heart would not allow you to render, were you in our place?

53
Louisa J. Hall
Birth in the Slave's Hut (1849)

The voice of her pangs had ceased,
    The cry of her sharp distress,
But the gloom on her brow increased,
    There was written—hopelessness.

"I have heard of a mother's joy,
    The joy of a new-made mother;
Could I crush this babe like a toy,
    Its breath in the grey dust smother!
Tenfold are the pangs I would bear
    To feel myself childless again,
Or dare with my own hand to tear
    The life from this creature of pain!

"Lo, they whisper, rejoice! rejoice!
    All, around my mistress fair,
When a new-born daughter's voice
    Wails out on the summer air,
And that babe with its welcome eyes
    A smile from the sick one wins;
But mine! as it helpless lies,
    The woe of its life begins.

"Have I knowledge? alas, but to learn
    How basely our nature is wronged,
And the fate of my child to discern
    As its future with curses comes throng'd.
In mercy, say not 'tis a daughter!
    Oh God, give me leave to destroy
By cord, by sharp knife, or by water,
    The thing thou didst mean for my joy!

"She is born, and I shrink from her cry;
    More wealth to my mistress is given—
She is born, there is *slave* in her eye;
    She is born; would it were into Heaven!
Kind Nature! what sayst thou to me?
    The love that is stronger than life

Crieth out with a voice like the sea—
    It rendeth my spirit with strife;
It crusheth the instinct of joy—
    It forbids me to thank thee, my God!
And awfully bids me destroy,
    And give the *slave's babe* to the sod!"

54
Frances Ellen Watkins [Harper]
The Slave Mother (1854)

Heard you that shriek? It rose
    So wildly on the air,
It seem'd as if a burden'd heart
    Was breaking in despair.

Saw you those hands so sadly clasped—
    The bowed and feeble head—
The shuddering of that fragile form—
    That look of grief and dread?

Saw you the sad, imploring eye?
    Its every glance was pain,
As if a storm of agony
    Were sweeping through the brain.

She is a mother pale with fear,
    Her boy clings to her side,
And in her kyrtle vainly tries
    His trembling form to hide.

He is not hers, although she bore
    For him a mother's pains;
He is not hers, although her blood
    Is coursing through his veins!

He is not hers, for cruel hands
    May rudely tear apart
The only wreath of household love
    That binds her breaking heart.

From *The Liberty Bell. By Friends of Freedom* (Boston: National Anti–Slavery Bazaar, 1849), 42–44.

From *Poems on Miscellaneous Subjects* (Boston: J. B. Yerrinton, 1854), 6–8, 7–9.

His love has been a joyous light
 That o'er her pathway smiled,
A fountain gushing ever new,
 Amid life's desert wild.

His lightest word has been a tone
 Of music round her heart,
Their lives a streamlet blent in one—
 Oh, Father! must they part?

They tear him from her circling arms,
 Her last and fond embrace:—
Oh! never more may her sad eyes
 Gaze on his mournful face.

No marvel, then, these bitter shrieks
 Disturb the listening air;
She is a mother, and her heart
 Is breaking in despair.

Eliza Harris (1854)

Like a fawn from the arrow, startled and wild,
A woman swept by us, bearing a child;
In her eye was the night of a settled despair,
And her brow was o'ershaded with anguish and
 care.

She was nearing the river—in reaching the
 brink,
She heeded no danger, she paused not to think!
For she is a mother—her child is a slave—
And she'll give him his freedom, or find him a
 grave!

'Twas a vision to haunt us, that innocent face—
So pale in its aspect, so fair in its grace;
As the tramp of the horse and the bay of the
 hound,
With the fetters that gall, were trailing the
 ground!

She was nerved by despair, and strengthen'd by
 woe,

As she leap'd o'er the chasms that yawn'd from
 below;
Death howl'd in the tempest, and rav'd in the
 blast,
But she heard not the sound till the danger was
 past.

Oh! how shall I speak of my proud country's
 shame?
Of the stains on her glory, how give them their
 name?
How say that her banner in mockery waves—
Her "star-spangled banner"—o'er millions of
 slaves?

How say that the lawless may torture and chase
A woman whose crime is the hue of her face?
How the depths of the forest may echo around
With the shrieks of despair, and the bay of the
 hound?

With her step on the ice, and her arm on her
 child,
The danger was fearful, the pathway was wild;
But, aided by Heaven, she gained a free shore,
Where the friends of humanity open'd their
 door.

So fragile and lovely, so fearfully pale,
Like a lily that bends to the breath of the gale,
Save the heave of her breast, and the sway of her
 hair,
You'd have thought her a statue of fear and despair.

In agony close to her bosom she press'd
The life of her heart, the child of her breast:—
Oh! love from its tenderness gathering might,
Had strengthen'd her soul for the dangers of
 flight.

But she's free!—yes, free from the land where
 the slave
From the hand of oppression must rest in the
 grave;
Where bondage and torture, where scourges and
 chains

Have plac'd on our banner indelible stains.

The bloodhounds have miss'd the scent of her
    way;
The hunter is rifled and foil'd of his prey;
Fierce jargon and cursing, with clanking of
    chains,
Make sounds of strange discord on Liberty's
    plains.

With the rapture of love and fullness of bliss,
She plac'd on his brow a mother's fond kiss:—
Oh! poverty, danger and death she can brave,
For the child of her love is no longer a slave!

55

Elizabeth C. Wright, Mrs. Williams, and Lucretia Mott

Women Speak Out at an Anti-Slavery Meeting in Philadelphia (1853)

Miss Elizabeth C. Wright, of Ceres, Pa., said she felt obliged to express her dissent to the sentiment uttered by the last speaker, in his remark that he loved Franklin Pierce as much as he loved William Lloyd Garrison. She believed that declaration affected the whole fundamental structure of human freedom. They had got to plant themselves on the fundamental rock of individual responsibility. They had got to prove that every man or woman in the wide world was master of himself or herself, and that no one else had the right to interfere with him or her, in any possible way, so long as they interfered with none others. That was the sum and substance of the whole thing. If they could say that they loved the great sinner, as a man, as well as they loved another, whom they believed upright

From *Proceedings of the American Anti-Slavery Society at Its Second Decade. Philadelphia, 1853* (New York: Anti-Slavery Society, 1854), 36–7, 73, 122–25, 127.

and holy, she did not see what was to become of the doctrine of individuality, or the responsibility we were all under to God. Our individual rights were no more to be trespassed upon than our responsibilities, for they must inevitably go together. The making a man a slave took away his right to discharge his duties. When God created us, he gave us not only these inalienable rights, and made us feel the consciousness, in our own souls, that these rights belonged to us, and to none others, but he gave us, at the same time, certain duties to perform, and made us capable of certain relations; and when we entered into those relations and duties, they were as self-evident as the rights by which we attained them. If a man, or any number of men, became the property, the personal chattels of another man, then all their responsibilities were merged in him; and God never gave a human soul to any mortal being great enough, expansive enough, to discharge the responsibilities of more than one soul. She felt that there was a great and terrible responsibility resting upon all who allowed those heavy burdens to be borne by others, which they would not allow themselves to touch with their little fingers. In a certain sense, the believed that "Resistance to tyrants is obedience to God;"—not resistance by carnal weapons, not resistance unto blood and death, but resistance with that strong moral force that is in every soul. She believed that principles were a part of God; and she believed, also, the mathematical axiom, that the whole is equal to the sum of all its parts, and, therefore, that every virtue is a part of God, and goes to make up the sum of the whole great Deity.

Miss Wright said she had been an Abolitionist all her life, in great good earnest, and she did not feel afraid of forfeiting any reputation that was good for any thing, by advocating God's own truth. (Applause.) When she used the words of Jesus, "All things whatsoever ye would that men should do to you, do ye even so to them," she did not believe she was guilty of heresy; neither did she think their friend Barker was when he said the same thing. She did not believe it was any heresy, if they went out and proclaimed to the world those self-evident truths (which seemed to be very much in need of evidence, to the great mass of the world) set forth in the Declaration of Independence, which proclaimed the common equality of all men.

Miss Wright concluded by saying that the idea she wished to advance was, that, in the sight of God, each man was just as great as another, unless, by obeying him more, having more virtue and more truth, he make himself greater; that, abstractly, whatever his position,

"A man's a man for a' that."

Mr. Whitson asked the speaker if she loved Garrison and Quincy better than Pierce.

Miss W. Yes.

Mr. Whitson. Why?

Miss W. Because I consider Garrison and Quincy right in their principles and actions, while those of Pierce I look upon as wrong.

Mr. Whitson. Suppose the views of Garrison and Quincy should change, and become like those of Pierce?

Miss W. Then they would cease to be Wm. Lloyd Garrison and Edmund Quincy. . . .

Mrs. Williams, of Wilmington, Del., (colored,) said she must be indulged in a few words. She spoke with much emotion and most impressively, remarking that she had attended but few Anti-Slavery meetings; but, she continued, I have been told that these men (pointing to Messrs. Garrison, Burleigh and others on the platform) are my enemies, and the enemies of the colored people. Within a fortnight, I heard a Methodist minister, in Wilmington, say that these men are all Infidels. Now I have seen and heard these men myself, and I say freely, that I have heard more truth this morning, I have had my intellect more enlightened as to the character of God, and my heart more stirred with the love of God, than by all the preaching of all the ministers I ever listened to in my life. I wish that all the world were here to see and hear for themselves. I believe that all good and honest men would be affected by the truth spoken here. The audience were deeply moved by Mrs. W's earnest lan-

guage, and she resumed her seat with the remark, "I couldn't help speaking; I should have burst, if I hadn't." . . .

Speech of Mrs. Lucretia Mott.

My Friends:

I am so often heard in this city, you are all so familiar with my voice, that I would fain give place, as long as any of our friends from a distance shall come forward to address you. I have had some most gratifying reminiscences since the opening of this Convention. I have looked back to the time of the formation of the Society, to the time of the issue of the Declaration of Sentiments of the Convention then assembled, twenty years ago. That Declaration has been read here; and I remember, at the time it was written or engrossed, and hung up in some of our parlors, William Lloyd Garrison came in, and, reading a part of it, exclaimed, "How will this sound some fifty or a hundred years hence—that such a truism as this, that every man has a right to himself, to his own body, to his own earnings, and that no man has a right to enslave or imbrute his brother, to hold him for one moment as a piece of property—that such truisms as these had to be declared in General Convention, had to be promulgated before the people, and before an *unbelieving* people, too?" . . .

It is well, while we bring into view the fact of the great wickedness and enormous atrocity in the world, that we should also take a view of the growth of Anti-Slavery sentiment, so that we may be cheered, that we may thank God and take courage, and go on conquering and to conquer, and not be at all weary in well-doing, but adhere to the great principles on which our movement was founded—the force, the potency, and the efficiency of moral appeal; that we may go on, in the confidence that the great heart of the people is right, and that it will respond to the truth, and that we may, with all hope of success, continue to appeal,—not, as has been said, in the elaborate arguments that seemed necessary at the beginning, not by appointing evening after evening for the discussion of the subject upon Scripture ground,—but to the deep sympathies of the popular heart. Why, I remember, in the beginning of this great enterprise, twenty years ago, it was proposed to declare the simple fact, that the slaveholder is a *man-stealer.* We had not been much accustomed to call this evil by its right name, and we feared the hard words. We were accustomed enough to calling a sheep-stealer a *sheep-stealer,* but a *man-stealer*—we did not like to apply such a term. But, after considerable discussion in the Convention, it was concluded, in order to modify the expression, and with a kind of tender courtesy to some of our Quaker friends, —who, I must say, although they had been accustomed to very plain language, were among the prominent ones to object to the word *man-stealer*—the language was modified by prefixing, perhaps in parentheses, the words, "according to Scripture," a *man-stealer,* (laughter,) so as to cover it up under an appeal to the veneration of the people. Then the pro-slavery divines presented themselves, and took the ground that Slavery was sanctioned by Scripture, and the Abolitionists came forward, and offered to discuss the question whether Slavery was or was not sanctioned by Scripture; and a great deal of time was spent in arguments and discussions of this kind. I have been rejoiced, in later years, to hear some of our New England friends say— "We have done wasting our time with these elaborate arguments and researches into Scripture, to prove a self-evident truth. It is enough for us now to affirm that Slavery is a sin; that the slave had the right to his freedom, and that it is no less the duty of the slaveholder instantly and unconditionally to emancipate him." This is evidence of progress, that we are not going back to find authorities to support us in our efforts for the deliverance of the wronged; that we are disposed to read the Bible with another pair of spectacles, through which, we may find in it co-operation with the right; and in this way we have learned what are the means we should use; that it should not be by these low arguments, by

bringing the subject up in a manner agreeable to the authorities of the age, the religion of the age, the politics of the age, or the social aspects of the time, but that we should stand simply and singly upon the inherent rights of man, on the self-evident truths that have been declared before the people, and which, being so self-evident, need no proof. We have advanced. We are willing now, in a great measure, to stand on the immutable principles of justice and right. Let us, then, not falter; let us go on. Plenty of Bible will be found in support of Freedom, as soon as it becomes a little more popular—just as it has been found in every scientific discovery, in every other advancement in morals. We need not fear. Plenty, too, of political truth will be found, and constitutional argument, if we go on with our spiritual arguments and weapons, making our appeal to the conscience and heart of the people. There will be no need of trying to bring the Bible or the Constitution to our support; for our enemies,—those who are now the pro-slavery party of the country,—will bring those instrumentalities,—those which are now their gods,—to the side of Freedom. Let us, then, go on, and not case away our confidence, which hath "great recompense of reward," if we will abide in the truth, and be satisfied that it is strong, and "mighty, through God, to the pulling down of the strongholds" of the iniquity of Slavery, and of wrong and oppression of every kind. . . .

I might say here a good deal of the Woman question—as to how the Anti-Slavery cause has brought forward woman, and of the many other instrumentalities that have been brought to operate upon this enterprise; but the hour is late, and I will not do it. I might not consider these extraneous topics, at a proper time; and I do say, that, in our desire to keep our platform directly and strictly to the subject, we must not go so far as to set such a limit as shall cramp the intellect and the heart of the advocates of Freedom, of those who would protest against this great, this monstrous evil of Slavery. There must be liberty; there must be an acknowledgment of the right to speak out our convictions, incidentally, in the course of any speech or remark, without all the time trembling lest we should be called to order.

56

HARRIET JACOBS
A Perilous Passage in a Slave Girl's Life (1861)

After my lover went away, Dr. Flint contrived a new plan. He seemed to have an idea that my fear of my mistress was his greatest obstacle. In the blandest tones, he told me that he was going to build a small house for me, in a secluded place, four miles away from the town. I shuddered; but I was constrained to listen, while he talked of his intention to give me a home of my own, and to make a lady of me. Hitherto, I had escaped my dreaded fate, by being in the midst of people. My grandmother had already had high words with my master about me. She had told him pretty plainly what she thought of his character, and there was considerable gossip in the neighborhood about our affairs, to which the open-mouthed jealousy of Mrs. Flint contributed not a little. When my master said he was going to build a house for me, and that he could do it with little trouble and expense, I was in hopes something would happen to frustrate his scheme; but I soon heard that the house was actually begun. I vowed before my Maker that I would never enter it. I had rather toil on the plantation from dawn till dark; I had rather live and die in jail, than drag on, from day to day, through such a living death. I was determined that the master, whom I so hated and loathed, who had blighted the prospects of my youth, and made my life a desert, should not, after my long struggle with him, succeed at last in trampling his victim under his feet. I would do any thing, every thing, for the sake of

From *Incidents in the Life of a Slave Girl. Written by Herself* (Boston: Published for the Author, 1861), 82–89.

defeating him. What *could* I do? I thought and thought, till I became desperate, and made a plunge into the abyss.

And now, reader, I come to a period in my unhappy life, which I would gladly forget if I could. The remembrance fills me with sorrow and shame. It pains me to tell you of it; but I have promised to tell you the truth, and I will do it honestly, let it cost me what it may. I will not try to screen myself behind the plea of compulsion from a master; for it was not so. Neither can I plead ignorance or thoughtlessness. For years, my master had done his utmost to pollute my mind with foul images, and to destroy the pure principles inculcated by my grandmother, and the good mistress of my childhood. The influences of slavery had had the same effect on me that they had on other young girls; they had made me prematurely knowing, concerning the evil ways of the world. I knew what I did, and I did it with deliberate calculation.

But, O, ye happy women, whose purity has been sheltered from childhood, who have been free to choose the objects of your affection, whose homes are protected by law, do not judge the poor desolate slave girl too severely! If slavery had been abolished, I, also, could have married the man of my choice; I could have had a home shielded by the laws; and I should have been spared the painful tasks of confessing what I am now about to relate; but all my prospects had been blighted by slavery. I wanted to keep myself pure; and, under the most adverse circumstances, I tried hard to preserve my self-respect; but I was struggling alone in the powerful grasp of the demon Slavery; and the monster proved too strong for me. I felt as if I was forsaken by God and man; as if all my efforts must be frustrated; and I became reckless in my despair.

I have told you that Dr. Flint's persecutions and his wife's jealousy had given rise to some gossip in the neighborhood. Among others, it chanced that a white unmarried gentleman had obtained some knowledge of the circumstances in which I was placed. He knew my grandmother, and often spoke to me in the street. He became interested for me, and asked questions about my master, which I answered in part. He expressed a great deal of sympathy, and a wish to aid me. He constantly sought opportunities to see me, and wrote to me frequently. I was a poor slave girl, only fifteen years old.

So much attention from a superior person was, of course, flattering; for human nature is the same in all. I also felt grateful for his sympathy, and encouraged by his kind words. It seemed to me a great thing to have such a friend. By degrees, a more tender feeling crept into my heart. He was an educated and eloquent gentleman; too eloquent, alas, for the poor slave girl who trusted in him. Of course I saw whither all this was tending. I knew the impassable gulf between us; but to be an object of interest to a man who is not married, and who is not her master, is agreeable to the pride and feelings of a slave, if her miserable situation has left her any pride or sentiment. It seems less degrading to give one's self, than to submit to compulsion. There is something akin to freedom in having a lover who has no control over you, except that which he gains by kindness and attachment. A master may treat you as rudely as he pleases, and you dare not speak; moreover, the wrong does not seem so great with an unmarried man, as with one who has a wife to be made unhappy. There may be sophistry in all this; but the condition of a slave confuses all principles of morality, and, in fact, renders the practice of them impossible.

When I found that my master had actually begun to build the lonely cottage, other feelings mixed with those I have described. Revenge, and calculations of interest, were added to flattered vanity and sincere gratitude for kindness. I knew nothing would enrage Dr. Flint so much as to know that I favored another; and it was something to triumph over my tyrant even in that small way. I thought he would revenge himself by selling me, and I was sure my friend, Mr. Sands, would buy me. He was a man of more generosity and feeling than my master, and I thought my freedom could be easily obtained from him. The crisis of my fate now came so near that I was desperate. I shuddered to think of being the mother of children that should be owned by my old tyrant. I knew that as soon as a new fancy took him, his victims were sold far off to get rid of them; especially if they had children. I had seen several women sold, with his babies at the breast. He never allowed his offspring by slaves to remain long in sight of himself and his wife. Of a man who was not my master I could ask to have my children well supported; and in this case, I felt confident I should obtain the boon. I also felt quite sure that they would be made free. With all these thoughts revolving in my mind and seeing no other way of escaping the doom I so much dreaded, I made a headlong plunge. Pity me, and pardon me, O virtuous reader! You never knew what it is to be a slave; to be entirely unprotected by law or custom; to have the laws reduce you to the condition of a chattel, entirely subject to the will of another. You never exhausted your ingenuity in avoiding the snares, and eluding the power of a hated tyrant; you never shuddered at the sound of his footsteps, and trembled within hearing of his voice. I know I did wrong. No one can feel it more sensibly than I do. The painful and humiliating memory will haunt me to my dying day. Still, in looking back, calmly, on the events of my life, I feel that the slave woman ought not to be judged by the same standard as others.

The months passed on. I had many unhappy hours. I secretly mourned over the sorrow I was bringing on my grandmother, who had so tried to shield me from harm. I knew that I was the greatest comfort of her old age, and that it was a source of pride to her that I had no degraded myself, like most of the slaves. I wanted to confess to her that I was no longer worthy of her love; but I could not utter the dreaded words.

As for Dr. Flint, I had a feeling of satisfaction and triumph in the thought of telling *him*. From time to time he told me of his intended arrangements, and I was silent. At last, he came and told me the cottage was completed, and ordered me to go to it. I told him I would never enter it. He said, "I have heard enough of such talk as that. You shall go, if you are carried by force; and you shall remain there."

I replied, "I will never go there. In a few months I shall be a mother."

He stood and looked at me in dumb amazement, and left the house without a word. I thought I should be happy in my triumph over him. But now that the truth was out, and my relatives would hear of it, I felt wretched. Humble as were their circumstances, they had pride in my good character. Now, how could I look them in the face? My self-respect was gone! I had resolved that I would be virtuous, though I was a slave. I had said, "Let the storm beat! I will brave it till I die." And now, how humiliated I felt!

I went to my grandmother. My lips moved to make confession, but the words stuck in my throat. I sat down in the shade of a tree at her door and began to sew. I think she saw something unusual was the matter with me. The mother of slaves is very watchful. She knows there is no security for her children. After they have entered their teens she lives in daily expectation of trouble. This leads to many questions. If the girl is of a sensitive nature, timidity keeps her from answering truthfully, and this well-meant course has a tendency to drive her from maternal counsels. Presently, in came my mistress, like a mad woman, and accused me concerning her husband. My grandmother, whose suspicions had been previously awakened, believed what she said. She exclaimed, "O Linda! has it come to this? I had rather see you dead than to see you as you now are. You are a disgrace to your dead mother." She tore from my fingers my mother's wedding ring and her silver thimble. "Go away!" she exclaimed, "and never come to my house, again." Her reproaches fell so hot and heavy, that they left me no chance to answer. Bitter tears, such as the eyes never shed but once, were my only answer. I rose from my seat, but fell back again, sobbing. She did not speak to me; but the tears were running

down her furrowed cheeks, and they scorched me like fire. She had always been so kind to me! *So* kind! How I longed to throw myself at her feet, and tell her all the truth! But she had ordered me to go, and never to come there again. After a few minutes, I mustered strength, and started to obey her. With what feelings did I now close that little gate, which I used to open with such an eager hand in my childhood! It closed upon me with a sound I never heard before.

Where could I go? I was afraid to return to my master's. I walked on recklessly, not caring where I went, or what would become of me. When I had gone four or five miles, fatigue compelled me to stop. I sat down on the stump of an old tree. The stars were shining through the boughs above me. How they mocked me, with their bright, calm light! The hours passed by, and as I sat there alone a chilliness and deadly sickness came over me. I sank on the ground. My mind was full of horrid thoughts. I prayed to die; but the prayer was not answered. At last, with great effort I roused myself, and walked some distance further, to the house of a woman who had been a friend of my mother. When I told her why I was there, she spoke soothingly to me; but I could not be comforted. I thought I could bear my shame if I could only be reconciled to my grandmother. I longed to open my heart to her. I thought if she could know the real state of the case, and all I had been bearing for years, she would perhaps judge me less harshly. My friend advised me to send for her. I did so; but days of agonizing suspense passed before she came. Had she utterly forsaken me? No. She came at last. I knelt before her, and told her the things that had poisoned my life; how long I had been persecuted; that I saw no way of escape; and in an hour of extremity I had become desperate. She listened in silence. I told her I would bear any thing and do any thing, if in time I had hopes of obtaining her forgiveness. I begged of her to pity me, for my dead mother's sake. And she did pity me. She did not say, "I forgive you;" but she looked at me lovingly, with her eyes full of tears. She laid her old hand gently on my head, and murmured, "Poor child! Poor child!"

57

HARRIET TUBMAN
The Underground Railroad
(1863)

Last fall, when the people here became very much alarmed for fear of an invasion from the rebels, all my clothes were packed and sent with others to Hilton Head, and lost; and I have never been able to get any trace of them since. I was sick at the time, and unable to look after them myself. I want, among the rest, a *bloomer* dress, made of some coarse, strong material, to wear on *expeditions*. In our late expedition up the Combahee river, in coming on board the boat, I was carrying *two pigs* for a poor sick woman, who had a child to carry, and the order "double quick" was given, and I started to run, stepped on my dress, it being rather long, and fell and tore it almost off, so that when I got on board the boat there was hardly any thing left of it but shreds. I made up my mind then I would never wear a long dress on another expedition of the kind, but would have a *bloomer* as soon as I could get it. So please make this known to the ladies if you will, for I expect to have use for it very soon, probably before they can get it to me.

You have without doubt seen a fully account of the expedition I refer to. Don't you think we colored people are entitled to some credit for that exploit, under the lead of the brave Colonel Montgomery? We weakened the rebels somewhat on the Combahee river, by taking and bringing away *seven hundred and fifty-six* head of their most valuable live stock, known up in your region as "contrabands," and this, too, without the loss of a single life on our part, though we had good reason to believe that a number of rebels bit the dust. Of these seven hundred and

fifty-six contrabands, nearly or quite all the able-bodied men have joined the colored regiments here.

I have now been absent two years almost, and have just got letters from my friends in Auburn, urging me to come home. My father and mother are old and in feeble health, and need my care and attention. I hope the good people there will not allow them to suffer, and I do not believe they will. But I do not see how I am to leave at present the very important work to be done here. Among other duties which I have, is that of looking after the hospital here for contrabands. Most of those coming from the mainland are very destitute, almost naked. I am trying to find places for those able to work, and provide for them as best I can, so as to lighten the burden on the Government as much as possible, while at the same time they learn to respect themselves by earning their own living.

58

SUSAN B. ANTHONY,
ERNESTINE ROSE, MRS. HOYT,
SARAH H. HALLECK, ANGELINE
G. WELD, AND LUCY STONE
Loyal Women of the Nation
Debate Their Role in
a Time of War (1863)

The call for a meeting of the Loyal Women of the Nation:

In this crisis of our country's destiny, it is the duty of every citizen to consider the peculiar blessings of a republican form of government, and decide what sacrifices of wealth and life are demanded for its defence and preservation. The policy of the war, our whole future life, depends on a clearly-defined idea of the end

From *Commonwealth*, July 1863.

From *History of Woman Suffrage, Vol. 2, 1861–1876*, ed., Elizabeth Cady Stanton, Susan B. Anthony, and Matilda Joslyn Gage (New York: Fowler and Wells, 1886), 53, 56–62, 64–66.

proposed, and the immense advantages to be secured to ourselves and all mankind, by its accomplishment. No mere party or sectional cry, no technicalities of Constitution or military law, no mottoes of craft or policy are big enough to touch the great heart of a nation in the midst of revolution. A grand idea, such as freedom or justice, is needful to kindle and sustain the fires of a high enthusiasm.

At this hour, the best word and work of every man and woman are imperatively demanded. To man, by common consent, is assigned the forum, camp, and field. What is woman's legitimate work, and how she may best accomplish it, is worthy our earnest counsel one with another. We have heard many complaints of the lack of enthusiasm among Northern women: but, when a mother lays her son on the altar of her country, she asks an object equal to the sacrifice. In nursing the sick and wounded, knitting socks, scraping lint, and making jellies, the bravest and best may weary if the thoughts mount not in faith to something beyond and above it all. Work is worship only when a noble purpose fills the soul. Woman is equally interested and responsible with man in the final settlement of this problem of self-government; therefore let none stand idle spectators now. When every hour is big with destiny, and each delay but complicates our difficulties, it is high time for the daughters of the revolution, in solemn counsel, to unseal the last will and testament of the Fathers—lay hold of their birthright of freedom, and keep it a sacred trust for all coming generations.

To this end we ask the Loyal Women of the Nation to meet in the church of the Puritans (Dr. Cheever's), New York, on Thursday, the 14th of May next.

Let the women of every State be largely represented both in person and by letter.
On behalf of the Woman's Central Committee,

ELIZABETH CADY STANTON.
SUSAN B. ANTHONY.

. . . Susan B. Anthony presented a series of resolutions,* and said:

There is great fear expressed on all sides lest this war shall be made a war for the negro. I am willing that it shall be. It is a war to found an empire on the negro in slavery, and shame on us if we do not make it a war to establish the negro in freedom—against whom the whole nation, North and South, East and West, in one mighty conspiracy, has combined from the beginning.

Instead of suppressing the real cause of the war, it should have been proclaimed, not only by the people, but by the President, Congress, Cabinet, and every military commander. Instead of President Lincoln's waiting two long years before calling to the side of the Government the four millions of allies whom we have had within the territory of rebeldom, it should have been the first decree he sent forth. Every hour's delay, every life sacrificed up to the proclamation that called the slave to freedom and to arms, was nothing less than downright murder by the Gov-

---

*Resolved, 1. That the present war between Slavery and Freedom is but one phase of the irrepressible conflict between the aristocratic doctrine that power, not humanity, is statute-maker, and the democratic principle that self-government is the inalienable right of the people.

Resolved, 2. That we heartily approve that part of the President's Proclamation which decrees freedom to the slaves of rebel masters, and we earnestly urge him to devise measures for emancipating all slaves throughout the country.

Resolved, 3. That the national pledge to the freedmen must be redeemed, and the integrity of the Government in making it vindicated, at whatever cost.

Resolved, 4. That while we welcome to legal freedom the recent slaves, we solemnly remonstrate against all State or National legislation which may exclude them from any locality, or debar them from any rights or privileges as free and equal citizens of a common Republic.

Resolved, 5. There never can be a true peace in this Republic until the civil and political rights of all citizens of African descent and all women are practically established.

Resolved, 7. That the women of the Revolution were not wanting in heroism and self-sacrifice, and we, their daughters, are ready in this war to pledge our time, our means, our talents, and our lives, if need be, to secure the final and complete consecration of America to freedom.

ernment. For by all the laws of common-sense—to say nothing of laws military or national—if the President, as Commander-in-Chief of the Army and Navy, could have devised any possible means whereby he might hope to suppress the rebellion, without the sacrifice of the life of one loyal citizen, without the sacrifice of one dollar of the loyal North, it was clearly his duty to have done so. Every interest of the insurgents, every dollar of their property, every institution, however peculiar, every life in every rebel State, even, if necessary, should have been sacrificed, before one dollar or one man should have been drawn from the free States. How much more, then, was it the President's duty to confer freedom on the four million slaves, transform them into a peaceful army for the Union, cripple the rebellion, and establish justice, the only sure foundation of peace! I therefore hail the day when the Government shall recognize that it is a war for freedom. We talk about returning to the old Union—"the Union as it was," and "the Constitution as it is"—about "restoring our country to peace and prosperity—to the blessed conditions that existed before the war!" I ask you what sort of peace, what sort of prosperity, have we had? Since the first slave-ship sailed up the James River with its human cargo, and there, on the soil of the *Old Dominion*, sold it to the highest bidder, we have had nothing but war. . . .

Woman must now assume her God-given responsibilities, and make herself what she is clearly designed to be, the educator of the race. Let her no longer be the mere reflector, the echo of the worldly pride and ambition of man. (Applause). Had the women of the North studied to know and to teach their sons the law of justice to the black man, regardless of the frown or the smile of pro-slavery priest and politician, they would not now be called upon to offer the loved of their households to the bloody Moloch of war. And now, women of the North, I ask you to rise up with earnest, honest purpose, and go forward in the way of right, fearlessly, as independent human beings, responsible to God alone for the discharge of every duty, for the faithful use of every gift, the good Father has given you. Forget conventionalisms; forget what the world will say, whether you are in your place or out of your place; think your best thoughts, speak your best words, do your best works, looking to your own conscience for approval.

Mrs. Hoyt, of Wisconsin: Thus far this meeting has been conducted in such a way as would lead one to suppose that it was an anti-slavery convention. There are ladies here who have come hundreds of miles to attend a business meeting of the Loyal Women of the North; and good as anti-slavery conventions are, and anti-slavery speeches are, in their way, I think that here we should attend to our own business. . . .

. . . Mrs. Rose called for the reading of the resolutions, which after a spirited discussion, all except the fifth, were unanimously adopted.

Mrs. Hoyt, of Wisconsin, said: *Mrs. President*—I object to the passage of the fifth resolution, not because I object to the sentiment expressed; but I do not think it is the time to bring before this meeting, assembled for the purpose of devising the best ways and means by which women may properly assist the Government in its struggle against treason, anything which could in the least prejudice the interest in this cause which is so dear to us all. We all know that Woman's Rights as an *ism* has not been received with entire favor by the women of the country, and I know that there are thousands of earnest, loyal, and able women who will not go into any movement of this kind, if this idea is made prominent. (Applause). I came here from Wisconsin hoping to meet the earnest women of the country. I hoped that nothing that would in any way damage the cause so dear to us all would be brought forward by any of the members. I object to this, because our object should be to maintain, as women properly may, the integrity of our Government: to vindicate its authority; to re-establish it upon a far more enduring basis. We can do this if we do not involve ourselves in any purely political matter, or any *ism* obnoxious to the people. The one idea should be the maintenance of the authority of the Government as it is, and the integrity of the Republican idea. For this, women may properly work, and I hope this resolution will not pass.

SARAH H. HALLECK, of Milton, N. Y.: I would make the suggestion that those who approve of this resolution can afford to give way, and allow that part of it which is objectionable to be stricken out. The negroes have suffered more than the women, and the women, perhaps, can afford to give them the preference. Let it stand as regards them, and blot out the word "woman." It may possibly be woman's place to suffer. At any rate, let her suffer, if, by that means, *man*kind may suffer less.

A VOICE: You are too self-sacrificing.

ERNESTINE L. ROSE: I always sympathize with those who seem to be in the minority. I know it requires a great deal of moral courage to object to anything that appears to have been favorably received. I know very well from long experience how it feels to stand in a minority of one; and I am glad that my friend on the other side (Mrs. Halleck) has already added one to make a minority of two, though that is by far too small to be comfortable. I, for one, object to the proposition to throw woman out of the race for freedom. (APPLAUSE). And do you know why? Because she needs freedom for the freedom of man. (APPLAUSE). Our ancestors made a great mistake in not recognizing woman in the rights of man. It has been justly stated that the negro at present suffers more than woman, but it can do him no injury to place woman in the same category with him. I, for one, object to having that term stricken out, for it can have no possible bearing against anything that we want to promote: we desire to promote human rights and human freedom. It can do no injury but must do good, for it is a painful fact that woman under the law has been in the same category with the slave. Of late years she has had some small privileges conceded to her. Now, mind, I say *conceded;* for publicly it has not yet been recognized by the laws of the land that she has a right to an equality with man. In that resolution it simply states a fact, that in a republic based upon free-

dom, woman, as well as the negro, should be recognized as an equal with the whole human race. (APPLAUSE).

ANGELINE G. WELD: *Mrs. President*—I rejoice exceedingly that that resolution should combine us with the negro. I feel that we have been with him; that the iron has entered into our souls. True, we have not felt the slave-holder's lash; true, we have not had our hands manacled, but our *hearts* have been crushed. . . . Woman was then too undeveloped to demand anything else. But woman is full-grown to-day, whether man knows it or not, equal to her rights, and equal to the responsibilities of the hour. I want to be identified with the negro; until he gets his rights, we never shall have ours. (APPLAUSE).

SUSAN B. ANTHONY: This resolution brings in no question, no *ism*. It merely makes the assertion that in a true democracy, in a genuine republic, every citizen who lives under the government must have the right of representation. You remember the maxim, "Governments derive their just powers from the consent of the governed." This is the fundamental principle of democracy; and before our Government can be a true democracy—before our republic can be placed upon lasting and enduring foundations— the civil and political rights of every citizen must be practically established. This is the assertion of the resolution. It is a philosophical statement. It is not because women suffer, it is not because slaves suffer, it is not because of any individual rights or wrongs—it is the simple assertion of the great fundamental truth of democracy that was proclaimed by our Revolutionary fathers. I hope the discussion will no longer be continued as to the comparative rights or wrongs of one class or another. The question before us is: Is it possible that peace and union shall be established in this country; is it possible for this Government to be a true democracy, a genuine republic, while one-sixth or one-half of the people are disfranchised?

MRS. HOYT: I do not object to the philosophy of these resolutions. I believe in the advancement of the human race, and certainly not in a retrograde movement of the Woman's Rights question; but at the same time I do insist that nothing that has become obnoxious to a portion of the people of the country shall be dragged into this meeting. (APPLAUSE). The women of the North were invited here to meet in convention, not to hold a Temperance meeting, not to hold an Anti-Slavery meeting, not to hold a Woman's Rights Convention, but to consult as to the best practical way for the advancement of the loyal cause. To my certain knowledge there are ladies in this house who have come hundreds of miles, who will withdraw from this convention, who will go home disappointed, and be thrown back on their own resources, and form other plans of organization; whereas they would much prefer to co-operate with the National Convention if this matter were not introduced. This movement must be sacred to the one object of assisting our Government. I would add one more remark, that though the women of the Revolution did help our Government in that early struggle, they did not find it necessary to set forth in any theoretical or clamorous way their right to equal suffrage or equal political position, though doubtless they believed, as much as any of us, in the advancement of woman.

A LADY: I want to ask the lady who just spoke if the women of the Revolution found it necessary to form Loyal Leagues? We are not bound to do just as the women of the Revolution did. (APPLAUSE AND LAUGHTER.) . . .

THE PRESIDENT (Lucy Stone): Every good cause can afford to be just. The lady from Wisconsin, who differs from some of us here, says she is an Anti-Slavery woman. We ought to believe her. She accepts the principles of the Woman's Rights movement, but she does not like the way in which it has been carried on. We ought to believe her. It is not, then, that she objects to the idea of the equality of women and negroes, but because she does not wish to have anything "tacked on" to the Loyal League, that to the mass of people does not seem to belong there. She seems to me to stand precisely in the position of those good people just at the close

of the war of the Revolution. The people then, as now, had their hearts aching with the memory of their buried dead. They had had years of war from which they had garnered out sorrows as well as hopes; and when they came to establish a Union, they found that one black, unmitigated curse of slavery rooted in the soil. Some men said, "We can have no true Union where there is not justice to the negro. The black man is a human being, like us, with the same equal rights." They had given to the world the Declaration of Independence, grand and brave and beautiful. They said, "How can we form a true Union?" Some people representing the class that Mrs. Hoyt represents, answered, "Let us have a Union. We are weak; we have been beset for seven long years; do not let us meddle with the negro question. What we are for is a Union; let us have a Union at all hazards." There were earnest men, men of talent, who could speak well and earnestly, and they persuaded the others to silence. So they said nothing about slavery, and let the wretched monster live.

To-day, over all our land, the unburied bones of our fathers and sons and brothers tell the sad mistake that those men made when long ago they left this one great wrong in the land. They could not accomplish good by passing over a wrong. If the right of one single human being is to be disregarded by us, we fail in our loyalty to the country. All over this land women have no political existence. Laws pass over our heads that we can not unmake. Our property is taken from us without our consent. The babes we bear in anguish and carry in our arms are not ours. The few rights that we have, have been wrung from the legislature by the Woman's Rights movement. We come to-day to say to those who are administering our Government and fighting our battles, "While you are going through this valley of humiliation, do not forget that you must be true alike to the women and the negroes." We can never be truly "loyal" if we leave them out. Leave them out, and we take the same backward step that our fathers took when they left out slavery. If justice to the negro and to woman is right, it can not hurt our loyalty to the country and the Union. If it is not right, let it go out of the way; but if it is right, there is no occasion that we should reject it, or ignore it. We make the statement that the Government derives its just powers from the consent of the governed, and that all human beings have equal rights. This is not an *ism*—it is simply an assertion that we shall be true to the highest truth.

A MAN IN THE AUDIENCE: The question was asked, as I entered this house, "Is it right for women to meet here and intermeddle in our public affairs?" It is the greatest possible absurdity for women to stand on that platform and talk of loyalty to a Government in which nine-tenths of the politicians of the land say they have no right to interfere, and still oppose Woman's Rights. The very act of standing there is an endorsement of Woman's Rights.

A VOICE: I believe this is a woman's meeting. Men have no right to speak here.

THE GENTLEMAN CONTINUED: It is on woman more than on man that the real evils of this war settle. It is not the soldier on the battlefield that suffers most; it is the wife, the mother, the daughter. (Applause, Cries of "Question, question").

A VOICE: You are not a woman, sit down.

SUSAN B. ANTHONY: Some of us who sit upon this platform have many a time been clamored down, and told that we had no right to speak, and that we were out of our place in public meetings; far be it from us, when women assemble, and a man has a thought in his soul, burning for utterance, to retaliate upon him. (LAUGHTER AND APPLAUSE).

The resolution was then put to vote.

A VOICE: Allow me to inquire if men have a right to vote on this question?

THE PRESIDENT: I suppose men who are used to business know that they should *not* vote here. We give them the privilege of speaking.

The resolution was carried by a large majority.

IV. Contesting Woman's Rights

THE WOMEN'S RIGHTS MOVEMENT THAT EMERGED by the mid-nineteenth century had its origins in the struggle for the abolition of slavery, a fact with which Margaret Fuller, one of the major intellectuals of the nineteenth century, opens her groundbreaking essay, "The Great Lawsuit" (1843). Fuller argues, five years before the "official" beginning of the woman's rights movement, that such a movement will face much resistance—that the nation is not ready to accept efforts that will allegedly "break up family union" by releasing women from the private into the public sphere. The ideas Fuller articulated in "The Great Lawsuit" (which was published in a journal she edited called *The Dial* and subsequently expanded into *Woman in the Nineteenth Century*) combined Transcendental spirituality and calls for practical agitation—and they had a direct influence on the first Woman's Rights Convention.

By all accounts, the movement to gain rights for women began in 1848 in Seneca Falls, New York. The call for the first meeting was put out by Elizabeth Cady Stanton, Mary Ann McClintock, Lucretia Mott, Martha Wright, and Jane C. Hunt, who had begun talking about women's right in McClintock's kitchen. They resolved to call a woman's rights convention a week later, on July 19 and 20, and even on such short notice, more than 200 women and about forty men came to the meeting. When the organizers wrote the statement for the convention, "Declaration of Sentiments and Resolutions" (1848), they turned to the founding document of the nation for inspiration—but they made some changes: "We hold these truths to be self-evident," they wrote, "that all men *and women* are created equal."

The aim of the woman's rights movement was to eliminate the sex's dependent and inferior position under the law. From the beginning feminist leaders demanded the right to vote and the rights of citizenship, elaborating a fundamental political reform that initially caused dissension within the nascent movement. Of the resolutions submitted by Elizabeth Cady Stanton at the Seneca Falls Convention, it was the ninth resolution—that which demanded the right of suffrage—which met with opposition, and it was only passed (though not unanimously) after a protracted discussion.

Lucretia Mott, while herself one of the organizers of the Seneca Falls Convention, initially opposed the demand for the vote. She publicly supported suffrage, but clearly wanted to maintain a distance from electoral politics. She argues in "Discourse on Woman" (1849)—a speech delivered in Philadelphia—that while women's abstract right to the franchise is the same as men's, women should not be encouraged to take an active role in electoral politics because the corruption of political life is unworthy of Christian men as well as women. She does hold out a hope, though, that perhaps women's entry into politics would elevate civic life.

Despite the fact that the call for women's right to vote was initially a cause of controversy within the woman's rights movement, it quickly became preeminent—elevated above other reforms to such an extent that antebellum feminism has often been labeled the suffrage movement. As "Resolutions of the Seventh National Woman's Rights Convention in New York" (1856) makes clear, feminists considered "the one cardinal demand for the right of suffrage" as both the symbol and the guarantee of all other rights. Public support, however, was much slower on the issue of female suffrage than on more specific legal changes proposed by woman's rights activists, such as the reform of marriage and property laws, and it would not be until 1920 that all women were given the franchise.

Early feminist activists based their arguments for legal, economic, and social equality between the sexes on natural rights—the Enlightenment idea that one is born with specific rights and that the state has the duty to protect those pre-existent rights. In Stanton's rewriting of the Declaration of Independence as the "Declaration of Sentiments," unanimously adopted by the Seneca Falls Convention, she insists that women, as well as men, are "endowed by their Creator with certain inalienable rights," including the right to the elective franchise. Women had certain natural rights, in other words, of which man-made laws were unjustly depriving her. One of the resolutions of the Seneca Falls Convention was that any law that interferes with woman's own conscience is "contrary to the great precept of nature," and therefore null and void.

The argument of natural rights was inextricable from the allegedly "natural" difference between the sexes, and antebellum feminists were forced to address the belief that men had certain rights that women did not because of their inherently superior strength and aggression. In "Justice for Women" (1850), Paulina W. Davis, the president elect of the First National Woman's Rights Convention in Worcester, attacks the argument that some rights should be enjoyed only by those who have the "natural" strength to win them from tyranny. Davis argues for a shift from the law of force to that of "justice": men may have achieved their rights by physical rebellion, but women—as the physically weaker sex—demand to be given their un-alienable rights as their just due. Similarly, Frances D. Gage, in "Woman's Natural Rights" (1851), an address to the Second National Woman's Rights Convention in Akron, insists that women be given their natural rights in a "revolution without armies," suggesting a massive cultural shift from the law of strength to the law of justice and truth.

Both Davis's and Gage's acceptance of women's physical weakness and superior morality is representative of most antebellum woman's rights activists, who—despite their insistence on legal equality—typically held entrenched assumptions about women's biological, cultural, and moral difference from men. Therefore, women's rights activists did not entirely oppose the so-called "domestic feminists"—those women who argued for women's rights within the domestic sphere, rights based on women's spiritual and moral superiority to men. Sarah Josepha Hale's enormously influential magazine, *Godey's Lady's Book*, was a primary vehicle for domestic feminist arguments. It reflected Hale's own belief that women were the undisputed ruler of the spiritual realm and the home, that "sacred residence." Haddie Lane's story "Woman's Rights" (1850) is paradigmatic of *Godey's* feminism and reveals how ladies' magazines served as alternative (albeit more conservative) feminist spaces to the more radical political arena of the woman's rights conventions.

After suffrage, the reform of marriage law was a cornerstone of the mainstream woman's rights movement. The convention at Seneca Falls asserted that men have rendered married women "civilly dead," ensuring that they have no control over their property, their earnings, their children, or even their own actions. In part because feminists met with some success in marriage reform, it became increasingly central to the movement. As "Resolving to Reform Marriage Laws" (1853) makes apparent, three of the resolutions passed at the Woman's Rights Convention in Rochester addressed inequities in the legal status of married women.

Along with attempting to change marriage as it was institutionalized in the legal code—through lobbying and petitioning state legislatures—some feminists chose to confront the inequalities of marriage at an individual level. In "The Marriage of Lucy Stone under Protest" (1855), Stone and Henry Blackwell declare that, although they are entering into marriage, they do not consider themselves bound by its laws, and they specifically refute each injustice which such laws enact upon women.

Very few feminists went as far as Mary S. Gove (Nichols) in their public statements about marriage. Nichols was a health reformer, practicing physician, and one of the only female "free love" advocates in antebellum America. She argues in "Woman, an Individual" (1854) for woman's absolute "self-ownership" and "self-sovereignty." A radical for her time, Nichols claims that the only laws each woman should follow are the laws of her "self," and if those laws conflict with marriage law, the latter should be disregarded. Nichols was virtually alone in dealing with the sexual abuses of marriage and in showing how an indissoluble marriage tie binds women to "prostitution" and wrecks their health—including destroying their natural sexual and maternal instincts. Never a part of the mainstream woman's rights movement, Nichols' insistence that a woman had the right to leave her marriage when she chose, and to pick whomever she wanted as the father of her children, caused many feminists to shun her. As the debate on marriage at the Woman's Rights Convention in 1860 reveals, no mainstream feminist wanted to risk being labeled a proponent of "free love."

Radicals like Nichols aside, the woman's movement contained a range of views about marriage. In "Debating Marriage and Divorce Laws" (1860), Antoinette Brown Blackwell, Ernestine Rose, and Susan B. Anthony—at the Tenth National Woman's Rights Convention, in New York—express divergent opinions about both the relevance of marriage to the movement and about what should be changed in existing laws. The issue of making divorce more accessible to women sparked a debate at the convention in which an idealistic Blackwell claims that marriage is a permanent contract between equals sanctioned both by God and by men and women's innate need of each other; presenting a countering view, the more pragmatic Rose argues that the realities of social inequality and human weakness mean that marriages are rarely ideal and that feminists should consider the daily abuse of women within the institution. Some participants in the convention introduced motions to exclude any discussion of marriage, proposing that such discussion was not germane to the issue of women's rights; Anthony strenuously disagreed.

Despite some internal conflict about the institution of marriage and the relevance of its reform to the woman's rights movement, feminists did succeed in bringing about changes in the law. In 1848 and 1860, New York passed the most comprehensive pieces of women's rights legislation in the United States thus far—Married Women's Property Acts, which granted women the right not only to control their own property but also to keep their separate earnings. "Appeal to the Women of New York" (1860) builds upon this success, urging women to keep working for other necessary rights such as the vote and the right to trial by a jury of their peers.

Perhaps one of the most sweeping feminist documents of the antebellum period is Elizabeth Cady Stanton's "Address to the New York Legislature" (1854), a speech which eloquently articulates all the elements of the legal program of the early woman's rights movement: the demand for the vote and other basic rights of citizenship, such as the right to a jury of one's peers; and a demand for reform of all aspects of family law. Stanton, however, reveals both her own bias and that of the predominantly white and middle-class movement when she positions herself, in front of the legislature, as one of the "daughters of revolutionary heroes of '76"—as "moral, virtuous, and intelligent"—and thus worthy to be classed with the "proud white man" rather than with "negroes" in terms of citizenship status. Her speech, for all its scope, does not elaborate the concerns of either working-class women or African-American women.

Up to and after the Civil War, the issue of race caused increasing divisions within the woman's rights movement. Generally, when mainstream antebellum feminists discussed rights, they meant the rights of middle-class white women like themselves—hence their attention to the laws of property and inheritance, which were of concern only to women of economic means. The only visible and vocal Africa-American woman in the feminist movement before the Civil War was Sojourner Truth, a regular speaker at woman's rights conventions; she was, in fact, the only black woman present at the First National Woman's Rights Convention held in Worcester in 1850. By both her very presence and the content of her speeches, such as "A'n't I a Woman?" (1851), Truth forced the white women around her to consider black women when they talked of "woman's" rights. When Truth prepared to speak at the Woman's Rights Convention in Akron in 1851, some women begged the chair of the convention not to allow her to do so for fear that newspapers would confound the cause of women with the cause of slaves—revealing the narrow-mindedness of some woman's rights activists. The title of Truth's speech was quite appropriate; slaves, in some women's minds at least, were not women.

The extent to which woman's rights activists should be concerned with slavery and with the position of African-Americans is the subject of heated debate in "Rights for All Women of Whatsoever Color" (1854) and Anne E. McDowell's "Woman's Rights and Slavery" (1856). The former is a letter to the *Una*, the first feminist newspaper to spring from the woman's rights movement (founded in 1853 and edited by Paulina Wright Davis). The writer is responding to a letter written by "Isola," printed in an earlier number of the paper, which argues that woman's rights activists should not waste energy fighting slavery when "the happiness of future generations of white women" is at stake. The writer of "Rights for all Women," who is strongly supported by the editor of *Una,* insists that feminists should fight for *all* women, of whatever color. Anne E. McDowell, the editor of another feminist newspaper, *The Woman's Advocate*, begins her editorial by quoting a review of her paper printed in the Lancaster *Ledger* in South Carolina. The reviewer scathingly criticizes her for diverting her attention from woman's rights to anti-slavery, and McDowell counters by graphically illustrating how slavery necessarily involves the inequality and degradation of women.

One of the first women to voice a fundamental critique of the class system and of the economic position of women was Caroline Healey Dall, who, in "Woman's Right to Labor" (1859)—one of her many lectures—argues that the fundamental injustice of women was not their lack of political rights but of economic opportunity. Dall specifically attacks middle-class female philanthropists who "work for nothing, like the angels," and who thus devalue all women's work and drive down wages for women who must work to survive. In her analysis of how women's actions (as well as those of men and the capitalist system in general) affect other women, Dall is one of a minority of feminists who articulates differences among women based on class. As feminist thought continued to strengthen and to diversify after the Civil War and toward the end of the nineteenth century, divisions along both race and class lines would continue to deepen—deepening, in turn, the theoretical and practical weight of feminism.

59

MARGARET FULLER
The Great Lawsuit (1843)

. . . Of all its banners, none has been more steadily upheld, and under none has more valor and willingness for real sacrifices been shown, than that of the champions of the enslaved African. And this band it is, which, partly in consequence of a natural following out of principles, partly because many women have been prominent in that cause, makes, just now, the warmest appeal in behalf of woman.

Though there has been a growing liberality on this point, yet society at large is not so prepared for the demands of this party, but that they are, and will be for some time, coldly regarded as the Jacobins of their day.

"Is it not enough," cries the sorrowful trader, "that you have done all you could to break up the national Union, and thus destroy the prosperity of our country, but now you must be trying to break up family union, to take my wife away from the cradle, and the kitchen hearth, to vote at polls, and preach from a pulpit? Of course, if she does such things, she cannot attend to those of her own sphere. She is happy enough as she is. She has more leisure than I have, every means of improvement, every indulgence."

"Have you asked her whether she was satisfied with these indulgences?"

"No, but I know she is. She is too amiable to wish what would make me unhappy, and too judicious to wish to step beyond the sphere of her sex. I will never consent to have our peace disturbed by any such discussions."

"'Consent'—you? it is not consent from you that is in question, it is assent from your wife."

"Am I not the head of my house?"

"You are not the head of your wife. God has given her a mind of her own."

"I am the head and she the heart."

From *The Dial* 6 (July 1843).

"God grant you play true to one another then. If the head represses no natural pulse of the heart, there can be no question as to your giving your consent. Both will be of one accord, and there needs but to present any question to get a full and true answer. There is no need of precaution, of indulgence, or consent. But our doubt is whether the heart consents with the head, or only acquiesces in its decree; and it is to ascertain the truth on this point, that we propose some liberating measures."

Thus vaguely are these questions proposed and discussed at present. But their being proposed at all implies much thought, and suggests more. Many women are considering within themselves what they need that they have not, and what they can have, if they find they need it. Many men are considering whether women are capable of being and having more than they are and have, and whether, if they are, it will be best to consent to improvement of their condition.

The numerous party, whose opinions are already labelled and adjusted too much to their mind to admit of any new light, strive, by lectures on some model-woman of bridal-like beauty and gentleness, by writing or lending little treatises, to mark out with due precision the limits of woman's sphere, and woman's mission, and to prevent other than the rightful shepherd from climbing the wall, or the flock from using any chance gap to run astray.

Without enrolling ourselves at once on either side, let us look upon the subject from that point of view which to-day offers. No better, it is to be feared, than a high house-top. A high hill-top, or at least a cathedral spire, would be desirable.

It is not surprising that it should be the Anti-Slavery party that pleads for woman, when we consider merely that she does not hold property on equal terms with men; so that, if a husband dies without a will, the wife, instead of stepping at once into his place as head of the family, inherits only a part of his fortune, as if she were a child, or ward only, not an equal partner.

We will not speak of the innumerable instances, in which profligate or idle men live upon the earnings of industrious wives; or if the wives leave them and take with them the children, to perform the double duty of mother and father, follow from place to place, and threaten to rob them of the children, if deprived of the rights of a husband, as they call them, planting themselves in their poor lodgings, frightening them into paying tribute by taking from them the children, running into debt at the expense of these otherwise so overtasked helots. Though such instances abound, the public opinion of his own sex is against the man, and when cases of extreme tyranny are made known, there is private action in the wife's favor. But if woman be, indeed, the weaker party, she ought to have legal protection, which would make such oppression impossible.

And knowing that there exists, in the world of men, a tone of feeling towards women as towards slaves, such as is expressed in the common phrase, "Tell that to women and children;" that the infinite soul can only work through them in already ascertained limits; that the prerogative of reason, man's highest portion, is allotted to them in a much lower degree; that it is better for them to be engaged in active labor, which is to be furnished and directed by those better able to think, &c. &c.; we need not go further, for who can review the experience of last week, without recalling words which imply, whether in jest or earnest, these views, and views like these? Knowing this, can we wonder that many reformers think that measures are not likely to be taken in behalf of women, unless their wishes could be publicly represented by women?

That can never be necessary, cry the other side. All men are privately influenced by women; each has his wife, sister, or female friends, and is too much biassed by these relations to fail of representing their interests. And if this is not enough, let them propose and enforce their wishes with the pen. The beauty of home would be destroyed, the delicacy of the sex be violated, the dignity of halls of legislation destroyed, by

an attempt to introduce them there. Such duties are inconsistent with those of a mother; and then we have ludicrous pictures of ladies in hysterics at the polls, and senate chambers filled with cradles.

But if, in reply, we admit as truth that woman seems destined by nature rather to the inner circle, we must add that the arrangements of civilized life have not been as yet such as to secure it to her. Her circle, if the duller, is not the quieter. If kept from excitement, she is not from drudgery. Not only the Indian carries the burdens of the camp, but the favorites of Louis the Fourteenth accompany him in his journeys, and the washerwoman stands at her tub and carries home her work at all seasons, and in all states of health. . . .

Under these circumstances, without attaching importance in themselves to the changes demanded by the champions of woman, we hail them as signs of the times. We would have every arbitrary barrier thrown down. We would have every path laid open to woman as freely as to man. Were this done, and a slight temporary fermentation allowed to subside, we believe that the Divine would ascend into nature to a height unknown in the history of past ages, and nature, thus instructed, would regulate the spheres not only so as to avoid collision, but to bring forth ravishing harmony. . . .

A writer in a late number of the New York Pathfinder, in two articles headed "Femality," has uttered a still more pregnant word than any we have named. He views woman truly from the soul, and not from society, and the depth and leading of his thoughts is proportionably remarkable. He views the feminine nature as a harmonizer of the vehement elements, and this has often been hinted elsewhere; but what he expresses most forcibly is the lyrical, the inspiring and inspired apprehensiveness of her being.

Had I room to dwell upon this topic, I could not say anything so precise, so near the heart of the matter, as may be found in that article; but, as it is, I can only indicate, not declare, my view.

There are two aspects of woman's nature,

expressed by the ancients as Muse and Minerva. It is the former to which the writer in the Pathfinder looks. It is the latter which Wordsworth has in mind, when he says,

"With a placid brow,
Which woman ne'er should forfeit, keep
thy vow."

The especial genius of woman I believe to be electrical in movement, intuitive in function, spiritual in tendency. She is great not so easily in classification, or re-creation, as in an instinctive seizure of causes, and a simple breathing out of what she receives that has the singleness of life, rather than the selecting or energizing of art.

More native to her is it to be the living model of the artist, than to set apart from herself any one form in objective reality; more native to inspire and receive the poem than to create it. In so far as soul is in her completely developed, all soul is the same; but as far as it is modified in her as woman, it flows, it breathes, it sings, rather than deposits soil, or finishes work, and that which is especially feminine flushes in blossom the face of earth, and pervades like air and water all this seeming solid globe, daily renewing and purifying its life. Such may be the especially feminine element, spoken of as Femality. But it is no more the order of nature that it should be incarnated pure in any form, than that the masculine energy should exist unmingled with it in any form.

Male and female represent the two sides of the great radical dualism. But, in fact, they are perpetually passing into one another. Fluid hardens to solid, solid rushes to fluid. There is no wholly masculine man, no purely feminine woman.

History jeers at the attempts of physiologists to bind great original laws by the forms which flow from them. They make a rule; they say from observation what can and cannot be. In vain! Nature provides exceptions to every rule. She sends women to battle, and sets Hercules spinning; she enables women to bear immense burdens, cold, and frost; she enables the man, who feels maternal love, to nourish his infant like a mother. Of late she plays still gayer pranks. Not only she deprives organizations, but organs, of a necessary end. She enables people to read with the top of the head, and see with the pit of the stomach. Presently she will make a female Newton, and a male Syren.

Man partakes of the feminine in the Apollo, woman of the Masculine as Minerva.

Let us be wise and not impede the soul. Let her work as she will. Let us have one creative energy, one incessant revelation. Let it take what form it will, and let us not bind it by the past to man or woman, black or white. Jove sprang from Rhea, Pallas from Jove. So let it be.

If it has been the tendency of the past remarks to call woman rather to the Minerva side,—if I, unlike the more generous writer, have spoken from society no less than the soul,—let it be pardoned. It is love that has caused this, love for many incarcerated souls, that might be freed could the idea of religious self-dependence be established in them, could the weakening habit of dependence on others be broken up.

Every relation, every gradation of nature, is incalculably precious, but only to the soul which is poised upon itself, and to whom no loss, no change, can bring dull discord, for it is in harmony with the central soul.

If any individual live too much in relations, so that he becomes a stranger to the resources of his own nature, he falls after a while into a distraction, or imbecility, from which he can only be cured by a time of isolation, which gives the renovating fountains time to rise up. With a society it is the same. Many minds, deprived of the traditionary or instinctive means of passing a cheerful existence, must find help in self-impulse or perish. It is therefore that while any elevation, in the view of union, is to be hailed with joy, we shall not decline celibacy as the great fact of the time. It is one from which no vow, no arrangement, can at present save a thinking mind. For now the rowers are pausing on their oars, they wait a change before they can pull together. All tends to illustrate the thought of a wise contemporary. Union is only possible to those who are units. To be fit for relations in time, souls, whether of man or woman, must be able to do without them in the spirit.

It is therefore that I would have woman lay aside all thought, such as she habitually cherishes, of being taught and led by men. I would have her, like the Indian girl, dedicate herself to the Sun, the Sun of Truth, and go no where if his beams did not make clear the path. I would have her free from compromise, from complaisance, from helplessness, because I would have her good enough and strong enough to love one and all beings, from the fullness, not the poverty of being. . . .

But men do *not* look at both sides, and women must leave off asking them and being influenced by them, but retire within themselves, and explore the groundwork of being till they find their peculiar secret. Then when they come forth again, renovated and baptized, they will know how to turn all dross to gold, and will be rich and free though they live in a hut, tranquil, if in a crowd. Then their sweet singing shall not be from passionate impulse, but the lyrical overflow of a divine rapture, and a new music shall be elucidated from this many-chorded world.

Grant her then for a while the armor and the javelin. Let her put from her the press of other minds and meditate in virgin loneliness. . . .

A profound thinker has said "no married woman can represent the female world, for she belongs to her husband. The idea of woman must be represented by a virgin."

But that is the very fault of marriage, and of the present relation between the sexes, that the woman does belong to the man, instead of forming a whole with him. Were it otherwise there would be no such limitation to the thought.

Woman, self-centered, would never be absorbed by any relation; it would be only an experience to her as to man. It is a vulgar error that love, *a* love to woman is her whole exist-

ence; she also is born for Truth and Love in their universal energy. Would she but assume her inheritance, Mary would not be the only Virgin Mother. Not Manzoni alone would celebrate in his wife the virgin mind with the maternal wisdom and conjugal affections. The soul is ever young, ever virgin.

And will not she soon appear? The woman who shall vindicate their birthright for all women; who shall teach them what to claim, and how to use what they obtain? Shall not her name be for her era Victoria, for her country and her life Virginia? Yet predictions are rash; she herself must teach us to give her the fitting name.

60

ELIZABETH CADY STANTON, LUCRETIA MOTT, MARTHA C. WRIGHT, MARY ANN MCCLINTOCK, AND JANE C. HUNT

Declaration of Sentiments and Resolutions at the First Woman's Rights Convention in Seneca Falls (1848)

Declaration of Sentiments

When, in the course of human events, it becomes necessary for one portion of the family of man to assume among the people of the earth a position different from that which they have hitherto occupied, but one to which the laws of nature and of nature's God entitle them, a decent respect to the opinions of mankind requires that they should declare the causes that impel them to such a course.

We hold these truths to be self-evident: that

From *The First Convention Ever Called to Discuss the Civil and Political Rights of Women, Seneca Falls, N.Y., July 19, 20, 1848* (n.p., n.d.), 1–6.

all men and women are created equal; that they are endowed by their Creator with certain inalienable rights, that among these are life, liberty, and the pursuit of happiness; that to secure these rights governments are instituted, deriving their just powers from the consent of the governed. Whenever any form of government becomes destructive of these ends, it is the right of those who suffer from it to refuse allegiance to it, and to insist upon the institution of a new government, laying its foundation on such principles, and organizing its powers in such form as to them shall seem most likely to effect their safety and happiness. Prudence, indeed, will dictate that governments long established should not be changed for light and transient causes; and accordingly, all experience hath shown that mankind are more disposed to suffer, while evils are sufferable, than to right themselves by abolishing the forms to which they were accustomed. But when a long train of abuses and usurpations, pursuing invariably the same object evinces a design to reduce them under absolute despotism, it is their duty to throw off such government, and to provide new guards for their future security. Such has been the patient sufferance of the women under this government, and such is now the necessity which constrains them to demand the equal station to which they are entitled.

The history of mankind is a history of repeated injuries and usurpations on the part of man toward woman, having in direct object the establishment of an absolute tyranny over her. To prove this, let facts be submitted to a candid world.

He has never permitted her to exercise her inalienable right to the elective franchise.

He has compelled her to submit to laws, in the formation of which she had no voice.

He has withheld from her rights which are given to the most ignorant and degraded men—both natives and foreigners.

Having deprived her of this first right of a citizen, the elective franchise, thereby leaving her without representation in the halls of legislation, he has oppressed her on all sides.

He has made her, if married, in the eye of the law, civilly dead.

He has taken from her all right in property, even to the wages she earns.

He has made her, morally, an irresponsible being, as she can commit many crimes with impunity, provided they be done in the presence of her husband. In the covenant of marriage, she is compelled to promise obedience to her husband, he becoming, to all intents and purposes, her master—the law giving him power to deprive her of her liberty, and to administer chastisement.

He has so framed the laws of divorce, as to what shall be the proper causes of divorce; in case of separation, to whom the guardianship of the children shall be given; as to be wholly regardless of the happiness of women—the law, in all cases, going upon a false supposition of the supremacy of man, and giving all power into his hands.

After depriving her of all rights as a married woman, if single and the owner of property, he has taxed her to support a government which recognizes her only when her property can be made profitable to it.

He has monopolized nearly all the profitable employments, and from those she is permitted to follow, she receives but a scanty remuneration.

He closes against her all the avenues to wealth and distinction, which he considers most honorable to himself. As a teacher of theology, medicine, or law, she is not known.

He has denied her the facilities for obtaining a thorough education—all colleges being closed against her.

He allows her in Church, as well as State, but a subordinate position, claiming Apostolic authority for her exclusion from the ministry, and, with some exceptions, from any public participation in the affairs of the Church.

He has created a false public sentiment, by giving to the world a different code of morals for men and women, by which moral delinquencies which exclude women from society, are not only tolerated but deemed of little account in man.

He has usurped the prerogative of Jehovah himself, claiming it as his right to assign for her a sphere of action, when that belongs to her conscience and to her God.

He has endeavored, in every way that he could, to destroy her confidence in her own powers, to lessen her self-respect, and to make her willing to lead a dependent and abject life.

Now, in view of this entire disfranchisement of one-half the people of this country, their social and religious degradation,—in view of the unjust laws above mentioned, and because women do feel themselves aggrieved, oppressed, and fraudulently deprived of their most sacred rights, we insist that they have immediate admission to all the rights and privileges which belong to them as citizens of the United States.

In entering upon the great work before us, we anticipate no small amount of misconception, misrepresentation, and ridicule; but we shall use every instrumentality within our power to effect our object. We shall employ agents, circulate tracts, petition the state and national legislatures, and endeavor to enlist the pulpit and the press in our behalf. We hope this Convention will be followed by a series of Conventions, embracing every part of the country.

Firmly relying upon the final triumph of the Right and the True, we do this day affix our signatures to this declaration.

Lucretia Mott, Elizabeth Cady Stanton, Eunice Newton Foote, Mary Ann McClintock, Martha C. Wright, Jane C. Hunt, Amy Post, Catharine A. F. Stebbins, Mary H. Hallowell, Charlotte Woodward, Sarah Hallowell.

Richard P. Hunt, Samuel D. Tilman, Elisha Foote, Frederick Douglass, Elias J. Doty, James Mott, Thomas McClintock.

This Declaration was unanimously adopted and signed by 32 men and 68 women.

Resolutions

Whereas the great precept of nature is conceded to be, "that man shall pursue his own true and substantial happiness." Blackstone, in his Commentaries, remarks, that this law of Nature being coeval with mankind, and dictated by God himself, is of course superior in obligation to any other. It is binding over all the globe, in all countries, and at all times; no human laws are of any validity if contrary to this, and such of them as are valid, derive all their force, and all their validity, and all their authority, mediately and immediately, from this original; therefore,

Resolved, That such laws as conflict, in any way, with the true and substantial happiness of woman, are contrary to the great precept of nature, and of no validity; for this is "superior in obligation to any other."

Resolved, That all laws which prevent woman from occupying such a station in society as her conscience shall dictate, or which place her in a position inferior to that of man, are contrary to the great precept of nature, and therefore of no force or authority.

Resolved, That woman is man's equal—was intended to be so by the Creator—and the highest good of the race demands that she should be recognized as such.

Resolved, That the women of this country ought to be enlightened in regard to the laws under which they live, that they may no longer publish their degradation, by declaring themselves satisfied with their present position, nor their ignorance, by asserting that they have all the rights they want.

Resolved, That inasmuch as man, while claiming for himself intellectual superiority, does accord to woman moral superiority, it is preeminently his duty to encourage her to speak, and teach, as she has an opportunity, in all religious assemblies.

Resolved, That the same amount of virtue, delicacy, and refinement of behavior, that is required of woman in the social state, should also be required of man, and the same transgressions should be visited with equal severity on both man and woman.

Resolved, That the objection of indelicacy and impropriety, which is so often brought against woman when she addresses a public audience, comes with a very ill-grace from those who encourage, by their attendance, her appearance on the stage, in the concert, or in feats of the circus.

Resolved, That woman has too long rested satisfied in the circumscribed limits which corrupt customs and a perverted application of the Scriptures have marked out for her, and that it is time she should move in the enlarged sphere which her great Creator has assigned her.

Resolved, That it is the duty of the women of this country to secure to themselves their sacred right to the elective franchise.

Resolved, That the equality of human rights results necessarily from the fact of the identity of the race in capabilities and responsibilities.

Resolved, therefore, That, being invested by the Creator with the same capabilities, and the same consciousness of responsibility for their exercise, it is demonstrably the right and duty of woman, equally with man, to promote every righteous cause, by every righteous means; and especially in regard to the great subjects of morals and religion, it is self-evidently her right to participate with her brother in teaching them, both in private and in public, by writing and by speaking, by any instrumentalities proper to be used, and in any assemblies proper to be held; and this being a self-evident truth, growing out of the divinely implanted principles of human nature, any custom or authority adverse to it, whether modern or wearing the hoary sanction of antiquity, is to be regarded as a self-evident falsehood, and at war with the interests of mankind.

The only resolution which met opposition was the 9th, demanding the right of suffrage which, however, after a prolonged discussion was adopted. All of the meetings throughout the two days were largely attended, but this, like every step in progress, was ridiculed from Maine to Louisiana.

61

LUCRETIA MOTT
Discourse on Woman, Speech Delivered in Philadelphia (1849)

. . . I have no prepared address to deliver to you, being unaccustomed to speak in that way; but I felt a wish to offer some views for your consideration, though in a desultory manner, which may lead to such reflection and discussion as will present the subject in a true light.

In the beginning, man and woman were created equal. "Male and female created he them, and blessed them, and called their name Adam." He gave dominion to both over the lower animals, but not to one over the other.

"Man o'er woman
He made not lord, such title to himself
Reserving, human left from human free."

The cause of the subjection of woman to man, was early ascribed to disobedience to the command of God. This would seem to show that she was then regarded as not occupying her true and rightful position in society.

The laws given on Mount Sinai for the government of man and woman were equal, the precepts of Jesus make no distinction. Those who read the Scriptures, and judge for themselves, not resting satisfied with the perverted application of the text, do not find the distinction, that theology and ecclesiastical authorities have made, in the condition of the sexes. In the early ages, Miriam and Deborah, conjointly with Aaron and Barak, enlisted themselves on the side which they regarded the right, unitedly going up to their battles, and singing their songs of victory. We regard these with veneration. . . .

Why should not woman seek to be a reformer? If she is to shrink from being such an iconoclast as shall "break the image of man's lower worship," as so long held up to view; if

From *Discourse on Woman, by Lucretia Mott. Delivered at the Assembly Buildings, December 17, 1849. Being a Full Phonographic Report, Revised by the Author* (Philadelphia: T. B. Peterson, 1850), 4–5, 7–8, 12–13, 14–20.

she is to fear to exercise her reason, and her noblest powers, lest she should be thought to "attempt to act the man," and not "acknowledge his supremacy;" if she is to be satisfied with the narrow sphere assigned her by man, nor aspire to a higher, lest she should transcend the bounds of female delicacy; truly it is a mournful prospect for woman. We would admit all the difference, that our great and beneficent Creator has made, in the relation of man and woman, nor would we seek to disturb this relation; but we deny that the present position of woman, is her true sphere of usefulness: nor will she attain to this sphere, until the disabilities and disadvantages, religious, civil, and social, which impede her progress, are removed out of her way. These restrictions have enervated her mind and paralysed her powers. While man assumes, that the present is the original state designed for woman, that the *existing* "differences are not arbitrary nor the result of accident," but grounded in nature; she will not make the necessary effort to obtain her just rights, lest it should subject her to the kind of scorn and contemptuous manner in which she has been spoken of.

So far from her "ambition leading her to attempt to act the man," she needs all the encouragement she can receive, by the removal of obstacles from her path, in order that she may become a "true woman." As it is desirable that man should act a manly and generous part, not "mannish," so let woman be urged to exercise a dignified and womanly bearing, not womanish. Let her cultivate all the graces and proper accomplishments of her sex, but let not these degenerate into a kind of effeminacy, in which she is satisfied to be the mere plaything or toy of society, content with her outward adornings, and with the tone of flattery and fulsome adulation too often addressed to her. True, nature has made a difference in her configuration, her physical strength, her voice, &c.—and we ask no change, we are satisfied with nature. But how has neglect and mismanagement increased this difference! It is our duty to develop these natural powers by suitable exercise, so that they may

be strengthened "by reason of use." In the ruder state of society, woman is made to bear heavy burdens, while her "lord and master" walks idly by her side. In the civilization to which we have attained, if cultivated and refined woman would bring all her powers into use, she might engage in pursuits which she now shrinks from as beneath her proper vocation. The energies of men need not then be wholly devoted to the counting house and common business of life, in order that women in fashionable society, may be supported in their daily promenades and nightly visits to the theatre and ball room. . . .

The question is often asked, "What does woman want, more than she enjoys? What is she seeking to obtain? Of what rights is she deprived? What privileges are withheld from her?" I answer, she asks nothing as favor, but as right, she wants to be acknowledged a moral, responsible being. She is seeking not to be governed by laws, in the making of which she has no voice. She is deprived of almost every right in civil society, and is a cypher in the nation, except in the right of presenting a petition. In religious society her disabilities, as already pointed out, have greatly retarded her progress. Her exclusion from the pulpit or ministry—her duties marked out for her by her equal brother man, subject to creeds, rules, and disciplines made for her by him—this is unworthy her true dignity. In marriage, there is assumed superiority, on the part of the husband, and admitted inferiority, with a promise of obedience, on the part of the wife. This subject calls loudly for examination, in order that the wrong may be redressed. . . .

I would not, however, go so far, either as regards the abject slave or woman; for in both cases they may be so degraded by the crushing influences around them, that they may not be sensible of the blessing of Freedom. Liberty is not less a blessing, because oppression has so long darkened the mind that it cannot appreciate it. I would therefore urge, that woman be placed in such a situation in society, by the yielding of her rights, and have such opportunities for growth and development, as shall raise her from this low, enervated and paralysed condition, to a full appreciation of the blessing of entire freedom of mind.

It is with reluctance that I make the demand for the political rights of woman, because this claim is so distasteful to the age. Woman shrinks, in the present state of society, from taking any interest in politics. The events of the French Revolution, and the claim for woman's rights are held up to her as a warning. But let us not look at the excesses of women alone, at that period; but remember that the age was marked with extravagances and wickedness in men as well as women. Indeed, political life abounds with these excesses, and with shameful outrage. Who knows, but that if woman acted her part in governmental affairs, there might be an entire change in the turmoil of political life. It becomes man to speak modestly of his ability to act without her. If woman's judgment were exercised, why might she not aid in making the laws by which she is governed? . . .

Far be it from me to encourage woman to vote, or to take an active part in politics, in the present state of our government. Her right to the elective franchise however, is the same, and should be yielded to her, whether she exercise that right or not. Would that man too, would have no participation in a government based upon the life-taking principle—upon retaliation and the sword. It is unworthy a Christian nation. But when, in the diffusion of light and intelligence, a convention shall be called to make regulations for self-government on Christian, non-resistant principles, I can see no good reason, why woman should not participate in such an assemblage, taking part equally with man.

Walker, of Cincinnati, in his Introduction to American Law, says: "With regard to political rights, females form a positive exception to the general doctrine of equality. They have no part or lot in the formation or administration of government. They cannot vote or hold office. We require them to contribute their share in the way of taxes, to the support of government, but allow them no voice in its direction. We hold them amenable to the laws when made, but allow them no share in making them. This language, applied to males, would be the exact definition of political slavery; applied to females, custom does not teach us so to regard it." Woman, however, is beginning so to regard it.

"The law of husband and wife, as you gather it from the books, is a disgrace to any civilized nation. The theory of the law degrades the wife almost to the level of slaves. When a woman marries, we call her condition coverture, and speak of her as a *femme covert*. The old writers call the husband baron, and sometimes, in plain English, lord. * * * The merging of her name in that of her husband is emblematic of the fate of all her legal rights. The torch of Hymen serves but to light the pile, on which these rights are offered up. The legal theory is, that marriage makes the husband and wife one person, and that person is the *husband*. On this subject, reform is loudly called for. There is no foundation in reason or expediency, for the absolute and slavish subjection of the wife to the husband, which forms the foundation of the present legal relations. Were woman, in point of fact, the abject thing which the law, in theory, considers her to be when married, she would not be worthy the companionship of man."

I would ask if such a code of laws does not require change? If such a condition of the wife in society does not claim redress? On no good ground can reform be delayed. . . .

May these statements lead you to reflect upon this subject, that you may know what woman's condition is in society—what her restrictions are, and seek to remove them. In how many cases in our country, the husband and wife begin life together, and by equal industry and united effort accumulate to themselves a comfortable home. In the event of the death of the wife, the household remains undisturbed, his farm or his workshop is not broken up, or in any way molested. But when the husband dies, he either gives his wife a *portion* of their joint accumulation, or the law apportions to her a *share;* the homestead is broken up, and she is dispossessed of that which she earned equally with him; for what she lacked in physical strength, she made up in constancy of labor and toil, day and evening. . . .

On no good ground can the legal existence of the wife be suspended during marriage, and her property surrendered to her husband. In the intelligent ranks of society, the wife may not in point of fact, be so degraded as the law would degrade her; because public sentiment is above the law. Still, while the law stands, she is liable to the disabilities which it imposes. Among the ignorant classes of society, woman is made to bear heavy burdens, and is degraded almost to the level of the slave.

There are many instances now in our city, where the wife suffers much from the power of the husband to claim all that she can earn with her own hands. In my intercourse with the poorer class of people, I have known cases of extreme cruelty; from the hard earnings of the wife being thus robbed by the husband, and no redress at law. . . .

But the demand for a more extended education will not cease, until girls and boys have equal instruction, in all the departments of useful knowledge. We have as yet no high school for girls in this state. The normal school may be a preparation for such an establishment. In the late convention for general education, it was cheering to hear the testimony borne to woman's capabilities for head teachers of the public schools. A resolution there offered for equal salaries to male and female teachers, when equally qualified, as practised in Louisiana, I regret to say was checked in its passage, by Bishop Potter; by him who has done so much for the encouragement of education, and who gave his countenance and influence to that convention. Still the fact of such a resolution being offered, augurs a time coming for woman, which she may well hail. At the last examination of the public schools in this city, one of the alumni delivered an address on Woman, not as is too common, in eulogistic strains, but directing the attention to the injustice done to woman in her position in society, in a variety of ways. The unequal wages she receives for her constant toil, &c., presenting facts calculated to arouse attention to the subject.

Women's property has been taxed, equally with that of men's, to sustain colleges endowed by the states; but they have not been permitted to enter those high seminaries of learning. Within a few years, however, some colleges have been instituted, where young women are admitted, nearly upon equal terms with young men; and numbers are availing themselves of their long denied rights. This is among the signs of the times, indicative of an advance for women. The book of knowledge is not opened to her in vain. Already is she aiming to occupy important posts of honor and profit in our country. We have three female editors in our state—some in other states of the Union. Numbers are entering the medical profession—one received a diploma last year; others are preparing for a like result. . . .

In conclusion, let me say, "Credit not the old fashioned absurdity, that woman's is a secondary lot, ministering to the necessities of her lord and master! It is a higher destiny I would award you. If your immortality is as complete, and your gift of mind as capable as ours, of increase and elevation, I would put no wisdom of mine against God's evident allotment. I would charge you to water the undying bud, and give it healthy culture, and open its beauty to the sun—and then you may hope, that when your life is bound up with another, you will go on equally, and in a fellowship that shall pervade every earthly interest."

62

PAULINA W. DAVIS

Justice for Women, Address to
the Woman's Rights Convention
in Worcester (1850)

. . . Human rights, and the reasons on which they
rest, are not difficult of comprehension. The
world has never been ignorant of them, nor insensible to them; and human wrongs and their
evils are just as familiar to experience and as
well understood; but all this is not enough to
secure to mankind the possession of the one, or
to relieve them from the [felt] burden and suffering of the other. A creed of abstract truths, or a
catechism of general principles, and a completely digested list of grievances combined, are
not enough to adjust a practical reform to its
proper work, else Prophets and Apostles and
earnest world-menders in general would have
been more successful, and left us less to wish
and to do.

It is one thing to issue a declaration of rights
or a declaration of wrongs to the world, but
quite another thing wisely and happily to commend the subject to the world's acceptance, and
so to secure the desired reformation. . . .

. . . The reformation which we purpose, in
its utmost scope, is radical and universal. It is
not the mere perfecting of a progress already in
motion, a detail of some established plan, but it
is an epochal movement—the emancipation of
a class, the redemption of half the world, and a
conforming re-organization of all social, political, and industrial interests and institutions.
Moreover, it is a movement without example
among the enterprises of associated reformations, for it has no purpose of arming the oppressed against the oppressor, or of separating

the parties, or of setting up independence, or of
severing the relations of either.

Its intended changes are to be wrought in
the intimate texture of all societary organizations, without violence, or any form of antagonism. It seeks to replace the worn out with the
living and the beautiful, so as to reconstruct
without overturning, and to regenerate without destroying; and noting of the spirit, tone,
temper, or method of insurrection, is proper or
allowable to us and our work. . . .

The first principles of human rights have
now for a long time been abstractly held and
believed, and both in Europe and America whole
communities have put them into practical operation in some of their bearings. Equality before the law, and the right of the governed to
choose their governors, are established maxims
of reformed political science; but in the countries most advanced, these doctrines and their
actual benefits are as yet enjoyed exclusively by
the sex that in the battle-field and the public
forum has wrenched them from the old time
tyrannies. They are yet denied to Woman, because she has not yet *so* asserted or won them
for herself; for political justice pivots itself upon
the barbarous principle that "Who would be free,
themselves must strike the blow." Its furthest
progress toward magnanimity is to give *arms* to
helplessness. It has not yet learned to give *justice*. For this rule of barbarism there is this much
justification, that although every human being
is naturally entitled to every right of the race,
the enjoyment and administration of all rights
require such culture and conditions in their subject as usually lead him to claim and struggle
for them; and the contented slave is left in slavery, and the ignorant man in darkness, on the
inference that he cannot use what he does not
desire. This is indeed true of the animal instincts,
but it is false of the nobler *soul;* and men must
learn that the higher faculties must be first awakened, and then gratified, before they have done
their duty to their race. The ministry of *angels*
to dependent humanity is the method of Divine
Providence, and among men the law of heaven

From *The Proceedings of the Woman's Rights Convention,
Held at Worcester, October 23d & 24th, 1850* (Boston: Prentiss
and Sawyer, 1851), 6–11.

is, that the "elder shall serve the younger." But let us not complain that the hardier sex over-value the force which heretofore has figured most in the world's affairs. "They know not what they do," is the apology that crucified woman-hood must concede in justice and pity to the wrong doers. In the order of things, the mate-rial world was to be first subdued. For this coarse conflict, the larger bones and stronger sinews of manhood are especially adapted, and it is a law of muscles and of all matter that might shall overcome right. This is the law of the vegetable world, and it is the law of the animal world, as well as the law of the animal instincts and of the physical organization of men; but it is not the law of spirit and affection. *They* are of such a na-ture as to charge themselves with the atonement for all evils, and to burden themselves with all the sufferings which they would remove.

This wisdom is pure, and peaceable, and gentle, and full of mercy and of good fruits.

Besides the feebler frame, which under the dynasty of muscles is degraded, there remains, even after justice has got the upper hand of force in the world's judgments, a mysterious and un-defined difference of sex that seriously embar-rasses the question of equality; or, if that is granted in terms, of equal fitness for avocations and positions which heretofore have been the monopoly of men. Old ideas and habits of mind survive the facts which produced them, as the shadows of night stretch far into the morning, sheltered in nook and valleys from the rising light; and it is the work of a whole creation-day to separate the light from the darkness.

The rule of difference between the sexes must be founded on the traits which each esti-mates most highly in the other; and it is not at all wonderful that some of woman's artificial in-capacities and slaveries may seem to be neces-sary to some of her excellencies, just as the chivalry that makes man a butcher of his kind still glares like a glory in the eyes of admiring womanhood, and all the more because it seems so much above and unlike her own powers and achievements. Nature does not teach that men

and women are unequal, but only that they are unlike; an unlikeness so naturally related and dependent that their respective differences by their balance establish, instead of destroying, their equality.

Men are not in fact, and to all intents, equal among themselves, but their theoretical equal-ity for all the purposes of justice is more easily seen and allowed than what we are here to claim for women. Higher views, nicer distinctions, and a deeper philosophy are required to see and feel the truths of woman's rights; and besides, the maxims upon which men distribute justice to each other have been battle-cries for ages, while the doctrine of woman's true relations in life is a new science, the revelation of an advanced age,—perhaps, indeed, the very last grand movement of humanity towards its highest des-tiny,—too new to be yet fully understood, too grand to grow out of the broad and coarse gen-eralities which the infancy and barbarism of so-ciety could comprehend.

The rule of force and fraud must be well nigh overturned, and learning and religion and the fine arts must have cultivated mankind into a state of wisdom and justice tempered by the most beneficent affections, before woman can be fully installed in her highest offices. We must be gentle with the ignorance and patient under the injustice which old evils induce. Long suffer-ing is a quality of the highest wisdom, and char-ity bearest all things for it hopeth all things. It will be seen that I am assuming the point that the redemption of the inferior, if it comes at all, must come from the superior. The elevation of a favored caste can have no other providential purpose than that, when it is elevated near enough to goodness and truth, it shall draw up its dependents with it.

But, however this may be in the affairs of men as they are involved with each other, it is clearly so in the matter of woman's elevation. The tyrant sex, if such we choose to term it, holds such natural and necessary relations to the victims of injustice, that neither rebellion nor revolution, neither defiance nor resistance, nor any mode of assault or defence incident to party antagonism, is either possible, expedient, or proper. Our claim must rest on its justice, and conquer by its power of truth. We take the ground, that whatever has been achieved for the race belongs to it, and must not be usurped by any class or caste. The rights and liberties of one human being cannot be made the property of another, though they were redeemed for him or her by the life of that other; for rights cannot be forfeited by way of salvage, and they are in their nature unpurchasable and inalienable.

We claim for woman a full and generous investiture of all the blessings which the other sex has solely or by her aid achieved for itself. We appeal from men's injustice and selfishness to their principles and affections.

For some centuries now, the best of them have been asserting, with their lives, the liberties and rights of the race; and it is not for the few endowed with the highest intellect, the largest frame, or even the soundest morals, that the claim has been maintained, but broadly and bravely and nobly it has been held that wherever a faculty is given, its highest activities are chartered by the Creator, and that all objects alike—whether they minister to the necessities of our animal life or to the superior powers of the human soul and so are more imperatively needed, because nobler than the bread that perishes in the use—are, of common right, equally open to ALL; and that all artificial restraints, for whatever reason imposed, are alike culpable for their presumption, their folly, their cruelty.

It is pitiable ignorance and arrogance for either man or woman now to prescribe and limit the sphere of woman. It remains for the greatest women whom appropriate culture, and happiest influences shall yet develope, to declare and to prove what are woman's capacities and relations in the world.

I will not accept the concession of any equality which means identity or resemblance of faculty and function. I do not base here claims upon any such parallelism of constitution or attainment. I ask only freedom for the natural unfold-ing of her powers, the conditions most favorable for her possibilities of growth, and the full play of all those incentives which have made man her master, and then, with all her natural impulses and the whole heaven of hope to invite, I ask that she shall fill the place that she can attain to, without settling any unmeaning questions of sex and sphere, which people gossip about for want of principles of truth, or the faculty to reason upon them. . . .

63

HADDIE LANE
Woman's Rights (1850)

"Haddie," said my Aunt Debbie, laying aside the stocking she had been knitting, and interrupting me in a most animated discussion with Cousin Tom, "Haddie, what do you mean by the words 'Woman's Rights?' They have passed your lips at least a dozen times within the last ten minutes."

"Why, auntie, I was just wishing to exercise my 'rights' as Tom's physician, and I was vowing to give him such a dose of ratsbane as would rid the world for ever of such a pest."

"I am sorry, my Haddie, to hear you speak jestingly on such a grave subject; but get your bonnet, and join me in a walk through the village, and you will find, I hope, before we return, that you have numerous and noble rights. You will learn that which will make you tremble for yourself, lest you should misuse your talents."

Greatly wondering what Aunt Debbie could mean, I was soon equipped, and found her waiting in the hall. As we descended the steps together, I noticed a shade of sadness on her brow, her lips had lost their usual smile, and there was a slight tremor in her voice when she spoke. . . .

"Now, Haddie, for a race to the top of the hill," said Aunt Debbie.

I soon attained the summit, and called to

From *Godey's Lady's Book* 40 (April 1850).

my aunt to follow. We had stood there some time, drinking in the splendid sunset, when we heard voices in the adjoining wood.

"The wood-cutters, John Holm and his son, I suppose," said my aunt.

The sounds, which had at first been those of cheerful conversation, now became louder and angry.

"Oh! aunt, they are quarreling," I exclaimed.

Aunt Debbie stepped boldly into the forest. Guided by the sounds, we soon emerged from the tangled thicket into an open glade. There stood the two disputants. The old man's countenance was crimson with rage; the son stood with uplifted arm and quivering lip. His glittering axe shone in his hand. In an instant, Aunt Debbie was between them, a hand on the arm of each.

"Are ye men!" said she. "Would you sully this bright glade with an act of violence? Old man, would you strike your son—that boy who was once your pride? Your white hairs should have taught you wisdom. Do not stir up his anger, lest he be too sorely tempted. Son, would you stain your gleaming axe with your father's blood? Remember that he is your *father*. That word alone should secure your respect. But he has toiled for you; his frame has been bent with labor, his hair has whitened with toil for you— for you, his ungrateful son."

The young man's arm relaxed its hold, and his axe fell to the earth. But the old man still grasped his, and his face wore a sterner frown.

"John," my aunt continued, "can you imagine your sainted wife looking down from heaven, and beholding you with arm uplifted against her son, her living image?"

At the mention of his wife, the old man burst into a flood of tears; and, sitting down on the newly-fallen tree, he buried his face in his hands and wept bitterly.

"Now go to him," said Aunt Debbie, touching the young man's arm; "go tell him you are penitent; ask his forgiveness, and all will be well."

He walked towards his father, and we left them. As we threaded our way through the thicket, now blinded by a branch from some impertinent tree, now scratched by a briar, now starting at a squirrel, I thought to myself—"Still another right—a peacemaker. Who but woman, helpless, unresisting woman is so formed to glide in gently among angry men, to calm their ruffled spirits, to weaken the strong arm and the hand heavy with passion? Who but woman can show them the noblest revenge—the revenge of kindness? A right so fearful must make every true woman tremble at the thought. Heaven send us strength to use it!"

As we descended the hill, I recognized the long avenue of cedars on our right, as leading to the house of Squire Carlton, as the magistrate was called. I had had many a fine race down that avenue with Fany Carlton; but I had not seen or heard anything of her for two years. True, before I left my native village for a fashionable boarding-school in a distant city, we two had plighted a solemn promise never to forget each other, and to write a long letter once a week; but amid the busy life of a school-girl and the excitement of new faces and new friends, I had forgotten, and Fanny was too proud to intrude her letters where she deemed herself neglected. My aunt, in answer to the questions which fell fast from my lips, informed me that Mr. Carlton had been for a long time afflicted with the gout; that his temper, never remarkable for urbanity, had now become very irritable; that Fanny had given up her friends, her studies, and her amusements, devoting her whole time to her father, who repaid this devotion with reproofs and harshness.

"I see them, Aunt Debbie," I cried, "there on the lawn."

It was, indeed, Fanny; but my playmate was greatly altered—she had grown tall. Her complexion was exquisitely clear; and her hair, instead of falling to her waist in those careless curls which seemed like a gleam of sunshine floating through the air, was turned smoothly back from her forehead, and gathered into a knot behind.

Her slight figure bent under the weight of the stately old man who leaned on her arm. They had observed us, and were coming slowly to meet us.

"We will wait for them here at the gate," said Aunt Debbie; "it is too late to go in."

I assented, and was stooping to gather some of the white violets with which the ground was covered, when an exclamation from my aunt startled me. Fanny and her father had approached nearly to where we stood, when the old man's foot struck against some obstacle in the path. He with difficulty suppressed a loud cry of pain; but, lifting his arm quickly, gave his daughter a blow so heavy that she reeled forward, and would have fallen but for a friendly cedar which stood near. She had been hastening towards us, her face beaming with pleasure; but at this shameful blow her color faded; an expression of pain crossed her face, and, bending upon me a look in which disappointment was mingled with mortification, she waved her hand and turned towards the house. We stood in silence, as if rooted to the spot. Mr. Carlton walked as fast as his foot would allow, muttering curses and imprecations; while Fanny seemed to have forgotten the blow, so tenderly did she support the old man, and so skillfully did she direct his steps.

"Wait a minute," said Aunt Debbie, after they had entered the house; "Fanny will soon be back, I fancy." And scarcely had the words passed her lips, when Fanny was at our side.

After the usual greetings, she reverted to her father's fall, blaming her own carelessness, but without mentioning her blow. She held her handkerchief to her forehead to hide the swelling. Aunt Debbie pressed her to spend the following day with us; but she declined, pleading an engagement.

"But you will come soon to see me?" said I; "on Saturday I shall expect you."

"I am afraid, dear Haddie," said she, confusedly, "that I cannot come at all; my father's indisposition requires my constant attention. I am dong penance, Haddie; I used to be such a rover. But my father likes me near him; and he has so few enjoyments, that I am glad I can help him to forget his sufferings."

A servant now came to inform Fanny that Mr. Carlton requested to see her immediately. With a smile and a half-suppressed sigh, she left us.

"Can this be one of woman's rights, Aunt Debbie?" I exclaimed.

"Yes, Haddie. Fanny is learning a lesson of self-denial, of patience; and though it may seem an unenviable right to you to be able to 'bless them that curse you,' we must think of 'the great reward' which Fanny will obtain in heaven." . . .

That night, when Aunt Debbie entered my chamber to bestow the good-night kiss, I accosted her with—

"Aunt Debbie, you did not tell me all of woman's rights—one right you omitted."

"What was it, my darling?"

"Hold down your head; I will tell you, if you will promise not to say anything to Tom."

"Well, I promise—only don't strangle me. What is it, my dear?"

"The—the *right* of *conquest,* aunty."

"Oh, fie! what a naughty girl!" and Aunt Debbie tripped lightly from the room.

64

FRANCES D. GAGE

Woman's Natural Rights, Address to the Woman's Rights Convention in Akron (1851)

I am at a loss, kind friends, to know whether to return you thanks, or not, for the honor conferred upon me. And when I tell you that I have never in my life attended a regular business meeting, and am entirely inexperienced in the forms and ceremonies of a deliberative body, you

From *History of Woman Suffrage, Vol. 1, 1848–1861*, ed., Elizabeth Cady Stanton, Susan B. Anthony, and Matilda Joslyn Gage (New York: Fowler and Wells, 1881), 111–13.

will not be surprised that I do not feel remark-ably grateful for the position. For though you have conferred an honor upon me, I very much fear I shall not be able to reflect it back. I will try.

When our forefathers left the old and beaten paths of New England, and struck out for themselves in a new and unexplored coun-try, they went forth with a slow and cautious step, but with firm and resolute hearts. The land of their fathers had become too small for their children. Its soil answered not their wants. The parents shook their heads and said, with doubt-ful and foreboding faces: "Stand still, stay at home. This has sufficed for us; we have lived and enjoyed ourselves here. True, our mountains are high and our soil is rugged and cold; but you won't find a better; change, and trial, and toil, will met you at every step. Stay, tarry with us, and go not forth to the wilderness."

But the children answered: "Let us go; this land has sufficed for you, but the one beyond the mountains is better. We know there is trial, toil, and danger; but for the sake of our chil-dren, and our children's children, we are will-ing to meet all." They went forth, and pitched their tents in the wilderness. An herculean task was before them; the rich and fertile soil was shadowed by a mighty forest, and giant trees were to be felled. The Indians roamed the wild, wide hunting-grounds, and claimed them as their own. They must be met and subdued. The savage beasts howled defiance from every hill-top, and in every glen. They must be destroyed. Did the hearts of our fathers fail? No; they en-tered upon their new life, their new world, with a strong faith and a mighty will. For they saw in the prospection a great and incalculable good. It was not the work of an hour, nor of a day; not of weeks or months, but of long struggling, toil-ing, painful years. If they failed at one point, they took hold at another. If their paths through the wilderness were at first crooked, rough, and dangerous, by little and little they improved them. The forest faded away, the savage disap-peared, the wild beasts were destroyed, and the

hopes and prophetic visions of their far-seeing powers in the new and untried country were more than realized.

Permit me to draw a comparison between the situation of our forefathers in the wilder-ness, without even so much as a bridle-path through its dark depths, and our present posi-tion. The old land of moral, social, and political privilege, seems too narrow for our wants; its soil answers not to our growing, and we feel that we see clearly a better country that we might inhabit. But there are mountains of established law and custom to overcome; a wilderness of prejudice to be subdued; a powerful foe of selfishness and self-interest to overthrow; wild beasts of pride, envy, malice, and hate to de-stroy. But for the sake of our children and our children's children, we have entered upon the work, hoping and praying that we may be guided by wisdom, sustained by love, and led and cheered by the earnest hope of doing good.

I shall enter into no labored argument to prove that woman does not occupy the position in society to which her capacity justly entitles her. The rights of mankind emanate from their natural wants and emotions. Are not the natural wants and emotions of humanity common to, and shared equally by, both sexes? Does man hunger and thirst, suffer cold and heat more than woman? Does he love and hate, hope and fear, joy and sorrow more than woman? Does his heart thrill with a deeper pleasure in doing good? Can his soul writhe in more bitter agony under the consciousness of evil or wrong? Is the sun-shine more glorious, the air more quiet, the sounds of harmony more soothing, the perfume of flowers more exquisite, or forms of beauty more soul-satisfying to his senses, than to hers? To all these interrogatories every one will an-swer, No!

Where then did man get the authority that he now claims over one-half of humanity? From what power the vested right to place woman—his partner, his companion, his helpmeet in life—in an inferior position? Came it from na-ture? Nature made woman his superior when she made her his mother; his equal when she fitted her to hold the sacred position of wife. Does he draw his authority from God, from the language of holy writ? No! For it says that "Male and female created he *them,* and gave *them* dominion." Does he claim it under law of the land? Did woman meet with him in council and voluntarily give up all her claim to be her own lawmaker? Or did the majesty of might place this power in his hands?—The power of the strong over the weak makes man the master! Yes, there, and there only, does he gain his authority.

In the dark ages of the past, when ignorance, superstition, and bigotry held rule in the world, might made the law. But the undertone, the still small voice of Justice, Love, and Mercy, have ever been heard, pleading the cause of humanity, pleading for truth and right; and their low, soft tones of harmony have softened the lion heart of might, and, little by little, he has yielded as the centuries rolled on; and man, as well as woman, has been the gainer by every concession. We will ask him to yield still; to allow the voice of woman to be heard; to let her take the position which he wants and emotions seem to require; to let her enjoy her natural rights. Do not answer that woman's position is now all her natural wants and emotions require. Our meeting here together this day proves the contrary; proves that we have aspirations that are not met. Will it be answered that we are factious, discontented spirits, striving to disturb the public order, and tear up the old fastnesses of society? So it was said of Jesus Christ and His followers, when they taught peace on earth and good-will to men. So it was said of our forefathers in the great struggle for freedom. So it has been said of every reformer that has ever started out the car of progress on a new and untried track.

We fear not man as an enemy. He is our friend, our brother. Let woman speak for herself, and she will be heard. Let her claim with a calm and determined, yet loving spirit, her place, and it will be given her. I pour out no harsh invectives against the present order of things—against our fathers, husbands, and brothers; they

do as they have been taught; they feel as society bids them; they act as the law requires. Woman must act for herself.

Oh, if all women could be impressed with the importance of their own action, and with one united voice, speak out in their own behalf, in behalf of humanity, they could create a revolution without armies, without bloodshed, that would do more to ameliorate the condition of mankind, to purify, elevate, ennoble humanity, than all that has been done by reformers in the last century.

65

SOJOURNER TRUTH

A'n't I a Woman? Address to the Woman's Rights Convention in Akron (1851)

Wall, chilern, whar dar is so much racket dar must be somethin' out o' kilter. I tink dat 'twixt de niggers of de Souf and de womin at de Norf, all talkin' 'bout rights, de white men will be in a fix pretty soon. But what's all dis here talkin' 'bout?

Dat man ober dar say dat womin needs to be helped into carriages, and lifted ober ditches, and to hab de best place everywhar. Nobody eber helps me into carriages, or ober mud-puddles, or gibs me any best place! . . . And a'n't I a woman? Look at me! Look at my arm! (and she bared her right arm to the shoulder, showing her tremendous muscular power). I have ploughed, and planted, and gathered into barns, and no man could head me! And a'n't I a woman? I could work as much and eat as much as a man—when I could get it—and bear de lash as well! And a'n't I a woman? I have borne thirteen chilern, and seen 'em mos' all sold off to slavery, and when I cried out with my mother's grief, none but Jesus heard me! And a'n't I a woman?

From *History of Woman Suffrage, Vol. 1, 1848–1861,* ed., Elizabeth Cady Stanton, Susan B. Anthony, and Matilda Joslyn Gage (New York: Fowler and Wells, 1881), 116.

Den dey talks 'bout dis ting in de head; what dis dey call it? ("Intellect," whispered some one near.) Dat's it, honey. What's dat got to do wid womin's rights or nigger's rights? If my cup won't hold but a pint, and yourn holds a quart, wouldn't ye be mean not to let me have my little half-measure full? . . .

Den dat little man in black dar, he say women can't have as much rights as men, 'cause Christ wan't a woman! Whar did your Christ come from? . . . Whar did your Christ come from? From God and a woman! Man had nothin' to do wid Him. . . .

If de fust woman God ever made was strong enough to turn de world upside down all alone, dese women togedder (and she glanced her eye over the platform) ought to be able to turn it back, and get it right side up again! And now dey is asking to do it, de men better let 'em. . . . 'Bleeged to ye for hearin' on me, and now ole Sojourner han't got nothin' more to say.

66

Resolving to Reform Marriage Laws, at the Woman's Rights Convention in Rochester (1853)

. . . *Resolved,* That, inasmuch as universal experience proves the inseparable connection between dependence and degradation—while it is plain to every candid observer of society that women are kept poor, by being crowded together, to compete with and undersell one another in a few branches of labor, and that from this very poverty of women, spring many of the most terrible wrongs and evils, which corrupt and endanger society; therefore do we invite the earnest attention of capitalists, merchants, traders, manufacturers, and mechanics, to the ur-

gent need, which everywhere exists, of opening to women new avenues of honest and honorable employment, and we do hereby call upon all manly men to make room for their sisters to earn an independent livelihood.

Resolved, That, whereas, the custom of making small remuneration for woman's work, in all departments of industry, has sprung from her dependence, which dependence is prolonged and increased by this most irrational and unjust habit of half pay; therefore do we demand, in the name of common sense and common conscience, that women equally with men, should be paid for their services according to the quality and quantity of the work done, and not the sex of the worker.

Resolved, That, whereas, the State of New York, in the acts of 1848 and 1849, has honorably and justly placed married women on the footing of equality with unmarried women, in regard to the receiving, holding, conveying, and devising of all property, real and personal, we call upon the Legislature of the State to take the next step—so plainly justified by its own precedents—of providing that husbands and wives shall be joint owners of their joint earnings—the community estate passing to the survivor at the death of either party.

Resolved, That, whereas, the evident intent of the Legislature of the State of New York has for many years been progressively to do away with the legal disabilities of women, which existed under the savage usages of the old common law, therefore we do urgently call upon the Legislature of this State, at its next session, to appoint a joint committee to examine and revise the statute, and to propose remedies for the redress of all legal grievances from which women now suffer, and suitable measures for the full establishment of women's legal equality with men.

Resolved, That, whereas, under the common law, the father is regarded as the guardian, by nature, of his children, having the entire control of their persons and education, while only upon the death of the father, does the mother

From *History of Woman Suffrage,* Vol. 1, 1848–1861, ed., Elizabeth Cady Stanton, Susan B. Anthony, and Matilda Joslyn Gage (New York: Fowler and Wells, 1881), 581–82.

become the guardian by nature; and, whereas, by the revised statutes of New York it is provided, that where an estate in lands shall become vested in an infant, the guardianship of such infant, with the rights, power, and duties of a guardian in soccage, shall belong to the father, and only in case of the father's death, to the mother; and, whereas, finally and chiefly, by the revised statutes of New York, it is provided, that every father may, by his deed or last will, duly executed, dispose of the custody and tuition of his children, during their minority, "to any person or persons in possession or remainder"; therefore, do we solemnly protest against the utter violation of every mother's rights, authorized by existing laws, in regard to the guardianship of infants, and demand, in the name of common humanity, that the Legislature of New York so amend the statutes, as to place fathers and mothers on equal footing in regard to the guardianship of their children. Especially do we invite the Legislature instantly to pass laws, entitling mothers to become their children's guardians, in all cases where, by habitual drunkenness, immorality, or improvidence, fathers are incompetent to the sacred trust.

Resolved, That, whereas, according to the amendments of the Constitution of the United States, it is provided that "in all criminal cases, the accused shall enjoy the right to a speedy and public trial, by an impartial jury," and that "in suits at common law, where the value in controversy shall exceed twenty dollars, the right of trial by jury shall be preserved"; and, whereas, according to the revised statutes of New York, it is provided, that "no member of this State can be disfranchised or deprived of any of the rights or privileges, secured to any citizen thereof, unless by the law of the land, or the judgment of his peers"; therefore, do we demand, that women, as "members" and "citizens" of this State, equally with men, should be entitled to claim a trial by "an impartial jury of their peers." And especially do we remonstrate against the partial, mean, and utterly inequitable custom, everywhere prevalent, that in questions of divorce,

men, and men alone, should be regarded as "an impartial jury."

67

LUCY STONE AND HENRY B. BLACKWELL

The Marriage of Lucy Stone Under Protest (1855)

While acknowledging our mutual affection by publicly assuming the relationship of husband and wife, yet in justice to ourselves and a great principle, we deem it a duty to declare that this act on our part implies no sanction of, nor promise of voluntary obedience to such of the present laws of marriage, as refuse to recognize the wife as an independent, rational being, while they confer upon the husband an injurious and unnatural superiority, investing him with legal powers which no honorable man would exercise, and which no man should possess. We protest especially against the laws which give to the husband:

1. The custody of the wife's person.

2. The exclusive control and guardianship of their children.

3. The sole ownership of her personal, and use of her real estate, unless previously settled upon her, or placed in the hands of trustees, as in the case of minors, lunatics, and idiots.

4. The absolute right to the product of her industry.

5. Also against laws which give to the widower so much larger and more permanent an interest in the property of his deceased wife, than they give to the widow in that of the deceased husband.

6. Finally, against the whole system by which "the legal existence of the wife is sus-

From *History of Woman Suffrage,* Vol. 1, *1848–1861,* ed., Elizabeth Cady Stanton, Susan B. Anthony, and Matilda Joslyn Gage (New York: Fowler and Wells, 1881), 260–61.

pended during marriage," so that in most States, she neither has a legal part in the choice of her residence, nor can she make a will, nor sue or be sued in her own name, nor inherit property.

We believe that personal independence and equal human rights can never be forfeited, except for crime; that marriage should be an equal and permanent partnership, and so recognized by law; that until it is so recognized, married partners should provide against the radical injustice of present laws, by every means in their power.

We believe that where domestic difficulties arise, no appeal should be made to legal tribunals under existing laws, but that all difficulties should be submitted to the equitable adjustment of arbitrators mutually chosen.

Thus reverencing law, we enter our protest against rules and customs which are unworthy of the name, since they violate justice, the essence of law.

68

ELIZABETH CADY STANTON
Address to the New York Legislature (1854)

The tyrant, Custom, has been summoned before the bar of Common-Sense. His majesty no longer awes the multitude—his sceptre is broken—his crown is trampled in the dust—the sentence of death is pronounced upon him. All nations, ranks, and classes have, in turn, questioned and repudiated his authority; and now, that the monster is chained and caged, timid woman, on tiptoe, comes to look him in the face, and to demand of her brave sires and sons, who have struck stout blows for liberty, if, in this change of dynasty, she, too, shall find relief. Yes,

From *History of Woman Suffrage, Vol. 1, 1848–1861*, ed., Elizabeth Cady Stanton, Susan B. Anthony, and Matilda Joslyn Gage (New York: Fowler and Wells, 1881), 595–605.

gentlemen, in republican America, in the nineteenth century, we, the daughters of the revolutionary heroes of '76, demand at your hands the redress of our grievances—a revision of your State Constitution—a new code of laws. Permit us then, as briefly as possible, to call your attention to the legal disabilities under which we labor.

1st. Look at the position of woman as woman. It is not enough for us that by your laws we are permitted to live and breathe, to claim the necessaries of life from our legal protectors—to pay the penalty of our crimes; we demand the full recognition of all our rights as citizens of the Empire State. We are persons; native, free-born citizens; property-holders, taxpayers; yet are we denied the exercise of our right to the elective franchise. We support ourselves, and, in part, your schools, colleges, churches, your poor-houses, jails, prisons, the army, the navy, the whole machinery of government, and yet we have no voice in your councils. We have every qualification required by the Constitution, necessary to the legal voter, but the one of sex. We are moral, virtuous, and intelligent, and in all respects quite equal to the proud white man himself and yet by your laws we are classed with idiots, lunatics, and negroes; and though we do not feel honored by the place assigned us, yet, in fact, our legal position is lower than that of either; for the negro can be raised to the dignity of a voter if he possess himself of $250; the lunatic can vote in his moments of sanity, and the idiot, too, if he be a male one, and not more than nine-tenths a fool; but we, who have guided great movements of charity, established missions, edited journals, published works on history, economy, and statistics; who have governed nations, led armies, filled the professor's chair, taught philosophy and mathematics to the savants of our age, discovered planets, piloted ships across the sea, are denied the most sacred rights of citizens, because, forsooth, we came not into this republic crowned with the dignity of manhood! Woman is theoretically absolved from all allegiance to the laws of the State. Sec. 1, Bill of Rights, 2 R. S., 301, says that no authority can, on any pretence whatever, be exercised over the citizens of this State but such as is or shall be derived from, and granted by the people of this State.

Now, gentlemen, we would fain know by what authority you have disfranchised one-half the people of this State? You who have so boldly taken possession of the bulwarks of this republic, show us your credentials, and thus prove your exclusive right to govern, not only yourselves, but us. Judge Hurlburt, who has long occupied a high place at the bar in this State, and who recently retired with honor from the bench of the Supreme Court, in his profound work on Human Rights, has pronounced your present position rank usurpation. Can it be that here, where we acknowledge no royal blood, no apostolic descent, that you, who have declared that all men were created equal—that governments derive their just powers from the consent of the governed, would willingly build up an aristocracy that places the ignorant and vulgar above the educated and refined—the alien and the ditch-digger above the authors and poets of the day—an aristocracy that would raise the sons above the mothers that bore them? Would that the men who can sanction a Constitution so opposed to the genius of this government, who can enact and execute laws so degrading to womankind, had sprung, Minerva-like, from the brains of their fathers, that the matrons of this republic need not blush to own their sons! . . .

True, the unmarried woman has a right to the property she inherits and the money she earns, but she is taxed without representation. And here again you place the negro, so unjustly degraded by you, in a superior position to your own wives and mothers; for colored males, if possessed of a certain amount of property and certain other qualifications, can vote, but if they do not have these qualifications they are not subject to direct taxation; wherein they have the advantage of woman, she being subject to taxation for whatever amount she may possess.

(Constitution of New York, Article 2, Sec. 2). But, say you, are not all women sufficiently represented by their fathers, husbands, and brothers? Let your statute books answer the question.

Again we demand in criminal cases that most sacred of all rights, trial by a jury of our own peers. The establishment of trial by jury is of so early a date that its beginning is lost in antiquity; but the right of trial by a jury of one's own peers is a great progressive step of advanced civilization. No rank of men have ever been satisfied with being tried by jurors higher or lower in the civil or political scale than themselves; for jealousy on the one hand, and contempt on the other, has ever effectually blinded the eyes of justice. . . . The nobleman can not make just laws of the peasant; the slaveholder for the slave; neither can man make and execute just laws for woman, because in each case, the one in power fails to apply the immutable principles of right to any grade but his own.

Shall an erring woman be dragged before a bar of grim-visaged judges, lawyers, and jurors, there to be grossly questioned in public on subjects which women scarce breathe in secret to one another? Shall the most sacred relations of life be called up and rudely scanned by men who, by their own admission, are so coarse that women could not meet them even at the polls without contamination? and yet shall she find there no woman's face or voice to pity and defend? Shall the frenzied mother, who, to save herself and child from exposure and disgrace, ended the life that had but just begun, be dragged before such a tribunal to answer for her crime? How can man enter into the feelings of that mother? How can he judge of the agonies of soul that impelled her to such an outrage of maternal instincts? How can he weigh the mountain of sorrow that crushed that mother's heart when she wildly tossed her helpless babe into the cold waters of the midnight sea? Where is he who by false vows thus blasted this trusting woman? Had that helpless child no claims on his protection? Ah, he is freely abroad in the dignity of manhood, in the pulpit, on the bench, in the professor's chair. The imprisonment of his victim and the death of his child, detract not a tithe from his standing and complacency. His peers made the law, and shall law-makers lay nets for those of their own rank? Shall laws which come from the logical brain of man take cognizance of violence done to the moral and affectional nature which predominates, as is said, in woman? . . .

2d. Look at the position of woman as wife. Your laws relating to marriage—founded as they are on the old common law of England, a compound of barbarous usages, but partially modified by progressive civilization—are in open violation of our enlightened ideas of justice, and of the holiest feelings of our nature. If you take the highest view of marriage, as a Divine relation, which love alone can constitute and sanctify, then of course human legislation can only recognize it. Men can neither bind nor loose its ties, for that prerogative belongs to God alone, who makes man and woman, and the laws of attraction by which they are united. But if you regard marriage as a civil contract, then let it be subject to the same laws which control all other contracts. Do not make it a kind of half-human, half-divine institution, which you may build up, but can not regulate. Do not, by your special legislation for this one kind of contract, involve yourselves in the grossest absurdities and contradictions.

So long as by your laws no man can make a contract for a horse or piece of land until he is twenty-one years of age, and by which contract he is not bound if any deception has been practiced, or if the party contracting has not fulfilled his part of the agreement—so long as the parties in all mere civil contracts retain their identity and all the power and independence they had before contracting, with the full right to dissolve all partnerships and contracts for any reason, at the will and option of the parties themselves, upon what principle of civil jurisprudence do you permit the boy of fourteen and the girl of twelve, in violation of every natural law, to make a contract more momentous in importance than any other, and then hold them to it, come what may, the whole of their natural lives, in spite of disappointment, deception, and misery? Then, too, the signing of this contract is instant civil death to one of the parties. The woman who but yesterday was sued on bended knee, who stood so high in the scale of being as to make an agreement on equal terms with a proud Saxon man, to-day has no civil existence, no social freedom. The wife who inherits no property holds about the same legal position that does the slave on the Southern plantation. She can own nothing, sell nothing. She has no right even to the wages she earns; her person, her time, her services are the property of another. She can not testify, in many cases, against her husband. She can get no redress for wrongs in her own name in any court of justice. She can neither sue nor be sued. She is not held morally responsible for any crime committed in the presence of her husband, so completely is her very existence supposed by the law to be merged in that of another. . . . By the common law of England, the spirit of which has been but too faithfully incorporated into our statute law, a husband has a right to whip his wife with a rod not larger than his thumb, to shut her up in a room, and administer whatever moderate chastisement he may deem necessary to insure obedience to his wishes, and for her healthful moral development! He can forbid all persons harboring or trusting her on his account. He can deprive her of all social intercourse with her nearest and dearest friends. If by great economy she accumulates a small sum, which for future need she deposit, little by little, in a savings bank, the husband has a right to draw it out, at his option, to use it as he may see fit.

There is nothing that an unruly wife might do against which the husband has not sufficient protection in the law. But not so with the wife. If she have a worthless husband, a confirmed drunkard, a villain, or a vagrant, he has still all the rights of a man, a husband, and a father. Though the whole support of the family be thrown upon the wife, if the wages she earns be paid to her by her employer, the husband can receive them again. If, by unwearied industry and perseverance, she can earn for herself and children a patch of ground and a shed to cover them, the husband can strip her of all her hard earnings, turn her and her little ones out in the cold northern blast, take the clothes from their backs, the bread from their mouths; all this by your laws may he do, and has he done, oft and again, to satisfy the rapacity of that monster in human form, the rum-seller.

But the wife who is so fortunate as to have inherited property, has, by the new law in this State, been redeemed from her lost condition. She is no longer a legal nonentity. This property law, if fairly construed, will overturn the whole code relating to woman and property. The right to property implies the right to buy and sell, to will and bequeath, and herein is the dawning of a civil existence for woman, for now the "femme covert" must have the right to make contracts. So, get ready, gentlemen; the "little justice" will be coming to you one day, deed in hand, for your acknowledgment. When he asks you "if you sign without fear or compulsion," say yes, boldly, as we do. Then, too, the right to will is ours. Now what becomes of the "tenant for life"? Shall he, the happy husband of a millionaire, who has lived in yonder princely mansion in the midst of plenty and elegance, be cut down in a day to the use of one-third of this estate and a few hundred a year, as long he remains her widower? And should he, in spite of this bounty on celibacy, impelled by his affections, marry again, choosing for a wife a woman as poor as himself, shall he be thrown penniless on the cold world—this child of fortune, enervated by ease and luxury, henceforth to be dependent wholly on his own resources? Poor man! He would be rich, though, in the sympathies of many women who have passed through just such an ordeal. But what is property without the right to protect that property by law? It is mockery to say a certain estate is mine, if, without my consent, you have the right to tax me when and how you please, while I have no voice in making the tax-gatherer, the legisla-

tor, or the law. The right to property will, of necessity, compel us in due time to the exercise of our right to the elective franchise, and then naturally follows the right to hold office.

3d. Look at the position of woman as widow. Whenever we attempt to point out the wrongs of the wife, those who would have us believe that the laws can not be improved, point us to the privileges, powers, and claims of the widow. Let us look into these a little. Behold in yonder humble house a married pair, who, for long years, have lived together, childless and alone. Those few acres of well-tilled land, with the small, white house that looks so cheerful through its vines and flowers, attest the honest thrift and simple taste of its owners. This man and woman, by their hard days' labor, have made this home their own. Here they live in peace and plenty, happy in the hope that they may dwell together securely under their own vine and fig-tree for the few years that remain to them, and that under the shadow of these trees, planted by their own hands, and in the midst of their household gods, so loved and familiar, they may take their last farewell of earth. But, alas for human hopes! the husband dies, and without a will, and the stricken widow, at one fell blow, loses the companion of her youth, her house and home, and half the little sum she had in bank. For the law, which takes no cognizance of widows left with twelve children and not one cent, instantly spies out this widow, takes account of her effects, and announces to her the startling intelligence that but one-third of the house and lot, and one half the personal property, are hers. The law has other favorites with whom she must share the hard-earned savings of years. In this dark hour of grief, the coarse minions of the law gather round the widow's hearth-stone, and, in the name of justice, outrage all natural sense of right; mock at the sacredness of human love, and with cold familiarity proceed to place a moneyed value on the old arm-chair, in which, but a few brief hours since, she closed the eyes that had ever beamed on her with kindness and affection; on the solemn clock in the corner, that told the hour he passed away; on every garment with which his form and presence were associated, and on every article of comfort and convenience that the house contained, even down to the knives and forks and spoons—and the widow saw it all—and when the work was done, she gathered up what the law allowed her and went forth to seek another home! This is the much-talked-of widow's dower. Behold the magnanimity of the law in allowing the widow to retain a life interest in one-third the landed estate, and one-half the personal property of her husband, and taking the lion's share to itself! Had she died first, the house and land would all have been the husband's still. No one would have dared to intrude upon the privacy of his home, or to molest him in his sacred retreat of sorrow. How, I ask you, can that be called justice, which makes such a distinction as this between man and woman? . . .

4th. Look at the position of woman as mother. There is no human love so strong and steadfast as that of the mother for her child; yet behold how ruthless are your laws touching this most sacred relation. Nature has clearly made the mother the guardian of the child; but man, in his inordinate love of power, does continually set nature and nature's laws at open defiance. The father may apprentice his child, bind him out to a trade, without the mother's consent—yea, in direct opposition to her most earnest entreaties, prayers and tears.

He may apprentice his son to a gamester or rum-seller, and thus cancel his debts of *honor*. By the abuse of this absolute power, he may bind his daughter to the owner of a brothel, and, by the degradation of his child, supply his daily wants; and such things, gentlemen, have been done in our very midst. Moreover, the father, about to die, may bind out all his children wherever and to whomsoever he may see fit, and thus, in fact, will away the guardianship of all his children from the mother. The Revised Statutes of New York provide that "every father, whether of full age or a minor, of a child to be born, or of any living child under the age of twenty-one

years, and unmarried, may by his deed or last will, duly executed, dispose of the custody and tuition of such child during its minority, or for any less time, to any person or persons, in possession or remainder." 2 R. S., page 150, sec 1. Thus, by your laws, the child is the absolute property of the father, wholly at his disposal in life or at death. . . .

By your laws, all these abominable resorts are permitted. It is folly to talk of a mother moulding the character of her son, when all mankind, backed up by law and public sentiment, conspire to destroy her influence. But when woman's moral power shall speak through the ballot-box, then shall her influence be seen and felt; then, in our legislative debates, such questions as the canal tolls on salt, the improvement of rivers and harbors, and the claims of Mr. Smith for damages against the State, would be secondary to the consideration of the legal existence of all these public resorts, which lure our youth on to excessive indulgence and destruction.

Many times and oft it has been asked us, with unaffected seriousness, "What do you women want? What are you aiming at?" Many have manifested a laudable curiosity to know what the wives and daughters could complain of in republican America, where their sires and sons have so bravely fought for freedom and gloriously secured their independence, trampling all tyranny, bigotry, and caste in the dust, and declaring to a waiting world the divine truth that all men are created equal. What can woman want under such a government? Admit a radical difference in sex, and you demand different spheres—water for fish, and air for birds.

It is impossible to make the Southern planter believe that his slave feels and reasons just as he does—that injustice and subjection are as galling as to him—that the degradation of living by the will of another, the mere dependent on his caprice, at the mercy of his passions, is as keenly felt by him as his master. If you can force on his unwilling vision a vivid picture of the negro's wrongs, and for a moment touch his soul, his logic brings him instant consolation. He says, the slave does not feel this as I would. Here, gentlemen, is our difficulty: When we plead our cause before the law-makers and savants of the republic, they can not take in the idea that men and women are alike; and so long as the mass rest in this delusion, the public mind will not be so much startled by the revelations made of the injustice and degradation of woman's position as by the fact that she should at length wake up to a sense of it.

If you, too, are thus deluded, what avails it that we show by your statute books that your laws are unjust—that woman is the victim of avarice and power? What avails it that we point out the wrongs of woman in social life; the victim of passion and lust? You scorn the thought that she has any natural love of freedom burning in her breast, any clear perception of justice urging her on to demand her rights.

Would to God you could know the burning indignation that fills woman's soul when she turns over the pages of your statute books, and sees there how like feudal barons you freemen hold your women. Would that you could know the humiliation she feels for [her] sex, when she thinks of all the beardless boys in your law offices, learning these ideas of one-sided justice—taking their first lessons in contempt for all womankind—being indoctrinated into the incapacities of their mothers, and the lordly, absolute rights of man over all women, children, and property, and to know that these are to be our future presidents, judges, husbands, and fathers; in sorrow we exclaim, alas! for that nation whose sons bow not in loyalty to woman. The mother is the first object of the child's veneration and love, and they who root out this holy sentiment, dream not of the blighting effect it has on the boy and the man. The impression left on law students, fresh from your statute books, is most unfavorable to woman's influence; hence you see but few lawyers chivalrous and high-toned in their sentiments toward woman. They can not escape the legal view which, by constant reading, has become familiarized to their minds: "*Femme covert,*" "dower," "widow's claims," "protection," "incapacities," "incumbrance," is written on the brow of every woman they meet.

But if, gentlemen, you take the ground that the sexes are alike, and therefore, you are our faithful representatives—then why all these special laws for woman? Would not one code answer for all of like needs and wants? Christ's golden rule is better than all the special legislation that the ingenuity of man can devise: "Do unto others as you would have others do unto you." This, men and brethren, is all we ask at your hands. We ask no better laws than those you have made for yourselves. We need no other protection than that which your present laws secure to you.

In conclusion, then, let us say, in behalf of the women of this State, we ask for all that you have asked for yourselves in the progress of your development, since the *Mayflower* cast anchor beside Plymouth rock; and simply on the ground that the rights of every human being are the same and identical. You may say that the mass of the women of this State do not make the demand; it comes from a few sour, disappointed old maids and childless women.

You are mistaken; the mass speak through us. A very large majority of the women of this State support themselves and their children, and many their husbands too. Go into any village you please, of three or four thousand inhabitants, and you will find as many as fifty men or more, whose only business is to discuss religion and politics, as they watch the trains come and go at the depot, or the passage of a canal boat through a lock; to laugh at the vagaries of some drunken brother, or the capers of a monkey dancing to the music of his master's organ. All these are supported by their mothers, wives, or sisters.

Now, do you candidly think these wives do not wish to control the wages they earn—to own the land they buy—the houses they build? to have at their disposal their own children, without being subject to the constant interference and tyranny of an idle, worthless profligate? Do you suppose that any woman is such a pattern of devotion and submission that she willingly stitches all day for the small sum of fifty cents, that she may enjoy the unspeakable privilege, in obedience to your laws, of paying for her husband's tobacco and rum? Think you the wife of the confirmed, beastly drunkard would consent to share with him her home and bed, if law and public sentiment would release her from such gross companionship? Verily, no! Think you the wife with whom endurance has ceased to be a virtue, who, through much suffering, has lost all faith in the justice of both heaven and earth, takes the law in her own hand, severs the unholy bond, and turns her back forever upon him whom she once called husband, consents to the law that in such an hour tears her child from her—all that she has left on earth to love and cherish? The drunkards' wives speak through us, and they number 50,000. Think you that the woman who has worked hard all her days in helping her husband to accumulate a large property, consents to the law that places this wholly at his disposal? Would not the mother whose only child is bound out for a term of years against her expressed wish, deprive the father of this absolute power if she could?

For all these, then, we speak. If to this long list you add the laboring women who are loudly demanding remuneration for their unending toil; those women who teach in our seminaries, academies, and public schools for a miserable pittance; the widows who are taxed without mercy; the unfortunate ones in our work-houses, poor-houses, and prisons; who are they that we do not now represent? But a small class of the fashionable butterflies, who, through the short summer days, seek the sunshine and the flowers; but the cool breezes of autumn and the hoary frosts of winter will soon chase all these away; then they, too, will need and seek protection, and through other lips demand in their turn justice and equity at your hands.

69

MARY S. GOVE [NICHOLS]
Woman, an Individual (1854)

. . . It has been said by Abolitionists, "the very kernel and life of slavery is, that the negro is not recognized as a man, belonging to himself, having inalienable rights." This is true. The first of all questions to be answered respecting women and negroes is this, Are they human beings, responsible to God for their acts, having certain inalienable rights, amongst which are "life, liberty, and the pursuit of happiness"? If we can obtain no affirmative answer to this question; if any number of persons decide that these two classes of human beings are appendages to another, higher, stronger, and wiser class, why then I have nothing farther to say to those who thus decide, whether they are women, negroes, or white men. It is said that government derives its authority from the consent of the governed. I have no plea to make for those women, or those negroes, who desire masters. I see the need of masters for such.

Those to whom I wish to appeal are they who believe that women and negroes are human individuals, responsible to God, and to be governed by His laws, and not to be subjected to the forcible requirements of other human beings. When the right of self-ownership and individual responsibility is established for woman all who are enslaved, then all bonds are really broken. This right is conceded by many to negroes, but by very few to woman.

There is now in this free country only the faint dawn of a legal existence for woman.

Few are aware of the legal disabilities under which women live, and fewer still see in how many ways they are regarded as property. In order to test the general recognition of woman as an appendage of man, to be governed and

From T. L. Nichols and Mary S. Gove, *Marriage* (Cincinnati: Valentine Nicholson, 1854), 190–91, 193–94, 197–99, 201–4, 206–7.

protected by him, let us for one moment consider her as an independent being, sustaining herself, and bestowing herself in love upon the man who seems in her judgment to be most divinely hers—conceive of her doing this without reference to law or public opinion—considering herself competent to decide who shall be the recipient of her love and the father of her babe. It is barely possible that society might forgive a woman once for so bestowing herself in love, if she was in no wise a cost, or charge, or if she ministered to some popular want—if she were a great actress, or a great singer, or a skillful physician. But if we contemplate her separating herself from this man whom she voluntarily chose, and whose babes she has borne, to unite herself in the same way to another man, what will be the judgement of society? In the first instance that I have supposed, it is hardly possible that a woman could be forgiven in this country, for thus assuming the ownership of herself. In the second case forgiveness would be an utter impossibility. . . .

The parallel between marriage and slavery has been more perfect than it is now. Formerly, in most of these States, a married woman had no right of property. This is true now in many of the States. The slave has no right of property. Indeed, the first condition of liberty is the right to possess and use property. The time has been when I earned all that my husband possessed. My earnings went into his hands, and he would not allow me six cents unless the purpose for which I wanted it pleased him. I was allowed to work, to lecture for the education and elevation of woman, on condition that I would render into the hands of this man whom the law called my husband, every penny that I earned. The slave does no more than this. He works and renders his wages to his master. The slave does not own his children. They are the property of his master. I did not own mine. The law declared them and the money that I earned the property of this husband. He could choose the place of my abode or service; he could oblige me to bear his children, and he could take my children and

my earnings and do what he pleased with both, and all according to law. Now what more can the master do with his slave than this? Is not the parallel complete? One answers, "no, because you consented to be married, and the slave did not consent to be sold." I answer, I was as much kidnapped as thousands of slaves and married women have been, and will be again—and I gave as little my consent to the transaction.

I was persuaded into a promise to marry, and was made to believe that hell was the reward of broken vows. My promise was given when appeals had been made to my benevolence, and I was assured that I might avert great evil if I gave this promise. Under a false excitement I gave my word, and then dared not break it. The day that I married I had no hope but in the death of one of the parties to this miserable *union*—and many, very many have gone to the altar as sad and hopeless as I was. There was no escape for me. I would have been considered mad, or wicked to the last degree, if I had had the courage to avow my real feeling—my detestation of the man to whom I was married.

. . . What is a woman to do with freedom when it is only liberty to starve body, and soul? When she is owned by a man who can maintain her, though he is loathsome almost as death to her; when her health is utterly lost in bearing his children, and in being the legal victim of his lust; when her children are not hers, but his, according to inexorable law; when she has no power to work, and no means of sustenance but from this owner; when public opinion will brand her with shame, most probably, if she leaves her husband, and most certainly if she enter upon ever so true and loving relations with another man;—what is such a woman to do but to live a false and unholy life? She may have the joy of loving God and her children, but purity and virtue are not for such as she is. A new thought has dawned upon the world—that of fidelity to one's self. The thought of freedom for man has been a glorious inspiration. The earth has been baptized in blood, in the assertion of this thought. The freedom of woman is now to be asserted and achieved. Everywhere fidelity to a husband, though he be a most hateful being, is required of woman. A new gospel and a new requirement comes to her in this day—the gospel of freedom, and the requirement that she be faithful to herself; that she go not shuddering and loathing to the bed of the drunkard, or any diseased monster, or any honest and good man whom she does not love, because the law and public opinion require this sacrifice, this so-called fidelity to the marriage bond. But the question comes, "How can I be true? How can I do otherwise than to submit to this terrible violation? I have no means to live. I am at this man's mercy. He owns my children, and the property that I earned when I had health, before I was his victim, or that I inherited from my father. He has my good name in his keeping. What can I do for life, for babes which are more than life, for my friends? What can I do but submit to degradation and disease?" . . .

It is for me to assert my right to myself; to assert individual sovereignty for woman, as for man; and to give the facts which constitute the pathology of marriage. Although I consider marriage mostly in its results to women and children, I by no means forget that all parties to a false institution are of necessity sufferers. Men are bound to disease and misery; to the burden of supporting the weak and sick; often they go weary and comfortless to the grave, or drown sorrow in drunkenness. I suppose the lot of man is really as hard and bitter as that of woman, but I know woman's life of suffering and endurance better than I do man's—I have more facts to give in her history than in his. I ask for the freedom of all, for the good of all, not for "the greatest good of the greatest number." The human race is one—and I labor and pray for no less an object than the redemption of the human race, and the planet which is our home.

. . . The love of purity, the distinction between good and evil, is violated in woman from the cradle. Everybody kisses the baby, and an infant who rejects and chooses is very rare and very disagreeable to the democratic taste of our community. I have known a grandmother drive a child of two years from her presence because the infant did not wish to kiss her, and refused to do the false thing. The general idea and feeling, whether we know it or not, is that woman is property. She has no right to herself if she is married. Nine tenths of the children born in marriage are not desired by the mother, often not by the father, though it is a great blessing that great love is born with them. Women have not, as a universal fact, the passion that asks the sexual indulgence. Vast numbers of the women of civilization have neither the sexual nor maternal passion. All women want love and support. They do not want to bear children, or to be harlots for this love or this support. In marriage as it at present exists, the instinct against bearing children and against submitting to the amative embrace, is almost as general as the love for infants after they are born. The obliteration of the maternal and sexual instincts in woman is a terrible pathological fact. It has not been defined by theologians, physicians, or political economists. People know no more its meaning than they know the meaning of purity in woman.

A healthy and loving woman is impelled to material union as surely, often as strongly, as man. Would it not be great injustice in our Heavenly Father to so constitute woman as to suffer the pangs of childbirth with no enjoyment of the union that gives her a babe. The truth is that healthy nerves give pleasure in the ultimates of love with no respect to sex; and the same exhausted and diseased nerves, that deny to woman the pleasures of love, give her the dreadful pangs of childbirth.

The apathy of the sexual instinct in woman is caused by the enslaved and unhealthy condition in which she lives. Many inherit from mothers, who are victims in unloving marriage, the diseased amativeness that makes them early subject to masturbation; and this habit destroyed the health of the nervous system. Others inherit an apathetic state that does not impel them to any material union. Healthy and loving women are destroyed by being made bond-women, having no spontaneity, and bearing children more rapidly than they ought, and in unhealthy condition.

I have in my mind now a fact that will shock moralists sufficiently. A lady had borne a large number of children in a hateful marriage in great suffering, and had never known any pleasure in the sexual union. Her husband was at last induced by principle, by a sense of her rights, and sorrow for her great suffering, to protect her in bearing a child to a man she did love. With this child of love she knew no pain, and had the heaven-ordained happiness that sin only has severed from the ultimates of love.

Will the world forever cling to its crimes and diseases, and crucify those who tell the truth?

I might have suppressed this instance, and have given many illustrations of the same truth drawn from happy and unhappy marriages, but I choose to show my utter contempt and abhorrence of the law of man when it contravenes the Higher Law, the law of Health and Purity. These opinions, "scandalous" and revolutionary as they are, and shocking as they must seem to moralists who obey arbitrary laws, are sacred to me. If I am mad, and speak not the words of truth and soberness, my fidelity to God and the faith in my own soul, must win the respect of honest men and women, whilst libertines, without law or according to law, must curse me by a necessity of their nature.

A delicate, nervous, and unhealthy girl marries. Every right-judging person may know that she has no ability to bear children. She may live to have half a dozen abortions or miscarriages, and to be subjected to more amative abuse than any paid harlot, to have less liberty of refusal and of self-protection, as much loathing, and not even the chance of choice that the unmarried prostitute has; and yet the murder of this woman, and the numberless violations of her purity and her person, have the sanction of the law and the church. There is but one drop of comfort in the bitter cup she is compelled to drink. She is self-justified in her degradation and destruction. She is the victim of a "Divine Institution," and believes in the righteousness of her life and death, as the slaves of an Eastern despot consider it an honor to be slain by the sword of royalty. . . .

[Gove ends by quoting from an article she submitted to the *New York Tribune,* but which Horace Greeley—the editor—refused to publish.]

"There is a large and increasing class of women in our land who know what purity is. They know that it is not an exhausted nervous system, which prompts to no union—which enables them to walk quietly in the common thoroughfare of custom. They know, also, that it is not fidelity to a legal bond, where there is no love—where there is force on one side and fear on the other—where rascals are born by immutable God's law, and where diseases are engendered that make the grave an earnestly coveted refuge from 'lawful' whoredom.

"Could any Woman, worthy the name—any other than a legal slave—*choose* to bear worse children than those we hang out of our way— than those who become seducers out of marriage, and destroyers in it?

"In the Medical College, at Albany, there is an exposition of indissoluble marriage, which should be studied by all those who begin to see that a legalized union may be a most impure, unholy, and, consequently, unhealthy thing. In glass vases, ranged in a large cabinet in this medical museum, are uterine tumors, weighting from half a pound to twenty four pounds. A viscus that in its ordinary state weighs a few ounces, is brought, by the disease caused by amative excess—in other words, licentiousness and impurity—to weigh more than twenty pounds. Be it remembered, these monstrosities were produced in lawful and indissoluble wedlock. The wives and mothers who perished of these evils, and left this terrible lesson to the world, knew only of legal purity. *They* lived in obedience to the Law of Marriage—pious, virtuous, reputable, ignorant women. God grant that their suffering be not in vain! God grant that they may be the Teachers of Purity, who being dead yet speak!

"In an age hardly past, 'Honor God and the King' was the great commandment. In this age, 'Honor God and a Husband' holds the same place. Men have learned that the first contains a solecism; Women are learning the same lesson of the last."

70

Rights for All Women of Whatsoever Color (1854)

The following article, in answer to Isola's letter, in the July number of the Una, is so much more spirited than our own remarks, and withal is so entirely to the purpose, that we withhold ours and give it place, endorsing most of its sentiments cordially. We do not quite admit that the wail of any bleeding heart, even though it be a *very selfish one,* sullies the garments of the child, Una.

We know, and our position compels us to the knowledge of the fact, that there are women among us so crushed, so loathing their lives, that even chattel slavery looks, in the distance, like a boon to be desired; and we cannot forbid them an utterance, though we may see them in the wrong and pity their blindness, their ignorance, perhaps the weakness that does not break the bonds which are hateful to them.

DORCHESTER, MASS., JULY, 1854.
To the Editor of the Una:

Dear Madam:—A firm believer in the wrongs of women and in the necessity and possibility of her demanding and obtaining her *Rights,* I hailed with great joy the advent of your paper. I have been a diligent reader of its pages and have striven by all means in my power to extend its circulation: *always* have I been an "Abo-

From *The Una,* August 1854.

litionist," therefore I confess the first numbers of the Una were read with jealous and anxious care, to be sure, that while it advocated "Woman's Rights," it was nowhere narrow or sectional, that it was indeed doing battle for the elevation of *all* Women of whatsoever *color,* clime or condition; that while true to its prime object, it did not hesitate to grasp hands with every cause that is grounded on "One God, one Humanity, one Law, one Love from all for all."

Up to this month I have never found the Una "wanting;" everywhere and always, have I rejoiced to find it, outspoken for oppressed humanity, whatever shape that oppression may have assumed and in your letters, when from home, you have never failed of expressing your word of condemnation for the vices and follies which have come under your observation. From all this, I must believe that *you* do not, *you cannot,* endorse the following sentiments, which I quote from the July number of the "Una:"

"It seems to me that the few women

'Faithful only found among the faithless,'

who have so bravely espoused our cause—a cause which to us is one of life or Death—emphatically the '*bread* question,' should have directed all their efforts to the abolishment of *white* slavery. *One* of the heads of Hydra was surely as much as so small a force should have attacked at once. We *need, this side* of Mason and Dixon line, *all that could be done.* The black slave, when old or disabled, has a sure support; she is in happy ignorance of her own degradation. It must be that our friends know not the magnitude, the length and depth of the evil they have so nobly undertaken to combat. On those women, to whom God has given the will and talent and opportunity, must depend the happiness of future generations of white women in this country. Why go abroad for the enemy when he is in our midst?"

I quote the above shamefully selfish sentiments, from an article from "Elmira, New York," signature, "Isola." The Italics are "Isola's" also—a fitting signature for such sentiments! I trust for the honor of the cause we advocate, she *is alone, insulated,* in such narrow, ignoble thoughts; well may one ask, "Why go *abroad* for the enemy when he is in *our midst?*" Let her indeed tear from her own soul, this terrible selfishness before she presumes to lift a finger in this "movement!"

"*One* of the heads of Hydra * * *." Let me tell her and all others (if indeed there *are any others*) who feel that *only* this one "Head," the wrongs of "White Women *this side* the Mason and Dixon line," is all they can possibly attack; if by any chance their one-sided blows are successful and this mighty sin *seems* vanished, they will quickly find all their labors useless, for God will never permit to *them* an "Iolaus" to finish their work, but forth for the uncauterized wound shall spring, not *two,* (as in the ancient Myth,) but *two dozen* heads, each more dreadful than the *one* they had striven to crush.

It must have a strange sound in the ears of foreign subscribers to the Una, that the "Woman Movement," in this country, "should be directed to the abolishment of *white* slavery *this side* of Mason and Dixon's line;" pray are *we* peculiarly degraded above all other women, that all the talents and power of the noble workers in this cause must be spent on us alone? I fancy there are many *white* women *the other side* of that terrible line, for whom a little of our sympathy and share of our labors would not be spent in vain. May not *even* the *free* colored women, who are among *us,* catch here and there a crumb, which may chance to fall from the full loaf, we are struggling to clutch for ourselves? I suppose "Isola" will say, "no, *only* white slaves!" but this is just after the pattern set us by the Revolutionary Sires, who gave this same cruel *no,* as pay to the black *men* who helped them fight their battles for Liberty in '76.

"The black slave, when old or disabled, has a sure support." If this were true, (it is not) I would ask, has not also the old and disabled *white* woman *this* side of Mason and Dixon's line a sure support? Surely she has, for all other means failing her, the Alms House is a "*sure*" home; and, for one, I should prefer the very meanest one in

the Free States, or a death from starvation on the public highway, to the best "support" the most humane of all the slave holders can give to the most valued of his slaves. I should at least know that my own body belonged to me, and that is better than "*bread;*" and death from starvation and the soul's *homeward* flight through *free* air, is infinitely to be preferred to *life without* Liberty.

"She is in happy ignorance of her own condition." Ah! indeed, is she really? If this is a reason for us to be silent, for them, then also is it a reason why we should evermore hold our peace, on the wrongs of "*White*" Women; for if they are not in "happy ignorance," they are at least *unwilling* to have redress, and will suffer any amount of misery rather than in any way be identified with, or acknowledge the justice and need of the "Woman's Rights Cause." I say this is true of two-thirds of the women this side of Mason and Dixon's line, and I think any laborer or leader in the movement will bear me out in this assertion.

If then ignorance, or willful hugging of the chains of slavery *be* happiness, shall we keep silent? nay, but the stones of the street would cry out for very shame! "Happy ignorance."—Then why do so many of them flee away from such "sure" homes, and escape through all sorts of perils to Canada, thus reducing themselves to the unfortunate condition of us "*White*" Slaves?— When we come to stand before God, and the "books are opened" and each one gives in the final account, and the voice of the "Inexorable One" sounds in our ears: "Where is thy Black Sister?" will it suffice to answer *there?* "Thou knowest Oh Lord! we were very "few" and could attack but "one head of the Hydra;" besides she was in "happy ignorance" of her situation" and had a "sure support in her old age;" "What is it to us? We were not our black sister's keeper!" Then shall *many* fugitives testify (and at *that Bar, color* makes no difference in the reception of testimony,) against the "happy ignorance" and more than one "Old Prue," prove the falseness of a "sure" home in old age. Then shall the Judge say,

"Inasmuch as ye did it not unto these, ye did not unto me. I know you not."

It is just precisely because "our friends" *do know* "the magnitude * * *" of the evil they have undertaken to combat, and because they also know that the "happiness and misery of future generations" of *black* women are just as dear to God as that of "white women," do they spend their "will, talents and opportunity" for *both*.

I have no faith in the sincerity or earnestness of any advocate of the "Woman's Rights Movement," who ignores the cause of the slave, and refuses the sympathy and aid within her or his power to give. . . .

In conclusion allow me to say, though grieved to see no note of dissent from the Editor's pen, and deeply pained that the child Una should thus early have so foul a spot on her hitherto fair garments, I cannot believe that any of the noble women, who lead in this cause, and *most* of those who follow have any sympathy with the sentiments contained in "Isola's" letter, upon which I have taken the liberty to comment in this article; but I could not refrain from expressing my indignant scorn. I feel that such utterances should not go forth in the Una unnoticed and unreproved.

For myself I must say, were I convinced that the Una does indeed endorse such sentiments, that this movement does in any way countenance the pro-slavery party, " I would have none of it. I would wash my hands clean from it!"—If I must give up one, if I find *myself* unable "to grapple but with one head of the Hydra," I shall not hesitate which to give up. May God forget me, when I forget the slave! May my tongue "cleave to the roof of my mouth," when I refuse to speak in their behalf!

In working for the slave I know I emancipate myself, I do more for the freedom of white women, than I possibly could in *any other way,* if at the *same time* I turned my back on the anti-slavery cause. Not yet are the words coined, which are strong enough to express the undying hate I bear the American slave system or the sympathy and pity I feel for its victims. I believe

the Woman's Rights party will never get what we ask for until this System is abolished, and we breathe free of a slave atmosphere. . . .

71
ANNE E. MCDOWELL
Woman's Rights and Slavery (1856)

From the *Lancaster* (S.C) *Ledger* we clip the following notice of the "Advocate":—

"This is the title of a paper established in Philadelphia about a year ago. It is edited and all the type set up by females. We had formed a very good opinion of this paper; . . . it professed, as its title purports, to be the advocate of the rights of women. We had no objection to this; in very fact, we have been among those who would elevate her to her proper position, and not suffer her to be prostrated and ignored, as some of the 'lords of creation' would have her. So far, then, we saw no reason to question the right of Miss McDowell, the editress, to be the advocate of her own sex. But when Miss McDowell comes out as the advocate of the abolition of slavery, we have a right to speak. She is departing from the avowed principle she at first started with.— What business has she, the advocate of woman's rights, with the subject of slavery? Does she know anything about slavery? . . . Has Miss McDowell ever seen slavery in South Carolina? We know how negroes are treated in South Carolina, and we have seen the poor, half-starved devils at the North, and, for Miss McDowell's information, now tell her that the South Carolina negro slave is a prince to the half-fed, half-clothed free negro.

We have nothing else against the Advocate: it is a neatly printed and very readable paper, but we insist that its *fair* editress has nothing to do with such *black* subjects."

From *The Woman's Advocate*, February 1856.

Our brother of the Ledger is correct in his supposition that our paper is the advocate of the rights of woman. "Give her of the fruit of her hands, and let her own works praise her in the gates," is the motto we have adopted, and which we have earnestly endeavored to incorporate in every article we have written. It is no fault of ours if he has not, until lately, been aware of our hatred of oppression. We have never sought to conceal it, but we have not meddled with the subject of southern slavery, because evils of as greater magnitude, and appealing more particularly to our personal sympathies, were to be found around us. The southern slave has many and able champions, while the northern working girl is fighting her way unaided amidst the sneers, insults, and ridicule of the so-called philanthropists of the other sex. Still we feel earnestly for all victims of tyranny, whether they be slaves of the cotton lords, or the slaves of the cotton loom. Our compassion is equally excited by the story of the black slave dragging out her weary life in constant terror of her brutal overseer, as by that of the slave of the needle in continual fear of beggary or starvation. It is equally heart-rending to know that there are thirty thousand women in the city of New Orleans, where persons can be sold at any moment to the highest bidder, as to read that thirty thousand women in the city of New York have been driven by poverty to the same awful fate.

The profession and practice of the Ledger differ widely, for in the article above quoted, this passage occurs—"We have ever been among those who would elevate woman to her proper position, and not suffer her to be prostrated and ignored as some of the lords of creation would have her," and in another column of the same paper we find the following:—

FOR SALE A LIKELY NEGRO GIRL.—

I will sell at Lancaster, C.H., on Sales day, February 4, 1856, a negro girl, Amanda, belonging to Elijah Horton of Alabama. Titles unquestionable, negro sound and likely, and sold by me at request of Elijah Horton and his attorney in fact.

Terms cash, or a credit of a few days.
J. H. WITHERSPOON.

Is it not shameful? "Title unquestionable, negro sound and likely." He asks, "What business has she, the advocate of woman's rights, with the subject of slavery?" We answer the right that every human heart has to sorrow for suffering, misery, degradation; that every woman's heart has to lighten, by sympathy, the grief and burden of her sister woman; the right that every northern heart has to speak out boldly for the cause of truth and humanity. The question is as absurd as it is impertinent. Again he asks, do we know anything of slavery. We answer, being a native of a slave State, where slavery exists only in its mildest form, we are conversant with everything that can be said in its favor. We have witnessed the attachment and devotion of slaves to the owners, and the heart-[indecipherable word] sobs and despairing moans of a mother torn from her children, and pray to God our eyes may never look upon such a scene again. . . .

72

Resolutions of the Seventh National Woman's Rights Convention in New York (1856)

1. *Resolved,* That the close of a Presidential election affords a peculiarly appropriate occasion to renew the demands of woman for a consistent application of Democratic principles.

2. *Resolved,* That the Republican Party, appealing constantly, through its orators, to female sympathy, and using for its most popular rallying cry a female name, is peculiarly pledged by

From *History of Woman Suffrage,* Vol. 1, 1848–1861, ed., Elizabeth Cady Stanton, Susan B. Anthony, and Matilda Joslyn Gage (New York: Fowler and Wells, 1881), 633–34.

consistency, to do justice hereafter in those States where it holds control.

3. *Resolved,* That the Democratic Party must be utterly false to its name and professed principles, or else must extend their application to both halves of the human race.

4. *Resolved,* That the present uncertain and inconsistent position of woman in our community, not fully recognized either as a slave or as an equal, taxed but not represented, authorized to earn property but not free to control it, permitted to prepare papers for scientific bodies but not to read them, urged to form political opinions but not allowed to vote upon them, all marks a transitional period in human history which can not long endure.

5. *Resolved,* That the main power of the woman's rights movement lies in this: that while always demanding for woman better education, better employment, and better laws, it has kept steadily in view the one cardinal demand for the right of suffrage; in a democracy the symbol and guarantee of all other rights.

6. *Resolved,* That the monopoly of the elective franchise, and thereby all the powers of legislative government by man, solely on the ground of sex, is a usurpation, condemned alike by reason and common-sense, subversive of all the principles of justice, oppressive and demoralizing in its operation, and insulting to the dignity of human nature.

7. *Resolved,* That while the constant progress of law, education, and industry prove that our efforts for women in these respects are not wasted, we yet proclaim ourselves unsatisfied, and are only encouraged to renewed efforts, until the whole be gained.

73

CAROLINE H. DALL
Woman's Right to Labor, Lecture Delivered in Boston (1859)

. . . I ask for woman, then, free, untrammelled access to all fields of labor; and I ask it, first, on the ground that she needs to be fed, and that the question which is at this moment before the great body of working women is "death or dishonor:" for lust is a better paymaster than the mill-owner or the tailor, and economy never yet shook hands with crime.

Do you object, that America is free from this alternative? I will prove you the contrary within a rod of your own doorstep.

Do you assert, that, if all avenues were thrown open, it would not increase the quantity of work; and that there would be more laborers in consequence, and lower wages for all?

Lower wages for *some,* I reply; but certainly higher wages for women; and they, too, would be raised to the rank of partners, and personal ill treatment would not follow those who had position and property before the law.

You offer them a high education in vain till you add to it the stimulus of a free career. In this lecture, I undertake to prove to you, that a large majority of women stand in such relations to their employers, that they are compelled to death or a life of shame. Why not choose death, then?

So I asked once of a woman thus pressed to the wall. "Ah, madam!" she answered, "I chose it long ago for myself; but what shall I do for my mother and child?"

The superior has a right to every advantage which he can honestly gain, as well as the infe-

From *Woman's Right to Labor; or, Low Wages and Hard Work. In Three Lectures, Delivered in Boston, November, 1859* (Boston: Walker, Wise, and Co., 1860), 4–11, 14–15, 57–9.

rior; but he has no right to increase any natural difference in his favor, if he believe it to exist, by laws or customs which cripple the inferior. If, as political economists tell us, it is chiefly by man, collectively taken, that the property of society is created; and if, on that very ground, man's interest has the first claim to consideration,—does it not follow, that every friend of woman will try to induce her to become a capitalist, and open to her, as her first path to safety, the way to honorable independence? And, in this connection, I must repeat what some of you have often heard me say, that a want of respect for labor, and a want of respect for woman, lies at the bottom of all our difficulties, low wages included.

I will not admit that the argument of the political economist has, as yet, any rightful connection with the price of woman's work. "The price of labor will always rise or fall," he says, "as the number of laborers is small or large; and it is because there are too many women for a few avenues of labor that the wages are so low." If man believes this, let him help us to open new avenues, and so reduce the number in any one. But I claim that he has increased the natural difference in his own favor, supposing that there be any such, by laws and customs which cripple woman; and that his own lust of gain stands in the way of her daily bread. Just so in hydraulics, men tell us, that water rises everywhere to the level of its source; but you may raise it a thousand feet higher by the aid of your forcing-pump, or drop it from a siphon a thousand feet below. And a forcing-pump and a siphon has man imposed upon the natural currents of labor. If, in my correspondence with employers last winter, one man told me with pride that he gave from eight to fifty cents for the making of pantaloons, including the heaviest doeskins, he *forgot* to tell me what he charged his customers for the same work. Ah! on those bills, so long unpaid, the eight cents sometimes rises to thirty, and the fifty cents *always* to a dollar or a dollar and twenty-five cents.

The most efficient help this class of work-

women could receive would be the thorough adoption of the cash system, and the establishment of a large workshop in the *hands of women* consenting to moderate profits, and superintended by those whose position in society would win respect for labor. When I said, six months ago, that ten Beacon-street women, engaged in honorable work, would do more for this cause than all the female artists, all the speech-making and conventions, in the world, I was entirely in earnest.

It is pretty and lady-like, men think, to paint and chisel: philanthropic young ladies must work for nothing, like the angels. *Let* them, when they rise to angelic spheres; but, here and now, every woman who works for nothing helps to keep her sister's wages down,—helps to keep the question of death or dishonor perpetually before the women of the slop-shop.

Why? Because she helps to depress the estimate of woman's ability. What is persistently given for nothing is everywhere thought to be worth nothing. I throw open a door here for some stifled sufferer at the West End: let her open a clothing establishment, and employ her own sex; let her make money by it, and watch for the end. When an Employment Society or a Needlewoman's Friend becomes bankrupt in purse, it is bankrupt in morals and argument as well. The wheels of the world move on the grooves of good management, of success. Set these once firmly underneath, and the outcry against our moral Fultons will be hushed.

In country villages and farming districts, there is a great deal of harmful competition with the girls of the slop-shops, which can never be ended until it is considered respectable for women openly to earn money. The stitching of wallets, hat-linings, and shoe-bindings, the more delicate labor on linen collars and shirt-bosoms, is carried on now not merely by so-called benevolent societies who want to build churches, lecture-rooms, and so on, but by rich farmers' wives, who keep or do not keep servants, in the long, summer afternoons and winter evenings, because it is work that can be done privately, and is sought to supply them with jewelry and dress. If they will not educate their minds by profitable reading, it is earnestly to be desired they should work, but openly, for money, and at such trades as naturally fall to their lot. Herb and fruit drying, distilling, preserving, pickling, market-gardening, may yet lay the foundations of ample fortune for many a woman. I have passed a summer amid lovely landscapes, where the woman found neither fruit nor vegetables for their table, but let the brown earth plead to them in vain; while they stitched, stitched, stitched the long hours away, every broken needle bearing witness against the broken lives of women who needed in distant cities, where they stood homeless and starving, the work their sisters pilfered, sitting at their ease beside the hearth-stone. Their ignorance was their excuse. Let it not be ours. . . .

Out of two thousand women who work for their daily bread in New York, five hundred and thirty-four receive a dollar a week. "How many men," asks Dr. Chapin, "would keep off death and conquer the Devil on such wages? One woman had to do it by making caps at two cents each! Think of this, women who like to buy things cheap: for, if the veil could be lifted from your eyes, *you* would see—the angels *do* see— on your gay, white dresses many a crimson stain; and among the dewy flowers with which you wreathe your hair, the grass that grows on graves!"

Seven thousand eight hundred and fifty ruined women walk the streets of New York,— five hundred ordinary omnibus-loads. They are chiefly young women under twenty, and the average length of the lives they lead is just four years. Every four years, then, seven thousand eight hundred and fifty women are drawn from their homes, many of them from simple, rural hearths, to meet this fate. What drives them to it? The want of bread. . . .

I have shown you that a very large number of women are compelled to self-support; that the old idea, that all men support all women, is an absurd fiction; and, if you require other evi-

dence than mine, you may find it in the English courts, under the working of the new Divorce Bill. Nearly all the women who have applied for divorces have proved that the subsistence of the family depended upon them. Out of six million of British women over twenty-one years of age, one-half are industrial in their mode of life, and more than two millions are self-supporting in their industry like men. Put this fact fully before your eyes.

Driven to self-support, you have seen, also, that low wages and comparatively few and over-crowded avenues of labor compel women to vicious courses for their daily bread. The streets of Paris, London, Edinburgh, New York, and Boston, tell us the same painful story; and in glaring, crimson letters, rises everywhere the question,—"Death or dishonor?" I have shown you that there is encouragement for moral effort, because these women escape from vice as fast as they find work to do. "Have they strength for the conflict?" you ask, "or desire to enter such fields?" Find your answer in what they have done from the earliest ages, with the foot of Confucius and Vishnu, of capital and interest, upon their necks. In the lovely lives of Bertha and Ann Gurney, and the powerful attraction of Sarah Scofield, you have found pleasanter pictures whereon to rest your eyes. Let no man taunt woman with inability to labor, till the coal-mines and the metal-works, the rotting cocoons and fuzzing-cards, give up their dead; till he shares with her, equally at least, the perils of manufactures and the press of the market. As partners, they must test and prove their comparative power.

74

ANTOINETTE BROWN BLACKWELL, ERNESTINE ROSE, AND SUSAN B. ANTHONY

Debating Marriage and Divorce Laws, at the Tenth National Woman's Rights Convention in New York (1860)

Rev. Antoinette Brown Blackwell followed, and prefaced her remarks by saying: "Ours has always been a free platform. We have believed in the fullest freedom of thought and in the free expression of individual opinion. I propose to speak upon the subject discussed by our friend, Mrs. Stanton. It is often said that there are two sides to every question; but there are three sides, many sides, to every question. Let Mrs. Stanton take hers; let Horace Greeley take his; I only ask the privilege of stating mine. (APPLAUSE). I have embodied my thought, hastily, in a series of resolutions, and my remarks following them will be very brief."

MRS. BLACKWELL continued:

I believe that the highest laws of life are those which we find written within our being; that the first moral laws which we are to obey are the laws which God's own finger has traced upon our own souls. Therefore, our first duty is to ourselves, and we may never, under any circumstances, yield this to any other. I say we are first responsible to ourselves, and to the God who has laid the obligation upon us, to make ourselves the grandest we may. Marriage grows out of the relations of parties. The law of our development comes wholly from within; but the relation of marriage supposes two persons as being united to each other, and from this relation originates the law. Mrs. Stanton calls mar-

From *History of Woman Suffrage,* Vol. 1, 1848–1861, ed., Elizabeth Cady Stanton, Susan B. Anthony, and Matilda Joslyn Gage (New York: Fowler and Wells, 1881), 723–35.

riage a "tie." No, marriage is a *relation;* and, once formed, that relation continues as long as the parties continue with the natures which they now essentially have. Let, then, the two parties deliberately, voluntarily consent to enter into this relation. It is one which, from its very nature, must be permanent. Can the mother ever destroy the relation which exists between herself and her child? Can the father annul the relation which exists between himself and his child? Then, can the father and mother annul the relation which exists between themselves, the parents of the child? It can not be. The interests of marriage are such that they can not be destroyed, and the only question must be, "Has there been a marriage in this case or not?" If there has, then the social law, the obligations growing out of the relation, must be life-long.

But I assert that every woman, in the present state of society, is bound to maintain her own independence and her own integrity of character; to assert herself, earnestly and firmly, as the equal of man, who is only her peer. This is her first right, her first duty; and if she lives in a country where the law supposes that she is to be subjected to her husband, and she consents to this subjection, I do insist that she consents to degradation; that this is sin, and it is impossible to make it other than sin. True, in this State, and in nearly all the States, the idea of marriage is that of subjection, in all respects, of the wife to the husband—personal subjection, subjection in the rights over their children and over their property; but this is a false relation. Marriage is a union of equals—equal interests being involved, equal duties at stake; and if any woman has been married to a man who chooses to take advantage of the laws as they now stand, who chooses to subject her, ignobly, to his will, against her own, to take from her the earnings which belong to the family, and to take from her the children which belong to the family, I hold that that woman, if she can not, by her influence, change this state of things, is solemnly obligated to go to some State where she can be legally divorced; and then she would be as solemnly bound to return again, and, standing for herself and her children, regard herself, in the sight of God, as being bound still to the father of those children, to work for his best interests, while she still maintains her own sovereignty. Of course, she must be governed by the circumstances of the case. She may be obliged, for the protection of the family, to live on one continent while her husband is on the other: but she is never to forget that in the sight of God and her own soul, she is his wife, and that she owes to him the wife's loyalty; that to work for his redemption is her highest social obligation, and that to teach her children to do the same is her first motherly duty. Legal divorce may be necessary for personal and family protection; if so, let every woman obtain it. This, God helping me, is what I would certainly do, for under no circumstances will I ever give my consent to be subjected to the will of another, in any relation, for God has bidden me not to do it. But the idea of most women is, that they must be timid, weak, helpless, and full of ignoble submission. Only last week, a lady who has just been divorced from her husband said to me—"I used to be required to go into the field and do the hardest laborer's work, when I was not able to do it; and my husband would declare, that if I would not thus labor, I should not be allowed to eat, and I was obliged to submit." I say the fault was as much with the woman as with the man; she should never have submitted. . . .

Of course, I would not have man or woman sacrificed—by no means. First of all, let every human being maintain his own position as a self-protecting human being. At all hazards, let him never sin, or consent to be sacrificed to the hurt of himself or of another; and when he has taken this stand, let him act in harmony with it. Would I say to any woman, "You are bound, because you are legally married to one who is debased to the level of the brute, to be the mother of his children?" I say to her, "No! while the law of God continues, you are bound never to make one whom you do not honor and respect, as well as love, the father of any child of yours. It is your

first and highest duty to be true to yourself, true to posterity, and true to society." (Applause). Thus, let each decide for himself and or herself what is right. But, I repeat, either marriage is in its very nature a relation which, once formed, never can be dissolved, and either the essential obligations growing out of it exist forever, or the relation may at any time be dissolved, and at any time those obligations be annulled. And what are those obligations? Two persons, if I understand marriage, covenant to work together, to uphold each other in all excellence, and to mutually blend their lives and interests into a common harmony. I believe that God has so made man and woman, that it is not good for them to be alone, that they each need a co-worker. . . .

The cure for the evils that now exist is not in dissolving marriage, but it is in giving to the married woman her own natural independence and self-sovereignty, by which she can maintain herself. . . .

ERNESTINE L. ROSE said:—Mrs. President—the question of a Divorce law seems to me one of the greatest importance to all parties, but I presume that the very advocacy of divorce will be called "Free Love." For my part (and I wish distinctly to define my position), I do not know what others understand by that term; to me, in its truest significance, love must be free, or it ceases to be love. In its low and degrading sense, it is not love at all, and I have as little to do with its name as its reality.

The Rev. Mrs. Blackwell gave us quite a sermon on what woman ought to be, what she ought to do, and what marriage ought to be; an excellent sermon in its proper place, but not when the important question of a Divorce law is under consideration. She treats woman as some ethereal being. It is very well to be ethereal to some extent, but I tell you, my friends, it is quite requisite to be a little material, also. At all events, we are so, and, being so, it proves a law of our nature. (APPLAUSE).

It were indeed well if woman could be what she ought to be, man what he ought to be, and marriage what it ought to be; and it is to be hoped that through the Woman's Rights move-ment—the equalizing of the laws, making them more just, and making woman more indepen-dent—we will hasten the coming of the millen-nium, when marriage shall indeed be a bond of union and affection. But, alas! it is not yet; and I fear that sermons, however well meant, will not produce that desirable end; and as long as the evil is here, we must look it in the face without shrinking, grapple with it manfully, and the more complicated it is, the more courageously must it be analyzed, combated, and destroyed. (Ap-plause).

Mrs. Blackwell told us that, marriage be-ing based on the perfect equality of husband and wife, it can not be destroyed. But is it so? Where? Where and when have the sexes yet been equal in physical or mental education, in position, or in law? When and where have they yet been rec-ognized by society, or by themselves, as equals? "Equal in rights," says Mrs. B. But are they equal in rights? If they were, we would need no con-ventions to claim our rights. "She can assert her equality." Yes, she can assert it, but does that as-sertion constitute a true marriage? And when the husband holds the iron heel of legal oppres-sion on the subjugated neck of the wife until every spark of womanhood is crushed out, will it heal the wounded heart, the lacerated spirit, the destroyed hope, to assert her equality? And shall she still continue the wife? Is that a mar-riage which must not be dissolved? (Applause).

According to Mr. Greeley's definition, viz., that there is no marriage unless the ceremony is performed by a minister and in a church, the tens of thousands married according to the laws of this and most of the other States, by a law-yer or justice of the peace, a mayor or an al-derman, are not married at all. According to the definition of our reverend sister, no one has ever yet been married, as woman has never yet been perfectly equal with man. I say to both, take your position, and abide by the consequences. If the few only, or no one, is really married, why do you object to a law that shall acknowledge the fact? You certainly ought not to force people

to live together who are not married. (Ap-plause). . . .

The papers have of late been filled with the heart-sickening accounts of wife-poisoning. Whence come these terrible crimes? From the want of a Divorce law. Could the Hardings be legally separated, they would not be driven to the commission of murder to be free from each other; and which is preferable, a Divorce law, to dissolve an unholy union, which all parties agree is no true marriage, or a murder of one, and an execution (legal murder) of the other party? But had the unfortunate woman, just be-fore the poisoned cup was presented to her lips, pleaded for a divorce, Mrs. Blackwell would have read her a sermon equal to St. Paul's "Wives, be obedient to your husbands," only she would have added, "You must assert your equality," but "you must keep with your husband and work for his redemption, as I would do for my husband"; and Mr. Greeley would say, "As you chose to marry him, it is your own fault; you must abide the consequences, for it is a 'divine institution, a union for life, which nothing but death can end.' " (Applause). . . .

But what is marriage? A human institution, called out by the needs of social, affectional hu-man nature, for human purposes, its objects are, first, the happiness of the parties immediately concerned, and, secondly, the welfare of soci-ety. Define it as you please, these are only its objects; and therefore if, from well-ascertained facts, it is demonstrated that the real objects are frustrated, that instead of union and happiness, there are only discord and misery to themselves, and vice and crime to society, I ask, in the name of individual happiness and social morality and well-being, why such a marriage should be bind-ing for life?—why one human being should be chained for life to the dead body of another? . . .

I therefore ask for a Divorce law. Divorce is now granted for some crimes; I ask it for oth-ers also. It is granted for a State's prison offense. I ask that personal cruelty to a wife, whom he swore to "love, cherish, and protect," may be made a heinous crime—a perjury and a State's prison offense, for which divorce shall be granted. Willful desertion for one year should be a sufficient cause for divorce, for the willful deserter forfeits the sacred title of husband or wife. Habitual intemperance, or any other vice which makes the husband or wife intolerable and abhorrent to the other, ought to be sufficient cause for divorce. I ask for a law of Divorce, so as to secure the real objects and blessings of married life, to prevent the crimes and immoralities now practiced, to prevent "Free Love," in its most hideous form, such as is now carried on but too often under the very name of marriage, where hypocrisy is added to the crime of legalized prostitution. "Free Love," in its degraded sense, asks for no Divorce law. It acknowledges no marriage, and therefore requires no divorce. I believe in true marriages, and therefore I ask for a law to free men and women from false ones. (APPLAUSE). . . .

Finally, educate woman, to enable her to promote her independence, and she will not be obliged to marry for a home and a subsistence. Give the wife an equal right with the husband in the property acquired after marriage, and it will be a bond of union between them. Diamond cement, applied on both sides of a fractured vase, re-unites the parts, and prevents them from falling asunder. A gold band is more efficacious than an iron law. Until now, the gold has all been on one side, and the iron law on the other. Remove it; place the golden band of justice and mutual interest around both husband and wife, and it will hide the little fractures which may have occurred, even from their own perception, and allow them effectually to re-unite. A union of interest helps to preserve a union of hearts. (LOUD APPLAUSE).

WENDELL PHILLIPS then said: I object to entering these resolutions upon the journal of this Convention. (APPLAUSE). I would move to lay them on the table; but my conviction that they are out of order is so emphatic, that I wish to go further than that, and move that they do not appear on the journals of this Convention. If the resolutions were merely the expressions

of individual sentiments, then they ought not to appear in the form of resolutions, but as speeches, because a resolution has a certain emphasis and authority. It is assumed to give the voice of an assembly, and is not taken as an individual expression, which a speech is.

Of course, every person must be interested in the question of marriage, and the branch that grows out of it, the question of divorce; and no one could deny, who has listened for an hour, that we have been favored with an exceedingly able discussion of those questions. But here we have nothing to do with them, any more than with the question of intemperance, or Kansas, in my opinion. This Convention is no Marriage Convention—if it were, the subject would be in order; but this Convention, if I understand it, assembles to discuss the laws that rest unequally upon women, not those that rest equally upon men and women. It is the laws that make distinctions between the sexes. Now, whether a man and a woman are married for a year or a life is a question which affects the man just as much as the woman. At the end of a month, the man is without a wife exactly as much as the woman is without a husband. The question whether, having entered into a contract, you shall be bound to an unworthy partner, affects the man as much as the woman. Certainly, there are cases where men are bound to women carcasses as well as where women are bound to men carcasses. (LAUGHTER AND APPLAUSE). We have nothing to do with a question which affects both sexes equally. Therefore, it seems to me we have nothing to do with the theory of marriage, which is the basis, as Mrs. Rose has very clearly shown, of divorce. . . .

ABBY HOPPER GIBBONS, of New York City, seconded the motion of Mr. Phillips, and said that she wished the whole subject of marriage and divorce might be swept from that platform, as it was manifestly not the place for it. . . .

SUSAN B. ANTHONY: I hope Mr. Phillips will withdraw his motion that these resolutions shall not appear on the records of the Convention. I am very sure that it would be contrary to all parliamentary usage to say, that when the speeches which enforced and advocated the resolutions are reported and published in the proceedings, the resolutions shall not be placed there. And as to the point that this question does not belong to this platform,—from that I totally dissent. Marriage has ever been a one-sided matter, resting most unequally upon the sexes. By it, man gains all—woman loses all; tyrant law and lust reign supreme with him—meek submission and ready obedience alone befit her. Woman has never been consulted; her wish has never been taken into consideration as regards the terms of the marriage compact. By law, public sentiment and religion, from the time of Moses down to the present day, woman has never been thought of other than as a piece of property, to be disposed of at the will and pleasure of man. And this very hour, by our statute-books, by our (so called) enlightened Christian civilization, she has no voice whatever in saying what shall be the basis of the relation. She must accept marriage as man proffers it, or not at all.

And then again, on Mrs. Phillips' own ground, the discussion is perfectly in order, since nearly all the wrongs of which we complain grow out of the inequality, the injustice of the marriage laws, that rob the wife of the right to herself and her children—that make her the slave of the man she marries.

I hope, therefore, the resolutions will be allowed to go out to the public, that there may be a fair report of the ideas which have actually been presented here, that they may not be left to the mercy of the secular press. I trust the Convention will not vote to forbid the publication of those resolutions with the proceedings.

REV. WM. HOISINGTON, the blind preacher: Publish all that you have said and done here, and let the public know it.

The question was then put on the motion of Mr. Phillips, and it was lost.

After which, the resolutions reported by the Business Committee were adopted without dissent.

75

ELIZABETH CADY STANTON, LYDIA MOTT, ERNESTINE ROSE, MARTHA C. WRIGHT, AND SUSAN B. ANTHONY
Appeal to the Women of New York (1860)

Once more we appeal to you to make renewed efforts for the elevation of our sex. In our marital laws, we are now in advance of every state in the Union. Twelve years ago New York took the initiative step, and secured to married women their property, received by gift or inheritance. Our last legislature passed a most liberal act, giving to married women their rights, to sue for damages of person or property, to their separate earnings and their children; and to the widow, the possession and control of the entire estate during the minority of the youngest child. Women of New York! You can no longer be insulted in the first days of your widowed grief by the coarse minions of the law at your fireside, coolly taking an inventory of your household gods, or robbing your children of their natural guardian.

While we rejoice in this progress made in our laws, we see also a change in the employment of women. They are coming down from the garrets and up from the cellars to occupy more profitable posts in every department of industry, literature, science and art.

In the church, too, behold the spirit of freedom at work. Within the past year, the very altar has been the scene of well fought battles; women claiming and exercising their right to vote in church matters, in defiance of precedent, priest or Paul. . . .

All this is the result of the agitation, technically called "*Woman's Rights*," through conventions, lectures, circulation of tracts and petitions,

From New York State Woman's Rights Committee, *Appeal to the Women of New York* (n.p., 1860), 1–4.

and by the faithful word uttered in the privacy of home. The few who stand forth to meet the world's cold gaze, its ridicule, its contumely and its scorn, are urged onward by the prayers and tears, crushed hopes and withered hearts of the sad daughters of the race. The wretched will not let them falter; and they who seem to do the work, ever and anon draw fresh courage and inspiration from the noblest women of the age, who, from behind the scene, send forth good words of cheer and heartfelt thanks.

Six years hence, the men of New York purpose to revise our State Constitution. Among other changes demanded, is the right of suffrage for women—which right will surely be granted, if through all the intervening years, every woman does her duty. Again, do we appeal to each and all—to every class and condition—to inform themselves on this question, that woman may no longer publish her degradation by declaring herself satisfied in her present position, nor her ignorance by asserting that she has "all the rights she wants."

Any person who ponders the startling fact that there are FOUR MILLIONS of African slaves in this Republic, will instantly put the question to himself "Why do these people submit to the cruel tyranny that our government exercises over them?" The answer is apparent—"simply because they are ignorant of their power." Should they rise *en masse,* assert and demand their rights, their freedom would be secure. It is the same with woman. Why is it that one-half the people of this nation are held in abject dependence—civilly, politically, socially, the slaves of man? Simply because woman knows not her power. To find out her natural rights, she must travel through such labyrinths of falsehood, that most minds stand appalled before the dark mysteries of life—the seeming contradictions in all laws, both human and divine. But, because woman cannot solve the whole problem of life to her satisfaction, because she cannot prove to a dem-

onstration the rottenness and falsehood of our present customs, shall she, without protest, supinely endure evils she cannot at once redress? The silkworm in its many wrappings, knows not it yet shall fly. The woman, in her ignorance, her drapery and her chains, knows not that in advancing civilization, she too, must soon be free, to counsel with her conscience and her God.

The religion of our day teaches that in the most sacred relations of the race, the woman must ever by subject to the man; that in the husband centres all power and learning; that the difference in position between husband and wife, is as vast as that between Christ and the church; and woman struggles to hold the noble impulses of her nature in abeyance to opinions uttered by a Jewish teacher, which, alas, the mass believe to be the will of God.

Woman turns from what she is taught to believe are God's laws, to the laws of man; and in his written codes she finds herself still a slave. No girl of fifteen could read the laws concerning woman, made, executed and defended by those who are bound to her by every tie of affection, without a burst of righteous indignation. Few have ever read or heard of the barbarous laws that govern the mothers of this *Christian Republic*—and fewer still care, until misfortune brings them into the iron grip of the law. It is the imperative duty of educated women to study the Constitution and statutes under which they live, that when they shall have a voice in the government, they may bring wisdom and not folly into its councils.

We now demand the ballot—trial by a jury of our peers—and and equal right to the joint earnings of the marriage copartnership. And, until the Constitution be so changed as to give us a voice in the government, we demand that man shall make all his laws on Property, Marriage and Divorce, to bear equally on man and woman.

Suggestions for Further Reading

Baker, Paula. "The Domestication of Politics: Women and American Political Society, 1780–1920." *American Historical Review* 89 (1984): 620–47.

Banner, Lois W. *Elizabeth Cady Stanton: A Radical for Woman's Rights.* Boston: Little, Brown, 1980.

Bardes, Barbara and Suzanne Gossett. *Declarations of Independence: Women and Political Power in Nineteenth-Century American Fiction.* New Brunswick: Rutgers Univ. Press, 1990.

Basch, Norma. *In the Eyes of the Law: Women, Marriage, and Property in Nineteenth-Century New York.* Ithaca: Cornell Univ. Press, 1982.

Boydston, Jeanne, Mary Kelley, and Anne Margolis. *The Limits of Sisterhood: The Beecher Sisters on Women's Rights and Woman's Sphere.* Chapel Hill: Univ. of North Carolina Press, 1988.

Douglas, Ann. *The Feminization of American Culture.* New York: Alfred A. Knopf, 1977.

DuBois, Ellen Carol. *Feminism and Suffrage: The Emergence of an Independent Women's Movement in America, 1848–1869.* Ithaca: Cornell Univ. Press, 1978.

Epstein, Barbara. *The Politics of Domesticity: Women, Evangelicism, and Temperance in Nineteenth-Century America.* Middletown, Conn.: Wesleyan Univ. Press, 1981.

Evans, Sara M. *Born for Liberty: A History of Women in America.* New York: The Free Press, 1989.

Flexnor, Eleanor. *A Century of Struggle: The Women's Rights Movement in the United States.* Cambridge: Harvard Univ. Press, 1959.

Foster, Frances Smith. *Written by Herself: Literary Production by African American Women, 1746–1892.* Bloomington: Indiana Univ. Press, 1993.

Dublin, Thomas. *Women at Work: The Transformation of Work and Community in Lowell, Massachusetts, 1826–1860.* New York: Columbia Univ. Press, 1979.

Giddings, Paula. *When and Where I Enter: The Impact of Black Women on Race and Sex in America.* New York: William Morrow, 1984.

Ginzberg, Lori D. *Women and the Work of Benevolence: Morality, Politics, and Class in the Nineteenth-Century United States.* New Haven: Yale Univ. Press, 1990.

Gordon, Linda and Ellen DuBois. "Seeking Ecstasy on the Battlefield: Danger and Pleasure in Nineteenth-Century Feminist Thought." *Feminist Studies* 9 (1983): 7–25.

Hersh, Blanche Glassman. *The Slavery of Sex: Feminist-Abolitionists in America.* Urbana: Univ. of Illinois Press, 1978.

Hewitt, Nancy A. *Women's Activism and Social Change: Rochester, New York, 1822–1872.* Ithaca: Cornell Univ. Press, 1984.

Kelley, Mary. *Private Woman, Public Stage: Literary Domesticity in Nineteenth-Century America.* New York: Oxford Univ. Press, 1984.

Lerner, Gerda. *The Grimké Sisters from South Carolina: Pioneers for Woman's Rights and Abolition.* New York: Schocken Books, 1966.

____. *The Majority Finds Its Past: Placing Women in History.* New York: Oxford Univ. Press, 1979.

Matthews, Glenna. *The Rise of Public Woman: Woman's Power and Woman's Place in the United States, 1630–1970.* New York: Oxford Univ. Press, 1992.

Melder, Keith E. *Beginnings of Sisterhood: The American Woman's Rights Movement, 1800–1850*. New York: Schocken Books, 1977.

Morris, Celia. *Fanny Wright: Rebel in America*. Cambridge: Harvard Univ. Press, 1984.

O'Neill, William L. *Everyone Was Brave: The Rise and Fall of Feminism in America*. Chicago: Quadrangle Books, 1969.

Ryan, Mary P. *Cradle of the Middle Class: The Family in Oneida County, New York, 1790–1865*. Cambridge: Cambridge Univ. Press, 1981.

____. *Women in Public: From Banners to Ballots, 1825–1880*. Baltimore: Johns Hopkins Univ. Press, 1990.

Sklar, Kathryn Kish. *Catharine Beecher: A Study in American Domesticity*. New Haven: Yale Univ. Press, 1973.

Smith, Daniel Scott. "Family Limitation, Sexual Control, and Domestic Feminism in Victorian America." *Feminist Studies* 1 (1973): 40–57

Smith-Rosenberg, Carroll. *Disorderly Conduct: Visions of Gender in Victorian America*. New York: Oxford Univ. Press, 1985.

Solomon, Martha M., ed. *A Voice of Their Own: The Woman Suffrage Press, 1840–1910*. Tuscaloosa: Univ. of Alabama Press, 1991.

Tompkins, Jane. *Sensational Designs: The Cultural Work of American Fiction, 1790–1860*. New York: Oxford Univ. Press, 1985.

Welter, Barbara. *Dimity Convictions: The American Woman in the Nineteenth Century*. Athens: Ohio Univ. Press, 1976.

White, Deborah. *Ar'n't I A Woman?: Female Slaves in the Plantation South*. New York: W. W. Norton, 1985.

Yellin, Jean Fagan. *Women & Sisters: The Antislavery Feminists in American Culture*. New Haven: Yale Univ. Press, 1989.

PART IV

The Post-Civil War Struggle for Political & Social Equality

I. Suffrage & Other Essential Rights

THE POST-CIVIL WAR QUEST FOR WOMEN'S SUFFRAGE BEGAN AMIDST BITTER DEBATE over whether, in the wake of the great armed conflict and the emancipation of slaves, the vote for women should be included in the Fifteenth Amendment to the Constitution, which (after ratification in 1870) guaranteed the ballot to black men—but not to women of any race. Sojourner Truth's speech, "Colored Men Will Be Masters Over the Women" (1867), makes the penetrating point that, without equal civil rights, black women would live in a state of virtual slavery, with black men replacing white masters. Truth—a former slave and feminist abolitionist and activist—thought that since the nation was already "stirred up" politically, women should press the issue and demand the vote immediately.

Other leading American feminists who fought for abolitionism, most notably Elizabeth Cady Stanton and Susan B. Anthony, opposed the Fifteenth Amendment precisely because of its exclusion of women. With the weekly newspaper *The Revolution* (founded in 1868 and originally edited by Stanton and Anthony) as its standard-bearer, this group of suffragists put forward a number of arguments as to why women should be given the responsibility of the vote. In "Suffrage for All, White and Black, Male and Female" (1868), Stanton points out the contradictions between abolitionist ideals of "individual rights" for blacks and the total disregard of one-half of that race; she also speaks of the great contributions "educated American women" could make to civic life during a time of unprecedented immigration—a rationale that would portend harsher nativist and racist comments as Stanton set feminism against the Republican Party's sole concern for the black vote.

While Stanton's appeal is directed primarily to whites, "A Letter to the Colored Men's State Convention in Utica, New York" (1868), by Susan B. Anthony, exhorts black men to include women in their demand for the ballot because, under the laws of the state, the degradations and grievances of "your wives and daughters—your mothers and sisters" are far greater than those of African-American men. And in "A Colored Woman's Voice" (1869), *The Revolution* reprinted a plea to a largely male convention in which the speaker betrays the moral fervency of suffragism as she invokes the liberatory spirit of Moses and the children of Israel along with Abraham Lincoln and the Emancipation Proclamation for the cause of the ballot. The feminist newspaper also reprinted "Debate on the Fifteenth Amendment at the Annual Meeting of the Equal Rights Association" (1869), during which white women (Paulina Davis and Anthony), a black man (Frederick Douglass), and a black woman (Frances Harper) contest the merits of postponing the realization of women's equal rights in order to ensure the rights of black men.

The split among women's rights activists reflected in the debate over the Fifteenth Amendment led to the division of what had been a relatively unified movment before the Civil War. In May of 1869, Elizabeth Cady Stanton and Susan B. Anthony founded the National Woman Suffrage Association (NWSA), an organization that began by re-directing its demands for immediate female suffrage from the state legislatures—the focus since the 1850s—to the United States Congress. In opposition to NWSA, Lucy Stone and her husband Henry Blackwell formed the American Woman Suffrage Association (AWSA) in 1869—a more moderate organization which supported the Fifteenth Amendment's guarantee of black male voting rights and which worked for the gradual enfranchisement of women at the state level. The differences between the NWSA and AWSA would divide the women's suffrage movement for the following twenty years.

After ratification of the Fifteenth Amendment, the NWSA petitioned Congress for a Sixteenth Amendment recognizing women's voting rights. In the petitions of 1876, taken from *History of Woman Suffrage* (1891–1922), the NWSA rationalizes its strategy of campaigning for the vote at the national level. The language of these petitions points out the NWSA's challenge to state "disenfranchisement" based on sex, an important argument in the post-Civil War period; believing that women are "born with" the vote (evoking natural rights doctrine), the NWSA claimed that it is only the abuse of state legislative power that has taken that inherent right away. In accordance with this theory, hundreds of women during the elections of 1871 and 1872 simply ignored prohibitions and went to the polls attempting to vote. Susan B. Anthony followed this strategy in her home town of Rochester, New York, where, much to her surprise, polling officials allowed her to vote. Later arrested, Anthony made an impassioned defense of her right to vote, as recorded in the trial transcript of *United States of America v. Susan B. Anthony* (1873).

Victoria Woodhull—a free love advocate, member of the International Workingmen's Association (a London-based Marxist organization), a financially-successful New York publisher, and militant suffragist—provided important constitutional justification for the idea of women's pre-existent right to vote. Testifying before a Congressional committee in January of 1871, Woodhull insisted that the Fourteenth and Fifteenth Amendments recognized women's citizenship and therefore implicitly included suffrage as a necessary part of that status. Woodhull acted on her intellectual convictions through her "Declaration of Candidacy for the Presidency of the United States" (1870); she went on to form the Equal Rights Party and castigate its political opponents for losing sight of the key issue: suffrage. In response, Laura Curtis Bullard, in "What Flag Shall We Fly?" (1870), published in *The Revolution*, belittles the narrow-mindedness of the *Woman's Journal*, insisting that the vote, while important, is only one tool in the fight for broader social change.

As the United States grew more diverse throughout the late-nineteenth century, so too did claims and interests of American women—those women, moreover, were no longer primarily from the northeastern section of the country. Lula Greene Richards and Emmeline B. Wells, for instance, edited a semi-monthly feminist newspaper in Salt Lake City, *The Woman's Exponent*. In their editorial, "Women's Rights and Polygamy" (1876), they attempt to expand understanding of women's freedom by claiming that the Mormon practice of plural marriage provides a wife with greater opportunity for personal freedom and development. In Topeka, Kansas, Emma and Ira Peck founded *The Farmer's Wife*, which claimed on its masthead, "Equal Rights to All, Special Privilege to None!" In her article for *The Farmer's Wife*, "A Kansas Farm" (1891), Fannie McCormick offers a feminist perspective far removed from the doctrinal debates between the NWSA and AWSA; and yet her discussion of the drudgery of housework, disenfranchisement, and the spiritual strength of womanhood connects not only with a great many American women, but also with the heart of the women's movement.

Many feminists realized during this time that gaining legal and social equality with men would mean challenging common cultural understandings of the separate roles of the sexes. At the turn-of-the-twentieth century, United States citizenship and the right to vote were tied closely to the notion of man's place and prominence in the public sphere, including the masculine ideal of hero-soldier and the willingness to risk one's life for country. In "The Physical Force Argument" (1895), Alice Stone Blackwell breaks apart this association, explaining that male suffrage has never actually been based on military service and that, in any case, the vote should not be denied to those who have been labeled mistakenly the weaker sex.

Alternatively, some women pushed for the vote and other rights so the sex could better realize conventional understandings of femininity. In "Voting Mothers" (1897), published in the *American Jewess*, Sara T. Drukker draws on a woman's traditional role as mother in arguing for the vote, reasoning that she can best fulfill her supreme duty of raising the young only if she herself has the advantage of being educated through political participation. Julia Ward Howe's speech "The Moral Initiative as Belonging to Women" (1893) offers a more complex view of sexual relations: like Drukker, she too believes women have a special social role of support and nurturance, an identity based on a distinct feminine quality of moral virtue; but Howe also recognizes that men systematically subordinate women and adds that they must take it upon themselves to free their sex.

In "Woman's Political Future" (1893), Frances W. Harper, an African-American author and activist, offers an over-arching critique of American political culture—a system infected by the corruption, self-interest, and violence (through lynching and other means) of white men. In response, Harper wants the vote to be given to those men and women who would meet certain educational and moral requirements, thereby opening the public sphere to women, who would in turn infuse it with high moral purpose and responsibility.

In "An Educational Suffrage Qualification Necessary" (1897), Elizabeth Cady Stanton contributes to a series of articles in *Woman's Journal* marking the fiftieth anniversary of the women's suffrage movement. Stanton seconds Harper's call for an education requirement, but notice in this article the added deprecation of the political influence of the new immigrant population, betraying the nativist impulses of some feminists of the late-nineteenth century. As Elizabeth Burrill Curtis points out in "The Present Crisis" (1897), the idea of an education and/or literacy requirement is a response to those who argue that giving women the vote would allow masses of uneducated and "ignorant" immigrants into civic life.

Woman's Journal also published arguments in 1897 against the education requirement. In "Educated Suffrage a Fetich" (1897), Harriet Stanton Blatch, Elizabeth Cady Stanton's daughter, rejects her mother's rationale, explaining that education and literacy have never been determinant of intelligence, moral character, or civic responsibility. Anna Gardner opposes a literacy test in "Educated Suffrage a Step Backward" (1897) along similar lines, adding that the United States would be ill-served by an electorate of educated elite.

In "'Common Sense' Applied to Woman Suffrage" (1894), Mary Putnam-Jacobi, one of the most accomplished medical doctors of her day, uses her powers of reason and analysis to argue for women's right to vote. While she draws her title from Thomas Paine's revolutionary tract *Common Sense* (1776), Putnam-Jacobi reflects an attitude toward suffrage distinctive of turn-of-the-century thought: expediency. While the right to vote had earlier been discussed as a "natural" right, or as an abstract ideal, Putnam-Jacobi insists that it is now a matter of political expediency, fulfilling the practical need of a group of citizens who have worked their way into the economic and social framework of the country.

Fannie Barrier Williams's essay, "Women's Influence in Politics" (1896), reflects another late-nineteenth century concern—the corruption and the domination of "machine politics" in the American electoral process, a party system which effectively erases the power of the individual voter. The piece goes on to say that through their affinity for reform, though, women could restore the political process to its democratic origins.

In "Suffrage in the South" (1900), Belle Kearney provides an historical overview of Southern women's evolving interest in gaining the vote. With the defeat of the Confederacy, women of all classes had to assume more public roles in Southern society, which awakened them to the possibilities of full civic participation. Women in the South had been slow to advocate women's rights before the turn of the century because, among other reasons, of the historical association between feminism and abolition.

76

SOJOURNER TRUTH
Colored Men Will Be Masters
Over the Women (1867)

My friends, I am rejoiced that you are glad, but I don't know how you will feel when I get through. I come from another field—the country of the slave. They have got their liberty—so much good luck to have slavery partly destroyed; not entirely. I want it root and branch destroyed. Then we will all be free indeed. I feel that if I have to answer for the deeds done in my body just as much as a man, I have a right to have just as much as a man. There is a great stir about colored men getting their rights, but not a word about the colored women; and if colored men get their rights, and not colored women theirs, you see the colored men will be masters over the women, and it will be just as bad as it was before. So I am for keeping the thing going while things are stirring; because if we wait till it is still, it will take a great while to get it going again. White women are a great deal smarter, and know more than colored women, while colored women do not know scarcely anything. They go out washing, which is about as high as a colored woman gets, and their men go about idle, strutting up and down; and when the women come home, they ask for their money and take it all, and then scold because there is no food. I want you to consider on that, chil'n. I call you chil'n; you are somebody's chil'n, and I am old enough to be mother of all that is here. I want women to have their rights. In the courts women have no right, no voice; nobody speaks for them. I wish woman to have her voice there among the pettifoggers. If it is not a fit place for women, it is unfit for men to be there.

I am above eighty years old; it is about time for me to be going. I have been forty years a slave and forty years free, and would be here forty years more to have equal rights for all. I suppose I am kept here because something remains for me to do; I suppose I am yet to help to break the chain. I have done a great deal of work; as much as a man, but did not get so much pay. I used to work in the field and bind grain, keeping up with the cradler; but men doing no more, got twice as much pay; so with the German women. They work in the field and do as much work, but do not get the pay. We do as much, we eat as much, we want as much. I suppose I am about the only colored woman that goes about to speak for the rights of the colored women. I want to keep the thing stirring, now that the ice is cracked. What we want is a little money. You men know that you get as much again as women when you write, or for what you do. When we get our rights we shall not have to come to you for money, for then we shall have money enough in our own pockets; and may be you will ask us for money. But help us now until we get it. It is a good consolation to know that when we have got this battle once fought we shall not be coming to you any more. You have been having our rights so long, that you think, like a slave-holder, that you own us. I know that it is hard for one who has held the reins for so long it give up; it cuts like a knife. It will feel all the better when it closed up again. I have been in Washington about three years, seeing about these colored people. Now colored men have the right to vote. There ought to be equal rights now more than ever, since colored people have got their freedom. I am going to talk several times while I am here; so now I will do a little singing. I have not heard any singing since I came here.

Address to the National Convention of the American Equal Rights Association, New York, May 9 1867. From *History of Woman Suffrage, Vol. 2, 1861–1876*, ed., Elizabeth Cady Stanton, Susan B. Anthony, and Matilda Joslyn Gage (New York: Fowler and Wells, 1886), 193–4.

77

ELIZABETH CADY STANTON
Suffrage for All, White and Black, Male and Female (1868)

. . . Just as the constituent elements of nitrogen and oxygen, make the necessary atmosphere in which man can breathe and live, and the exhausting of either is certain death, so are the male and female elements in their true proportions as necessary for our moral life, and this negation of womanhood is the degradation of our common humanity. Hence, when we had it in our power to put one race on an equal footing at the south, as an abolitionist we protested against the enfranchisement of the black man alone, seeing that the bondage of the women of that race, by the laws of the south, would be more helpless than before. What to her the loosing of the white man's chains, if the ignorant laborer by her side, who has learned no law but violence, her equal to-day, is henceforth to become her master? To us the black women of the south are as precious in the scale of being as the men. Woman suffers in slavery a degradation man can never know. The strongest appeals made by abolitionists in the past against slavery have been on woman's wrongs, and now, when the day of emancipation comes, shall man enter into all the rights, privileges and immunities of citizenship while the woman by his side is left without the sceptre of power, the ballot, for her protection? Wendell Phillips says that emancipation is mockery to the black man without the ballot? Have not the women of this nation suffered enough from man's unjust legislation, to know that such emancipation as he offers the black woman is a mockery also? Those slaves have worked and suffered side by side, shared each other's sorrows, fears, and anxieties through centuries of heathenism and bondage; and now shall abolitionists consent that another race of men shall find their liberties over this fresh holocaust of

From *The Revolution*, April 19, 1868.

womanhood? No, no. We have no reason to suppose that the black man understands the principles of equity, or will practice the christian virtues better than his Saxon masters. And our demands on the Woman's Rights platform for the last twenty years are proof sufficient that man cannot legislate wisely and justly for the woman by his side. Abolitionists show us "the cold shoulder" because they know we see their vulnerable points. After discussing "individual rights" thirty years, and claiming suffrage for the black man as "a natural right" when they ask, with the republican party, "manhood suffrage" merely, they compromise the best interests of the race they would serve, throw over board one-half "their clients," stultify their past declarations, and prove false to their education and high calling, as the statesmen of the hour. This is not with us a question of personality as between the individual black man and Saxon woman, but a principle of government. It is not a question of necessary precedence for one or the other. If people were enfranchised by car-loads at the Capitol of the nation, it might be a question who should go first, but suffrage for all in this hour of reconstruction could be more easily and logically secured than for a new class. Our demand has long been suffrage for all, white and black, male and female, of legal age and sound mind.

. . . The most pitiful spectacle this country presents, is that of educated American women consenting, in this hour of our country's danger, to this incoming tide of ignorance, poverty and vice, from every quarter of the globe, to legislate for them at the polls, without demanding that it be outweighed with the wealth, virtue and intelligence of their own sex. And this indifference to a nation's life, to the interests of 30,000,000 of people, to the institutions of a continent, drapes itself under the false guise of Christian philanthropy. Would not the education, elevation and enfranchisement of 15,000,000 women do more to hasten advancing civilization than that of 2,000,000 black men? The questions bear no proportion to each other. The partial results of the one on national welfare,

are wholly lost in the magnitude and far-reaching consequences of the other. To-day the ship of state is tempest-tossed on an uncertain sea. The men at the helm, lacking the spiritual intuitions of women by their side, are steering without chart or compass. A voice from out the threatening clouds calls out: "It is not good for man to be alone." Seeing the nation's danger and man's need, shall woman, with the charts spread out before her, knowing all the dangerous coasts and isles, meekly remain in the vessel's hold, while ignorant hands lay hold the ropes and sails, capable of giving no new light or inspiration to those already bewildered there? To us it would be the height of wisdom for such women to rush on deck and say, let not another man come up to touch the ropes until those more skilled have tried what they can do. Suppose the question were to be settled to-day, shall we enfranchise such men as Chase, Wade, Sumner, Beecher, Garrison and Phillips to govern this country, or shall all these be set aside, and the government placed in the hands of the southern *freedwomen:* Of course, we should all choose the former class. So we say to-day, educated women first, ignorant men afterward. E. C. S.

78

SUSAN B. ANTHONY
Letter to the Colored Men's State Convention in Utica, New York (1868)

A convention of colored people was held at Utica last week to demand right of Suffrage. Rev. J. W. Loguen was chosen President. Addresses were made by the President, by W. W. Brown of Boston, James Spellman of New York, Stephen Myers and others. A Declaration of Rights was issued, and the following letter was received and read:

From *The Revolution*, October 22, 1868.

Woman's Suffrage Association of America
No. 37 Park-row, Room No. 20
New York, Oct 1, 1868
To the President and members of the Colored Men's State Convention.

GENTLEMEN: Permit me in behalf of the colored women of the State of New York to urge upon you to extend your demand for the ballot to your wives and daughters—your mothers and sisters. By the laws of our State the grievances of colored women are a thousand fold greater than those of colored men. While colored men not possessed of the requisite $250 to make them voters are exempted from taxation, all colored *women* worth even $50 are compelled to pay taxes. That is, the colored man to-day is worth $200, and is exempt, he dies to-morrow, and his widow is immediately assessed as tax-payer. Then in all the trades and professions, your sisters and daughters have not only the obstacles that are everywhere thrown in your way, but also the prejudices and impediments everywhere thrown in woman's way, in addition. Now, Heaven, and all colored men know that the barriers that hedge *your* pathway on every side are most discouraging; I ask you, then, to remember the women by your side, and secure to them all you claim for yourselves. Now is the time to establish the government of our state, as well as the nation, on the *one Democratic Republican principle*—the *consent of the whole people*—black women and white, as well as black men must now be brought within the body politic.

Respectfully yours, SUSAN B. ANTHONY.

The letter of Miss Anthony was presented by Mr. Spelman, New York delegate, and after it was read, we understand a Mr. Rich of Troy moved to lay it on the table, and on a vote being taken it was almost unanimous. The President, Rev. J. W. Loguen and Mr. Spelman voted nay. Several attempts were made, we are told, by the friends of Woman Suffrage to bring the question before the convention again, but they were unsuccessful, a careful canvass of the members showed that they were bitterly opposed to it.

79

A Colored Woman's Voice
(1869)

The colored women, of all other American women, should be devoted to the cause of Suffrage. One appeared in the recent Chicago Convention to the following effect:

I present myself to you as a composition of humanity, for there flows through my veins a combination of the blood of four distinct nations, of which the greater part is Dutch, part Indian, part African, and the lesser part Irish. (Applause and laughter.) I am an American, because here I was born. I am true, because I love the dear old flag. I am on the right side of the question, because I believe woman was made a helpmate for man; that he is but half a man without woman (applause), and you need her help as well in political affairs as you do in private or domestic affairs. And, gentlemen, I warn you no longer to stand out in refusing the right for which we contend; in trying to withhold from these noble ladies here and their darker sisters the franchise they now demand. Miss Anthony and Mrs. Stanton, with their high moral and intellectual power, have shaken the states of New England, and the shock is felt here to-day. The echo comes back from St. Louis and all through the west; a sensation is aroused in England; and soon the whole world will be awakened to a sense of the value and importance of our cause. Woman has a power within herself, and the God that reigns above, who commanded Moses to lead the children of Israel from out the land of Egypt, from out the house of bondage, who walled the waters of the Red Sea, who endowed Samson with power to slay his enemies with the jaw-bone of an ass, who furnished Abraham Lincoln with knowledge to write the emancipation proclamation, whereby four millions of blacks were set free—that God, our God, is with and for us, and will hear the call of woman, and her

rights will be granted, and she shall be permitted to vote.

80

PAULINA DAVIS, FREDERICK DOUGLASS, SUSAN ANTHONY, AND FRANCES HARPER
Debate on the Fifteenth Amendment (1869)

Mrs. Paulina W. Davis then came forward. She would not be altogether satisfied to have the Fifteenth Amendment passed without the Sixteenth, for they would have a race of tyrants raised above them in the South, and the black women of that country would also receive worse treatment than if the Amendment was not passed. Take any class that have been slaves and you will find that they are the worst when free, and become the hardest masters. The colored women of the South say they do not want to get married to the negro, as their husbands can take their children away from them, and also appropriate their earnings. The black women are more intelligent than the men, because they have learned something from their mistresses. She then related a story of how the black men whip and abuse their wives in the South. One of her sister's servants whipped his wife every Sunday regularly. (LAUGHTER.) She thought that sort of men should not have the making of the laws for the governance of the women throughout the land. (APPLAUSE.)

Mr. Douglas then stepped forward and was received with great applause. He said that all disinterested spectators would concede that this Equal Rights meeting had been pre-eminently a Woman's Rights meeting. (APPLAUSE.) They had just heard an argument with which he could not agree—that the suffrage to the black men should

From *The Revolution*, March 4, 1869.

At the Annual Meeting of the Equal Rights Association, May 1869. From *The Revolution*, May 27, 1869.

be postponed to that of the women. Here is a woman who, since the day that the snake talked with our mother in the garden—from that day to this, I say, she has been divested of political rights. What may we not expect, according to that reasoning, when woman, when—(LOUD LAUGHTER AND APPLAUSE.)

Miss Anthony hereupon rose from her seat and made towards Mr. Douglass, saying something which was drowned in the applause and laughter which continued. Mr. Douglass was heard to say, however, "No, no. Susan," which again set the audience off in another audible smile, and Miss Anthony took her seat.

When silence was somewhat restored, Mr. Douglass continued, saying "You see when women get into trouble how they act. Miss Anthony comes to the rescue—(LAUGHTER)—and these good people have not yet learned to hear people through. (LAUGHTER.) When anything goes against them they are up right away. Now I do not believe the story that the slaves who are enfranchised become the worst of tyrants. (A Voice—"Neither do I."APPLAUSE.) I know how this theory came about. When a slave was made a driver he made himself more officious than the white driver, so that his master might not suspect that he was favoring those under him. But we do not intend to have any master over us. (APPLAUSE.)

The President then took the floor and argued that not another man should be enfranchised until enough women are admitted to the polls to outweigh those who have the franchise. (APPLAUSE.) She did not believe in allowing ignorant negroes and ignorant and debased Chinamen to make laws for her to obey. (APPLAUSE.)

Mrs. Harper (colored) asked Mr. Blackwell to read the fifth resolution of the series he submitted, and contended that that covered the whole ground of the resolutions of Mr. Douglass.

Miss Anthony—Then I move that that resolution be reconsidered.

Mr. Douglas—Oh! no; you cannot do that while the floor is occupied.

Mrs. Harper then proceeded with her remarks, saying that when it was a question of race she let the lesser question of sex go. But the white women all go for sex, letting race occupy a minor position. She liked the idea of working-women, but she would like to know if it was broad enough to take colored women?

Miss Anthony and several others—Yes, yes.

Mrs. Harper said that when she was at Boston, there were sixty women who rose up and left work because one colored woman went to gain a livelihood in their midst. (APPLAUSE.) If the nation could only handle one question, she would not have the black women put a single straw in the way if only the race of men could obtain what they wanted. (GREAT APPLAUSE.)

Mr. C. C. Burleigh attempted to speak, but was received with some disapprobation by the audience, and confusion ensued.

Miss Anthony said she protested against the Fifteenth Amendment because it *wasn't Equal Right*. It put two million more men in position of tyrants over two millions women who had until now been the *equals* of the men at their side.

81

Petitions for a Sixteenth Amendment (1876)

. . . The women generally came to the conclusion that if in truth there was no protection for them in the original constitution nor the late amendments, the time had come for some clearly-defined recognition of their citizenship by a sixteenth amendment.

The following appeal and petition were extensively circulated:

To the Women of the United States:

Having celebrated our centennial birthday

From *History of Woman Suffrage*, Vol. 3, 1876–1885, ed., Elizabeth Cady Stanton, Susan B. Anthony, and Matilda Joslyn Gage (Rochester, N.Y.: Susan B. Anthony, 1886), 58–60, 104.

with a national jubilee, let us now dedicate the dawn of the second century to securing justice to women. For this purpose we ask you to circulate a petition to congress, just issued by the National Association, asking an amendment to the United States Constitution, that shall prohibit the several States from disfranchising citizens on account of sex. We have already sent this petition throughout the country for the signatures of those men and women who believe in the citizen's right to vote. . . .

Having petitioned our law-makers, State and national, for years, many from weariness have vowed to appeal no more; for our petitions, say they, by the tens of thousands, are piled up in the national archives, unheeded and ignored. Yet it is possible to roll up such a mammoth petition, borne into congress on the shoulders of stalwart men, that we can no longer be neglected or forgotten. Statesmen and politicians alike are conquered by majorities. We urge the women of this country to make now the same united effort for their own rights that they did for the slaves of the South when the thirteenth amendment was pending. Then a petition of over 300,000 was rolled up by the leaders of the suffrage movement, and presented in the Senate by the Hon. Charles Sumner. But the statesmen who welcomed woman's untiring efforts to secure the black man's freedom, frowned down the same demands when made for herself. Is not liberty as sweet to her as to him? Are not the political disabilities of sex as grievous as those of color? Is not a civil-rights bill that shall open to woman the college doors, the trades and professions—that shall secure her personal and property rights, as necessary for her protection as for that of the colored man? And yet the highest judicial authorities have decided that the spirit and letter of our national constitution are not broad enough to protect woman in her political rights; and for the redress of her wrongs they remand her to the State. If our *Magna Charta* of human rights can be thus narrowed by judicial interpretations in favor of class legislation, then must we demand an amendment that, in

clear, unmistakable language, shall declare the equality of all citizens before the law.

Women are citizens, first of the United States, the second of the State wherein they reside; hence if robbed by State authorities of any right founded in nature or secured by law, they have the same right to national protection against the State, as against the infringements of any foreign power. If the United States government can punish a woman for voting in one State, why has it not the same power to protect her in the exercise of that right in every State? The constitution declares it the duty of congress to guarantee to every State a republican form of government, to every citizen, equality of rights. This is not done in States where women, thoroughly qualified, are denied admission into colleges which their property is taxed to build and endow; where they are denied the right to practice law and are thus debarred from one of the most lucrative professions; where they are denied a voice in the government, and thus, while suffering all the ills that grow out of the giant evils of intemperance, prostitution, war, heavy taxation and political corruption, stand powerless to effect any reform. Prayers, tears, psalmsinging and expostulation are light in the balance compared with that power at the ballot-box that coins opinions into law. If women who are laboring for peace, temperance, social purity and the rights of labor, would take the speediest way to accomplish what they propose, let them demand the ballot in their own hands, that they may have a direct power in the government. Thus only can they improve the conditions of the outside world and purify the home. As political equality is the door to civil, religious and social liberty, here must our work begin.

Constituting, as we do, one-half the people, bearing the burdens of one-half the national debt, equally responsible with man for the education, religion and morals of the rising generation, let us with united voice send forth a protest against the present political status of woman, that shall echo and reëcho through the land. In view of the numbers and character of those making the demand, this should be the largest petition ever yet rolled up in the old or the new; a petition that shall settle forever the popular objection that "women do not want to vote."

ELIZABETH CADY STANTON, *President.*

MATILDA JOSLYN GAGE, *Chairman Executive Committee.*

SUSAN B. ANTHONY, *Corresponding Secretary.*

Tenafly, N.J., November 10, 1876.

To the Senate and House of Representatives in Congress assembled:

The undersigned citizens of the United States, residents of the State of———, earnestly pray your honorable bodies to adopt measures for so amending the constitution as to prohibit the several States from disfranchising United States citizens on account of sex.

In addition to the general petition asking for a sixteenth amendment, Matilda Joslyn Gage, this year (1877) sent an individual petition, similar in form to those offered by disfranchised male citizens, asking to be relieved from her political disabilities. This petition was presented by Hon. Elias W. Leavenworth, of the House of Representatives, member for the thirty-third New York Congressional district. It read as follows:

To the Senate and House of Representatives of the United States in Congress assembled:

Matilda Joslyn Gage, a native born citizen of the United States, and of the State of New York, wherein she resides, most earnestly petitions your honorable body for the removal of her political disabilities and that she may be declared invested with full power to exercise her right of self government at the ballot-box, all State constitutions or statute laws to the contrary notwithstanding.

The above petition was presented January 24, and the following bill introduced February 5:

AN ACT *to relieve the political disabilities of Matilda Joslyn Gage:*

Be it enacted by the Senate and House of Representatives of the United States of America in congress assembled, that all political disabilities heretofore existing in reference to Matilda Joslyn Gage, of Fayetteville, Onondaga county, State of New York, be removed and she be declared a citizen of the United States, clothed with all the political rights and powers of citizenship, namely: the right to vote and to hold office to the same extent and in the same degree that male citizens enjoy these rights. This act to take effect immediately.

The following year a large number of similar petitions were sent from different parts of the country, the National Association distributing printed forms to its members in the various States. The power of congress to thus enfranchise women upon their individual petitions is as undoubted as the power to grant individual amnesty, to remove the political disabilities of men disfranchised for crime against United States laws, or to clothe foreigners, honorably discharged from the army, with the ballot. . . .

Hon. George F. Hoar of Massachusetts, February 4, presented in the Senate the 120 petitions with their 6,261 signatures, which, by special request of its officers, had been returned to the headquarters of the American Association, in Boston. In her appeal to the friends to circulate the petitions, both State and national, Lucy Stone, chairman of its executive committee, said:

The American Suffrage Association has always recommended petitions to congress for a sixteenth amendment. But it recognizes the far greater importance of petitioning the State legislatures. *First——*Because suffrage is a subject referred by the constitution to the voters of each State. *Second*——Because we cannot expect a congress composed solely of representatives of States which deny suffrage to women, to submit an amendment which their own States have not yet approved. Just so it would have been impossible to secure the submission of negro suffrage by a congress composed solely of representatives from States which restricted suffrage to white men. While therefore we advise our friends to circulate both petitions together for signature, we urge them to give special prominence to those which apply to their own State legislatures, and to see that these are presented and urged by competent speakers next winter.

82

United States of America v. Susan B. Anthony (1873)

. . . The Court, after listening to an argument from the District Attorney, denied the motion for a new trial.

THE COURT: The prisoner will stand up. Has the prisoner anything to say why sentence shall not be pronounced?

MISS ANTHONY: Yes, your honor, I have many things to say; for in your ordered verdict of guilty, you have trampled underfoot every vital principle of our government. My natural rights, my civil rights, my political rights, are all alike ignored. Robbed of the fundamental privilege of citizenship, I am degraded from the status of a citizen to that of a subject; and not only myself individually, but all of my sex, are, by your honor's verdict, doomed to political subjection under this so-called Republican government.

JUDGE HUNT: The Court can not listen to a rehearsal of arguments the prisoner's counsel has already consumed three hours in presenting.

MISS ANTHONY: May it please your honor, I am not arguing the question, but simply stating the reasons why sentence can not, in justice, be pronounced against me. Your denial of my citizen's right to vote is the denial of my right of consent as one of the governed, the denial of my right of representation as one of the taxed, the denial of my right to a trial by a jury of my peers as an offender against law, therefore, the

From *History of Woman Suffrage, Vol 2, 1861–1876,* ed., Elizabeth Cady Stanton, Susan B. Anthony, and Matilda Joslyn Gage (New York: Fowler and Wells, 1886), 687–9.

denial of my sacred rights to life, liberty, property, and—

JUDGE HUNT: The Court can not allow the prisoner to go on.

MISS ANTHONY: But your honor will not deny me this one and only poor privilege of protest against this high-handed outrage upon my citizen's rights. May it please the Court to remember that since the day of my arrest last November, this is the first time that either myself or any person of my disfranchised class has been allowed a word of defense before judge or jury—

JUDGE HUNT: The prisoner must sit down; the Court can not allow it.

MISS ANTHONY: All my prosecutors, from the 8th Ward corner grocery politician, who entered the complaint, to the United States Marshal, Commissioner, District Attorney, District Judge, your honor on the bench, not one is my peer, but each and all are my political sovereigns; and had your honor submitted my case to the jury, as was clearly your duty, even then I should have had just cause of protest, for not one of those men was my peer; but, native or foreign, white or black, rich or poor, educated or ignorant, awake or asleep, sober or drunk, each and every man of them was my political superior; hence, in no sense, my peer. Even, under such circumstances, a commoner of England, tried before a jury of lords, would have far less cause to complain than should I, a woman, tried before a jury of men. Even my counsel, the Hon. Henry R. Selden, who has argued my cause so ably, so earnestly, so unanswerably before your honor, is my political sovereign. Precisely as no disfranchised person is entitled to sit upon a jury, and no woman is entitled to the franchise, so, none but a regularly admitted lawyer is allowed to practice in the courts, and no woman can gain admission to the bar—hence, jury, judge, counsel, must all be of the superior class.

JUDGE HUNT: The Court must insist—the prisoner has been tried according to the established forms of law.

MISS ANTHONY: Yes, your honor, but by

forms of law all made by men, interpreted by men, administered by men, in favor of men, and against women; and hence, your honor's ordered verdict of guilty, against a United States citizen for the exercise of "that citizen's right to vote," simply because that citizen was a woman and not a man. But, yesterday, the same manmade forms of law declared it a crime punishable with $1,000 fine and six months' imprisonment, for you, or me, or any of us, to give a cup of cold water, a crust of bread, or a night's shelter to a panting fugitive as he was tracking his way to Canada. And every man or woman in whose veins coursed a drop of human sympathy violated that wicked law, reckless of consequences, and was justified in so doing. As then the slaves who got their freedom must take it over, or under, or through the unjust forms of law, precisely so now must women, to get their right to a voice in this Government, take it; and I have taken mine, and mean to take it at every possible opportunity.

JUDGE HUNT: The Court orders the prisoner to sit down. It will not allow another word.

MISS ANTHONY: When I was brought before your honor for trial, I hoped for a broad and liberal interpretation of the Constitution and its recent amendments, that should declare all United States citizens under its protecting aegis—that should declare equality of rights the national guarantee to all persons born or naturalized in the United States. But failing to get this justice—failing, even, to get a trial by a jury *not* of my peers—I ask not lenience at your hands—but rather the full rigors of the law.

JUDGE HUNT: The Court must insist— (Here the prisoner sat down.)

JUDGE HUNT: The prisoner will stand up. (Here Miss Anthony arose again.) The sentence of the Court is that you pay a fine of one hundred dollars and the costs of the prosecution.

MISS ANTHONY: May it please your honor, I shall never pay a dollar of your unjust penalty. All the stock in trade I possess is a $10,000 debt, incurred by publishing my paper—*The Revolution*—four years ago, the sole object of which

was to educate all women to do precisely as I have done, rebel against your man-made, unjust, unconstitutional forms of law, that tax, fine, imprison, and hang women, while they deny them the right of representation in the Government; and I shall work on with might and main to pay every dollar of that honest debt, but not a penny shall go to this unjust claim. And I shall earnestly and persistently continue to urge all women to the practical recognition of the old revolutionary maxim, that "Resistance to tyranny is obedience to God."

JUDGE HUNT: Madam, the Court will not order you committed until the fine is paid.

83

VICTORIA WOODHULL
Declaration of Candidacy (1870)

I now turn to the record of my own work. Having clearly satisfied my own mind that the existing Constitutions of my country conferred this franchise on all citizens, independently of the accident of sex, and that all rights attaching to the possession of the franchise followed necessarily on with its exercise, I determined to bring matters to an issue by claiming my rights in their highest form of expression, and declared myself a candidate for the Presidency in the following terms:—

[Reprinted from the *New York Herald* of April 2nd, 1870.]

The disorganized condition of parties in the United States at the present time affords a favourable opportunity for a review of the political situation and for comment on the issues which are likely to come up for settlement in the Presidential election in 1872. As I happen to be the most prominent representative of the only unrepresented class in the republic, and perhaps the most practical exponent of the prin-

From Victoria Woodhull, *The Argument for Women's Electoral Rights* (London: F. Norman and Son, 1887), 28–30.

ciples of equality, I request the favour of being permitted to address the public through the medium of the *Herald*. While others of my sex devoted themselves to a crusade against the laws that shackle the women of the country, I asserted my individual independence; while others prayed for the good time coming, I worked for it; while others argued the equality of woman with man, I proved it by successfully engaging in business; while others sought to show that there was no valid reason why women should be treated, socially and politically, as being inferior to man, I boldly entered the arena of politics and business and exercised the rights I already possessed. I therefore claim the right to speak for the unenfranchised women of the country, and believing as I do that the prejudices which still exist in the popular mind against women in public life will soon disappear, I now announce myself as candidate for the Presidency.

I am well aware that in assuming this position I shall evoke more ridicule than enthusiasm at the outset. But this is an epoch of sudden changes and startling surprises. What may appear absurd to-day will assume a serious aspect to-morrow. I am content to wait until my claim for recognition as a candidate shall receive the calm consideration of the press and the public. The blacks were cattle in 1860; a negro now sits in Jeff Davis' seat in the United States Senate. The sentiment of the country was, even in 1863, against negro suffrage; now the negro's right to vote is acknowledged by the Constitution of the United States. Let those, therefore, who ridiculed the negro's claim to exercise the right to "life, liberty and the pursuit of happiness," and who lived to see him vote and hold high public office, ridicule the aspirations of the women of the country for complete political equality as much as they please. They cannot roll back the rising tide of reform. The world moves.

. . . All that has been said and written hitherto in support of equality for woman has had its proper effect on the public mind, just as the anti-slavery speeches before secession were

effective; but a candidate and a policy are required to prove it. Lincoln's election showed the strength of the feeling against the peculiar institution; my candidature for the Presidency will, I confidently expect, develop the fact that the principles of equal rights for all have taken deep root. The advocates of political equality for women have, besides a respectable known strength, a great undercurrent of unexpressed power, which is only awaiting a fit opportunity to show itself. By the general and decided test I propose, we shall be able to understand the woman question aright, or at least have done much towards presenting the issue involved in proper shape. I claim to possess the strength and courage to be the subject of that test, and look forward confidently to a triumphant issue of the canvass. . . .

VICTORIA WOODHULL.

84

VICTORIA WOODHULL

Letter Accepting the Presidential Nomination of the Equal Rights Party (1872)

NEW YORK, JUNE 5, 1872.
Hon. J. D. Reymert, President of the Nominating Convention of the Equal Rights Party, and Associates:

GENTLEMEN AND LADIES: Your communication received this day, conveying the formal statement to me of the simple fact that the Equal Rights Party, recently represented in convention in this city, has nominated me as the chief standard-bearer of the party in the coming conflict, recalls the vivid sensations of gratitude, renewed responsibility and profound humility with which I was overwhelmed on that memorable evening when the spontaneous acclaim of a great, enthusiastic and admirable assembly of

From *Woodhull and Claflin's Weekly*, June 15, 1872.

male and female citizens, gave me the same information without waiting for the formalities of announcement. You speak almost as if this simple fact were one of the ordinary events of politics. But to my apprehension it is far more than that. It is not even a common-place historical event. The joint assemblage of all the reformers, of all schools, for the first time in the history of the great transition which human society is undergoing, blended and fused into the same spirit, coming to agree to stand upon the same platform of ideas and measures, and nominating by an outburst of inspiration a woman known to be representative of the most advanced and unmitigated radicalism, and because she was so known; and a negro, one of the boldest of the champions and defenders of human rights, a representative man and a representative woman of the two oppressed and repressed classes, for the two highest offices in the gift of a great people—such an occurrence rises in my mind into the sublimity and pregnant significance of the grander class of the events of history. . . .

In a word, it is the appropriate inauguration of the EQUAL RIGHTS PARTY; which, in its larger aspect, contemplates not American politics merely, or alone; but the establishment of justice throughout the world. It is also the subordination of party strife, among reformers themselves, to the unity of a common cause. . . .

The reformers have been kept asunder by various causes; and divided and weakened, they have been conquered. Their intensity in the perception of particular and different evils, and of their remedies, has tended to divide them. But they are coming now to perceive that the greatest of all evils, relatively to their conflict with the common enemy the organized injustice of society, is the diversity in their own views, carried to the extent of defeating their common action. The higher truth is unity in the midst of their diversity, the unity of a combined phalanx for action; with the freedom of absolute toleration. The organization of the Equal Rights party is the expression of the fact that the cohorts of reform have at length arrived at this solid center of united activity.

Another cause for the division of the ranks of reformers has been the different degrees of radicalism, by which they have been severally characterized. Those a little behind have feared to trust those a little in advance, until at length it is clearly seen that they are all travelling along the same road, and destined to reach the same goal—the absolute dissolution of the old order of social managements, and the erection of a totally new order, on the two bases of freedom and justice.

This point once gained, everything is gained. Reformers, instead of falling asunder like a rope of sand at every strain will be consolidated, by their co-operation, into a mighty strength, from the moment that they can no longer be frightened by any other degree of radicalism beyond where they severally stand. *They have evidently reached that point when they nominate me.* It has been the purpose of my life to administer to them *that test.* I have uttered as radical thoughts in behalf of social and individual freedom (short of encroachment), as I could find the power to frame into words; and you have called me to the front, not, I presume, in spite of the fact, but *in virtue* of the fact, as that I have been so plainspoken. At all events, I stand by all that I have uttered. If by retracting one word I have written or spoken in behalf of human emancipation *from all the slaveries,* except merely to remove misapprehensions, I could be proclaimed, to-morrow, Empress of the World, I would not retract. What I have said stands; and, by your nomination, I understand you to mean that you stand with it; not in the details, nor necessarily, in the form of utterance, but in the general spirit of ultra devotion to human rights. . . .

Still wars have been, and, perhaps, still are a necessity, and so of the violent affirmation of rights, until rights are conceded and peace inaugurated upon a right basis. The uses of political movements, and more especially this one of them, are to wipe away hindrances. It is chiefly in breaking down the old and ushering in the new, that I know that I have a special function to perform; and in doing this humanitarian work, my inspirations and my spiritual previsions reveal to me views which I look upon with dread. I do not hold my life dear, except for its value to this cause, but an ordinary courage might shrink from what I foresee will oppose itself to this movement. I know not that I understand, myself, the full meaning of scenes which open to my inner vision. Is it possible that the wealthy and well to do in our midst, who have fattened from the country's industries will be blinded to the signs of the times, and refuse justice to those "who have reaped down their fields," until, as with the slaveholders of the South, calamity overtakes them? Is it possible they can believe that the working men and the women are not in earnest in their demands, and that nothing but a bloody commune will convince them?

. . . I said the platform strikes directly at the heart of the system under which we live. By this I mean very much more than the present governmental structure. I mean the much farther reaching theory of the uses of government. Heretofore governments have been maintained almost wholly upon the idea that they are for the protection of property; hitherto legislation has altogether overlooked humanity, and proceeded as if there were no such thing as human rights, which were entitled to respect. It is now proposed to reverse completely this order of things and to make human rights the pivotal center around which legislation shall cluster, the rights of property ever remaining of secondary importance, or as the means only to greater and better ends. Under our present system people are, perhaps it may be, almost unconsciously compelled to make property the chief end and aim of life; are compelled to live, as if with death, all existence ceases. The reversal of all this will the reversal of the causes which compel it, and the people instead of living the theory of individual selfishness, will come up to the realization of the fact that each one is but a part of one

perfect whole, which includes all; and that the interests and well being of every individual member of the whole are best promoted when the interests and well being of the whole are made the governing motives. . . .

Not only has it claimed the sacred right of self-government, but also the almost equally important measure, that the people themselves shall be their own law-makers; and that our Congress and Legislatures shall be restricted to their legitimate duties as working committees, whose acts must be approved by, before becoming binding upon, the people. This single plank in this platform will, when carried out in practice, do more to abolish corrupt legislation than all the measures ever proposed by legislative bodies. All well informed persons, know that the people have nothing to do with present legislation; know that it is capital—wealth—in one form or another, that controls not only the law-making, but the law-executing power, as well. The people no longer require rings, lobbies and cliques to attend to their business, and in adopting the *referendum* as one of the demanded reforms they propose to wipe them out of existence.

Again, the people are becoming sick of legalized monopolies. They know of no reason why the government should grant chartered privileges to any man or any set of men which permit him or them to absorb all surplus earnings, while they toil on year after year eating the hard crusts of industrial dependence, their legalized masters rolling in luxuries they have not earned. Into this condition it is proposed to introduce a little of the leaven of equality and equity, so that every man, aye, and every woman also, shall be confirmed and protected in the possession of all the results of their labors. . . .

The Equal Rights party also recognizes the destiny of nations, and affirms its purpose to be, to work in consonance therewith. It accepts the prophecy of all ages, that the time shall come when, instead of a multitude of constantly opposing nations, the whole world shall be united under a single paternal government, whose citi-

zens shall become a common brotherhood own-
ing a common origin and inheriting a common
destiny.

I return, in conclusion, to what I have said
of the transitional nature of the impending political revolution. When this conflict shall be
concluded, either with or without actual bloodshed; when the spirit of conceding justice shall
have been secured, either by convincement or
force; the call will be made on all sides for constructive science and wisdom. Sociology is the
rising science of the day. The writings and living
thoughts of the great students of social phenom-
ena of all ages, in the strictly scientific point of
view, will become the common property of the
whole people. In the mean time let us do well
the preliminary work. Let there be, first, a *whole
people;* let there be freedom; let there be the
universal desire for the reign of justice; then
there will be a fitting preparation for the final
grand organization of all human affairs.

Finally, I gratefully accept the nomination
made of me, and pledge myself to every honorable means to secure, at the earliest possible day,
the triumph of the principles enunciated in the
platform, which being those of justice, and for
the welfare of humanity; I know they must
shortly succeed.

Your obedient servant,
      VICTORIA C. WOODHULL.

85
VICTORIA WOODHULL
Constitutional Equality (1871)

*To the Hon. the Judiciary Committees of the Senate
and the House of Representatives of the Congress of
the United States:*

. . . The public law of the world is founded upon
the conceded fact that sovereignty cannot be
forfeited or renounced. The sovereign power of
this country is perpetual in the politically-orga-
nized people of the United States, and can neither be relinquished nor abandoned by any
portion of them. The people in this Republic
who confer sovereignty are its citizens: in a
monarchy the people are the subjects of sovereignty. All citizens of a republic by rightful act
or implication confer sovereign power. All
people of a monarchy are subjects who exist
under its supreme shield and enjoy its immunities.

The subject of a monarch takes municipal
immunities from the sovereign as a gracious
favour; but the woman citizen of this country
has the inalienable "sovereign" right of self-government in *her own proper person.* Those who look
upon woman's status by the dim light of the common law, which unfolded itself under the feudal
and military institutions that establish right upon
physical power, cannot find any analogy in the
status of the woman citizen of this country, *where
the broad sunshine of our Constitution has enfranchised all.*

As sovereignty cannot be forfeited, relinquished, or abandoned, those from whom it
flows—the citizens—are equal in conferring the
power, and should be equal in the enjoyment of
its benefits and in the exercise of its rights and
privileges.

From *The Argument for Woman's Electoral Rights Under
Amendments XIV and XV of the Constitution of the United States*
(London: G. Norman & Son, 1887), 35–43.

One portion of citizens have no power to deprive another portion of rights and privileges such as are possessed and exercised by themselves. The male citizen has no more right to deprive the female citizen of the free, public, political expression of opinion than the female citizen has to deprive the male citizen thereof.

The sovereign will of the people is expressed in our written Constitution, which is the supreme law of the land. The Constitution makes no distinction of sex. The Constitution defines a woman born or naturalized in the United States, and subject to the jurisdiction thereof, to be a citizen. It recognizes the right of citizens to vote. It declares that the right of citizens of the United States to vote shall not be denied or abridged by the United States of by any State on account of "race, colour, or previous condition of servitude."

Women, white and black, belong to races; although to different races. A race of people comprises all the people, male and female. The right to vote cannot be denied on account of race. All people included in the term race have the right to vote, unless otherwise prohibited. . . .

With the right to vote sex has nothing to do. Race and colour include all people of both sexes. All people of both sexes have the right to vote, unless prohibited by special limiting terms less comprehensive than race or colour. No such limiting terms exist in the Constitution. . . .

The citizen who is taxed should also have a voice in the subject matter of taxation. "No taxation without representation" is a right which was fundamentally established at the very birth of our country's independence; and by what ethics does any free government impose taxes on women without giving them a voice upon the subject or a participation in the public declaration as to how and by whom these taxes shall be applied for common public use? . . .

Your Memorialist complains of the existence of State Laws, and prays Congress, by appropriate legislation, to declare them, as they are, annulled, and to give vitality to the Constitution under its power to make and al-

ter the regulations of the States contravening the same. . . .

The Supreme Court has the power, and it would be its duty so to declare the law; but thee Court will not do so unless such a point shall arise as shall make it necessary to determine a controversy, and hence a case must be presented in which there can be no rational doubt. All this would subject the aggrieved parties to much dilatory, expensive, and needless litigation, which your memorialist prays your Honourable Body to dispense with by appropriate legislation, as there can be no purpose in special arguments *ad inconveniente*, enlarging or contracting the import of the language of the Constitution.

Therefore, Believing firmly in the right of citizens to freely approach those in whose hands their destiny is placed, under the Providence of God, your memorialist has frankly, but humbly, appealed to you, and prays that wisdom of Congress may be removed to action in this matter for the benefit and the increased happiness of our beloved country

Most respectfully submitted,
VICTORIA WOODHULL
Dated New York, January 2, 1871

86

ELIZABETH CADY STANTON
Infanticide and Prostitution
(1868)

SOCIAL EVIL STATISTICS.—The annual inspection report of the Captains of the Metropolitan Police of New York city and Brooklyn, gives the number of houses of prostitution as 523; of houses of assignation, 92; and of prostitutes, 2,097. This estimate, however, must be considered as only approximative, on account of the migratory character of the women to whom it relates, and because many of them reside in tenement houses and other dwellings, where their

From *The Revolution*, February 5, 1868.

real character is unknown and it may be, unsuspected.—*Sun.*

CHILD MURDER.—The horrible developments published the other day respecting a notorious "boarding-house" in this city, where mothers, married or unmarried, can be delivered of their offspring in the strictest confidence, and relieved of all the bothers of maternity, awaken serious reflection as to what ought to be done for the repression of the terrible social evil of which such establishments are at once the outgrowth and the promoters. The evil, we are sorry to believe, is on the increase. The murder of children, either before or after birth, has become so frightfully prevalent that physicians, who have given careful and intelligent study to the subject, have declared that were it not for immigration the white population of the United States would actually fall off! In a populous quarter of a certain large Western city it is asserted, on medical authority, that not a single Anglo-American child has been born alive for the last three years. This is incredible; but, making all due allowance for exaggeration, it is plain enough that the murder of infants is a common thing among American women.—*Tribune.*

Scarce a day passes but some of our daily journals take note of the fearful ravages on the race, made through the crimes of Infanticide and Prostitution.

For a quarter of a century sober, thinking women have warned this nation of these thick coming dangers, and pointed to the only remedy, *the education and enfranchisement of woman;* but men have laughed them to scorn. Let those who have made the "strong-minded" women of this generation the target for the gibes and jeers of a heedless world repent now in sackcloth and ashes, for already they suffer the retribution of their folly at their own firesides, in their sad domestic relations. Wives sick, peevish, perverse; children deformed, blind, deaf, dumb and insane; daughters silly and wayward; sons waylaid at every corner of the streets and dragged down to the gates of death, by those whom God meant to be their saviors and support. Look at

these things no longer as necessary afflictions, sent to wean us from earth as visitations from Providence; but as the direct results of the violation of immutable laws, which it was our duty to study and obey. In the midst of all these miseries, let us regard ourselves as guilty sinners and not helpless saints. God does not wink, even at the sin of ignorance.

We ask our editors who pen those startling statistics to give us *their* views of the remedy. We believe the cause of these abuses lies in the degradation of woman.

Strike the chains from your women; for as long as they are slaves to man's lust, man will be the slave of his own passions.

Wonder not that American women do everything in their power to avoid maternity; for, from false habits of life, dress, food, and generations of disease and abominations, it is to them a period of sickness, lassitude, disgust, agony and death.

What man would walk up to the gallows if he could avoid it? And the most hopeless aspect of this condition of things is that our Doctors of Divinity and medicine teach and believe that maternity and suffering are inseparable.

So long as the Bible, through the ignorance of its expounders, makes maternity a curse, and women, through ignorance of the science of life and health find it so, we need not wonder at the multiplication of these fearful statistics.

87

Child Murder (1868)

Editors of Revolution:

In a late number of "THE REVOLUTION" I noticed an article under this head, wherein the statement was made that four hundred children were annually murdered in Androscoggin county, and in a later number an article from a teacher, wherein it was proposed to remedy this

From *The Revolution,* April 9, 1868.

evil by educating woman to the knowledge that there was life in the embryo. Now, I live in Androscoggin county, and am personally acquainted with the physician who made the statement and several of the women who go to make up the four-hundred; and though I do not wish to disturb the faith of any one in the virtue or goodness of woman; I must confess that I do not think this knowledge would deter one out of ten, if it did one out of a hundred; with us, from the commission of this deed. They do it with the knowledge that it endangers their own lives, but the cry is "Liberty or Death;" and could you look in upon the wretched homes where heart-broken women work day and night, for the most shameful pittance, to provide food for the little ones whom the brutal lusts of a drunken husband have forced upon them, you would not wonder that they did not choose to add to their number.

If our statesmen and philanthropists would abate this evil, let them give liberty to woman, freedom entire, and the education it is sure to bring.

The *Tribune* laments over this "conspiracy against marriage," but it is time to conspire against an institution which makes one human being the slave of another. It is time to conspire against all who forsake principle for party.

CONSPIRATOR.

E. Poland, Me., March 30, 1868.

88

MATILDA E. J. GAGE
Is Woman Her Own? (1868)

Editors of Revolution:

The short article on "Child Murder" in your paper of March 12th, touched a subject which lies deeper down into woman's wrongs than any other. This is the denial of the right to herself. In no historic age of the world has woman yet

From *The Revolution*, April 9, 1868.

had that. From the time when Moses, for the hardness of his heart, permitted the Jew husband to give his unpleasing wife a letter of divorcement—to Christ when the seven *male* sinners brought to him for condemnation the woman taken in adultery—down through the Christian centuries to this nineteenth, nowhere has the marital union of the sexes been one in which woman has had control over her own body.

Enforced motherhood is a crime against the body of the mother and the soul of the child.

Medical jurisprudence has begun to accumulate facts on this point, showing how the condition and *feelings* of the mother mould not only the physical and mental qualities of the child, but its moral nature.

Women keep silence upon many points, not breathing their thoughts to their dearest friends, because of their inner reticence, a quality they possess greatly in excess of men.

And, too, custom has taught them to bear in silence.

But the crime of abortion is not one in which the guilt lies solely or even chiefly with the woman. As a child brings more care, so also, it brings more joy to the mother's heart.

Husbands do not consult with their wives upon this subject of deepest and most vital interest, do not look at the increase of family in a physiological, moral, or spiritual light, but almost solely from a money standpoint. It costs. Tens of thousands of husbands and fathers throughout this land are opposed to large families. And yet, so deeply implanted is the sin of self-gratification, that consequences are not considered while selfish desire controls the heart.

Much is said of the wild, mad desire of the age for money. Money is but another name for power, it is but another name for bread, it is but another name for freedom, and those who possess it not are the slaves of those who do.

How many states in the Union grant the wife an equal right with the husband to the control and disposal of the property of the marital firm? But two. [What two? EDS. REV.]

How long is it since a married woman in this state had the right to the control of her own separate property? Barely twice ten years.

How long since she could control her own earnings, even those of a days' washing? Not yet ten.

History is full of the wrongs done the wife by legal robbery on the part of the husband. I need not quote instances; they are well known to the most casual newspaper reader. It is accepted as a self-evident truth, that those "who are not masters of any property, may easily be formed into any mould."

I hesitate not to assert that most of this crime of "child murder," "abortion," "infanticide," lies at the door of the male sex.

Many a woman has laughed a silent, derisive laugh at the decisions of eminent medical and legal authorities, in cases of crimes committed against her as a woman. Never, until she sits as juror on such trials, will or can just decisions be rendered.

This reason and that reasons have been pointed to by the upholders of equal rights, to account for the oppression of woman during past ages, but not one that I have ever heard offered has looked to the spiritual origin of that oppression.

89
Political Organization (1870)

The great necessity of the cause of WOMAN SUFFRAGE in America is an efficient organization in which every friend of the movement can work freely and without the need of protest.

To effect such an organization is not as easy as may at first appear. The advocates of woman's political equality differ utterly upon every other topic. Some are abolitionists; others, hostile to the equality of races. Some are evangelical Christians; others, Catholics, Unitarians, Spiritualists or Quakers. Some hold the most rigid theories

From *Woman's Journal*, January 8, 1870.

with regard to marriage and divorce; others are latitudinarian on these questions. Some are Republicans, others Democrats. In short, people of the most opposite views agree in desiring to establish Woman Suffrage, while they anticipate very different results from the reform, when effected.

Now the union of all these people is essential to success. But their diversities of opinion are only compatible with union, provided the question of Woman's legal and political equality is made *sole* and *paramount*. Unfortunately, many well-meaning people cannot, or will not so regard it. They insist upon dragging in their peculiar views upon theology, temperance, marriage, race, dress, finance, labor and capital—it matters not what. They demand a free platform and unlimited latitude of expression.

We have had quite enough of this unlimited range of discussion, this confusion of ideas which have no logical connection. No one can estimate the damage the cause of Woman's enfranchisement has already sustained, by the failure of its advocates to limit themselves to the main question. For ourselves, we propose to begin our reform at this very point. As advocates of equal rights, we protest against loading the good ship "Woman Suffrage" with a cargo of irrelevant opinions. There may be good reasons why every wise man and woman should advocate, or oppose the Fifteenth amendment. But they would be out of place in the editorial columns of a Woman Suffrage paper, or on the platform of a Woman Suffrage Convention. There may be excellent reasons why Mr. and Mrs. Richardson should be justified or ensured, and why Mr. McFarland should be hanged or acquitted, but they are not reasons which affect the question of Woman Suffrage. It may be a matter of philanthropic interest whether Hester Vaughan should be executed for infanticide, but it has nothing to do with the question whether Hester Vaughan should vote. One of the most powerful pulpit-orators who ever swayed the minds of men was solicited by a youthful aspirant for clerical influence to impart the secret of his success. He replied, "My secret is comprised in four words—'Stick to the text!'" We hope that the American Woman Suffrage Association will adopt, as the corner-stone of "the new departure," the motto—"Concentrate on Woman Suffrage!"

If it be objected that to limit the question to Suffrage alone is to narrow the platform of Woman's Rights, we reply that in practical questions which involve the united action of masses of men, distinctness and definiteness are primary conditions of success. A certain narrowness and precision are as essential to practical action as are breadth and comprehensiveness to theoretical speculation. This is the law of all political organizations. And Woman Suffrage *is* a political question. Who ever heard of discussing social questions in a Republican, or Democratic Convention? Or, in any way of identifying public men with opinions of private transactions, or of complicating the consideration of tariff or finance with the personal merits or demerits of any individual? In order to command the universal support which is essential to political success, Woman Suffrage must cease to be treated as a symbol of social innovations. It must be urged as a purely political question upon its own merits. In England it has always been kept separate. And the result has been a much more rapid advance in public opinion and influence there than here.

But the question of Suffrage is not really narrow. It underlies all else. Remember that the ballot is the symbol of Equality for Woman. As Wendell Phillips has said—"It is the Gibraltar of the Movement." Napoleon conquered Europe by bringing to bear upon the vital point, at the critical moment, an overwhelming preponderance of men and metal. We must conquer public opinion in America upon the same principle. Our vital point is Suffrage. And to concentrate the efforts of all the friends of Woman Suffrage in the United States, for this one great radical political reform, is the object of the AMERICAN WOMAN SUFFRAGE ASSOCIATION.

H. B. B.

90

LAURA CURTIS BULLARD
What Flag Shall We Fly? (1870)

It grieves us to find certain organs of the woman's movement narrowing down our great reform to the mere dimensions of a demand for the elective franchise. The *Woman's Journal,* for instance, lifts its hands in gentle shudder at the impropriety of what it regards THE REVOLUTION₃slatitudinarian discussions, and warns us to "stick to the point." What are these discussions, and what is this point? The discussions for which we are criticized run over the whole range of woman's needs and demands, rights and wrongs, opportunities and enterprises—including her work, her wages, her property, her education, her physical training, her social status, her political equality, her marriage, and her divorce. The "point" to which we are asked to stick is the single one of woman's suffrage.

We reject the advice—not because we do not respect its source, but because we do not believe in its wisdom.

In the first place, the *Woman's Journal,* in attempting to reduce the woman's movement to the square-inch of a ballot, writes itself down in 1870 as more conservative than the originators of the movement were in 1848. It turns back the sun on the dial. It makes not even the crab's progress, which is sidewise, but goes directly to the rear. This will be clearly seen by any one who takes pains to refer to the proceedings of the original woman's rights convention at Seneca Falls, held in July, 1848—more than twenty-two years ago. The utterances of that convention were far in advance of the customary editorial comments of the *Woman's Journal* of the present day. William Henry Channing's report on divorce, presented at Worcester in 1851, was as radical as any utterance that has been made since. Not only the original convention, but other similar assemblages which followed it in quick and

From *The Revolution*, October 27, 1870.

brilliant succession, dealt freely with the whole circle of those very questions which are now discussed in THE REVOLUTION, and against which the *Woman's Journal* warns womankind. The early pioneers never thought of conforming themselves to the one point, and one only, to which the *Woman's Journal* asks THE REVOLUTION to stick. On the contrary, the whole volume of woman's industrial, social, intellectual, moral and religious functions, duties, and relations was always and invariably opened in every convention in those brave days. We prefer the earlier plan of the radicals to the later modification of it by the conservatives. "No woman, having tasted old wine, straightway desireth new, for she saith the old is better."

In the second place, the *Woman's Journal* does not stick to its own point. That paper cannot possible advocate woman's suffrage without explaining why woman wants suffrage, namely, for the settlement of those identical questions which this sagacious critic forbids a woman's newspaper to discuss! Why does our Boston contemporary demand suffrage at all? Merely as a bauble, an ornament, a gewgaw? Nay, but a weapon, an instrument, a scepter. The *Woman's Journal,* like all the other advocates of the cause, demands woman's suffrage in order, for instance, to secure woman's title to her own property— and this opens the question of woman's right to hold and bequeath her own earnings; in order to increase woman's compensation for her toil— and this opens, directly or indirectly, the question of labor and capital; in order to arrest the growing evil of drunkenness—and this opens incidentally the question of temperance; in order to secure woman's admission to the learned universities—and this opens the question of the co-education of the sexes; in order to settle her disputed title to her own children—and this opens the question of the comparative authority of father and mother, in order to maintain for her a just personal freedom, as well after marriage as before—and this opens the question of her sovereignty over her own person; in order to provide for her, in too many sad and

agonizing instances, a necessary relief through divorce—and this opens the whole question of the just relations of the sexes. The woman's movement includes all that affects woman's welfare; and as suffrage is the symbol only of her political independence, suffrage therefore represents but a small portion of her universal enfranchisement.

In the third place, the theory propounded by the *Woman's Journal,* and which it offers for the acceptance of all similar papers as the true method of conducting our great reform, is open to the grave objection of always presenting this movement in the most disagreeable light in which it can possibly appear to woman's eyes. For this theory gives it wholly a political character; and women are, in the present state of society, more averse to the political than they are to any other phase of the woman's movement. We value the ballot as precious; we ask for it, and yearn to possess it; we wait anxiously, and with beating hearts, for the day when our Mother Country shall not be ashamed to call her daughters, as well as her sons, enfranchised citizens. But we are not dreamers or fanatics; and we know that the ballot, when we get it, will achieve for woman no more than it has achieved for man. And to drop all other demands for the sake of uniting to demand the ballot only, may seem the whole duty of the *Woman's Journal,* but is only a very small part of the mission of THE REVOLUTION. The ballot is not even half the loaf; it is only a crust—a crumb. The ballot touches only those interests, either of women or men, which take their root in political questions. But woman's chief discontent is not with her political, but with her social, and particularly with her marital bondage. The solemn and profound question of marriage—what should bind, and what should break, the bond—is of more vital consequence to woman's welfare, reaches down to a deeper depth in woman's heart, and more thoroughly constitutes the core of the woman's movement, than any such superficial and fragmentary question as woman's suffrage. The *Woman's Journal* attempts to contract a whole heaven of daylight into one diminutive focus. But the greatest reform of modern times—a movement whose issues reach to the whole circle of woman's joys and hopes, loves and sufferings, toils and sacrifices, consecration and martyrdom—refuses to be thus belittled to a single, albeit a shining, point.

In the fourth place, THE REVOLUTION cannot copy the example of the *Woman's Journal* in another respect; it cannot dwarf itself into being the organ of any association. We sympathize as heartily with the Union Woman's Suffrage Society as the *Woman's Journal* does with the American Woman Suffrage Association, but we do not undertake to speak for anybody save our own garrulous selves. It was the glory of Mr. Garrison's *Liberator* that he never would consent to square his columns to a measuring edge with the constitution and by-laws of the American Anti-Slavery Society. He discussed every topic connected directly or indirectly with the whole momentous theme of human freedom. THE REVOLUTION, in like manner, seeks to be the *Liberator* of womankind. It may be well enough to restrict an association or a convention to a narrow parliamentary adherence to the single topic named in its constitution or its call, and to conduct its proceedings under the ruling of Jefferson's Manual; but a journal like THE REVOLUTION, devoted to whatever concerns the welfare of women, must be free to pursue its theme in more directions than one. In undertaking the conduct of this newspaper, we took into our hands a harp of more than a single string. Instead, therefore, of sticking to the solitary point which the *Woman's Journal* indicates, we hereby dedicate these columns anew to each and all the multitudinous interests connected with the industrial, social, intellectual, civil, political, moral and religious progress of the disfranchised half of the American people.

91

LULA GREENE RICHARDS AND EMMELINE B. WELLS

Women's Rights and Polygamy (1876)

It is a well-authenticated fact and palpable to all the world, that there are thousands of women, who have no such substantial support to cling to, as an oak in the form of a husband, father or brother, and of those who have, there are many, who suffer more than those who have not, from intemperance and other causes, consequently it follows that as vines they would trail upon the earth, and very naturally be trod upon just as thousands of women are, who have been taught and encouraged in dependence instead of independence.

Circumstances and training it is said form the individual; certainly they tend to strengthen and develop important characteristics. Custom the irrepressible tyrant, has in the past constrained parents to train their boys for the battle of life, the girls to look forward to marriage as the one great aim of their existence. Now custom, alias fashion, argues men cannot afford wives they are too expensive a luxury; then women must necessarily look round for some avenue of support, some practical, paying kind of labor. These matters require serious thought, require words, require actions,—which will determine some positive demonstration of the subject in question.

Women cannot talk too much about these matters, if they do so understandingly to assist in enlightening themselves and others.

The world says Polygamy makes women inferior to men—we think differently. Polygamy, gives women more time for thought, for mental culture, more freedom of action, a broader field of labor, inculcates liberality and generosity, develops more fully the spiritual elements

From *The Woman's Exponent*, August 15, 1876.

of life, fosters purity of thought and gives wider scope to benevolence, leads women more directly to God the fountain of all truth, knowledge, light and intelligence.

If those who are anxious to promote higher development, would consider the true principles upon which to base marriage, they would look closely into the order of plural marriage, and some of the most momentous questions that are puzzling the world at the present time, might thus be properly adjusted. Then let women talk, and write, and reason, and think, and interchange their ideas with each other and with men. God has endowed woman with reasoning and intuitive powers—certainly He intended her to use her own agency.

92

FANNIE McCORMICK
A Kansas Farm (1891)

John Thompson arrived at home about 6 o'clock. Mary saw him coming afar off, as it were, and meeting him with a cheerful face, took a seat beside him and began a recital of the experiences of the day. At the supper table she continued the information that church services would be held in a school house only five miles away, on the following Sunday; also that Mrs. Green had told her that the neighbors living three miles west of them were a young couple from the State of New York; that the wife was a frail, delicate creature, who had been reared tenderly in an elegant home, was very homesick in a sod house, and Mary expressed a determination to visit her on the morrow.

. . . With the beginning of harvest comes the hardest time of the whole year for women folks on the farm. When the heads of wheat begin to turn brown, the housewives bestir themselves to lay in large stores of supplies to cook

From *The Farmer's Wife*, September 1891.

for harvest hands, and to try to secure help in the kitchen during the busy season.

Improved machinery for reaping grain lessens the number of hands required for harvesting, and the steam thresher increases the amount required at threshing time, but compensates somewhat by shortening the time of their stay. Threshers are looked upon as a sort of plague, or necessary evil and the common enemy of woman kind. They drop in unexpectedly before breakfast or just after supper, and always at dinner. The unsuspecting family may be taking a quiet breakfast when eight or ten men will walk in, wash their faces and sit down to the table. The horrified house-keeper knows full well that this means twenty men for dinner and for every meal until the great wheat stacks are exhausted, which takes sometimes two or three weeks.

New machinery has done much to lighten and lessen the work of men on the farm—riding plows, patent drills, self binders, headers and steam threshers all tend to do this; but machinery has as yet wrought but little benefit to farmers' wives. Dishwashing, cooking, scrubbing and ironing, like perpetual motion, seem to be beyond the skill of inventors. Women's work on the farm is constant, unceasing toil—a never-ending, recurring round of duties, "world without end." All the hard work consequence upon the harvest, which is mostly cooking, has to be done in hot weather, the hardest time of the whole year to do this kind of work, and also at a time when it is next to impossible to obtain help for the kitchen. Many a farmer's wife with a babe lying in the crib and two or three small children to be cared for, patiently gets through the herculean task all alone, except such help as the men folks can give morning and evening. The farmers' wives are not merely "helpmeets" in subduing the wilds of this western country, but have done their full share of solid, hard work as *equal partners;* and if there is a credit balance on either side, it is in favor of the women.

The women on the farms are intelligent as a class. They work, and read and think. They devote what leisure time they have to reading, instead of fashionable dress and society calls. Consequently they are well informed on the leading topics of the day; and many a woman now living on a Kansas farm, in her girlhood attended the best schools in the east. Yet these women are disfranchised. The legislature of Kansas passed a law called the "Municipal Suffrage Law," which granted to women living in cities the right to vote for municipal officers, but neglected to provide any privileges for this great army of women who reside in the country; and if in the campaign of 1890 the farmer women massed their strength and energy to elect the candidates on the People's ticket, no one can blame them. It spoke well for their political sagacity and excellent knowledge of "ways and means." Under an old law women are allowed to vote for school directors in the country.

On the morrow Mary went to visit Mrs. Gray, as she had proposed, and found her indeed homesick and ill. She spent the afternoon with her, and was so cheerful that even Mrs. Gray began to laugh and take a more hopeful view of life in Kansas. . . .

Faithfully Mary cared for her new friend, and entreated Mr. Gray to take his wife back to her eastern home for a while; but they thought the expense was too great to be incurred. A terrible storm came on and Mary could not get over to see her friend, but heard she was very ill, and before the week had passed, word was brought that Mrs. Gray *was dead.* On a damp bed in that sod house, for the rain had dripped through the roof so badly that an umbrella was raised to keep it off the sick, lay the lifeless form of this young mother and her dead babe lay beside her. Mary fell upon her knees beside the bed and wept bitterly. The neighbors gathered in and sang with subdued voices, "Shall we gather at the river," the minister said a few words about the sad dispensations of Providence, and then Mrs. Gray and the babe were burried in a lonely cemetery on the great prairie.

Travelers to California rush to the windows and platforms of their train to get a glimpse of what is called in the guide-book, the Maiden's

Grave. The story goes that years ago, while a wagon train was passing over the wilderness, a young girl died and was burried in some lonely spot, and travelers will brush aside a tear over what seems her sad, sad fate.

Oh, women who dwell in elegant mansions where there *are* lace curtains and soft carpets and beautiful surroundings of every kind, will you not drop a tear of sympathy for this young mother who perished for the lack of a warm, comfortable house, a skillful physician and a loving mother's care? The sod of the western prairie covers very many such graves, and in many an eastern home white haired parents are bowed with grief because their daughter is no more. Never until the recording angel opens the book, shall the heroic deeds and sacrifices of women who have striven to build up homes on this wild prairie be fully known or appreciated. Their names will be among the noblest names recorded and among the "blessed and holy" who "hath part in the first resurrection."

93

ALICE STONE BLACKWELL
The Physical Force Argument
(1895)

Miss M'Intyre says:

The suffragists claim that women are taxed without representation. Those advancing this argument exhibit their entire lack of understanding of the theories of taxation and suffrage, and prove that they, at least, are not yet ready to enter intelligently into politics.

"Those advancing this argument" include Abraham Lincoln, George William Curtis, and other statesmen deservedly esteemed. It seems a little presumptuous for Miss M'Intyre to say that such men have proved themselves unable to "enter intelligently into politics." Of course the sneer was meant to apply only to women

From *The Woman's Column*, May 4, 1895.

who use this argument; but since these women find themselves in company with many of the most distinguished men America has yet produced, they can afford to bear it with equanimity.

Miss M'Intyre proceeds to what she regards as the fundamental argument:

We have founded our government on manhood suffrage, not because our male citizens own more or less property, or any property at all, but because they are men; because behind the law must be the power of enforcing it. Without sufficient force to compel respect and observance, laws would be dead letters. To make laws that cannot be enforced is to bring a government into ridicule and contempt and to invite anarchy. The insuperable objection to woman suffrage is fundamental and functional, and Nature alone is responsible for it, since she has created man combatant and woman non-combatant.

If this theory were correct, all men who can fight would be admitted to the ballot box, and all men who cannot fight would be excluded. But the theory has not a vestige of foundation, either in history, or in the practice of other nations, or in our own. In Massachusetts to-day thousands of able-bodied men are excluded from suffrage because they cannot read and write. Tens of thousands who are not able-bodied vote at every election. In most European nations, the majority of men who can fight are not admitted to vote. In our own country, suffrage has at different times been conditioned upon property, intelligence, moral character, in some cases even upon religious opinions and church membership; but never upon the ability to bear arms.

By a kind of comic fatality, this argument that women must not vote because they cannot fight is especially apt to be used by men who could not fight themselves. Some peaceable, venerable old clergyman comes up and makes this objection before the Legislative committee; or some corpulent elderly physician, who would expire under a forced march of five miles. I have even had this objection made to me by a man who had been stone blind ever since he was three years old. He voted at every election, but he was fully convinced that a woman ought not to be permitted to vote because she could not shoulder a musket in time of war.

If no one were allowed to help choose the law-makers except those who can help to enforce the laws, women could not complain of being ruled out along with other non-combatants. But so long as the old, the infirm, the halt, the lame and the blind are freely admitted to vote, some better reason must be found for excluding women than the fact that they do not fight.

It may be said that we have to legislate for classes, not for individual exceptions; and that men as a class can fight, while women as a class cannot. But there are large classes of men who are regarded as unable to fight, and are legally exempt from military service, and who are nevertheless allowed to vote. All men over forty-five years of age are exempt from military service. So are all who are not physically robust. The U. S. Military Statistics taken at the time of our last war show that a large majority of the lawyers, ministers and editors examined for military service were found to be physically disqualified. Of unskilled laborers, on the other hand, only a very small fraction were found disqualified. Since professional men as a class cannot fight, while unskilled laborers can, does it follow that suffrage should be taken away from professional men and be limited to unskilled laborers?

Besides, this is not true that we do not legislate for exceptions. Men as a class are of sound mind; men as a class are unconvicted of crime; men as a class are able to read and write. But when a man is an exception, in anything that it regarded as essential to suffrage, he is treated as an exception, and is forbidden to vote.

Either the ability to fight is a necessary qualification for suffrage, or it is not. If it is, the men who lack it ought to be excluded. If it is not, the lack of it is no reason for excluding women. There is no escape from this conclusion.

94

SARA T. DRUKKER
Voting Mothers (1897)

. . . The age accepts but one code for both and, amid all this moral advance, the progress of woman has come. Passionate adoration and gallantry have been replaced by justice and human rights. No matter what opposition may be made, suffrage for women is the crowning glory of progress, and the cause will be gloriously known when the small arguments against it are forgotten.

Oh, Liberty, hide thy face! for thy soil still nourishes old fogies belonging to the age of tallow candles and not fin de siecle days of electric light, for they see things by the light of other days and not by the new light. Free and enlightened motherhood is the greatest blessing of our age. The saying, "If you want to reform a child you must begin with the grandmother," contains more truth than poetry. How can a mother who is not herself familiar with the fundamental principles upon which our government is founded, impart to her child, whose possibilities are born of her capacity, those qualities which go to make the loyal and patriotic citizen. Think of the possibilities of a race born of an enfranchised, awakened and developed motherhood. Our sons are voting citizens, says Charlotte Perkins; statesmen are all born of and reared by non-voting citizens, who cannot possibly be capable of transmitting the enlightened ideas, the breadth of vision, the power of calm judgment, which come with the exercise of this civic function in a free government. Besides, a non-voting class living with a voting class is at a perpetual disadvantage, and we can only hope to better conditions by the spread of practical knowledge. As most human ills arise from ignorance, so the woman who does not know her social and political wrongs will never ask for political rights. We, the women of the United States, living under the stars and stripes, are fortunate; we have in-

From *The American Jewess*, April 5, 1897.

herited fundamental rights which no written law can supersede or abrogate.

The best way of educating women in politics is to give them the responsibility of voting. Responsibility educates like nothing else does. "Man," says the superb American Wendell Phillips, "never grew to his stature without the weight of responsibility, and women will grow up the same way." In order to make our mothers practical citizens they must vote. They will gain a wider knowledge of men and of governmental law, and learn to judge less harshly of the crime and vice surrounding us on all sides.

It becomes clearer and clearer to students of social science as a waste of energy to punish criminals while permitting the existence of conditions that will breed crime. Justice studies the incentive of the criminal and devises means for its removal.

Woman's advice in the administration of law and justice can only be beneficial. Our votes can do more for us in one month than all our prayers and petitions have done for centuries. Who shall then deny the right of the mother to vote for the protection of her own child? It is a mistaken idea to suppose that the woman who has achieved national or world-wide fame is averse to a secluded and domestic life. All students of social science, and close observers know that those who do the routine work in any vocation seldom form comprehensive views of it.

95

JULIA WARD HOWE
The Moral Initiative as
Belonging to Women (1893)

. . . Now, what do I mean by this moral initiative as belonging to women? Is it a mere phrase that sounds metaphysical and means nothing? My

From *Julia Ward Howe and the Woman Suffrage Movement*, ed., Florence Howe Hall (Boston: Dana Estes and Co., 1913), 119–26, 133–35.

thought of it is simply this: the world has had much good to say of its women, and much evil, and both with reason. The first woman has been credited with all the woes which have befallen humanity, and with all the sins into which it has fallen. Buddhism considers the principle of evil in nature as resident in the female sex, and ascetics in all kinds have held the same view. The legends of the Mother of Christ have no doubt exercised a potent influence in elevating the moral position of the sex. Yet in romance and stage play to-day as well as in ordinary society pleasantry, the question is common: where is the woman who is at the bottom of the mischief?

I think that wise people now ask an opposite question. When we meet with a man who is without fear and without reproach, whose blameless life seems to have gone on from strength to strength, upbuilding the community, and honoring humanity by his own noble image and conduct, we are apt to ask where the woman is? And our thoughts go back to the helpless cradle in which his infancy was tended, even further, to the heart to which his own was the nearest thing on earth, to the breast from which he was fed with the essence of a pure life. Happy is the man whose mother has been a tower of strength to herself and her family! The first precious lessons it has been hers to give. . . .

This I call the moral initiative. The man's start in life, the nucleus of all that he is to believe, to aim at, and to do has been delivered to him like a sealed packet full of precious things by a mother who honors supremely all that honors humanity, who dreads and despises all that dishonors and deforms it.

No one will deny that this type of woman is most precious. The question will rather be how we may maintain and multiply it. And here the whole horizon of the past confronts us, as well as the veiled heaven of the future.

In this past we read that all that is slavish in human institutions is demoralizing, that while discipline forms and exalts, despotism degrades and deforms, appealing back to the lower in-

stincts which have their place in animal life: fear, cunning, low self-love, and the low attachments of mere habit and interest. From the tyrannies of the old order into the liberty wherewith Christ has made us free, the world is slowly passing, but all that detains humanity on its lower levels retards the progress of the race. Oh! that men, themselves enfranchised, should wish to detain their women in the bondage from which they themselves have been delivered. In true Christianity there is no moral distention of sex, neither male nor female. But in the political life even of free America, the man opens the door for himself and shuts it against his wife, opens the door for his son, and shuts it upon his daughter. And this I say, is demoralizing. It compels one half of the human race to look back toward the old barbarism, while the other insists upon looking forward to the new civilization. The man to whom the woman's freedom of soul is the first condition of his own, puts on that freedom a fatal barrier and defrauds himself thereby. His mother should be his superior, his wife should be his equal and companion. He invites them to acquiesce in a lower position, to exercise a self-control which he does not dream of exacting from himself, but also to sacrifice the self-respect out of which should spring this very power of self-control, of self-sacrifice, of subordinating the pleasurable to the ethical, the caprice of self-indulgence to the steady purposes of duty.

I do not say that any of these thoughts are new, but I do say that as life goes on and the world with it, they do present themselves to me with new power and completeness. In reviewing my days, I recall the noble women whom I have known, deep-hearted and wise-thoughted. I have revered them as individuals, as stars in a dark sky, as striking exceptions to the poor average of feminine attainment, intellectual and moral. But I see them now as partial revelations of a glorious whole. The germ of all that I have admired in any woman surely resides in every woman, and if you can reach the true woman in her you will call forth something of it. The world of men and of women are alike cheated by the frivolity in which most of us are bred and educated. We are taught to be content with taking the whole tone of our life from the careless pleasure of thoughtless men. Now I say, let there be an uprising among us. Let thoughtless men take, on the contrary, their altitude from our nobleness of mind. Let them recognize in us not only a moral sentiment which they must respect but a moral determination to which they must conform. Oh! women, let your sons see in you only what shall raise you in their esteem. And while you inspire them with tender respect, and train them to all that is generous and truth-loving, remember that you have a double duty to your daughters. They are to be the companions and inspirers of men. . . .

The dwarfed and degraded woman has without doubt often dwarfed and degraded the men who had to do with her. . . .

I find the remedy for these evils in the moral power of the woman herself, if she can be taught and trained to exert it. Let her call no man master, but seek to exercise that mastery of self which is the first condition of all the virtues. "Self-reverence, self-knowledge, self-control, These three alone lead life to sovereign power."

In our own time we have seen a temporary reaction against these sacred maxims, and a wild vindication of the supremacy of instinct. Sad tales of debauch and crime tell us to how low a pass men and women, acting as creatures devoid of conscience, can bring each other. Let us learn from these sex-tragedies their true lesson. The secondary morality will no longer answer for women. They need no man to interpret to them those suggestions of reserve and modesty with which nature seeks to protect them from the lawlessness of force. Only let them listen to these. Only let them add to these good promptings the salutary lessons of history and the uplifting influences of religion, and in place of the amiable weaknesses once in vogue, we shall find estimable strength and profitable wisdom.

Lastly, we have certainly learned that women must be free if freedom is to be enjoyed by men, and safeguarded for them. Ignorance is the first condition of enslavement, and ignorant women will always be the tools of the men who are the enemies of freedom. To all that society expects from women, let us then add the enlightened mind, the liberal and resolute will. This will secure to them the moral initiative.

96

FRANCES E. W. HARPER
Woman's Political Future (1893)

Not the opportunity of discovering new worlds, but that of filling this old world with fairer and higher aims than the greed of gold and the lust of power, is hers. Through weary, wasting years men have destroyed, dashed in pieces, and overthrown, but to-day we stand on the threshold of woman's era, and woman's work is grandly constructive. In her hand are possibilities whose use or abuse must tell upon the political life of the nation, and send their influence for good or evil across the track of unborn ages.

As the saffron tints and crimson flushes of morn herald the coming day, so the social and political advancement which woman has already gained bears the promise of the rising of the full-orbed sun of emancipation. The result will be not to make home less happy, but society more holy; yet I do not think the mere extension of the ballot a panacea for all the ills of our national life. What we need to-day is not simply more voters, but better voters. To-day there are red-handed men in our republic, who walk unwhipped of justice, who richly deserve to exchange the ballot of the freeman for the wristlets of the felon; brutal and cowardly men, who torture, burn, and lynch their fellow-men, men whose defenselessness should be their best de-

Address to the World's Congress of Representative Women, Chicago, May 13, 1893. From *The World's Congress of Representative Women*, ed., May Wright Sewall (Chicago and New York: Rand McNally, and Co., 1894), 433–36, 437.

fense and their weakness an ensign of protection. More than the changing of institutions we need the development of a national conscience, and the upbuilding of national character. Men may boast of the aristocracy of blood, may glory in the aristocracy of talent, and be proud of the aristocracy of wealth, but there is one aristocracy which must ever outrank them all, and that is the aristocracy of character; and it is the women of a country who help to mold its character, and to influence if not determine its destiny; and in the political future of our nation woman will not have done what she could if she does not endeavor to have our republic stand foremost among the nations of the earth, wearing sobriety as a crown and righteousness as a garment and a girdle. In coming into her political estate woman will find a mass of illiteracy to be dispelled. If knowledge is power, ignorance is also power. The power that educates wickedness may manipulate and dash against the pillars of any state when they are undermined and honeycombed by injustice.

I envy neither the heart nor the head of any legislator who has been born to an inheritance of privileges, who has behind him ages of education, dominion, civilization and Christianity, if he stands opposed to the passage of a national education bill, whose purpose is to secure education to the children of those who were born under the shadow of institutions which made it a crime to read.

To-day women hold in their hands influence and opportunity, and with these they have already opened doors which have been closed to others. By opening doors of labor woman has become a rival claimant for at least some of the wealth monopolized by her stronger brother. In the home she is the priestess, in society the queen, in literature she is a power, in legislative halls law-makers have responded to her appeals, and for her sake have humanized and liberalized their laws. The press has felt the impress of her hand. In the pews of the church she constitutes the majority; the pulpit has welcomed her, and in the school she has the blessed privilege of

teaching children and youth. To her is apparently coming the added responsibility of political power; and what she now possesses should only be the means of preparing her to use the coming power for the glory of God and the good of mankind; for power without righteousness is one of the most dangerous forces in the world.

Political life in our country has plowed in muddy channels, and needs the infusion of clearer and cleaner waters. I am not sure that women are naturally so much better than men that they will clear the stream by the virtue of their womanhood; it is not through sex but through character that the best influence of women upon the life of the nation must be exerted.

I do not believe in unrestricted and universal suffrage for either men or women. I believe in moral and educational tests. I do not believe that the most ignorant and brutal man is better prepared to add value to the strength and durability of the government than the most cultured, upright, and intelligent woman. I do not think that willful ignorance should swamp earnest intelligence at the ballot box, nor that educated wickedness, violence, and fraud should cancel the votes of honest men. The unsteady hands of a drunkard can not cast the ballot of a freeman. The hands of lynchers are too red with blood to determine the political character of the government for even four short years. The ballot in the hands of woman means power added to influence. How well she will use that power I can not foretell. Great evils stare us in the face that need to be throttled by the combined power of an upright manhood and an enlightened womanhood; and I know that no nation can gain its full measure of enlightenment and happiness if one-half of it is free and the other half is fettered. China compressed the feet of her women and thereby retards the steps of her men. The laments of a nation's weakness must ever be found at the hearthstone.

More than the increase of wealth, the power of armies, and the strength of fleets is the need of good homes, of good fathers, and good mothers. . . .

O women of America! into your hands God has pressed one of the sublimest opportunities that ever came into the hands of the women of any race or people. It is yours to create a healthy public sentiment; to demand justice, simple justice, as the right of every race; to brand with everlasting infamy the lawless and brutal cowardice that lynches, burns, and tortures your own countrymen.

97

Elizabeth Cady Stanton
An Educational Suffrage Qualification Necessary (1897)

. . . As all who prize this right sufficiently to labor to attain it can easily do so, an educational qualification in no way conflicts with our cherished idea of universal suffrage. According to our theory of government, all our citizens are born voters, but they must be of age before they can exercise the right. To say they must also read and write the English language intelligently is equally logical and fair. We do not propose to restrict any citizen now exercising this right, but to apply the restriction to all new claimants, at the dawn of the next century, who do not possess the educational qualification.

It will be a fitting time for us to celebrate our fiftieth year by taking so important a progressive step.

As an Association we should prepare, discuss, and pass a strong resolution to this end, and thus limit the foreign vote and stimulate our native population to fit themselves for the exercise of this right.

The greatest block in the way of woman's enfranchisement to-day is doubling the ignorant vote. An educational qualification would answer this objection. Some say that the ignorant classes need the ballot for their protection more than

the rich. Well, they have had it and exercised it, and what have they done to protect their own interests? Absolutely nothing, because they did not know in what direction these lay, or by what system of legislation they could be lifted out of poverty, vice and ignorance to enjoy liberty, justice and equality.

A gun is a good weapon for a man's protection against his enemy, but if he does not know how to use it, it may prove a danger rather than a defence. There is something lacking in our science of industrial economics when multitudes in this land of plenty are suffering abject poverty. Yet by their ignorant votes they have helped to establish the very conditions from which they suffer. The ballot is of value only in the hands that know how to use it: . . .

In establishing free schools, our forefathers said to us in plain words: "The stability of a republic depends on the virtue and intelligence of the people." I sincerely hope that an educational qualification for the suffrage will be the chief topic for discussion at the coming Washington Convention.

Elizabeth Cady Stanton.
26 West 61st Street, New York.

98

Elizabeth Burrill Curtis
The Present Crisis (1897)

On the eve of its fiftieth anniversary, the advocates of the Woman Suffrage movement may wisely pause to see how much is gained, and how far the past and present policy should be adhered to in the future.

During the half century the position of women before the law may be said to have changed so much that they are no longer perpetual minors, but have attained their majority, in everything but the one point of self-govern-

From *Woman's Journal*, October 2, 1897.

From *Woman's Journal*, October 2, 1897.

ment. This is much to have done, and the leaders of the movement have all but reached the summit of their desires.

But the change in the position of women is by no means the only change that the past fifty years have brought. Among a large minority at least, of our people, the idea is slowly gaining ground that possibly universal suffrage is not the best form of government, and that something more than merely being born is necessary to fit a human being to be a voter.

Many things have led to this conclusion, or rather this theory, for it is as yet too vague and nebulous to have reached the dignity of a conclusion. Chief among them are the result of the enfranchisement of the negroes and the tremendous influx of ignorant foreigners, but it is the woman suffrage movement that has finally driven the opponents of universal suffrage to declare themselves openly. For the opposition to women's entering into public life has mainly disappeared, in the face of what women have accomplished and the position which they hold, in America at least. The opponents now declare that no one has a natural right to vote, and that while disfranchisement is hard on certain women, it is better that they should suffer, and that the State should suffer for lack of their voices, than that a horde of ignorant women should be added to the present mass of ignorant voters. This, at least, is the only argument of weight that is presented on the side of the opponents of woman suffrage, and it is obvious that those holding such an opinion shift the ground which has hitherto, for the most part, been taken for granted—the assumption, namely, that a democracy implies universal manhood suffrage—universal, that is, with a few unimportant and obvious exceptions.

The question before the believers in women's right to vote is simply this: How far is this objection well-founded? and if they allow that there is no natural and inherent right to self-government, are they turning their backs on the sacred cause of democracy which they have maintained hitherto as the very life-blood of their movement?

It is certain that the time has come when this question must be faced, and decided squarely on its merits. It is obvious that there are men—and women too—who are utterly unfit for self-government. This is recognized by the naturalization laws as well as by the debarring of certain classes from the franchise, but it has never been asserted that such laws are undemocratic.

When the actor Bernard, through a fortunate accident found himself the guest of Washington at Mount Vernon, he smiled when, in the midst of his host's discourse on liberty, "a black entered the room, bearing a pitcher of fresh spring water." Washington, perceiving his guest's amusement and its cause, said at once that no one regretted the slavery of the negroes more than he, but that liberty, in their hands, would become a scourge, until they knew how to use it. The understanding of Washington, which stood unmoved, as has been declared, when "the foundations of empires were shaken," was surely not at fault here. We are learning day by day what is meant by power in the hands of those unfit to exercise it.

The contention that a certain standard must be reached before a man or woman shall be allowed to exercise the privilege of self-government is not undemocratic, although at first it may seem so, as has been said already. We admit the desirability of such a standard when we refuse to allow a man to vote before he has reached the age of twenty-one years, and when we exclude idiots and lunatics from the ballot. Yet the adoption of these limitations is by no means considered undemocratic, and there is no valid reason why the raising of the standard should be so considered, *as long as it is left within the reach of the great majority of the people.*

What, then, shall be the qualification which we demand? Tried by the above criterion, the property-owning qualification fails, because it is by no means within the power of every man, much less every woman, to acquire property. Nobody in this country will seriously suggest any test founded in mere birth, except that of sex, which is, of course, founded on nothing better. It were well if a certain standard of character could be adopted, but any such, other than the present disfranchisement of convicts, is almost impossible of attainment. There remains one method, broad enough to include the bulk of the population, and within the reach of every man or woman who is sincerely desirous of qualifying for self-government, viz., the power to read and write the English language.

We have long known that the safety of a country rests upon the intelligence as much as upon the character of its citizens, and it is for this reason that we have constantly maintained a system of public schools—not a perfect system, it is true, but the attempt shows our recognition of the fundamental principle alluded to above. An educational qualification for the ballot is simply extending this principle to its logical conclusion.

It is not asserted that the introduction of such a basis for self-government would necessarily do away with all the evils from which we are now suffering. No such preposterous claim is intended. It is simply held that the illiteracy of voters, native or foreign, is one of the greatest sources of the dangers which now menace us, and that its removal from the ranks of voters will go very far to lessen those dangers.

There is no class legislation in the proposed plan, for it is possible for all men and women to qualify themselves for self-government, if they desire to do so. Further, the mere fact that it is necessary to take certain steps in order to attain to the rank of a voter, will tend to give the ballot a value in the eyes of the citizen, even more than it at present possesses. It is usually found that a man cares more for those things which compel him to work, and there is no reason why there should be an exception to the rule in this case. Nor is any suggestion of disfranchisement made. It is a comparatively simple thing to demand that every man or woman, who comes of age after a certain date, shall be required to meet

the prescribed standard before being admitted to the privileges of a voter, and in this way all unfairness and injustice will be avoided.

. . . And it is most fitting that this step shall be taken by women for many reasons, chief among which is the fact of their not being now voters, which removes the suspicion of their having any axe to grind.

The question before us is how to attain the best government. If women can lead the way on the right road, even if but one step, they will have deserved well of the Republic both now and hereafter.

ELIZABETH BURRILL CURTIS.
Ashfield, Mass.

99

HARRIET STANTON BLATCH
Educated Suffrage a Fetich [sic] (1897)

In an open letter to Mrs. Stanton, Mrs. Harriet Stanton Blatch says:

"*My Honored Mother:* As you represent a growing body of opinion in America, and have addressed the wide constituency of the JOURNAL, I beg leave to express my thoughts in an equally public way.

People are ever raising to themselves fetiches to worship in government, as in everything else. No sooner is one Golden Calf—as, for instance that it is only the man with a moneybag who has a stake in the country—torn down, than another is erected. The idea of restricting the suffrage to those who can read and write is another fetich. Now, my dear mother, if you have the heart to reread the letter in which you invite us to fall down and worship this fetich, you will find that throughout you imply that if a person can *read and write,* he is "enlightened" and "educated," and if he cannot read and write he is

From *Woman's Journal*, October 9, 1897.

"ignorant." I am sure, if you will frankly appeal to your knowledge of the world, you will be forced to admit that many a person who could satisfy even you in the "intelligence" of his reading, nay, more, who could satisfy a board of examiners of his collegiate accomplishments, is lamentably ignorant; while many a man without a sign of the three Rs about him, is gifted with the sterling common sense and abiding honesty which the school of life's experience teaches.

But you go still further, and call every American citizen who was born in Europe, and who cannot read or write the *English* language, an "ignorant foreigner." Perhaps you forgot that the nations of Europe have their public school systems. Take Germany, for instance; probably not a son of the Fatherland arrives in New York who has not had quite as good a common school education as the average man of the proletariat born in the United States. I think I am right in saying that you cannot read, write, or speak a word of German. Now, I not only affirm that you would not be an "ignorant foreigner" if you landed in Germany, but I declare, if you were given the franchise there, you would be the most intelligent voter in the whole Empire on women's questions. Of course I do not mean to contend that every foreigner in America is as well-informed as you would be in Germany; but I do say that the proletariat, whether able to read or not, can give a more valuable opinion than any other class upon such a question, for example, as the housing of the poor. As our ability to feel our own needs is not bounded by our linguistic accomplishments, neither should our power to *remedy* them through government be so bounded. Because you overlook the fact that the conditions of the poor are so much harder than yours or mine, you are led to argue that "the ignorant classes do not need the suffrage more than the enlightened, but just the reverse." Every working man needs the suffrage more than I do, but there is another who needs it more than he does, just because conditions are more galling, and that is the working woman.

You warn us that "Wise men see what a strain it (the ignorant vote) is on our institutions." I here derive great comfort that you did not quote wise women in support of your contentions, but left the burden to men. As you omit to name these wise men, I cannot challenge their right to the title; but, certain it is, their wisdom is free of any historical basis. The heaviest strain on American institutions was the Civil War and all the upheaval that preceded it; but surely the "ignorant vote" was not then the disturbing cause. And has not a government by an aristocracy of "intellect" been tried? Why, my dear mother, right in our own country, a government of the "educated" ruled over a wide area for generations. Before the war, the whole southern section of the United States was ruled by its men who could "read and write." They had it all their own way, and what did they do with their power? No, no, we are ever vainly trying to get morals and character out of intellect, but they grow on quite other soil. I recommend to all worshippers of the "reading and writing" fetich, the re-perusal of "The Tempest," in which Shakespeare shows how the intellect can be awakened, and yet the man remain a Caliban in morals.

But do not understand that, if it were possible to separate the truthful, the upright, the conscientious and the loving from their weaker fellowmen, I would advocate a government of an aristocracy of the moral; for I would not, and on this ground, that government is not the end of man, but merely a method of expressing collective thought, and achieving concerted action. And the thought is not collective if any human being capable of thought is excluded. We cannot escape the law that society is never stronger than its weakest link. Hence the wisdom of having the weakest link brought out in full light of day, freely showing its weakness, so that flaws may be corrected. If the strong links never were made to feel the detriment to themselves, individually and collectively, of the existence of the weak, nothing would be done to improve the feeble. Let the illiterate man express himself;

he is not ignorant on all sides; and let the mistakes which arise from his limitations stand as stumbling blocks in the paths of the wise, so that his power for evil may bring conviction of his need for help.

Again, you assert that "if a foreigner can read and write the English language intelligently, he has taken the first step towards understanding the spirit of our institutions and the duties of citizenship." Let me assure you the spirit of freedom is not a treasure hidden in America, but is everywhere throbbing in the heart of growing democracy. I do not call the man ignorant or wanting in an understanding of republican principles who, under the grinding, economic conditions of the Old World, stints himself to lay by, little by little, his passage money across the Atlantic, hoping to find in America a broader freedom for himself; but I do call ignorant, and a real danger to the State, the educated man, born and bred in a republic, who devotes his highest energies to money getting and neglects his every duty as a citizen. Monarchy is the true government for the lazy; a republic calls for energy, and true it is that the actual voters will form the government. And if the "reading and writing," "intelligent," "enlightened," "educated," "wise," "moral" American won't soil his hands with politics, let him at least be thankful that he has the "ignorant" masses to give him that necessary thing—a government.

Yours ever devotedly,
HARRIET STANTON B'LATCH.

100
D. ANNA GARDNER
Educated Suffrage a Step Backward (1897)

A plea for universal suffrage in the dawn of the 20th century!

So long has universal suffrage been an accomplished fact in the United States in its application to men, that any opposition to the principle seems in ill accordance with the evolutionary changes in the growing wisdom of mankind. The proposal for its restriction by an educational qualification, as seen of late in the columns of the WOMAN'S JOURNAL, strikes many minds as reactionary—a progress backward. We can not afford to tamper with the corner-stone of the noble structure of freedom built on our National Declaration of Independence. We can not afford to deny the principle upon which it stands, just as it is beginning to be accepted, not only in our own land but the world over, for woman as an integral part of the human family, as well as for man.

The final success of the woman suffrage movement must depend entirely upon keeping step by step in harmony with the eternal principles of justice. Any swerving from that base, must in the end prove detrimental to the women's cause. Advocating measures of expediency such as limiting suffrage to educated women, should it avail to hasten their enfranchisement, would segregate from the whole body of the people the unlettered and ignorant, thereby legalizing a new class-distinction, clearly defined, arousing hostile interests. The illiterate woman would be deprived of the security and protection which the ballot affords to life, liberty, and property. Being already under the subjection of man, she would be doubly defenceless. . . .

It will be urged by the advocates of an educational test, that the barrier to suffrage is not

From *Woman's Journal*, October 30, 1897.

insuperable; that it requires only the rudiments of learning, which can be easily attained, to qualify as a voter. But the fact that learning could be readily acquired does not justify class legislation so dangerous in a republic.

The ability to read and write can not always be a just criterion of intelligence. The innate sense of right and wrong in the human mind, helped by mother wit, would render Sojourner Truth vastly superior to many a scholar as a voter. Without knowledge of the A B C's, a person may be clear-headed enough to discern political measures better than his educated neighbor. He could see that legislation would always be in favor of the legislating class, and vote for equal privileges. True patriotism, so valuable a quality, is not confined to the learned.

When education alone governs, the tendency must be to brain aristocracy, more to be deplored than the aristocracy of wealth or family. It has been shown by universal experience that there is no class of citizens, however highly educated, that can be safely entrusted with exclusive political power; though there must be found noble exceptions among individuals who, under all conceivable circumstances, would be magnanimously inclined to lift a disfranchised class to a higher plane of knowledge—to sustain popular institutions, especially the public schools. But the mass of voters generally would abuse concentrated political power.

Were it practical and consistent with democracy, it would be far more serviceable in uplifting civilization to disfranchise educated dishonesty—rascality in high places—than to withhold the vote from honest illiteracy, whether of man or woman. An unrepresented class is necessarily an oppressed class. . . .

The only just vote in a republic based on the consent of the governed, is an average vote of the rich and the poor, the educated and the uneducated alike. The interests of the whole people are safe only in the hands of the whole people. . . .

ANNA GARDNER.

Nantucket, Oct. 22, 1897.

101
M. PUTNAM-JACOBI
"Common Sense" Applied to Woman Suffrage (1894)

This fourfold strand of circumstance, this fourfold revolution in the industrial, legal, educational, and governmental position of women, has entirely changed the existing situation from that when the argument for equal suffrage was first outlined. Then the argument was sketched on thin and rarefied air; now it is embedded in solidities of accomplished fact. Then it only appealed to those whose ears were attuned to the finer vibrations beyond the diapasons of ordinary thought; to-day it is enforced by the practical exigencies of every-day life. Then it only based itself on the abstract principles dear to the elect souls,—among the great and good of all ages[*]; to-day the Thought has descended from the empyrean, it has taken flesh, it has become incarnate among the prosaic possibilities of men. It was a Thought; it has become an imminent Fact. It was a Right; it has become an Expediency. It was born a heavenly body of abstract Truth; it has become an earthly body of social and political Institution. . . .

No matter how well born, how intelligent, how highly educated, how virtuous, how rich, how refined, the women of to-day constitute a political class below that of every man, no matter how base born, how stupid, how ignorant, how vicious, how poverty-stricken, how brutal. The pauper in the almshouse may vote; the lady who devotes her philanthropic thought to making that almshouse habitable, may not. The tramp who begs cold victuals in the kitchen may vote; the heiress who feeds him and endows universities may not. The half civilized hordes pouring into our country through the open gates

---

[*]"And for company the great and good of all ages." —Emerson in the *American Scholar.*

From *"Common Sense" Applied to Woman Suffrage* (New York: The Knickerbocker Press, 1894), 60–2, 74–5, 81–6, 92.

of our seaport towns, the Indian if settled in sev-
eralty, the negro on the cotton plantation,—all,
now, or in a few years, have a vote. But the white
woman of purest blood, and who, in her own
person, or that of mother or grandmother, has
helped to sustain the courage of the Revolutionary war, to fight the heroic battle of abolition,
and to dress the wounds of the Rebellion,—this
woman must keep silence. Legislatures are distracted by controversies over the means to secure the "illiterate vote"; pasters are provided,
and symbols; and in the meanwhile, all the
women—who embrace half the education, half
the virtue, and but a fraction of the illiteracy or
crime of the community—remain excluded
from the franchise, buried behind this dense
cloud of often besotted ignorance. . . .

Because the idea of sovereignty has become
detached from all previously admitted attributes
of sovereignty, is no longer necessarily associated with any insignia of intrinsic power, the
conception of sovereignty itself has become lax,
feeble, confused.

Sovereignty, divided into a million frag-
ments, seems illusory, worthless. "Absurd,"
women are told, "to struggle for the right of
suffrage, when that means nothing. You might as
well pine for the privilege of riding in a crowded
omnibus, when you already have the right of
driving in your comfortable carriage. The right
to rule yourselves! No one rules himself, much
less any one else. What personal influence may
be exerted by tongue or pen, can be done by
the unenfranchised full as well as by those who
possess the illusory privilege of the ballot. I, who
am legally entitled to vote, do not vote half the
time. What, then, do you want to vote for?"

"No one rules!" Yet, according to the dictum of a master in political thought, the first
question to be decided in any community is:
Where rests the Sovereign Power? The answer,
according to the theory of democratic society,
is: With Public Opinion. According to the theory
of a Republic, the sovereignty lies, with such
Public Opinion as shall prove itself, through superior virtue and intelligence, to be not only

the best, but the strongest. For intelligence must
be stronger than ignorance, and virtue than vice,
wherever free play is really allowed to each.

This is the answer according to theory. The
answer according to fact must be that the Sovereign Power rests upon physical force. Otherwise it would be incomprehensible that Power,
thus defined, should remain confined to the sex
whose only universal superiority lay in physical
force; and that the sex which admittedly possessed in abundance the attributes of intelligence
and virtue should be excluded from all share in
the Sovereign Power.

This cynical answer has indeed been given;
given, *mirabile dictum,* even by clergymen, by
those whose profession dictates the constant
exaltation of mental over physical qualification
for the Sovereignty.

Nevertheless, not only the answer is not
true, but, what is more important for our purpose, no one really believes that in modern societies it is true. Every one knows that physical
force is at present the servant, and not, if it has
ever been, the master of intelligence. If, with
the advent of manhood suffrage, apparently unintelligent masses often obtain supreme control,
it can only be because intelligence has either
abdicated or declined. The control is not at all
due to the possession of a vast amount of latent
physical force, which by itself is as useless as the
river, which is as yet unturned into the mill race.

Who abdicates, but those who call the privilege of the ballot illusory?

The complex contradictions in the present
distributions of Sovereign Power are further intensified by the vulgarization of the general ideal.
It is one thing to say, "Some men shall rule," quite
another to declare, "All men shall rule," and that
in virtue of the most primitive, the most rudimentary attribute they possess, that namely of
sex. If the original contempt for masses of men
has ever diminished, and the conception of mankind been ennobled, it is because, upon the
primitive animal foundation, human imagination
has built a fair structure of mental and moral
attribute and possibility, and habitually deals

with that. This indeed is no new thing to do; for it was to this moral man that Pericles addressed his funeral oration; and of whom Lincoln thought in his speech at Gettysburg.

Of this moral man women—the sex hitherto so despised,—are now recognized to constitute an integral part. It is useless therefore to attempt to throw them out by an appeal to the primitive conditions of a physical force, to which no one appeals for any other purpose.

It is forgotten to-day that, until to-day, the incapacity of women for the suffrage was attributed, not merely to their deficiency in physical force, but to the profound mental and moral inferiority of her entire nature. Whether this theory was ultimately derived from the natural contempt of the primitive savage for every one whom he could knock down; or whether, as the Canon Law asserts, it is the natural punishment for the seduction of Adam by Eve, and the expression of the subsequent natural indignation of the human race, which owes to the same fact its existence and its fall; certain it is that this theory has prevailed throughout Christendom down to the second half of the nineteenth century, and is only just beginning to wane in its force and in its extraordinary practical efficiency.

During the long ages of class rule, which are just beginning to cease, only one form of sovereignty has been assigned to all men—that, namely, over all women. Upon these feeble and inferior companions all men were permitted to avenge the indignities they suffered from so many men to whom they were forced to submit. To-day, when all men rule, and diffused self-government has abolished the old divisions between the governing classes and the governed, only one class remains over whom all men can exercise sovereignty—namely, the women. Hence a shuddering dread runs through society at the proposal to also abolish this last refuge of facile domination. . . .

It is not, therefore, "abdication of sovereignty" which is proposed, demanded, or to be dreaded in extending the suffrage to women. It is simply the association of women with men,

for such functions of sovereignty as they are able to exercise, and whose dissociation from some others has for precedent a similar dissociation among the functions of the complex modern State.

102

FANNIE BARRIER WILLIAMS
Women's Influence in Politics (1896)

If the newspapers are to be believed, politics in our country, and especially in cities like Chicago, is fast becoming a sort of "trust," which controls, directs, or stifles a fair and free competition for public offices, and makes patriotism wholly subordinate to the practical considerations and interests of the trust business. Under the manipulations of the trust, or combination, or "machine," or whatever it may be called, a convention is simply an occasion for passively ratifying the plans of the political stockholders. The average man voter mildly submits to every plan or policy of the "machine," whether that policy be for the weal or woe of his country.

To the American women who are eager for all the political equalities of citizenship, this condition of politics ought to be especially significant, if not discouraging. Does woman's entrance into politics mean nothing more or better than the enlargement and firmer establishment of "machine politics"? Does her enfranchisement only mean a few more partisan votes for the respective parties, and a few more hallelujahs for the "grand principles," etc.? If so, it is difficult to see wherein the mere right to vote will either bless our country, purify American politics, or exalt womankind. In saying this, there is no intention to challenge the righteousness of women's claim to political equality with men. I merely wish to suggest that the cause of American women cannot well be advanced by the

From *Woman's Journal*, March 7, 1896.

suffrage, if such suffrage only means to them what it means to the average American citizen—a man citizen who shamefully delegates all his rights to think and believe to his political "bosses." If the average American voter, especially those who are so much opposed to woman suffrage, had any proper sense of the meaning and responsibility of politics, there could be no such degrading terms in American politics as "bosses," "machines," "machine-made candidates," "packed conventions," etc., *ad nauseam*.

Ideal partisanship may be a good thing, but samples of it are so rare that few American voters know what it is. Certainly, most of the women who are our spokesmen in political conventions and other gatherings have not found it. There is every reason to expect that women should be more conscientious and more independent as voters than men. It certainly can be said that women have an instinct for reform. Disinterested sympathy is one of the marked characteristics in most of the activities that engage the heart and the hand of the nineteenth century woman. In these activities she has displayed a degree of courage and independence that have been strong arguments as to her fitness to exert a wholesome influence in all kinds of reform work. Is there, then, any reason why she should cease to be a reformer and become one of the most uncompromising of partisans as soon as she enters the arena of politics? . . .

FANNIE BARRIER WILLIAMS
Chicago, Ill., Feb. 24, 1896.

103

BELLE KEARNEY
Suffrage in the South (1900)

. . . During the Southern Exposition in 1884, my second trip was made to New Orleans. The

From *A Slaveholder's Daughter* (1900; reprint ed., New York: Negro Universities Press, 1969), 107–8, 110–13, 118–20.

world had changed considerably to me since my first visit: my eyes had grown accustomed to larger visions. Since beginning to teach, every question that related to the attainments and possibilities of women was of intense interest to me; but especially her developed power of breadwinning.

Julia Ward Howe was lecturing in the city. She was the first woman I had ever heard speak before a public audience, except students on a school rostrum. Never can the eagerness be forgotten with which my feet hastened to the hall where she was to be heard, nor the absorption with which my listening ears drew in every word, nor the critical attention that was given to every detail of the speaker's appearance, from the lace cap that rested on her brainy head down to the toes of her common-sense boots.

She spoke on "Woman's Work." As she talked brilliantly and fluently my enchantment grew. The remark that she had visited several foreign countries and had addressed the women of each in their own tongue particularly impressed me. How far away those strange lands seemed! How wonderful to be looking at a person who had really seen them! Going to Europe had been the dream of my life, and here was a woman who had actually been there! For many years an earnest desire had possessed me to behold a genuinely strong-minded woman,—one of the truly advanced type. Beautiful to realize, she stood before me! and in a position the very acme of independence—upon a platform delivering a speech!

Since the development of my reasoning faculties I had believed in the rights of women, although in an article on that subject, written at the age of nineteen, I had affirmed "that we do not ask for the ballot." It would have been too shocking, and my radicalism at that period was in the chrysalis state. There was born in me a sense of the injustice that had always been heaped upon my sex, and this consciousness created and sustained in me a constant and ever increasing rebellion. The definite idea of the political emancipation of woman, as a happy and logical solution of the vexed question, did not present it-self to me in a positive guise until some time after my entrance upon the list of wage-earn-ers. . . .

The freedom of my home environment was perfect, but I recognized the fact that there were tremendous limitations of my "personal liberty" outside the family circle. An instance of it soon painfully impressed my consciousness. Three of my brothers, the comrades of my childhood, had become voting citizens. They were manly and generous enough to sympathize with my ballotless condition, but it was the source of many jokes at my expense among them. On a certain election day in November, they mounted their horses and started for the polls. I stood watching them as they rode off in the splendor of their youth and strength. I was full of love and pride for them, but was feeling keenly the disgrace of being a disfranchised mortal, simply on account of having been born a woman,— and that by no volition of my own. Surmising the storm that was raging in my heart, my sec-ond brother—who was at home from the West on a visit of over a year's duration—looking at me, smiling and lifting his hat in mock courtesy said: "Good morning, sister. You taught us and trained us in the way we should go. You gave us money from your hard earnings, and helped us to get a start in the world. You are interested infinitely more in good government and under-stand politics a thousand times better than we, but it is election day and we leave you at home with the idiots and Indians, incapables, paupers, lunatics, criminals and the other women that the authorities in this nation do not deem it proper to trust with the ballot; while we, lordly men, march to the polls and express our opinions in a way that counts."

There was the echo of a general laugh as they rode away. A salute was waved to them and a good-by smiled in return; but my lips were trembling and my eyes were dim with tears. For the first time the fact was apparent that a wide gulf stretched between my brothers and me; that there was a plane, called political equality, upon which we could not stand together. We had the same home, the same parents, the same facul-ties, the same general outlook. We had loved the same things and striven for the same ends and had been equals in all respects. *Now* I was set aside as inferior, inadequate for citizenship, not because of inferior quality or achievement but by an arbitrary discrimination that seemed as unjust as it was unwise. I too had to live under the laws; then why was it not equally my inter-est and privilege, to elect the officers who were to make and execute them? I was a human being and a citizen, and a self-supporting, producing citizen, yet my government took no cognizance of me except to set me aside with the unworthy and the incapable for whom the state was forced to provide.

That experience made me a woman suffrag-ist, avowed and uncompromising. Deep down in my heart a vow was made that day that never should satisfaction come to me until by personal effort I had helped to put the ballot into the hands of woman. It became a mastering purpose of my life.

The women of the South have not sought work because they loved it; they have not gone before the public because it was desirable for themselves; they have not arrived at the wish for political equality with men simply by a pro-cess of reasoning; all this has been thrust upon them by a changed social and economic envi-ronment. It is the result of the evolution of events which was set in motion by the bombard-ment of Fort Sumter.

At the close of the war when the entire South was lying prostrate and bleeding; her fer-tile fields left bare an desolate, her lovely homes ravaged by fire and sword; her young men slaughtered or disabled; her commercial streams choked and stagnated; her system of labor ut-terly and forever destroyed; her social affiliations blasted and every feature of life dazed and revo-lutionized, the women of that unhappy time arose in the majesty of their hitherto un-dreamed-of strength and with forceful calmness and unmurmuring determination, put their hands figuratively and literally to the plow and have never faltered nor looked back. Their heroism has not been known as it deserves. When, after the war, the men were dying all about them from the hardships that they had endured in the field of battle, the mother-heart of the South said, "Somebody must live for the sake of our children"—and the women lived and worked. Those of the better classes had been accustomed to the control and management of servants and households, often of large planting interests. They were full of resources, and their naturally flexible temperament made readjustment easier to them than to men. For a decade or more, the boys usually went to work at the time they should have entered college, partly from necessity, partly because many of them had served in the Confederate army and preferred work to the confinement of a student's life. The daughters were sent to college; every sacrifice was made for this end, until, after fifteen years, the superiority of culture of the young woman over the average young man was very noticeable. Improving circumstances gradually corrected this inequality: but the tide had set toward the advancement of women in the educational and industrial field.

. . . Modern reformations have gained foothold in the hearts and lives of Southern women that is astonishing to all who realize the intense conservatism that fettered them in other days.

The Woman's Christian Temperance Union was the golden key that unlocked the prison doors of pent-up possibilities. It was the generous liberator, the joyous iconoclast, the discoverer, the developer of Southern women. It, above all other forces, made it possible for women to occupy the advanced and continually advancing position they now hold; a position that is leading steadily to the highest pinnacle that can be reached in civil government, namely, the political emancipation of women. The hungry avidity with which the brainy, philosophical women of the South are taking hold of this great subject is something at which we cannot wonder. It is the natural outcome of their desperate

struggles for individual freedom. This sentiment for woman suffrage is not confined to one sex, by any means. I have always maintained, and do now insist, that Southern men, as a rule, are stronger advocates for the enfranchisement of women than men in any other section of the United States except in certain portions of the West. The old-time element of chivalry, which constituted so largely the make-up of the Southern gentleman, has been handed down through the generations and now begins to crystalize in the direction of equality before the law for men and women. Southern people are hospitable to reforms, whether they come in the guise of religion, philanthropy or politics, if justice and righteousness lie at the foundation. The movement for woman suffrage has advanced slowly in the South, because very slight effort has been made there to secure the ballot for women, and the thought is somewhat a new one to the masses. For years, in different Southern states I have heard prominent men say: "If women want to vote, it is all right. We have no objection. As human beings, they are entitled to the same privileges as we are, and require the same legal protection. We do not give them the ballot because they do not seem to desire it. Just as soon as they demand it, they will get it."

When the constitutional convention was held in Mississippi, a few years since, suffrage came very near being granted to the women of that state; and in South Carolina, soon after, the bill introduced in the legislature for woman's enfranchisement was lost by a remarkably small vote in the senate. In 1898, the state of Louisiana, by constitutional enactment, gave to all tax-paying women the right to vote upon all questions submitted to the tax-payers.

There are several states in the South that give women the right of suffrage to a limited degree, and whenever they have exercised that privilege they have been treated with the utmost deference by the male citizens who met them on an equal footing at the polls. Kentucky enjoys the distinction of being the first state in the nation to grant suffrage in any form to women.

This was done as early as 1838. Of course, there are thousands of men in the South, as elsewhere, who are heavily coated with an impenetrable crust of prejudice concerning the hoary creed of "woman's sphere," who would oppose bitterly any effort made for her enfranchisement, just as they would fight any other progressive measure. To this class belong the liquor dealers, the wily politicians of the lower stamp, the ultra-conservative ecclesiastics, the superfine "swells" and men who have risen from the humbler walks of life deprived of early advantages of education and the refinements of elevated home environments.

Exactly as there are opponents among men, so are there thousands of women in the South who have arrayed themselves in a belligerent attitude toward the movement that was instituted especially for their well-being. There are multitudes of others who are still in a deep sleep regarding the necessity of having the ballot, and are continuing to drone the old song in their slumbers: "I have all the rights I want;" but there are many of their sisters who are beginning to rub their eyes and look up with a glad surprise upon the new day that is breaking, while scores of others have shattered every shackle that bound them to the old conditions and have walked out boldly into the flood-tide of the most benignant evolution that the centuries have brought to them, and are working with heart and brain on fire to materialize into legislation the most potential gift that civilization can bestow.

II. Higher Education and the Professions

THE STATE OF WOMEN IN HIGHER EDUCATION PROGRESSED unevenly in the late-nineteenth century. While some Midwestern colleges (e.g., Oberlin and Antioch) and universities (e.g., Iowa and Wisconsin) had opened their doors to women at mid-century, many others, including the prestigious (what would later be called) Ivy League schools, remained entrenched in all-male traditions. At the same time, however, this period saw the founding of a number of women's colleges in the East, including Vassar, Mt. Holyoke, Smith, and Wellesley—institutions that would rapidly achieve national recognition.

The denial to women of access to higher education and the professions was based on a complex of biases, ranging from cultural expectations of a female's proper place in the home to biological arguments about women's physical frailty. In "Sex and Work" (1874), Antoinette Brown Blackwell, who in 1853 became the first ordained woman minister of a recognized religious denomination in the United States, challenges the notion that women are less evolved than men: while male brains are on average larger than those of females, Blackwell argues, women have more developed nervous systems—an integral element of human physiology. At a different level, Blackwell insists that "the Creator" would not have put women and men on different planes of evolution; while the two sexes have distinct capabilities, they both should be allowed to develop fully and freely.

In *Sex in Education* (1873), Dr. Edward Clarke, a member of Harvard University's Board of Overseers, addressed the issue of coeducation at Harvard. Clarke stated that, in his expert medical opinion, the rigorous intellectual exercise of a university education posed a grave danger to a woman's well-being, including overtaxing the brain and serious threat to reproductive capacities. Clarke's book met with overwhelming criticism from various quarters. Julia Ward Howe, for example, put together a collection of essays entitled *Sex and Education: A Reply to Dr. Clarke's "Sex in Education."* The responses by Elizabeth Stuart Phelps and Maria K. Elmore (1874) first question the value of an opinion of a physician on a matter so related to intellectual abilities; they go on to point out how successfully women have already filled a range of positions in industry, education, business, as well as the home—all without the dire consequences Clarke predicts, such as madness and even death.

The idea of innate physical-mental differences between the sexes found its most influential support in the work of the English naturalist Charles Darwin and his study *Descent of Man* (1871), which explains that centuries of male preeminence in the human struggle for existence guaranteed the superior bodily strength of men and also more developed qualities of bravery, courage, and leadership. Feminists, particularly as they themselves entered the scientific and medical professions, have attacked the findings and implications of Darwinian evolutionary thought since its emergence, as in Dr. Frances Emily White's article "Woman's Place in Nature" (1875). White acknowledges that the sexes have inherited different traits but argues that, with the advance of civilization, the sexually-specific characteristics of men have diminished in value while those of women (e.g., nurturance and moral strength) have become more important. White draws from her medical training to add specificity to feminist arguments based on women's moral difference.

Among the professions, law would prove to be unusually difficult for women to break into. In "The XIV Amendment and Our Case" (1873), Myra Bradwell—co-founder and editor of the *Chicago Legal News*—takes issue with the United States Supreme Court's affirmation of the Illinois Supreme Court's refusal to grant her a license to practice law in the state. Bradwell had argued that the Fourteenth Amendment to the Constitution and its provision that "the citizens of each state shall be entitled to all privileges and immunities of citizens in the several states" should guarantee her right to join the bar. In 1873, the Illinois legislature finally settled the issue, passing a law that "no person shall be precluded or debarred from any occupation, profession or employment (except military) on account of sex. (Provided that this act shall not be construed to affect the eligibility of any person to an elective office.)" In 1879, Belva A. Lockwood became the first woman admitted to practice before the Supreme Court of the United States. "My Efforts to Become a Lawyer" (1888) outlines her long and oftentimes heroic efforts to pursue her livelihood in the hyper-masculinized profession of American law.

In "Should Professional Women Marry?" (1874), Gertrude Stuart Baillie addresses the divisive issue of whether a young woman can fulfill both a professional career and also the domestic role of wife and mother. While the essay welcomes the growing number of women in the professions, notice how the traditional concept of marriage is privileged as something that should not be entered into without complete commitment, thereby suggesting that women (unlike men) need to choose between one or the other.

A corollary to women's increased access to the professions was greater need and opportunites for higher education. In "A Review of Higher Education of Women" (1892), Alice Freeman Palmer considers the merits and drawbacks of the three types of higher education available to women in the late-nineteenth century—co-educational institutions, separate women's colleges, and women's annexes to all-male universities. Freeman Palmer knew of what she spoke: an 1870 graduate of the University of Michigan, she went on to become one of the first presidents of Wellesley College; after marrying a senior faculty member of Harvard University, Freeman Palmer served as Dean of Women at the University of Chicago and also pushed for Harvard Annex to be recognized as Radcliffe College.

As all American women fought institutional biases against equal opportunity in higher education, African-American women had the added, greater burden of overcoming widespread social beliefs and pseudo-scientific theories regarding the intellectual inferiority of their race, as well as their sex. Black women thus had to fight obstacles raised not only by white men but also by black men and white women. Anna Julia Cooper writes in "The Higher Education of Colored Women" (1892) that black men, while forward thinking on other political issues, are partially responsible for holding back African-American women, as they accept the dominant view about public life as inappropriate for women. In "Higher Education of Colored Women in White Schools and Colleges" (1902), Pauline F. Hopkins focuses on how harmful "Anglo-Saxon woman" has been in marking herself as superior to other women, especially to black women; it is a "self-evident" truth that African-American women have the right to education, Hopkins writes, adding that they should ultimately be judged by their performance once given an equal chance.

104

ANTOINETTE BROWN BLACKWELL
Sex and Work (1874)

The nervous system is the brain system of the body, the mechanism especially adapted to all mental processes of thought, of feeling, of voluntary motion; to all those reflex activities which simulate voluntary movement; and to the promotion of all the organic processes of growth and nutrition. Nerves are literally the brain extended; ramified into every minutest part of the body; accompanying the blood vessels everywhere; branching into every muscle, and impelling the entire system to activity. They are formed of the identical peculiar white and grey matter of the brain, every fiber closely modeled after a uniform pattern of growth, as every twig, branch, trunk and root in an ordinary tree is one in structure.

Like arteries and veins, the nerves branch outwards from their centers to every toe and finger tip, and return again in distinct lines. The heart is the recognized great organ of the wonderful branching tree of hollow tubes, in which the blood of the system circulates; and the brain, of the even more marvelous and vital banyan-tree of nerves, which establishes its partially independent ganglia, or new roots in the spinal cord, and at all the important centers where they are needed to carry forward the endlessly complicated processes of active life. Nerves have long been recognized as having special feminine relations.

How incredibly singular, blind, and perverse, then, is the dogmatism which has insisted that man's larger brain, measured by inches in the cranium, must necessarily prove his mental superiority to Woman. First, let Dr. Brown-Sequard, or some other learned professor of the rapidly growing science of the nervous system, demonstrate the special significance of the

From *Woman's Journal*, April 18, 1874.

unique feminine plexus of nerves in the mammary glands, as related to the emotional, intuitional and moral nature of womanhood. Let us comprehend something more of the supplemental nerves which grow, and live, and die in the new uterus; which itself grows, and acts, and lives, and dies in the interest, not of the mother but of her unborn babe; yet which also profoundly influences her life, physical and psychical. Let us distinctly understand how the feminine brain system with all its adjuncts differs from the masculine; then, if the facts warrant the conclusion, let man's old-time claim to superiority be vaunted with equal confidence, but on the basis of a more enlightened understanding.

When we learn to balance mass of tissue, strength of action, amount or quantity in all its forms of being and doing in Man, against the more complex structure and the more rapid action of corresponding functions in Woman, we may conclude that the predominating greater velocity is a fair set off to the greater power. The more complex feminine structure, since it is entirely complete within a considerably smaller model, must be proportionately more delicate in workmanship; this may involve finer tissues and subtler processes throughout, and these may represent equivalent forces. The suggestion is credible.

All physiologists teach us that the feminine skin is thinner and more active, the circulation quicker, and the respiration more frequent; all satirists affirm that Woman's nerves have a sharper edge; it is orthodox to believe that her feelings are more acute, and her intuitions more rapid. What hinders then the conclusion that what man has gained in power he has lost in velocity? Or reverse the law. What Woman has gained in velocity, she has lost in power. Who is prepared to show that they are not started in life as equals on an identical plane of evolution?

It is hazardous to rely altogether upon an *a priori* dogmatism, learned or unlearned, which forces one to set up the assumption that the

Creator has been driven by partiality to model an unbalanced, unsymmetrical humanity, like an unshapely apple, one half large and desirable, but the other half small and unsavory.

No want of symmetry is involved if we accept the theory of variety in equivalents. Regarded as peers, equals in all the qualities of force, physical, mental and moral, the creative fatherhood is vindicated, and Woman ennobled; but Man not degraded. The *a priori* argument to me is completely reversed. Omnipotence might create one vessel to honor and another to dishonor; but Beneficence would be obliged to look far before it could find an adequate motive in that direction.

How the few really great men of the world reach out to shake hands with each other across an ocean or a continent, more rejoiced at a word from one of these, an equal, than with endless plaudits from the millions of inferiors! The appreciation and companionship of one's equals is everywhere the social element of highest value. Add to this the responsive, quickening influences which react with special enthusiasm between the sexes, and you have my highest ideal of the sustaining and thoroughly ennobling effects which rise from human sympathy. But Man, forever bowing his royal head, curving his moral neck, and dropping his eyes from their heavenward outlook down to Woman, is not an edifying social arrangement, nor can it be a pleasant means of grace to either party.

Even if Nature's creative forces be regarded as acting blindly, without moral forecast, yet what sufficient reason can we assign for supposing the sexes, so equally balanced numerically, to be so unequally balanced in all highest values? Fortunately, it is a question to be ultimately decided on the comparative evidence of nerve and muscle, and their quality and quantity of functions; on the balanced testimony of thought and feeling, of logic and intuition and similar equivalent forces. "The old man and his deeds" decreed himself the superior; the new woman by her deeds is asserting her equality; now on which side will Nature declare herself if scientifically interrogated?

At present we are inquiring only as to the capacity of the sexes to perform equivalent amounts of work uninjured. Man can lift a heavier weight; but Woman can watch more enduringly at the bedside of her sick child. Such at least is the current belief; and if physiology can show us that the added periodicity of function in her constitution, intimately connected as it is with the circulation of the blood in every artery and vein, must confer on her an added impulse towards the perpetual renewal of exhausted health through this surplus method of eliminating worn tissues and relieving overtaxed nerves, here is one point gained. That such is the result, every woman and every physician must testify. Whenever her work is endurance, whenever patient waiting and some degree of enforced muscular and mental inactivity is necessitated by her maternal functions, before and after the birth of children, then extraordinary organic processes re-establish the balance. Nature, by unlike but kindred methods, has instituted a special system of provisions for the preservation and renewal of the health of Woman. These provisions are adapted alike to overwork and to underwork, as the evil arising in either case is a disturbed action to the whole system. They are as admirably adjusted to the over use of the intellectual and emotional faculties as to excessive muscular activity. They are special provisions related not simply to maternal functions; but are needed also by the generally more rapid activity of the more excitable feminine temperament.

My conclusion, therefore, is that an equivalent amount of work, mental or physical, though it will be performed in somewhat different ways by men and women, other things being equal, could often be borne more successfully by the average woman than by the average man.

105

ELIZABETH STUART PHELPS
AND MARIA A. ELMORE
Sex and Education (1874)

ELIZABETH STUART PHELPS

. . . Meanwhile it remains possible for any of us to say, in deprecation of the notion of womanhood advanced by Dr. Clarke, two things.

1. The physician is not the person whose judgment upon a matter involving the welfare of women can possibly be final. His testimony, worth what it may be worth, should seek and fall into its proper place in the physical aspects of such a question; but it shall *stay* in its place. It is but a link in a chain. It is only a tint in a kaleidoscope. A question so intricate and shifting as that which involves the exact position of woman in the economy of a cursed world is not to be settled by the most intimate acquaintance with the proximate principles of the human frame, with the proportions of the gray and white matter in the brain, or with the transitional character of the tissues and the exquisite machinery of the viscera. The psychologist has yet his word to say. The theologian has a reason to be heard. The political economist might also add to experience knowledge. The woman who is physically and intellectually a living denial of every premise and of every conclusion which Dr. Clarke has advanced, has yet a right to an audience. Nor is he even the man whose judgment as to the *health* of women can be symmetrical. No *clinical* opinion, it will be remembered, bearing against the physical vigor of any class of people, is or can be a complete one. The physician knows sick women almost only. Well women keep away from him, and thank Heaven. . . . Thousands of women will not believe what the author of "Sex in Education" tells them, *simply because they know better.* Their own unlearned experience stands

From *Sex and Education: A Reply to Dr. E. H. Clarke's "Sex in Education,"* ed., Julia Ward Howe (Boston: Roberts Brothers, 1874), 127–31, 131–33, 134–36, 174–77, 179–82.

to them in refutation of his learned statements. They will give him theory for theory. They can pile up for him illustration on illustration. Statistics they have none; but no statistics has he. They and the Doctor are met on fair fight.

Many a woman who stands at the factory loom eleven hours and a half a day, from year's end to year's end, from the age of eight to the age of forty-eight, knows better than he tells her. Every lady lecturer in the land, who unites the most exhausting kind of brain and body labor in her own experience, day and night after day and night, for the half of every year, and unites it in defiance of Dr. Clarke's prognostications, knows better. Every healthy woman physician knows better; and it is only the woman physician, after all, whose judgment can ever approach the ultimate uses of the physicist's testimony to these questions.

It should be said: 2. Almost every fact brought forward by Dr. Clarke goes to illustrate the exact opposite of his almost every conclusion in respect to the effect of *mental* labor upon the female physique. With the serene, not to say dogmatic conviction of the physician whose own patients represent the world to him, he has copied for us from his note-books a series of cases exemplifying the remarkable unanimity with which girls, *after* leaving school, break down in health. . . . he calls our consideration to his list of cases, arguing detachedly, by the way, and ingeniously constructing for our benefit very much such a syllogism as this.

Sumption.—All women ought to be incapable of sustained activity.

Subsumption.—Some women whom I have known are incapable of sustained activity. Miss X. became an invalid soon after leaving school. Miss Y. was injured by gymnastic exercises, fell under my care, and will never be well. Miss Z. became an invalid soon after leaving school, and being for some time under my treatment was sent to an insane asylum.

Therefore,

Conclusion: All women are incapable of sustained activity, but proved especially incapable of sustained brain activity; and, since it would cost Harvard College several millions of dollars to admit them, co-education is a chimera, and old maids a monstrosity at which physicians may sneer, and by which young women should take warning.

Or, to put it in another form, more compactly,

As long as girls are in school they are (with exceptions so rare that I have had great difficulty in finding them) in excellent health.

When girls leave school, they fall sick.

Therefore it is sustained study which injures girls.

Here, now, is the point of fair dispute. Why do girls so often become invalids within a few years after leaving school?

. . . Women sick because they study? Does it not look a little more as if women were sick because they *stopped* studying?

Worn out by intellectual activity?

Let us suppose that they might be exhausted by the change from intellectual activity to intellectual inanition. Made invalids because they go to school from fourteen to eighteen? Let us conceive that they might be made invalids because they *left* school at eighteen! Let us draw upon our imagination to the extent of inquiring whether the nineteenth-century girl—intense, sensitive, and developing, like her age, nervously and fast—might not be made an invalid by the plunge from the "healing influences" of systematic brain exertion to the broken, jagged life which awaits a girl whose "education is completed." Made an invalid by exchanging the wholesome pursuit of sufficient and worthy aims for the unrelieved routine of a dependent domestic life, from which all aim has departed, or for the whirl of false excitements and falser contents which she calls society. Made an invalid by the abrupt slide from "thinking," as poor Lamb had it, "that life was going to be something," to the discovery that it has "unaccountably fallen from her before its time." Made an invalid by the sad and subtle process by which a girl is first inspired to the ideal of a life in which her per-

sonal culture has as honest and honorable a part of her regard as (and as a part of) her personal usefulness; and then is left to find out that personal culture substantially stopped for her when she tied the ribbon of her seminary diploma. Made an invalid by the prejudice that deprives her of the stimulus which every human being needs and finds in the pursuit of some one especial avocation, and confines that avocation for her to a marriage which she may never effect, and which may never help the matter if she does. Made an invalid by the change from doing something to doing nothing. Made an invalid by the difference between being happy and being miserable. Made an invalid, in short, for *just the reasons* (in whatever manner, the manner being a secondary point) *why a man would be made an invalid* if subjected to the woman's life when the woman's education is over. That wretched, mistaken life, that nervous, emotive, aimless, and exhausting life which women assume at the end of their school career would have killed Dr. Clarke, had it been his lot, quite too soon for his years and experience to have matured into the writing of "Sex in Education."

MARIA A. ELMORE

Dr. Clarke talks as though women in every thing but college life had perfect liberty to change at will their position from the erect to the reclining; as though nothing else required four weeks' labor in a month; as though a regular, sustained, and uninterrupted course of work was something of which they have never had any experience; and as though identical education of the sexes was the only regimen that ignored the periodic tides and reproductive apparatus of their organization.

We would like to have Dr. Clarke inform us what regimen there is that does not ignore them?

While but very few women are called by a chapel-bell to a standing prayer, thousands and tens of thousands in America are called by the bell of "that university, which has a water-wheel at the bottom," to all-day standing tasks at the noisy loom, and this followed from half-past six in the morning till half-past six at night, with the intermission only of half, three-quarters, or the whole of an hour at noon, throughout every working-day in the year.

Has Dr. Clarke written a book on "Sex in Manufacturing Establishments"? If he hasn't, he ought to.

Women stand behind the counter, obliged to be at their post just such a time every morning, and to wait on customers, if need be, the livelong day. Are they excused from work every fourth week? Can they sit, stand, or recline at their pleasure? Are they exempted from tending to the wants of their employers' patrons because they feel indisposed? Nay, in many instances are they not required to be on their feet all the time, even when there are no customers?

Has Dr. Clarke written a book on "Sex in Clerkships"?

Women have, year out and year in, busily plied the needle in tailors' and dressmakers' shops, having no opportunity to change at will their position from the sitting to the standing, walking, or reclining.

Has Dr. Clarke written a book on "Sex in Workshops," or "Sex in Sewing"?

School-teachers are expected to be in their school-rooms promptly on the hour every school-day in the year, ready to discharge their duties to their pupils. Where is the school-board that ever allowed its female teachers to take a week's vacation every month? Where is that man who would have a young woman teach in his ward or neighborhood who should make application to him in this wise: "Sir, I am very desirous of becoming a teacher. I want a school, and will do all in my power to bring it to a standard of high moral excellence and worth. But I must tell you that I cannot teach for four consecutive weeks. I can teach only three weeks at a time: the fourth I must have to myself. Mighty and powerful demands are then made upon my constitution, and it requires all the strength and energy I can command to meet them. To attempt at such times to manage and instruct an unruly and rollicking set of young urchins would derange the tides of my organization, divert blood from the reproductive apparatus to my head, and consequently add to my piety at the expense of my blood." . . .

Does that regimen which men are ever prescribing for woman, namely, marriage, grant her one week's cessation from labor out of every four? Can a mother, when weary and overtasked, relinquish the work and care of her family, and engage her thoughts upon nothing save that of her own physical weaknesses, and how to relieve them?

No, woman may work in the factory, in the store, in the workshop, in the field, in the dining-saloon, at the wash-tub, at the ironing-table, at the sewing-machine,—do all these things, and many more equally hard, from Monday morning till Saturday night every week in the year; may wear their lives out toiling for their children, and doing the work for their families that their husbands ought to do, and nobody raises the arm of opposition; but just now, because there is a possibility and even probability that in matters of education women will be as honorably treated as men, lo! Dr. Clarke comes forth and tells us it ought not to be so, because, forsooth, the periodical tides and reproductive apparatus of her organization will be ignored!

If there are any spheres of labor or of action that have with earnest solicitude more carefully and faithfully looked after the health of the girls and women who every day repair within their walls than have many of our seminaries of learning, we have yet to learn the fact.

So long as men are willing that women should do all or any of the things herein specified, beside the thousand and one things to which we have no space to allude; so long as men are willing she should enter marriage, a regimen which imposes more duties, responsibilities, trials, burdens, cares, and sorrows than any other can, which taxes health, strength, blood, and nerve infinitely more than any thing else she can ever do; so long as they are willing that she should endure the wear and tear of wifehood and motherhood, the severest and most trying ordeals through which human beings are ever called to pass, and, in comparison to the burdens which it inflicts upon her physical organization, all others are of a straw's weight; so long as men are willing that woman should act, work, labor, earn her living in these various capacities, not one of which gives her more opportunity to favor herself than it gives man, is it not insulting for a physician to single out one individual phase of action, and declare that it is a sin for woman to share equally with man in the advantages it affords, because it don't pay so much attention to the subject of catamenia as he things it ought?

Will Dr. Clarke please tell us why colleges, or places of learning of any kind, should be denied to woman on the ground that an insufficient amount of deference is given to her physiological nature, any more than other institutions which overlook it entirely?

106

FRANCES EMILY WHITE, M.D.
Woman's Place in Nature (1875)

. . . How does she differ from man, and to what extent do these differences modify or determine her place in life? In other words, how does that differentiation of the human germ which we designate as feminine, influence the organism as a whole? Will these questions admit of complete solution? Probably not; no great question has ever yet been fully answered—and, although the human organism may be divided, for purposes of study, into numerous sets of apparatus, each having a definite office in the general economy— as the digestive apparatus, the reproductive, the intellectual, etc.—the correlation of all the forces and functions of the body is so intimate and subtle that true philosophy makes no attempt to measure the exact and separate influ-

From *Popular Science Monthly* 6 (January 1875).

ence of any one force or function upon the rest, or upon the organism as a whole. Hence, to estimate the influence of sex in any given organism is impossible upon general principles, and evidently so in the case under consideration, from the fact that there is no standard of comparison. To assume man as the standard would be obviously absurd, for he is as distinctively differentiated as is woman, and it is impossible for a scientific imagination to conceive of a common type of the human species excluding the idea of sex; the attempt would demonstrate the impossibility of separating the mental conception of its two phases—just as it would be impossible to conceive of a magnetic needle without polarity. . . . Recognizing the difficulties which beset this investigation, then, the most that can be hoped for is the attainment of some broader and deeper truth than appears on the surface of the present disturbances in the social world; the only legitimate inquiry seems to be in regard to the influences and conditions which have resulted in the woman of to-day; and the practical questions related to it: Is there a tendency toward any important change in these influences and conditions, and, if so, in what direction? From what has gone before, my readers will have already inferred that the study of this subject will unavoidably include that of its natural complement, and that, should we succeed in obtaining answer to these questions, others of equal interest will find solution.

While the distinction of sex has for its manifest object the continuation of the race, that it is of deeper significance than this—that it has important bearings upon race-development as well as race-preservation—is indicated by a mass of evidence of so great weight as to carry with it the force of a demonstration. In Darwin's "Descent of Man" we have an accumulation of statements of facts gathered from vast fields of observation by many of the foremost naturalists of the age; and his deductive interpretations of these facts seem to have been accepted by a majority of the leading naturalists and physicists of the day. Such being the case, we are warranted in making this work the basis of our inquiry, thus looking at the subject from the side of natural history. Should some additional deductions and interpretations be brought out, it is hoped that they will not be found either forced or imaginary.

In order to a clear understanding of the line of reasoning employed, we must distinguish between the terms "natural selection" and "sexual selection," as used by Darwin. The traits resulting from these two processes are under a different law of heredity—those arising through natural selection being transmitted alike to the young of both sexes, while the results of sexual selection are inherited mainly by the adults of the corresponding sex. It will be seen that these are important laws, and that they furnish a key to our inquiry into the conditions and influences which have resulted in the woman of to-day. Under the operation of this second law (quoting from the "Descent of Man"), "it is the male which, with rare exceptions, has been chiefly modified—the female remaining more like the young of her own species, and more like the other members of the same group. . . .

Following Darwin's argument—"the greater eagerness of the male has thus indirectly led to the more frequent development of secondary sexual characters in the male than in the female"—secondary sexual characters being those not directly concerned in reproduction. Among these are the greater size, strength, courage, and pugnacity of the male, which most naturalists admit to have been acquired or modified by sexual selection—not depending on any superiority in the general struggle for life, but on certain individuals of one sex, generally the male, having been successful in conquering other males, and thus having left a larger number of offspring to inherit their superiority.

In the human species, the differences between the sexes are marked. The greater size and strength of man are apparent. His broader shoulders, more powerful muscles, greater physical courage and pugnacity, may be plainly claimed, by Darwin and his adherents, as man's inheritance from a long line of ancestry, of which the vanishing-point is in the remote past, among the lowest forms of life.

Whether or not this relationship be accepted, the same principles which have prevailed among lower animals must have been operative in the progress and development of the human race.

During the long ages when man was in a condition of barbarism, it must have been the strongest and boldest hunters and warriors who would succeed best in the struggle for existence, thus improving the race through the operation of natural selection, and the survival of the fittest; while the stronger passions accompanying these traits would lead to their success in securing the wives of their choice.

They would necessarily, by means of the same advantages, leave a more numerous progeny than their less successful rivals. It is here that the laws of sexual selection and heredity come in to maintain and increase the differences between the sexes. Who can doubt that a difference in mental characteristics would result from such causes? The greater necessity for exertion on the part of men would inevitably result in the development of more robust intellects. "Mere bodily size and strength would do little for victory unless associated with courage, perseverance, and determined energy." . . .

Let us now glance at the converse of these vivid pictures of the advantages accruing to man through habits and conditions rising from primary sexual characters, and endeavor to learn whether the habits and conditions necessarily attaching to the female have been the source of any gain either to herself or to the race as a whole.

The less degree of hardship and exposure to which she has been subjected have doubtless tended to develop in her the physical beauty in which she is generally acknowledged to be man's superior, while the fact that women have long been selected and prized for their beauty will have tended, on the principle of sexual selection, to increase the differences originally acquired through natural selection.

. . . Woman, unable to obtain an influence by those means so readily at the command of man, will have naturally resorted to milder measures, both for securing any desired object, and in self-defense; and music, appealing as it does to the gentler and more tender emotions, will have been often employed in arousing the better nature of him at whose mercy her inferior strength has placed her. Thus she will have held the ruder passions of man in check, and, in taming his wilder nature, will have developed an increasing gentleness both of feelings and of manners in the entire race.

During the battles of rival males, the female will have occupied the less active but more dignified position of arbiter and judge. Not being in the heat of the conflict, she will have had opportunity to observe the strategy of each, and to weigh their comparative merits. By this exercise of the faculties of observation, comparison, judgment, and reason, her intellectual powers will have been "continually put to the test and selected during" womanhood. Unfairness in the conduct of the battle will doubtless have roused her indignation, and compelled her better feelings in favor of the more honorable combatant. Sympathy for the vanquished will sometimes have taken the place of exultation in the superior prowess of the victor, and admiration for mere muscular power will have had to contend with these finer emotions.

While man has been engaged in contests with the common enemy, during which his fiercest passions will have been aroused, woman has been subjected to the discipline of family life. To meet emergencies successfully, to provide for the sick, to maintain order and discipline in the household, which, at an early period in human history, included slaves as well as children, will have required mental powers of a high order. At the same time she will have developed a milder character through the exercise of the beneficent traits of maternal love, and solicitude for the absent husband and father. These feelings of tenderness and love will have gradually prepared the way for the development of the devotional sentiment, and will have thus furnished a basis for the deeper religious nature which has become a part of woman's birthright. . . .

Thus it appears that while sexual selection and intellectual development have gone hand-in-hand, it is no less true that the moral and emotional sides of human nature have been developed by the operation of the same laws mainly through the female portion of the race. . . .

But, if I have read their teachings aright, neither man nor woman can justly take any individual pride, the one in his intellectual, the other in her moral superiority; rather they must see themselves as "Parts and proportions of a wondrous whole;" as the accompanying movements which make up the harmony of the grand diapason of the human race.

And there is that just adaptation of the different parts which is essential to and constitutes harmony. Bacon says that the causes of harmony are equality and correspondence; and Pope completes our argument with the line—"All discord, harmony not understood." There can be, then, no real conflict of interests between man and woman, since there is a mutual dependence of each upon the other, bringing mutual good. Neither can it be a misfortune to be a woman, as so many at the present day would have us believe, although her position may be in some respects subordinate to that of man.

In fact, the subordination of man to woman, different in kind from its converse, is equally apparent; both seem to be matters of common consciousness. It may be readily seen how, in early times, when muscular strength and general physical power were held in the highest esteem, that the position of woman should have been a subordinate one. Animal courage, endurance of physical hardships, the strength, cunning, and agility, which enabled men to cope with wild beasts and with each other, were the traits of character most prized, because most conservative of life in those barbarous times; hence the idea that, woman's position is naturally a subordinate one, has acquired the force of a primal intuition, and might almost be claimed as a "datum of consciousness." But, as the necessities of existence have been gradually modified by civilization, both the character and degree of her subordination have notably changed.

Those qualities, regarded as preëminently feminine, have risen in common estimation, and mere muscular superiority, and even intellectual power, are now put to the test of comparison with the higher moral qualities.

It is true that the laws of most countries still discriminate in a manner unfavorable to women. Legislation has been largely upon the ideal basis of every woman being under the protection of some man, and of all men being the true defenders of all women, and this is evidently traceable to the conviction, already alluded to, that a subordinate position belongs naturally to woman. Lecky says that "the change from the ideal of paganism to the ideal of Christianity was a change from a type which was essentially male to a type which was essentially feminine." As the race shall continue to approach the level of its lofty ideal, the subordination of woman, as well as that of man, will continue to lessen, since both have their chief foundation in the lower traits of character, the force in the one case being superior strength combined with power of will, and, in the other, superior beauty with the desire to fascinate. As these influences are gradually losing their power of despotic sway, woman, in place of acting as the slave, the toy, or the tyrant of man, is becoming not only his companion, but the custodian of the moral and religious interests of society, man looking at her as the natural critic and judge of the moral aspects of his conduct.

While the varying characteristics of the two sexes are thus seen to be inherent and inevitable (the secondary sexual characters having largely grown out of those which are primary and essential), it does not follow that they are necessarily indicative of the "sphere" of each for all time. While it is doubtless true, in a certain sense, that "that which has been is that which shall be," nevertheless, change (in accordance with law) underlies the very idea of evolution,

and as it has been and is now, so it ever shall be, that the sphere of woman will be determined by the kind and degree of development to which she shall attain. Like man, she need know no other limitation; but when we look around upon the great industries of life, mining, engineering, manufacturing, commerce, and the rest, and consider how little direct agency woman has had in bringing them to their present state of progress, we are compelled to believe that she must not look toward direct competition with man for the best unfolding of her powers, but rather, while continuing to supplement him, as he does her, in the varied interests of their common life, that her future progress, as in the past, will consist mainly in the development of a higher character of womanhood through the selection and consequent intention of those traits peculiar to her own sex.

107

MYRA BRADWELL
The XIV Amendment and Our Case (1873)

We have heretofore published a telegraphic report of the opinion of a majority of the Judges of the Supreme Court of the United States, delivered by MILLER, J., affirming the judgment of the Supreme Court of Illinois, refusing to grant us a license to practice law, upon the sole ground that we were a woman. We have since received an official copy of the opinion of the court, also the opinion of BRADLEY, J., concurred in by FIELD, J., and an official notification that the late lamented CHIEF JUSTICE CHASE, for whose opinion we always had the greatest respect, dissented entirely from the opinion of the court. These opinions will be found elsewhere in this issue. Although we do not believe the construction of the XIV amendment, as given by a majority of the court, and their definition of the

From *Chicago Legal News*, May 10, 1873.

privileges and immunities of citizens of the United States are sound, we take great pleasure in saying that the opinion delivered by JUDGE MILLER is confined strictly to the points at issue, and is just such an one as might be expected from an able and experienced jurist entertaining the views that JUDGE MILLER does upon these constitutional questions. He does not for a moment lower the dignity of the judge by traveling out of the record to give his individual views upon what we commonly term "*Woman's Rights.*"

We regard the opinion of JUDGE BRADLEY as in conflict with his opinion delivered in what are known as the New Orleans Slaughter-house Cases, reported 3 CHICAGO LEGAL NEWS, 17. In that case JUDGE BRADLEY said: "*There is no more sacred right of citizenship than the right to pursue unmolested a lawful employment in a lawful manner. It is nothing more or less than the sacred right of labor.*" In speaking of pursuits that required the granting of licenses, the judge said: "Public policy may require that these pursuits should be regulated and supervised by the local authorities in order to promote the public health, the public order and the general well being, but they are open to all proper applicants, and none are *rejected except those who fail to exhibit the requisite qualifications.*" * * * "All these systems of regulation are useful and entirely competent to the governing power, and are not at all inconsistent with the great rights of LIBERTY OF PURSUIT, which is one of the *fundamental* privileges of an American citizen." If, as JUDGE BRADLEY says, the *liberty of pursuit* is one of the fundamental privileges of an American citizen, how can he then, and be consistent, deprive an American citizen of the right to follow any calling or profession under laws, rules and regulations that shall operate equally upon all, simply because such citizen is a woman?

108

BELVA A. LOCKWOOD
My Efforts to Become A Lawyer
(1888)

From a child, the bent of my mind has been one of extreme practicality. That knowledge only has been prized which I could immediately turn to account in every-day life, and in the pursuit of such knowledge I have been undaunted by conventions. I have never been able to enter into the prejudices of the centuries past, that have had no foundation in reason, in nature, or in nature's laws, nor to discover that the limitations of woman's sphere as heretofore dictated by the customs of society were worthy of serious consideration. My only thought was to do those things which in the nature of human affairs seemed the things to be done, and to do them in the best and most expeditious manner. Hence I was not careful as to the nature of my work, so that it was means to an end, and never for a moment stopped to consider whether the labor was such as women were accustomed to do, but only whether I had the ability to perform it.

. . . In February, 1866, I sold out my school property in Owego, and came to Washington, for no other purpose than to see what was being done at this great political centre,—this seething pot,—to learn something of the practical workings of the machinery of government, and to see what the great men and women of the country felt and thought. As I came without any great amount of money in my purse, with no claim to being a public benefactor, with no vote on any important question, and was not a newspaper scribe, I had no pass on the railroad, no free board at the hotels, and hardly a passport into aristocratic society (if such distinction is known to Washington life), and therefore soon found that some exertion would be necessary to sustain myself while I was making my proposed investigations. To this end I accepted a

From *Lippincott's Monthly Magazine*, February 1888.

position in a young ladies' school with barely enough salary for my maintenance, but with all the time after one o'clock P.M. to myself. This was satisfactory, as it gave me ample time for investigation; and during the five months that I spent in this school I listened to the debates in Congress and the arguments in the United States Supreme Court, investigated the local government of the District, visited her public buildings, studied her historic reminiscences, her works of art, and finally the geology and geography of the surrounding country.

In my college course I had studied and had become deeply interested in the Constitution of the United States, the law of nations, political economy, and other things that had given me an insight into political life. I had early conceived a passion for reading the biographies of great men, and had discovered that in almost every instance law has been the stepping-stone to greatness. Born a woman, with all of a woman's feelings and intuitions, I had all of the ambitions of a man, forgetting the gulf between the rights and privileges of the sexes. In my efforts to discover new avenues of labor I met with some ludicrous and some serious experiences,—many of which were known only to myself. Andrew Johnson was at this time President of the republic, and William H. Seward Secretary of State. There was a vacancy in the consulship at Ghent. Conceiving that I could fill this position, I had the audacity to make application for it. Preparatory to a prospective appointment, I reviewed my German, read all the authors that I could find on International Law in the United States Supreme Court Library, and procuring through my member of Congress a copy of the Consular Manual, made myself quite familiar with its contents, so that I fully believed that I was competent to perform the service required of a consular officer, never once stopping to consider whether the nation to which I should be accredited would receive a woman.

To my disappointment and chagrin, no notice was ever taken of my application, and I was too weak-kneed to renew it. The fact that An-

drew Johnson soon afterwards became involved in many complications with Congress, which ended in his impeachment by that body, may account in a measure for the lack of interest taken by him and by the public at large in my humble aspirations.

. . . All my leisure hours were employed in study. And now, possessing myself of an old copy of the Four Books of Blackstone's Commentaries, I gave myself daily tasks until I had read and re-read them through. In the midst of these labors I committed the indiscretion so common to the women of this country, and, after fifteen years and more of widowhood, married the Rev. Ezekiel Lockwood, on the 11th of March, 1868.

But this marriage did not cure my mania for the law. The school was given up, and during the following year I read Kent's Commentaries, occupying all the spare moments in the midst of my domestic work. In the autumn of 1869, on the opening of the Columbian College Law Class, I attended with my husband, by invitation of its President, Dr. Samson, the opening lecture of the course, delivered by him. I almost went to the second lecture, and before the third presented myself for matriculation in the class and offered to pay the entrance-fee. This was refused, and I was thereupon informed that the question of my admission would be submitted to the faculty. One week, two weeks, elapsed, when one day I received a letter running thus:

"COLUMBIAN COLLEGE, Oct. 7, 1869.
"MRS. BELVA A. LOCKWOOD:

"MADAM,—The Faculty of Columbian College have considered your request to be admitted to the Law Department of this institution, and, after due consultation, have considered that such admission would not be expedient, as it would be likely to distract the attention of the young men.

"Respectfully,
"GEO. W. SAMSON, *Pres.*"

I was much chagrined by this slap in the face, and the inference to be drawn from it, that my rights and privileges were not to be considered a moment whenever they came in conflict with those of the opposite sex. My husband counselled that I should keep silence about it, as his relations with Dr. Samson, as ministers and co-laborers in the same church, had hitherto been friendly. But the truth would out. The newspaper men got hold of it, as newspaper men will, and came to me and demanded to see the letter, declaring that the action of Dr. Samson was a matter of public interest. My husband protested; but I read them the letter, retaining the original, which I still have.

Next year the National University Law School was opened, and, ostensibly as a part of its plan to admit women to membership on the same terms as young men, I was invited, with other ladies, to attend the classes, and gladly accepted. At this first session, fifteen ladies matriculated, partly as a novelty, I suppose, but certainly without any adequate idea of the amount of labor involved. Many of them left with the close of the first quarter; but some continued through the year, and a few of them held on until the middle of the second year. Only two persons, Lydia S. Hall and myself, completed the course. At first, besides the regular class-recitations, we were admitted to the lectures with the young men, although the recitations had been separate. This was a compromise between prejudice and progress. It was not long before there commenced to be a growl by the young men, some of them declaring openly that they would not graduate with women. The women were notified that they could no longer attend the lectures, but would be permitted to complete the course of studies. As Commencement day approached, it became very evident that we were not to receive our diplomas, nor be permitted to appear on the stage with the young men at graduation. This was a heavy blow to my aspirations, as the diploma would have been the entering wedge into the court and saved me the weary contest which followed.

For a time I yielded quite ungracefully to the inevitable, while Lydia S. Hall solaced herself by marrying a man named Graffan and leaving the city. She was not a young woman at that time, but a staid matron, past forty; and after her departure I entirely lost sight of her, and suppose she became "merged," as Blackstone says, in her husband. I was not to be squelched so easily.

. . . I now [got] a little bolder, and to a certain extent desperate, and addressed the following letter to President Grant, then President *ex officio* of the National University Law School:

"No. 432 Ninth Street. N.W.,
"Washington, D.C., September 3, 1873.
"To His Excellency U. S. Grant, *President U.S.A.*:
    "Sir,—You are, or you are not, President of the National University Law School. If you are its President, I desire to say to you that I have passed through the curriculum of study in this school, and am entitled to, and *demand,* my diploma. If you are not its President, then I ask that you take your name from its papers, and not hold out to the world to be what you are not.
    "Very respectfully,
    "Belva A. Lockwood."

This letter contained about as much bottled-up indignation as it was possible for one short missive to conceal under a respectful guise. I received no direct answer, but next week I was presented by the Chancellor of the University, W. B. Wedgewood, with my diploma duly signed, and a few days after I was admitted to the bar.

On my admission, the clerk remarked, "You went through to-day, Mrs. Lockwood, like a knife. You see the world moves in our day." Justice Cartter said, "Madam, if you come into this court we shall treat you like a man." Justice Arthur McArthur remarked, "Bring on as many women lawyers as you choose: I do not believe they will be a success." These comments did not affect me, as I already had my hands full of work,

and cases ready to file in anticipation of my admission. My friends had confidence in my ability; and the attention that had been called to me
in the novel contest I had made not only gave
me a wide advertising, but drew towards me a
great deal of substantial sympathy in the way of
work. Besides this, I had already booked a large
number of government claims, in which I had
been recognized by the heads of the different
Departments as attorney: so that I was not compelled, like my young brothers of the bar who
did not wish to graduate with a woman, to sit in
my office and wait for cases. I have been now
fourteen years before the bar, in an almost con-
tinuous practice, and my experience has been
large, often serious, and many times amusing. I
have never lacked plenty of good paying work;
but, while I have supported may family well, I
have not grown rich. In business I have been
patient, painstaking, and indefatigable. There is
no class of case that comes before the court that
I have not ventured to try, either civil, equitable,
or criminal; and my clients have been as largely
men as women. There is a good opening at the
bar for the class of women who have taste and
tact for it.

But neither my ambitions nor my troubles
ceased with my admission to the District bar.
On or about the 1st of April, 1874, having an
important case to file in the Court of Claims, I
asked one A. A. Hosmer, a reputable member
of the bar of that court, to move my admission
thereto, having previously filed with the clerk
my power of attorney in the case, and a certificate from the clerk of the District Court of my
good standing therein, as required by the rule
of that court.

At precisely twelve o'clock the five justices
of that dignified court marched in, made their
solemn bows, and sat down. Without ceremony,
after the formal opening of the court by the
clerk, and the reading of the minutes of the last
session, my gracious attorney moved my admission. There was a painful pause. Every eye in the
court-room was fixed first upon me, and then
upon the court; when Justice Drake, in mea-

sured words, announced, "*Mistress Lockwood, you
are a woman.*" For the first time in my life I began
to realize that it was a crime to be a woman; but
it was too late to put in a denial, and I at once
pleaded guilty to the charge of the court. Then
the chief justice announced, "This case will be
continued for one week." I retired in good order, but my counsel, who had only been employed for that occasion, deserted me, and
seemed never afterwards to have backbone
enough to keep up the fight.

On the following week, duly as the hand of
the clock approached the hour of twelve, I again
marched into the court-room, but this time almost with as much solemnity as the judges, and
accompanied by my husband and several friends.
When the case of Lockwood was reached, and I
again stood up before that august body, the solemn tones of the chief justice announced, "Mistress Lockwood, you are a *married woman!*" Here
was a new and quite unexpected arraignment,
that almost took my breath away for the moment; but I collected myself, and responded,
with a wave of my hand towards my husband,
"Yes, may it please the court, but I am here with
the consent of my husband," Dr. Lockwood at
the same time bowing to the court. My pleading and distressed look was of no avail. The solemn chief justice responded, "This cause will be
continued for another week."

Seeing that a fierce contest was imminent,
I forthwith employed a member of this bar, one
Charles W. Horner, to appear and plead my
cause. He was a man who loved justice, and who
feared neither the court nor conservatism. He
prepared an able argument, presented it to the
court on the following Monday, and, after patient attention, was allowed to file the same with
the clerk, while the cause of "Lockwood" was
continued for one more week. Next Monday,
Judge Peck, who had been sitting in the cause,
had died and of course there was an adjourn-
ment for another week. Upon the convening of
the court at this time the cause was given to
Judge Nott to deliver the opinion of the court;
and three weeks were devoted to this work. I

had time to reflect, to study up on my law, to ponder upon the vast disparity between the sexes, and, if I had possessed any nice discrimination, to see the utter folly of my course. But I would not be convinced.

Three weeks later, I was again present on the solemn assembling of that court. It took Judge Nott one hour and a half to deliver his opinion, which closed as follows:

"The position which this court assumes is that under the laws and Constitution of the United States a court is without power to grant such an application, and that a woman is without legal capacity to take the office of attorney."

Of course this was a squelcher, and with the ordinary female mind would have ended the matter; for it was concurred in without a dissenting voice by the four other judges on that august bench.

. . . At last, in October, 1876, full of hope and expectation, and in company with the Hon. A. G. Riddle, whom I had asked to introduce me, I presented myself before the bar of the United States Supreme Court for admission thereto. Again I had reckoned without my host. My attorney made the presentation, holding my credentials in his hand. Those nine gowned judges looked at me in amazement and dismay. The case was taken under advisement, and on the following Monday an opinion rendered, of which the following is the substance: *"As this court knows no English precedent for the admission of women to the bar, it declines to admit, unless there shall be a more extended public opinion, or special legislation.*"* No pen can portray the utter astonishment and surprise with which I listened to this decision. My reverence for the ermine vanished into thin air. I was dazed, and kept repeating to myself, "No English precedent! How about Queens Eleanor and Elizabeth, who sat in the *aula regia* and dispensed the duties of chief chancellor of the English realm in person? How about Anne,

* Justice Miller dissented from this opinion, and the chief justice himself, but if his decision was ever reduced to writing, he never allowed it to be printed. It was in vain that I sought a copy of it from the clerk.

Countess of Pembroke, who was hereditary sheriff of Westmoreland, and who at the assizes at Appleby sat with the judges on the bench?" "A more extended public opinion,"—how was I to make it? "Special legislation,"—how was I to obtain it, with a family to support, and a sick husband on my hands? I went home, and again took up the thread of my law cases before the district bar, but determined not to let this matter rest.

What next? When Congress assembled in December, I appealed to the Hon. Benjamin F. Butler to draft and introduce in that body a bill for the admission of women to the bar of the United States Supreme Court. This was my first bid for the *special legislation*. The bill was carefully drawn, introduced, recommended by the House Judiciary for passage, debated, and ingloriously lost on its third reading.

. . . I prepared and asked the Hon. John M. Glover to introduce into the House of Representatives, in December, 1877, the following bill:

"Be it enacted by the Senate and House of Representatives of the United States of America in Congress assembled:

"That any woman duly qualified who shall have been a member of the highest court of any State or Territory, or of the Supreme Court of the District of Columbia, for the space of three years, and shall have maintained a good standing before such Court, and who shall be a person of good moral character, shall, on motion, and the production of such record, be admitted to practise before the Supreme Court of the United States."

I was soon called to make an argument before the House Committee on the Judiciary, after which the bill was favorably reported without a dissenting voice, and passed the House early in the session by a two-thirds majority.

On reaching the Senate, it was referred to the Senate Judiciary and committed to the Hon. Aaron A. Sargent, of California. Conceiving that the bill as it passed the House was not broad enough, he amended it, but his amendment was lost, and the Judiciary Committee made an adverse report on the bill. I had done a great deal of lobbying and had used a great many arguments to get the bill through, but all to no avail; With consummate tact, Mr. Sargent had the bill recommitted, but it went over to the next session. I worked diligently through the second session of the Forty-fifth Congress for the passage of my bill, but the Judiciary Committee made a second adverse report on the bill, and this time Mr. Sargent had the forethought to have the bill calendared, so that it might come up on its merits.

But another misfortune overtook me: Mr. Sargent was taken ill before my bill was reached, and compelled to go to Florida for his health. What was I to do now? Here was my work for years about to be wrecked for want of a foster-mother in the Senate to take charge of it. I knew pretty well the status of every member of that body, for I had conversed with all of them, both at this and at the previous session; and in this extremity I went to the Hon. Joseph E. McDonald, of Indiana, and besought him to take charge of the bill. At first he declined, because, as he said, it was Mr. Sargent's bill, and when I insisted, he bade me go to the Hon. George F. Hoar. I found that gentleman somewhat unwilling to take the entire responsibility of the bill. I was not satisfied to leave anything that I ought to do undone, and so returned to Mr. McDonald, told him that I feared Mr. Sargent's health was such that he would not return in time, and besought him to take upon himself the responsibility of urging and securing the passage of the bill, saying that Senator Hoar would assist him, and Senator Sargent also, when he returned. From the time he assumed this responsibility Senator McDonald was vigilant in the interest of the bill, and as the Forty-fifth Congress drew to a close, used what influence he could to get the bill up. It was in a precarious position. A single objection would carry it over. When it was about to be reached, I grew anxious, almost desperate,—called out everybody who was opposed to the bill, and begged that it might be permitted to come up on its merits, and that a fair vote might be had on it in the Senate.

I have been interested in many bills in Congress, and have often appeared before committees of Senate and House but this was by far the strongest lobbying that I ever performed. Nothing was too daring for me to attempt. I addressed Senators as though they were old familiar friends, and with an earnestness that carried with it conviction. Before the shadows of night had gathered, the victory had been won. The bill admitting women to the bar of the United States Supreme Court passed the Senate on the 7th of February 1879. It was signed by the President, Rutherford B. Hayes, some days later.

On the 3d of March, 1879, on motion of the Hon. A. G. Riddle, I was admitted to the bar of the United States Supreme Court. The passage of that bill virtually opened the doors of all the Federal courts in the country to the women of the land, whenever qualified for such admission. I was readily admitted to the District Courts of Maryland and Massachusetts after this admission to the Supreme Court.

On the 6th of March, 1879, on motion of the Hon. Thomas J. Durant, I was admitted to the bar of the United States Court of Claims. Thus ended the great struggle for the admission of woman to the bar. Most of the States in the Union have since recognized her right thereto, and notably the State of Pennsylvania, as in the case of Carrie B. Kilgore, who has recently been admitted to the Supreme Court of the State.

Belva A. Lockwood.

109
GERTRUDE STUART BAILLIE
Should Professional Women Marry? (1894)

Among the various women's clubs no question has been so often asked, so much discussed, as

From *Woman's Medical Journal* 2 (February 1894).

that of marriage of those women who go to make up the great professional and business world. It has been discussed by men in every station of life from the minister, to the lawyer, doctor, philanthropist, moralist and novelist, the conservative and the radical, yet the most pronounced positivist among them dare not answer emphatically in either the negative or affirmative.

It is said by some, that the higher education of women, though they consider it an excellent and praiseworthy movement, has resulted in training them for functions which belong exclusively to the sterner sex, and that during this process they gradually become more or less womanly and lose those charms of person and sentimentality which are supposed to be the birthright of every woman. Not only this, but her higher development mentally, is purchased at the cost of her physical deterioration, inasmuch as her sexuality is enfeebled or destroyed, and sexuality, Dr. Edson and Mr. Grant Allen informs us, is the base of everything.

Now, in the absence of what the physiologists term a natural desire for the propagation of the species, the Positivists claim it is almost criminal for women to marry. Firstly, because if she has adopted any profession and is in consonance with it, each day finds her more engrossed in her work, with less time and thought to give to her husband and his welfare. Secondly, she lives in absolute abhorrence lest she may be called upon to perform the duties of motherhood and for which she is so ill-fitted. Thus, a marriage with a woman who has risen above the animal, is to the Positivist's mind, anything but a consummation.

. . . The purport of this paper is rather to show that women in professional or business life have no claim to "recklessness," apparent or real, but on the other hand, possess the same natural instincts as their mothers before them, with the exception, that their liberal education has stored their minds with the fundamental truths of nature. They are not stunted ascetics by any means, but they have learned to make their bodies subservient to their wills.

The reasons for professional women preferring to remain single, are many and obvious, and are not always due, as the critics would have us believe, to a lack of physical impulse.

Of course, no one who has kept apace with the latter half of this nineteenth century, will attempt to deny, that a momentuous revolution is taking place in all the so-called spheres of women. Progression has largely destroyed the domestic character of former times, consequently, the old idea, that every woman should be a wife, is disappearing as rapidly as those customs which heretofore deprived them of the same pecuniary and educational advantages of men.

The professional women themselves, are, after all, in the best position to reply to the query in question, seventy percent of whom agree that a negative answer is the only true one.

Parenthetically, the above is doubtless too sweeping an assertion, as the writer happens to be acquainted with several women engaged in active work, professional and otherwise, who lead an ideal married life. "But why," asks the skeptic, "Do those women who have achieved eminence and renown invariably remain single?" Because, as Rosa Bonheir has wisely said, "No woman can serve two masters." A woman of lofty ambitions, high ideals, endowed with great talent and capacity, is sure, sooner or later, to become a small power in her way. She may be artist, novelist, physician, anything, but she begins by courting her profession and ends in being wedded to it. Should she marry, she would be none the less an artist, but she would be surrounded by numerous other cares, which as must eventually come to every married woman, and either her work or her family will feel the neglect. The nightingales sing sweetest before they are mated, after that, their songs cease, for their mirth has turned into solicitude for their little ones.

Mrs. E. D. E. N. Southworth recently admitted, she never could have accomplished so much in literature, had she not been left a widow in early life.

Two of America's most famous women novelists have refused many offers of marriage, not because they advocated asceticism, but for the best of reasons, viz.: they could not conscientiously give their hand where their heart was not, for their heart was given to their work.

One of the most successful physicians in this country, whose contributions to medical journalism are read with avidity by the medical profession abroad, as well as at home, asserts that women physicians, least of all, should hesitate to enter the matrimonial state. She, whose office it is to launch upon the sea of life frail nameless barks, who has learned to soothe the cradle of reposing age, to heal the sick and combat dread pestilence, she least of all, cannot work well under the yoke of matrimony. She lives by and for the people and hence must ever be in readiness to answer their summons, which, should she be married, it might not always be propitious to do. Whether the advice of the physician referred to, has been followed, I am not prepared to say, but statistics show, that there are fewer marriages among women in medicine, than any other profession.

Another reason why women who are in daily contact with the world and its ways hesitate before they exchange their freedom for a wedding ring, is, that they have learned self-control and gained a balance which is of inestimable value to them in dealing with the practical affairs of life. They are no longer compelled to sacrifice themselves to their own emotions. Again, they are convinced of their ability to take care of themselves, and they have heard how men—husbands of friends—do not always "come to time" in the role of provider. Thus, is it to be wondered at, that they prefer celibacy, with the title of "old maid," rather than to fly to matrimonial evils they know not of!

There are so many channels open, through which women can influence the race, and while generous recognition is given to the power, importance and nobility of purpose of the married women, this is not her only field.

In one of his tirades against women and higher education, Mr. Grant Allen alludes in a very caustic manner to the self-supporting spin-

ster, usually a school teacher, whom he terms "a deplorable accident of the passing moment." And what, pray, would become of the school system of either this country or England, if it were not for these very "accidents," whose self-sacrifice, patient endurance, and especial fitness for the great responsibilities put upon them, to teach them how to lead and direct the young ideas of both nations? How many more children owe their success in life, rather to their school than home training!

To recapitulate, some of the formidable causes that are responsible for the celibacy of professional women, "We find," they say, "that intellectually, we are the equals of the majority of men whom we meet. That as we are able to support ourselves comfortably, and have a keen appreciation of freedom of *being,* as well as *seeming,* we have no desire to reject our newly-found liberty for what would handicap and hamper us in our individual vocations."

Women, to-day, occupy an important position in human development. That they stand upon a morally higher level than men, modern sociology has long conceded, and herein lies another stern fact that repels the educated woman contemplating marriage.

Until men reach the same plane of morality, have the same worthy aspirations, and thereby bridge the chasm that stands between them and women who are a distinct product of the best evolutionary forces, they should raise no dissenting voice if women are less interested in them as possible lovers.

There has been no attempt made to discuss this question of marriage for professional women with a fullness adequate to its importance. In matters of this type it is hard to write with clearness and impartiality. Then, too, the query is one that every woman will answer according to her own dictates of heart or mind, and the complexity of the whole problem depends altogether upon the environment.

110

Alice Freeman Palmer
A Review of the Higher Education of Women (1892)

. . . The advanced education of young women is exposed to all the uncertainties which beset the education of men, but it has perplexities of its own in addition. After fifty years of argument and twenty-five of varied and costly experiment, it might be easy to suppose that we were still in chaos, almost as far from knowing the best way to train a woman as we were at the beginning. No educational convention meets without a session devoted to the difficulties in "the higher education of women"; so important has the subject become, and so hard is it to satisfy in any one system the variety of its needs. Yet chaos may be thought more chaotic than it really is. In the din of discussion it would not be strange if the fair degree of concord already reached should sometimes be missed. We are certainly still far from having found the one best method of college training for girls. Some of us hope we may never find it, believing that in diversity, no less than in unity, there is strength. But already three tolerably clear, consistent, and accredited types of education appear which it will be the purpose of this paper to explain. The nature of each with its special strengths and weaknesses will be set forth in no spirit of partisanship, but in the belief that a cool understanding of what is doing at present among fifty thousand college girls may make us wiser and more patient in our future growth. What, then, are the three types, and how have they arisen? . . .

Co-education involves, as its name implies, the education of a company of young men and women as a single body. To the two sexes alike are presented the same conditions of admission, of opportunities during the course, of requirements for the degrees, of guardianship, of discipline, of organization. The typical features are

identical classrooms, libraries, and laboratories, occupied at the same time, under the same instructors; and the same honors for like work.

. . . In estimating the worth of such a system as this, we may say at once that it does not meet every need of a woman's nature. No system can, no system that has yet been derived. A woman is an object of attraction to men, and also in herself so delicately organized as to be fitted peculiarly for the graces and domesticities of life. The exercise of her special function of motherhood demands sheltered circumstances and refined moral perceptions. But then, over and above all this, she is a human being—a person, that is, who has her own way in the world to make, and who will come to success or failure, in her home or outside it, according as her judgment is fortified, her observations and experiences are enlarged, her courage is rendered strong and calm, her moral estimates are trained to be accurate, broad and swift. In a large tract of her character—is it the largest tract?—her own needs and those of the young man are identical. Both are rational persons, and the greater part of the young man's education is addressed to his rational personality, rather than to the peculiarities of his sex. Why, the defenders of co-education ask, may not the same principles apply to women? Why train a girl specifically to be a wife and mother when no great need is felt for training a boy to be a husband and father? In education, as a public matter, the two sexes meet on common ground. The differences must be attended to privately.

At any rate, whatever may be thought of the relative importance of the two sides—the woman side, and the human side—it will be generally agreed that the training of a young woman is apt to be peculiarly weak in agencies for bringing home to her the importance of direct and rational action. The artificialities of society, the enfeebling indulgence extended to pretty silliness, the gallantry of men glad ever to accept the hard things and leave to her the easy—by these influences any comfortably placed and pleasing girl is pretty sure to be surrounded in her early teens. The co-education-alists think it wholesome that in her latter teens and early twenties she should be subjected to an impartial judgment ready to estimate her without swerving and tell her as freely when she is silly, ignorant, fussy, or indolent as her brother himself is told. Co-education, as a system, must minimize the different needs of men and women; it appeals to them and provides for them alike, and then allows the natural tastes and instincts of each scope for individuality. The strengths of this system, accordingly, are to be found in its tendency to promote independence of judgment, individuality of tastes, common sense and foresight in self-guidance, disinclination to claim favor, interest in learning for its own sake; friendly, natural, unromantic, non-sentimental relations with men. The early fear that co-education would result in class-room romances has proved exaggerated. These young women do marry; so do others; so do young men. Marriage is not in itself an evil, and many happy homes have been founded in the belief that long and quiet acquaintance in intellectual work, and intimate interests of the same deeper sort, form as solid a basis for a successful marriage as ball-room intercourse or a summer at Bar Harbor.

The weaknesses of this system are merely the converse of its strengths. It does not usually provide for what is distinctively feminine. Refining home influences and social oversight are largely lacking; and if they are wanting in the home from which the student comes, it must not be expected that she will show, on graduation, the graces of manner, the niceties of speech and dress, and the shy delicacy, which has been encouraged in her more tenderly nurtured sister.

The woman's college is organized under a different and far more complex conception. The chief business of the man's college, whether girls are admitted to it or not, is to give instruction of the best available quality in as many subjects as possible; to furnish every needed appliance for the acquirement of knowledge and the encouragement of special investigation. The woman's college aims to do all this, but it aims, also, to make for its students a home within its own walls, and to develop other powers in them than the merely intellectual. . . . In short, the arrangements of the woman's college, as conceived by founders, trustees, and faculty, have usually aimed with conscious directness at building up character, inspiring to the service of others, cultivating manners, developing taste, and strengthening health, as well as providing the means of sound learning.

It may be said that a similar up-building of the personal life results from the training of every college that is worthy of the name; and fortunately it is impossible to enlarge knowledge without, to some extent, enlarging life. But the question is one of directness or indirectness of aim. The woman's college puts this aim in the foreground side by side with the acquisition of knowledge. By setting its students apart in homogeneous companies, it seeks to cultivate common ideals. Of its teaching force, a large number are women who live with the students in the college buildings, sit with them at table, join in their festivities, and in numberless intimate ways share and guide the common life. Every student, no matter how large the college, has friendly access at any time to several members of the faculty, quite apart from her relations with them in the class-room. In appointing these women to the faculty no board of trustees would consider it sufficient that a candidate was an accomplished specialist. She must be this, but she should be also a lady of unobjectionable manners and influential character; she should have amiability and a discreet temper, for she is to be a guiding force in a complex community, continually in the presence of her students, an officer of administration and government no less than of instruction. Harvard and Johns Hopkins can ask their pupils to attend the lectures of a great scholar, however brusque his bearing or unbrushed his hair. They will not question their geniuses too sharply, and will trust their students to look out for their own proprieties of dress, manners, and speech. But neither Wellesley nor any other woman's college could find a place in its faculty for a woman Sophocles or Sylvester. Learning alone is not enough for women. . . .

This detailed explanation of the peculiarities of the girls' college renders unnecessary any long discussion of its strengths and weaknesses. According to the point of view of the critic these peculiarities themselves will be counted means of invigoration or of enfeeblement. Living so close to one another as girls here do, the sympathetic and altruistic virtues acquire great prominence. Petty selfishness retreats or becomes extinct. An earnest, high-minded spirit is easily cultivated, and the break between college life and the life from which the student comes is reduced to a minimum.

It is this very fact which is often alleged as the chief objection to the girls' college. It is said that its students never escape from themselves and their domestic standard, that they do not readily acquire a scientific spirit, and become individual in taste and conduct. Is it desirable that they should? That I shall not undertake to decide. I have merely tried to explain the kinds of human work which the different types of higher training schools are best fitted to effect for women. . . .

The third type is the "annex," a recent and interesting experiment in the education of girls, whose future it is yet difficult to predict. Only a few cases exist, and as the Harvard Annex is the most conspicuous, by reason of its dozen years of age and nearly 200 students, I shall describe it as the typical example. In the Harvard Annex, groups of young women undertake courses of study in classes whose instruction is furnished entirely by members of the Harvard faculty. No college officer is obliged to give this instruction, and the Annex staff of teachers is, therefore, liable to considerable variation from year to year. Though the usual four classes appear in its curriculum, the large majority of its students devote themselves to special subjects. A wealthy girl turns from fashionable society to pursue a single course in history or economics; a hard-worked teacher draws inspiration during a few

afternoons each week from a famous Greek or Latin professor; a woman who has been long familiar with French literature explores with a learned specialist some single period in the history of the language. Because the opportunities for advanced and detached study are so tempting, many ladies living in the neighborhood of the Annex enter one or more of its courses. There are consequently among its students women much older than the average of those who attend the colleges.

The business arrangements are taken charge of by a committee of ladies and gentlemen, who provide class-rooms, suggest boarding-places, secure the instructors, solicit the interest of the public—in short, manage all the details of an independent institution; for the noteworthy feature of its relation to its powerful neighbor is this, that the two, while actively friendly, have no official or organic tie whatever. . . .

The Harvard Annex is, then, to-day a woman's college, with no degrees, no dormitories, no woman instructors, and with a staff of teachers made up from volunteers of another college.

. . . It is impossible to estimate either favorably or adversely the permanent worth of an undertaking still in its infancy. Manifestly, the opportunities for the very highest training are here superb if they happen to exist at all. In this, however, is the incalculable feature of the system. The Annex lives by favor, not by right, and it is impossible to predict what the extent of favor may at any time be. A girl hears that an admirable course of lectures has been given on a topic in which she is greatly interested. She arranges to join the Annex and enter the course, but learns in the summer vacation that through pressure of other work, the professor will be unable to teach in the Annex the following year. The fact that favor rules, and not rights, peculiarly hampers scientific and laboratory courses, and for its literary work obliges the Annex largely to depend on its own library. Yet when all these weaknesses are confessed—and by none are they confessed more frankly than by the wise and devoted managers of the Annex them-selves—it should be said that hitherto they have not practically hindered the formation of a spirit of scholarship, eager, free and sane to an extraor-dinary degree. The Annex girl succeeds in re-maining a private and unobserved gentlewoman, while still, in certain directions, pushing her studies to an advanced point seldom reached elsewhere. . . .

The preceding survey has shown how in co-education a woman's study is carried on inside a man's college, in the woman's college outside it, in the annex beside it. Each of these situa-tions has its advantage. But will the community be content to accept this; permanently to forego the counter advantages, and even after it fully realizes the powers and limitations of the differ-ent types, firmly to maintain them in their dis-tinctive vigor? Present indications render this improbable. Already co-educational colleges in-cline to more careful leadership for their girls. The separate colleges, with growing wealth, are learning to value intrepidity, and are carrying their operations close up to the lands of the Ph.D. The annex swings in its middle air, some-times inclining to the one side, sometimes to the other. And outside them all, the great body of men's colleges continually find it harder to maintain their isolation, and extend one privi-lege after another to the seeking sex.

The result of all these diversities is the most instructive body of experiment that the world has seen for determining the best ways of bring-ing woman to her powers. While the public mind is so uncertain, so liable to panic, and so doubt-ful, whether, after all, it is not better for a girl to be a goose, the many methods of education assist one another mightily in their united war-fare against ignorance, selfish privileges, and antiquated ideals. It is well that for a good while to come woman's higher education should be all things to all mothers if by any means it may save girls. Those who are hardy enough may con-tinue to mingle their girls with men; while a parent who would be shocked that her daugh-ter should do anything so ambiguous as to enter

a man's college may be persuaded to send her to a girl's. Those who find it easier to honor an old university than the eager life of a young col-lege, may be tempted into an annex. The im-portant thing is that the adherents of these differing types should not fall into jealousy, and belittle the value of those who are performing a work which they themselves cannot do so well. To understand one another kindly is the busi-ness of the hour—to understand and to wait.

111
ANNA JULIA COOPER
The Higher Education of Colored Women (1892)

. . . Only the BLACK WOMAN can say "when and where I enter, in the quiet, undisputed dignity of my womanhood, without violence and with-out suing or special patronage, then and there the whole *Negro race enters with me.*" Is it not evi-dent then that as individual workers for this race we must address ourselves with no half-hearted zeal to this feature of our mission. The need is felt and must be recognized by all. There is a call for workers, for missionaries, for men and women with the double consecration of a fun-damental love of humanity and a desire for its melioration through the Gospel; but superadded to this we demand an intelligent and sympathetic comprehension of the interests and special needs of the Negro.

. . . Mrs. Mary A. Livermore, a woman whom I can mention only to admire, came near shaking my faith a few weeks ago in my theory of the thinking woman's mission to put in the tender and sympathetic chord in nature's grand symphony, and counteract, or better, harmonize the diapason of mere strength and might.

She was dwelling on the Anglo-Saxon ge-nius for power and his contempt for weakness,

From *A Voice From the South* (Xenia, Ohio: Aldine, 1892), 31, 53–5, 73–9.

and described a scene in San Francisco which she had witnessed.

The incorrigible animal known as the American small-boy, had pounced upon a simple, unoffending Chinaman, who was taking home his work, and had emptied the beautifully laundried contents of his basket into the ditch. "And," said she, "when that great man stood there and blubbered before that crowd of lawless urchins, to any one of whom he might have taught a lesson with his two fists, *I didn't much care.*"

This is said like a man! It grates harshly. It smacks of the worship of the beast. It is contempt for weakness, and taken out of its setting it seems to contradict my theory. It either shows that one of the highest exponents of the Higher Education can be at times untrue to the instincts I have ascribed to the thinking woman and to the contribution she is to add to the civilized world, or else the influence she wields upon our civilization may be potent without being necessarily and always direct and conscious. The latter is the case. Her voice may strike a false note, but their whole being is musical with the vibrations of human suffering. Her tongue may parrot over the cold conceits that some man has taught her, but her heart is aglow with sympathy and loving kindness, and she cannot be true to her real self without giving out these elements into the forces of the world. . . .

The high ground of generalities is alluring but my pen is devoted to a special cause: and with a view to further enlightenment on the achievements of the century for THE HIGHER EDUCATION OF COLORED WOMEN, I wrote a few days ago to the colleges which admit women and asked how many colored women had completed the B. A. course in each during its entire history. These are the figures returned: Fisk leads the way with twelve; Oberlin next with five; Wilberforce, four; Ann Arbor and Wellesley three each, Livingstone two, Atlanta one, Howard, as yet, none.

I then asked the principal of the Washington High School how many out of a large number of female graduates from his school had chosen to go forward and take a collegiate course. He replied that but one had ever done so, and she was then in Cornell.*

Others ask questions too, sometimes, and I was asked a few years ago by a white friend, "How is it that the men of your race seem to outstrip the women in mental attainment?" "Oh," I said, "so far as it is true, the men, I suppose, from the life they lead, gain more by contact; and so far as it is only apparent, I think the women are more quiet. They don't feel called to mount a barrel and harangue by the hour every time they imagine they have produced an idea."

But I am sure there is another reason which I did not at that time see fit to give. The atmosphere, the standards, the requirements of our little world do not afford any special stimulus to female development.

It seems hardly a gracious thing to say, but it strikes me as true, that while our men seem thoroughly abreast of the times on almost every other subject, when they strike the woman question they drop back into sixteenth century logic. They leave nothing to be desired generally in regard to gallantry and chivalry, but they actually do not seem sometimes to have outgrown that old contemporary of chivalry—the idea that women may stand on pedestals or live in doll houses, (if they happen to have them) but they must not furrow their brows with thought or attempt to help men tug at the great questions of the world. I fear the majority of colored men do not yet think it worth while that women aspire to higher education. . . . The three R's, a little music and a good deal of dancing, a first rate dress-maker and a bottle of magnolia balm, are quite enough generally to render charming any woman possessed of tact and the capacity for worshipping masculinity.

My readers will pardon my illustrating my point and also giving a reason for the fear that is in me, by a little bit of personal experience.

---

* Graduated from Scientific Course, June, 1890, the first colored woman to graduate from Cornell.

When a child I was put into a school near home that professed to be normal and collegiate, i.e. to prepare teachers for colored youth, furnish candidates for the ministry, and offer collegiate training of those who should be ready for it. Well, I found after a while that I had a good deal of time on my hands. I had devoured what was put before me, and, like Oliver Twist, was looking around to ask for more. I constantly felt (as I suppose many an ambitious girl has felt) a thumping from within unanswered by any beckoning from without. Class after class was organized for these ministerial candidates (many of them men who had been preaching before I was born). Into every one of these classes I was expected to go, with the sole intent, I thought at the time, of enabling the dear old principal, as he looked from the vacant countenances of his sleepy old class over to where I sat, to get off his solitary pun—his never-failing pleasantry, especially in hot weather—which was, as he called out "Any one!" to the effect that "*any* one" then meant "*Annie* one."

Finally, a Greek class was to be formed. My inspiring preceptor informed me that Greek had never been taught in the school, but that he was going to form a class *for the candidates for the ministry,* and if I liked I might join it. I replied—humbly I hope, as became a female of the human species—that I would like very much to study Greek, and that I was thankful for the opportunity, and so it went on. A boy, however meager his equipment and shallow his pretentions, had only to declare a floating intention to study theology and he could get all the support, encouragement and stimulus he needed, be absolved from work and invested beforehand with all the dignity of his far away office. While a self-supporting girl had to struggle on by teaching in the summer and working after school hours to keep up with her board bills, and actually to fight her way against positive discouragements to the higher education; till one such girl one day flared out and told the principal "the only mission opening before a girl in his school was to marry

one of those candidates." He said he didn't know but it was. And when at last that same girl announced her desire and intention to go to college it was received with about the same incredulity and dismay as if a brass button on one of those candidate's coats had propounded a new method for squaring the circle or trisecting the arc.

Now this is not fancy. It is a simple unvarnished photograph, and what I believe was not in those days exceptional in colored schools, and I ask the men and women who are teachers and co-workers for the highest interests of the race, that they give the girls a chance! . . .

The earnest well trained Christian young woman, as a teacher, as a home-maker, as wife, mother, or silent influence even, is as potent a missionary agency among our people as is the theologian; and I claim that at the present state of our development in the South she is even more important and necessary.

112

PAULINE F. HOPKINS

Higher Education of Colored Women in White Schools and Colleges (1902)

Can the Negro woman learn anything? Is she capable of the highest mental culture? are questions which have been conclusively answered in the series of articles closing with this number.

We have seen that every slave State had laws against the education of the Blacks, and that the present regime of State government in the South land is in opposition to the highest educational development for the race.

We have seen, too, that the Anglo-Saxon woman, in convention assembled, has sought to place the indelible stamp of hopeless intellec

From *The Colored American Magazine,* October 1902.

tual inferiority upon the Negro race in spite of voluminous testimony to the contrary. There is none so blind as they who will not see; none so hard to convince as they who wish to believe the worst of their fellow beings.

Is the course adopted toward the unfortunate Negroes of this country according to the teaching and spirit of the Gospel which is so proudly and austerely heralded to heathen nations at an annual cost of millions? We look in vain for a trace of the graciousness attributed to the female character or the meek gentleness of Christ, in the position assumed by the Anglo-Saxon woman toward her dark-skinned sister. In the struggle for supremacy now going on in the world of women, the first principles of development are lost sight of. Whatever is divine in ourselves is most fully developed by the endeavor to make it beneficial to our neighbor. Herein is scope, and motive, and reward for the most patient effort of self-culture. In the wonderful scheme of God's earthly government, the doing of good to others is the direct means of achieving success in life for ourselves. All science, commerce, industry, spread blessings abroad, leading to fame and fortune if pursued for the benefits spread abroad. Women's education and work are no exception to this rule. For the sake of our country and its future dearest interests women of every nationality should be encouraged and invited to bear a part in the Christian duty of doing good to our neighbor, and should be trained to understand that duty and to do it.

In denying the intellectual capacity of the Negro woman, our fair-skinned sisters have forgotten that they themselves have but just gained intellectual equality in the great world of endeavor.

. . . It was reserved, however, for the nineteenth century to witness the higher and much fuller development of the female intellect. This century gave the world Queen Victoria who may be considered the leading figure in the advancement of all womanly excellence. In literature woman has achieved a high position. In science a few great names demonstrate the capacity of the sex for high attainments in astronomy, mathematics, political economy, psychology and moral philosophy.

In mechanic arts they have exhibited skill in manipulation; in trade and commerce trained women have exhibited decided abilities. But in the Crimean War, the Civil War and the war in Germany, the remarkable executive ability of woman was fully demonstrated on the battlefield and in hospitals.

The Negro woman having risen from no greater depths, though enslaved, than the Anglo-Saxon woman, feels her womanhood stir within her and boldly advances to scale the heights of intellectual advancement, feeling that the door has been opened for her to take an active, intelligent and resolute part in the march of human progress. It seems almost as if the inspiration of the times had created a new race of colored women, a new tide set in, new forces called into play, a new era in the world's history and through all this the moral and social regeneration of a race. The command of God to the woman of color is: "Behold, I have set before thee an open door, and no man can shut it." So, let us press forward in faith believing.

If we look closely into the mass of all that has been lately written and spoken against us, it resolves itself into two main heads: first, the question as to the right of the woman of color to live in the world on the same terms as a white woman does—to work as she does, to be paid as she is, to elevate herself, intellectually and socially as she does—to make use, in short, of all that is elevating in life; and, second, the question as to the colored woman's competency so to do.

As to the first question, we do not discuss a right. We assume it. Assertion would weaken our position. That we have the right is a self-evident truth. It rests with our enemies to prove why we should not enjoy the privileges we claim. "The burden of proof," says Mills, "is supposed to be with those who are against liberty; who contend for any restriction or prohibition, either any limitation of the general freedom of human action, or any disqualification or disparity of privilege, affecting one person or kind of persons, as compared with others. The *a priori* presumption is in favor of freedom and impartriality."

As to the question of competence, it must be settled by the law of natural selection and the application of the same practical tests that settle this question for the Anglo-Saxon woman. The only proof of competence is performance. The world belongs to them who take it, black or white.

The great advantage in co-education of the races lies in the self-reliance engendered in students of the weaker race, the perfect development of a manly or womanly spirit, and, in women more particularly, refinement of manner and the inculcation of the highest ideals in morality—in social life and in the home.

Most of the institutions for the higher education of women have a corps of teachers endowed with rare attainments and possessed of the purest principles of Christian womanhood.

The benign influence poured upon susceptible youth by the close association between teachers and pupils in four years of academical life can hardly be estimated, especially for a race where every effort has been made to degrade its womanhood. We are happy to record that undaunted by the cruelty of caste prejudice, many young colored women have entered the sacred precincts of celebrated institutions of letters, and successfully combatting great obstacles have demonstrated to the world their peculiar fitness for service in the sacred inner courts of intellectual preeminence, regardless of race. In these schools our women have occupied unique positions, the great searchlight of publicity being constantly cast upon their every action. Thus they have become pioneers in the field of letters; indeed, in every field of human life where great personal effort rebounds to the good of humanity.

We do not wish to be misunderstood; we do not imply that our race schools are not doing excellent work; it is the great opportunity of presenting an object lesson to the on-looking world, which lies within the grasp of the colored student in white institutions.

III. Clubwomen

HISTORIANS DISAGREE OVER THE FEMINIST STATUS OF WOMEN'S CLUBS: socially exclusive and (in some ways) politically reactionary, these organizations also produced solidarity and sisterhood among women in an increasingly unsettled modern urban world; and while many organizations founded themselves as literary study clubs—one of the first being Sorosis (1868)—others would take on activist roles, infusing traditionally domestic concerns into public spheres of debate and politics.

Thousands if not millions of mid- to late-nineteenth century American women rallied around the call for temperance and prohibition of liquor, a key point of reform in its own right and also a fountainhead for further activism on issues ranging from suffrage and prison reform to prostitution. Drawing on the same strategy as antebellum temperance literature—which appealed to the emotions of its readers—the article "Woman's Suffering from Intemperance" (1869) from the *Agitator* details the connections between the predominantly male habit of excessive drink and domestic violence and abuse of women and children.

The push for prohibition would be spearheaded by The Woman's Christian Temperance Union (WCTU); founded in Cleveland in 1874, it would grow by the mid-1880s into the largest women's organization in the United States. As described by Francis Willard in "Aims and Methods of the W.C.T.U." (1883), temperance "crusaders" confronted the issue of alcohol abuse at its source, as women marched *en masse* to saloons demanding the destruction of liquor—their tactics reminiscent of those antebellum moral reformers who had forced their way into brothels. Willard served as president of the W.C.T.U. from 1879 to 1898. Her extraordinary talents as administrator, orator, and political strategist were responsible, in large part, for the growth and success of the W.C.T.U.; she sought continually to expand the organization's concerns and efforts past the goal of prohibition.

The leaders of women's clubs distinguished the form and function of the organizations from that of their male counterparts. While men's clubs offered members private space and time for socializing and camaraderie, women explained that they founded clubs for public, philanthropic, and civic-minded purposes. Jane C. Croly—a prominent journalist and founder of both Sorosis and the General Federation of Women's Clubs (1890)—makes this point in "The History of the Woman's Club Movement in America" (1898), adding that the rise of these organizations led to the social and political awakening of American women. In "The Work of Women's Clubs" (1891–2), a broad historical account of the movement, Alice Hyneman Rhine also emphasizes the good works of the clubs; she adds, however, that few have been successful in connecting with lower classes in American society.

Because African-American women were explicitly barred from most non-black women's clubs, they developed a separate network of organizations—institutions that took on the role of pulling up the race from both the ravages of slavery and the continued hardships of economic destitution and social prejudice in the South and every other part of the country. In their speech "The Organized Efforts of the Colored Women of the South to Improve Their Condition," Sarah J. Early and Hallie Q. Brown used the occasion of the 1893 World's Columbian Exposition in Chicago to mark the progress of Black women in the South. A crucial part of that progress, they argue, is the critical role women's organizations played in caring for the least fortunate among them and also in spreading Christian gospel through mission work in the United States and abroad.

In "The Club Movement Among Colored Women of America" (1900), Fannie Barrier Williams writes that a primary purpose of the black organizations is the uplift of the race through the virtues of education, domesticity, and the ideal of womanhood itself. African-American women should recognize a moral responsibility to their race, Barrier Williams explains, and that effort can be best made through women's clubs. Barrier Williams adds that white women's clubs have inspired black women, but at the same time black clubs have developed independently and are designed to serve the specific needs of African-American women. Separate black women's clubs organized themselves under the National Association of Colored Women (NACW) in 1896.

In the forum "What Role is the Educated Woman to Play in Uplifting Her Race?" (1902), Rosetta Sprague (daughter of the abolitionist and activist Frederick Douglass) emphasizes, like Fannie Barrier Williams, that black women need to develop and refine life in the home. Mary Church Terrell discusses how women can fight Jim Crow laws and lynching in the South and, in general, weigh in on other legal-political matters of the day; but she too focuses on sophistication of the home as both a practical way to improve the material conditions of African-American life and as a symbol of racial development since the end of slavery. Church Terrell (the first president of the NACW) insists that club women need to pay attention to working-class black women because their poverty, illiteracy, and "depravity" necessarily reflect on the race as a whole. Finally, Rosa D. Bowser (a journalist) reiterates the need for more attention to domesticity and motherhood. With their common emphasis on the centrality of African-American homes and homelife, each writer suggests different ways in which domestic concerns necessitate and legitimate black women's public activity and organization.

113

Woman's Suffering from Intemperance (1869)

Who can tell what women have suffered from the vice of intemperance, during the ages? How it has blasted the choicest hopes of life—ruined the tenderest associations—turned the happiest homes into dreary wastes! The history of this vice is written in unrealized hopes, and broken hearts, and murdered affections. None are more familiar with the dreadful history than the wives and daughters of drunkards. They have watched and wept, while others have been thoughtless and sleeping—they have suffered, and continued to hope for better days, when every one else has given up all as lost.

When the agent of the New York State Temperance Society visited all the jails and the poorhouses in that state, a few years ago, in search of temperance statistics, he said: "In no poor-house have I failed to find the wife or widow, and the children of the drunkard! In one poor-house, of one hundred and ninety persons, received during the year, there were nineteen wives of drunken husbands, and seventy-one children of drunken fathers. In almost every jail were husbands confined for whipping their wives, or otherwise abusing their families. In one nine, in another fourteen, in another sixteen, had been in prison for this offense, during the last year; in another three out of four who were then in prison, were confined for whipping their wives."

But when we reflect that but a very small proportion of these brutes in human shape are legally punished, and that a large amount of domestic suffering arising from this source, is often kept private, the aggregate exceeds the power of human mind to compute. Yet the sale of that which occasions all this dreadful suffering, is not only tolerated by custom, but is sanctioned by law.

Could we collect all the wives and children

From *The Agitator*, April 3, 1869.

of drunkards in one vast amphitheater—place in an outer circle all the makers and vendors of intoxicating drinks, and next to them all the ministers and professors of religion who favor this accursed business, and all the editors and reporters of newspapers who give their influence in the same direction, and could we fasten them here until each mother and child, each wife and daughter had told the story of her suffering and shame—of her downward course from affluence or competency, from respectability and domestic happiness, to poverty and wretchedness, it would not make too prominent the awful wickedness of the traffic in intoxicating drinks, which is everywhere realized.

But a thousand such hearings would not sufficiently portray the sufferings of women, arising from this business. If we could gain the attention of the intemperate, and of those who are acquiring an appetite for strong drink, which bye and bye they can neither resist nor overcome, we would say to them, if you are entirely indifferent about your own future condition and prospects in life, do for humanity's sake, remember and pity your mothers and sisters—your wives and daughters. There is no deeper ingratitude in the world, than that displayed by a young man, who deliberately surrenders to the seductions of intemperance, and thus fills his own mother with sorrow and shame, who not only brought him into the world, but had watched over him with tenderness through the long days and sleepless nights, of his infancy and childhood. And the young man who will deliberately acquire this habit, has but little manhood left. Nor has the father, who will pursue an intemperate course of life, and thus heap mortification and shame on his sons and daughters, and tempt them to deny his acquaintance, and their relation to him.

Said an intelligent and educated young man to me, a few years ago—"When I see my own father returning home drunk, I feel as though I would like to go off in the woods alone, and hate myself to death." And many a sensitive daughter has felt that she would gladly die to escape so fearful a sight, and the bitter shame that comes from the conviction that she is "a drunkard's daughter." If there were no other inducement to lead a man to put forth all the strength he possesses to control his appetite for drink, one would suppose this must certainly do it. And yet how powerless a motive it proves in most cases!

T. H. T.
Malcomb, Ill.

114

FRANCES E. WILLARD
Aims and Methods of the WCTU (1883)

Thus have I tried to set forth the sequel of that modern Pentecost called the "Woman's Crusade." That women should thus dare was the wonder after they had so long endured, while the manner of their doing left us who looked on, bewildered between laughter and tears. Woman-like, they took their knitting, their zephyr work or their embroidery, and simply swarmed into the drink-shops, seated themselves, and watched the proceedings. Usually they came in a long procession from their rendezvous at some church where they had held morning prayer-meeting; entered the saloon with kind faces, and the sweet songs of church and home upon their lips, while some Madonna-like leader with the Gospel in her looks, took her stand beside the bar, and gently asked if she might read God's word and offer prayer.

Women gave of their best during the two months of that wonderful uprising. All other engagements were laid aside; elegant women of society walked beside quiet women of home, school and shop, in the strange processions that soon lined the chief streets, not only of nearly

From *Woman and Temperance: or, The Work and Workers of the Woman's Christian Temperance Association* (Hartford, Conn.: Park Publishing Co., 1883), 469–75.

every town and village in the state that was its birthplace, but of leading cities there and elsewhere; and voices trained in Paris and Berlin sang "Rock of Ages, cleft for me," in the malodorous air of liquor-rooms and beer-halls. Meanwhile, where were the men who patronized these places? Thousands of them signed the pledge these women brought, and accepted their invitation to go back with them to the churches, whose doors, for once, stood open all day long; others slunk out of sight, and a few cursed the women openly; but even of these it might be said, that those who came to curse remained to pray. Soon the saloon-keepers surrendered in large numbers, the statement being made by a well-known observer that the liquor traffic was temporarily driven out of two hundred and fifty towns and villages in Ohio and the adjoining states, to which the Temperance Crusade extended. There are photographs extant representing the stirring scenes when, amid the ringing of church-bells, the contents of every barrel, cask and bottle in a saloon were sent gurgling into the gutter, the owner insisting that women's hands alone should do this work, perhaps with some dim thought in his muddled head of the poetic justice due to the Nemesis he thus invoked. And so it came about that soft and often jeweled hands grasped axe and hammer, while the whole town assembled to rejoice in this new fashion of exorcising the evil spirits. In Cincinnati, a city long dominated by the liquor trade, a procession of women, including the wives of leading pastors, was arrested and locked up in jail; in Cleveland, dogs were set on the crusaders, and in a single instance, a blunderbuss was pointed at them, while in several places, they were smoked out, or had the hose turned on them. But the arrested women marched through the streets singing, and held a temperance meeting in the prison; the one assailed by dogs laid her hands upon their heads and prayed; and the group menaced by a gun marched up to its mouth singing, "Never be afraid to work for Jesus." The annals of heroism have few pages so bright as the annals of that strange crusade, spreading as if by magic, through all the Northern States, across the sea and to the Orient itself. Everywhere it went, the attendance at church increased incalculably, and the crime record was in like manner shortened. Men say there was a spirit in the air such as they never knew before; a sense of God and of human brotherhood.

But after fifty days or more, all this seemed to pass away. The women could not keep up such work; it took them too much from their homes; saloons re-opened; men gathered as before behind their sheltering screens, and swore "those silly women had done more harm than good," while with ribald words they drank the health of "the defunct crusade."

Perhaps the most significant outcome of this movement was the knowledge of their own power gained by the conservative women of the churches. They had never even seen a "woman's rights convention," and had been held aloof from the "suffragists" by fears as to their orthodoxy; but now there were women prominent in all church cares and duties eager to clasp hands for a more aggressive work than such women had ever before dreamed of undertaking.

Nothing is more suggestive in all the national gatherings of the Woman's Christian Temperance Union, that sober second thought of the crusade, then the wide difference between these meetings and any held by men. The beauty of decoration is specially noticeable; banners of silk, satin and velvet, usually made by the women themselves, adorn the wall; the handsome shields of states; the great vases bearing aloft grains, fruits and flowers; the moss-covered well with its old bucket; or the setting of a platform to present an interior as cozy and delightful as a parlor could afford, are features of the pleasant scene. The rapidity of movement with which business is conducted, the spontaneity of manner, the originality of plan, the perpetual freshness and ingenuity of the convention, its thousand unexpectednesses, its quips and turns, its wit and pathos, its impromptu eloquence and its perpetual good nature—all these elements,

brought into condensed view in the National Conventions, are an object-lesson of the new force and unique method that womanhood has contributed to the consideration of the greatest reform in Christendom. It is really the crusade over again; the home going forth into the world. Its manner is not that of the street, the court, the mart, or office; it is the manner of the home. Men take one line, and travel onward to success; with them discursiveness is at a discount. But women in the home must be mistresses, as well as maids of all work; they have learned well the lesson of unity in diversity; hence by inheritance and by environment, women are varied in their methods; they are born to be "branchers-out." Men have been in the organized temperance work not less than eighty years—women not quite fifteen. Men pursued it at first along the line of temperance, then total abstinence; license, then prohibition; while women have already over forty distinct departments of work, classified under the heads of preventive, educational, evangelistic, social, and legal. Women think in the concrete. The crusade showed them the drinking man, and they began upon him directly, to get him to sign the pledge and seek "the Lord behind the pledge." The crusade showed them the selling man, and they prayed over him and persuaded him to give up his bad business, often buying him out, and setting him up in the better occupation of baker, grocer, or keeper of the reading-room into which they converted his saloon after converting him from the error of his ways.

But oftentimes the drinking man went back to his cups, and the selling man fell from his grace; the first one declaring, "I can't break the habit I formed when a boy," and the last averring, "Somebody's bound to sell, and I might as well make the profit." Upon this the women, still with their concrete ways of thinking, said, "To be sure, we must train our boys and not ours only, but everybody's; what institution reaches all?—the Public Schools." How well they wrought, under the leadership of Mrs. Mary H. Hunt, has been told on earlier pages.

To the inane excuse of the seller that he might as well do it since somebody would, the quick and practical reply was, "To be sure; but suppose the people could be persuaded not to let anybody sell? why, then that would be God's answer to our crusade prayers." So they began with petitions to municipalities, to Legislatures and to Congress, laboriously gathering up, doubtless, not fewer than ten million names in the great aggregate, and through the fourteen years. Thus the Women's Christian Temperance Union stands as the strongest bulwark of prohibition, state and national, by constitutional amendment and by statute. Meanwhile, it was inevitable that their motherly hearts should devise other methods for the protection of their homes. Knowing the terrors and the blessings of inheritance, they set about the systematic study of heredity, founding a journal for that purpose. Learning the relation of diet to the drink habit, they arranged to study hygiene also; desiring children to know that the Bible is on the side of total abstinence, they induced the International Sunday-school Convention to prepare a plan for lessons on this subject; perceiving the limitless power of the Press, they did their best to subsidize it by sending out their bulletins of temperance facts and news items, thick as the leaves of Vallombrosa, and incorporated a publishing company of women.

It is curious to watch the development of the women who entered the saloons in 1874 as a gentle, well-dressed, and altogether peaceable mob. They have become an army, drilled and disciplined. They have a method of organization, the simplest yet the most substantial known to temperance annals. It is the same for the smallest local union as for the national society with its ten thousand auxiliaries. Committees have been abolished, except the executive, made up of the general officers, and "superintendencies" substituted, making each woman responsible for a single line of work in the local, state and national society. This puts a premium upon personality, develops a negative into a positive with the least loss of time, and increases beyond all computation the aggregate of work accomplished. Women with specialties have thus been multiplied by tens of thousand, and the temperance reform introduced into strongholds of power hitherto neglected or unthought of. Is an exposition to be held, or a state or county fair? there is a woman in the locality who knows it is her business to see that the W. C. T. U. has an attractive booth with temperance literature and temperance drinks; and that, besides all this, it is her duty to secure laws and by-laws requiring the teetotal absence of intoxicants from grounds and buildings. Is there an institution for the dependent or delinquent classes? there is a woman in the locality who knows it is her duty to see that temperance literature is circulated, temperance talking and singing done, and that flowers with appropriate sentiments attached are sent the inmates by young ladies banded for that purpose. Is there a convocation of ministers, doctors, teachers, editors, voters, or any other class of opinion-manufacturers announced to meet in any town or city? there is a woman thereabouts who knows it is her business to secure, through some one of the delegates to these influential gatherings, a resolution favoring the temperance movement, and pledging it support along the line of work then and there represented. Is there a Legislature anywhere about to meet, or is Congress in session? there is a woman near at hand who knows it is her business to make the air heavy with the white, hovering wings of petitions gathered up from everywhere asking for prohibition, for the better protection of women and girls, for the preventing of the sale of tobacco to minors, for the enforcement of the Sabbath, or for the enfranchisement of women.

Thus have the manifold relationships of the mighty temperance movement been studied out by women in the training-school afforded by the real work and daily object-lessons of the W. C. T. U. Its aim is everywhere to bring woman and temperance in contact with the problem of humanity's heart-break and sin; to protect the home by prohibiting the saloon, and to police the state with men and women voters committed to the enforcement of righteous law. The women saw, as years passed on, that not one, but three curses were pronounced upon their sons by the nineteenth century civilization: the curse of the narcotic poisons, alcohol and nicotine; the curse of gambling; the curse of social sin, deadlier than all, and that these three are part and parcel of each other. And so, "distinct like the billows, but one like the sea," is their unwearied warfare against each and all. They have learned, by the logic of defeat, that the mother-heart must be enthroned in all places of power before its edicts will be heeded. For this reason they have been educated up to the level of the equal suffrage movement. For the first time in history, the women of the South have clasped hands with their Northern sisters in faith and fealty, wearing the white ribbon emblem of patriotism, purity and peace, and inscribing on their banners the motto of the organized crusade, "For God and Home and Native Land."

"No sectarianism in religion," "no sectionalism in politics," "no sex in citizenship"—these are the battle-rules of this relentless but peaceful warfare. We believe that woman will bless and brighten every place she enters, and that she will enter every place on the round earth. We believe in prohibition by law, prohibition by politics, and prohibition by woman's ballot. After ten years' experience, the women of the crusade became convinced that until the people of this country divide at the ballot-box on the foregoing issue, America can never be nationally delivered from the dram-shop. They therefore publicly announced their devotion to the Prohibition party, and promised to lend it their influence and prayers, which, with the exception of a very small minority, they have since most sedulously done. Since then they have not ceased beseeching voters to cast their ballots first of all to help elect an issue, rather than a man. For this they have been vilified as if it were a crime; but they have gone on their way, kindly as sunshine, steadfast as gravitation, and persistent as a hero's faith. While their enemy has brewed

beer, they have brewed public opinion; while he distilled whisky, they distilled sentiment; while he rectified spirits, they rectified the spirit that is in man. They have had good words of cheer alike for North and South, for Catholic and Protestant, for home and foreign born, for white and black, but gave words of criticism for the liquor traffic and the parties that it dominates as its servants and allies.

While the specific aims of the white ribbon women everywhere are directed against the manufacture, sale and use of alcoholic beverages, it is sufficiently apparent that the indirect line of their progress is, perhaps, equally rapid, and involves social, governmental, and ecclesiastical equality between women and men. By this is meant such financial independence on the part of women as will enable them to hold men to the same high standards of personal purity in the habitutdes of life as they have required of women, such a participation in the affairs of government as shall renovate politics and make home questions the paramount issue of the state, and such equality in all church relations as shall fulfill the gospel declaration, "There is neither male nor female, but ye are all one in Christ Jesus."

The cultivation of specialties, and the development of *espirit de corps* among women, all predict the day when, through this mighty conserving force of motherhood introduced into every department of human activity the common weal shall be the individual care; war shall rank among the lost arts; nationality shall mean what Edward Bellamy's wonderful book, entitled "Looking Backward," sets before us as the fulfillment of man's highest earthly dream; and Brotherhood shall become the talismanic word and realized estate of all humanity.

115

JANE C. CROLY

History of the Woman's Club Movement in America (1898)

. . . The woman has been the one isolated fact in the universe. The outlook upon the world, the means of education, the opportunities for advancement, had all been denied her; and that "community of feeling and sense of distributive justice which grows out of cooperative interests in work and life, had found small opportunity for growth or activity."

The opportunity came with the awakening of the communal spirit, the recognition of the law of solidarity of interests, the sociologic advance which established a basis of equality among a wide diversity of conditions and individualities, and opportunities for all capable of using them. This great advance was not confined to a society or a neighborhood; it did not require subscription to a tenet, or the giving up of one's mode of life. It was simply the change of a point of view, the opening of a door, the stepping out into the freedom of the outer air, and the sweet sense of fellowship with the whole universe that comes with liberty and light.

The difference was only a point of view, but it changed the aspect of the world.

This new note, which meant for the woman liberty, breadth, and unity, was struck by the woman's club.

To the term "club," as applied to and by women, may be fitly referred the words in which John Addington Symonds defines "Renaissance." "This," he remarks, "is not explained by this or that characteristic, but as an effort for which at length the time had come." It means the attainment of the conscious freedom of the woman spirit, and has been manifested first most strongly and most widely in this country because here that spirit has attained the largest measure of freedom.

The woman's club was not an echo; it was not the mere banding together for a social and economic purpose, like the clubs of men. It became at once, without deliberate intention or concerted action, a light-giving and seed-sowing centre of purely altruistic and democratic activity. It had no leaders. It brought together qualities rather than personages; and by a representation of all interests, moral, intellectual, and social, a natural and equal division of work and opportunity, created an ideal basis of organization, where every one has an equal right to whatever comes to the common centre; where the centre itself becomes a radiating medium for the diffusion of the best of that which is brought to it, and into which, all being freely given, no material considerations enter.

This is no ideal or imaginary picture. It is the simplest prose of every woman's club and every club woman's experience during the past thirty years.

It has been in every sense an awakening to the full glory and meaning of life. It is also a very narrow and self-absorbed mind that only sees in these openings opportunities for its own pleasure, or chances for its own advancement, on its own narrow and exclusive lines. The lesson of the hour is help for those that need it, in the shape in which they need it, and kinship with all and everything that exists on the face of God's earth. If we miss this we miss the spirit, the illuminating light of the whole movement, and lose it in the mire of our own selfishness.

The tendency of association upon any broad human basis is to destroy the caste spirit, and this the club has done for women more than any other influence that as yet has come into existence. A club that is narrowed to a clique, a class, or a single object is a contradiction in terms. It may be a society or a congregation of societies, but it is not a club. The essence of a club is its many-sided character, its freedom in gathering together and expressing all shades of difference,

From *The History of the Woman's Club Movement in America* (New York: Henry G. Allen & Co., 1898), 12–13, 18–19, 24–25, 26, 33.

its equal and independent terms of membership, which puts every one upon the same footing and enables each one to find or make her own place. The most opposite ideas find equal claims to respect. Women widest apart in position and habits of life find much in common, and acquaintance and contact mutually helpful and advantageous. Club life teaches us that there are many kinds of wealth in the world—the wealth of ideas, of knowledge, of sympathy, of readiness to be put in any place and used in any way for the general good. These are given, and no price is or can be put upon them, yet they ennoble and enrich whatever comes within their influence.

We are only at the threshold of a future that thrills us with its wonderful possibilities—possibilities of fellowship, where separation was; of love, where hatred was; of unity, where division was; of peace, where war was; of light, physical, mental, and spiritual, where darkness was; of agreement and equality, where differences and traditions had built up walls of distinction and lines of caste. This beautiful thing needs only to be realized in thought to become an actual fact in life, and those who do realize it are enriched by it beyond the power of words to express.

Women have been God's own ministers everywhere and at all times. In varied ways they have worked for others until the name of woman stands for the spirit of self-sacrifice.

Now, He bids them bind their sheaves and show a new and more glorious womanhood; a new unit—the completed type of the mother-woman, working with all, as well as for all. . . .

116
ALICE HYNEMAN RHINE
The Work of Women's Clubs (1891–2)

A somewhat silent but active revolution is in progress among the women of the United States, by which the old conditions that consigned them to inferiority and subjection to men, are gradually being changed. American women are leading their sex throughout the world to a higher life by their work in every State of the Union. One of the principal means by which this revolution, or "reformation" as some call it, is to be finally effected, will be through the women's clubs that are becoming so numerous.

To whatever extent women's clubs may grow, there need be no fear that they will be used for any thing but good. The distinction that nature has made between the dispositions of women and men, together with the treatment to which women have been subjected throughout the ages, has acted upon their habits of thought in such manner that now, when women band themselves together to achieve some common end, their impulses lead them so strongly to be helpful that their united work takes on an entirely different character in many ways from the associated work of their brethren. In nothing is this divergence shown so plainly as in the clubs of the two sexes. While the clubs of men consist usually of luxuriously appointed apartments, with card-rooms, bars, restaurants, bowling-alleys, and billiard-rooms for the comfort and enjoyment of the members only, women's clubs always have a basis of philanthropy, even when instituted for merely social purposes. . . .

That the work women do in their clubs is always vital, is shown by the haste with which they make their societies into what have been called "cradles of reform." There are clubs the work of which lies mainly in the line of attempt-

From *The Forum* 1 2 (1 8 9 1 – 2).

ing the reformation of those of their sex who have fallen victims to intemperance in drink. This is the work of the Charity Club of Boston, Mass. Most of them have no special line of philanthropy laid down, but have their committees on education, philanthropy, political and social science, ethical culture, reform, literature, lectures, entertainments, and the like. How women contrive to mix up economics with their other club work is well demonstrated by the Old and New Club of Malden, Mass. The chief object of this organization is "mutual improvement;" and the members say that this purpose is best carried out by giving every member an equal chance in carrying on the business of the club. So rotation in office is one of its rules. As the club has a hundred members, and the meetings are conducted in strict accordance with parliamentary law, considerable experience is acquired in performing public duties. "This," says Mrs. Harriet H. Robinson, one of the principal founders of the club, "is necessary, as we do not know how soon any of us may be called to take an active part in the events of the time, and it behooves us to prepare ourselves, and to help other women to be ready also." She holds that the "mission of the women's clubs is to fit the sex for the larger duties which are so surely coming into their lives." These words seem significant of New England, the home of the "Pilgrim Mothers," where one expects to find, by the laws of heredity, high thinkers and active doers; yet this temper is confined to no one part of the country, but is the general characteristic of women's clubs everywhere.

. . . It might be expected that the work of so many clubs would be based on diversified lines of activity, and that these would represent the thought of the several geographical sections. In the East the clubs do a vast amount of philanthropic work, which has widened from purely economic labors to industrial performance. As the conditions of life became harder for women in America, and more of them were forced to become bread-winners, the clubs added to their list of aims the free teaching of old and new avo-cations. In the Southern towns, where the stress of poverty too often exists, associated bodies of women are frequent, whose aims are philanthropic, benevolent, and educational; but the conservatism, and almost Oriental timidity, of the sex in that portion of the country, prevents them from naming their gatherings by so radical a name as "clubs." There are, however, exceptions, such as the New Orleans Woman's Club, which is as advanced as any women's organizations elsewhere. Its objects are the removal of the line of caste (women of every rank in life belonging to it, and enjoying each other's companionship), and intellectual growth, which is helped by means of lectures, classes in music, art, literature, languages, and industrial teaching. In the West, where the settlements of men are more sparse, and food is plentiful, the clubs are rarely philanthropic. The most of them are of a social and literary character. Because public amusements are fewer, and libraries less accessible, the women of the Western towns devote their energies to aiding these factors of civilization. In almost every case, an association of women in Kansas, Wisconsin, Iowa, or elsewhere, means a club for the promotion and guidance of pleasure among the young, and the collecting, studying, and circulating of good books. In many cases the club is utilized as a means of pursuing the education given by colleges, or that part which relates to literature. Thus the Ladies' Afternoon Club of Janesville, Wis., makes a study of the great empires of the world as comprised in the history of their art, ethnology, philology, religions, and literatures. In far-off North Dakota, during the midst of the great blizzard of 1884 a literary club was started. Its first attempt was to try to gain a comprehensive idea of the life, manners, and customs of the city of London from its beginning to the present day. As ten pages of a good book properly read are said to give a liberal education, so students reading on these lines are likely to get far advanced on the questions of present as well as past times.

One token of the broader culture that

women gained through this associated work was, that it made so large a number of clubs as 117 ready to answer the call of Sorosis for co-operative effort. This evidence of a solidarity of sentiment among women for centralizing their endeavors, was as unexpected to the outside world as it was grateful to the promoters of the scheme of a national federation. Men had so often asserted that women lacked the power of combining for large definite purposes, that they had come to believe themselves unable to work together, except in the small ways involving personal or doctrinal mattes. And yet observation of what women have done in the way of co-operative work in the past twenty-five years proves them to have a natural gift for administration and organization. Despite their so recent experience in legislative matters, they seem to have grasped intuitively the necessity of centralizing their forces. The constant tendency in all their associated work has been to group local clubs under one head, to unite these again under some central or State control, and then to form a national council, and in some cases international departments.

. . . The calling together of these councils, with much of the radical thought expressed in them, was the work of the woman suffrage societies. These formerly despised bands, that were confined to a small section of New England, have spread, until there is scarcely a State in the Union without its woman's rights organizations, in which its members meet on the true club idea of uniting for the purpose of gaining one common end.

In later years the woman suffrage societies have had their power still further strengthened by the support of the Woman's Christian Temperance Union. This organization, which is the largest incorporated society of women in the United States, soon saw the policy of helping to gain the franchise for the sex. "Only," said they, "through woman's ballots will America be delivered nationally from the dram-shops." To realize what this assistance means, it is simply necessary to consider that the Woman's Chris-

tian Temperance Union has regularly organized societies in forty-four States of the Union and in every Territory except Alaska. It counts ten thousand local unions with a membership and following, inclusive of children of about half a million. It owns its own publishing-house, which is a stock company; and its business manager, editors, directors, and stock-holders are all women. It sends out yearly enough temperance literature to give occupation to 146 employees, who are mostly women. Singularly enough, the Woman's Christian Temperance Union, which is to-day one of the most perfectly systematized of organizations, is the outgrowth of that mob of sentimental enthusiasts who perpetrated the "Woman's Crusade,"—a crusade wherein, amid the peal of churchbells and the singing of hymns, soft jewelled hands and hard ones met in the work of turning the contents of saloons into the gutters. It was from the experience gained in this fight, that women learned the value of organization, and that difficult issues must be met before the temperance movement could succeed. One of their discoveries was, that they must begin at the beginning, with the children; and they have triumphed so far, that laws have been secured in thirty of the States, requiring a place in the curriculum of the public schools for the study of the relation to liquor of hygiene. Thus, while the aims of the "white ribbon party" are specifically directed against the use, manufacture, and sale of intoxicants, an indirect line in their progress involves the employment of social, educational, and political means as aids to its ends.

Another modern organization, and one with which the women's suffrage and temperance societies affiliate, is the Woman's Alliance, organized in Illinois in 1888. Unlike those societies that were each founded for the purpose of carrying out a special idea, the Alliance is cosmopolitan in its character. The club motto is "Justice to children—loyalty to women;" and its work, as might be expected, is altogether economic. One great distinction between the Alliance and other organizations of women is, that men give it their moral support. In Chicago it is said to be backed with the twenty-five thousand votes of the Trades Unions and Labor Assemblies. It has brought about, among other measures, the appointment in Chicago of the only police-women in the world. The duties of these are to inspect establishments where women and children are employed; and a silver star, which is their badge, admits them everywhere. In spite of the mayor, the Alliance secured the admission of an extra woman on the Board of Education, and has been successful generally with the things with which it concerns itself. Every thing about the Alliance shows that the women are not wedded to conservative ideas. Organizations of men join it by sending women delegates; and the platform is broad enough for such different bodies to meet on it, as masonic lodges, labor unions, Christian science associations, aid societies, and the like. In all their work the modern thought is uppermost, of practical things to be done to benefit humanity as a whole in its social estate. Standing committees organize the members according to the political divisions of the city; and these do such valuable work as attending the county court on those days when homeless children are assigned to private institutions, seeing to the sanitation of schoolhouses, insane-asylums, and jails. The success of the Alliance in accomplishing factory reforms, and similar reforms, is a proof of what good work can be done when men and women act together for the same things in the same directions, in place of pulling separately and in different ways. . . .

It is through this dominant thought of doing something active for bettering the condition of women, and consequently the rest of mankind, that—after many years of struggle, first by the woman suffrage societies, then by the Woman's Christian Temperance Union, and later by the agitation in the clubs—the sex has gained the right to vote on school matters in twenty-eight States in the Union; that women can serve in hospitals as physicians and nurses; that women have been allowed to protect the unfortunate of their own sex as matrons in police-stations, or,

as in Chicago, in the city jails. In two States the right of equal suffrage has been granted, and in several others permission to vote on matters connected with municipal reform. Colleges which in former times denied them the privilege of entrance have opened wide their doors to let them gain the knowledge they desire. These are some of the actual gains of a class of beings to whom was denied the right, at one time, to learn the alphabet.

Nor, in her anxiety to reach up to the higher branches of learning, has woman neglected the lower. Froebel clubs have been started for the teaching of the kindergarten system for the use of mothers; and numerous societies support free kindergartens for the purposes of raising to higher levels the children of the coming generations. This spirit of helpfulness has become so imbued with the life of the nation, that, turn which way one will, the outcome is embodied in material shape of some kind. And where the clubs have done nothing else, they have brought a sweeter, broader life to hundreds of women whose hearts and minds were running dry from lack of motive in existence, beyond that of working to live. To these the clubs have brought that soft mellowed happiness which comes only to those who spend themselves in the service of others.

The sole drawback to the beautiful work of the women's clubs is, that their influence as yet scarcely reaches far enough to take in the caste most in need of their labors, and that is the proletariat. Those who do come near enough to them have already been subject to some degree of cultivation. But for the great majority outside the clubs, and needing their help, there is only the hope of that reflex action which comes in the course of years. Some there are who have learned that the philanthropist must go out from her associations, and live the life of those she would serve. And this, too, is being done. In New York there is a club called the "College Settlement Girls," which has taken up its residence in the slums of the city, and whose members are endeavoring by their example and presence to bring something of the sweetness of their own culture—derived from Vassar, Wellesley, Smith and Bryn Mawr Colleges—into the lives of their less fortunate neighbors. There are also other noble souls agitating, educating, and organizing under the banner of that social and economical re-organization, based upon scientific and philosophical principles, which will lead to incalculably great results.

Nothing is more lovely than this spirit of altruism which has taken possession of the time, and is leading woman, as she never was led before, to care of her sister-woman in the sense not only of duty, but of love, and which is urging her to bring about in so many ways a universal sisterhood of women, a reign of peace and happiness to all on earth.

117

SARAH J. EARLY AND HALLIE Q. BROWN

The Organized Efforts of the Colored Women of the South to Improve Their Condition (1893)

. . . Step by step, as the dark cloud of ignorance and superstition is dispelled by the penetrating rays of the light of eternal truth, men begin to think, and thought brings revolution, and revolution changes the condition of men and leads them into a happier and brighter existence. So have the great revolutions of the age affected the condition of the colored people of the Southern States, and brought them into a more hopeful relation to the world. When they emerged from the long night of oppression, which shrouded their minds in darkness, crushed the energies of their soul, robbed them of every inheritance save their trust in God, they found themselves

From *The World's Congress of Representative Women*, ed., May Wright Sewall (Chicago and New York: Rand McNally, 1894), 719–21, 722, 723, 724, 726, 728–29.

penniless, homeless, destitute, with thousands of aged and infirm and helpless left on their hands to support, and poverty and inexperience prevailing everywhere. To improve their social condition was the first impulse of their nature. For this purpose they began immediately to organize themselves into mutual aid societies, the object of which was to assist the more destitute, to provide for the sick, to bury the dead, to provide a fund for orphans and widows. These societies were the beginning of their strength, the ground work of their future advancement and permanent elevation. They were constructed with admirable skill and harmony. Excellent charters were secured, and the constitution and by-laws were adhered to with remarkable fidelity. The membership increased rapidly, and the funds in the treasuries grew daily. The women, being organized separately, conducted their societies with wonderful wisdom and forethought. Their influence for good was felt in every community, and they found themselves drawn together by a friendly interest which greatly enhanced the blessings of life. Their sick and dead and orphans have been properly cared for. Thus our people have shown a self-dependence scarcely equaled by any other people, a refined sensibility in denying themselves the necessities of life to save thousands of children from want and adults from public charity; in screening them from the stinging arrows of the tongue of slander and the carping criticisms of a relentless foe.

These organizations number at least five thousand and carry a membership of at least a half-million women. They have widened into State societies, and some of the strongest bodies into national organizations, meeting in annual assemblies to transact business and to discuss their future well-being. They have in some States built and sustained orphans' homes, and in others purchased their own cemeteries. They have built commodious halls for renting purposes; they have assisted in building churches and other benevolent institutions. They have granted large death benefits, and thus provided homes for many orphan children, and have deposited large sums in savings banks for future use. Should the question be asked what benefit has accrued from these organized efforts, we answer, much in every way. Their organizations have bound the women together in a common interest so strong that no earthly force can sever it. Organization has taught them the art of self-government, and has prepared the way for future and grander organizations. By their frequent convocations and discussions their intellectual powers have been expanded and their judgment has been enlightened. Organization has given hope for a better future by revealing to colored women their own executive ability. It has stimulated them to acquire wealth by teaching them to husband their means properly. It has intensified their religion by giving them a more exalted idea of God through a constant survey of his goodness and mercies toward them. It has refined their morality through adherence to their most excellent constitutions and by-laws. It has assisted in raising them from a condition of helplessness and destitution to a state of self-dependence and prosperity; and now they stand a grand sisterhood, nearly one million strong, bound together by the strongest ties of which the human mind can conceive, being loyal to their race, loyal to the government, and loyal to their God.

Having thus provided for their future well-being, their attention was turned to the spread of the gospel. With hearts glowing with the love of God, they longed to assist in building up his kingdom on earth. Many devout women joined themselves into missionary societies to obtain means with which to send the gospel to other parts of the world more destitute than their own. They were auxiliary to the churches of various denominations, and multiplied until their scanty donations amounted to sums sufficient to accomplish much good in the Master's cause. On the women's part in the African Methodist Episcopal church they have donated the sum of thirty thousand dollars, and a like amount in each of the five other leading denominations. The Pres-

byterian Home and Foreign Missionary Society sustains missions in West Africa, the West Indies, the Bermuda Islands, South America, and the islands of Hayti and St. Thomas. The home missions of the various denominations occupy the time of more than one thousand ministers. About the year 1890 the women of the African Methodist Episcopal church formed a mite missionary society, which has its auxiliary branches all over the Union. They now labor assiduously for the advancement of the foreign missions they had prayed for. They believe in him who blessed the widow's mite, and who pronounced a divine benediction on the modest disciple who had done what she could. . . .

The colored women of the Southern States have not been indifferent to the necessity of guarding their homes against the pernicious influences of the drinking system. They have begun to fortify themselves against the most powerful of all enemies—strong drink. Woman's Christian temperance unions have been formed in all Southern States, into which many hundreds have gathered, who work with much patience and diligence. Hospital work, prison work, social purity, and flower mission work, and the distribution of literature among all classes of persons have been performed faithfully, and many erring and destitute souls have felt the tenderness and shared the bounty of the benevolent hearts and ready hands of the colored women of the Woman's Christian Temperance Unions.

These organizations have accomplished much in forming temperance sentiment among the people and in the churches, and have helped materially in changing votes at the polls for prohibition. . . .

If we compare the present condition of the colored people of the South with their condition twenty-eight years ago, we shall see how the organized efforts of their women have contributed to the elevation of the race and their marvelous advancement in so short a time. When they emerged from oppression they were homeless and destitute; now they are legal owners of real estate to the value of two hundred and sixty-three millions of dollars. Then they were penniless, but now they have more than two millions in bank. In several States they have banks of their own in successful operation, in which the women furnish the greater number of deposits. Then they had no schools, and but few of the people were able to read; now more than four millions of their women can read. Then they had no high schools, but now they have two hundred colleges, twenty-seven of which are owned and conducted by their own race.

These feeble efforts at organization to improve our condition seem insignificant to the world, but this beginning, insignificant as it may seem, portends a brighter and nobler future. If we in the midst of poverty and proscription can aspire to a noble destiny to which God is leading all his rational creatures, what may we not accomplish in the day of prosperity? . . .

DISCUSSION OF THE SAME SUBJECT BY HALLIE Q. BROWN OF ALABAMA.

For two hundred and fifty years the negro woman of America was bought and sold as a chattel. The sacred ties of wife and mother were broken and disdained. Side by side with the men of her race she toiled in the dank rice-swamps, in the cotton-fields, and the lone cane-brakes. She tilled the soil of her so-called master, enlarged his estates, heaped his coffers with shining gold, and filled his home with the splendors of the world.

In character she was patient, sympathetic, and forgiving. She was counted but little higher than the brute creation that surrounded her, and was said to possess neither a brain nor a soul. Scourged by the hard hand of the slave-driver, and suffering every privation, there fell upon her a helplessness born of despair; but with an implicit trust and an unswerving faith in God, she caught the glinting light from the peak of freedom's day.

. . . Twenty-five years of progress find the Afro-American woman advanced beyond the most sanguine expectations. Her development

from darkest slavery and grossest ignorance into light and liberty is one of the marvels of the age. Her friends and enemies united in declaring that she would die out under the higher refining influences of Christian civilization; but through unremitting exertions she has climbed to elevated planes, accepting all which dignifies and refines, and flourishing under it.

The negro woman has made greater progress educationally than in any other direction. We favor this as an intelligent choice, a wise decision, for what trade, profession or vocation in life may be entered upon without the basis of scholastic education? Moreover, it prepares her for her important duty in home economy, since she must mold the men of the future. . . .

I have come to this Congress to represent the women of the black belt of Alabama, black not on account of its numerous dark-skinned inhabitants, but black because of its ignorance, superstition, and degradation. Ten years ago B. T. Washington founded a school at Tuskegee which has served as the one beacon-light in all that land of darkness. More than six hundred pupils have studied there.

Three hundred earnest girls bade me God-speed as I left them to come to this Congress. And if you would have a slight idea of the work they can do, they instructed me to say that you should look at the gown their representative wears, made by girls who six months ago could handle only the hoe and the plow. The whistle of the engine, the ring of the hammer, the buzz of the saw, the spinning of the wheel serve as music and inspiration to this school.

The gospel of honorable manual labor sinks into the mind with every stitch that is taken, with every nail that is driven. The dignity of labor is taught with every lesson in domestic economy, cooking, dressmaking, tailoring, nurse-training, and carpentry.

What more is needed?

Time and an equal chance in the race of life.

Ages of savagery and centuries of bondage weakened the intellect and dwarfed the faculties. The proper development of the mind, like the formation of character must come by a slow and steady growth. What are thirty years in the history of a nation? It is but a day since Freedom blew her blast proclaiming liberty to the slave. The sound of the cannon's breath has scarcely died upon the passing breeze; the smoke of the battle-field has hardly cleared away; the earth seems yet to tremble "neath the mighty tread of Sherman's march to the sea."

Talk not of the negro woman's incapacity, of her inferiority, until the centuries of her hideous servitude have been succeeded by centuries of education, culture, and refinement, by which she may rise to the fullness of the stature of her highest ideal.

God speed the day when the white American woman, strengthened by her wealth, her social position, and her years of superior training, may clasp hands with the less fortunate black woman of America, and both unite in declaring that "God hath made of one blood all nations of men for to dwell on all the face of the earth."

118

Fannie Barrier Williams
The Club Movement Among Colored Women of America (1900)

Afro-American women of the United States have never had the benefit of a discriminating judgment concerning their worth as women made up of the good and bad of human nature. What they have been made to be and not what they are, seldom enters into the best or worst opinion concerning them.

In studying the status of Afro-American women as revealed in their club organizations, it ought to be borne in mind that such social

From *A New Negro for a New Century*, ed., Booker T. Washington (Chicago: American Publishing Co., 1900), 379, 382–83, 384, 396–97, 427–28.

differentiations as "women's interests, children's interests, and men's interests" that are so finely worked out in the social development of the more favored races are but recent recognitions in the progressive life of the negro race. Such specializing had no economic value in slavery days, and the degrading habit of regarding the negro race as an unclassified people has not yet wholly faded into a memory.

The negro as an "alien" race, as a "problem," as an "industrial factor," as "ex-slaves," as "ignorant" etc., are well known and instantly recognized; but colored women as mothers, as home-makers, as the center and source of the social life of the race have received little or no attention. These women have been left to grope their way unassisted toward a realization of those domestic virtues, moral impulses and standards of family and social life that are the badges of race respectability. They have had no special teachers to instruct them. No conventions of distinguished women of the more favored race have met to consider their peculiar needs. There has been no fixed public opinion to which they could appeal; no protection against the libelous attacks upon their characters, and no chivalry generous enough to guarantee their safety against man's inhumanity to woman. Certain it is that colored women have been the least known, and the most ill-favored class of women in this country.

Thirty-five years ago they were unsocialized, unclassed and unrecognized as either maids or matrons. They were simply women whose character and personality excited no interest. If within thirty-five years they have become sufficiently important to be studied apart from the general race problem and have come to be recognized as an integral part of the general womanhood of American civilization, that fact is a gratifying evidence of real progress.

In considering the social advancement of these women, it is important to keep in mind the point from which progress began, and the fact that they have been mainly self-taught in all those precious things that make for social order, purity and character. They have gradually become conscious of the fact that progress includes a great deal more than what is generally meant by the terms culture, education and contact.

The club movement among colored women reaches into the sub-social condition of the entire race. Among white women clubs mean the forward movement of the best women in the interest of the best womanhood. Among colored women the club is the effort of the few competent in behalf of the many incompetent; that is to say that the club is only one of many means for the social uplift of a race. Among white women the club is the onward movement of the already uplifted.

The consciousness of being fully free has not yet come to the great masses of the colored women in this country. The emancipation of the mind and spirit of the race could not be accomplished by legislation. More time, more patience, more suffering and more charity are still needed to complete the work of emancipation. . . .

With this training the more intelligent women of the race could not fail to follow the example and be inspired by the larger club movement of the white women. The need of social reconstruction became more and more apparent as they studied the results of women's organizations. Better homes, better schools, better protection for girls of scant home training, better sanitary conditions, better opportunities for competent young women to gain employment, and the need of being better known to the American people appealed to the conscience of progressive colored women from many communities.

The clubs and leagues organized among colored women have all been more or less in direct response to these appeals. Seriousness of purpose has thus been the main characteristic of all these organizations. While the National Federation of Woman's Clubs has served as a guide and inspiration to colored women, the club movement among them is something deeper than a mere imitation of white women.

It is nothing less than the organized anxiety of women who have become intelligent enough to recognize their own low social condition and strong enough to initiate the forces of reform. . . .

It will thus be seen that from 1890 to 1895 the character of Afro-American womanhood began to assert itself in definite purposes and efforts in club work. Many of these clubs came into being all unconscious of the influences of the larger club movement among white women. . . .

Colored women everywhere were quick to see the possible benefits to be derived from a National conference of representative women. It was everywhere believed that such a convention, conducted with decorum, and along the lines of serious purpose might help in a decided manner to change public opinion concerning the character and worth of colored women. This agitation had the effect of committing most of the clubs to the proposal for a call in the summer of 1895. While public-spirited Afro-American women everywhere were thus aroused to this larger vision in plans for race amelioration, there occurred an incident of aggravation that swept away all timidity and doubt as to the necessity of a National conference. Some obscure editor in a Missouri town sought to gain notoriety by publishing a libelous article in which the colored women of the country were described as having no sense of virtue and altogether without character. The article in question was in the form of an open letter addressed to Miss Florence Belgarnie of England, who had manifested a kindly interest in behalf of the American negro as a result of Miss Ida B. Wells' agitation. This letter is too foul for reprint, but the effect of its publication stirred the intelligent colored women of America as nothing else had ever done. The letter, in spite of its wanton meanness, was not without some value in showing to what extent the sensitiveness of colored women had grown. Twenty years prior to this time a similar publication would scarcely have been noticed, beyond the small circles of the few who could read, and were public-spirited. In 1895 this open and vulgar attack on the character of a whole race of women was instantly and vehemently resented, in every possibly way, by a whole race of women conscious of being slandered. Mass meetings were held in every part of the country to denounce the editor and refute the charges.

. . . It, perhaps, should be confessed that in spite of the actual good already realized, the club movement is more of a prophecy than a thing accomplished. Colored women organized have succeeded in touching the heart of the race, and for the first time the thrill of unity has been felt. They have set in motion moral forces that are beginning to socialize interests that have been kept apart by ignorance and the spirit of dependence.

They have begun to make the virtues as well as the wants of the colored women known to the American people. They are striving to put a new social value on themselves. Yet their work has just begun. It takes more than five or ten years to effect the social uplift of a while race of people.

The club movement is well purposed. There is in it a strong faith, an enthusiasm born of love and sympathy, and an ever-increasing intelligence in the ways and means of affecting noble results. It is not a fad. It is not an imitation. It is not a passing sentiment. It is not an expedient, or an experiment. It is rather the force of a new intelligence against the old ignorance. The struggle of an enlightened conscience against the whole brood of social miseries born out of the stress and pain of a hated past.

119

R. D. SPRAGUE, MARY CHURCH TERRELL, ROSA D. BOWSER
What Role Is the Educated Negro Woman To Play in the Uplifting of Her Race (1902)

R. D. SPRAGUE

. . . Barring the barriers that avarice has placed in our way in the past or the growing egotism of our brothers in white at this stage of our progress, the women of the Negro race should put themselves in contact with all the women of this land and espouse all worthy efforts for the advancement of the human race.

The educated Negro woman will find that her greatest field for effective work is in the home. The attributes that are necessary in forming an upright character are each of them facts, the acceptance of them making or marring the character as they are accepted or ignored.

In view of this thought I cannot see that any different role should be adopted by us than by women in general in this land.

Industry, honesty and morality are the cardinal attributes to become acquainted with in forming an irreproachable character, and each and all of them must be dwelt upon in the home. Already the mothers all over the country are uniting themselves in the one thought—*the home.* No less should our women esteem it essential to place themselves in line with the progressive mothers in our common country. In advancing such a thought we are confronted with the fact that the development of the homes of this land has not been a day's work, and the improvement of the character of the homes will test the energies of the women who preside over them. The home life of the Negro has taken on a new sig-

From *Twentieth Century Negro Literature. Or A Cyclopedia of Thought on the Vital Topics Relating to the American Negro*, ed., D.W. Culp (Toronto: J.L. Nichols and Co., 1902), 167–69, 170, 171, 173–75, 176, 177–78, 181.

nificance during the past thirty or more years, and the zeal required to show the parents today their duties in the rearing of their children should be untiring. We have a few among us that are interested workers for the maintenance of good government in the home. . . .

It is a source of regret and deep concern to a number of our women that there is so little attention paid to the labors of "The woman's Christian Temperance Union," when we reflect that through the medium of rum, and, I may add, red beads, African homes were devastated. We wonder at the apathy of our women in the matter of temperance. The homes of the race can but be humble and poverty-stricken so long as the men and women in them are intemperate. The educated women among us need to set the pace in discountenancing the social glass in their homes. In this transition stage toward a higher plane of civilization we need every faculty pure and undefiled to do the work that will lift us to a merited place in our land. Surely our women must see the necessity of urgent endeavor against a traffic fraught with so much that is inimical to the promotion of good citizenship and purer and better homes. . . .

The motto of the National Association of Colored Women, "Lifting as we climb," is in itself an inspiration to great activity in all moral reforms; and with a spirit of devotion for the welfare of humanity we embraced the work of the Woman's Christian Temperance Union in their motto, "For God and Home and Native Land." . . .

MARY CHURCH TERRELL

. . . Questions affecting our legal status as a race are sometimes agitated by our women. In Tennessee and Louisiana colored women have several times petitioned the legislature of their respective States to repeal the obnoxious Jim Crow car laws. In every way possible we are calling attention to the barbarity of the convict lease system, of which Negroes and especially the female prisoners are the principal victims, with the hope that the conscience of the country may

be touched and this stain on its escutcheon be forever wiped away. Against the one room cabin we have inaugurated a vigorous crusade. When families of eight or ten men, women and children are all huddled promiscuously together in a single apartment, a condition common among our poor all over the land, there is little hope of inculcating morality and modesty. And yet in spite of the fateful heritage of slavery, in spite of the manifold pitfalls and peculiar temptations to which our girls are subjected, and though the safeguards usually thrown around maidenly youth and innocence are in some sections entirely withheld from colored girls, statistics compiled by men not inclined to falsify in favor of my race show that immorality among colored women is not so great as among women in some foreign countries who are equally ignorant, poor and oppressed.

Believing that it is only through the home that a people can become really good and truly great the National Association has entered that sacred domain. Homes, more homes, better homes, purer homes is the text upon which sermons have been and will be preached. There has been a determined effort to have heart to heart talks with our women that we may strike at the root of evils, many of which lie at the fireside. If the women of the dominant race, with all the centuries of education, culture and refinement back of them, with all the wealth of opportunity ever present with them, feel the need of a mother's congress, that they may be enlightened upon the best methods of rearing their children and conducting their homes, how much more do our women, from whom shackles have but yesterday been stricken, need information on the same vital subjects. And so the association is working vigorously to establish mothers' congresses on a small scale, wherever our women can be reached.

. . . Some of our women are now urging their clubs to establish day nurseries, a charity of which there is an imperative need. Thousands of our wage-earning mothers with large families dependent almost entirely upon them for support are obliged to leave their children all day, entrusted to the care of small brothers and sisters, or some good-natured neighbor who promises much, but who does little. Some of these infants are locked alone in the room from the time the mother leaves in the morning, until she returns at night. Not long ago I read in a Southern newspaper that an infant thus locked alone in a room all day, while its mother went out to wash, had cried itself to death. When one reflects upon the slaughter of the innocents which is occurring with pitiless persistency every day and thinks of the multitudes who are maimed for life or are rendered imbecile because of the treatment received during their helpless infancy, it is evident that by establishing day nurseries colored women will render one of the greatest services possible to humanity and to the race.

Nothing lies nearer the heart of colored women than the children. We feel keenly the need of kindergartens and are putting forth earnest efforts to honey-comb this country with them from one extremity to the other. The more unfavorable the environments of children the more necessary is it that steps be taken to counteract baleful influences upon innocent victims. How imperative is it then that as colored women we inculcate correct principles and set good examples for our own youth whose little feet will have so many thorny paths of temptation, injustice and prejudice to tread. So keenly alive is the National Association to the necessity of rescuing our little ones whose evil nature alone is encouraged to develop and whose noble qualities are deadened and dwarfed by the very atmosphere which they breathe, that its officers are trying to raise money with which to send out a kindergarten organizer, whose duty it shall be to arouse the conscience of our women and to establish kindergartens wherever means therefor can be secured.

Through the children of to-day we believe we can build the foundation of the next generation upon such a rock of morality, intelligence and strength, that the floods of proscription,

prejudice and persecution may descend upon it in torrents and yet it will not be moved. We hear a great deal about the race problem and how to solve it. The real solution of the race problem lies in the children, both so far as we who are oppressed and those who oppress us are concerned. Some of our women who have consecrated their lives to the elevation of their race feel that neither individuals nor organizations working toward this end should be entirely satisfied with their efforts unless some of their energy, money or brain is used in the name and for the sake of the children.

The National Association has chosen as its motto: Lifting as We Climb. In order to live strictly up to this sentiment, its members have determined to come into the closest possible touch with the masses of our women, through whom the womanhood of our people is always judged. It is unfortunate, but it is true, that the dominant race in this country insists upon gauging the Negro's worth by his most illiterate and vicious representatives rather than by the more intelligent and worthy classes. Colored women of education and culture know that they cannot escape altogether the consequences of the acts of their most depraved sisters. They see that even if they were wicked enough to turn a deaf ear to the call of duty, both policy and self-preservation demand that they go down among the lowly, the illiterate and even the vicious, to whom they are bound by the ties of race and sex, and put forth every possible effort to reclaim them. By coming into close touch with the masses of our women it is possible to correct many of the evils which militate so seriously against us and inaugurate the reforms, without which, as a race, we cannot hope to succeed. . . .

Carefully and conscientiously we shall study the questions which affect the race most deeply and directly. Against the convict lease system, the Jim Crow car laws, lynchings and all other barbarities which degrade us, we shall protest with such force of logic and intensity of soul that those who oppress us will either cease to disavow the inalienability and equality of human rights, or be ashamed to openly violate the very principles upon which this government was founded. By discharging our obligation to the children, by coming into the closest possible touch with the masses of our people, by studying the labor question as it affects the race, by establishing schools of domestic science, by setting a high moral standard and living up to it, by purifying the home, colored women will render their race a service whose value it is not in my power to estimate or express. The National Association is being cherished with such loyalty and zeal by our women that there is every reason to hope it will soon become the power for good, the tower of strength and the source of inspiration to which it is destined.

And so lifting as we climb, onward and upward we go, struggling and striving and hoping that the buds and blossoms of our desires will burst into glorious fruition ere long. With courage born of success achieved in the past, with a keen sense of the responsibility which we must continue to assume we look forward to the future, large with promise and hope. Seeking no favors because of our color or patronage because of our needs, we knock at the bar of justice and ask for an equal chance.

ROSA D. BOWSER

In all the ages of the world woman has been the central figure around which all joys and sorrows, all inspirations, all aspirations, and all accomplishments have circled. In all conditions of life, in all climes, in all Christian epochs, in all countries, she holds this position indisputable among the nations of the earth. For without her there would be no home circles, without the home circles there would be no races nor nations. Her office, of divine institution for the perpetuation of the human family, should not be lightly regarded by any class of people. Woman's primary duty is the systematic and wise ordering of the household. The infant looks into its mother's face and there receives its first impressions. These impressions are stamped upon the mind and heart of the child. The mother notices all the little disorders and griefs of the child from its birth throughout its life. The conscientious mother is ever ready to console, advise and sympathize in all grievances and perplexities which may confront her offspring. Hence there is great need for proper instruction to wives, mothers, and, in fact, to all women in anticipation of the responsibilities of a home, and the obligations of motherhood. It has been well said that the training of children should begin with their grandparents. The character of the homes of the land, the moral and immoral bearing of every settlement, town, and city in a large measure depend upon the class of women—upon the idiosyncrasies of wives, mothers, and women in general, who by nature mould the sentiment of every department of human control. That society is ruled by women cannot be questioned. The age of complete dependence of women upon the stronger sex, has so far passed as to be foreign to the minds of the present generation. Not that the gentler sex is averse to the protection and tender solicitudes of the father, husband and brother, but it is of such common occurrence that women are thrown upon their own resources in the maintenance of the home, that they of necessity rather than from choice assume a degree of independence in various avenues of life. . . .

Such are the women needed to-day. Women who teach by doing. Women who can take a basket of soap on the arm, and in a gentle, winning way present it to homes that need it, while at the same time extol its merits in a pleasant manner. Women are needed who can teach the lesson of morality, cleanliness of soul and body, and the hygienic and economic management of the humble home, by showing them how to perform these acts, and furnish examples. Women who can arouse their sense of propriety to such a degree that by frugal habits they may abandon the one-room cabin in which a family of eight or ten eat, cook, sleep, wash and iron, for the neat two, three, or four-room well ventilated cottage. The laundry tub may be an excellent substitute when no better can be provided, but they will be taught to see the need of a genuine bath tub in every home. They will be taught that honest labor is no disgrace; that, however, much education one may acquire, the deftness of the hands to execute the mandates of the mind tends rather to elevate the possessor, and hastens the day of a full developed man or woman with mind, heart, and hand trained to the best service—thereby dignifying labor. Above all, the thought must be impressed indelibly upon the hearts and consciences of the youth that the men can be no better than the women. Men are what the women make them. If a woman is refined, and exhibits a modest, dignified bearing, men can not fail to appreciate her demeanor and conduct themselves accordingly. While, on the other hand, boisterous, uncouth conduct upon the part of women will encourage boldness toward them, disrespect for them, and win the contempt of the men of a community for such women. Hence, wherever uplifting influence is needed, the result of the labor depends upon the compliant nature of the element upon which they are working, whose persuasive power is more efficacious in directing the *upward* and *downward* trend of the masses. The women who can best appreciate this fact have the very grave responsibility of keeping the lesson constantly before the people—"Lest we forget, lest we forget." The so-called Negro problem must be solved by the Negro.

IV. Women and Labor

AFTER THE CIVIL WAR AMERICAN FEMINISM BECAME increasingly concerned with economic rights and social welfare, as a growing number of women became wage earners. As a rapidly expanding industrial economy began to draw still more young women away from home and family, many recognized the need to protect and expand the interests of the woman worker since capitalism devalued female labor and male-run unions and other labor organizations regularly excluded women. Feminists also began more vocally to value paid labor as a means not just of economic independence but also of self-fulfillment. In "Opening for New Employments for Women" (1869), Virginia Penny speaks of the primacy of work to the identity of women, urging others to push their way into new occupations, and arguing that both business and the state should encourage and support women's training and employment.

In the "The Working Women's Association" (1868), Elizabeth Cady Stanton describes the goals of the organization by the same name, founded by Susan B. Anthony in New York City in 1868. Higher wages and the establishment of trade unions were the two central concerns of the working women themselves, although Anthony thought the association would lend strength to what she considered the all-important push for the ballot.

Another purpose of the Working Women's Association would be to address the practical, everyday problems of workers who found themselves alone in the city; the Association also wanted to "elevate" workers, a goal that sometimes put the middle-class organizers in the position of patronizing working women. "The Working Women's Association and the Case of Hester Vaughan" (1868) describes the efforts taken for a destitute immigrant who, after being sexually overcome by "brute force," was convicted of infanticide and sentenced to death. In its first public act, the Working Women's Association petitioned the Governor of Pennsylvania to pardon Hester Vaughan. Leaders of the Association argued that Vaughan was a perfect example of the horrors to which working women were subjected: inability to find any work other than domestic service and the sexual double standard that caused Vaughan to bear all the blame for her pregnancy. Vaughan was finally pardoned.

In the mid- to late-nineteenth century, groups of working women not uncommonly appealed to government bodies for consideration and assistance. "A Petition of the Working Women to the Massachusetts Legislature: A Modest and Strong Appeal" (1869) goes as far as asking the state to build housing for single women wage earners; the petitioners—a group of Boston sewing women—carefully versed this bold request in the language of dependency, appealing to the legislature's paternalistic sensibility. As women, these workers wanted families, the petition added, but since women far outnumbered men they had to fend for themselves. Predictably, the legislature denied the petition.

While most labor unions of late-nineteenth-century America kept their doors closed to women workers, the Knights of Labor—which began as a secret society of tailors in Philadelphia in 1869 and would grow into the most important union of the nineteenth century—started to accept female members in 1879. In 1885, the national convention of the Knights (called the "General Assembly") created a committee to "collect statistics on women's work," and the following year it established a Department of Woman's Work with Leonora Barry as the General Investigator. In the three and a half years she held the post, Barry travelled throughout the United States and then summarized and presented her findings to the General Assembly, as in "A Report of the General Investigator of Woman's Work and Wages to the Knights of Labor" (1888).

Except for gains in the Knights of Labor, women workers at the end of the nineteenth century found it difficult to make inroads into organized labor. The American Federation of Labor (AFL), a national association of trade unions founded in 1886, offered women hope, however, as it appointed female organizers in 1891 and, to some extent, opened itself up to the interests of women workers. In "Woman and Labor" (1896), Eva McDonald Valesh—a regular contributor to and managing editor of the AFL journal, *The American Federationist*—makes a strong case for the inclusion of women in organized labor, arguing that the well-being of many young women depends on the organizational support and increasing political clout of the male-run association.

Feminist leaders at the end of the nineteenth century drew from the on-going legacy of women among the paid work force to support the claim that American women deserved the vote. Harriot Stanton Blatch and Florence Kelley make this point in their speeches "Women, Work and Citizenship," given in 1898 before the National American Woman Suffrage Association convention in Washington D.C., emphasizing that, as integral and productive members of society, women needed the ballot.

A collective identity and consciousness of women as workers developed as more and more women in the late-nineteenth century started to support themselves through wage labor. Rebecca's "Letter From a Working Girl" (1886)—a popular column in the New York City labor newspaper *John Swinton's Paper*—betrays both pride of independence among the sewers and also the need for greater organizational support, so they may receive "fair wages and decent treatment." In "Why Do People Look Down On Working Girls?" (1891), Lucy A. Warner champions the qualities of young working women, pointing out that only circumstance separates her from her better educated, middle-class sisters.

Along with the push for better conditions of employment, workers and middle-class reformers opened clubs and supervised boarding houses, attempting to infuse domestic values into the lives of young single women. In 1881, Grace H. Dodge, from an old, well-to-do New York family, opened the first "Working Girls Club"—a group of factory workers from the silk industry who met weekly for conversation and discussion of such topics as proper "lady-like" dress, language, and behavior. Dodge's idea had spread widely by 1885, when she founded the Association of Working Girls Societies. Dodge also published advice manuals for young working women; in "Working and Saving" (1887), she extols the virtues of thrift and self-reliance.

In "Women Wage Workers: With Reference to Directing Immigrants" (1893), Julia Richman speaks of the revolutionary advances working women have made in the United States, adding that Jewish immigrants have made the most progress in travelling from the old world to the new. Richman goes on to examine the different strata of employment open to American women, detailing which positions are most commonly filled by immigrant workers.

Many feminist arguments about the need to better women's working conditions reflected the predominantly middle-class standing of the movement's leaders. In a startling essay, however, Kate Richards essay develops an identity as a working socialist. "How I Became a Socialist Agitator" (1908) chronicles her fascinating, wide-ranging experiences as a girl growing up on a Kansas ranch, to her religious and temperance work in the slums of Kansas City, to learning a trade as a machinist and the evolution of her working-class consciousness. After meeting Mother Jones at a labor rally, Richards devoted herself to socialism and specifically to the organization of labor.

A common source of tension in the late-nineteenth century writings of working women is the subject of love and marriage—that institution consistently held to be diametrically opposed to women's earning a living on their own. In "Work and Wages" (1869), Anna Dickinson criticizes the idea and propensity of women taking a husband for financial security, arguing that if equal wage scales existed women would not have to sacrifice their autonomy to loveless marriage. Mary A. Livermore seconds this point in her essay "Superfluous Women" (1883), adding that women desperately need access to higher education and new forms of labor so they may free themselves from dependency on men. In "Matrimony as a Last Resort" (1897), Lucinda B. Chandler takes the point of Dickinson and Livermore a step further by likening marriage for material comfort to prostitution; she wonders why nobody is shocked by this practice. Finally, Eliza S. Turner answers the question "Should Women Work Outside Their Homes?" (1895) by pointing out that work *inside* the home is becoming less and less taxing and rewarding, suggesting that a woman of intelligence and "spirit" would find little to do.

Charlotte Perkins Gilman, one of the most prolific feminist writers in American history, offers in "Women and Economics" (drawn from her 1898 master work of the same title), a broadly-gauged, sociological and anthropological analysis of women's social subordination through their material dependency on men.

120

Virginia Penny
Opening of New Employments for Women (1869)

Selfishness and prejudice have closed, and kept closed, many of the employments in which women might have engaged. They have been monopolized by men, and men have been enabled to sustain their monopoly by public opinion. But they have suffered from the results of their injustice in the loss of health, strength, and manliness.

A wider scope is needed for the employment of active, intelligent females. Even some of the few branches of industry open to women have been done away, within the last few years, by the invention of machinery. The general use of sewing machines, and the introduction of stencil plates for maps, have thrown a large number of women out of employment. The mass of women, in moderate circumstances, seem to be hedged in more and more from year to year.

Mrs. Stephens writes, "Look at the employments vouchsafed to our women. How few they are; how scanty and how worthless! That which no man will touch is always good enough for a woman. Look at their pay when they labor diligently and faithfully all their lives long, poor creatures, in the hope of saving a little for the day of sorrow! And these employments are vouchsafed, and these prices are paid by *men,* and among men—men who would have the women of their country believe that they have a hearty desire to promote the welfare, and the comfort, and the goodness of woman. God forgive them."

Says the author of "Woman and Work," "We hear cries that the world is going wrong for want of women; that Moral Progress cannot be made without their help; that Science wants the light

From *Think and Act: A Series of Articles Pertaining to Men and Women, Work and Wages* (Philadelphia: Claxton, Remsen, & Haffelfinger, 1869), 19–26.

of their delicate perceptions; that Moral Philosophy wants the light of their peculiar points of view; Political Economy their directness of judgment and sympathy with the commonalty; Government the help of their power of organizing; and Philanthropy their delicate tact. Hospitals must have them, asserts one; Watches must be made by them, cries another; Workhouses, Prisons, Schools, Reformatories, Penitentiaries, Sanctoriums are going to rack and ruin for want of them; Medicine needs them; the Church calls for them; the Arts and Manufactures invite them."

One great corresponding cry rises from a suffering multitude of women, saying, "We want work." It is unjust to say, sneeringly, if women wish to work, why do they not?

Some exclaim, O, keep woman to woman's work! We say so too, as far as it is practicable. Is there not enough work in the United States to keep all employed that are willing to labor, and wish to? We dare not say there is not a man or woman that wants remunerative employment but what can obtain it. No; we know it is not so. In our large cities there is many a genteel young woman that would be glad to obtain employment for her board; and there are hundreds, yes, thousands, of women thrown upon their own resources by the war who were tenderly reared, and possessed all the comforts, and even luxuries, of life.

"Blind, indeed, must they be who cannot see that there is a pressing from the ranks of domestic service as wives and servants; that there is another current, large and strong, for which a way must be opened. If it is not done, it will force itself into various channels. That is, in fact, already taking place. The departments of wood-engraving, plaster statuary, watch-making, &c., are being entered. Teachers, shopkeepers, and factory operatives have, for a long time, received file after file of women to their ranks. And what woman would force them back when it is that work, starvation, or ruin?"

The opening of a new field of labor in one country to women makes easier the way for its introduction into other countries. There are some women of great genius and daring courage, who tread down all difficulties, and dash aside all opposition, to make their way into and through an occupation suitable, but hitherto closed, to woman. Agricultural, trading, and manufacturing interests have received an impetus from the quick and vigorous exercise of woman's talents.

A woman should be able to acquire a standing in society by honorable exertion. It would be well for a woman to feel that she has the whole world to work in. If she has health, and is properly trained for a pursuit, she can somewhere find work to do; of a large portion of the earth is nothing more than a moral chaos, a wilderness of business. But women ought not to expect to occupy important places without proper training. They should be willing to pass through a series of gradations, such as is common with men, and also to acquire business habits.

To enter and prosecute new branches of female employment will awaken latent energy and talent, and do away with much idleness that now exists. "They who are always so willing to assist others, to their own detriment, should now, in turn,—for their wants call loudly for it,—be assisted and encouraged to strike out a new path by which they could assist themselves. There must be a change for the better in the efforts of women. Many are degraded by their poverty; and their degradation is the cause of nearly all the crime that is committed."

It is difficult to decide what occupations are most suitable for women without further trial, so little attention has been given to the subject. Schools for teaching girls some of the mechanic arts should be established in every town and city. Is not the Government or state as justifiable in taxing the population for the establishment of schools, where the industrial arts shall be taught, as the branches of a book education? One is essential to the existence; the other, though desirable, can be dispensed with. The rising generation of females will probably have more

advantages in the selection and prosecution of suitable employments than the present.

With us, in the United States, there is even a greater deficiency in the variety of employments than with the nations of Europe. It has probably arisen from the greater demand for women in domestic life, and the lower wages paid for men's labor in Europe.

We have been told that there are about four times as many occupations open to women in New York as in any other city of the country. In the United States, pride and prejudice are not able to raise as great barriers as in older countries, whose foundations were laid during the mediaeval age. Here, rank is not so distinctly defined by the grades that accident makes. Here, the hearts of the higher classes are not kept so within the bounds of their own choice circles, but run through the ramifications of a far-reaching humanity.

If a woman has education, health, judgment, some knowledge of human nature, and a small capital, she might, in favorable times for business, earn a livelihood in almost any suitable branch she selects. She certainly can when there are not already enough engaged in it. But it will be necessary for success that she give her time and undivided attention to her business, and she will be better qualified, if prepared for it early in life.

Perhaps it would be difficult for women in large cities to commence in those branches of business hitherto unoccupied by their sex. It might require more capital than in smaller places. Yet so many changes are constantly taking place in business establishments, in some cities, that a woman might enter at some favorable juncture. In the western towns that are springing up and growing so rapidly, women with a small capital, and a knowledge of business, and the wants of the people, could, with success, enter into some paying business.

Mrs. Jameson mentions a reformatory prison she visited in Europe, "governed chiefly by women—and the women, as well as the men, who directed it, were responsible only to the government." "There are offices, either entire, or half-sinecures, connected with our government affairs, that are well suited for women."

Women more frequently err from ignorance of their duties, and the way in which to perform them, than from any inherent evil. I believe there are very few women that would go astray if honest employments were provided for them at *living prices*. Much of the degradation, madness, and suicide, that we hear of among women, in the humbler walks of life, arises from a want of properly remunerated labor—from destitution—from a want of sympathy and guidance from those of their sex in the higher walks of life with whom they have to do. It is the utter loneliness, and uncertainty of a home, from day to day, that drives many to desperation.

A woman is apt to grow selfish with no one but herself to think of—to grow bitter in her feelings if conscious that she is unjustly debarred from her natural sphere of action.

A man's occupation furnishes him with a source of thought and activity; it exercises his talents, matures his judgment, cultivates foresight; it stimulates to the acquisition of knowledge; it prompts to an efficient use of his powers and property; it promotes health and enlivens his spirits. The same effect would be produced on women that would devote themselves to the prosecution of some *intelligent* pursuit.

Educated women doomed to menial labor, (aside from that attending every one's own household,) feel that society has driven them to a position they were not made to occupy. And so the moral nature suffers. A constant sense of injustice preys upon the mind; while if some congenial pursuit were offered them they would enter it with eagerness, and pursue it with enthusiasm. If a boy belonging to a good family loses his father, and with him his support, or is deprived by adverse circumstances of an expected fortune, much sympathy and interest are elicited. Friends unite and counsel with him, and aid him pecuniarily while he prepares for business. How different is it with girls! There is rarely

any provision made for the future. They, perhaps, are forced into some trade, already filled, that must be hurriedly, and therefore indifferently, learned, or must subsist in a poor, shabby way, in an indifferent home, oppressed with care and anxiety for those of their family similarly situated.* Such facts are proof that new employments must be entered by women. The condition of affairs in all civilized countries demands it. It is a want of the times, and must be met. If not, hundreds, yea, thousands, of our sex sink into ruin. The condition of woman cannot be stationary. It must either advance or recede.

The precarious subsistence of dependent women cannot but excite the sympathy and interest of philanthropists. Some remedy should be devised to furnish them with more permanent and reliable sources of support. The *few* employments hitherto opened to women are crowded. Some cannot find employment, and many that can, eke out but a scanty subsistence. Why should not women have a variety of occupations as well as men? Why should they not exercise some choice in the selection of an occupation as well as men? The mind now vacant, or filled with idle fancies, might be profitably occupied in directing all its powers to the acquisition or prosecution of some useful employment. The industrial energies of women need to be turned into a proper channel—their talents profitably directed. There would not be so many suicides among the poor women of France and England if sufficient employment, at living rates, was offered hem. The opening of new employments will do much to prevent prostitution. The low wages paid females, the small number of occupations open to them, and the excess to which they are crowded, are filling our

---

* Many clergymen with good salaries, and having congregations in easy circumstances, are either ignorant of, or affect ignorance of, the condition of poor, hardworking, and of destitute educated women. And when they are convinced of existing errors in society, they talk and write as if such errors could not be remedied, or propose some visionary, impracticable, remedy. (See "Woman's Rights," by Rev. John Todd.)

prisons, our penitentiaries, and almshouses. Who will not try to save one soul at least? It will be a bright star in the crown of one's rejoicing.

It is necessary for women to have some definite idea of what their resources may be—to what branches of business they may fly with hope of success. The occupations of men have formed a circle; those of women have not been even the segment of a circle.

We need a more systematic arrangement of labor for women. In every city and large town there should be a market for labor just as there is a market for anything else. There should be, in the different callings pursued by human beings, enough employment for women suited to their natures and capacities. There should also be employment enough for men; but some in which they now engage is beneath their dignity as men, and unworthy their strength. They are pursuits that should be in the hands of women. A strong, healthy man behind the counter of a fancy store, in a millinery establishment, on his knees fitting ladies' shoes, at hotels laying the plates and napkins of a dinner table, is as much out of place, as a woman chopping wood, carrying in coal, or sweeping the streets.

By women having a variety of employments open to them they could command better prices for their work; for if one occupation did not pay they could learn another—one that did pay. We think a state of affairs would be brought about different from that in France. There all occupations are open to women, yet their wages are not more than half as high as men's. That is the result of a custom already established. Affairs might be differently arranged in a democratic government of the present time.

Women, in their ignorance of the nature of different occupations, and the fear of being ridiculed or rudely treated, often pass by those best suited to them, and engage in those altogether unfit, while the men are only too ready, and too willing, to seize the opportunity of entering into the duties of the lighter, and easier occupations. All the most intelligent and well-paid occupa-

tions, and some of the most enervating and ornamental, are engrossed by men, while the most poorly paid, laborious, and disagreeable work is done by women. Thousands of females sacrifice their tastes, and even their talents, every day of the world, for the purpose of earning an honest livelihood. But if more occupations were understood by women, there would be no need of such sacrifice. Any person who opens a new branch of industry to women confers one of the greatest blessings on the inhabitants of a large city. Let women step forward into new fields of labor as a matter of justice to themselves. American women should prepare themselves for the higher departments of labor, leaving the lower to foreigners, who have more bodily strength.

121

ELIZABETH CADY STANTON
The Working Women's Association (1868)

The Working Woman's movement in this city is already assuming an importance unlooked for by the few who met together scarce one month since in the office of "THE REVOLUTION," to discuss the necessity of doing something for the protection of woman's labor. We well remember the shrinking manners and uncertain speech of those who did come; fearing lest in asking for more they should lose all. Those who had suffered the most from low wages were the most timid in taking any steps for their own advantage that might call down on them the displeasure of their employers, and all alike failed to see that the right of suffrage laid at the foundation of all social and civil equality. As the meetings were held week after week, many were threatened with instant dismissal by their employers, if they made any reports of their work and wages, and many laboring men forbid their wives, sisters and daughters going to the office

From *The Revolution*, November 6, 1868.

of "The Revolution." Such a dread have the "white males" in general of the coming rebellion among the women of the land, that all affiliation with the "strong-minded" is forbidden as dangerous both to the family and the nation. But in spite of all opposition the meetings have gradually increased in numbers until our apartments are too small for their accommodation.

A Working Woman's Association was organized by Susan B. Anthony, which now numbers over two hundred members. They are to meet once a month to devise ways and means to open to themselves new and more profitable employments, that thus by decreasing the numbers in the few avocations now open to women, they can decrease the supply and raise the wages of those who remain. They propose, also, to demand an increase of wages in all those trades where they now work beside men for half pay. This can only be done by combination, for one person alone demanding higher wages can effect nothing, but 5,000 women in any one employment, striking for higher wages, would speedily bring their employers to terms. Out of the present Association will be formed co-operative unions in every branch of industry, with funds that will enable them to maintain themselves during the period of a strike. The men's typographical union have pledged the women to stand by them in their proposed demand for higher wages. As the gods help those who help themselves, we urge on all working women to rouse up from the lethargy of despair and make one combined, determined effort to secure for themselves an equal chance with men in the whole world of work. We urge women of wealth all over the country to devote themselves for a time to helping their own sex. Let the churches, the colleges, the schools where men preach and pray and vote and teach and pocket all the salaries, help themselves while Christian women study what Ruskin calls the three fine arts, how to feed, clothe and house the poor; and let them give every thought and effort to the protection,

education and elevation of the young girls of our laboring classes. It is a shame that so many women have large bequests to churches, where women are not permitted to speak or vote, and to colleges where girls are forbidden to enter. Let every man of wealth educate his daughter for some profitable and honorable post of life, that if left to depend on herself she need not fall into the ranks of the seamstress or the household drudge and thus crowd woman's present employments. Let women of wealth and brains step out of the circles of fashion and folly, and fit themselves for the trades, arts, and professions, and become employers, instead of subordinates; thus making labor honorable for all, and elevating their sex, by opening new avenues for aspiration and ambition. One of Miss Anthony's most cherished plans is to have a magnificent printing establishment, and a daily paper, owned and controlled and all the work done by women, thus giving employment to hundreds and making the world ring with the new evangel for woman.

The barbarisms perpetrated in our slop shops and in every department of labor where young girls are struggling for a virtuous living, by means of these associations and a daily organ, could then be brought to light and be heralded from pole to pole until the world should see the need of more humane and christian legislation for womankind. But while association will do much toward ameliorating some of the evils of our present social condition, so radical changes can be effected for woman's elevation until she holds the ballot, the citizens only shield of protection; in her own right hand.

E. C. S.

122
The Working Women's Association and the Case of Hester Vaughan (1868)

On the 6th of last August an editorial appeared in "THE REVOLUTION," calling public attention to the case of Hester Vaughan, under sentence of death for alleged infanticide. It was pronounced by it "judicial murder." On Thursday evening, Nov. 5th, Anna E. Dickinson, in her lecture at the Cooper Institute in behalf of the "Working Women's Association," in her usual graphic and feeling manner, described the girl's terrible wrongs and sufferings, and in this way aroused a large amount of interest in her behalf. Mrs. Stanton then treated the narrative to an editorial article in "THE REVOLUTION," which was very extensively copied by the press in all parts of the country. After this, several members of the "Working Women's Association," as well as many outside of this organization, called at the office of "THE REVOLUTION," 37 Park Row, to see what steps could be taken in the wretched woman's behalf. Nothing was decided upon until Eleanor Kirk, at the suggestion of R. J. Johnston, arose, in the next meeting of the Working Woman's Association and moved that the very first public step taken by this new Society should be to petition Gov. Geary for the pardon and release of Hester Vaughan. . . .

MRS. KIRK'S REPORT

   . . . Imagine, if you please, a girlish figure; a sweet, intelligent face; soft, brown eyes; broad forehead; warm, earnest mouth, and you have a slight idea of Hester Vaughan. Her story is quickly told. She was born in Gloucestershire, England; well reared by respectable parents; married a man, a native of Wales, and came to this country full of hope and enthusiasm for the future. A few weeks, and Hester was deserted. Some other woman had a prior claim, it is sup-

posed, and the scamp has never since been heard of. Then came the tug of war for Hester Vaughan, as for every other woman who, from what cause soever, finds herself compelled to fight the battle of life alone. Think of this young girl, a stranger in a strange land, with neither friend or relative to advise or comfort. For several weeks she lived out as servant in a family at Jenkintown; was then recommended as dairy maid to another family, and here misfortune befel her. Overcome, not in a moment of weakness and passion, but by superior strength—*brute force*—Hester Vaughan fell a victim to lust and the gallows. That man also went his way. Three months after this terrible occurrence, Hester removed to Philadelphia and hired a room there. She supported herself by little odd jobs of work from different families, always giving the most perfect satisfaction. During one of the fiercest storms of last winter she was without food or fire or comfortable apparel. She had been ill and partially unconscious for three days before her confinement, and a child was born to Hester Vaughan. Hours passed before she could drag herself to the door and cry out for assistance, and when she did it was to be dragged to a prison where she now lies with the near prospect of a halter. Is it not terrible that this victim of a man's craven lust should be thus fouly dealt with, while her seducer walks the earth free and unmolested? In this connection let me say that no amount of coaxing or entreaty will induce Hester Vaughan to name the man who thus cruelly wronged her. Since that time he has married. "If he were alone," said Hester, "I would ring his name through the whole country, but nothing will induce me to send terror and disgrace into the heart of an innocent, trusting woman." Glorious Hester Vaughan! True as steel to her own sex. Dr. Lozier will inform you how she came to be accused of infanticide. This comes under the head of medical testimony, and as I am entirely at sea on that subject I can only give as my belief from all that I saw and heard at Philadelphia, that Hester Vaughan is no more guilty of infanticide than I am.

From *The Revolution*, December 10, 1868.

. . . I had an interview with Judge Ludlow, the man who pronounced the sentence of death upon poor Hester. "I do not think her a bad woman naturally," said the Judge; "she has an excellent face, but there was no other course open for me but the broad course of condemnation; she was, in the opinion of the jury, guilty of the murder of her child. Mrs. Kirk," he continued, quite earnestly; "you have no idea how rapidly the crime of 'infanticide' is increasing. Some woman must be made an example of. It is for the establishment of a principle, ma'am." "Establishment of a principle" indeed. I suggested to the Judge that he inaugurate the good work by hanging a few men, but, strange to relate, he has not been able to see it in that light. Women of New York, women of America, turn your backs upon libertines. The victims of the fiends, you will see upon all sides as you go from your respective houses. . . .

MEMORIAL.

To His Excellency the Governor of the State of Pennsylvania:

The Working Women's National Association, through their Committee, whose name are hereto appended, after careful investigation of the case of Hester Vaughan, now confined in a Pennsylvania prison for the alleged crime of INFANTICIDE, would respectfully represent that, as they believe she was condemned on insufficient evidence and with inadequate defence, justice demands a stay of proceedings and a new trial; or, if that be impracticable, they most earnestly pray your Excellency to grant her an unconditional pardon.

RESOLUTIONS.

Whereas, The right of trial by a jury of one's peers is recognized by the governments of all civilized nations as the great palladium of rights, of justice, and equality to the citizen: therefore,

Resolved, That this Association demand that in all civil and criminal cases, woman shall be tried by a jury of her peers; shall have a voice in making the law, in electing the judge who pro-

nounces her sentence, and the sheriff who, in case of execution, performs for her that last dread act.

Resolved, That the existence of the Death Penalty, odious as it is when man is the victim, is doubly so in a case like this of Hester Vaughan—a young, artless, and inexperienced girl—a consideration that should startle every mother into a sense of her responsibility in making and executing the laws under which her daughters are to live or perish.

Resolved, That, as capital punishment is opposed to the genius of our institutions and the civilization of the age, we demand that the gallows—that *horrible relic of barbarism*—be banished from the land; for human life should be held alike sacred by the individual and the state.

123

A Petition of the Working Women to the Massachusetts Legislature: A Modest and Strong Appeal (1869)

To the Honorable the Senate and the House of Representatives of the Commonwealth of Massachusetts (which may God protect and prosper in General Court assembled.

We, the undersigned, workingwomen of the city of Boston, dependent for our daily bread upon the daily labor of our own hands, humbly make known to your honorable body that we are insufficiently paid for our labor, scantily clothed, poorly fed, and badly lodged.

That the mere physical health of many of us is becoming, or has already become, thoroughly undermined by habits of prolonged work, performed under the constant influence of deleterious conditions.

That many of us suffer in our moral natures through the lack of proper society with each other and with those whose influence would have

From *The Workingman's Advocate*, April 24, 1869.

a tendency to strengthen us and elevate us, we being prevented, by a natural pride, from showing ourselves, with such clothing as we have at command, either at church or in the company of persons whom we respect.

That we are, to a great extent, deprived of the consolations of the Christian religion, by being occupied throughout the week with incessant toil, thus being compelled, through sheer necessity, to bring up the arrears of our household duties by working on the Lord's day.

That many of our sisters are actually forced to make up for the insufficiency of their earnings, by a recourse to avocations ruinous to themselves and dangerous to the whole community.

That we are harshly judged by persons in prosperity, who do not stop to reflect that we are called upon to face trials, necessities and temptations, to which the wives, sisters and daughters of the members of your honorable body are never subjected, and that, in this way, our progressive isolation from redeeming moral influences is becoming more and more marked.

We are poor, ignorant women, with insufficient education, and without proper training. We do not presume to dictate any plan for our own relief. You know better than we do what the circumstances of our case requires. It is the humble prayer of your petitioners, that you should think for us, care for us, and take counsel from your own kind hearts to do for us better than we know how to ask.

We, nevertheless, pray your honorable body to cause to be purchased, in the neighborhood of Boston, a tract of good cultivated land; and to lay out the same in suitable lots, some of half an acre, some of an acre, and so on, to lots of three and five acres, with a good (but the cheapest possible) house on each lot. It is our desire that these lots should be let on lease to poor workingwomen of Boston, to whom the State would be willing to furnish rations, tools, seeds and instruction in gardening, until such time as the women would be able to raise their own food, or otherwise become self-supporting; the payment of rent to commence with the third year only, and the rent to be then so graduated, and so applied as purchase money, that each woman might, in a reasonable time, pay off, in the form of rent, the entire cost to the State of the lot on which she lives, with all other necessary incidental expenses, and become the sole proprietress of the lot in fee simple; or, if it be thought preferable, each lot may be held in trust by the State of the sole use and benefit of the woman who has paid for it under the form of rent, to pass to her female heirs in the event of her death. And it is our further desire that these homesteads may be exempted from all taxation and from all process for debt, and that the title to them may be nontransferable to any male person whatever.

We know that difficulties will at once suggest themselves to your minds; but we think that all serious objection to our plan may be easily answered. Is it our fault that the women of Massachusetts greatly outnumber the men? that we are precluded, by our relative weakness, from success in business competition with the men, we being formed by nature to help the men, and not to compete with them? It is evidence of great distress when women call for guarantees for separate existence; and it is not at all their fault that they cannot, at this day and hour, find for themselves husbands and homes.

We are assured that our petition, when you hear it, will awaken pity in your hearts, and that you will not receive it with indifference and neglect.

It it any worse for women to be collected together in a separate village by themselves, where they may exercise a moral influence upon each other, where their whole natures are invigorated by working upon the soil and in the open air, than it is for these same women to be scattered, as they now are, in the by-streets of a large city, where they have no collective responsibility, and where they are subjected to nameless and numberless necessities, trials, and temptations? Give us good and kind husbands and suitable homes, make our condition something distantly approximating to that of your own wives, and we withdraw this petition. It is not of our own choice that we ask you to secure to us the mere conventional existence we propose. It is no better for women to be alone than it is for man; and if by the inscrutable decrees of so allwise Providence, our existence is frustrated, and we live but half lives, not fulfilling our whole destinies as women upon the earth, are we unreasonable in asking that our condition shall be made as tolerable as circumstances permit?

We have further to request that, if you deign to give us a hearing, you will call some of our number before you, and cross-question us, thus eliciting the required testimony. We are poor, ignorant women, unable to arrange our own ideas, or to properly state our own case; but we think we can answer your questions.

We hope no one will be allowed except at our own express desire, to speak before your committee in our name.

Such time as you may be disposed to give us will be occupied, we hope, with an investigation of the matter presented by this petition, and not by discussions of universal philanthropy.

And now, praying that the Eternal Lawmaker, who alone hath inherent immortality who is the invisible and only wise God, may have you continually in holy keeping, and incline your hearts to give a favorable answer to this our humble petition, we, who have no vote, no voice in public affairs, remain, as always, loyal subjects of the glorious old Commonwealth of Massachusetts.

124

L. M. BARRY

A Report of the General Investigator of Woman's Work and Wages to the Knights of Labor (1888)

PHILADELPHIA, PA., October 15, 1888.
To the Officers and Members of the General Assembly of the K. of L., Greeting:

GENERAL MASTER WORKMAN, BROTHERS AND SISTERS:—Once again we are assembled for the purpose of reviewing the past and deliberating on measures for the future welfare of our constituency. With your other servants I herewith submit my annual report, with such suggestions and recommendations as my observations and judgment warrant me in believing to be for the best interest of all concerned. Ere I have concluded many may say I have done more lecturing than investigating. I have neglected neither wherever I found an opportunity to carry them out. I found by repeated trial and failure that to investigate the condition of women as thoroughly as I could wish was, as a Knight of Labor, simply impossible, as not only did employers refuse me the opportunity, but cautious friends of the employed warned them against ever holding conversation with the General Investigator, lest some error be made public for which they would receive blame and consequent discharge.

I did not feel justified in spending the time and money of my constituents in playing the spy or detective, as since we have set the ball of exposing the wrongs and injustice done workingwomen a rolling others have entered the field in this line, and with what success all must be satisfied who have followed the footsteps of Nell Nelson, Ethel Allan and our own dear Eva

An Address at the General Assembly of the Knights of Labor, Philadelphia, October 15, 1888. From *Proceedings of the Knights of Labor*, 1888.

Gay. Neither did I feel justified in going around among industries and gathering from officials or employers such information as they would give, knowing that such knowledge could be gleaned form the reports of our Labor Bureaus and State Factory Inspectors.

My understanding of the duties implied in my office was that I was to do everything in my power that would in my judgment have a tendency to educate and elevate the workingwomen of America and ameliorate their condition. Therefore, when I spoke to a public audience of American citizens, exposing existing evils and showing how, through the demands of Knighthood, they could be remedied, I felt that I was fulfilling the duties of my office. When I found a body of workingmen who were so blind to what justice demanded of them on behalf of women as to pass unanimously a resolution excluding women from our organization, I felt I was performing a sacred duty toward women by trying to enlighten those men and showing their mistake. When I found an opportunity of laying before other organizations of women the cause of their less fortunate sisters and mould a favorable sentiment, I felt I was doing that which is an actual necessity, as woman is often unconsciously woman's oppressor. With these, my honest convictions, I place my work of the past year in your hands, ready and willing to accept your decision and abide by the same.

. . . On February 24 visited Chicago. In the evening visited a Colored Waiters' Local, and on February 26 held a public meeting. February 28, lectured at Evanston, Ill. At the conclusion of my address our friend and co-worker in humanity's cause, Mrs. Elizabeth Boynton Harbourt, gave her townsmen a short address, filled with words of love, cheer and comfort, which was highly appreciated. February 29, Chicago. Held a public meeting. This was my last and also my most successful meeting in this city. Chicago is a good field for organizers and educators, but with deep regret it must be admitted that up to the time of my visit both these important matters were neglected, especially in

the interest of women. Being very sick while there I was unable to do much by way of investigation. However, I visited the manufacturing house of Marshall Field & Co.; the operatives worked on the top floor, but went up and down by way of elevator; room was nice, clean, warm and well-lighted. It was at the time of their annual shut down, but I found several girls sitting in groups—some crocheting, others embroidering, and all doing something for themselves. The girls occupied this room through the kindness of employers, as it saved them the expense of burning fuel in their own rooms. In a large retail store known as "The Fair" children of all ages from apparently nine years up to fifteen, are employed. Each was well drilled in the parrot-like answer to the query, "How old are you?" "Past fourteen." The older employees refused to give any information whatever about their wages or the system under which they worked. Another establishment had one of its departments in a basement, where salesmen and women, who were largely in the majority, worked all day with incandescent lights, not one ray of sunshine or fresh air, except such as was circulated through the rooms by means of pipes in the side. Here again I tried to glean some information, but failed, finding at least some women who did not love to talk. I was told on good authority that the reason for this was the employer would go to each girl in turn and tell her that, owing to her superior qualities, he would pay her more than any other, naming the amount, but upon condition that she would not mention it to her neighbor. Thus each imagined herself more favored than others and no confidences were exchanged, when in reality all got the same, the prevailing wages being from $2.50 to $5 per week, the highest ranging from $6 to $10, according to experience. There are employed in Chicago, including domestics, 80,000 women and girls at following industries: Shirtmakers, laundresses, children's shirt operatives, cloakmakers, buttonmakers, bookbinding, corsetmakers, furriers, regalias and costumes, shoeworkers, dressmakers, gents' neckwearmakers, cigarmakers (some factories being run exclusively by women), suspendermakers, tobaccoworkers, type-writers, printing-office operatives, hosiery and knit goods, gloves and mittens, 1,000 employed in tinshops, including many small girls, painters and decorators on china, glass, etc., coreworkers in iron and brass foundries, millinery, scouring, dying and feather cleaning, paper-box factories, paper-bag factory, confectionery, rag and junk shops (this work is mostly done by foreigners; it is very filthy and all done piece-work), photographers, actresses, gilders, waiters, cooks and the professions make up the army of women wage-workers.

. . . The violation of every law in regard to the employment of women and children in Pennsylvania is to be met with on every hand, and it is my sincere and earnest request that every Knight of Labor in Pennsylvania will give his support to the bill which I have prepared and will have presented at the session of the coming State Legislature for the establishment of a Factory Inspector law on behalf of the little ones of this rich and thriving State, 200,000 of whom are deprived of the privileges of common school education, and 125,000 of whom are employed in its workshops, factories, mines and mercantile industries. There are many evils attendant upon the employment of children, particularly girls, which leads to misery, ignorance and despair. A custom is rapidly increasing in this country which means shame, dishonor and humiliation to womanhood, and I here and now appeal to every father within sound of my voice to be watchful and wary of his little daughter, if she be employed in any large establishment, or small one either, where she is made to understand that the price of her position is, that she "stand in with the boss." Many may ask why I do not give name and locality. First, because those who resent such pernicious approaches shrink from giving publicity to their humiliation, and those who do submit will not make their misfortunes public until, perhaps, they can no longer hide their shame. In very many instances facts were given that were blood-curdling, but no affidavit would be made, and neither myself or the Order was in a position to stand a libel suit, with all the power of wealth against us wherewith to influence a decision against honor and truth.

125

EVA McDONALD VALESH
Woman and Labor (1896)

The American Federation of Labor is the body best fitted to investigate woman's work, and apply the proper remedy for existing abuses. History proves, over and over again, that the toiling masses receive no permanent benefit, except that which they achieve for themselves. No class of people can understand and sympathize with the needs of working women like those who stand side by side with them in the factory, and who know, by actual experience, what their home life must be.

Among some classes of people, there is a misconception of the position occupied industrially by the woman of to-day. Well-meaning but inaccurate, writers are constantly telling us that woman is rapidly advancing to that higher level of social, intellectual and moral equality, which is her natural right, but which has been withheld so long that a majority of even the most liberal people forget that the inherent right always existed, and always will exist no matter how deeply buried by custom and prejudice. As a convincing proof of this advancement, we are shown in the countless avenues of employment now open to woman. It is assumed as axiomatic that all of these occupations afford at least a comfortable maintenance, and, consequently, free woman from that state of dependence which proves an effectual barrier to true progress. If it were true that the industrial development of this century offered woman a free choice between the home and the workshop, or, in other words, if it offered even pecuniary independence in re-

From *The American Federationist*, February 1896.

turn for work performed, the question would then be shorn of its most perplexing features. In fact, it could be trusted to work itself out, and would need no special attention from a body of representative working people.

Unfortunately, these assumptions of philanthropists are in a large degree false, and the facts point to exactly the opposite conclusion. There is a small class of women who, through exceptional natural abilities and careful training, are able to achieve both pecuniary independence and a broader development than was formerly possible to any woman, no matter how fortunately situated. The class to which I refer are simply exceptions to the general rule. It is both unfair and misleading to cite such isolated cases as typical ones.

In order to intelligently consider the question of "Woman's Work," we must clearly understand what her environments are in the industrial world. Knowing the causes and conditions of her employment, it will be comparatively easy to correct abuses which the present industrial system fosters. Let us distinctly understand:

1. That woman, as a rule, does not enter the factory or workshop of her own sweet will. She is forced there by the existing system of production, which finds her labor both cheap and plentiful, and that she is less apt to rebel against bad conditions than man.

2. That the introduction of machinery and consequent sub-division of labor makes the employment of woman possible. The resulting evils must not be charged to the invention of machinery, but to an abuse of its proper function—viz., that of saving labor and ensuring more leisure to those engaged in the production of wealth.

3. Woman enters the industrial field under the same conditions as man. That is, no favor is shown here on account of physical disadvantages. She works as long hours, under the same sanitary conditions, and often for lower pay than man. She is, however, still held strictly accountable to the absurd social code which sets up one standard of morality for men and another for women. In addition, although forced to labor, the ballot is still withheld, so that she has no voice in shaping legislation which may affect her condition.

4. Every woman employed displaces a man and adds one more to the idle contingent that are fixing wages at the lowest limit. With the surplus of male labor in the market, there is no more excuse for employing women than Chinamen. The employer's reason for employing either is the same—cheapness.

5. The number of women employed in various industries grows greater from year to year; the number at present being estimated at nearly four millions.

In the face of these tendencies, it must be clear that whatever has tended to ameliorate the condition of male laborers, must have an equally good effect when applied to women working under the same conditions. Organization and education have been the two great factors in industrial improvement.

You are asked to apply these same two remedies to the condition of workingwomen. . . .

The trade union, evolved from centuries of conflict, has proved the only real solution of the labor problem. The time has come in the development of woman when she must take advantage of the opportunities offered by organization. The working woman imperatively needs shorter hours of labor, a higher standard of wages, better sanitary surroundings and more opportunities for education. These practical reforms must be accomplished before the more abstract questions can even be approached. In fact, these few reforms will remove the worst features now attendant upon woman's work. The organization of women into trade unions will gradually accomplish these and many other beneficial results.

In view of the prominence assumed by woman's work, the question must soon be taken up by the organized trade unions of the country. The American Federation of Labor is specially fitted to take the initiative in such work. After the work of organization is properly started, the working women will awake to a sense of its importance, and will not only carry it on without further assistance, but will form a valuable auxiliary to the trade unions already in existence.

126

HARRIOT STANTON BLATCH AND FLORENCE KELLEY
Women, Work, and Citizenship (1898)

Mrs. Harriot Stanton Blatch (Eng.) treated of Woman as an economic factor.

It is often urged that women stand greatly in need of training in citizenship before being finally received into the body politic. . . . As a matter of fact women are the first class who have asked the right of citizenship after their ability for political life has been proved. I have seen in my time two enormous extensions of the suffrage to men—one in America and one in England. But neither the negroes in the South nor the agricultural laborers in Great Britain had shown before they got the ballot any capacity for government; for they had never had the opportunity to take the first steps in political action. Very different has been the history of the march of women toward a recognized position in the State. We have had to prove our ability at each stage of progress, and have gained nothing without having satisfied a test of capacity. . . . .

The public demand for "proved worth" suggests what appears to me the chief and most convincing argument upon which our future claims must rest—the growing recognition of the

Address at the National-American Woman Suffrage Association Convention, Washington, D.C., February 13–19, 1898. From *History of Woman Suffrage*, Vol. 4, 1883–1900, ed., Elizabeth Cady Stanton, Susan B. Anthony, and Matilda Joslyn Gage (Rochester, N.Y.: Susan B. Anthony, 1900), 311–13.

economic value of the work of women. . . . . There has been a marked change in the estimate of our position as wealth producers. We have never been "supported" by men; for if all men labored hard every hour of the twenty-four, they could not do all the work of the world. A few worthless women there are, but even they are not so much supported by the men of their family as by the overwork of the "sweated" women at the other end of the social ladder. From creation's dawn our sex has done its full share of the world's work; sometimes we have been paid for it, but oftener not.

Unpaid work never commands respect; it is the paid worker who has brought to the public mind conviction of woman's worth. The spinning and weaving done by our great-grandmothers in their own homes was not reckoned as national wealth until the work was carried to the factory and organized there; and the women who followed their work were paid according to its commercial value. It is the women of the industrial class, the wage-earners, reckoned by the hundreds of thousands, and not by units, the women whose work has been submitted to a money test, who have been the means of bringing about the altered attitude of public opinion toward woman's work in every sphere of life.

If we would recognize the democratic side of our cause, and make an organized appeal to industrial women on the ground of their need of citizenship, and to the nation on the ground of its need that all wealth producers should form part of its body politic, the close of the century might witness the building up of a true republic in the United States.

Mrs. Florence Kelley, State Factory Inspector of Illinois, showed the Working Woman's Need of the Ballot.

No one needs all the powers of the fullest citizenship more urgently than the wage-earning woman, and from two different points of view—that of actual money wages and that of her wider needs as a human being and a member of the community.

The wages paid any body of working people are determined by many influences, chief among which is the position of the particular body of workers in question. Thus the printers, by their intelligence, their powerful organization, their solidarity and united action, keep up their wages in spite of the invasion of their domain by new and improved machinery. On the other hand, the garment-workers, the sweaters' victims, poor, unorganized, unintelligent, despised, remain forever on the verge of pauperism, irrespective of their endless toil. If, now, by some untoward fate the printers should suddenly find themselves disfranchised, placed in a position in which their members were politically inferior to the members of other trades, no effort of their own short of complete enfranchisement could restore to them that prestige, that good standing in the esteem of their fellow-craftsmen and the public at large which they now enjoy, and which contributes materially in support of their demand for high wages.

In the garment trades, on the other hand, the presence of a body of the disfranchised, of the weak and young, undoubtedly contributes to the economic weakness of these trades. Custom, habit, tradition, the regard of the public, both employing and employed, for the people who do certain kinds of labor, contribute to determine the price of that labor, and no disfranchised class of workers can permanently hold its own in competition with enfranchised rivals. But this works both ways. It is fatal for any body of workers to have forever hanging from the fringes of its skirts other bodies on a level just below its own; for that means continual pressure downward, additional difficulty to be overcome in the struggle to maintain reasonable rates of wages. Hence, within the space of two generations there has been a complete revolution in the attitude of the trades-unions toward the women working in their trades. Whereas forty years ago women might have knocked in vain at the doors of the most enlightened trade-union, to-day the Federation of Labor keeps in the field paid organizers whose duty it is to enlist in the unions as many women as possible. The workingmen have perceived that women are in the field of industry to stay; and they see, too, that there can not be two standards of work and wages for any trade without constant menace to the higher standard. Hence their effort to place the women upon the same industrial level with themselves in order that all may pull together in the effort to maintain reasonable conditions of life.

But this same menace holds with regard to the vote. The lack of the ballot places the wage-earning woman upon a level of irresponsibility compared with her enfranchised fellow workingman. By impairing her standing in the community the general rating of her value as a human being, and consequently as a worker, is lowered. In order to be rated as good as a good man in the field of her earnings, she must show herself better than he. She must be more steady, or more trustworthy, or more skilled, or more cheap in order to have the same chance of employment. Thus, while women are accused of lowering wages, might they not justly reply that it is only by conceding something from the pay which they would gladly claim, that they can hold their own in the market, so long as they labor under the disadvantage of disfranchisement? . . . .

Finally, the very fact that women now form about one-fifth of the employees in manufacture and commerce in this country has opened a vast field of industrial legislation directly affecting women as wage-earners. The courts in some of the States, notably in Illinois, are taking the position that women can not be treated as a class apart and legislated for by themselves, as has been done in the factory laws of England and on the continent of Europe, but must abide by that universal freedom of contract which characterizes labor in the United States. This renders the situation of the working woman absolutely anomalous. On the one hand, she is cut off from the protection awarded to her sisters abroad; on the other, she has no such power to defend her interests at the polls, as is the heritage of her brothers at home. This position is untenable, and there can be no pause in the agitation for full political power and responsibility until these are granted to all the women of the nation.

127
REBECCA
Letter from a Working Girl
(1886)

Mr. Editor:—I can scarcely suppose that a poor sewing girl like me, even though I did have (before father died) a pretty good education, and even though I have been a reader of *John Swinton's Paper* so long, can have any ideas to suggest worthy of your printing. But as you publish what I send you, I will venture to write a few lines more.

Is it possible to improve the condition of the great number of sewing girls in this and our adjoining cities? It is a deep problem. The lot of a woman in any condition of life is full of trials and sorrows, and even the queenly occupant of a throne suffers, as well as any humble operator on a sewing machine. But is it possible to organize us poor girls so as to secure to us, who are now subject to so much injustice, caprice and humiliation, fair wages and decent treatment? No and yes. If left to ourselves it will never be done; we can never, I fear, originate an agreement to act together. The impulse must come from outside. Some of the men who are accustomed to such things must undertake it. There is an abundance of impulse and feeling among the working girls. They know that they are wronged, robbed and crushed. They have not, excepting a very, very few of us, any idea that the condition of things can ever be improved. They scarcely give the idea a moment's consideration. Their hope is not to remedy, but to escape from it. Young women have their individual

lives to lead, full of hopes and fears, ambitions and rivalries, despondencies and heart-breakings. A writer in the *Ledger* said, the other day, that we women are "dominated by our affections" and are not as capable of cool business calculations as men. It would be well, then, if some of those successful, manly Unions of which I read in your paper would undertake the organization.

Then, every care should be taken to avoid exciting jealousies at the very beginning. Girls differ, as men do, in nationality, religion, education and many other matters. There are even shop rivalries; there are grades of work, superior and inferior; there are twenty things to disagree about. The effort should be made to include all needle women. It will be very difficult, but it is not impossible. The girls in each large shop might be a party by themselves, perhaps.

The worst of our situation is, that we work so many hours as to have little time for organization. To be sure some of us may find time to go to a ball and dance all night, or to parade with beaux. You cannot expect to change these things. One evening, occasionally, they may be able to give, however.

A sewing girls' Union would have much trouble with the bosses and with those contemptible creatures, the forewomen. I see by your paper that it is very often the overseers and foremen who make the trouble for men employed, and who compel the men to strike. In our trade these slave-drivers are terrible. They are spies upon the workers and toadies to the boss. It will never do to let them know our purposes, or to trust to their honor.

From *John Swinton's Paper*, April 4, 1886.

128

LUCY A. WARNER

Why Do People Look Down on Working Girls? (1891)

How it Looks From a Working Girl's Standpoint

Why do people look down on Working Girls? This is the question that we girls ask each other over and over again. It is not a hard question, but it has never yet been answered to our satisfaction.

Is it because we lack natural ability? Do working girls lack natural ability? Go into the places where we work and see the delicate and difficult work that we are doing—work that requires the help of eye and hand and brain, and, when you have gone the rounds, if you should give us your candid opinion, would not that opinion be that working girls are not deficient in natural ability? Are working men and the sons of working men lacking in natural ability? For answer, we point you to the men prominent in scientific, literary, religious, and business circles. No, working men are not lacking in natural ability. Neither are working women. There is no copyright on brains. God is no respecter of persons, and so, to us working girls, He has entrusted one, two, and, to some, even five talents.

Is it because we lack education? That we do lack education, we admit. We have the brains. Give us the time and opportunity to use them. We are hungering and thirsting for knowledge. Make it easier for us to satisfy that thirst and hunger. It is true that there are some among us who would not improve the opportunity to obtain a higher education and greater culture if such opportunity were ours. But is not that also true of those in a higher station than we? A man now prominent in literary circles once said of his wife: 'My wife has had time since her marriage to have obtained a college education.' My

From *Far and Near*, January 1891.

cultured friend, you who have just received your well-earned diploma at Wellesley or Vassar, are there not ladies in 'your set' who have had equal opportunities with yourself and yet have not improved those opportunities? There are many working girls who are spending every leisure moment in study, not because they think others will respect them more, but because such study is to them a delight.

Is it because we lack virtue? Are working girls, as a class, virtuous? Years ago, a man who knew whereof he affirmed, wrote: 'Not even the famed Hebrew maiden as she stood on the giddy turret, more sacredly guarded her honor than does many a half-starved sewing woman in the streets of New York.' And we who have comfortable homes and who receive fair wages, can the same be said of us? Yes, we are as proud of our honor, we are as careful of our reputation as our sisters who dress in 'purple and fine linen and fare sumptuously every day.' It is true, there are exceptions, but has not the immoral working girl her rivals among a class of women who should be her teachers in all pure and noble living?

Is it because we work? What an absurd idea! People 'look down' on us because we work? Why, the lawyer and the doctor and the clergyman and the professor and the merchant all work, and work hard, too, and every one looks *up* to them. 'Of course,' says a bright, young lady, 'we expect men to work and support their families, but ladies do not work.' Don't they? We have lady artists and musicians, lady docters, lawyers and lecturers, trained nurses and teachers. If it isn't *work* that they are doing, what is it? 'But,' says the same young lady, 'have you never discovered that there is a difference between brain work and manual labor?' Yes, we have discovered it, to our sorrow. The teacher considers herself superior to the sewing girl, and the sewing girl thinks herself above the mill girl, and the mill girl thinks the girl who does general housework a little beneath her, and Miss Flora McFlimsey, 'who toils not, neither does she spin,' thinks herself superior to them all. Is one kind of work more honorable than another? Is any honest work degrading?

My friend, have you ever considered that 'brain work' enters into every department of manual labor? An intelligent girl will do better work anywhere than an ignorant one. Isn't it a work of art to make a dress? It is just as necessary that a cook should mix her bread with 'brains' as it is that an artist should mix her colors with the same materials.

Dear sister workers, we who work in shop and store and factory, and in countless homes all over the United States, if it is because we work that people look down on us, then let us pray that the Lord will change their opinion, and go quietly about our business, for, among the 'nobility of labor' there is an illustrious company, at whose head stands the Carpenter of Nazareth, by Whom labor was forever glorified.

LUCY A. WARNER,
(Help Each Other Club.)

129
GRACE H. DODGE
Working and Saving (1887)

Dear Girls:

We are all workers—busy bodies; and I think there is not one of us who could not say, "It seems as if woman's work was never done." Some of us have home cares, and from the making of the fire before six o'clock until nine or ten at night, when the children or family are in bed, we have few idle moments. We find so much to do even in our small rooms or houses. Others of us are due at seven o'clock at factory or shop, and have eight or nine hours of manual work, with only lunch time off. When we get home, if there is no housework there is sewing or planning for clothes, and if we find time for any recreation or fun, we are wondrous busy up

From *A Bundle of Letters to Busy Girls On Practical Matters* (New York: Funk and Wagnall's, 1887), 88–92.

to a late hour. Again, there are some of us who use our fingers, and as dressmakers it is sew, sew, sew until we get tired of needles and thread. Still there are among us those who have brain work combined with hand effort, and as teachers, telegraph operators, stenographers, clerks, or bearing still heavier responsibility, we come to night tired both in body and in mind. Some are ashamed of being called workingwomen, but why should we be? Is it not a grand thing to be a worker, and to have ability to work? Nowadays hundreds of girls are proud of being workers who might stay at home and be supported by father or mother. They wish to feel able to care for themselves. No honest work degrades us, rather uplifts and strengthens us. I like to feel myself a worker, and to count as true friends many who labor from early to late in shop or factory. From the beginning of this world of ours people have been workers, receiving only what they or their parents worked for. Some of those men or women whom you envy and think of as having a good time always, are much busier than you ever thought of being, and bear burdens of responsibility which you can hardly grasp even in thought. The motto taken by a Prince of Wales hundreds of years ago, and still borne by the present prince, translated contains only these two words, "I serve;" so, dear girls, if the Prince of Wales feels the need of such a motto, surely we, too, should think of ourselves as serving or working.

When we are at home we serve for love, from a sense of duty, but when we go out from home into any position we expect to serve for more than these things—for *money*.

Here, then, are the two points of our letter to-day—Work, Money; serving, and the wage received for said service.

The terms can be applied from the President of the United States, who serves his country and receives for his work a salary from the country, to a little cash-girl working for $1.50 per week. Some of us work hard and find our duties irksome; some make light of everything, and by their way of going about it make all effort easy.

First. Set your mind on the work, whatever it is, feeling it is necessary and cannot be shirked. Second. When the mind is fixed and it is to be done, try and take a cheer view of the work. There are two words which are often used, "Don't worry." Apply them to the work to be done, and put after them, "over it." Third. Endeavor by system and order to simplify the work. Bring your brains to it and try to lighten it by planning for it, keeping all implements, from pen, pencil, needle, thread, to machinery, in order. Know where your working tools are, and be able to lay your hands on them at any moment.

How often I have seen a girl stop in the midst of a rush of work at home, at the store, or in the work-room, and cry out as she hurried around, "Oh, where's my brush?" "Where's the cash-book?" "Where's my scissors?" That quarter of an hour's work is hard, and if the same difficulty continues, at night the girl is tired out and blames the work, when she should blame herself for carelessness and thoughtlessness. Fourth. Put your heart into your work. This means much the same as the first point, only the addition of love for it and a determination to really do it as well as one can. Heartily, as applied to a hand-shake, you understand; think of the same idea in doing what you have to do to-day and see if "heartiness" will not help it on. Fifth. Do the work as well as you can, and try and take pride in the doing. Sixth. Make the work yours for the time being, and even if it is done for others, feel it your own, and show interest in it. Seventh. Quiet, slow work usually tells better in the long run than that done with rapid, spasmodic effort, which, while it may accomplish much in an hour, cannot be continued for eight hours. The fable of the tortoise and the hare can be applied here. Eighth. It is hardly necessary to add the thought of faithful, thorough work. No one will ever succeed or be advanced who does not do earnest, true work. I have heard it said that one reason why women cannot compare with men as "wage-earners" is, that they do not do faithful, thorough work, for

they do not think of work as a life pursuit, but rather as a necessary means of tiding over those years before they marry, and have some man to do the money-earning for them.*

Girls, I would not like to think this true, but rather to feel that we women are so anxious to become skilful, thorough workers that we at all times are doing our utmost to fit ourselves for that duty which is ours. Happy women also, for we realize that we must work, and are doing the best we can in a cheery, earnest manner. . . .

130
JULIA RICHMAN
Women Wage Workers: With Reference to Directing Immigrants (1893)

This is an age of progress and, surrounded as we are to-day by every evidence of the astounding advance that the nineteenth century has carried in its train, I feel that I am flinging down a challenge that will, perhaps, bring me face to face with a volley of rhetorical bullets, when I assert that in no other country and in no other direction is this progress more noticeable than in the relative position to man and the affairs of the world that woman occupies to-day. This advance has been made in almost every grade in society, in almost every walk in life; but so far as my own personal observations have permitted me to go, so far as my own experiences have enabled me to judge, it is my belief that this change, this revolution, yes, this progress is more noticeable in the position held by the Jewish women of America (notably the descendants of European emigrants driven from their homes forty or fifty years ago), than in that of any other class in our cosmopolitan community.

An Address at the Jewish Women's Congress, Chicago, September 5, 1893. From *The Papers of the Jewish Women's Congress* (Philadelphia: The Jewish Publication Society of America, 1894), 91–6, 105–07.

Many conditions have conspired to bring about this change: the general advance in the education of women the desire to give children greater educational advantages than the parents enjoyed; the financial value of woman's work; the frequent necessity for women to contribute to the support of families; the growing conviction that there is not a sufficient number of marrying men to supply all the marriageable girls with good husbands—these are but a few, with only one of which it is my privilege to deal, viz., the financial value of woman's work.

Perhaps it was due to custom and tradition, perhaps due to our oriental origin, but notwithstanding the fact that there may have always been among us a certain number of Deborahs, Ruths and Esthers, in general, the wives and daughters of Jews were, and in many parts of the world unfortunately still are, regarded as man's inferiors, their chief mission in life being to marry, or rather to be given in marriage, to rear children, to perform household duties, and to serve their lords and masters.

This is an age of progress; and thousands of women, many of them good, true, pure, womanly women, have discovered for themselves, or have been led to discover, that there is, at best, only an uncertain chance of real happiness facing the woman who calmly settles down in her parents' home, to perform, in an inane, desultory way, certain little household or social duties, who lives on from day to day, from year to year, without any special object in life, and who sees no prospect of change, unless a husband should appear to rescue her from so aimless an existence. Having made this discovery they try to join, and frequently, in the face of opposition, succeed in joining the ever-increasing army of women wage-workers, striving to lead useful, if sometimes lonely lives, with the hope of making the world, or that little corner thereof into which their lines have fallen, a little better and a little brighter than they found it.

I speak of such as women wage-workers, although many of them labor for no more substantial pay than the approval of conscience, and the satisfaction of feeling that it is God's work, however imperfectly done, that they are doing. With this class others must deal; for me it is enough to thank those who I have met, for the inspiration their work has so often been to me, and to point out, humbly and modestly, how their future efforts may make life sweeter for the class whose work and condition must form the main topic of this paper—the immigrant wage-workers in America.

Who are our women wage-workers? From the writer or artist who receives thousands for a single work, to the poor overworked girl in some pest-hole, called a factory, killing herself by inches for a couple of dollars a week, there is so wide a range, divided into strata, sub-strata and veins leading to or from these sub-strata, that it is practically impossible to mark off, with well-defined lines, the different classes of woman's work. Perhaps the simplest classification on practical lines would be in general terms:

Women engaged in professional work.

Women engaged in domestic service.

Women engaged in store or factory work.

The professional workers, excluding writers, artists and all other classes requiring special talent in addition to long training, let us, for convenience, divide again into two classes; the one class, including teachers, governesses, companions, kindergartners, typewriters, stenographers, bookkeepers, trained nurses, etc., demands, first, a general education, in a greater or less degree, with a thorough knowledge of the English language; and, second, some special course of instruction, to which, in most cases, months, sometimes years must be devoted. The other class, a type best represented by dressmakers, milliners, manicures, masseuses and hair-dressers, demands little general education, in which a thorough knowledge of the English language is not an essential, a marketable value of which can usually be acquired by a special course of instruction, which can be completed in a few weeks.

This first class of professional work is, with very few exceptions, not open to immigrants, particularly not to the class with which American Jewish philanthropists have to deal, Russians, Poles, Hungarians and uneducated Germans. The exceptions would include those young women, who, by unusual educational advantages in Europe, may possibly have been fitted to give instruction in music, German, perhaps French, or in kindergarten methods; but the well-educated female immigrant is not plentiful, and the competition for positions of this nature is great, and I am afraid that discouragements drive such applicants too frequently into the factories and shops, where their surroundings are neither educating nor refining.

Into this second class of professional workers, I should direct as many capable immigrants as the demand for such work would justify. To be sure, some preparatory instruction must be furnished. Upon what lines this is to be done, I shall try to suggest later on.

The workers, whom, in general terms, I have placed under the head, "Women engaged in domestic service," are the cooks, laundresses, waitresses and chambermaids, children's nurses, seamstresses, ladies' maids and general houseworkers. And when we have found a sound, practical, reasonable plan for directing the tide of immigration into this channel, we shall have solved the most perplexing woman's problem of the day.

Good servants are in greater demand in all parts of the United States than any other class of labor, and yet, while thousands of homes, many of them good homes, are open to these homeless, friendless girls, we find them living in miserable tenements, slaving in dismal factories, forming corrupt associations, losing their health morally as well as physically, turning their faces away from a life incomparably better than the one they follow,—and why?

It is hardly proper that, in a paper prepared to advance the interests of immigrant working girls, I should put in a plea for the housekeeper of to-day. But the sight of the hundreds of homes which are annually broken up, because incompetent servants make housekeeping, if not marriage, a failure, the knowledge of how these housekeepers drift into the evils that the idleness of hotel or boarding-house life engenders, and the certainty that many a matrimonial craft has met shipwreck, the indirect if not the direct cause of which has been the servant question, force me to emphasize the fact, that it is not alone the poor and the ignorant that have need of our philanthropy. If, from the plan I shall attempt to outline later on, any good may come, it is not the immigrants alone, it is a whole generation of housekeepers who will be benefited.

And now we come to the third class, "Women engaged in store or factory work." Perhaps this class comprises more grades of work than could be classed under any other general head.

The manager of one large dry-goods house reports to me that he employs women as buyers, forewomen, dressmakers, milliners, saleswomen, cashiers, stock-girls, office-assistants, bundlers, operators, addressers and scrubwomen; while a manufacturer of tin toys uses female help exclusively for painting on tin, cutting tin, packing toys, making paper boxes, and working foot presses. There are almost as many grades of woman's work as there are branches in every style of factory work. A word, now and again, is all that I can say in reference to these.

Saleswomen in large establishments are, on the whole, fairly well paid; but this avenue is closed to the immigrant, until she shall have mastered the English language to such an extent that there is no room for misunderstanding between herself and her customer.

"Figures" in wholesale cloak and suit houses are well paid; their hours are short, their work never onerous, and "between seasons" they have little or no work to do. But, perhaps, no other class of working women in large cities is so directly placed in the way of temptation, and the mother who lets her daughter, particularly if she be attractive and vain, take a position as a "figure," has need of all our prayers added to her own to protect her girl. You, who are doing such zealous work among working girls, try to reach this class. God help them! They have need of you.

. . . Almost all the female immigrants who come to this shore, through lack of knowledge as to the means by which they can swing themselves above the discouraging conditions which face them, sink down into the moral and intellectual maelstrom of the American ghettos, becoming first household or factory drudges, and then drifting into one of three channels: that of the careless slattern, of the giddy and all-too-frequently sinful gad-about, or of the weary, discontented wife.

We must disentangle the individual from the mass. We must find a way or several ways of leading these girls, one by one, away from the shadows which envelop them, if not into the sunshine of happiness and prosperity, at least, into the softening light of content, born of pleasant surroundings, congenial occupations, and the inward satisfaction of a life well spent.

Working girls' clubs are doing a grand work, but these clubs never reach the lower strata. There must be something before and beyond the working girls' clubs, something that shall lay hold of the immigrant before she has been sucked down into the stratum of physical misery or moral oblivion, from which depths it becomes almost impossible to raise her.

In this age of materialism, in these days of close inquiry as to the "Why?" of every condition, it has been claimed that the ever-increasing proportion of unmarried women among the Jews of America is largely due to the independent position women make for themselves, first, by becoming wage-earners, and second, through the development of self-reliance brought about by societies, working girls' clubs and kindred movements. If marriage always meant happiness, and if celibacy always meant unhappiness, to make women independent and self-reliant would be a calamity. But, in the face of so much married unhappiness and so much unmarried contentment, it is hardly pessimistic to wish that there might be fewer marriages consummated,

until the contracting parties show more discrimination in their selection of mates.

The saddest of many sad conditions that face our poor Jewish girls is the class of husbands that is being selected for them by relatives. It is the rule, not the exception, for the father, elder brother, or some other near relative of a Jewish working girl, to save a few hundred dollars, by which means he purchases some gross, repulsive Pole or Russian as a husband for the girl. That her whole soul revolts against such a marriage, that the man betrays, even before marriage, the brutality of his nature, that he may, perhaps, have left a wife and family in Russia, all this counts for nothing. Marry him she must, and another generation of worthless Jews is the lamentable result.

I wish it distinctly understood that there is no desire on my part to disparage matrimony; indeed, happy wifehood and motherhood are to my mind the highest missions any woman can fulfill; but in leading these girls to see the horror of ill-assorted marriages, I intend to teach them to recognize the fact that many of them may never find suitable husbands; and recognizing this fact, they must fill up their lives with useful, perhaps even noble work. Should the possible husband fail to appear, their lives will not have been barren; should he come, will a girl make a less faithful wife and mother because she has teen taught to be faithful in other things?

And so I could go on showing how, in every direction, the harm and the evil grow, until the day will come when charity, even with millions at her disposal, will not be able to do good. It is easier to save from drowning than to resuscitate the drowned. Disentangle the individual from the mass; create a new mass of disentangled individuals, who shall become the leading spirits in helping their benighted sisters, and with God's help, the future will redeem the present and the past.

131

KATE RICHARDS
How I Became a Socialist
Agitator (1908)

My earliest memory is of a Kansas ranch, of the wide stretches of prairie, free herds roaming over the hills and couless, of cowpunchers with rattling spurs and wide hats, free and easy of speech and manner, but brave and faithful to their friends, four-footed or human; of the freedom and security and plenty of a well-to-do rancher's home.

Those were wonderful days and I shall never cease to be thankful that I knew them. Days that laid the foundation of my whole life, gave me health and strength and love of freedom, taught me to depend on myself, to love nature, to honor rugged strength of mind and body and to know no shams in life. Everything is very real, very much alive and in close touch with nature on the broad sweep of the prairie amid the longhorns.

The Wolf at the Door.

Then comes the memory of a Kansas drouth, followed by one of the periodical panics which sweep over our country. Days and weeks of hazy nightmare when father's face was gray and set, when mother smiled bravely, when he or we children were near, but when we sometimes found tears upon her cheeks if we came upon her unexpectedly. Of course, it was all beyond our comprehension. A horrible something that we could not fathom had settled down over our lives, but the day when the realness of it all was forced home came all too soon. The stock was sold, the home dismantled and one day father kissed us good-bye and started away to the city to find work. He who had always been master of his own domain, who had hewn his

From *The Socialist Woman*, October 1908.

destiny bare-handed from the virgin soil, forced to go out and beg some other man for a chance to labor, an opportunity to use his hands. Though I could not comprehend it then the bitterness of it all was seared upon my memory and I never see a strong man vainly seeking and begging for work that my whole soul does not revolt.

Goes to the City.

Then came the day when we left the ranch and went to the city to take up the life of a wage-worker's family in the poverty-cursed section of town. For, of course, no other was possible for us for father's wages were only nine dollars a week and nine dollars is not much to support a family of five. Of that long, wretched winter following the panic of 1887 the memory can never be erased, never grow less bitter. The poverty, the misery, the want, the wan-faced women and hunger pinched children, men tramping the streets by day and begging for a place in the police stations or turning footpads by night, the sordid, grinding, pinching poverty of the workless workers and the frightful, stinging, piercing cold of that winter in Kansas City will always stay with me as a picture of inferno, such as Dante never painted.

Of the years that followed when father had regained to some extent his economic foothold and poverty no longer pinched us though it encompassed us all about like a frightful dream that could not be shaken off, it is hard to write intelligently.

I, child-woman that I was, seeing so much poverty and want and suffering, threw my whole soul into church and religious work. I felt somehow that the great..good God who had made us could not have wantonly abandoned his children to such hopeless misery and sordid suffering. There was nothing uplifting in it, nothing to draw the heart nearer to him, only forces that clutched and dragged men and women down into the abyss of drunkenness and vice. Perhaps he had only overlooked those miserable children of the poor in the slums of Kansas City, and if we prayed long and earnestly and had enough of religious zeal he might hear and heed and pity. For several years I lived through that Gethsemane we all endure who walk the path from religious fanaticism to cold, dead, material cynicism with no ray of sane life philosophy to light it.

Temperance Work

I saw drunkenness and the liquor traffic in all the bestial, sordid aspects it wears in the slums, and with it the ever-close companion of prostitution in its most disgusting and degraded forms. I believed, for the good preachers and temperance workers who led me said, that drunkenness and vice caused poverty and I struggled and worked with only the heart breaking zeal that an intense young girl can work, to destroy them. But in spite of all we could do the corner saloon still flourished, the saloon-keeper still controlled the government of the city and new inmates came to fill the brothel as fast as the old ones were carried out to the Potter's field, and the grim grist of human misery and suffering still ground on in defiance to church and temperance society and rescue mission.

Gradually I began to realize that the great Creator of the universe had placed us here to live under fixed natural laws that were not changed at the whim of God or man and that prayers would never fill an empty stomach or avoid a panic. I also learned that intemperance and vice did not cause poverty, but that poverty was the mother of the whole hateful brood we had been trying to exterminate and that the increase of her offspring was endless. Dimly I began to realize that if we would win we must fight the cause and not the effects, and since poverty was the fundamental cause of the things I abhorred, I began to study poverty, its whys and wherefores, and to try to understand why there should be so much want in such a world of plenty.

Becomes a Mechanic.

About this time father embarked in the machine shop business and I added to my various experiences that of a woman forced into the business world there to have every schoolday illusion rudely shattered, and forced to see business life in its sordid nakedness. Possibly because I hated ledgers and daybooks and loved mechanics, and possibly because I really wanted to study the wage-worker in his own life, I made life so miserable for the foreman and all concerned that they finally consented to let me go into the shop as an apprentice to learn the trade of machinist. For more than four years I worked at the forge and lathe and bench side by side with some of the best mechanics of the city and some of the noblest men I have ever known. The work was most congenial and I learned for the first time what absorbing joy there can be in labor, if it be a labor that one loves.

Even before my advent into the shop I had begun to have some conception of economics. I had read "Progress and Poverty," "Wealth vs. Commonwealth." "Caesar's Column," and many such books. Our shop being a union one I naturally came in contact with the labor union world and was soon as deeply imbued with the hope trade unionism held out, as I had been with religious zeal. After a while it dawned upon me in a dim and hazy way that trade unionism was something like the frog who climbed up to the well side two feet each day and slipped back three each night. Each victory we gained seemed to give the capitalist class a little greater advantage.

Meets "Mother" Jones.

One night while returning from a union meeting, where I had been severely squelched for daring to remonstrate with the boys for voting for a man for mayor whom they had bitterly fought four months before in a long, hard strike, I heard a man talking on a street corner of the necessity of workingmen having a political party of their own. The man's words were balm to my ruffled spirits, for I had been unmercifully ridiculed for daring to talk politics to a lot of American Voting Kings; "a woman, the very idea!" I asked a bystander who the speaker was and he replied, "a Socialist." Of course, if he had called him anything else it would have meant just as much to me, but somehow I remembered the word. A few weeks later I attended a ball given by the Cigar Maker's union, and Mother Jones spoke. Dear old Mother! That is one of the mileposts in my life that I can easily locate. Like a mother talking to her errant boys she taught and admonished that night in words that went home to every heart. At last she told them that a scab at the ballot box was more to be despised than one at the factory door, that a scab ballot could do more harm than a scab bullet; that workingmen must support the political party of their class and that the only place for a sincere union man was in the Socialist party.

Here was that strange new word again coupled with the things I had vainly tried to show my fellow unionists. I hastily sought out "Mother" and asked her to tell what Socialism was, and how I could find the Socialist party. With a smile she said, "Why, little girl, I can't tell you all about it now, but here are some Socialists, come over and get acquainted." In a moment I was in the center of an excited group of men all talking at once, and hurling unknown phrases at me until my brain was whirling. I escaped by promising to "come down to the office tomorrow and get some books." The next day I hunted up the office and was assailed by more perplexing phrases and finally escaped loaded down with Socialist classics enough to give a college professor mental indigestion. For weeks I struggled with that mass of books only to grow more hopelessly lost each day. At last down at the very bottom of the pile I found a well worn, dog-eared, little book that I could not only read, but understand, but to my heart-breaking disappointment it did not even mention Socialism.

It was the Communist Manifesto, and I could not understand what relation it could have to what I was looking for.

Finds a Friend in J. A. Wayland.

I carried the books back and humbly admitted my inability to understand them or grasp the philosophy they presented. As the men who had given me the books explained and expostulated in vain, a long, lean, hungry looking individual unfolded from behind a battered desk in the corner and joined the group. With an expression more forceful than elegant he dumped the classics in the corner, ridiculed the men for expecting me to read or understand them, and after asking some questions as to what I had read gave me a few small booklets, Merrie England and Ten Men of Money Island, Looking Backward, and Between Jesus and Caesar, and possibly half a dozen more of the same type. The hungry looking individual was Comrade Wayland, and the dingy office the birthplace of the Appeal to Reason.

For a time I lived in a dazed dream while my mental structure was being ruthlessly torn asunder and rebuilt on a new foundation. That the process was a painful one I need not tell one who has undergone it, and most of us have. At last I awoke in a new world, with new viewpoints, and a new outlook. Recreated, I lived again with new aims, new hopes, new aspirations and the dazzling view of the new and wonderful work to do. All the universe pulsated with new life that swept away the last vestige of the mists of creed and dogma and old ideas and beliefs.

Marries a Fellow-Student.

For some time I worked with our group in Kansas City, and seven years ago when Walter Thomas Mills opened his training school for Socialist workers in Girard, Kansas, I was one of its students. There I found not only a conge-

nial group of comrades, the best and most forceful teacher I have ever known, but that crowning finishing touch of human life, love. In the
school as a fellow-student I met my husband.
Of our marriage at the home of Comrade
Wayland at the close of the school and our life
since that time little need be said. All who are at
all acquainted with the Socialist movement know
more or less of it for our story has been the story
of the Socialist movement, it has been our life.

Life of an Organizer.

Taking up the work of traveling speakers
and organizers the next day after our wedding
we have followed the stony, rough hewn path
from that day to this. From the coal fields of
Pennsylvania and West Virginia and Indian Territory, to the farms of Kansas and Iowa and Missouri, through the plains of Texas and into the
cotton fields of Oklahoma and Arkansas and Tennessee, from the Ghetto of New York to the
Rocky Mountains we have gone wherever and
whenever the economic pressure has made men
and women receptive to the philosophy of Socialism. We have stood on the street corner and
in the pulpit, at the shop door and in the college
assembly room, in the country school houses and
trades union hall, in the legislative chambers and
temples of justice, in all manner of places and
appealing to all manner of men we have worked
and have seen the Socialist movement grow from
a handful of men and women sneered at, de-
rided and ridiculed, into the mighty force it now
is.

Twice in the seven years my work in the
field has been interrupted by the cares of maternity and now a curly-haired boy of five and a
brown-eyed girl of two share our hearts and
make the fight seem all the more worth while.

Seven years, yes, seven long, weary,
toilworn, travel-tired years. Years when the path
was often dark and the road rough; when the
heart grew sick and the soul faint because the
world is deaf and dumb and blind, has eyes that
see not and ears that do not hear, hearts that do

not feel either their own needless suffering or
that of their fellowmen. Yet they have been glorious years, years of battle with the forces of
ignorance, years that have tried men's souls, that
have left many a noble comrade lying by the
wayside, dead upon the field of battle for economic justice, yet years of such achievement as
the world has never known, years filled with
success still unmeasured, of revolutionary forces
we can not even guess. Our thought in so short
a time has dominated the thought of the world,
our literature setting the standards, our philosophy shaping the political forces of the nations
and round the world glows the spark of human
brotherhood, ready to spring at our call into living flame.

132
Anna Dickinson
Work and Wages (1869)

There is no argument so powerful as the argument of success, and the people will never recognize the rights that women claim, until they
have successfully achieved them. It is an Italian
proverb that the world belongs to those who take
it, and it is true that it is not for those who pray
or plead for it, but for those who lay strong hands
upon it, and make it their own. And this general
law of humanity must apply to women as well
as to men, unless it be claimed, as it is in effect
by some insurance companies, that women are
not human beings. Men can be insured against
accident as well as death, but women only against
death. The gist of the whole matter is that there
is a misconception of the sphere of woman; and
it is the commonly received idea that it is not
desirable for women to take, or possess any part
of the world. She shall taste of its oil and wine,
but must not cultivate the plants. She is to sit
enshrined in some man's heart, and partake of
the good things there offered.

From *The Agitator*, March 13, 1869.

That would be well, if the heart were good and the offerings abundant; but in looking into those hearts of men one is often disagreeably surprised at their barrenness. As for the gifts, it reminded one of searching for pounds, in a pocket where nothing could be found but a few shillings. Yet having granted all the good that could be claimed for the abundant offerings in the hearts of mankind—their undivided love, protection, and the like it does not follow that her position is better when freed from turmoil and work, and from the responsibility of the need of action. It is not good for one person to do the thinking of another, of one conscience to carry the responsibilities of another conscience, of one life to attend to the work of another life.

It is commonly considered that it is the chief end of existence for one woman to be supported by one man, and the more helpless the woman is, the more attractive and adorable she becomes. The women are told that if they step out into [missing text] and become the competitors of men they must give up the admiration and love which are now bestowed upon them, but they would be rendered more lovable, rather than less, by thus trying to help themselves. You can nowhere find among those who always consume and never produce, perfectly sound and healthy beings. A celebrated physician has lately said that a man cannot be in perfect health unless his body and brain are actively worked, and this is true of women as well as men. I have seen women who have lived only to please and be pleased, and when their days of pleasure were passed, they were not alive, though they were not dead.

The encouragement of this false idea of woman's sphere is constantly forcing girls to marry without love. They go to the altar, not because their hearts force them, but because the exigencies of their pockets, and the sentiments of society compel them. The expression, "she has made a good match," more often means a wealthy husband than a good one, and girls are taught to regard the acquisition of a husband, as the trade and profession by which they are to derive their support.

The results of marriages entered into without the strongest love are unhappy in the extreme, and the consequence of inculcating so erroneous an idea of the purpose of marriage fills the palaces of iniquity, and leads girls who have failed to find husbands, oftentimes to exchange the greatest of their possessions, the charm and crown of their womanhood, for the money which they are ashamed to earn by honest work. Girls who are trained to believe that work is dishonorable have every element of self-respect destroyed in their souls and they are helpless when they need help the most. This idea that labor is dishonorable re-acts from women to men, and there are hundreds of men in every large city, who work in clerkships and the professions for half the pay that mechanics get. Women control society, and when it is found that women honor those men most, who have the least to do with manual labor, there is a general withdrawal from work by the hands. Make labor honorable for women, and it will be all the more honorable for men.

What is wanted is that woman shall have a chance to do well-paid, as well as ill-paid work, and to have an opportunity to earn $50 or $500 a week, as well as a few cents. There are plenty of women who might have been ministers, physicians, lawyers, architects, and a hundred other things, honorable, useful and remunerative, if they had only received the necessary training. The question is, shall woman be allowed to travel in the paths that lead to profit and honor, or shall she be forced along those ways leading to poverty and degradation? We are told that home is the sphere in which God placed woman. Well, grant it. What shall we do with those who have no homes, and those whose homes are the homes of brutality and vice? If the Almighty has invested woman with genius, it is not for man to limit its sphere. It is arrogating the purposes of the Infinite to fix the boundaries of intellect, be it male or female. When all human laws are primarily meant for the amelioration of mankind, why should we refuse to strike at the root of one-half the crime in our large cities, by closing the doors upon those women who must either have encouragement to work, or perish in infamy? It is the want of preliminary training, and the want of a fair field for the exercise of that training, which sends so many girls and women to lives of sin, and deaths of misery.

In Washington, there are a great number of female government clerks, who receive $900 a year, and at the same time young men as clerks, who receive from $1,200 to $3,000 a year. These women have mostly families to support, while the young men have not; and yet the latter have raised the cry that the cause of morality in Washington would be served by dismissing all the women. It is plain to any one but a man, that the throwing these helpless women on the world would be a very sure way to increase immorality. I wish the male clerks would start for the prairies of the West and leave their places for employed and well qualified women.

The physicians say that it would never do for women to go to college, and attend medical lectures with young men, and that they would be contaminated and most seriously by visiting the hospitals for medical work. Women can serve as nurses at two dollars a day, but they must not take the large [missing text] physicians. The same is said by lawyers and others. Women were never accused of abandoning their sphere, so long as they did servile and poorly paid work. A gentleman said to me the other day that he should think much more of me if I were in my proper sphere at home. I told him that unless I were doing what I am, I and seven others would have no home. I was never accused of abandoning my sphere when I tended store, worked in the mint and taught school, and the trouble now is that those who criticise me and my course, think that if I was out of the way some nice young man could have my place upon the lecture platform, and receive the money I now receive.

133
MARY LIVERMORE
Superfluous Women (1883)

To all the arguments for woman's better industrial training, and to all the movements now in progress for its accomplishment, there is constantly interposed the objection that it interferes with the marriage of women. The objection definitely stated is this: that if women are trained to self-support, and are able to maintain themselves by their own labor, they will not marry, but will ignore their "fore-ordained work as mothers and nurses of children." . . .

In my own country I have seen women sawing and splitting wood; on their hands and knees, hours before daylight, scrubbing the floors and stairs of offices, in hotels, and public buildings; staggering under loads, sometimes of fuel, and sometimes of material to be worked up at home; sometimes, amid coal and iron manufactures, shovelling coke and coal into freight-cars, and doing other like hard manual work, to which, indeed, in many instances, they seemed adapted physically. Where the wife and mother performs all the household labor for a family of four, six, or more persons,—husband and children,—cooking, washing, ironing, making, mending, nursing the sick, and caring for the house, she is compelled to labor very severely. And this is the condition of the majority of the married women of America.

. . . I do not complain that women must toil, and toil severely. Greater harm befalls them in indolence than is encountered in severe, honest industry. I only ask that they shall have a physical and industrial training that shall lighten severe labor, and give them fair remuneration. But this is the point. Magazine-articles and pamphlets and books were never written to complain that woman is compelled to work; nor to trumpet

From *What Shall We Do With Our Daughters?* (Boston: Lee and Shepard, Publishers, 1883), 132, 134–35, 135–36, 138–40, 166–69, 202–05.

an alarm concerning the terrible dangers this work will inflict on her prospective maternity, until, as Van de Warker announces, she began "to invade all the higher forms of labor," or as Eliot expresses it in clumsy phraseology, "to prepare, by superior education, to engage in clerkships, telegraphy, newspaper-writing, school-teaching, etc." The gravamen of these accusations is, that woman "labors for bread in the same field with man." It is, seemingly, "the superior education," "the higher forms of labor," and the equality of work that have caused the amazing scientific and literary affliction of the day, which is calling upon the world for condolence. Women have always been toilers from a time coincident with the beginning of history, and, undoubtedly, anterior to that; but no tears have been shed for them, save what they have wept themselves, until they began to enter higher fields of labor, and to receive better compensation. Lo! then the floodgates of grief are hoisted, and there is mourning that will not be comforted.

Nor are women refusing to marry, or "remaining unmarried," because "they are now able to support themselves;" nor yet, as Eliot asserts in "The North-American Review," because they are the victims of "impracticable theories," expecting "to become the idols of men, and to receive every thing, and to do nothing," "to be helped, and not to be helpful;" nor yet because, according to the same authority, "not one woman in ten is a fairly healthy creature;" nor because, being "sick in body," "women are sensitive, nervous, possibly fretful and unhappy." If all these criticisms of women are just, and if every charge is proved true, they tell very little on marriage.

. . . It is true there are communities where women are in excess of men, as in Massachusetts where they outnumber men by more than sixty thousand. The exhortation of Horace Greeley, "Go West, young man, go West!" has been largely heeded by the young men of the Eastern States, mainly those most enterprising and energetic. They have emigrated in such numbers, that while there is in the whole country,

according to the United States census, an excess of men, there are large communities in the East where there is an excess of women. It is very evident in such communities that there will be large numbers of unmarried women, unless the surplusage of women should emigrate,—Heaven only knows where,—or Utah be re-enacted in New England. The laws forbid the latter, if it were not forbidden by a high civilization. And the women, who have a right to decide concerning the former, very naturally choose to remain among their friends and kindred. No theory therefore is necessary to account for the non-marriage of tens of thousands of Eastern women. The facts explain it. And these same facts form an imperative reason why "superior education," and "higher forms of labor," should be conceded to them, as also every other needed aid; for they are to be self-dependent and self-supported.

It is also true that the better class of women, the more thoughtful and the more refined, demand more in marriage at the present time than was formerly thought essential. Not more in the way of worship or luxury or indolence; but the theory of the wife's equality with the husband has rooted itself in the minds of most women; and the old-time doctrine of marital domination and wifely submission still has zealous advocates among men. "Suppose woman finds too late, that she is doomed (in marriage) to walk with a soulless brute, then what? Let her soberly accept her lot." This was the advice given by a doctor of divinity five or six years ago to the graduating class of Packer Institute, Brooklyn, N.Y. He assumed that the young ladies then graduating were all bound to the marriage altar, that their marriage was inevitable; and he proceeded to teach them that their "lot" was "wifely submission under all circumstances." This may be good advice for a doctor of divinity to give, but it is very poor advice for a woman to follow; and only a minority of a minority will follow it, in our republic, in this age of the world. . . .

The spheres of both men and women are

to be defined by their tastes and their capacities, as well as by their physiology. All that they are in themselves should enter into the settlement of the problem, as well as their various environments. No *doctrinaire,* no physiologist, no church, and no pope can propound an arbitrary theory concerning the sphere of women which it is worth while for women to aim to realize. For there is no Procrustean bed of correct length on which to measure them, drawing them out, or cutting them off, as they are too long or too short. Above the titles of wife and mother, which, although dear, are transitory and accidental, there is the title of human being, which precedes and out-ranks every other. Womanhood comes in advance of wifehood and motherhood, and rises above it, as manhood is more than husbandhood or fatherhood; and the woman who lives up to a noble ideal of womanhood cannot make her life a failure, albeit she may be no man's wife, and no child's mother.

Let it be granted, that in an ideal state every man will have a wife, and every woman a husband; that the husband will be the bread-winner, and the wife the bread-maker; that the work of the man will be to obtain the livelihood, and that of the woman to make the home. We are far enough from an ideal state at present; and, while working up to it, it is wisdom to provide for the necessities that press upon us to-day. Woman was made for man, as man for woman,—no more and no less. But both are to live for God and humanity. When they unite in marriage they have equal rights and mutual responsibilities; and while living for each other they are to tend towards a higher ideal,—that of the Infinite Perfection. No more demoralizing doctrine was ever taught, and none more belittling to woman, than that propounded by Milton in the oft-quoted line,—

"He for God only: she for God in him,"—
a doctrine which Eve seems to have accepted;
for we soon find her addressing the weak Adam
in this fulsome strain,—
"God is thy law; thou, mine: to know no more
Is woman's happiest knowledge and her praise."

The world is outgrowing this ethical nonsense; and women, married and single, are more and more held to a stern accountability for their deeds, words, and influence. And this is as it should be.

Who are the women whom the social scientists insult with the adjective "superfluous," at whom misogynists sneer as "old maids," and whom sociologists brand as "social failures"? A glance at them reveals the fact, that in many instances they are the most useful women in society. Were they expatriated to-morrow the resultant misery to many classes—notwithstanding the good work wrought by modern institutions—would be almost as great as that which followed the immediate dissolution of the monasteries in the time of the Reformation. . . .

WHO ARE "SUPERFLUOUS WOMEN"?

Superfluous women! There are plenty of them, and of superfluous men also, who might drop out by the ten thousand during a night, and the world would not know at the breakfast-hour that it had lost any thing. Nor would it lose any thing, save a minimum of the weight on its back, or of the drag on its wheels. But you will not always find superfluous women among the unmarried. *They* are the superfluous women, whether married or unmarried, whose lives are days of idle pleasure, and who are victims of *ennui,* unrest, and morbid fancy, because they despise the activities of the age into which they are born. Truly has Elizabeth Barrett Browning said,—

"The honest, earnest man must stand and work;
    The woman also—otherwise she drops
    At once below the dignity of man,
    Accepting serfdom."
The world has no need of women who feel themselves degraded to the level of servitude when compelled to engage in practical work.

They are superfluous women, who, with imbecile renunciation, hasten to wash their reputations of the taint of "strong-mindedness;" whose intellects are "accidents of the body," and, "like the candles inside Chinese lanterns, are of use only to light up, and show off to advantage, the pretty devices outside." They are superfluous women, who are so indifferent to duty, so lacking in high principle, so devoid of tender feeling, that they are capable of accepting any man in marriage—an octogenarian, an imbecile, a debauchee—if his establishment, his equipage, and bank-account are satisfactory; these being of more value than the man who offers them, and whose adjuncts they are. They are superfluous women, who, anchored in the haven of a husband's love, and surrounded by the severely earned luxury of his toil, are steeped in selfishness, rebelling against motherhood, scouting philanthropy, and answering the plea of their less fortunate sisters with the shameful iteration, "I will not be disturbed! I have all the rights I want!" They are superfluous women, who live for what they call "society," their weak natures knowing no loftier aspiration than to be admitted to a gilded social circle higher than they; whose whole duty is comprised in swift obedience to the dictates of folly and fashion; to whom the tittle-tattle of gossip is as the nectar of the gods, and whose instinct for scandal and intrigue is as keen as the scent of the vulture for the battle when it rages.

It is the false teaching of society—a demoralizing public sentiment—that is responsible for these women. As long as women are taught to believe that a life of ease is better than work; that they are born into the world to be the dependents of men, whose inferiors they are; that it is their mission to please and amuse men, and not to stimulate them to high endeavor; as long as courage and capacity, self-poise and independence, are regarded as qualities ennobling men, but de-womanizing women,—so long will low ideals of womanhood prevail, necessarily dragging down the standard of manhood. While society in its highways and byways, in its drawing-rooms and workshops, by hints and suggestions, through novels and essays, lectures, sermons, and editorials, in season and out of season, dins in the ears of young women, "Marry!

marry! for the unmarried woman fails of the end for which she was created!" we may expect them to rush into marriage without thought or preparation, and to regard it as a man does business or trade. We may also expect that the unmarried woman will be regarded with disfavor, that her position will be considered less honorable than that of the wife; thus perpetuating an estimate of woman that belongs to a rude age, when population was sparse, development low, and the wants of the world were physical.

134

LUCINDA B. CHANDLER
Matrimony as a Last Resort (1897)

On reading the statement under the above heading in December issue of FAMILY CULTURE, I sighed as I have many times before, and was amazed as I have been many times, that a woman who had probably been reared in a decent home, and who evidently had enjoyed refining influences and associations, could enter into a marriage which she cannot justify, and only excuse for mercenary reasons.

The saddest phase of the case and similar cases is, that neither the woman nor society looks upon such a relation as out of order or impure.

The idea that a sanction by civil law, and a ceremony by priest or magistrate can make holy (whole) a union of man and woman in matrimony, is the error that is the root of much social impurity, both in and out of marriage. The idea that the selection of one as a matrimonial partner on a basis of convenience, or considerations of material interest, is a means of promoting social morals if the falsehood is pronounced by the priest, "What God has joined together let not man put asunder," has borne the pernicious fruit of illegitimate parenthood, and

From *Family Culture*, January 1, 1897.

furnished material for divorce courts and many forms of disorder.

If a man needs a housekeeper and a woman needs a home and a means of support, there is no need that she should prostitute herself by a mercenary marriage which calls for a defence. A woman could become a housekeeper without being under any obligation to community, or to her own sense of honor to defend herself. If women would refuse to sell themselves in marriage for a home, both the estate of matrimony and the merits of housekeeping would be lifted to higher standing.

That a woman recognizes the necessity or propriety of offering a defence for her marriage shows clearly that she is outraging her higher sense of truth to her better nature, and loyalty to womanly honor and purity. And the pity of it is that the moral sense of the people generally are nowise shocked by such legalized prostitution. If a higher standard of personal and social purity is ever established, the foundation must be laid in the sacredness of a union that can be recognized by a ceremonial, but cannot be created or sanctified by it.

Till prostitution under marriage vows ceases, prostitution outside legal sanction will continue. And till co-operation provides opportunity for all members of the social organism to win subsistence by honest industry, the weaker womanhood must sell themselves either in or outside of marriage.

135

Eliza S. Turner

Should Women Work Outside Their Homes? (1895)

On this question, lately discussed by the Guild Lyceum, a member then absent would like to add a word:

Time was when the distinctive partition of

From *The WorkingWoman's Journal*, December 7, 1895.

occupations between the sexes was an absolute necessity, and consequently needed no legislation nor argument to secure it. In the mere brute struggle for existence, which was the condition of all, tribe against tribe, and often family against family, those who could fight best took the fighting, while their wives staid at home and cared for the children, cooked, wove, made garments, and tilled the ground when any of that was done. And long since fighting, and hunting have ceased to be the sole business of men, they have continued to occupy a large proportion of their activity.

"Man for the field and woman for the hearth,

He for the sword, and for the needle she."

"This," argue many, "has always been so, and consequently always will, it is human nature." And so it is, but not the whole of our human nature. As life becomes gradually less chaotic and disorderly, man is left with time to discover in himself other and finer needs and powers, and as the world outside the tent or hovel becomes a safer place for woman to move about in, she too begins to realize the possession of needs and capacities hitherto undreamed of, and in both cases they are not less, but more human than of old. The fact is, there is nothing more likely to lead us into mistakes than to say of the general sentiment of any given time, on any given subject, "This is human nature; this must be our immutable guide."

It is the nature of some of the savage tribes, I think the Fijians, when a parent has outlived his or her influence, to boost the aged party into a tree, and as he clings to the highest branch within reach, to form a circle round it, and with jovial dance and song, invite him to descend, singing a chorus kept especially for these occasions, "The fruit is ripe, it must come down," enforcing their urgency with stones and other persuasives. When he does fall, they finish the glad occasion by cooking and eating him. Well, that is human nature, as far as the Fijians have got, and I suppose that if one of our race should suggest that there might be other ways of dealing with the aged, they would be shocked at such a violation of their God-given instincts. The oak tree is as truly natural as the little hard acrid seed from which it has been evolved; but if the dwarf loving Japanese gardeners had succeeded in putting them all into diminutive pots at a certain stage of their growth, who could ever have dreamed the destiny intended for them by nature? Neither is it for any theorist to say to us women, "You are now very pretty saplings, needing only a little pruning from us; but you have gone far enough; to grow any more would violate our ideals of oak nature; so we will fit you all in your little pots, that you may change no more forever."

But to go back to the concrete question— "Would it be better, on the whole; for women to occupy themselves exclusively with home duties?" The writer has an idea that it probably would. But what sort of home? In the old times it meant the cradle and spinning wheel and cook stove, and these alone; and for centuries domestic conditions changed so slowly that it was natural to think this was all it would ever be; but in the last fifty years and with greatly accelerating speed in the last twenty, the sewing machine and the ready made clothing and the gas and electric cooker have begun to revolutionize the craft of housekeeping; and to-day the air is full of premonitions of still more wonderful changes, such as may affect most importantly the domestic conditions of life. Who can prophesy what may be the home of the coming century? In it housekeeping may have become so easy that a woman of spirit would be ashamed to give her whole life to its management.

But if she have children, would it be possible to devote too large a proportion of her time to them?

We know not a few women with children, whose fathers are dead, or in some way incapacitated or unwilling to support them, who have gone out into the world to earn the means to give them the education they could not otherwise get; if they be all exceptions they are so frequent as to make it worth while to consider

them in laying down our rules; if she can stay at home, it ought to be such a sphere as will allow her to fit herself to train and protect and guide her children with intelligence and as they grow older she needs to keep herself in touch with the outside world for their sakes to be able to answer their questions understandingly, to have a mind and judgment of her own, to the end that she may keep her hold on their affection and respect. A mother who is only nurse and cook for her children is but a poor specimen of a parent.

But, without looking so far afield, considering only the present phase of our civilization, there are many thousands of young women whose circumstances are such that they must be bread winners or starve; and there are thousands more who have a sort of option of living as dependents on fathers or brothers, having to forego most of the pleasures and many of the almost necessities of life, never having a cent except as a gift from the one bread-winner—to choose between this and going out to earn a living for themselves. In these days, when most girls have ideas of their own, she who stays in a home where she is not sufficiently needed to make her feel that she pays her way, is apt to be discontented, restless, suffering a sense of humiliation; in a word, unhappy. The writer has known, in spite of Charles Read's theories to the contrary, many cases of this kind, where the sense of independence, even coupled with hard work, has changed the worker into a happy instead of a miserable woman.

And having once tasted the sweets of freedom, how are we to make her happy when the time shall come for her to withdraw into a home of her own? By leaving her still free, except as the laws of her woman's nature, (not some outworn ideal of femineity) shall bind her. If, on the contrary, she leave her independent life, be it ever so hard, to become again a dependent, if her husband is the sort of man of whom people say, "He dresses his wife well or ill," or if she can say, "I think the children ought to be corrected of such or such a fault, but 'he' won't allow it;"

or if he can say, "I never allow my servants to have followers;" or if, when she needs a new dress she has to wait until he has time to go with her and buy it for her, and take out his purse and pay for it; and if, supposing she wants to go to another counter to get some hooks and eyes, he hands her half a dollar and she brings him back the change, the woman once accustomed to judge for herself must be unhappy.

Or even if it is not so bad as this, if he gives her five dollars freely when she explains what she wants it for and seldom interferes with her housekeeping; if he only, when she shows an interest in something outside her own four walls, good-naturedly snub her, perhaps in the presence of her children, and asks if she has got to the bottom of her mending basket, even so she is likely to be unhappy. It will be only when the new man (for it is time for some of them to try to be new men), perceives that the true home is one where man and wife, although differing, are equals, that home will be all it is capable of being. Sometime he will come to understand how many things there are beyond her darning basket, about which, as a homekeeper, she ought to concern herself; he will perceive that not only the kitchen drain pipe, but the general drainage of the city, is her business as well as his own; that not only the fib told by Tommy, but the corruption at the ballot-box, is lowering the moral atmosphere for her own children; that not only the management of the school where Tommy goes, but the management of all the city schools, is her business; that not only the safety of the world for her own precious daughter, but for other people's daughters, is something which demands her thought; in short, gives the ideal home maker a sphere large enough to include all the interests which really affect the welfare of the individual home, and we shall pray for the time to come when every woman, not compelled by any artificial theory, but left to her own desire, will gravitate thereto.

ELIZA S. TURNER.

136
CHARLOTTE PERKINS GILMAN
Women and Economics (1898)

. . . In view of these facts, attention is now called to a certain marked and peculiar economic condition affecting the human race, and unparalleled in the organic world. We are the only animal species in which the female depends on the male for food, the only animal species in which the sex-relation is also an economic relation. With us an entire sex lives in a relation of economic dependence upon the other sex, and the economic relation is combined with the sex-relation. The economic status of the human female is relative to the sex-relation.

. . . The economic status of the human race in any nation, at any time, is governed mainly by the activities of the male: the female obtains her share in the racial advance only through him.

Studied individually, the facts are even more plainly visible, more open and familiar. From the day laborer to the millionaire, the wife's worn dress or flashing jewels, her low roof cr her lordly one, her weary feet or her rich equipage,—these speak of the economic ability of the husband. The comfort, the luxury, the necessities of life itself, which the woman receives, are obtained by the husband, and given her by him. And, when the woman, left alone with no man to "support" her, tries to meet her own economic necessities, the difficulties which confront her prove conclusively what the general economic status of the woman is. None can deny these patent facts,—that the economic status of women generally depends upon that of men generally, and that the economic status of women individually depends upon that of men individually, those men to whom they are related. But we are instantly confronted by the commonly

From *Women and Economics: A Study of the Economic Relation between Men and Women as a Factor in Social Evolution* (Boston: Small, Maynard, and Co., 1898), 5, 9–22, 29–30, 37–39, 49, 181–87, 237, 241–45, 247 received opinion that, although it must be admitted that men make and distribute the wealth of the world, yet women earn their share of it as wives. This assumes either that the husband is in the position of employer and the wife as employee, or that marriage is a "partnership," and the wife an equal factor with the husband in producing wealth.

Economic independence is a relative condition at best. In the broadest sense, all living things are economically dependent upon others,—the animals upon the vegetables, and man upon both. In a narrower sense, all social life is economically interdependent, man producing collectively what he could by no possibility produce separately. But, in the closest interpretation, individual economic independence among human beings means that the individual pays for what he gets, works for what he gets, gives to the other an equivalent for what the other gives him. I depend on the shoemaker for shoes, and the tailor for coats; but, if I give the shoemaker and the tailor enough of my own labor as a housebuilder to pay for the shoes and coats they give me, I retain my personal independence. I have not taken of their product, and given nothing of mine. As long as what I get is obtained by what I give, I am economically independent.

Women consume economic goods. What economic product do they give in exchange for what they consume? The claim that marriage is a partnership, in which the two persons married produce wealth which neither of them, separately, could produce, will not bear examination. A man happy and comfortable can produce more than one unhappy and uncomfortable, but this is as true of a father or son as of a husband. To take from a man any of the conditions which make him happy and strong is to cripple his industry, generally speaking. But those relatives who make him happy are not therefore his business partners, and entitled to share his income.

Grateful return for happiness conferred is not the method of exchange in a partnership. The comfort a man takes with his wife is not in the nature of a business partnership, nor are her frugality and industry. A housekeeper, in her place, might be as frugal, as industrious, but would not therefore be a partner. Man and wife are partners truly in their mutual obligation to their children,—their common love, duty, and service. But a manufacturer who marries, or a doctor, or a lawyer, does not take a partner in his business, when he takes a partner in parenthood, unless his wife is also a manufacturer, a doctor, or a lawyer. In his business, she cannot even advise wisely withough training and experience. To love her husband, the composer, does not enable her to compose; and the loss of a man's wife, though it may break his heart, does not cripple his business, unless his mind is affected by grief. She is in no sense a business partner, unless she contributes capital or experience or labor, as a man would in like relation. Most men would hesitate very seriously before entering a business partnership with any woman, wife or not.

If the wife is not, then, truly a business partner, in what way does she earn from her husband the food, clothing, and shelter she receives at his hands? By house service, it will be instantly replied. This is the general misty idea upon the subject,—that women earn all they get, and more, by house service. Here we come to a very practical and definite economic ground. Although not producers of wealth, women serve in the final processes of preparation and distribution. Their labor in the household has a genuine economic value.

For a certain percentage of persons to serve other persons, in order that the ones so served may produce more, is a contribution not to be overlooked. The labor of women in the house, certainly, enables men to produce more wealth than they otherwise could; and in this way women are economic factors in society. But so are horses. The labor of horses enables men to produce more wealth than they otherwise could. The horse is an economic factor in society. But the horse is not economically independent, nor is the woman. If a man plus a valet can perform more useful service than he could minus a va-let, then the valet is performing useful service. But, if the valet is the property of the man, is obliged to perform this service, and is not paid for it, he is not economically independent.

The labor which the wife performs in the household is given as part of her functional duty, not as employment. The wife of the poor man, who works hard in a small house, doing all the work for the family, or the wife of the rich man, who wisely and gracefully manages a large house and administers its functions, each is entitled to fair pay for services rendered.

To take this ground and hold it honestly, wives, as earners through domestic service, are entitled to the wages of cooks, housemaids, nursemaids, seamstresses, or housekeepers, and to no more. This would of course reduce the spending money of the wives of the rich, and put it out of the power of the poor man to "sup-port" a wife at all, unless, indeed, the poor man faced the situation fully, paid his wife her wages as house servant, and then she and he combined their funds in the support of their children. He would be keeping a servant: she would be help-ing keep the family. But nowhere on earth would there be "a rich woman" by these means. Even the highest class of private housekeeper, useful as her services are, does not accumulate a for-tune. She does not buy diamonds and sables and keep a carriage. Things like these are not earned by house service.

But the salient fact in this discussion is that, whatever the economic value of the domestic industry of women is, they do not get it. The women who do the most work get the least money, and the women who have the most money do the least work. Their labor is neither given nor taken as a factor in economic ex-change. It is held to be their duty as women to do this work; and their economic status bears no relation to their domestic labor, unless an inverse one. Moreover, if they were thus fairly paid,—given what they earned, and no more,—all women working in this way would be reduced to the economic status of the house servant. Few

women—or men either—care to face this con-dition. The ground that women earn their liv-ing by domestic labor is instantly forsaken, and we are told that they obtain their livelihood as mothers. This is a peculiar position. We speak of it commonly enough, and often with deep feel-ing, but without due analysis.

In treating of an economic exchange, ask-ing what return in goods or labor women make for the goods and labor given them,—either to the race collectively or to their husbands indi-vidually,—what payment women make for their clothes and shoes and furniture and food and shelter, we are told that the duties and services of the mother entitle her to support.

If this is so, if motherhood is an exchange-able commodity given by women in payment for clothes and food, then we must of course find some relation between the quantity or qual-ity of the motherhood and the quantity and qual-ity of the pay. This being true, then the women who are not mothers have no economic status at all; and the economic status of those who are must be shown to be relative to their mother-hood. This is obviously absurd. The childless wife has as much money as the mother of many,— more; for the children of the latter consume what would otherwise be hers; and the ineffi-cient mother is no less provided for than the efficient one. Visibly, and upon the face of it, women are not maintained in economic pros-perity proportioned to their motherhood. Motherhood bears no relation to their economic status. Among primitive races, it is true,—in the patriarchal period, for instance,—there was some truth in this position. Women being of no value whatever save as bearers of children, their favor and indulgence did bear direct relation to maternity; and they had reason to exult on more grounds than one when they could boast a son. To-day, however, the maintenance of the woman is not conditioned upon this. A man is not al-lowed to discard his wife because she is barren. The claim of motherhood as a factor in economic exchange is false to-day. But suppose it were true. Are we willing to hold this ground, even in theory? Are we willing to consider motherhood as a business, a form of commercial exchange? Are the cares and duties of the mother, her travail and her love, commodities to be exchanged for bread?

It is revolting so to consider them; and, if we dare face our own thoughts, and force them to their logical conclusion, we shall see that nothing could be more repugnant to human feeling, or more socially and individually injurious, than to make motherhood a trade. Driven off these alleged grounds of women's economic independence; shown that women, as a class, neither produce nor distribute wealth; that women, as individuals, labor mainly as house servants, are not paid as such, and would not be satisfied with such an economic status if they were so paid; that wives are not business partners or co-producers of wealth with their husbands, unless they actually practise the same profession; that they are not salaried as mothers, and that it would be unspeakably degrading if they were,—what remains to those who deny that women are supported by men? This (and a most amusing position it is),—that the function of maternity unfits a woman for economic production, and, therefore, it is right that she should be supported by her husband.

The ground is taken that the human female is not economically independent, that she is fed by the male of her species. In denial of this, it is first alleged that she is economically independent,—that she does support her self by her own industry in the house. It being shown that there is no relation between the economic status of woman and the labor she performs in the home, it is then alleged that not as house servant, but as mother, does woman earn her living. It being shown that the economic status of woman bears no relation to her motherhood, either in quantity or quality, it is then alleged that motherhood renders a woman unfit for economic production, and that, therefore, it is right that she be supported by her husband. Before going farther, let us seize upon this admission,—that she *is* supported by her husband.

Without going into either the ethics or the necessities of the case, we have reached so much common ground: the female of genus homo is supported by the male. Whereas, in other species of animals, male and female alike graze and browse, hunt and kill, climb, swim, dig, run, and fly for their livings, in our species the female does not seek her own living in the specific activities of our race, but is fed by the male.

Now as to the alleged necessity. Because of her maternal duties, the human female is said to be unable to get her own living. As the maternal duties of other females do not unfit them for getting their own living and also the livings of their young, it would seem that the human maternal duties require the segregation of the entire energies of the mother to the service of the child during her entire adult life, or so large a proportion of them that not enough remains to devote to the individual interests of the mother.

Such a condition, did it exist, would of course excuse and justify the pitiful dependence of the human female, and her support by the male. As the queen bee, modified entirely to maternity, is supported, not by the male, to be sure, but by her co-workers, the "old maids," the barren working bees, who labor so patiently and lovingly in their branch of the maternal duties of the hive, so would the human female, modified entirely to maternity, become unfit for any other exertion, and a helpless dependant.

Is this the condition of human motherhood? Does the human mother, by her motherhood, thereby lose control of brain and body, lose power and skill and desire for any other work? Do we see before us the human race, with all its females segregated entirely to the uses of motherhood, consecrated, set apart, specially developed, spending every power of their nature on the service of their children?

We do not. We see the human mother worked far harder than a mare, laboring her life long in the service, not of her children only, but of men; husbands, brothers, fathers, whatever male relatives she has; for mother and sister also;

for the church a little, if she is allowed; for society, if she is able; for charity and education and reform,—working in many ways that are not the ways of motherhood.

It is not motherhood that keeps the housewife on her feet from dawn till dark; it is house service, not child service. Women work longer and harder than most men, and not solely in maternal duties. The savage mother carries the burdens, and does all menial service for the tribe. The peasant mother toils in the fields, and the workingman's wife in the home. Many mothers, even now, are wage-earners for the family, as well as bearers and rearers of it. And the women who are not so occupied, the women who belong to rich men,—here perhaps is the exhaustive devotion to maternity which is supposed to justify an admitted economic dependence. But we do not find it even among these. Women of ease and wealth provide for their children better care than the poor woman can; but they do not spend more time upon it themselves, nor more care and effort. They have other occupation.

In spite of her supposed segregation to maternal duties, the human female, the world over, works at extra-maternal duties for hours enough to provide her with an independent living, and then is denied independence on the ground that motherhood prevents her working!

If this ground were tenable, we should find a world full of women who never lifted a finger save in the service of their children, and of men who did *all* the work besides, and waited on the women whom motherhood prevented from waiting on themselves. The ground is not tenable. A human female, healthy, sound, has twenty-five years of life before she is a mother, and should have twenty-five years more after the period of such maternal service as is expected of her has been given. The duties of grandmotherhood are surely not alleged as preventing economic independence.

The working power of the mother has always been a prominent factor in human life. She is the worker *par excellence*, but her work is not

such as to affect her economic status. Her living, all that she gets,—food, clothing, ornaments, amusements, luxuries,—these bear no relation to her power to produce wealth, to her services in the house, or to her motherhood. These things bear relation only to the man she marries, the man she depends on,—to how much he has and how much he is willing to give her. The women whose splendid extravagance dazzles the world, whose economic goods are the greatest, are often neither houseworkers nor mothers, but simply the women who hold most power over the men who have the most money. The female of genus homo is economically dependent on the male. He is her food supply.

. . . Very early in the development of species it was ascertained by nature's slow but sure experiments that the establishment of two sexes in separate organisms, and their differentiation, was to the advantage of the species. Therefore, out of the mere protoplasmic masses, the floating cells, the amorphous early forms of life, grew into use the distinction of the sexes,—the gradual development of masculine and feminine organs and functions in two distinct organisms. Developed and increased by use, the distinction of sex increased in the evolution of species. As the distinction increased, the attraction increased, until we have in all the higher races two markedly different sexes, strongly drawn together by the attraction of sex, and fulfilling their use in the reproduction of species. These are the natural features of sex-distinction and sex-union, and they are found in the human species as in others. The unnatural feature by which our race holds an unenviable distinction consists mainly in this,—a morbid excess in the exercise of this function.

It is this excess, whether in marriage or out, which makes the health and happiness of humanity in this relation so precarious. It is this excess, always easily seen, which law and religion have mainly striven to check. Excessive sex-indulgence is the distinctive feature of humanity in this relation.

. . . When, then, it can be shown that sex-distinction in the human race is so excessive as not only to affect injuriously its own purposes, but to check and pervert the progress of the race, it becomes a matter for most serious consideration. Nothing could be more inevitable, however, under our sexuo-economic relation. By the economic dependence of the human female upon the male, the balance of forces is altered. Natural selection no longer checks the action of sexual selection, but co-operates with it. Where both sexes obtain their food through the same exertions, from the same sources, under the same conditions, both sexes are acted upon alike, and developed alike by their environment. Where the two sexes obtain their food under different conditions, and where that difference consists in one of them being fed by the other, then the feeding sex becomes the environment of the fed. Man, in supporting woman, has become her economic environment. Under natural selection, every creature is modified to its environment, developing perforce the qualities needed to obtain its livelihood under that environment. Man, as the feeder of woman, becomes the strongest modifying force in her economic condition. Under sexual selection the human creature is of course modified to its mate, as with all creatures. When the mate becomes also the master, when economic necessity is added to sex-attraction, we have the two great evolutionary forces acting together to the same end; namely, to develop sex-distinction in the human female. For, in her position of economic dependence in the sex-relation, sex-distinction is with her not only a means of attracting a mate, as with all creatures, but a means of getting her livelihood, as is the case with no other creature under heaven. Because of the economic dependence of the human female on her mate, she is modified to sex to an excessive degree. This excessive modification she transmits to her children; and so is steadily implanted in the human constitution the morbid tendency to excess in this relation, which has acted so universally upon us in all ages, in spite of our best efforts to restrain it. It is not the normal sex-tendency, common to all creatures, but an abnormal sex-tendency, produced and maintained by the abnormal economic relation which makes one sex get its living from the other by the exercise of sex-functions. This is the immediate effect upon individuals of the peculiar sexuo-economic relation which obtains among us.

. . . But it is in our common social relations that the predominance of sex-distinction in women is made most manifest. The fact that, speaking broadly, women have, from the very beginning, been spoken of expressively enough as "the sex," demonstrates clearly that this is the main impression which they have made upon observers and recorders. Here one need attempt no farther proof than to turn the mind of the reader to an unbroken record of facts and feelings perfectly patent to every one, but not hitherto looked at as other than perfectly natural and right. So utterly has the status of woman been accepted as a sexual one that it has remained for the woman's movement of the nineteenth century to devote much contention to the claim that women are persons! That women are persons as well as females,—an unheard of proposition!

. . . Human motherhood is more pathological than any other, more morbid, defective, irregular, diseased. Human childhood is similarly pathological. We, as animals, are very inferior animals in this particular. When we take credit to ourselves for the sublime devotion with which we face "the perils of maternity," and boast of "going down to the gates of death" for our children, we should rather take shame to ourselves for bringing these perils upon both mother and child. The gates of death? They are the gates of life to the unborn; and there is no death there save what we, the mothers, by our unnatural lives, have brought upon our own children. Gates of death, indeed, to the thousands of babies late-born, prematurely born, misborn, and still-born for lack of right motherhood. In the primal physical functions of maternity the human female cannot show that her supposed specialization to these uses has improved her fulfilment of them, rather the opposite. The more freely the human mother mingles in the natural industries of a human creature, as in the case of the savage woman, the peasant woman, the working-woman everywhere who is not overworked, the more rightly she fulfils these functions.

The more absolutely woman is segregated to sex-functions only, cut off from all economic use and made wholly dependent on the sex-relation as means of livelihood, the more pathological does her motherhood become. The over-development of sex caused by her economic dependence on the male reacts unfavorably upon her essential duties. She is too female for perfect motherhood! Her excessive specialization in the secondary sexual characteristics is a detrimental element in heredity. Small, weak, soft, ill-proportioned women do not tend to produce large, strong, sturdy, well-made men or women. When Frederic the Great wanted grenadiers of great size, he married big men to big women,—not to little ones. The female segregated to the uses of sex alone naturally deteriorates in racial development, and naturally transmits that deterioration to her offspring. The human mother, in the processes of reproduction, shows no gain in efficiency over the lower animals, but rather a loss, and so far presents no evidence to prove that her specialization to sex is of any advantage to her young. The mother of a dead baby or the baby of a dead mother; the sick baby, the crooked baby, the idiot baby; the exhausted, nervous, prematurely aged mother, —these are not uncommon among us; and they do not show much progress in our motherhood.

Since we cannot justify the human method of maternity in the physical processes of reproduction, can we prove its advantages in the other branch, education? Though the mother be sickly and the child the same, will not her loving care more than make up for it? Will not the tender devotion of the mother, and her unflagging attendance upon the child, render human motherhood sufficiently successful in comparison with that of other species to justify our peculiar method? We must now show that our motherhood, in its usually accepted sense, the "care" of the child (more accurately described as education), is of a superior nature.

Here, again, we lack the benefit of comparison. No other animal species is required to care for its young so long, to teach it so much. So far as they have it to do, they do it well. The hen with her brood is an accepted model of motherhood in this respect. She not only lays eggs and hatches them, but educates and protects her young so far as it is necessary. But beyond such simple uses as this we have no standard of comparison for educative motherhood. We can only study it among ourselves, comparing the child left motherless with the child mothered, the child with a mother and nothing else with the child whose mother is helped by servants and teachers, the child with what we recognize as a superior mother to the child with an inferior mother. This last distinction, a comparison between mothers, is of great value. We have tacitly formulated a certain vague standard of human motherhood, and loosely apply it, especially in the epithets "natural" and "unnatural" mother.

But these terms again show how prone we still are to consider the whole field of maternal action as one of instinct rather than of reason, as a function rather than a service. We do have a standard, however, loose and vague as it is; and even by that standard it is painful to see how many human mothers fail. Ask yourselves honestly how many of the mothers whose action toward their children confronts you in street and shop and car and boat, in hotel and boardinghouse and neighboring yard,—how many call forth favorable comment compared with those you judge unfavorably? Consider not the rosy ideal of motherhood you have in your mind, but the coarse, hard facts of motherhood as you see them, and hear them, in daily life.

Motherhood in its fulfilment of educational duty can be measured only by its effects. If we take for a standard the noble men and women whose fine physique and character we so fondly attribute to "a devoted mother," what are we to say of the motherhood which has filled the world with the ignoble men and women, of depraved physique and character? If the good mother makes the good man, how about the bad ones? When we see great men and women, we give credit to their mothers. When we see inferior men and women,—and that is a common circumstance,—no one presumes to question the motherhood which has produced them. When it comes to congenital criminality, we are beginning to murmur something about "heredity"; and, to meet gross national ignorance, we do demand a better system of education. But no one presumes to suggest that the mothering of mankind could be improved upon; and yet there is where the responsibility really lies. If our human method of reproduction is defective, let the mother answer. She is the main factor in reproduction. If our human method of education is defective, let the mother answer. She is the main factor in education.

To this it is bitterly objected that such a claim omits the father and his responsibility. When the mother of the world is in her right place and doing her full duty, she will have no ground of complaint against the father. In the first place, she will make better men. In the second, she will hold herself socially responsible for the choice of a right father for her children. In the third place, as an economic free agent, she will do half duty in providing for the child. Men who are not equal to good fatherhood under such conditions will have no chance to become fathers, and will die with general pity instead of living with general condemnation. In his position, doing all the world's work, all the father's, and half the mother's, man has made better shift to achieve the impossible than woman has in hers. She has been supposed to have no work or care on earth save as mother. She has really had the work of the mother and that of the world's house service besides. But she has surely had as much time and strength to give to motherhood as man to fatherhood; and not until she can show that the children of the

world are as well mothered as they are well fed can she cast on him the blame for our general deficiency.

There is no personal blame to be laid on either party. The sexuo-economic relation has its inevitable ill-effects on both motherhood and fatherhood. But it is to the mother that the appeal must be made to change this injurious relation. Having the deeper sense of duty to the young, the larger love, she must come to feel how her false position hurts her motherhood, and for her children's sake break away from it. Of man and his fatherhood she can make what she will.

. . . No, the human race is not well nourished by making the process of feeding it a sex-function. The selection and preparation of food should be in the hands of trained experts. And woman should stand beside man as the comrade of his soul, not the servant of his body.

. . . As society develops, its functions specialize; and the reason why this great race-function of cooking has been so retarded in this natural growth is that the economic dependence of women has kept them back from their share in human progress. When women stand free as economic agents, they will lift and free their arrested functions, to the much better fulfilment of their duties as wives and mothers and to the vast improvement in health and happiness of the human race.

Co-operation is not what is required for this, but trained professional service and such arrangement of our methods of living as shall allow us to benefit by such service. When numbers of people patronize the same tailor or baker or confectioner, they do not co-operate. Neither would they co-operate in patronizing the same cook. The change must come from the side of the cook, not from the side of the family. It must come through natural functional development in society, and it is so coming. Woman, recognizing that her duty as feeder and cleaner is a social duty, not a sexual one, must face the requirements of the situation, and prepare herself to meet them. A hundred years ago this could not have been done. Now it is being done, because the time is ripe for it.

If there should be built and opened in any of our large cities to-day a commodious and well-served apartment house for professional women with families, it would be filled at once. The apartments would be without kitchens; but there would be a kitchen belonging to the house from which meals could be served to the families in their rooms or in a common dining-room, as preferred. It would be a home where the cleaning was done by efficient workers, not hired separately by the families, but engaged by the manager of the establishment and a roof-garden, day nursery, and kindergarten, under well-trained professional nurses and teachers, would insure proper care of the children. The demand for such provision is increasing daily, and must soon be met, not by a boarding-house or a lodging-house, a hotel, a restaurant, or any makeshift patching together of these; but by a permanent provision of the needs of women and children, of family privacy with collective advantage. This must be offered on a business basis to prove a substantial business success; and it will so prove, for it is a growing social need.

There are hundreds of thousands of women in New York City alone who are wage-earners, and who also have families; and the number increases. This is true not only among the poor and unskilled, but more and more among business women, professional women, scientific, artistic, literary women. Our school-teachers, who form a numerous class, are not entirely without relatives. To board does not satisfy the needs of a human soul. These women want homes, but they do not want the clumsy tangle of rudimentary industries that are supposed to accompany the home. The strain under which such women labor is no longer necessary. The privacy of the home could be as well maintained in such a building as described as in any house in a block, any room, flat, or apartment, under present methods. The food would be better, and would cost less; and this would be true of the service and of all common necessities.

In suburban homes this purpose could be accomplished much better by a grouping of adjacent houses, each distinct and having its own yard, but all kitchenless, and connected by covered ways with the eating-house. No detailed prophecy can be made of the precise forms which would ultimately prove most useful and pleasant; but the growing social need is for the specializing of the industries practised in the home and for the proper mechanical provision for them.

The cleaning required in each house would be much reduced by the removal of the two chief elements of household dirt,—grease and ashes.

Meals could of course be served in the house as long as desired; but, when people become accustomed to pure, clean homes, where no steaming industry is carried on, they will gradually prefer to go to their food instead of having it brought to them. It is a perfectly natural process, and a healthful one, to go to one's food. And, after all, the changes between living in one room, and so having the cooking most absolutely convenient; going as far as the limits of a large house permit to one's own dining-room; and going a little further to a dining-room not in one's own house, but near by,—these differ but in degree. Families could go to eat together, just as they can go to bathe together or to listen to music together; but, if it fell out that different individuals presumed to develop an appetite at different hours, they could meet it without interfering with other people's comfort or sacrificing their own. Any housewife knows the difficulty of always getting a family together at meals. Why try? Then arises sentiment, and asserts that family affection, family unity, the very existence of the family, depend on their being together at meals. A family unity which is only bound together with a table-cloth is of questionable value.

There are several professions involved in our clumsy method of housekeeping. A good cook is not necessarily a good manager, nor a good manager an accurate and thorough cleaner, nor a good cleaner a wise purchaser. Under the free development of these branches a woman could choose her position, train for it, and become a most valuable functionary in her special branch, all the while living in her own home; that is, she would live in it as a man lives in his home, spending certain hours of the day at work and others at home.

. . . The organization of household industries will simplify and centralize its cleaning processes, allowing of many mechanical conveniences and the application of scientific skill and thoroughness. We shall be cleaner than we ever were before. There will be less work to do, and far better means of doing it. The daily needs of a well-plumbed house could be met easily by each individual in his or her own room or by one who liked to do such work; and the labor less frequently required would be furnished by an expert, who would clean one home after another with the swift skill of training and experience. The home would cease to be to us a workshop or a museum, and would become far more the personal expression of its occupants—the place of peace and rest, of love and privacy—than it can be in its present condition of arrested industrial development. And woman will fill her place in those industries with far better results than are now provided by her ceaseless struggles, her conscientious devotion, her pathetic ignorance and inefficiency.

Suggestions for Further Reading

Blair, Karen J. *The Clubwoman as Feminist: True Womanhood Redefined, 1868–1914*. New York: Holmes & Meier Publishers, 1980.

Blewett, Mary H. *Men, Women, and Work: A Study of Class, Gender, and Protest in the Nineteenth-Century New England Shoe Industry*. Urbana: Univ. of Illinois Press, 1988.

Bordin, Ruth. *Woman And Temperance: The Quest for Power and Liberty, 1873–1900*. New Brunswick, N.J.: Rutgers Univ. Press, 1990.

Buhle, Mari Jo. *Women and American Socialism, 1870–1920*. Urban: Univ. of Illinois Press, 1983.

DuBois, Ellen Carol. *Feminism and Suffrage: The Emergence of an Independent Women's Movement in America, 1848–1869*. Ithaca, N.Y.: Cornell Univ. Press, 1978.

Epstein, Barbara. *The Politics of Domesticity: Women, Evangelicism, and Temperance in Nineteenth-Century America*. (Middletown, Conn.: Wesleyan Univ. Press, 1981).

Flexner, Eleanor. *Century of Struggle: The Woman's Rights Movement in the United States*. Cambridge, Mass.: Harvard Univ. Press, 1958).

Giddings, Paula. *When and Where I Enter: The Impact of Black Women on Race and Sex in America*. (New York: William Morrow and Company, 1984)

Kenneally, James J. *Women and American Trade Unions*. St. Albans, Vermont: Eden Press Women's Publications, 1978.

Kessler-Harris, Alice. *Out to Work: A History of Wage-Earning Women in the United States*. New York: Oxford Univ. Press, 1982.

Kraditor, Aileen S. *The Ideas of the Woman Suffrage Movement, 1890–1920*. New York: Columbia Univ. Press, 1965.

Meyorowitz, Joanne J. *Women Adrift: Independent Wage Earners in Chicago, 1880–1930*. Chicago: Univ. of Chicago Press, 1988.

Pleck, Elizabeth. *Domestic Tyranny: The Making of American Social Policy Against Family Violence from Colonial Times to the Present*. New York: Oxford Univ. Press, 1987.

Roth Walsh, Mary. *"Doctors Wanted, No Women Need Apply": Sexual Barriers in the Medical Profession, 1835–1975*. New Haven: Yale Univ. Press, 1977.

Scott, Anne Firor. *Natural Allies: Women's Associations in American History*. Urbana: Univ. of Illinois Press, 1992.

Smith-Rosenberg, Carroll, and Charles Rosenberg. "The Female Animal: Medical and Biological Views of Woman and Her Role in Nineteenth-Century America." *Journal of American History* 60 (1973): 332–56.

Solomon, Barbara. *In the Company of Educated Women: A History of Women in Higher Education in America*. New Haven: Yale Univ. Press, 1985.

Wiener, Lynn Y. *From Working Girls to Working Mother: The Female Labor Force in the United States, 1820–1980*. Chapel Hill: Univ. of North Carolina Press, 1985.

Index

This book is set in Eric Gill's typeface Perpetua
and designed by Gregory M. Britton.